AREA HANDBOOK
for
MALAYSIA

Co-Authors

John W. Henderson

Helen A. Barth
Judith M. Heimann
Philip W. Moeller
Francisco S. Soriano
John O. Weaver

Research and writing were completed on

December 23, 1969

Published October 1970

(This phamphlet supersedes DA Pam 550–45, July 1965.)

DA Pam 550–45

Library of Congress Catalog Card Number: 71–608971

For sale by the Superintendent of Documents, U.S. Government Printing Office
Washington, D.C. 20402—Price $4.

FOREWORD

This volume is one of a series of handbooks prepared by Foreign Area Studies (FAS) of the American University, designed to be useful to military and other personnel who need a convenient compilation of basic facts about the social, economic, political, and military institutions and practices of various countries. The emphasis is on objective description of the nation's present society and the kinds of possible or probable changes that might be expected in the future. The handbook seeks to present as full and as balanced an integrated exposition as limitations on space and research time permit. It was compiled from information available in openly published material. Extensive bibliographies are provided to permit recourse to other published sources for more detailed information. There has been no attempt to express any specific point of view or to make policy recommendations. The contents of the handbook represent the work of the authors and FAS and do not represent the official view of the United States government.

An effort has been made to make the handbook as comprehensive as possible. It can be expected, however, that the material, interpretations, and conclusions are subject to modification in the light of new information and developments. Such corrections, additions, and suggestions for factual, interpretive, or other change as readers may have will be welcomed for use in future revisions. Comments may be addressed to:

The Director
Foreign Area Studies
The American University
5010 Wisconsin Avenue, N.W.
Washington, D.C. 20016

PREFACE

Fundamental changes have taken place in the structure of Malaysia, as well as in its foreign relations, since the *Area Handbook for Malaysia and Singapore* was prepared in 1965. Among the major developments that have required a revision of the original handbook have been Singapore's separation and its establishment as an independent state, the end of the so-called Confrontation between Indonesia and Malaysia, and the first moves toward reduction of the British and other Commonwealth defense presence in the area.

In addition to these basic institutional changes, there have been many more subtle alterations in economic, social, and political patterns. Communal strife, for example, has increased, and the question of whether or not the multiethnic elements of the society could be brought into harmony and permanent stability remained as perhaps the most formidable problem confronting the nation's leaders as the 1970's approached. In another major developing trend, the government has assumed an increasingly important role in developing the economy.

This book attempts to bring the previous handbook up to date as of the end of the decade of the 1960's. Its purpose is to provide in compact, convenient, balanced, and objective form an integrated exposition and analysis of the dominant social, political, and economic aspects of Malaysian society. It is designed to give readers an understanding of the dynamics of the component elements of the society and an insight into the ideas and feelings of its people, as well as the role of the country in the world around it.

This revision has drawn liberally on the 1965 handbook, which was written by a team headed by Bela C. Maday. Other members of the team were Susan E. Callaway, Gustave A. Mellander, Elaine M. Themo, and John O. Weaver.

English usage in the revised edition follows *Webster's Third New International Dictionary of the English Language* (unabridged). Malay language usage has followed Wilkinson's *Malay-English Dictionary*, 8th edition, 1961. Malaysian place names and official names are transliterated in accordance with Malaysian official usage whenever this could be determined from available sources. In other cases spellings of place names have followed decisions of the Board on Geographic Names, United States Department of the Interior. Malaysian usage has been followed so far as possible in the spelling of loan words and names derived from Arabic and Sanskrit.

This book has followed the official Malaysian convention in using *Malay* to describe the major indigenous ethnic group and its language. When referring to citizens without regard to ethnic designation, the term *Malaysian* is used. The portion of the Malay Peninsula occupied by Malaysia is referred to as West Malaysia, and the Malaysian states of Sabah and Sarawak on Borneo are called East Malaysia.

COUNTRY SUMMARY

1. COUNTRY: Malaysia, formed in 1963 through a federation of the Federation of Malaya, an independent country, the crown colonies of Sabah and Sarawak on Borneo, and the crown colony of Singapore. Singapore separated in 1965.

2. POPULATION: Estimated to be 10.3 million in 1969. About 85 percent lived in West Malaysia, heavily concentrated along the western coast. About 40 percent of population under the age of 15. Ethnic composition was estimated as 44 percent Malays, about 36 percent Chinese, 10 percent Indians and Pakistanis, and the remainder composed of 16 indigenous ethnic groups. Among the major groups are the Ibans, Land Dayaks, Kadazans, and Bajaus of East Malaysia, and the Senoi of West Malaysia. First national census due in 1970.

3. GEOGRAPHY: Divided into two main segments separated by hundreds of miles of sea. West Malaysia occupies the Southern third of the Malay Peninsula. East Malaysia, along with Brunei, a protectorate of Great Britain, occupies the northern strip of the island of Borneo. *Area.* 128,430 square miles, with 39.7 percent in West Malaysia, 37.5 percent in Sarawak, and 22.8 percent in Sabah. *Topography.* Coastal strips, relatively narrow in East Malaysia and on east coast of West Malaysia, with mountainous interiors. Forests and plantations cover about 90 percent of the land area.

4. CLIMATE: Humid and tropical, marked by wet and hot winter and summer monsoons. Average rainfall is just over 100 inches in West Malaysia and 150 inches in East Malaysia. Daily temperatures vary between 70°F. and 90°F. in coastal areas and between 55°F. and 80°F. in mountain regions.

5. LANGUAGES: Bahasa Malaysia, known in English as Malay, was adopted as the official language in 1967. The Constitution provides for the use of English as the official language in East Malaysia until 1973 and throughout the country as the language of the courts until otherwise decided. Other languages in popular use include Chinese and Tamil and tribal languages and dialects.

6. RELIGION: Official religion is Islam, with adherents representing about 44 percent of the population. About 34 to 40 percent are Buddhist, Taoist, or Confucian. Other religons are Christianity and animist cults. Fundamental belief in mysticism is prevalent.

7. EDUCATION: Literacy rate estimated at about 51 percent in West Malaysia and about 25 percent in East Malaysia at the beginning of the 1960's. During the 1960's literacy rate increased at a fairly rapid rate, but statistical measurement awaited census. Public and private schools provide primary through university education. Six years of education compulsory in West Malaysia for all those within walking distance of a school.

8. HEALTH: Infant mortality rate in 1969 estimated at about 48 per 1,000 in West Malaysia and about 43 per 1,000 in East Malaysia. Death rate in the late 1960's was about 8.1 per 1,000. Life expectancy about 58 years. Greatest causes of death were tuberculosis, pneumonia, malignant neoplasms, and degenerate heart and connected diseases. Anemia, bronchitis, and infectious and parasitic diseases also were important causes of death.

9. GOVERNMENT: Parliamentary democracy with a Supreme Head elected for a term of 5 years by and from the Conference of Rulers, a group of nine hereditary rulers. Parliamentary rule was suspended after civil unrest followed the 1969 general elections, and effective power administered by National Operations Council. Constitution provides special position for Malays.

10. JUSTICE: Constitution provides for an independent judiciary with two High Courts, one for West Malaysia and one for East Malaysia, and a Federal Court, composed of a Lord President, the two chief justices of the High Courts, and four others judges. Courts subordinate to the High Courts provided under federal law. The Lord President and judges of the Federal Court and the chief justices and judges of the High Courts appointed by the Supreme Head on the advice of the Prime Minister, after consulting the Conference of Rulers. Many matters of civil justice are under the jurisdiction of Islamic religious courts.

11. ADMINISTRATIVE DIVISION: *Civil*. Country is federation of 13 states. Eight are headed by hereditary Malay rulers, one is headed by a ruler chosen by and from local Malay chiefs, and the others are headed by federally appointed governors. Each has a chief minister, executive council, and unicameral legislative assembly. States were broken into districts, each headed by a district officer. Districts were broken into *mukims*. *Mukims* may be composed of sparsely populated tracts of land or of one or several *kampongs* (villages). *Military*. For territorial defense Malaysia is divided into five areas, each representing a numbered Malaysian Infantry Brigade (MIB).

12. ECONOMY: Major goal of government since independence has been industrialization of the economy. Cooperation with private enterprise with minimum government direct participation but increas-

ingly dynamic and direct role for government was in planning at the end of the 1960's. Agriculture provided 56 percent of the country's exports by value. The largest contribution to gross domestic product made by commercial activity (34 percent).

13. FINANCE: *Currency*. Unit is the Malaysian dollar (3.06 Malaysian dollars equal (US$1). It is issued as a nonconvertible paper unit having legal tender. Denominations in common circulation include M$1, M$10, M$50, and M$100; coins in circulation include 1 cent, 5 cents, 10 cents, 20 cents, and 50 cents. *Banks*. Bank Negara Malaysia is the central bank and head of the banking system. Since 1967 it has been the only source of currency. Credit creation controlled through regulation of bank reserve ratios. In 1968 there were 38 commercial banks.

14. EXPORTS: Principal exports are rubber, tin, saw logs, sawn timber, palm oil, and iron ore. Total value of exports in 1968 was about M$4.1 billion. Major markets were Japan, Singapore, the United States, the United Kingdom, the Soviet Union, and Australia.

15. IMPORTS: Principal imports are consumer goods and needs of export enterprises, including food, beverages, tobacco, manufactured goods, machinery, transportation equipment, and mineral fuels. Total value in 1968 was M$3.5 billion. Major sources of imports were Japan, Singapore, the United States, the United Kingdom, the Federal Republic of Germany (West Germany), and Australia.

16. INDUSTRY: Industry concentrated in the urban areas of West Malaysia and consisted mainly of processing plants and light industry. Industry contributed about M$2 billion, or 23.3 percent of the gross domestic product in 1967. Manufacturing contributed 11.1 percent; mining, 5.4 percent; construction, 4.7 percent; and public utilities, 2.1 percent. Installed electric capacity in 1967 was 694,000 kilowatts.

17. LABOR: About 2.7 million workers employed or actively seeking employment in 1967. About 50 percent of labor force engaged in agriculture. Unemployment in West Malaysia at about 8.8 percent, but labor scarcity in East Malaysia. Largest labor organization is Malaysian Trade Union Congress (MTUC), representing 36 percent of all unions and about 73 percent of all union members in West Malaysia. Total union membership in West Malaysia for 1967 was nearly 307,000.

18. COMMUNICATIONS: *Radio and Television*. Radio Malaysia has 12 radio stations in West Malaysia and four stations in East Malaysia. Nine television stations in West Malaysia, and service scheduled for East Malaysia by 1970. *Telecommunications and Postal*

Service. Operated by the government. Telephone system, with over 120,000 phones in service in the late 1960's, brought the greatest revenues. Expansion of country's microwave system in progress in 1969. Linked by Southeast Asia Commonwealth Cable (SEACOM) to Japan, United States, and United Kingdom. Contract for interaction communication satellite link signed in 1969. *Press.* Active and relatively free press. Most newspapers, periodicals, and book publishing houses privately owned.

19. RAILROADS: Government operated. About 1,300 miles of single, meter-gauge track in West Malaysia in 1969, mainly along coasts and in urban, industrial areas. One railroad in East Malaysia.

20. ROADS: Road system in West Malaysia included about 10,000 miles in late 1960s. Expansion of road system in East Malaysia scheduled to achieve total of 3,200 miles by late 1960's; 80 percent of roads in West Malaysia are paved.

21. PORTS: Principal ports are: Penang, Butterworth, Port Swettenham, Malacca, and Dungan in West Malaysia; Sandakan and Kota Kinabalu in Sabah; and Kuching and Sibut in Sarawak.

22. AIRFIELDS: Major cities of West Malaysia and many towns and administrative centers of East Malaysia are well linked by domestic and international service. Malaysia-Singapore Airlines (MSA) owned jointly by governments of Brunei, Malaysia, and Singapore. Subang International Airport serves capital and offers facilities for jet traffic.

23. INTERNATIONAL AGREEMENTS, MEMBERSHIPS, AND TREATIES: Member of United Nations and its specialized agencies; ASEAN (Association of Southeast Asian Nations); ASPAC (Asian and Pacific Council); the Colombo Plan; and the Asian Development Bank.

24. AID PROGRAMS: Not a major recipient of aid. Technical assistance under Colombo Plan. FAO (Food and Agriculture Organization), IBRD (International Bank for Reconstruction and Development), IFC (International Finance Corporation), and ADB (Asian Development Bank) were institutional sources of aid. Commonwealth countries also have furnished assistance.

25. ARMED FORCES: Regular military establishment has three separate and coequal components, with a total manned strength of less than 40,000. Includes land, air, and sea forces. Reserve groups and several quasi-military police forces also maintained.

MALAYSIA

TABLE OF CONTENTS

SECTION   IV. NATIONAL SECURITY

LIST OF ILLUSTRATIONS

LIST OF TABLES

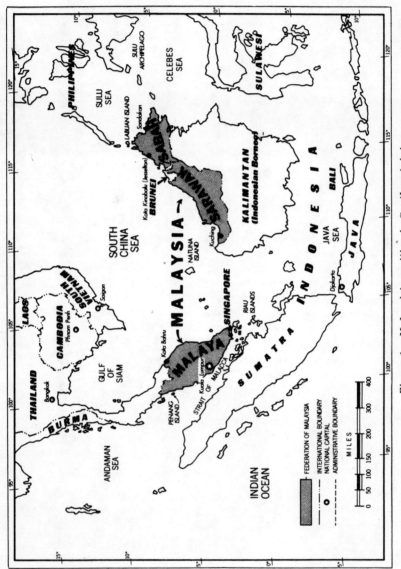

Figure 1. Malaysia's position in Southeast Asia.

SECTION I. SOCIAL

CHAPTER 1

GENERAL CHARACTER OF THE SOCIETY

Nation-building has been the preoccupation of the country's leaders since 1963 when the new political entity of Malaysia was created out of a group of former British dependencies, with the Federation of Malaya, which already had become an independent state in 1957, as the nucleus. This nation-building process has proved to be an exceptionally difficult one because of the plural nature of Malaysian society and the disparate historical, economic, and political backgrounds of the country's major components. The difficulties have been compounded by several years of armed hostility emanating from Indonesia on the south, by the separation of Singapore within 2 years of Malaysia's founding, and the unremitting subversion of a minority of Chinese abetted by the Communist regime on the China mainland.

The establishment of an independent Singapore with its predominantly Chinese population created serious political problems for the country, since it disturbed an already shaky political balance that had been established mainly along ethnic-religious lines. The separation left the Malays with a substantial plurality in the country as a whole while Chinese political power declined. After the separation it was officially estimated that the Chinese, Indian, and Pakistani components of the population were about equal in combined numbers to the Malay population, while other indigeneous and aboriginal groups made up less than 10 percent of the national total.

In late 1969 Malaysia had not yet had a census. Precise delineation of ethnic groups was not possible, so that the proportions of the various elements of the population could only be estimated. There was no doubt, however, that ethnic divisions formed the chief basis for the sharp political schisms that led to severe violence in 1969 and that offered potential for further explosive reactions in the future.

Because of Malaysia's strategic position in Asia, lack of internal political stability has been a matter of considerable concern to its neighbors, such as Singapore and Indonesia, and to such Western

1

allies as Australia and New Zealand. Meanwhile, the government has followed an independent course externally, limiting its political alignments to membership in the British Commonwealth and to regional association with its Asian neighbors. At the same time the government, despite its insistence upon a neutral status, has maintained determined hostility toward communism. Controversy with the Philippines over the latter's claim to Sabah, part of East Malaysia, has been a complicating factor in regional relationships.

Malaysian national society and political values have been created only by welding together groups not naturally homogeneous. Cultural and religious infiltration, immigration for economic reasons, foreign economic and commercial exploitation, colonial policy, and the will for independence have interreacted.

Unlike some former colonial dependencies, Malaysia won independence without violent revolution, and the peaceful departure of former colonial masters has left a political attitude different from that which some other colonies have inherited. Instead, antagonism to communism and the identification of communism with the Chinese have become more of a preoccupation, which has added to the dangerous divisions that exist between the Malays and the Chinese.

The country is divided into two major segments. The lower third of the Malay Peninsula, which divides the South China Sea from the Andaman Sea, a part of the Indian Ocean, is West Malaysia; the states of Sarawak and Sabah, forming a strip along the northern rim of Borneo, comprise the second segment, East Malaysia. Within the Borneo segment are two small enclaves forming the sultanate of Brunei, a British-protected state.

Slightly more than 10 million people were officially estimated in 1969 to inhabit the two major Malaysian segments, most of them along the coasts of the Peninsula and the rim of the island of Borneo. Both geographic areas are the product of Britain's voluntary divestiture of empire, which was stimulated in Malaysia by strong political sentiment favoring independence. Separation of Singapore after Malaysia's formation left the country with 13 states, of which eight were hereditary Malay sultanates (Johore, Kedah, Kelantan, Pahang, Perak, Perlis, Selangor and Tregganu), one elected royal head of state (Negri Sembilan), two former members of the British Straits Settlements (Malacca and Penang), and the two former British crown colonies of Sabah (formerly British North Borneo) and Sarawak.

For hundreds of years, particularly before the discovery of the Western Hemisphere by Europeans, the Strait of Malacca formed a corridor between India and the Pacific, between the Arab countries

2

and the East, and between Europe and the spice-growing lands of the Orient. Malaysia still dominates the trade routes and the straits connecting these regions. The Malay Peninsula also formed a land connection from the straits and islands to the mainland of Asia. Modern-day Malaysia has two land borders, one shared with Thailand in the north and the other with Indonesia on Borneo. In addition, some of Malaysia's islands and those of the Philippines and Indonesia are located within sight of one another.

Because of its geographic position, the Malay Peninsula was exposed to successive waves of Hindu, Islamic, and European cultures. Malays adapted each of these to their own underlying Malay and aboriginal society. European influence included first Portuguese, then Dutch, and finally British. The British influence has left a marked imprint on the modern social order through, among other contributions, legal institutions, language, and the development of a modern civil service system. The country was subjected also to waves of Chinese and Indian immigration. While Islam retained its Malay following, the Chinese brought Buddhist, Taoist, and Confucian beliefs. Thus many social systems exist side by side. For example, some affairs are regulated by customary law, some by Islamic law, and some by Western-style jurisprudence.

In general, Malaysian society is rural and agricultural, with the Chinese tending to concentrate in urban centers and Malays favoring rural settlements, fishing villages, and smallholder agricultural production. Much rubber estate labor has been drawn from the Indian immigrants, while tin mining and certain other industries as well as retail trade have attracted immigrants from China. With new emphasis on industrialization since independence there is a greater trend to urbanization, with marked changes in social patterns generally.

The architects of Malaysia realized that it would take much time and great effort to harmonize their country's ethnic and cultural diversities. They knew that the development of multiracial nationalism embracing the entire country would encounter difficulties in the ethnically heterogeneous components, especially between the Malays and Malay-related groups, which consider themselves "indigenous," and the Chinese, Indians, and Pakistanis, whom the Malays consider "immigrants."

The Malays have in common their language, their religion, and a basic Indonesian-Malay culture seen in the nature of village life and individual characteristics. Many of their actions and relationships are defined by *adat*, the customary law or "way of doing things" that combines Islamic law with ancient Malay custom and Hindu elements. For the Malays work is a means of living, not a way of life, and accumulation of wealth is a goal neither for its own sake nor for prestige. Cooperation is more highly valued than is competition.

The distinction conferred by noble birth is basic in Malay society. Within the aristocracy, birth determines rank in the social hierarchy, and the sultan of the state is the head of both the government and the religious structure. Royalty and members of the aristocracy are his advisers, and this relationship is reflected throughout Malay society in the prestige attached to government service.

The life of the Chinese presents a series of contrasts to that of the Malays. The proportion of Chinese in Malaysia is greater than it is in any country outside of China. The Chinese have relatively few roots in Malaysia's older past. Their primary ties are to the family and secondly to associations based on dialect and geographic origin in China or on business interests. They retain their own language and sponsor their own cultural activities. Work and profit are virtues of the highest order, and material accumulation and display represent the primary means of fulfilling one's obligation to ancestors and of achieving personal and family prestige.

The Indians and Pakistanis live primarily within the communities of estate workers in West Malaysia, although some work as laborers, clerks, and merchants in the cities. Like the Chinese, they tend to keep to themselves, although they have made some inroads into Malaysian life through the labor movement in which they predominate. Most, however, use their own languages, preserve their Hindu, Sikh, or Islamic religion and traditions, and join organizations to promote ethnic interests and social life.

The indigenous people of non-Malay origin in West Malaysia continue their isolated life and perpetuate their own characteristic culture. The indigenous communities of East Malaysia find it difficult to adjust to the comparatively more complex society of Malaysia as a nation. They lack a single primary language, and local dialect differences divide even those communities that otherwise share a common tradition. Some of the indigenous people profess Islam and some have adopted Christianity, but the majority still hold to animistic beliefs and practices.

Political control and offices of the federal government remained in the hands of Malays on the eve of 1970. Under the 1957 Constitution of the Federation of Malaya, which was extended to cover Malaysia in 1963, the form of government remained a constitutional monarchy, in which the offices of the Supreme Head of the nation (Yang di-Pertuan Agong), the Deputy Supreme Head (Timbalan Yang di-Pertuan Agong), and the prime minister were open to

4

Muslim Malays only. The structure of the Federal Parliament further favored membership of the Malays.

Although the component states retained their own constitutions and governments, the federal government assumed many responsibilities beyond handling the national matters of internal and external security. Also, as a measure to protect indigenous East Malaysians against Chinese and Malay domination, Sarawak and Sabah retained autonomy regarding immigration and land tenure affairs.

Malaysia's per capita income and foreign reserve position were among the highest in Southeast Asia in late 1969, but the distribution of wealth was uneven. The Chinese dominate the modern economy. They supply much of the capital and nearly all of the labor in tin mining. With Europeans, they own and manage the rubber estates, handle most of the overseas trade, and nearly monopolize internal commerce. At the lower end of the scale are indigenous small farmers and fishermen, and even further removed are nomadic hunters and food gatherers of the hinterland.

The federal government has made significant attempts to establish Malay as the official national language and to promote a unified school system as the prerequisite for a stronger national solidarity. Because English-language education in the past proved to be a strong unifying force, it was hoped that Malay education would function in the same manner but, particularly as it affects the Chinese, it has become highly controversial. In the sphere of economics the First Malaysia Plan for 1966 to 1970 is intended to promote equalization of economic differences through the strategic allocation of funds.

Mutual distrust and suspicion, which provoked postelection riots leading to imposition of martial law and rule through an emergency body with extraordinary powers, continued to smolder in late 1969. The leadership, which blamed much of the unrest on communism, had as its major task the development of unity—a unity that the government acknowledged was still incomplete by year's end.

CHAPTER 2

PHYSICAL ENVIRONMENT AND POPULATION

Malaysia is divided into two main segments on either side of the southernmost portion of the South China Sea (see fig. 1). One of these is West Malaysia, which occupies the southern one-third of the Malay Peninsula. The Peninsula juts southward from the mainland of Asia almost to Sumatra, thus separating the South China Sea and the Gulf of Siam from the Andaman Sea and the Indian Ocean. It thereby dominates the main East-West trade routes passing through the Pacific Ocean.

The other major segment of the country, separated by some hundreds of miles of sea, is made up of the two contiguous states of Sabah (formerly British North Borneo) and Sarawak. These states occupy a continuous strip across the northern portion of the island of Borneo, although there are two small enclaves within Sarawak that constitute Brunei, a protected state of Great Britain.

This physical location shaped the country's history, economy, religion, and social makeup for hundreds of years as it was alternately courted, fought over, exploited, and governed by a succession of European and Asian powers (see ch. 3, Historical Setting). The country's geographical location also has thrust upon the young nation a key role in affairs of modern Asia.

Both geographic segments of the country are characterized by sparse population and vast stretches of uninhabited jungle, much of which has not yet been explored. Towering mountains, lush green forests, white beaches, majestic palms, and rushing rivers combine to create great scenic beauty. Although some coastal areas consist of swamplands, in 1968 it was estimated that about 70 percent of the land area was covered with dense tropical forests.

The total area of the country has been calculated by the government to be 128,430 square miles, with 48,342 in Sarawak and 29,388 in Sabah. There never has been a complete census for all of the country, but the 1967–68 estimates of the government and of the United Nations placed the population at 10,331,000, of which 8,840,000 were in West Malaysia and about 1,491,000 in East Malaysia. The annual rate of increase has been estimated variously at from 3 to 3.5 percent annually, one of the world's highest.

Population density has been estimated at 158 persons per square mile in West Malaysia, which contains an estimated 85 percent of the population within 40 percent of the nation's land area, but only 18 persons per square mile in Sabah and 17 in Sarawak. These figures are somewhat deceptive, however, since the people are concentrated in a few particularly favorable locations, and there the density is much higher. For example, the west coast of the Malay Peninsula is more developed than the east coast because the Strait of Malacca is sheltered and, consequently, has better sea communications. Much of the population lives on the coasts, which extend for 3,000 miles in West Malaysia. In 1969 the government was planning for the first national census to be taken in 1970.

Located just above the equator, the country has a hot and humid tropical climate characteristic of the monsoon belt. Temperatures are generally uniform from place to place and season to season with a mean of 81°F. Rainfall is abundant, with wide local variations.

Malaysia has an abundance of valuable natural resources, most of which exist as potential rather than as producing assets. The largest foreign exchange earners in 1968 were rubber, tin, lumber, and oil palm (see ch. 22, Foreign Economic Relations). Although a few oil wells have been developed in northern Sarawak, their output has not yet reached major proportions. The presence of rich oil-producing fields in Brunei has resulted in expectations that new deposits might be located in areas of Sarawak not yet fully explored.

THE LAND

West Malaysia

The Malay Peninsula is the long, narrow backbone of a range of mountains extending southward from Thailand and Burma. West Malaysia occupies its southern portion and is connected to Singapore at its southern tip by a manmade causeway. West Malaysia has but one land boundary—that in the north abutting Thailand. It is bounded on the east by the South China Sea and on the south and west by the narrow Strait of Malacca, which separates it from the Indonesian island of Sumatra.

West Malaysia, roughly oval in shape, measures approximately 480 miles in its longest north-south dimension and some 200 miles at its widest east-west axis, with a total area of 50,700 square miles. Its land boundary with Thailand is 314 miles long. Penang, a few miles off the northwestern mainland, is an economically important island, whose harbor of George Town is a busy trading port. Other islands are significant because of their scenic beauty and their value as bases for fishing craft.

The mountain chain that forms the backbone of the Malay Peninsula continues southward from Thailand through Malaya for about 300 miles. Its highest peak is Gunong Korbu (Buffalo Mountain), in the State of Perak, rising to a height of 7,160 feet. The range, about 30 to 40 miles wide, divides West Malaysia into two unequal parts— the larger to the east of the range and the smaller and more populous, constituting the west coastal area of settlement, to the west of it. A long spur, the Bintang Range, divides the valley of the Perak River from the basin of the Muda River. The foothills on both sides of the mountain range are characterized by numerous rugged hills of limestone, almost all of which, especially in the north, contain caves.

East of the main range, and separated from it by valleys, is a secondary mountain highland along the boundary between the states of Kelantan and Trengganu (see fig. 2). Generally lower than the main range, it nevertheless contains the highest elevation in West Malaysia, Gunong Tahan (7,186 feet), on the boundary between the states of Pahang and Kelantan.

Seaward from the mountains, in the west, south, and east, are the coastal lowlands. The most significant of these, from the point of view of continuity, ease of communications and, hence, number of inhabitants, is on the west coast. It varies in width from roughly 10 to 50 miles and is generally level to rolling. Few hills attain an elevation of more than 500 feet; slopes increase abruptly on nearing the mountains. The east-coast lowland is more irregular, less densely populated, and less important from the point of view of productivity and commerce. In the north this plain is some 40 miles in width and then tapers to no more than 5 miles as the east-coast range approaches the sea; farther south it becomes wider again, but swamps and lagoons extending as much as 20 miles inland reduce the importance of the area from the point of view of settlement and economic usefulness. There is also a plain dotted with low hills at the foot of the southern end of the main range, embracing western Pahang State and interior parts of Negri Sembilan and Johore states.

Before the Europeans built highways and railroads in Malaya, the many rivers were the only arteries to the interior and had a profound influence on the pattern of settlement. Settlement of the inland areas, not only by Malays but also by the early Chinese immigrants, generally proceeded from the sea up the rivers (see ch. 3, Historical Setting).

The Pahang River, which extends for about 285 miles, is West Malaysia's longest river. Like several of the other large streams, it is known by various names in different parts of its course. The Perak

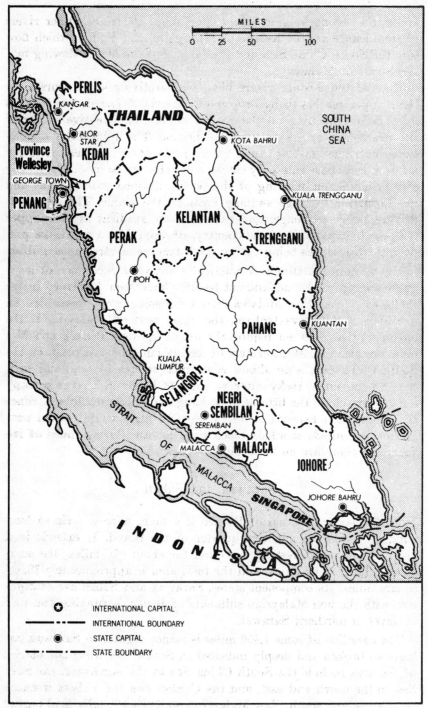

MILES

0   25   50   100

PERLIS
KANGAR

THAILAND

SOUTH
CHINA
SEA

KEDAH
ALOR
STAR

KOTA BAHRU

Province
Wellesley

GEORGE TOWN

PENANG

KUALA TRENGGANU

KELANTAN

PERAK

TRENGGANU

IPOH

PAHANG

KUANTAN

KUALA
LUMPUR

SELANGOR

NEGRI
SEMBILAN

STRAIT

SEREMBAN

OF

MALACCA

MALACCA

MALACCA

JOHORE

SINGAPORE

JOHORE BAHRU

I N D O N E S I A

⊛ INTERNATIONAL CAPITAL
——— INTERNATIONAL BOUNDARY
⊙ STATE CAPITAL
—·—·— STATE BOUNDARY

Figure 2. Administrative divisions of West Malaysia, 1969

River, the second longest, extends for about 200 miles. Other rivers of significance are the Kelantan, Trengganu, and Endau, which flow into the South China Sea, and the Muar and the Muda, flowing into the Strait of Malacca.

Most of the western rivers have comparatively short courses. In their upper reaches many drop more than 4,000 feet in less than 15 miles before reaching the flat coastal plain. The extensive silting of the riverbeds near the sea limits navigation. The light Malay double-ended outrigger sailing canoe (*prahu*) can enter some estuaries for a few miles; above this, only canoes and rafts can be used. The silting also brings about flooding of the poorly drained coastal areas and the formation of large swampy areas on the plains. The eastward-flowing rivers are longer and have a flatter gradient in their upper reaches. In nearly all of the country, draining has a trellislike pattern, the hill slopes being cut by small transverse streams or gullies.

The western coastline is a practically unbroken succession of mangrove swamps and mudflats, but harbors have been developed in the sheltered areas. The Malacca Strait in some ways resembles an inland sea. Port Swettenham, the chief port of Malaysia, is the only port that does not require the use of lighters. Penang and Malacca are also important centers of navigation. The east coast, on the South China Sea, is an almost continuous stretch of sand and surf, with an occasional rocky outcrop; there is, however, a large swampy coastal stretch on the littoral of Pahang and northeast Johore. Since the east coast is exposed to heavy seas and high winds, coastal navigation is limited; sandbars block river mouths during much of the year, and there are no important harbors.

Sarawak and Sabah

The Malaysian section of Borneo is a long, narrow strip of land running across the northern quarter of the island. It extends in a northeasterly-southwesterly direction for about 670 miles; the maximum width is 160 miles; and the total area is approximately 78,000 square miles. Its component states, Sarawak and Sabah are contiguous, with the non-Malaysian sultanate of Brunei occupying two tiny enclaves in northern Sarawak.

The coastline of some 1,400 miles is rather regular in Sarawak but becomes broken and deeply indented in Sabah. Maritime boundaries of the area include the South China Sea to the northwest, the Sulu Sea to the north and east, and the Celebes Sea for a short distance on the east and south. East Malaysia also has a 900-mile land border with Kalimantan (Indonesian Borneo), which occupies the rest of the island. Because of the wild, rugged, and unexplored country through which it passes, the actual border has never been surveyed, and the area is constantly under cloud cover so that even aerial photography has not succeeded in determining a definite line. Indigenous peoples of the area are unaware of any boundary and move freely from one region to another (see fig. 3).

The Sarawak portion of the border is defined by the watershed differentiating rivers that flow west and northwest to the South China Sea from those that flow south or east to the Java and Celebes seas. The Sabah portion is less naturally marked but follows a line running due west from a point just south of Tawau in Sabah until it intersects the Sarawak line.

Topographically, Sarawak slopes upward, southeastward from the sea, across a flat coastal plain, and through a narrow belt of undulating hills, before rising sharply and abruptly to the mountainous mass that crests at the border with Kalimantan. The mountainous interior is not well defined as to height or form. It is, rather, an area of irregular masses of dissected highlands; of practically unexplored ravines, gorges, and plateaus; and of involved, unconnected ranges with a mean elevation of about 5,000 feet. Occasionally, peaks rise above the normal terrain level to altitudes of over 7,000 feet. Mount Murud, for example, near the junction of Sarawak, Sabah, and Kalimantan, is the state's loftiest at 7,950 feet.

From this rugged and forbidding interior the land drops steeply to a belt of undulating hills that runs the full length of Sarawak. The hills themselves are usually less than 1,000 feet above sea level but are broken by a few mountain groups of about 2,500 feet, some of which extend to the coast and terminate in sea-formed cliffs. The most prominent of those that reach the coast in Sarawak are the Santubong Mountains, which jut into the sea just north of the capital city of Kuching. The presence of these short ranges lends a character to the region not apparent in its designation as a belt of low, undulating hills. Actually, the terrain is very rugged, with steep hills and narrow valleys or gorges where the rivers have cut through in sharply descending rapids.

The coastal region is a flat alluvial plain only a few feet above sea level. Typically 20 to 40 miles wide, its width varies from less than a mile at Miri in the north to over 100 miles at some points farther south. It consists mainly of swampland and alluvial deposits of soft mud or a deep and extensive mantle of peat. The soil is unsuitable for agriculture because of the poor drainage of the peat swamps and also because about a third of its area is subject to regular salt-water tidal or fresh-water river flooding. Some moderately productive wet paddy land can be found on the banks of river deltas.

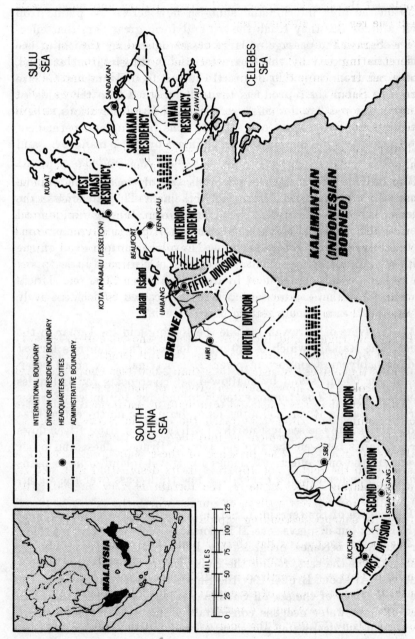

Figure 3. *Administrative divisions and boundaries of East Malaysia, 1969.*

INTERNATIONAL BOUNDARY
DIVISION OR RESIDENCY BOUNDARY
HEADQUARTERS CITIES
ADMINISTRATIVE BOUNDARY

SULU
SEA

CELEBES
SEA

SANDAKAN

SANDAKAN
RESIDENCY

TAWAU
RESIDENCY

TAWAU

SABAH

KUDAT

WEST
COAST
RESIDENCY

KENINGAU

INTERIOR
RESIDENCY

BEAUFORT

KOTA KINABALU (JESSELTON)

KALIMANTAN
(INDONESIAN
BORNEO)

Labuan Island

LIMBANG

FIFTH DIVISION

BRUNEI

MIRI

FOURTH DIVISION

SARAWAK

THIRD DIVISION

SIBU

SECOND DIVISION

SIMANGGANG

FIRST DIVISION

KUCHING

SOUTH
CHINA
SEA

MALAYSIA

MILES

0   25   50   75   100   125

13

The South China Sea off Sarawak is extremely shallow and, coupled with the regular coastline, affords no significant harbors. Moreover, the rivers, heavily laden with silt from their precipitous drop off the high interior and sluggish flow across the plain, drop their alluvium as they reach the sea and form great bars that effectively obstruct the passage of large vessels upstream. Typical of the difficulties imposed by this characteristic is the situation at Miri, where refineries cannot load directly into seabound tankers but are forced to pump their products through pipelines into the holds of vessels anchored 3 miles offshore. Higher coastal elevations, where the hills extend to the sea, can support some farming and permanent settlements, but the muddy beaches fringed by thick mangroves and nipa palm swamps discourage economic activity elsewhere.

The rivers of Sarawak are numerous and of considerable volume because of the abundance of rainfall in the area. They all arise in the interior and descend through deep gorges over foaming rapids until they reach the flat coastal plain, where they change character completely and meander gently to the sea. Despite the rapid drop off the heights there are no spectacular waterfalls, and there is little opportunity for the development of hydroelectric power. The one significant waterfall that has been discovered was located by accident early in the 1960's in a remote section of the north.

Major rivers of Sarawak include the Rajang and the Lupar in the south. The Rajang, which is 350 miles long, is the country's largest and probably most important river. It is navigable by small ocean vessels for 60 miles and by shallow-draft river boats for 150 miles from its mouth. The Lupar extends inland for 142 miles. Farther north the Baram River, 250 miles long, drains the north-central area and empties into the sea just north of Miri; the Limbang River flows for 122 miles between the two enclaves of Brunei. These and other rivers are the only effective avenues for travel inland. Jungle paths connect their headwaters, but only a few trails pass over the watershed into Kalimantan.

The nature of the terrain in Sabah is superficially similar to that of Sarawak but displays several important differences. The coastline, for example, becomes progressively more irregular from west to east until, in the east, facing the Sulu Sea, it is boldly and deeply indented. At about Brunei Bay the Sunda Shelf, which accounts for the shallowness of the sea off Sarawak, reaches its northern limit so that offshore water deepens considerably, and eastern Sabah offers many excellent deepwater ports and anchorages. On the South China Sea, Labuan Island, 35 miles from the mainland entrance at Brunei Bay, has a fine sheltered harbor that is the major terminus for seaborne traffic destined for Sarawak and Brunei as well as Sabah.

The mountains of Sabah also have significant differences from those of Sarawak. The interior mass, particularly where it borders Kalimantan, is the same complex arrangement of highly dissected ranges and occasional peaks reaching altitudes of over 7,000 feet, but the ranges lie much closer to the sea and tend to become more orderly. The coastal plain in the west along the South China Sea reaches inland only 10 to 20 miles and then gives way abruptly to the only truly continuous range in Malaysian Borneo. This backbone, known as the Crocker Range, is really the southwestward extension of the same chain that created the Philippine Islands. It averages somewhat higher than elevations in Sarawak, particularly in its northern reaches, where spectacular Mount Kinabalu (13,455 feet) towers over everything else in the country. No other peak in Sabah reaches 8,000 feet.

East of the Crocker Range, a series of parallel but lower ranges extend from the elevated interior core to the Sulu Sea. Each of these ranges is separated by a wide valley into the lower reaches of which the sea has flowed, creating the long, deep bays of the east coast. The ridges themselves continue on as a series of peninsulas, including Kudat and Benkoka, which enclose Maruda Bay in the extreme north, and the Sandakan, Dent, and Simporna extensions, which define Labuk, Sandakan, Darvel, and Cowie bays in the east.

Like Sarawak, Sabah is drained by a fine system of rivers. Those in the west, with one exception, empty into the South China Sea and are relatively short because the mountains are so near the coast. The exception is the Padas River, which has cut a deep gorge through the Crocker Range and drains a large section of interior lowland. All western rivers carry heavy loads of silt that are deposited on the narrow coastal plain to form many areas of good agricultural land. The other rivers of Sabah drain into the Sulu or Celebes seas. The 350-mile-long Kinabatangan is the largest and the most significant river of Sabah. Rising in the southern part of the Crocker Range, it flows generally east-west through the middle of Sabah until it empties into Sandakan Bay. It can be used by launches for about 120 miles from the coast to reach the rich plantations and forest valleys through which it flows. The Sugut, Labuk, and Segama rivers are also important routes by which native craft gain access to the agricultural products of their valleys and the timber resources of the interior.

CLIMATE AND VEGETATION

Both segments of Malaysia lie in the same latitudes, are subject to the same movement of airmasses, and have almost identical climates. Some local variations in temperature and rainfall are evident because of elevation or proximity to the sea, but both are tropical and have heavy rainfall, oppressive humidity, and year-round uniformity of temperature. Sarawak and Sabah are slightly wetter and hotter than the continental segment, but the differences are minor.

The year is divided into two seasonal monsoon periods, corresponding to winter and summer in more northerly latitudes. Both monsoons are wet and hot, and the major difference between them is the direction from which the rains arrive. The more robust period is that of the northeast monsoon, which prevails from the beginning of October until the end of February. Its strong, regular winds sweep southward at a rapid pace until they reach about 5° latitude, where they become stalled, or even retreat slightly, so that the rains that accompany them often persist for days. The southwest monsoon blows from mid-April to about mid-October and is slightly milder but less predictable. It is a period of sudden squalls and thunderstorms of great intensity that in Sabah have been known to raise rivers as much as 50 feet above normal level in a few hours.

Total annual rainfall varies somewhat between the two segments, as does the relative amount occurring in each monsoon. The annual mean rainfall in West Malaysia is just over 100 inches, with precipitation primarily during the southwest monsoon; in East Malaysia the annual mean is about 150 inches, the major portion of which is received during the northeast monsoon. Within the two segments some variations can also be noted. On the Peninsula local averages range from 64 inches a year at Jelebu in the State of Negri Sembilan to over 200 inches in the Larut Hills near Taiping in the State of Perak. Whereas the west coast is wettest during the southwest monsoon, the higher elevations of the interior receive most of their rainfall during the short, 8-week transition period between monsoons. Within Sarawak and Sabah, climatological stations at Kuching and Sibu reported a difference of over 53 inches in areas that are only 100 miles apart. Farther north, at Long Akah, in the mountains of the upper Baram River, an annual mean rainfall of 236 inches makes it the wettest place in Malaysia.

Temperatures in Malaysia's two segments also show remarkable similarity, varying between 70°F. and 90°F. in the coastal areas and ranging from 55°F. to 80°F. in the mountains. Rarely do they rise above 95°F. or drop below 68°F. anywhere, although an absolute maximum of 97°F. was recorded at Sibu in Sarawak during May 1962. Absolute minimum temperatures are unknown, since coldest spots are found in remote mountain heights where weather readings are not taken. In all areas and at all times of the year, humidity remains extremely high both day and night.

16

Under the favorable influence of its hot, humid climate, Malaysia is a land of lush and verdant plant life. Woody varieties constitute most of the growth, but lianas, ferns, low shrubs, flowering bushes, and countless epiphytic plants abound in all areas. Cleared land exists only in major settlement areas along the coast or on the banks of rivers for varying distances inland. Much of the land that has been cleared has been replaced by palm and rubber tree plantations so that, if these regions are added to those naturally covered, the total forested area reaches about 90 percent of total land area.

The type of vegetation in the forests is as varied as it is extensive. Along the coastal areas mangrove and nipa palms are dominant. In the hill country the true tropical rain forest is found. Above 4,000 feet smaller trees and much vegetation of the tropical shrub type take over, giving way at 5,000 feet to the moss forests, so called because mosses and liverworts form a cover over other, more dwarfed vegetation. Although elevated, the moss forests, like those at lower altitudes, are dank, and the ground underfoot is constantly moist and dripping. Above the moss forests is a rich growth of mountain grasses and shrubs.

All wild forests are commonly referred to as "jungle," a term that is not entirely accurate. The mangrove and nipa areas are really swamp forests, which are treacherous underfoot and almost impenetrable. The major portion of the rain forest is characterized by towering, bare-trunked trees, usually hardwoods. Most of the trees are about 100 feet high, forming their canopies from about 70 feet upward, through which occasional giants rise as high as 200 feet. Trees are so close and the canopy is so dense that the floor of the forest is in perpetual shade, and only a thinly scattered undergrowth of flowers and low shrubs can exist. In other areas of the rain forest, where the soil was derived from underlying strata of limestone, the trees are less tall; the canopy is more open; and the undergrowth is so luxuriant that a true jungle exists.

Throughout the rain forest almost every tree supports some other form of plant that is not parasitic but lives on, rather than off of, its host. Hundreds of species of orchids, ranging from brilliant single blossoms with six-inch leaves to others that grow in clusters on spikes three feet long, have been cataloged. Thousands of types of ferns, mosses, gingers, and climbing vines cling to the trees. Even the broad-leaved banana tree often follows the trunk of a taller tree in an upward search for light. One of the more interesting forest growths is the pitcher plant, some varieties of which often reach 16 inches across. Brightly patterned, the pitcher, or body of the plant, secretes a sugary substance at its lip. Attracted by the color and sweetness, insects coming to feed tumble down the slippery inside of the pitcher and are trapped, drowned, and finally devoured in a digestive fluid that fills the bottom.

In addition to the exotic forms of plant life, Malaysia's forests contain vast stands of valuable hardwoods and other useful products that represent an asset of major importance to the national economy. A lack of transport and extractive and processing facilities, however, has severely limited their development, and only a fraction of their value is exploited. Forest potential, moreover, has been subject to constant erosion by demands for more cleared land to accommodate the constantly increasing population, by the felling of timber for quick profit, and by the destructive migratory farming practices of many areas.

MINERAL RESOURCES

A great variety of minerals is known to exist in Malaysia. Tin in West Malaysia and to a lesser extent oil in Sarawak most significantly affect the economy of the country. The tin deposits of Malaysia are among the world's richest and most extensive (see ch. 19, Industry). Other mineral resources in West Malaysia include sizable quantities of iron ore from hematite deposits in Perak, Trengganu, and Johore; a poor grade of coal useful only for local heating; a little gold from Pahang; minor quantities of tungsten from Kedah and Trengganu; and a promising and developing output of bauxite from Johore. Of less commercial importance are minor quantities of china clay, monazite, pebble corundum, and copper sulfide.

At one time northern Borneo was thought to be an area rich in mineral deposits, probably because gold was found in southern Sarawak as long ago as the 18th century. Dreams of a bountiful El Dorado, however, never materialized. Gold was significant in the last half of the 19th century but has been declining most of the time since then.

Antimony, mercury, and coal also had brief periods of importance before the turn of the century but, except for coal, were reduced to virtual insignificance within a few years. Oil in fairly good quantities is derived from wells at Miri in northern Sarawak. The first well began to produce in 1916, and by 1930 the oilfield was producing over 50 million barrels a day. Production was interrupted by World War II and has never fully recovered.

Other minerals found in Malaysian Borneo, all of which are minor in value or occurrence, include antimony, bauxite, dolomite, iron ore, mercury, nickel, copper, cobalt sulfide, zinc, gypsum, and talc. Extremely small quantities of diamonds, sapphires, and silver have been found.

WILD ANIMAL LIFE

The dense, virtually uninhabited forests of Malaysia teem with wildlife. Many species are common to both segments of the country; others can be found in only one. Nearly all are protected by game and wildlife laws in an effort to preserve many of the species from extinction through the depredations of hunters commissioned to collect specimens for zoos or of local residents who kill them for food.

Among the big game of West Malaysia are wild elephants, often a destructive nuisance to farmers, and the large Malayan tiger that often preys on plantation workers. West Malaysia is noted for a large variety of deer, among them the cow-sized sambhur deer, or rusa, and the magnificent seladang (wild ox). West Malaysia's forests also contain tapir and wild cattle; wild pigs are common and are avidly hunted as a source of meat.

Many kinds of monkeys, small wildcats, civet cats, tarsiers, huge pythons, and an uncounted number of brightly plumaged birds also abound. In the reptile category many crocodiles, lizards (including the monitor), and poisonous snakes are common to the forest and swamp areas. Among the snakes the king cobra, or hamadryad, is among the most deadly. It often reaches a length of 15 feet and is one of the few snakes in the world that will launch an unprovoked attack on human beings.

The variety of wildlife in East Malaysia is even greater than on the mainland. Elephants are found only in Sabah. The seladang, sambhur deer, wild cattle, wild pigs, tarsiers, civet cats, snakes (including the python and the king cobra), crocodiles, lizards, and thousands of varieties of birds are native to Sarawak, and several animals are unique to it.

The mangrove swamp forests of Sarawak are the habitat of the unique proboscis monkey. Extremely delicate and shy, it avoids human beings and is one of the few animals in the area that is thriving and increasing. The contrary is true of Sarawak's noisy gibbon ape, which is fast disappearing as the natives hunt it for food.

The rhinoceros is fast disappearing, and there are fewer than 1,000 still at large because of the persistent, although illegal, hunting carried out by the Dayak tribesmen. Perhaps the most famous of Sarawak's animals is the once-numerous orangutan. Because they are so widely sought as zoo attractions, orangutans have been decimated in recent years and now survive mainly in Sumatra and Sarawak. Strict protection is afforded the orangutan, but authorities estimate that there are less than 500 left in Malaysian Borneo.

The only dangerous land animal in Malaysian Borneo is the honey bear. It is a great favorite as a pet when young, but becomes ferocious at maturity and will attack and claw the unwary when angry or aroused.

One of the largest and most varied bird populations in the world is found in northern Borneo. Among them are hornbills, parrots, broadbills, the sweet-voiced bulbul, 10 kinds of pigeons, 20 kinds of woodpeckers, and many other species. Most dramatic are the millions of bats and swifts that inhabit the limestone caves of the hill country. One cave alone, that at Niah in Sarawak, is said to house 1 million bats and 4 million swifts. These birds are a lucrative source of income. The nests of the swifts, made of saliva from special glands, are highly prized through the Orient as the basic ingredient of bird's nest soup. The droppings of both the swifts and the bats have covered the floor of their caves with a deep layer of guano, unexcelled as a fertilizer.

Apart from a few species of dugong, which inhabit an area off the extreme southern tip of Sarawak, and several varieties of the common dolphin, which live in the muddy estuaries of river mouths, marine life is not well cataloged. Most renowned of Malaysia's sea life is the big green turtle, which is used in making soup. Nowhere else in the world do these turtles appear in such quantities. They lay their eggs on three small islands off Sarawak and then disappear for several years at a time. A large program of tagging these strange beasts is under way in an effort to learn more about their habits. The tag from one was discovered on a beach near Vancouver, Canada, but there has been no explanation for their mysterious disappearances.

POPULATION

Available population figures are imprecise in the absence of a census. They have been calculated at different times and on different and incompatible bases. The latest census for West Malaysia was taken in 1957; one for Sarawak was conducted in 1960, and one for Sabah, in 1965. On the bases of these censuses and estimated annual population growth rates, the total population of Malaysia was calculated most recently in 1968 as more than 10.3 million.

Concentration

The people are concentrated in areas that were developed under the impetus of the colonial economy. Settlement patterns within each segment are similar in that the greatest densities are found along coastal areas and in the river valleys.

In West Malaysia about three-fourths of the people occupy the western portion, and the greatest concentration is along the western coast, where all districts (subdivisions of states and settlements) have at least 100 persons per square mile. These areas, which, with the exception of the valley of the Kinta River and the environs of Kuala Lumpur, are no more than 30 miles in width, are the sites of the most intensive mining and the most extensive rubber estates, and they have the best and most used transportation facilities.

A second important population concentration in West Malaysia exists in the ricegrowing area of the northeast, though it accounts for only about 7 percent of West Malaysia's population. In the interior, densities average less than 25 persons per square mile, but in some very small areas where economic development has taken place it may reach as high as 100.

Sarawak's population distribution also is uneven. The greater portion is concentrated in and around the three urban centers of Kuching, Sibu, and Miri; most of the rest is scattered along the coast, particularly in the south. The interior, except for a few concentrations in upstream river valleys, is virtually uninhabited.

Population concentration in Sabah is similar to that of Sarawak. People are concentrated in small urban areas of the coast, particularly in the west, and to a smaller extent in trade centers of the farming regions in interior river valleys. Away from the rivers, the interior is largely virgin forest with only an occasional cluster of indigenous tribal huts.

Ethnic Distribution

The Malaysian population is a complex mixture of ethnic groups with the bulk of the population divided among Malays, Chinese, and Indians-Pakistanis (see ch. 4, Ethnic Groups and Languages). The government estimates that in West Malaysia about 50 percent of the population is of Malay origin, about 37 percent Chinese, and 11 percent Indians and Pakistanis. Eurasians and Europeans account for most of the remainder. Unofficial sources estimate the ethnic Chinese population of Sarawak as 31 percent and that of Sabah 23 percent. The remainder includes a few Malays and is made up predominantly of Dayaks, Kadazans (the largest racial group in Sabah), and other Borneo ethnic groups. These groups constitute about half the population of Sarawak and form almost two-thirds of the population in Sabah.

Distribution by Sex and Age

Sex distribution among the various ethnic groups is currently fairly well stabilized and in 1964 stood at an estimated 1,099 males to every 1,000 females. Formerly, the disparity between the sexes was more pronounced because of the large-scale male immigration in search of jobs and new economic opportunities. As these men remained to become permanent inhabitants, they sent for their families, and gradually the sex ratio was reduced to its present value.

There is a large preponderance of young people throughout the nation. The latest semiofficial estimates indicate that more than 40 percent of the population was under 15 years of age in 1967.

Rates of Increase

Rates of population increase vary among the individual states and the various ethnic groups. Very little of the increase has been caused by immigration, which began to be restricted for all areas after the passage of the Aliens Ordinance Act in 1939. Subsequent legislation in 1946 and 1953 further defined categories of individuals permitted to enter, and immigration since then has been virtually nil. The annual rate of increase, therefore, is a function of natural growth as the spread between birth and death rates in all regions constantly widens. Birth rates are uniformly high, averaging about 38.1 per 1,000 throughout the country in the period from 1963 to 1966. Death rates, meanwhile, have been almost halved since the end of World War II, dropping to an average of 8.1 per 1,000 in the period from 1963 to 1966.

Urbanization

The Chinese are predominantly urban, but some live in settlements of the tin and rubber belts or operate market gardens close to urban areas. There is also a large urban group of Indians, with the majority concentrated in the cities of Penang, Kuala Lumpur, and Ipoh. Most of the others are associated with rubber cultivation and the estate economy. The Malays, on the other hand, are rural. In both segments of Malaysia, they inhabit the agricultural regions of the coasts and the small holding rubber areas, and they have a clear predominance in all ricelands both in the lowlands and in the hills. Where they do cluster in groups, the major unit of settlement is the *kampong* (Malay village), not the town.

The largest and most important cities and towns of the country, with the possible exception of Kuching, the capital of Sarawak, are located on the Malay Peninsula. In Sarawak and Sabah concentrations of more than 1,000 people are classified as urban centers.

Kuching is the most significant of these with a 1964 population estimated at about 60,000. Other major towns descend in population size to Beaufort in Sabah, with a total population of only 1,576.

CHAPTER 3

HISTORICAL SETTING

Although Malaysia's major parts were not joined under one government until 1963, there are a number of features common to all parts of Malaysia that have helped in shaping the nation's history over a period of centuries. Throughout history, for example, the country has suffered from poor soil fertility and productivity, sparse population, and extreme difficulty of overland communication through tropical swamps and jungles. To support population densities great enough to enjoy a level of civilization above that of rural subsistence agriculture, the people of the urban settlements from the earliest times have had to depend on food imported from abroad. Political stability and economic development have depended upon the ability to obtain and feed an adequate labor supply.

Malaysians have used the waterways to provide what the land failed to give. Downriver chiefs extracted tribute and labor from upriver villages by controlling the river traffic. A strategic position astride the East-West trade routes, and especially the Peninsula's position alongside the narrow Strait of Malacca, encouraged rivermouth chiefs to attempt to profit from the East-West trade in transit as well as from the exchange of upriver jungle produce for rice and other imports.

Foreigners, both Asian and European, also sought to control the shipping through the strait and, in the process, exercised powerful influences on the territory. Among the most important effects of these foreign contacts were the spread of Islam, the introduction of a concept of empire that resulted in indigenous empires developing in Malacca and Brunei, and finally a century of British control that left its influence in the political, social, economic, and military institutions of modern Malaysia.

Sharing the same racial and linguistic background with neighboring peoples in Indonesia and the southern Philippines, Malaysia's indigenous coastal peoples moved easily from place to place along the shores facing the Java and South China seas until 19th-century European colonial regimes divided the area into separate spheres of influence. Most of the so-called indigenous people are in fact migrants from Indonesia and the Philippines within the past four centuries, and migrants from these areas are still easily absorbed. The tribal people of the interior of the Peninsula and in Borneo are less easily absorbed into the coastal population, having strikingly different cultures that have not felt the full effect of the foreign influences which conditioned coastal society.

The second half of the 19th century brought, on a massive scale, migration of Chinese laborers and, in West Malaysia, Indian laborers. This migration has resulted in the unassimilated "minority" of Chinese who constitute 35 to 40 percent of the country's population. This in turn meant that economic development of Malaysia's resources was achieved without the full participation of the indigenous community. At the same time, the Chinese were prevented from gaining political power commensurate with their economic power. Indirect rule by the British and paternalistic regulations, aimed at protecting the less sophisticated indigenous population, kept alive the prestige and power of an indigenous elite that has to some extent carried over to modern times. Indigenous nationalism was, as a result, slow to demand the end of British rule, since the European was regarded as the protector of indigenous interests against the Chinese.

Independence came for the Federation of Malaya in 1957 after a relatively brief period of preparation for self-government. The independent government inherited from the colonial period two major problems that have confronted the successor government of Malaysia—a need to create national harmony out of diverse ethnic groups and a need to diversify an economy overly dependent upon the world prices of a few primary products.

EARLY PERIOD

Evidence of human residence in parts of Malaysia goes back more than 35,000 years. There is widespread evidence of a Mesolithic culture beginning about 10,000 years ago. The people of this culture are thought to have been small, dark-skinned Veddoids similar to the Melanesians and to some of the aboriginal peoples still living a stone-age existence in the inland jungles of the Malay Peninsula. These Veddoids were cavedwellers who hunted, fished, and collected jungle produce. They buried their dead and engaged in ritual cannibalism and possibly headhunting.

About 2500 to 1500 B.C., a Neolithic people, believed to have migrated from southwest China, moved down the Peninsula and also beyond it to the Indonesian archipelago. These proto-Malays were good woodworkers and carvers. They grew food crops, including yams and possibly rice; they had pottery and stone jewelry and may have worn bark-cloth clothing. Of the same racial stock as the proto-Malays are the deutero-Malays, who are credited with having introduced the Bronze-Iron Age to Southeast Asia. Beautiful and intricately decorated bronze drums and bells have been unearthed in various parts of West Malaysia testifying to the ubiquity and skill of these early migrants.

In the first century A.D., the more advanced portion of the populace, who for the most part dwelt near the coast, had an irrigated rice agriculture, mixed gardening, and domesticated cattle. They had the ability to work metals and considerable navigational skill. They lived in bamboo houses raised on stilts. Their social system included matriarchal descent and an important place for women. Their religious practices involved ancestor and phallic worship, horizontal and vertical megaliths, burials in jars or horizontal cists, and a tendency to categorize things dualistically—for example, high versus low, mountain versus sea.

Malaysian culture was never uniform, however. Depending upon accessibility to foreign influence and other factors, there were, and have continued to be, great variations in culture among different ethnic groups and tribes.

THE HINDU-BUDDHIST PERIOD, SECOND TO FIFTEENTH CENTURIES A.D.

The Indian traders who visited Malaya in the first centuries A.D. inaugurated a process of cultural influence that was to continue for more than a thousand years. From India came many of the Malays' basic political ideas and practices, art forms, and popular legends. Indian traders introduced, successively, Hinduism, Buddhism, and Islam. Indian influence came in waves, and the Indian contributions to Malaysian culture represent several periods of history and geographic regions.

Indianized city-states began to develop in Southeast Asia at the start of the Christian Era as the result of trade contacts. Although there is no evidence of large-scale settlement, control, or invasion by Indians, Indian concepts adopted by the indigenous Southeast Asian elite soon became the basis of political organization in the trading communities. This organization transformed independent subsistence villagers into citizens of city-states and kingdoms, subject to a ruling class, indigenous or foreign, who lived off the trade profits and justified the new hierarchical social structure by reference to Hindu and Buddhist religious doctrines.

The first Southeast Asian city-state of lasting importance was Funan, a trading settlement on the Mekong Delta. Smaller city-states also sprang up. One of these was Kedah, on the west coast of the Peninsula. A vassal to Funan, Kedah was, by the seventh century, the last port of call in Southeast Asia for Chinese pilgrims on their way to the Buddhist holy places in India. By the third century A.D., Chinese were trading at an entrepôt in the Malacca Strait, perhaps on the island of Singapore.

In the seventh century Funan fell to the Khmers of Cambodia. Kedah soon became a vassal of a new empire, Sri Vijaya, which was growing on the profits of the trade through the Malacca Strait. Sri Vijaya's capital was in southern Sumatra, but gradually the empire incorporated the coasts of peninsular Malaya and parts of western Borneo, the isthmian city-states that had formerly been Funan's vassals, and, for a time, parts of Java (see fig. 4).

Through its control of the Malacca Strait and its suzerainty over the region's seaports, Sri Vijaya became the richest and most powerful kingdom in Southeast Asia. It also became a major center for the propagation of Mahayana Buddhism. A seventh-century Chinese pilgrim reported finding 1,000 Buddhist monks studying in Sri Vijaya's Sumatran capital near modern Palembang.

All traffic through the Malacca Strait paid duty at the Sri Vijayan ports. A Chinese account of the time states that "if some foreign ship passing Sri Vijaya should not enter the port, an armed party would certainly board it and kill the sailors to the last man."

Perhaps in reaction to the highhandedness of the Sumatra-based empire, King Rajendra Chola I of the Chola dynasty of southern India led a raid on Sri Vijaya's capital and on the vassal states on the Malay Peninsula. Kedah, which had become a leading city of Sri Vijaya, never fully recovered from this attack.

The trade of Sri Vijayan days was essentially luxury trade. Arabs came to the northwest of the Peninsula to buy tin and jungle produce in exchange for Western goods such as glassware and cloth. The Chinese trade with maritime Southeast Asia, an area the Chinese called Nanyang (Southern Seas), was more exotic. Ivory, rhinoceros horn (used in Chinese traditional medicine), hardwood, and camphor from Southeast Asia were exchanged for Chinese wine, rice, silk, and porcelain.

In the 11th century there developed a lucrative and well-organized East-West trade to provide Europe with Moluccan spices. Arab traders carried the trade between Venice and Cambay in western India through the Red Sea and the Persian Gulf. Gujerati Indians from Cambay and other southern Indian ports operated the trade

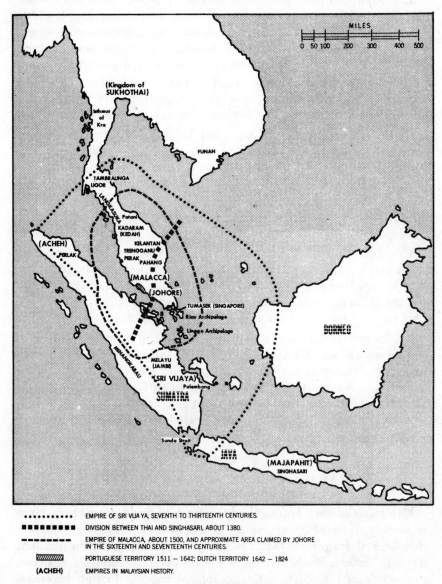

MILES
0 50 100 200 300 400 500

(Kingdom of
SUKHOTHAI)

Isthmus
of
Kra

FUNAN

TAMBRALINGA
LIGOR
Patani
KADARAM
(KEDAH)
KELANTAN
TRENGGANU
PERAK PAHANG
(MALACCA)
(JOHORE)
TUMASEK (SINGAPORE)
Riau Archipelago
Lingga Archipelago

(ACHEH)
PERLAK

MINANGKABAU

MELAYU
(JAMBI)
(SRI VIJAYA)
Palembang
SUMATRA

BORNEO

Sunda Strait

JAVA
(MAJAPAHIT)
SINGHASARI

.... EMPIRE OF SRI VIJAYA, SEVENTH TO THIRTEENTH CENTURIES.

▪▪▪▪▪▪▪▪ DIVISION BETWEEN THAI AND SINGHASARI, ABOUT 1380.

- - - - - - EMPIRE OF MALACCA, ABOUT 1500, AND APPROXIMATE AREA CLAIMED BY JOHORE
IN THE SIXTEENTH AND SEVENTEENTH CENTURIES.

▨▨▨▨ PORTUGUESE TERRITORY 1511 – 1642; DUTCH TERRITORY 1642 – 1824

(ACHEH) EMPIRES IN MALAYSIAN HISTORY.

*Figure 4. Important periods in Malaysian history through the
nineteenth century.*

across the Indian Ocean to the northern coast ports of East Java, the
chief collection point for spices from Indonesia's eastern islands.

By the 13th century the demand in the West for goods from China
increased and exceeded China's demand for Western goods. In order
to maintain the balance of trade with China, the Indian and Arab

29

traders expanded their trade with indigenous Malaysians. The Indian traders exchanged Western goods for Southeast Asian jungle produce, which found a ready market in China. By 1225 a new port on the east coast of the Malay Peninsula, possibly in the present-day state of Trengganu, had become the chief emporium of this Indian, Arab, and Chinese trade. Malaysian jungle produce, including tree resins, hornbill ivory, and edible birds' nests from the caves of Borneo, formed an important part of the trade between China and the West.

By the end of the 13th century, Sri Vijaya had gone into eclipse, and the land empire of the Khmers in the north of the Peninsula had fallen to the Thais. A new city-state, established by a Sumatran prince on the island that is now Singapore at the end of the 13th century, was raided alternately by the Thais and by the new southern power, the Javanese empire of Majapahit, throughout the 14th century.

The trade through the Strait of Malacca was constantly harassed by pirates inhabiting the old Sri Vijayan Sumatran ports including Palembang. When the Mongol dynasty fell in the mid-14th century and the Ming emperor banned private Chinese trade in the Nanyang, Chinese outlaws joined the other pirates of the strait.

By the end of the 14th century, the Thais had extended their control to most of the Malay Peninsula. A Javanese attempt to capture Singapore was repulsed, and Java could no longer exact allegiance from the Sumatran ports. New Muslim city-states were growing on Sumatra's northeast coast that were engaged in an effort to establish safe ports along the pirate-infested strait between Sumatra and the Malay Peninsula.

MALACCA'S GOLDEN AGE, 1400–1511

Malaysian history before the beginning of the 15th century must be mainly deduced by arranging in meaningful order the scant archaeological fragments that have survived the centuries in a damp, tropical climate. Much of what is known of early Malaysia has been gleaned from the occasional comments of passing foreign travelers, most of them Chinese.

With the start of the 15th century, however, Malaysia entered into the fully historical period with the rise of the entrepôt of Malacca, celebrated in Malaya's first known indigenous chronicle, the *Sejarah Melayu* (Malay Annals). The *Sejarah Melayu* was written before 1536 and is still a useful source for Malaysian social history despite some evident distortions.

Covering much of the same period are historical summaries written by the Portuguese who conquered Malacca in the 16th century. There are also two detailed first-hand accounts by Chinese officials who accompanied the emperor's envoy, Admiral Cheng Ho, to Malacca during the early days of the Malacca sultanate. Although there are conflicting details in these various accounts, the century during which Malacca was under Malay rule is fully described. With the addition of historical romances, such as the famous *Hikayat Hang Tuah* (Tale of Hang Tuah), the first original romance in the Malay language that dates back to the 16th century or earlier, the flavor and character of this time have been preserved. Although the sultanate lasted in Malacca only a century, its customs and organizations survive, especially in the traditions of the Malay royal courts.

For all Malaysians who regard themselves as culturally Malay, 15th-century Malacca still provides cultural heroes, dynastic ancestors, patterns of statecraft, and traditional examples of ideal public and private behavior. For the Malays of Malaysia (some 44 percent of the population) modern civilization began here.

The Founding of Malacca

Shortly before the end of the 14th century, a Sumatran-born refugee from Majapahit Java fled to Singapore. His name, Sri Parameswara, meaning Prince Consort, suggests that he had married above himself, possibly a Javanese or Sumatran princess.

Singapore at that time was being ruled by a relative of the Thai king. Parameswara promptly murdered the ruler and, with his band of followers, took over the town. The Thai king sent, one source recounts, "3,000 troops and war elephants" to avenge the murder and retake the town. Parameswara and his group, which now included adventurers collected along the way and bands of indigenous aborigines who lived a sea-nomad existence along the Peninsula's coasts, retreated from Singapore, which was thoroughly devasted by this siege.

In approximately 1400 the refugees took over a small fishing village at the mouth of the Melaka River and started to operate a trading port of the Sri Vijayan type. It was a good time to start a new trading port; China's overland routes to the West had been blocked by Tamerlaine, and the new Ming emperor who came to the throne of China in 1402 was anxious to open a sea route to the West. In 1403 the emperor sent the first of seven expeditions to Southeast Asia to arrange for a new system of controlling the traffic through the strait. Thailand, China's vassal, was instructed not to molest Malacca. More important for Malacca's success, in 1407 Admiral Cheng Ho and a fleet of 62 vessels and 37,000 men destroyed the pirate's den in Palembang, removing a serious threat to Malaccan power. Grateful Malaccan kings went to China four times between 1411 and 1433 to demonstrate their loyalty as vassals of the emperor, although to avoid trouble they continued paying tribute to the Thais until 1446.

The Muslim city-states of north Sumatra benefited from the strait being made clear for trade again. Parameswara (or possibly his son), by converting to Islam and marrying a princess of the north Sumatran port of Pasai, became the ally of the Sumatran Muslim traders who soon moved their headquarters to Malacca.

Malacca's chief asset was its location; it was convenient for controlling the trade through the strait and provided safe anchorage where the monsoons met. Malacca's rulers wisely kept the toll and customs charges reasonable, and it was relatively easy to police the 40 miles between Malacca and the Sumatran coast to prevent ships bypassing the entrepôt.

The Golden Age

Although as time went on Malacca received tribute from vassals, the bulk of her wealth came from a 6-percent duty on foreign trade and lesser taxes on domestic trade, including sales in the local food markets and even licenses for peddlers. Of the foreign trade, the most important was the trade between the Gujerati Indian traders, now converted to Islam, and Javanese traders who met in Malacca to exchange Western manufactures, chiefly cloth, for Moluccan spices.

One effect of the prominence of the zealously missionizing Gujeratis in the Malacca trade was the spread of Islam throughout the archipelago, especially among the coastal populations who were most directly involved in the spice trade. Islam became the religion of the commercial fraternity. Another shared feature of the Malacca population was a facility in the Malay language, which became the lingua franca of trade and from which developed the national language of Malaysia, Bahasa Malaysia (see ch. 4, Ethnic Groups and Languages).

Malacca, however, was by no means a social melting pot. Rather, it was a large foreign settlement subdivided into smaller foreign enclaves on the sparsely settled Malay coast. Gujeratis, Malays, Javanese, Sumatrans, Bugis (from the Celebes), Borneans, Filipinos, Persians, Arabs, and Chinese each lived apart. A *capitan* (headman) chosen by each enclave from among its members represented the community in its dealings with outsiders. Above the *capitans* came the four *shahbandars*, (harbormasters and controllers of customs). Each *shahbandar* dealt with the traders from prescribed areas; one *shahbandar* dealt with the Gujeratis, and another dealt with the Sumatrans, the Javanese, and the people of the islands to the east. Frequently, the harbormaster was of the nationality of one of the groups with whom he dealt. Above the *shahbandars* was the Malay court, headed by Parameswara's successors.

Although after 1446 the ruler of Malacca bore the Muslim title of sultan, the court officials continued to use Sanskrit titles, and court ritual showed the persisting influence of Hindu ideas. As the personification of the state, the sultan drew upon many Hindu symbols of divine kingship, such as the royal umbrella, the sacred *kris* (dagger), and the reservation to royalty of the colors yellow and white, symbols that had become part of court ritual in the city-states of Southeast Asia since the time of Funan.

As this elaborate ritual developed around the throne of the sultan, the actual wielding of power tended to come under the control of the chief minister (*bendahara*). The *bendahara* more or less inherited his claim to the office, as did the sultan's other chief officers, the treasurer, the admiral, and the military commander. Below this inner council of four there were eight other major chiefs, and below them 32 territorial chiefs.

These courtiers lived well on the proceeds of the various taxes and presents from traders. In return, they held together the mosaic of small and mutually suspicious transient communities so that trade could take place for everyone's profit.

The *bendahara* during the period of Malacca's greatest wealth and power was Tun Perak. He was the power behind the throne during the reigns of four sultans from 1456 to 1498. He led Malacca's forces against land and sea invasions by the Thais and made vassals of the ports of central and southern Sumatra. Pahang, Kedah, Perak, Johore, and Trengganu became part of the empire before Tun Perak's death in 1498 (see fig. 4). As Malacca successfully wrested territory from the Thais, Islam spread on the Peninsula, taking root among the people as an expression of opposition to Buddhist Thailand.

Sultan Mansur Shah (1459-77) reigned at the height of Malacca's power. He was a devout Muslim, and during his reign Malacca became a center for the study of the Sufi mystic sect of Islam.

One problem that was to plague Malacca and subsequent Malay sultanates was that of the royal succession. A king generally nominated one of his sons, by no means always the eldest, to the post of *raja muda* (crown prince) during his lifetime. This choice, however, was not binding on his subjects. At the funeral of a sultan, the senior chiefs of the kingdom gathered and made the final choice among candidates whose royal blood entitled them to consideration. The chiefs often passed over the dead sultan's favorite and conferred the title on a pretender who, they anticipated, would be grateful to and dependent upon his electors. It was a system upon which intrigue thrived and usually resulted in weak elderly sultans and strong petty chieftains.

Potential troublemakers among the pretenders were sent away from the capital to govern outlying posts of the empire. In this way, for example, a dynasty of rulers in Pahang was founded by sons of Sultan Mansur Shah who had been passed over by the chiefs.

The establishment of new dynasties and intermarriage with old ones ensured the spread of Islam among the ruling families of Malaysia. The court of Brunei in northwest Borneo became Muslim at this time. Majapahit, with whom Brunei had had close connections, had been gradually declining. In converting to Islam, Brunei severed its ties forever with the Javanese empire.

On Mansur Shah's tombstone, dated A.D. 1477, appears the verse, "The world is but transitory; the world has no permanence; the world is like a house made by a spider." The transitoriness of Mansur Shah's Malacca became clear shortly after the death of his *bendahara*, Tun Perak, in 1498.

TRADERS, PIRATES, AND MIGRANTS AFTER THE FALL OF MALACCA

The Portuguese

During the time of Malacca's sultanate, the trade between Southeast Asia and Europe was in the hands of Muslim traders as far as Venice, which was the sole distributor of Asian goods in Europe. The Portuguese in the early 16th century sought to damage the Muslim trade and break the control of Venice over the European market.

By 1509 they had partly destroyed the Muslim monopoly on the India-Arabia leg of the trade route, and a peaceful attempt to establish a trading post at Malacca was unsuccessful. In 1511 Affonso d'Albuquerque led a large fleet from the Portuguese fort at Goa eastward to Malacca and, after a long battle, captured the town. The sultan fled, first to Pahang and then to Johore, and the Portuguese began immediately to fortify their new emporium.

Within the thick stone walls of the fort, called A Famosa (the Famous One), a Eurasian, Christian, Portuguese-speaking community emerged that continued into the 20th century. Portuguese Malacca, like the sultanate that preceded it, was dependent on imports from abroad for food. The Javanese provided the bulk of the rice during the Portuguese period, although at the beginning they were hostile and sent a fleet of 100 ships to attack Malacca in 1513.

A Famosa was attacked almost continually during the 130 years of Portuguese control. From Johore, the new center of the displaced Malacca sultanate, there were serious attacks leading to vigorous Portuguese counterattacks for a century after the Portuguese takeover. In the period from 1540 to 1640 an aggressive and zealously Muslim dynasty in Acheh (Atjeh), North Sumatra, sought to gain a monopoly over the Strait of Malacca and alternately attacked Johore and Malacca. Alliances between the two Muslim kingdoms, Johore and Acheh, were occasionally attempted to destroy the Europeans, but mutual suspicion kept the two sultanates apart.

Brunei

Another Malay sultanate, Brunei on Borneo, fared better in the Portuguese era. Brunei was much like Malacca, a Muslim state with Hindu rituals and an elegant court given to display of wealth. Never as powerful as Malacca, it had only one *shahbandar*. At the height of its power in the 16th century, Brunei claimed all northern Borneo and the Sulu archipelago in the southern Philippines, and it even received tribute from Manila for a few years.

The Portuguese kept on friendly terms with Brunei, and their ships stopped there en route to the Moluccan spice gardens. Brunei had habitually sent gold and jungle produce to Malacca to be exchanged there for cloth and beads from India and the West. The Portuguese city inherited that trade, but the bulk of Brunei's trade was with Chinese merchants, many of whom had moved from Malacca to Patani in the Thai part of the Malay Peninsula, which became in the 17th century the chief entrepôt for the Chinese goods in Southeast Asia.

The Dutch

As the 16th century came to a close, another European power entered the contest for control of the Malacca Strait. The Dutch had for a century handled the European distribution of the Portuguese Eastern trade, collecting their goods in Lisbon. In 1594 the Spaniards closed Lisbon to the Dutch, who now had to obtain Eastern produce directly from the source.

By 1619 the Dutch East India Company had established its headquarters on Java and attempted to form alliances with Acheh and

Johore to destroy Malacca. Dutch fleets tried to cut off rice supplies from Java and Sumatra on their way to Malacca. In 1640, after more than 20 years of harassment and attacks, the Dutch, allied with Johore, laid siege to the walled community. A breach on the land side of the famous fort admitted the invaders to the starving town after a siege of 6 months.

Malacca's period as a major trade emporium was over. During the Portuguese era it had been declining, with some of the trade following the Muslim traders to northern Sumatra and to the Riau Islands of the Johore sultanate. The Dutch, with their new entrepôt Batavia (modern-day Djakarta) in Java, regarded Malacca more as a fortress on the strait to maintain Dutch trade monopoly of spices, pepper, gold, and tin than as a trading port.

The Sulu Sultanate

Brunei's power also waned in the 17th century. Attacks by Bruneis and Sulus on the Spanish settlements in the Philippines resulted in the sacking and burning of Brunei Town in 1645 by Spaniards. With Brunei weakened, Sulu gained its independence.

At the end of the 17th century, the rivalry of two heirs to the Brunei sultanate brought on a civil war. One of the pretenders asked the sultan of Sulu for military aid in return for that portion of what is now Sabah running from the island of Sebatik on the east coast to Kimanis on the west coast. Although Sulu's ally won the war, it later became unclear whether the promised cession actually took place or whether the Sulus unilaterally claimed the promised territory as their reward. This question of overlapping claims was to become important in the late 19th century when some adventurous Western businessmen sought to obtain a grant of the disputed territory. Some of the ramifications of this dispute also carried over into the 20th-century controversy between Malaysia and the Philippines over title to the area.

The Bugis and the Minangkabau

Dutch trade policies had a more deleterious effect on indigenous trade than had the Portuguese. Whereas the Portuguese were interested primarily in monopolizing the Eastern trade reaching Europe by controlling the shipping from the East to the West, the Dutch were determined to take over the trade between the Asian ports as well. Garrisons and blockades in Kedah and Perak were built by the Dutch to prevent tin shipments from slipping past them, and in 1667 the seagoing *prahus* (small sailing craft) of the Bugis people of the Celebes were cut off from their traditional control of the Celebes-to-Java spice trade by a Dutch garrison in Makassar.

The frustrated Bugis turned to piracy and migrated to other parts of the archipelago. Many settled in Selangor, West Malaysia. Ambitious and aggressive, the Bugis were ready to fill the power vacuum that occurred in the Johore empire at the beginning of the 18th century.

Johore, the direct descendant of the Malacca sultanate, had squandered its wealth gained from its entrepôt at Riau in a 20-year war with the Sumatran state of Jambi, but the Bugis found Johore's empire (which included the tip of the Peninsula and the Riau and Lingga islands) an excellent base from which to attack Malacca and the Dutch shipping monopoly. Another foreign Malay group, the Minangkabau of Sumatra, many of whom had migrated to farm the hinterland of Malacca since the time of the Portuguese, were also determined to gain political power on the Peninsula.

The two foreign Malay groups allied to take the throne of Johore in 1717, after the last heir to the Malacca dynasty had died in 1699 and the *bendahara* had come to the throne. There was bad faith on both sides of the alliance, and by 1721 the Bugis had effective control of the Johore empire. A puppet sultan, the son of the former *bendahara*, was installed under the authority of a Bugis regent with a new royal title, *yam tuan muda* (deputy king).

Conflict between the Minangkabau and Bugis broke out again in Kedah in 1724 when they intervened on opposite sides in a dynastic war. Again the Bugis were the victors, and for more than 40 years they extracted war-debt payments from Kedah. The Bugis fought the Minangkabau again in Perak, and in 1740 they established a Bugis dynasty in Selangor.

The Dutch grew concerned over the increasing Bugis power and especially over their attempts in Perak and elsewhere to break the Dutch monopoly on tin. In midcentury the sultan of Johore offered the Dutch trade and tin monopolies if the Dutch would rid him of his Bugis overlord. The Dutch and the Bugis fought each other intermittently for nearly 30 years until finally the Bugis power was broken, and the Dutch established a garrison at the Bugis stronghold at Riau. The sultan of Johore now had a Dutch, instead of a Bugis, overlord.

EARLY BRITISH FOOTHOLDS

Borneo

In the second half of the 18th century, the British East India Company was engaged in importing tea from China for a growing European market. China, however, had less interest in the goods the

British traders had to sell, and the balance of payments deficit had to be met with silver bullion. To stop the bullion drain, the British East India Company sought to establish trading centers on islands off the coast of northern Borneo. There Western goods could be exchanged for tropical produce, which had a good market in China.

The plan did not succeed. The British settlement in Balembangan was attacked and destroyed in 1775, and the following year the British withdrew from Labuan as well.

Penang

Attempts to establish a trading port and naval harbor on the west coast of the Malay Peninsula also began at this time. In 1771 Francis Light, an ex-naval officer and private trader, began negotiations with the sultan of Kedah for rights to establish a trading post in the Kedah harbor. The sultan was willing to grant such a port to the British East India Company in return for protection against his enemies, the Thais, the Burmese, and the Bugis of Selangor; for a number of reasons, however, the negotiations failed. In 1786 Francis Light tried again with the new sultan of Kedah and obtained the offer for the company of the almost unpopulated island of Penang off the Kedah coast in return for his promise of company protection against military attacks on Kedah and a generous stipend for the sultan.

Although the British assumed their right under this agreement and occupied Penang, they signed no treaty. At about the same time, the Bugis drove the Dutch from Selangor and Johore, and in 1790 they allied with Kedah, Trengganu, Johore, and several Sumatran kingdoms in a grand scheme to attack the Dutch north of Malacca and to aid Kedah against the British in Penang. Sufficient strength to achieve either goal was lacking, and the attack on Penang was easily repulsed. The subsequent treaty in 1791 recognized the cession of Penang in return for a stipend, but did not include any promise of assistance to the sultan of Kedah.

Francis Light himself was perhaps the chief reason that the British acquired and kept Penang. If it had not been for his personal friendship with the Kedah sultan, Kedah might have accepted Dutch suzerainty at this time. Light had rashly promised the sultan military assistance originally, but he in fact led the Penang militia against an invasion attempt by the Kedah sultan when it became clear that the British East India Company would not honor Light's promise.

For the first 8 years of its existence, the new residency at Penang, officially subject to the governor general of the British East India Company in Bengal, was, as Light himself described it, "under the sole administration of one person."

Under Light's administration the population grew from almost nothing to 25,000, which included 3,000 Chinese, plus Indians, Thais, Burmese, Arabs, and Malays. From the time of Penang's establishment as a British post, Chinese began to come to Malaya, particularly those portions of it under British rule, in large numbers. In 1788 Chinese constituted over two-fifths of Penang's population and were soon to become the majority group.

By 1794, the year Light died of malaria, the import and export trade at Penang was substantial, and pepper, grown on the island at Light's suggestion, began to find a place in the world market. In 1800 the food supply for Penang was ensured by the cession of Province Wellesley, a strip of rice-growing land on the mainland of Kedah across from Penang Island.

Malacca

The next British acquisition in Malaysia was Malacca. In 1795, at the request of the Dutch government in exile, which was allied with the British against France, the British occupied Malacca. The occupation of Malacca was envisioned by both Dutch and British as a temporary measure, part of a policy carried out throughout the Dutch empire to prevent Dutch property from falling into French hands. The Dutch garrison from Riau was withdrawn at this time also, and the Bugis *yam tuan muda* promptly reasserted his power over the Johore-Riau sultan.

The turmoil in Europe dragged on, and as it did, Penang continued to grow and prosper. By 1805 the British East India Company, jealous for Penang's future, began to consider the destruction of Malacca's fort and the removal of its population so that when the time came to return Malacca to its Dutch owners, Penang's supremacy would be assured. In 1807 the fort was destroyed, but the plan to destroy the settlement was abandoned largely as the result of the remonstrances of a young clerk in the Penang administration, Thomas Stamford Raffles, whose eloquence and knowledge concerning the Malay-speaking areas of Southeast Asia made a favorable impression on the governor general of the company in Bengal, Lord Minto. Raffles was shortly thereafter rewarded by Lord Minto with control over Java and her dependencies, which were easily wrested from the control of a French-appointed governor.

Singapore

For reasons connected with the balance of power after the war in Europe was over, the British cooperated in returning the Dutch to supremacy in the Indonesian archipelago in 1818. The Dutch reasserted their trade monopolies and forbade British shipping in any port of the Dutch East Indies except Batavia.

Raffles, after having had the control of a substantial empire governed from Java, was removed to the small and unflourishing Sumatran port of Bengkulu (Bencoolen), where the British East India Company had a trading post. From Bengkulu, Raffles, a longtime advocate of free trade and an expanding British Empire, watched with misgivings as the Dutch began to reestablish their trade monopoly.

With the lukewarm support of the new governor general in Bengal, who knew his directors would not tolerate conflict with the Dutch, Raffles sailed to the island of Singapore in January 1819. He was authorized to investigate possible sites for a British trading post more conveniently located for the strait traffic than Bengkulu but not to compete with the Dutch, who had just reopened their Riau garrison.

The island of Singapore at this time was sparsely populated. There were a few Chinese inland and a riverside clustering of the houseboats of Malaysia's aboriginal sea gypsies. Along the shore there was a small settlement of Malays ruled by a *temenggong* (a traditional Malay official title), who claimed allegiance to the elder son of the former sultan of the Johore empire, then resident in Bintang in Riau. This elder brother had been passed over for the title of sultan by the real ruler of Riau-Johore, the Bugis overlord, now calling himself *raja muda*.

The Bugis government had treaty arrangements with the Dutch that granted the Dutch exclusive trading rights; thus, it suited Raffles' purpose that the nobleman in charge of Singapore should not be vassal to the Bugis-dominated sultan. Accordingly, Raffles arranged for the installation of the elder son as Sultan Hussein of Johore, thus dividing the sultanate between two rivals. The newly installed sultan and the *temenggong* then granted the British East India Company the right to establish a trading post in Singapore in return for an annual stipend to the two rulers.

In 1824 Great Britain's ascendancy on the Peninsula of Malaya was recognized in the Anglo-Dutch Treaty, which divided rights to establish settlements or make treaties in the Malay-speaking world between the British and the Dutch. Great Britain gained Dutch Malacca and the promise of noninterference from Singapore northward while giving up Bengkulu, the inferior port in West Sumatra, and any territorial ambitions south of Singapore. The split which Raffles had created in the Johore empire by installing a second sultan was confirmed by this treaty. The island portion of the empire was in the Dutch sphere of influence, while Singapore and mainland Johore were in the British sphere.

Another result of this treaty was that it created a lasting political division between the Indonesian archipelago and the Malay Peninsula. Sumatra, which had participated actively in the affairs of the Malay Peninsula since Sri Vijayan times, now began a separate history under Dutch colonialism.

NINETEENTH-CENTURY MALAYSIA

The Straits Settlements

Singapore, Penang, and Malacca, called the Straits Settlements, were important to the British for the command of the strait and as links in the long chain of bastions protecting the shipping lanes from Gibraltar to Hong Kong. They were also important as trading centers where the exchange of Eastern and Western goods could take place.

In both respects, Singapore was more successful than the other Straits Settlements because its location was best for controlling the strait, and by 1825 Singapore had double the trade of Penang and Malacca together. It was the British East India Company's first unqualified success at establishing a trade center in the area, the original purpose for which the company had been founded two centuries earlier.

A free-trade area, Singapore was soon the greatest trading port in Southeast Asia. In 1832 Singapore became the administrative capital of all the Straits Settlements.

Unwilling to abandon its free-trade policy and tax the entrepôt trade, the company depended for its revenue upon so-called tax farms. The tax farmers were businessmen, almost always Chinese, who were granted the right to collect taxes on gambling, luxury goods, and imports for local use. The tax farmer retained any sums received above the amounts promised to the government. It was the least expensive way to collect revenue and, since the taxes were collected on items used predominantly by the Chinese, such as opium, whiskey, and pork, and on gambling, a large Chinese community was welcomed in the Straits Settlements.

Like the Dutch and the Portuguese before them, the British were interested primarily in trade and not in acquiring territory on the Peninsula. A small, costly, and ill-advised war against the Minangkabau settlers in Malacca's hinterland, Naning, provided proof that the British East India Company had nothing to gain and much to lose by interfering in the Malay Peninsula.

The Thais, 1816–63

The first permanent British settlement in Malaysia, Penang, had been granted to the British East India Company by the sultan of Kedah in the hope of protection against his enemies, chiefly the Bugis and the Thais. In 1823 the Thais, unsatisfied with Kedah's cooperation in its efforts to gain Perak, sent an expedition into Kedah that destroyed much life and property. The sultan begged Penang in vain for the aid that Frances Light had promised but which the company had never endorsed.

To the British East India Company, with its major investments in India, Thai friendship was more important than that of Kedah, whereas to interfere for Kedah's protection would be very expensive. In a treaty with Thailand in 1826, the company sacrificed Kedah to the Thais in exchange for a promise that the Thais would no longer molest Perak. The Thais then attempted to assert control over the eastern coast, and soon Kelantan and Trengganu were vassals. An attempt to gain control over Pahang, however, was unsuccessful, and by 1863 the Thai wave of expansion southward in the Malay Peninsula was over. The Thais retained their suzerainty over Kedah (including what later became Perlis), Kelantan, and Trengganu until 1909.

The Malay States Before 1874

Life in the Malay states was little changed at first by the establishment of the Straits Settlements. In 1850 the population of all the Malay states of the Peninsula did not exceed 300,000. The Borneo territories, later to become Sarawak and Sabah, had very sparse populations. Only the Straits Settlements had substantial populations, with the majority Chinese. In 1857 there were 70,000 Chinese in Singapore alone.

Malay society in the 19th century consciously retained as much as possible of the Malacca system. Malays were divided into two classes, the rulers and the ruled. The ruling class, including royal heirs and nonroyal aristocrats, was headed by the state's sultan, whose capital was at a strategic place along the main river mouth of the area.

Surrounded by elaborate protocol and ritual going back to Malacca times and earlier, the sultan was charged with the defense of the state against outsiders. Within the portion of the state over which his strategic riverine position gave him control, the sultan acted as the district chief, collecting tribute in crops, minerals, and jungle produce. Other district chiefs, appointed by the sultan in return for their allegiance and a portion of their income, collected from the trade of major tributaries and nearby rivers.

A sultan ruled for life but, as at the time of Malacca, his son did not necessarily inherit the title. At the funeral of the reigning sultan, the district chiefs met to select the new one from among a number of royal candidates; the chiefs usually preferred a weak or aged ruler who could be expected not to interfere seriously with the chiefs' administration of their districts, and civil wars over the succession were a frequent occurrence.

The chiefs depended less on their noble birth and letters of appointment from the sultan than on their armed followers to enforce their authority over the villages in their districts. A successful chief collected a substantial labor force—an entourage of relatives, hired mercenaries, debt bondsmen, and pagan slaves—to enforce his rule and provide the amenities of civilization.

A small but prestigious immigrant group to be found at the trading ports and elsewhere along the coast was the Arab community, composed primarily of persons of mixed Arab-Malay parentage. Often wealthy traders, they had additional prestige because of their association with the land of Islam's origin. Many of these Arabs prefaced their names with the honorific "Sherif" or "Syed," titles reserved for direct descendants of the Prophet Muhammad.

The Muslims of part Arab or Indian descent were less easily assimilated into the Malay community than were, for example, the Bugis and Minangkabau. Their wealth and intellectual attainments were admired, but their bias toward urban residence and shopkeeping in the British-governed Straits Settlements made them foreign culturally.

In the early 19th century, most Chinese lived in the Straits Settlements. Although there were small Chinese enclaves at district capitals and other larger settlements inland on the Peninsula, there was little to induce Chinese to settle in large numbers away from the big entrepôt towns. This situation changed in midcentury when large tin deposits were discovered in the west of the Peninsula, in Perak, Selangor, and Sungei Ujong (part of what later became the State of Negri Sembilan).

Malay district chiefs in tin-bearing areas invited Chinese entrepreneurs in the Straits Settlements to develop the mines in return for rent and royalties. The Chinese entrepreneurs imported indentured laborers from South China because the local labor supply was insufficient for their needs. Soon there were Chinese mining settlements at mine sites scattered throughout the interior of the western Malay states; these settlements were entirely separate from the rural Malay villages surrounding them. Many of Malaysia's inland towns and cities, including the capital at Kuala Lumpur, grew out of these Chinese mining settlements.

The miners lived a hard pioneer life. Malaria and other jungle fevers produced a high death rate, especially when a new mine site was opened. The miners came without their wives or families, but in other ways they brought their South China village structure with them. They established self-governing communities modeled on South China clan and village organization called *kongsis*.

The *kongsi* provided the miners with food, lodging, law and order, and a militia for its defense. An elected headman, the *capitan*, took charge of management of the mines and relations with the miners' landlord, the Malay district chief. When times were bad, the *capitan*, who was often one of the major investors, could live off the profits of the *kongsi* store; when there was no money for wages, the miners would sometimes be offered shares in the company instead of cash. The *kongsi* endurance and ability to survive times of poor returns kept tin mining a predominantly Chinese industry until the 1920's, when European superior capital resources became important as the result of new mining techniques. Chinese labor and capital developed Malaysia's tin resources to the point where Malaysia became the world's chief supplier of tin.

Other features of *kongsi* society were less productive. The organizations had a semireligious aspect that involved sworn loyalty to the brotherhood of *kongsi* members and secret rituals that could not be disclosed to the non-*kongsi* members on pain of death. Politically, the *kongsis* were connected to a South China underground movement that had begun as an effort to restore the Ming dynasty but had to some extent degenerated into banditry and organized crime. This tradition of outlawry was continued in the Malaysian *kongsis*, or secret societies as they were often called.

Although the Malay chiefs were pleased to receive the rents and royalties from the mines and enlisted the support of *kongsi* militias in the frequent wars over dynastic succession, they found the Chinese settlements a mixed blessing, especially when wars between rival *kongsis* broke out. The *kongsis* were beyond the power of Malay chiefs to control. By 1870 there were 40,000 Chinese in the Larut mines of Perak, and in many parts of West Malaysia Chinese miners outnumbered Malays.

Disputes over land concessions and taxes involving rival Malay chiefs and rival *kongsis* and involvement of Chinese militias on both sides of dynastic wars resulted in widespread disorders throughout the tin-mining areas. The Malay political hierarchy also suffered sudden changes as petty chieftains downstream from newly developed mines found themselves more rich and powerful than their sultans.

British Intervention in the Malay States

In the 1870's British policy in the Malay states changed. Until then the officially proclaimed policy was noninterference in the affairs of the Malay states, except where "necessary for the supression of piracy or the punishment of aggression on our people or territories." By 1874, however, the British government policy became one of employing its influence "to rescue, if possible, these fertile and productive countries from the ruin which must befall them if the present disorders continue unchecked."

The wars over the mines in western Malaysia were largely responsible for this change in policy. Chinese born in the Straits Settlements, and therefore British subjects, were demanding protection of their interests in the Malay states. Improved communications with Europe, especially after the Suez Canal opened in 1869, meant an increase in European business interests, including British investments that needed protection. There was also the fear that foreign interests might gain control of the Malay states if Great Britain hesitated.

Another factor in creating a more activist policy was the establishment of a crown colony composed of the Straits Settlements and Labuan Island in 1867. The interest of the British crown in the Malay territories was greater now that the Straits Settlements were under its direct authority and not, as formerly, a mere appendage to the Indian empire. Singapore's role in Western trade with China and Indonesia was being reduced by the new port at Hong Kong and by the Dutch shipping network directly connecting the Netherlands with her colonies. The handling of the west-coast tin exports from Malaya offered a new source of income to the Straits Settlements.

Great Britain extended its influence over the Malay states by a combination of persuasion, pressure, and an occasional show of force rather than by actual conquest. The Pangkor Treaty of 1874, which became the model for similar agreements signed later with the states of Selangor, Negri Sembilan, and Pahang, bound the sultan of Perak to accept British protection and to have no dealings with foreign powers except through Great Britain. In internal affairs the advice of a British resident had to be asked and followed except in matters concerning Malay religion and custom.

The Chinese *kongsi* war in Perak was also brought to an end at Pangkor through the arbitration of Great Britain's first Chinese-language officer in the Malay states, W.A. Pickering. After the extension of protection to Malay states of Selangor and Negri Sembilan, the *kongsi* wars subsided.

In exchange for accepting British advice, the sultans received very substantial stipends, as did other royal claimants and aristocratic chieftains. Efforts were made to maintain intact the forms of the Muslim monarchies, although basic changes were made, for example, in the way taxes were collected and justice administered.

State councils were established by the residents in the protected states. Headed by the sultan, the typical council membership included the resident, the major Malay chiefs, and the leading Chinese and, later, Western businessmen. The councils, to some extent a formalization of the Malay tradition of consultation between a sultan and his territorial chiefs, discussed all problems as they arose and approved estimates of revenue and expenditure and the appointment of lesser chiefs and village headmen (*penghulu*).

The resident, in theory responsible to the governor of the Straits Settlements but in practice virtually autonomous within his state, took the initiative in all matters except those concerning Malay religion and custom. A successful resident always tried to win genuine support and help from the Malay counselors by tact and patience, especially when venturing into areas regarded by the Malays as reserved to their control, such as slavery and customary criminal law.

By centralizing the power of each state in the hands of the resident, nominally the sultan, and at the same time remunerating the territorial chiefs and maintaining their formal prestige, the British brought an end to most of the causes for war that had previously troubled the states. For the villagers the abolition of feudal taxes, slavery, and the arbitrary rule of the territorial chiefs led to a more settled and peaceful life. In the protected states the villagers no longer felt the need to flee an oppressive chieftain. A penal code, based on British practice in India, was established, and European and Malay magistrates were appointed to administer it.

By the 1890's it became apparent that greater coordination of policy in the several states was necessary if they were to develop similar institutions. Sir Frank Swettenham, the resident in Perak, was largely responsible for developing a plan to federate the states and gaining its acceptance by the several sultans.

The federation came into effect in 1896. Included were the protected states of Perak, Selangor, Pahang, and the confederation of Negri Sembilan—which had been reformed with British advice the previous year—but not the Straits Settlements, over which the British ruled directly. In the Federated Malay States each ruler retained a theoretical sovereignty, even if he surrendered many of his functions to the British residents. Thus, the Malays in each state were subjects of the sultan, whereas residents of the Straits Settlements could become British subjects. Although the vaguely worded federation treaty had promised no lessening of the sultan's authority, it led, in effect, to considerable centralization. Under the first resident general of the federation, Sir Frank Swettenham, a central administration was developed at Kuala Lumpur; the decisions of its departments were implemented in each of the states. Laws were often drafted by a British legal adviser, approved by the resident general, and automatically passed by the state councils. During this era in Malaya the civil servants, recruited by examination in Great Britain, exercised much of the authority usually belonging to legislative or executive bodies.

Under the British resident, British district officers administered the districts within each state and, within each district, administration was executed by salaried Malay *penghulu* appointed by the British after consultation with the Malay community. The *penghulu* were responsible for maintaining law and order in their territories.

Material prosperity increased greatly in the next decade. Revenues nearly tripled; exports nearly doubled; population increased; and roads, railroads, hospitals, schools, postal services, and savings banks appeared where none had been before. In 1900 the Institute for Medical Research was founded at Kuala Lumpur, and within a few years a concerted campaign against malaria was under way. British capital holders began to invest in the tin mines and in estate agriculture. A major innovation, one to play an important part in Malaya's future, was the introduction of rubber cultivation. The first seedlings had been smuggled from Brazil to Great Britain and brought to Malaya in the 1870's. By 1905 considerable acreage was planted in rubber, and from then on, with the continued increase in world demand, new land was put into rubber cultivation even faster. The estate owners faced a serious labor shortage, as had the owners of tin mines before them. Indian laborers were brought in to tap the rubber trees, as well as to work in railroad construction and on coffee plantations. By 1911, when the first census was taken, Malaya's plural society had been created. The population was composed of nearly 1.5 million Malays, over 900,000 Chinese, and 267,000 Indians. No restrictions were placed on immigration until 1930, when the world depression led to serious unemployment among Malay's alien workers.

The British Come to Sarawak and Sabah

By the 19th century the sultanate of Brunei had declined from its former greatness. Although theoretically the ruler of a territory covering all of northern and western Borneo, from the Sibuku River in the east to Cape Datu in the west, the sultan was unable to enforce his rule much beyond his capital city at Brunei Town. The sultan of Sulu also claimed ownership of part of north Borneo eastward from the Kimanis River and, although he could not enforce his rule over much of the territory, Brunei's power was strongest in the west and was negligible in the areas claimed by Sulu.

In 1842 the sultan of Brunei ceded a large tract of land embracing the Sarawak River area to a young British adventurer, James Brooke, as reward for the help Brooke had given in putting down a rebellion against the sultan's district chief in the area. Brooke was appointed the new district chief, or raja, of Sarawak, by the sultan. Within a few years he eliminated piracy and headhunting in his dominions with the occasional help of gunboats of the British Navy. In 1845 the "White Raja's" regime survived a Malay rebellion led by the ousted district chief, and by 1853 Sarawak was independent of Brunei.

In the decade after 1850 a number of Chinese gold miners migrated to Sarawak from Dutch Borneo, joining the smaller community of Chinese gold miners in Bau, 20 miles from Kuching. In a bid for political power, the Chinese *kongsi* struck Kuching in 1857 and forced the raja to flee his residence. A combined force of Malays and Land Dayaks led by the raja's nephew put down the rebellion, but Brooke suspicion of Chinese political and secret-society activity continued to the end of Brooke rule a century later (see ch. 4, Ethnic Groups and Languages).

Headhunting was an essential feature of Iban and other Borneo religions and cultures, and piracy, including, by Brook definition, all seaborne opposition, was prevalent. In fighting these and in responding to requests for relief from the oppression of Brunei's appointed district chiefs, James Brooke and his heir, Charles Brooke, greatly expanded the borders of Sarawak. By the 1880's Brunei was surrounded by Sarawak territory except on the seaside (see fig. 5). The sultan generally favored cessions to the Brookes since he thus received annual payments that were greater than those he had previously received from his district chiefs.

Under the Brooke regime, the country was not open to commercial exploitation or large-scale migration in the manner of Malaya. This was largely because the raja felt a paternal concern that his subjects not be overwhelmed. Commerce and cash crops, however, were soon in the hands of Chinese merchants and farmers, and revenues for the raja came mainly from tax farms on Chinese opium, gambling, and other luxuries, as in the Straits Settlements. A handful of British residents and district officers governed according to the raja's personal instructions. Malay traditional leaders provided some measure of political backing as advisers, and Malays and other indigenous leaders filled minor administrative positions.

Enforcement of Brooke rule was achieved by letting loose upon disobedient tribal communities punitive expeditions of fearsome bands of Iban volunteers led by the Brookes. This unusual method of policing their territory earned the raja notoriety in Great Britain, which never gave its unqualified support to the Brookes' highly personal autocracy.

The Sarawak people, however, enjoyed a measure of physical security, which had previously been totally absent, and a modest amount of economic develoment without severe disruption of the way of life of the tribal interior peoples.

British control did not come to Sabah until 1881, when the British government granted a royal charter to the British North Borneo Company. The company, formed by a group of British and Austrian entrepreneurs, had already received grants from the sultans of Brunei and Sulu for their overlapping claims in northern Borneo and had bought out the rights to other earlier business ventures in the area.

The acquisition of the territory brought immediate objections from the Spanish, Dutch, and German governments, all of which claimed certain rights in the area, which were eventually quieted. The Spanish claim was revived by the Philippines in the 20th century (see ch. 14, Foreign Relations).

The royal charter was essentially one of restraint rather than privilege. The British North Borneo Company was to remain British in character and domicile; all directors and officials were to be British subjects; territory was not to be alienated without the consent of the British government; foreign affairs were to be controlled by the British government; slavery was abolished; religious freedom was guaranteed; general commercial monopoly was prohibited; and the appointment of the governor was made subject to British approval. Great Britain assumed, in fact, the role of protector.

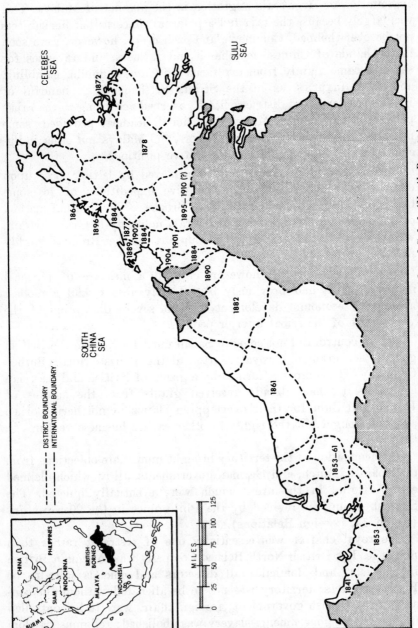

Figure 5. *Territorial expansion of Sarawak and Sabah (North Borneo).*

Two major tasks faced the company: the economic development of the country and its territorial consolidation. Land and loans were offered to various groups to encourage development, and the immigration of Chinese was encouraged in order to provide a labor supply. Serious attempts were made to exploit what were considered the three major assets—timber resources, mineral deposits, and an abundance of arable land. Although timber proved to be an asset, mineral deposits were disappointing, and development of the land resources for tobacco plantations became, after 1890, the salvation of the company for a period of 20 years. A serious economic crisis was averted by the development of a boom in the production of rubber in the early 20th century, and rubber became the mainstay of the country's economy. A west coast railroad linking Kota Kinabalu (formerly Jesselton), Weston, and Melalap, completed in 1905, opened up land ideal for rubber production. A degree of economic security resulted from these developments, which were also accompanied by a rise in population.

Territorial consolidation occurred mainly between 1884 and 1902 and involved the absorption of coastal enclaves through pressure either directly on local chieftains or on the sultan of Brunei (see fig. 5). The extensive hinterland, a kind of *terra incognita*, fell to company control by default. In 1905, through the sale of the Lawas district to Sarawak, the boundary with that state was defined. Between 1890 and 1906 the company also administered the crown colony of Labuan.

Determined to keep on good terms with the Colonial Office in London, the chartered company modeled its administration on Malayan practices. With little money and few men, it kept the peace and abolished piracy and headhunting. As in Sarawak, the government was benevolent and paternalistic, although the gains in self-government and social services were modest.

Consolidation of British Rule

At the turn of the century the British were consolidating their control over the Malaysian territories (see fig. 6). In 1888 Sarawak, Sabah, and Brunei had accepted the protection of the crown, and in the next two decades Sarawak's and Sabah's boundaries acquired the shapes that they had in late 1969. In 1906 the sultan of Brunei accepted a British resident, thereby interposing the British government between what was left of Brunei and the continuing territorial ambitions of Sarawak. This had an unexpected result when, a few years later, northern Borneo's major oilfields were developed in territory that Brunei had been on the verge of ceding to Sarawak.

The Brunei resident, with the help of civil servants borrowed from the Malayan Civil Service, ran the government on behalf of the sultan.

In 1909 the Federated Malay States government was further centralized by the creation of a federal council in Kuala Lumpur, which came gradually to take over much of the legislative initiative previously exercised by the state councils. The great rubber boom had begun, and the large-scale British investment required a more efficient government than separate state councils could provide. Improved transportation and communications within the Peninsula made centralized administration possible for the first time.

The new priority placed on modern technical knowledge and skills left little place in the administration for Malays, whose skills were primarily political. The Malay establishment objected to the increase in centralized administration, since it lessened further the influence on British policy of the indigenous Malay state leadership. Pro-Malay sentiment among the British civil servants also opposed the increased centralization of the government of the Federated States. They felt that since the Malays were not partaking in the phenomenal economic development of their country, they should at least be allowed consideration in political matters.

The decentralizing faction grew in strength when the Thai government signed a treaty with Great Britain in 1909 transferring the states of Perlis, Kedah, Kelantan, and Trengganu from Thai to British protection. These four states and the southernmost state, Johore, refused to enter into the federation and became known as the Unfederated Malay States. Gradually, these states agreed to accept British "advisers," whose authority was somewhat less than that of the residents of the Federated States.

Other developments in Malaya during this period were largely continuations of trends begun in the previous century. Railroads, roads, and communications were extended into the Unfederated States. Social services increased throughout the Peninsula. Malays, Indians (who had been imported in quantity after 1870 to work in the rubber estates), and Chinese were given slightly more opportunity to advise the government of their opinions, but neither the fact of nor the demand for representative government existed.

THE GROWTH OF NATIONAL AWARENESS

Malaya was slow to develop a sense of nationalism, and for most of its history there was little hostility to Great Britain. The growth of a nationalist spirit was retarded by the existence of various types

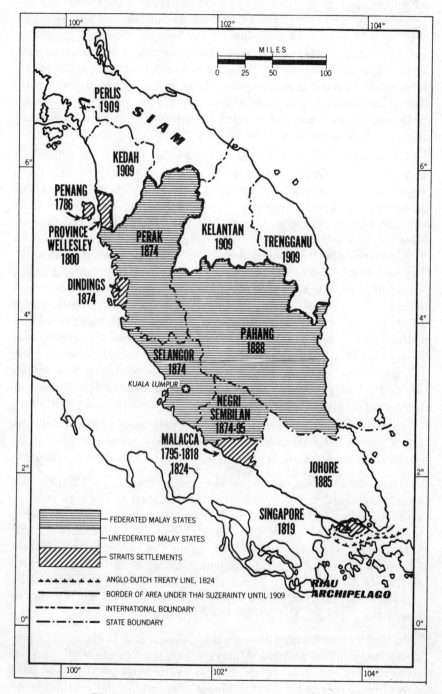

MILES

| 0 | 25 | 50 | 100 |

FEDERATED MALAY STATES
UNFEDERATED MALAY STATES
STRAITS SETTLEMENTS

ANGLO-DUTCH TREATY LINE, 1824
BORDER OF AREA UNDER THAI SUZERAINTY UNTIL 1909
INTERNATIONAL BOUNDARY
STATE BOUNDARY

SIAM

PERLIS
1909

KEDAH
1909

PENANG
1786

PROVINCE
WELLESLEY
1800

PERAK
1874

KELANTAN
1909

TRENGGANU
1909

DINDINGS
1874

PAHANG
1888

SELANGOR
1874

KUALA LUMPUR

NEGRI
SEMBILAN
1874-95

MALACCA
1795-1818
1824-

JOHORE
1885

SINGAPORE
1819

RIAU
ARCHIPELAGO

Figure 6. Extension of British Rule in Malaya.

53

of government in the country, by the separate state traditions and loyalties, by relative prosperity, and by the serious problem of ethnic divisions. Moreover, in principle, if not in fact, the British officials in the Malay states were merely advising the indigenous governments. The sultans, the royal heirs, and many of the senior Malay aristocrats received stipends generous enough to live in great comfort and maintain a stylish court life. Malay interests were also protected in other ways; for example, citizenship and landownership regulation gave preference to Malays.

Along with protection of Malay privileges, the British attempted to prevent any disturbance to the Malay farmer's way of life. Land reservation regulations were aimed at preventing Malays from alienating their land to foreign ethnic groups. In order to maintain their subsistence agriculture and to protect the Malays from the fluctuations of the world market, Malay farmers in certain areas were forbidden to plant rubber and were required to plant rice instead. Fearing that overeducation, especially English-language education, would alienate the Malays from their traditional rural heritage and produce a nation of clerks, the British provided English-language education for only a small upper stratum to prepare young royal and aristocratic heirs for entry into the lower rungs of the prestigious Malayan Civil Service or for positions of nominal power in the indigenous state government. Free vernacular education was set up for rural Malays, but it was kept at a rudimentary level aimed at producing a "sturdy peasantry" rather than an educated populace.

No such paternalism governed British policies toward the Indians and Chinese. The British assumed that they were not permanent settlers and therefore provided no government schooling for them.

While it was true, as in earlier times, that most Chinese and Indians returned home eventually, after the start of the 20th century an increasing number stayed to become permanent residents. Being urban dwellers primarily, they were able to take advantage of private English-language schools set up in the cities, many of them Christian missionary establishments. Chinese and Indians with facility in English easily found jobs in the railways, postal services, public works, and other technical services, as well as serving as clerks for the large British business concerns.

In the 20th century, although the Chinese and Indians were predominantly urban and the Malays rural, the "foreigners" were no longer largely confined to the Straits Settlements as they had been a century earlier. By 1911 Chinese immigrants far outnumbered Malays in Perak, Selangor, and Negri Sembilan. In the same states in the period from 1906 to 1920, the number of Indian laborers who, either on contract or of their own initiative, came to work on the burgeoning rubber estates, increased from 27,000 to 158,500.

In reaction to the encroachment of foreign populations, the Malays rallied behind their traditional leaders, the royalty, nobility, and the Muslim institutional hierarchy. The Muslim bureaucracy had grown in size and importance since the intervention of the British. Religion was the only clear field for indigenous authority, and the sultans had built up elaborate hierarchies of officials, providing by this royal patronage the only nonfarming employment open to Malay commoners. As a result of this patronage, a close alliance developed between the religiously conservative Muslim officials and the Malay courts.

In the early 20th century, when a Muslim reform movement based on the teachings of an Egyptian religious philosopher, Mohammed Abduh, divided the Muslim world into modernists and conservatives, the modernists in Malaya found themselves pitted against not only the conservative religious leaders but also against their patrons, the Malay secular establishment (see ch. 10, Religion). The challenge of the reform movement, therefore, soon acquired social overtones.

The modernist movement, as a religious reform movement for a more purified Islam designed to bring Malay society to grips with modern life, was strongest among city Muslims and was led largely by members of the foreign Muslim groups, the Arabs, and the Jawi Peranakan (community of mixed Muslim Indian and Malay descent) of Singapore and Penang. The modernist appeal gradually broadened to include secular social reform and came under the influence of Indonesian nationalists who introduced Marxism and ideas of Pan-Malay cooperation into modernist thought.

In general, the foreigners were more radical than the indigenous Malays, but an indigenous nonaristocratic group of intellectuals, mostly teachers at the government vernacular schools and journalists, eventually emerged. In 1938 a radical group of writers and teachers, many of them graduates of the Tanjong Malim Teachers Training College, which for many years was the only Malay-language secondary school, formed the Young Malay Union (Kesatuan Melayu Muda). This was the first indigenous organization of Malays to oppose the traditional aristocratic elite. Heavily influenced by the nationalist movement growing up in Indonesia, the Young Malay Union was strongly anticolonialist. From this organization would develop the leadership of radical Malay parties, such as the Party Ra'ayat, that have continued into the 1960's to support close relations with Indonesian Malays and substantive social change (see ch. 13, Political Dynamics).

The majority of Malays, however, were loyal to their sultans and to the conservative Muslim leadership that they patronized. Malay nationalism looked to the English-educated sons of Malay royalty for protection against the threats posed by the immigrant communities. In the late 1930's Malay state associations emerged and served as vehicles for this socially conservative, pro-British political conciouness. From these Malay associations there later developed the United Malays National Organization, the major Malay political organization of the post-World War II period.

Among the Chinese in West Malaysia, nationalism became a real force in the 1920's and 1930's. The Kuomintang, the Nationalist Party of China, received much of its early support from the Nanyang Chinese. At one time the British considered it dangerous to allow Sun Yat-sen, the founder of the Chinese Republic, to remain in Penang. When the Nationalists split into Communist and non-Communist wings, this split also occurred among the Chinese of Malaya. The new Chinese nationalism, combined with an increase in availability of Chinese women to marry, drew the migrants into a new interest in their homeland. The rebirth of interest in Chinese culture, which gave rise to the founding of private schools taught in the Chinese national language, increased the cohesion of the overseas Chinese community and widened the gap between it and the other peoples of Malaysia.

The Indians, most of them retaining close ties to their homeland, were also participating at long range in the independence movement at home. This Indian nationalism was also fostered by private Indian-language schools.

In Sarawak and Sabah no true nationalism developed during the pre-World War II period, but a sense of communal identity did emerge. There were, as in West Malaysia, various regulations designed to protect Malays and tribal peoples, and the integration of the various ethnic groups was not attempted. The different communities were represented by their own chiefs when dealing with the Westerners, and the customary law of each group was taken into account whenever possible in determining policy affecting the various communities.

Gradually, the Chinese, as the result of nationalist developments in China, began to feel an ethnic identity that transcended province of origin or dialect group. With peace, more stable populations, and improved communications, the Muslims grew closer together, transcending local loyalties, and non-Muslims began to see themselves as belonging to broader groupings than merely their village or longhouse (see Glossary).

In the 20th century, for the first time, the people of the Malay and Borneo states felt the direct impact of world trade conditions on their lives. By the 1920's the economy had become dependent on a few primary products: in Malaya, chiefly rubber and tin; in Sarawak, rubber, pepper, and oil; and in Sabah, rubber and timber. A large share of government revenue was derived directly from export duties on these products and indirectly from taxes on luxuries and other imports used primarily by people employed in the export industries. Sharp fluctuations in the price of rubber after World War I and a drop in the prices of all primary products in the world depression of 1929 had severe effects on government finances and on the people themselves. The migrations from China and India halted, and many Chinese and Indians had to be repatriated. Nonetheless, Malaysia had in 1941 more than double the population of 30 years earlier, and all were living a more prosperous and peaceful life than had been possible before the British came.

THE JAPANESE OCCUPATION

Malaya and Singapore

On December 8, 1941, when Japan declared war on Great Britain, Singapore's sea defense included only two capital vessels, which were soon sunk. The Japanese moved easily from Thailand to Kedah and on down the Peninsula; on February 15, 1942, the British surrendered.

In occupying Malaya, the Japanese diverged from the tactics used in other parts of Southeast Asia in that they made no pretense of permitting Malayan self-government. Malaya and Sumatra were briefly combined in an attempted union. The Japanese made few changes in government on the Peninsula and, for the most part, the Malays neither opposed nor actively aided the invaders. In 1943 Kedah, Perlis, Trengganu, and Kelantan were returned by the Japanese, for the duration of the war to the Thais, who placed Thai governors at the head of the existing state administrations. The civil servants in Malaya continued to function much as they had done under the British; they had, however, slightly more authority during the war than before it, with the result that the eventual return of the British was felt to be a loss.

Although the whole population suffered during the war years, particularly because the cessation of rice imports led to widespread malnutrition, the most marked hardships were borne by the Chinese community. Thousands of Chinese were killed in the first days of occupation, and many thousands more fled to the interior, where they became squatters on the fringes of the jungle. The British, in preparing to leave Malaya, had given rapid training in the arts of sabotage to the members of the only group sufficiently organized and anti-Japanese to carry on armed resistance — the Chinese of the Malayan Communist Party. These men formed and led the Malayan People's Anti-Japanese Army (MPAJA) and developed a civilian support group called the Anti-Japanese Union; the membership of both of these was almost entirely Chinese, and the Chinese who settled at the jungle's edge formed an essential part of the latter group, providing supplies and a means of communication to the armed groups that remained in the jungle.

In 1943 British intelligence officers made contact with the MPAJA, and an agreement was reached whereby it would take orders from the Supreme Commander for the Allied Powers (Japan) in return for arms, ammunition, and explosives. By the end of the war there were some 6,000 men in the resistance army; they had carried on few operations, however, and had inflicted few casualties on the Japanese. Mainly because the British plans for a military campaign in Malaya were made unnecessary by the surrender of Japan, the actual return of the British in September 1945 was ill-prepared. In the interim between the Japanese surrender and the British return, the men of the MPAJA emerged from their jungle camps and were welcomed as heroes of the war by much of the population. They provided a sort of government over some areas and carried out a summary justice on those they regarded as collaborators. When the British returned, the MPAJA agreed to surrender its arms, but many weapons were hidden for later use.

Sabah and Sarawak

Resistance against the Japanese was carried on also by the people of Sabah and Sarawak. In Sabah the biggest single action took place on October 9, 1943, when a few hundred Chinese, Sulus, and Bajaus killed all 50 Japanese in the Kota Kinabalu area. Japanese retribution was fierce, and during the remainder of the occupation executions, death marches, and disease overtook much of the Asian population and annihilated the Allied prisoners of war.

At the start of the occupation Sarawak's monarch was out of the country, and the civil servants left in charge were without instructions. With the arrival of the Japanese in Kuching on Christmas Day 1941, the entire government collapsed. The civil servants were put in prison camps, and the Japanese took charge. As the occupation continued, food and other basic imports grew more scarce, and the town populations suffered hardship; attempts to resist the Japanese, generally led by Chinese, were easily crushed. In the beginning of 1945 Allied guerilla leaders parachuted into the Sarawak interior to organize the indigenous resistance that preceded the Allied liberation of Borneo beginning in June.

THE REESTABLISHMENT OF BRITISH RULE

When the British returned to their Malaysian territories, they found them devastated by war. Sabah's major cities, Kota Kinabalu and Sandakan, had been leveled by Allied bombs during the fight for liberation. Hunger was widespread, and throughout the territories racial animosities had intensified.

Great Britain's status had been irrevocably altered by the war. The success of the Japanese in East and West Malaysia was a defeat for British prestige and a boost to Asian and communal nationalism. With the growth of nationalism also came demands for better economic and social conditions.

The Federation of Malaya

During the war the British Colonial Office had drawn up plans for the Malayan Union to be imposed on British Malaya (the Malay States of the Peninsula and the Straits Settlements) when the Japanese were driven out. The union, involving great concessions by the Malay rulers and the state governments to a British-led central government, was conceived with little discussion and considerable haste and was implemented by the MacMichael treaties between Great Britain and the Malay rulers in 1946.

The imposition of centralization upon the Malay states with allegiance to the British crown replacing that sworn to the individual sultans was a threat not only to the long-recognized prerogatives of the ruling class but also to the special position of all ethnic Malays, since the plan called for the incorporation of Penang and Malacca, with their large Chinese and Indian populations, into the union and the granting of Malayan citizenship to all on an equal basis. Singapore, with its 1 million Chinese, was omitted from the union as a concession to Malay sentiment.

The Malayan Union came into legal effect in April 1946, but unexpectedly strong Malay resistance induced the British to delay its implementation. The resistance was led by the new United Malays National Organization (UMNO), founded and led by Dato Onn bin Ja'afar, a Johore Malay. Months of discussions between British and local leaders resulted in the abandonment of the centralized government scheme. On February 1, 1948, the Federation of Malaya came into being. The Federation of Malaya was a revival of the method used by the British to govern the Federated Malay States. A British high commissioner appointed by the crown ruled as the representative of the crown and the Malay rulers. An appointed executive council advised the high commissioner, and the Federal Legislative Council included representatives from the state and Straits Settlements councils. The Federation included the nine Malay states and the two Straits Settlements of Penang and Malacca. It returned to the states many of their traditional rights; to the rulers, their prerogatives, and to the Malays, the assurance by its citizenship provisions that the Chinese would not in the near future become politically dominant.

The Emergency

In the year the Federation came into being, the Malayan Communist Party began an insurrection. Partly because the Communists' former tactics in Malaya, mainly the infiltration of labor unions, were being successfully opposed by British policy and partly because of the change in tactics of Asian Communist groups, the Malayan Communist Party began to follow a policy of terrorism. Their targets were local, mainly police stations and communications lines, and many Chinese Kuomintang leaders and European planters were murdered. On June 16, 1948, the British authorities declared a state of emergency.

Gradually, the guerrillas were driven into isolated jungle areas, but the operations against them were a tremendous drain on the country's economy. To cut the guerrilla's supplies of food and equipment, the government was obliged to resettle in fenced and protected New Villages nearly half a million persons, among them thousands of Chinese families who since World War II had been squatters on the jungle's fringes.

The Emergency, as the guerrilla war was called, lasted 12 years, claimed 11,000 lives, and cost the Malayan government the equivalent of US$567 million. The nadir came in 1951 when a convoy protecting the British high commissioner, Sir Henry Gurney, was ambushed in daylight on one of the main roads of Malaya and Sir Henry was killed.

The Path to Independence

The British had promised in the Federation Agreement of 1948 to grant eventual self-rule to Malaya. Nevertheless, the colonial government insisted upon evidence of national unity before granting independence. This evidence seemed lacking, even though a vigorously implemented antiguerrilla program begun shortly after Gurney's death was improving the security situation and despite the fact that the economy had recovered, passing its prewar peak in 1950. What the British feared most was the outbreak of communal strife such as that which accompanied the 1947 British withdrawal from India.

Certainly, evidence of racial harmony was lacking. The immediate postwar period had given evidence of strong communal animosities. Politics, both legal and illegal, were in the hands of communally organized groups. The non-Communist Chinese formed the Malayan Chinese Association in 1949. The Indians had formed their party, the Malayan Indian Congress, 3 years earlier. Dato Onn bin Ja'afar tried to broaden his national organization, the UMNO, to include non-Malays and failed. In 1951, when municipal elections were held as Malaya's first step toward democratic self-government, the communalist parties defeated all those organized on multiracial lines.

Having failed to convert the UMNO to his views, Onn left the UMNO and founded a new party, the Independence of Malaya Party, open to all "Malayans," that is, citizens of Malaya. To contest Onn's new party in the Kuala Lumpur municipal elections of 1952, a pragmatic, British-educated scion of Kedah royalty, Tengku (Prince) Abdul Rahman, the new leader of UMNO, formed an alliance with the Malayan Chinese Association, putting up Malay candidates in Malay wards and Chinese candidates in Chinese wards. The partnership won the election and, calling itself the Alliance Party, won 94 out of 124 seats contested in various local elections held all over Malaya between 1952 and 1954.

The Alliance was an outstanding success for interracial cooperation, if not the cultural fusion that Onn would have wished. To the British, the Alliance's successes brought the possibility of independence within reach. In 1955 the Malayan Indian Congress joined the Alliance Party, and Abdul Rahman led this coalition to a spectacular victory, 51 out of 52 elected seats in the 99-member Federal Legislative Council. The Alliance had campaigned on a platform of independence within 4 years and improvements in social services, labor, and economic policies. An answer to the controversial question of who would have full citizenship privileges in an independent Malaya was avoided.

The British government meanwhile attempted to strike at the bases of communal conflict by advancing the economy of the rural Malays through development projects and improving the non-Malays' political position by liberalizing the requirements for citizenship and granting non-Malays, for the first time, limited entry into the Malayan Civil Service.

After the showing of support for interracial cooperation provided by the 1955 elections, the British prepared to leave. The guerrilla war had reduced in intensity, and the economy was in good shape. A Commonwealth commission under Lord Reid was formed to establish the outlines of a federal state with a strong central government based on parliamentary democracy. The commission was instructed to see that their proposals protected the "special position of the Malays and the legitimate interests of other communities."

During the year-long consultations to determine the provisions of the constitution, the Alliance presented a united front. It was kept together by the knowledge that a split in the coalition might seriously delay independence. Within the party caucus, the Malayan Chinese Association was at a disadvantage compared to the United Malays when arguing constitutional issues. Tradition and British policy favored the Malays in the political arena and, because of the Emergency, loyal Chinese were constantly required to show proof of their loyalty to Malaya. There was, however, a genuine determination on all sides to find acceptable compromises. The great trust that non-Malays had in the fairmindedness of the Tengku, who as party chairman had the burden of reconciliation and pacification, proved crucial during this period.

The resultant document, the 1957 Constitution of the Federation of Malaya, was intended to reflect the balance between Malays and non-Malays that had brought the Alliance repeated political success since 1952 (see ch. 12, The Governmental System). It provided for the retention of special privileges for Malays in the civil service, scholarships, businesses, licenses, and the reservation of some land for their exclusive use, while assuring that the rights of non-Malays could not be hindered by prejudicial legislation or government intervention. On August 31, 1957, Merdeka Day, the Federation of Malaya attained independence (*merdeka*) within the Commonwealth of Nations.

Malaya's independence movement was remarkable for the speed with which it achieved its goal and for the nonparticipation of Communists. When independence came, the guerrilla war, although greatly reduced in force, had still 3 years to run, and the independent government from its inception has retained a strong anti-Communist posture.

On Malaya's Merdeka Day, Singapore was moving toward full internal self-government within 2 years. In the Borneo territories constitutional developments moved at a slower pace.

Postwar Colonialism in British Borneo

The third "White Raja," Charles Vyner Brooke, returning to Borneo in 1946, felt unable to give Sarawak the reconstruction and development it needed and ceded the country to Great Britain over Malay opposition. The British North Borneo Company felt similarly incompetent to rehabilitate its devastated territory and ceded it to the crown. The British then joined it to their island colony of Labuan to make a new crown colony, the status given to Sarawak. Brunei remained separate under the indirect rule of a British resident, whose advice the sultan was obliged to follow.

Few signs of political consciousness had been displayed by the people in any of the Borneo states before 1941, although the raja of Sarawak had granted a constitution that year. As in Malaya, the Japanese occupation awoke an interest in greater political participation. One result of the new political consciousness was the anticession movement in Sarawak, which opposed absorption into Great Britain as the replacement of the Brooke monarchy that had been tailored to Sarawak. The anticession movement was largely responsible for a number of guarantees written into the cession agreement between the raja and the British crown providing for the continuation of former policies in regard to the rights and privileges of the indigenous peoples, the continuation of the former legal system and code, and the maintenance of most of the articles of the former constitution.

Both Sarawak and Sabah, unable to finance their own reconstruction programs, received large allotments from the British government that totaled in some instances nearly half the entire governmental expenditures of the two colonies. Brunei, on the other hand, made prosperous by its oilfields, did not require economic relief and made loans and grants to the other two colonies and to Malaya.

During the two decades following the return of the British to Malaya which brought independence to the Federation of Malaya and internal self-government to Singapore, the British were also anxious to advance the degree of self-government in the Borneo territories. In 1959 Brunei was relieved of its obligation to follow British advice in all matters except foreign affairs and defense. Local elections to district and municipal councils, which in turn elected some members to the state legislature, took place in Sarawak in December 1959. Sabah, although it had appointed members to legislative councils who participated in lawmaking as representatives of the various ethnic groups, had no elections of any kind until 1962.

THE CREATION OF MALAYSIA

Regional association, or at least cooperation, in Southeast Asia has been a common topic of debate in most of the affected countries since World War II. Suggestions ranged from bilateral cooperation to an association of all formerly British territories, including Hong Kong, into a regional political entity. The first attempt at a formal association, which would have reached even beyond the area of Southeast Asia, concerned Australia, Ceylon, India, Indonesia, Pakistan, the Philippines, and Thailand in 1950 and met with failure mostly because of disagreement on the form of association and on leadership. Less ambitious plans proposing association among the Malayan states, Indonesia, Pakistan, and the Philippines or among the Malayan states, Thailand, and the Philippines seemed to have more possibilities for success.

A strong stimulant for regional cooperation originated in the realization of the politically fragmented area's susceptibility to outside pressure concurrent with the gradual withdrawal of European powers. Especially serious consideration was given to China's uncontrolled population explosion, to its growing industry, and to its rapidly increasing military potential.

Perhaps the first formal initiative to consolidate the Malayan states and the Straits Settlements was made by Singapore, which submitted such a proposition even before Malayan independence in 1957 and again after it achieved internal self-government in 1959. The principal Malayan objection to such a proposal was based on fear of Chinese domination within the proposed union. If Singapore's 1.1 million Chinese (enumerated in the 1957 census) were added to Malaya's 2.3 million Chinese, they would have outnumbered the 3.1 million Malays. In addition to their numerical strength, the Chinese represented stronger political and labor organizations with pronounced leftist and Communist factions.

To reduce Malayan fears, Singapore tried to develop a Malayan consciousness among its Chinese citizens. Many of the Chinese felt themselves to belong to Malaya, and it was feared that if isolated they might reorient themselves toward China. In terms of internal politics, the leftist People's Action Party (PAP), under the leadership of Lee Kuan Yew, supported "independence through merger," whereas the Workers' Party, led by David Marshall, stood for "independence before merger." Only the Socialist Party opposed merger altogether because British rule in Singapore enabled it to continue its "anticolonial struggle" and subversion on the Peninsula.

In the second half of 1960 prime ministers Tengku Abdul Rahman of the Federation of Malaya and Lee Kuan Yew of the State of Singapore held a series of talks with Duncan Sandys, secretary of Commonwealth relations of the United Kingdom. As a result, the scope of the proposed association was enlarged to include the three Bornean territories of Sarawak, Brunei, and North Borneo (Sabah) and thereby provide an ethnic composition for the projected federation in which the indigenous people would have maintained their majority. In arriving at this method of ethnic balances, the assumption was made that the interests of the Malays and the indigenous people of Borneo were very similar. This assumption was later to be challenged by leaders of indigenous non-Muslim communities in Sabah and Sarawak. When the plan was made public on May 27, 1961, it became the focus of domestic political controversies in all five territories and later evolved into an issue of international dimensions.

The announcement sharpened the lines of demarcation between antimerger and promerger forces in Singapore. The crisis was climaxed in a referendum on September 1, 1962, in which the government provided a choice between three different forms of merger but none for the expression of opposition to it. In the compulsory vote, 25 percent of the electorate cast blank ballots to express disapproval of the merger, but 71 percent endorsed one of the government's alternative plans.

Great Britain supported federation because it believed that Singapore as a city-state could not survive long. It was even more convinced that the economically underdeveloped and politically unsophisticated crown colonies of Sarawak and Sabah and the tiny protected state of Brunei could not stand on their own feet after British withdrawal. The British argued that complete independence would upset the economic balance and result in permanent political instability, thereby making the territories easy prey to an outside aggressor. By offering continuous cooperation and protection, the British also hoped to maintain most of their vital military bases and their economic interests. The British were also concerned about the rapid increase of the Chinese in Borneo, many of whom held loyalties to Communist China.

As in Malaya and Singapore, the governments of Sarawak and Sabah and most of the educated population favored federation. Although some opposition was expressed in the beginning by certain political and religious leaders who feared Malay and Muslim domination in the new state, it dwindled down to the political extremists when special provisions to safeguard Bornean interests were promised by Malaya and Singapore. To ascertain public sentiment, a joint British-Malay group of investigators, the Cobbold Commission, was dispatched to Sarawak and Sabah in 1962 and found that two-thirds of the population favored merger. Based upon the recommendations of the commission, the United Kingdom made preparations for the transfer of these two crown colonies to the federation of Malaysia.

The situation was quite different in the Brunei protectorate. Here a militant nationalist group had long planned an independent Brunei kingdom that, on historical grounds, would have incorporated Sarawak and Sabah. The dynamic leader of the nationalists, Inche A.M. Azahari, was in Manila on December 7, 1962, when the North Kalimantan National Army (Tentara Nasional Kalimantan Utara) staged a revolt and planned to capture the sultan and force him to sanction their objectives. Although Azahari's army received enthusiastic support from its followers in the Limbang district of Sarawak, the narrow strip between the two enclaves formed by Brunei, the assistance from sympathizers in Sarawak and Sabah did not meet expectations, and the 100,000 Indonesian "volunteers" allegedly promised by President Sukarno to join in the establishment of the Unitary State of Kalimantan Utara never arrived. The sultan escaped capture and, with British and Malayan help, defeated the revolt within a few days. Some of Azahari's followers escaped to the jungles to the south and threatened the security of the territories through guerrilla activities. Azahari himself continued his mission, first from Manila and later from Djakarta.

Formidable opposition to federation came also from the Chinese-dominated Sarawak United People's Party founded in 1959 and strongly supported by labor and Chinese farmers. The party was suspected by the British administration of cooperating with the clandestine Communist organization, a small but powerful group that infiltrated the ranks of the party, the labor organizations, local Chinese newspapers, and secondary schools. Party opposition to merger stimulated a closer cooperation of the pro-Malaysia forces. Pro-federation Chinese and Malays joined with Dayaks and other indigenous peoples in forming the Sarawak Alliance Party which, in the June 1963 district elections, won, together with independent pro-Malaysian candidates, 73 percent of the votes. No such struggle ensued in Sabah, where the pro-Malaysia North Borneo Alliance Party won 90 percent of the votes in that territory's first election in December 1962.

Merger as a domestic issue was still not resolved when objections to the creation of Malaysia were raised by two governments, those of the Philippines and of Indonesia. The Philippine objection centered around a claim to Sabah put forward on the ground that it was part of the former Sulu sultanate to which the Philippines were the rightful heirs and which was only leased to the British. The claim seemed seriously to threaten the plans for regional cooperation embodied in the Association of Southeast Asia (ASA), which Malaya, Thailand, and the Philippines joined on July 31, 1961. Philippine President Diosdado Macapagal suggested a Malayan confederation composed of his country and the prospective Malaysian components in 1962.

The Confrontation with Indonesia

Indonesia did not at first support the Philippine claim but, after the abortive Brunei revolt, it denounced Malaysia as a "neocolonialist plot" that was "against our wishes and our revolution." President Sukarno vowed to block the creation of Malaysia or, if unsuccessful, to "crush" it by every means at his disposal.

Having experienced a long war with the Dutch for Indonesia's national liberation, Sukarno, his government, and many Indonesians were suspicious of Malaya's peaceful transition to independence. Sukarno accused the easygoing Tengku Abdul Rahman of being a tool of the colonialists. Malayan cooperation with a colonial power against Asian Communists during the Emergency, asylum given to Sumatran rebels against the Indonesian central government in the late 1950's, and acquiescence in the smuggling of Indonesian foreign-exchange goods across the the Strait of Malacca added to Indonesia's resentment of Malaysia.

In a choice between an armed revolutionary revolt, either Azahari's or the one led by the clandestine Communist organization, and a peaceful handover of British colonies to the Federation, Sukarno's sympathies went automatically to the revolutionaries. The time was opportune. The Indonesian Communists opposed Malaysia. The campaign for West New Guinea against the Dutch had just concluded, and the Indonesian army needed reasons not to reduce strength. A new national cause might also serve to distract popular attention from Indonesia's worsening economic situation. Sukarno called Indonesia's opposition to Malaysia *konfrontasi* (confrontation), but it soon became an undeclared war on the Federation and the Borneo territories.

Adverse foreign reaction and hope that a joint Philippine-Indonesian action might delay the creation of Malaysia caused Sukarno to strike reconciliatory tones and to give theoretical consent to the Federation in May 1963. Negotiators of the three countries met in Manila in June and agreed to propose to their respective governments the creation of a consultative arrangement for collective defense within the framework of MAPHILINDO (Malaysia, the Philippines, and Indonesia) and the submission of the Borneo problem to the United Nations (UN) for assessment of public opinion in the territories of Sarawak and Sabah.

Prime Minister Rahman accepted the UN proposal and, in theory, also MAPHILINDO; nevertheless, he proceeded with federation plans and, on July 9, signed the final agreement with the United Kingdom setting the slate of the formation of Malaysia for August 31, 1963. The announcement of the agreement infuriated Sukarno, who thereupon pledged to activate his "crush Malaysia" campaign by military action if necessary. At a summit meeting arranged to avoid open warfare, Prime Minister Rahman and President Sukarno met in Manila late in July, where, through the intermediary role of President Macapagal, Rahman agreed to postpone federation for 2 weeks to allow the UN sufficient time for assessment. In mid-August nine UN delegates began their work to assess the attitude of the peoples of Sarawak and Sabah toward federation.

The UN team reported that two-thirds of the people favored federation, basing their report on review of the results of recent elections and on interviews with 4,000 persons. Meanwhile, the final terms of merger were worked out between the respective governments, first in Kuala Lumpur and then later in London. Allowances were made for the differences between the various components of Malaysia in terms of economic and political development and ethnic composition; specific requests were honored and in part incorporated in the new Constitution (see ch. 12, The Governmental System). At the last minute Brunei declined to join the federation, partly because the sultan was dissatisfied with the determination of his precedence among the heads of governments, which also determined his succession to the seat of Yang di-Pertuan Agong, or Supreme Head of Malaysia (see ch. 12, The Governmental System). Controversy about the division of revenue received from oil also contributed to the sultan's stand. Neither Brunei's negative decision nor the confrontation with Indonesia, however, prevented the Federation of Malaya, the state of Singapore, and the crown colonies of Sarawak and Sabah from raising the flag of Malaysia on September 16, 1963.

Indonesia's Confrontation intensified within hours. On September 17 Indonesian demonstrators, encouraged by their government, attacked the Malaysian and British embassies in Djakarta. The ambassadors from Indonesia and the Philippines had left Kuala Lumpur the day before Malaysia came into being, and diplomatic contact among the three nations was not resumed until January 1964 when the foreign ministers met in Bangkok at the urging of the United States special envoy, Attorney General Robert F. Kennedy. The intervening period produced increasing numbers of Indonesian-inspired incidents along the Kalimantan-East Malaysian borders. The Indonesian "volunteers" were joined by Chinese members of the clandestine Communist organization (CCO) in Sarawak.

The Bangkok talks quickly collapsed, as did a summit conference of Macapagal, Sukarno, and Rahman in Tokyo in June 1964. Great Britain, New Zealand, and Australia sent troops and other military aid in accordance with their defense agreements to help the Malaysian army. A diplomatic boost came in December 1964 when Malaysia was elected to one year's rotating membership on the Security Council of the UN over Indonesia's objection.

In one sense the war was a help to Malaysia in that it served to unite the nation against an aggressor. It was, however, expensive and diverted funds from economic development plans that had been envisaged as necessary to bring the rural Malays and the Bornean indigenous people nearer to economic equality with the Chinese. In general, however, Malaysia's economy was booming. Tin had an exceptionally good year in 1965; Sabah's economic growth was remarkable; investment in manufacturing was increasing; and the cost of living was relatively steady.

The cutoff in trade from Indonesia during the Confrontation was serious for Singapore, although smuggling by Indonesians prevented Sukarno's trade embargo from being completely effective. More than 100,000 Singaporeans were thrown out of work by the loss of the Indonesian trade. Penang and Sarawak were also affected, though less substantially.

Singapore's Secession

In addition to the problems created by the Confrontation in 1964, Malaysia also had to cope with conflict developing between Singapore and Malaya. In the agreement of 1963, upon which Malaysia was based, worked out by the Malayan and Singapore heads of government, Tengku Abdul Rahman and Lee Kuan Yew, Singapore accepted substantial underrepresentation in the lower house of the Federal Parliament (Dewan Ra'ayat) in exchange for keeping most of its revenue and handling its own education and labor affairs. The agreement also provided that Singapore citizens, though legally Malaysian citizens, could not participate as full citizens in peninsular Malaysia without fulfilling stringent naturalization requirements.

Lee, however, did not appear to regard this agreement as confining him politically to Singapore. A British-educated Chinese who combined academic brilliance and political dynamism, Lee had led his socialist People's Action Party (PAP) to a great victory in Singapore's 1959 elections with Communist help. Since then he had crushed the Communist power, reassured timid foreign investors, and had established a capable, relatively corruption-free, and popular government on the island. An election held the week after merger confirmed Lee's control over Singapore's electorate. As a socialist, he had contempt for the conservative Chinese component of the Alliance government, the Malayan Chinese Association, whose leadership seemed willing to permit the retention of special privileges of Malays for the indefinite future. As a politician, he saw the association as blocking the PAP's path to further political expansion in the country at large.

The PAP entered nine candidates in the peninsular elections of 1964 for seats in the Malaysian Federal Parliament against candidates of the Malayan Chinese Association. Its leaders hoped that if enough PAP candidates won the Tengku might in time contemplate severing connections with the Malayan Chinese Association and creating a UMNO-PAP alliance.

The Malaysian Alliance leadership felt that Lee had violated the spirit of the Malaysia Agreement by not being satisfied with the 15 seats already alloted to Singapore in that agreement. The election results were a sweeping victory for the Alliance. Only one PAP candidate won a seat, and the Alliance's other opponents also sustained losses. Lee's party, with 16 seats, was the major opposition party against 89 Alliance seats. There was now little hope that Singapore could play a more active role than the limited one the Tengku envisioned for it, that of the New York City of Malaysia.

The Alliance's success in the election had come in response to a call to all citizens of all nationalities to show their loyalty to a beleaguered country by supporting the Alliance regime. The government stress on the necessity for national loyalty continued during the critical months that followed the election.

In mid-1964 several attempts were made to land Indonesian troops by sea and air on the Peninsula of Malaya. In July and again in September, serious race riots broke out in Singapore between Chinese and Malays. In January 1965 the government arrested three east-coast Malay opposition leaders, who later confessed to involvement in Indonesia-backed fifth column activity. The Indonesian Confrontation continued without any sign of abatement.

Thus, the Alliance regarded Lee as acting disloyally when he began to call for greater equality of rights for all Malaysian citizens in speeches delivered in Malaysia and abroad in 1965. To the Tengku and his government, who felt that no true equality could exist until the Malays and other indigenous peoples were given a chance to catch up with the wealthier and more highly qualified Chinese, Lee appeared to be reneging on the 1963 agreement that had been incorporated in the Constitution.

In May 1965 the PAP led the organizing of a Malaysian Solidarity Convention in Singapore. At this convention, Singapore Malay members of the PAP appealed for the support of rural peninsular Malays against the Alliance's alleged partnership of Malay UMNO aristocrats and Chinese exploitative capitalists. Several East Malaysian non-Alliance parties sent delegations. At a UMNO convention in Kuala Lumpur in the same month, Lee was burned in effigy.

Bitter debates in the Federal Parliament followed, in which Lee attempted to push for greater speed in removing special privileges for Malays and the creation of a "Malaysian nation." In rebuttal, Alliance members argued that racial harmony was needed first and should precede any attempt to create a noncommunal national society.

Lee's actions during the summer of 1965 suggest that he had agreed to the 1963 terms as the minimum acceptable concession and that he considered himself, the popular leader of a state that was 80 percent Chinese, obligated to work continually to improve the position of Chinese within the Malay-Chinese partnership. To the Tengku and UMNO, however, the 1963 agreement terms were not open for renegotiation. Incorporated in the agreement of 1963 was the compromise worked out by the Malays and Chinese of Malaya in 1957, a delicate balance of opposing forces within an Alliance that had brought political stability. The Malayan Chinese Association leaders agreed with Rahman that Malaya's Chinese, a minority, would lose ground if Chinese pressure for further political power drove Malay support away from Rahman's moderates and into the camp of the Malay chauvinists (see ch. 13, Political Dynamics).

Early in August the Tengku returned from 12 months abroad and, in secret meeting with Lee and members of both the federal and Singapore cabinets, arranged for the peaceful departure of Singapore from Malaysia. On August 9, 1965, Singapore became an independent and sovereign state. The two countries signed an agreement including the promise to work out arrangements for joint defense and mutual assistance.

Simultaneous announcements by Lee and Tengku Abdul Rahman broke the news of separation to a surprised public. The Tengku gave his reasons in a speech before the Federal Parliament that day: "We had pledged to form Malaysia with Singapore, but, having given it a trial, we found that if we persist in going on with it, in the long run there will be more trouble in Malaysia than what Singapore is worth to us."

Lee, speaking to the press, later that morning, referred to the severance of ties as a cause for anguish: "All my life I have believed in Malaysia, merger, and the unity of these two territories." Later, however, Singapore leaders began to speak of the benefits achieved from their new autonomy.

The two Borneo states that had joined with Singapore and Malaya to form Malaysia were not consulted before Singapore's secession. The news came as a surprise and produced anxiety in the two states. In particular, the non-Muslims, who constitute a majority in both states, were distressed by the news.

Early in the post-Singapore period, hope for an eventual end to the Confrontation came when a pro-Communist coup attempt on September 30, 1965, in Djakarta backfired, resulting in an anti-Communist domestic purge. Gradually, it became clear that Indonesia was undergoing a fundamental change of direction, and on August 11, 1966, a peace treaty between Indonesia and Malaysia ended the undeclared war.

The termination of the Confrontation did not bring an end to the Philippine claim to Sabah, however. By 1968 relations between the Philippines and Malaysia, which had moved briefly toward an interest in cooperation, were suspended (see ch. 14, Foreign Relations).

Communal friction also continued in the post-Confrontation period. In mid-November 1967 riots broke out in Penang. Touched off by a Labor Party call for a general strike to protest the way the government handled the monetary crisis caused by Great Britain's devaluation of the pound, the rioting soon provoked communal responses (see ch. 22, Foreign Economic Relations). For a month there were curfews in various parts of the country. The economy also suffered in 1967, partly as the result of falling rubber prices.

The Malayan federal parliamentary elections in 1969 provided the Alliance Party with the smallest majority it had ever had. With 66 seats, 23 less than in 1964, UMNO politicians blamed the Malayan Chinese Association, who were responsible for losing 14 of the Alliance seats, 13 of them to the Democratic Action Party.

The following day the election results triggered a wave of racial violence between Malays and Chinese in Kuala Lumpur and elsewhere in Malaysia more serious than any since independence. Most of the victims were Chinese.

A state of emergency was declared, and scheduled East Malaysian elections were postponed. The normal government arrangements were suspended, and the deputy prime minister, Tun Abdul Razak, whom the Tengku had been grooming as his successor, acted as chairman of the National Operations Council. He was put in charge of government operations with advice from Prime Minister Rahman and emergency power granted him by Malaysia's constitutional monarch, the Yang di-Pertuan Agong.

CHAPTER 4

ETHNIC GROUPS AND LANGUAGES

The estimated 10.3 million population of Malaysia in 1969 was comprised of about 44 percent Malays (over 50 percent in West Malaysia), about 36 percent Chinese, 10 percent Indians and Pakistanis, and the remainder mostly made up of native tribal groups whose ancestors inhabited the area long before the Malays, Chinese, or Indians arrived. The tribal groups are usually found in small, highly localized enclaves in the interior; elements of the other ethnic groups are present throughout the country, although their uneven distribution creates significantly different population profiles in each area.

The Malays are concentrated in West Malaysia. In East Malaysia they are less numerous, ranking only third in size as a group. Culturally and politically, the Malays are the most influential segment of the population.

The Chinese are the second largest group and have significant numbers in all parts of the nation. They form 37 percent of the population in West Malaysia, 31 percent of that in Sarawak, and 23 percent of that in Sabah. The Chinese also manifest a uniformity that, together with their domination of trade and commerce, makes them a powerful and influential group in the economic life of the country.

The number of Indians is not significant in any area and, except for considerable prominence in labor unions, they do not exert much national influence. The native tribal peoples are most numerous in East Malaysia but form only a minor portion of the inhabitants in the western segment. Their great diversity in respect to origins, language, and culture, combined with their small numbers, renders them generally ineffective as a group.

Many languages are spoken in the country, most of them with a number of variations and dialects associated with particular regions or ethnic subgroups. The most widely spoken are Bahasa Malaysia (Malay, the national language), Chinese, Tamil (Indian), and English. In addition, several other languages and many dialects are spoken in the mountainous regions of both East and West Malaysia, and some Indian tongues other than Tamil are used by immigrants from northern India.

In each locality speakers of different languages may be found living side by side, so that many persons are conversant in more than one language or dialect of the same language. English, Mandarin Chinese, and Malay are used as vehicles for communication outside local groups. Intercommunications among various Chinese dialect groups are through Mandarin, but English is often used between them and other peoples. Only Bahasa Malaysia approaches the status of a common language, and its use as such is constantly promoted by the government.

Literacy is confined largely to Bahasa Malaysia, Chinese, and English, although written forms exist for some of the tribal languages. Iban is the most important among the written tribal languages, but a few persons are literate in other local dialects. The non-Malay speaker who learns to read usually does so in Bahasa Malaysia rather than in his own language, even when there is a written form for it. Literacy in Chinese is limited almost exclusively to the Chinese population and is greatest in urban areas where it is important in commercial circles. Literacy in English also is found primarily in towns and is achieving importance in administrative and commercial affairs and in the educational systems of both East and West Malaysia.

ETHNIC GROUPS

The great ethnic diversity that characterizes Malaysian society reflects a history of original habitation and later colonization by successive migratory waves of many varying groups. The process began in prehistoric times with the southward movement of tribes from mainland Southeast Asia into what is now West Malaysia, where they occupied coastal areas, sometimes penetrating inland a few miles along river banks. These peoples were the original inhabitants of the land and the ancestors of the non-Muslim, non-Malay native groups of West Malaysia. They included several tribes of Negritos called the Semang, another group known as the Senoi, and a third group referred to as the Jakun. In East Malaysia the number of separate groups was more numerous, and these groups were generally of later, nonmainland origin. The most significant among them were the Iban (Sea Dayak) and the Land Dayak in Sarawak and the Kadazan (Dusun) in Sabah.

These people were followed, about 2500 B.C., by northward migrations of Malay speakers from Indonesia into both the Malay Peninsula and Indonesian Borneo. The new arrivals settled in coastal areas, pushing the original inhabitants into the interior, where most of them remained as closed enclaves preserving their own physical and cultural identity. A significant exception to this displacement involved the Jakun, who adopted the Hinduized or Islamized culture of the newcomers and, although retaining their group name, came to be known also as proto-Malays.

Continuing migratory waves of people from Sumatra, Java, Celebes, and lesser Indonesian islands occurred sporadically and with varying intensity over the several succeeding centuries. These later arrivals were all Malayo-Polynesian speakers, who added to the number and variety of local Malay groupings and greatly increased the ratio between them and the original native peoples. They gave a deeper Malay cultural shading to society in general but did not otherwise alter the basic structure or ethnic composition or the population (see ch. 3, Historical Setting).

The situation remained essentially unchanged in this form until various groups of Europeans (English, Portuguese, Spanish, and Dutch) began to appear during the 16th century A.D. in an attempt to control trade in and through the area. The Europeans by themselves did not radically upset the historic ethnic balance in Malaysia, because their numbers were relatively small; but their development of trade, commerce, industry, and natural resources created expanding economic opportunities that attracted additional migrations, not only from Indonesia but also from China and India. The Indonesians were speedily assimilated and absorbed into the Malay community, but the Chinese and Indians constituted the first significant influx of new ethnic elements that had occurred for centuries. These immigrations became substantial in the latter part of the 19th century and completely altered the population pattern of the country. In West Malaysia the Chinese and the Indians ultimately outnumbered all resident groups except the Malays; in East Malaysia the immigration of Indians was insignificant, but the Chinese expanded, until by 1900 they had become second in size only to the combined total of the various native non-Malay tribes (see ch. 3, Historical Setting).

In addition, a few other ethnic groups, such as Arabs, Burmese, Thai, and Filipinos, arrived during the later immigrations. These people were in the minority and remain numerically insignificant, although the Arabs have had great influence in religious matters (see ch. 10, Religion).

The ethnic composition of the population of present-day Malaysia therefore is a loosely homogenized mixture of peoples grouped into three broad categories. The first category consists of numerous native tribal groups and subgroups whose members, descended from earliest inhabitants of their areas, have persistently maintained their own unique physical and cultural identities.

The second category is that of the Malays. Identity as a Malay is extremely elusive and often arbitrary, but a Malay may be superficially defined as any Muslim who practices the Indonesian form of Malay culture, speaks Malay, and is accepted as a Malay within the community. The single most important element distinguishing a Malay from a non-Malay is the Islamic religion. These elements are included in the Malaysian Constitution's definition of Malays (see ch. 10, Religion). Some Malays, prompted perhaps by a concern for social status, define an authentic Malay as one whose ancestors were in the area during the latter part of the 18th century, regardless of his previous origin. This limiting time factor, however, is not popularly accepted nor legally established.

The third category includes the Chinese, Indians, Europeans, and other recent arrivals who represent cultures derived from their homelands and alien to Malaysia.

In East Malayasia the term *Malay* is less circumscribed than it is in the western segment of the nation, popularly referring to all who profess Islam, whether they be Malay speakers or recent converts. Most Malays are descendants of peoples who were in northern Borneo before the arrival of Islam; and, although Muslim proscriptions and values have created important distinguishing changes among them since conversion, the changes have occurred within the framework of a broad traditional culture common to all indigenous peoples of Sarawak and Sabah.

The Malays form an important, although not numerically dominant, segment of the population, and almost every town and settlement has its Malay community. They are predominantly coastal dwellers who live in individual huts near the water rather than in the longhouses (multifamily dwellings) of the interior peoples. In addition to immigrations from Indonesia, there has been much internal migration, as Malays in both Sarawak and Sabah do not appear to have strong attachment to any traditional locality. Fishing plays an important part in their subsistence activities, as does the cultivation of sago and wet rice. These more sedentary subsistence activities result in larger and more permanent villages than those of non-Malays.

The Malays

The modern Malay community is a composite formed of a core group augmented by later additions of groups collectively called the *anak dagang* or foreign Malays. The core group is a fusion of the early Sumatran immigrants, who introduced the Hinduized or Islamized culture that is now known as Malay culture, and descendants of the Jakun, or proto-Malays, who were already in the area and lost separate identity by adopting the culture of the newcomers. The *anak dagang* include later Islamized Jakun and all subsequent Muslim immigrants who needed only to learn the Malay dialect and adopt the Malay culture to be accepted into the community.

The mixture of Malay and proto-Malay physical types in all segments is well advanced, but distinctive features of each remain and can be easily recognized. Examples of the total range of variation may be found in any group, even among members of the same family, but are not considered important, because identity as a Malay is determined by custom, social organization, language, and economic pursuits rather than by biological heritage.

The assimilation of the *anak dagang* into established Malay regional communities was easily accomplished and followed their mastery of the Malay dialect of the Peninsula, the compulsory attendance of their children in Malay schools, their common adherence to Islam, and their basically similar cultures. Speed of assimilation varied according to the origin of the immigrants and the attitudes of the community or district in which they settled. Generally, immigrants from Sumatra, who settled in Negri Sembilan, were readily absorbed, but those from Java and Celebes tended to create villages and neighborhoods isolated from the rest of the community in Selangor, Perak, Johore, and Penang.

In 1969 approximately 85 percent of the Malays lived in rural areas as poor peasants or in coastal regions as fishermen. There has been considerable internal migration among them, however, consisting of movements of the agricultural segment into less densely populated or newly developed regions (such as from Penang to Kedah, Perak, and Selangor; from Malacca, Negri Sembilan, and Perak to Selangor and Johore; and from Kelantan and Trengganu to Pahang), an to a lesser extent from rural areas to urban centers, such as Kuala Lumpur. Consequently, although regional groupings remain well defined, differentiated by many dialects that are not always mutually intelligible, Malays as a group are not wholly localized.

In West Malaysia the original pattern of Malay settlements on the lowlands and coastal areas was set by the rivers, which not only formed the easiest line of communications but also provided water for wet rice cultivation, the basis of their agriculture. Settlements were focused around the mouths of rivers, from which expansion proceeded along the coasts of upriver. A raja or sultan (see Glossary) held absolute power over each concentration, which was separated from its neighbors by forested areas. As these rulers increased their power, local dialects and cultural variations developed and crystallized, particularly in those groups that remained relatively isolated, such as in Kedah, Perak, Pahang, Trengganu, and Kelantan. By the 11th century these regional groupings were well established, and the pattern for the present basic divisions among Malays was laid.

The rise of the State of Malacca after 1400 and its territorial expansion after 1450 caused the spread of Malacca-Johore Malays, mainly Sumatran immigrants, along the coasts of the states of Negri Sembilan, Selangor, Perak, and Pahang. The Portuguese invasion of 1511 marked the end of the Malaccan era, and the period from 1511 to about 1800 witnessed the settlement of parts of Perak, Selangor, Negri Sembilan, Johore, and Kedah by new migratory waves from Indonesia. The Dutch conquest of Sumatra (1816–1908) resulted in additional immigration of Sumatran and Javanese peoples to the more permissively governed British-protected states of Malaya (see ch. 3, Historical Setting).

The Malays in East Malaysia, although basically farmers, are attracted to salaried and wage-earning occupations as well, and many are employed in the government services. Like their counterparts in West Malaysia, they have an aristocratic tradition with a system of hereditary rank encompassing four or five stages from ex-slaves and commoners to members of the titled upper class. An individual, nevertheless, may achieve higher social status through acquired wealth or prestige. Because of their wider horizons and experience in government, upper-class Malays have come closer to a consciousness of ethnic unity and regional political entity than other ethnic groups in East Malaysia.

The Chinese

The Chinese, the second largest ethnic group, hold a predominant place in the economy of both West and East Malaysia. They own and operate most of the commercial organizations, control virtually all the retail trade, provide a large part of the general labor force, and dominate the technical and service industries. Because of their economic position, the Chinese have become the object of some antipathy on the part of Malays and have been greatly restricted in the amount of land they can acquire and in their continued immigration.

Socially, the Chinese tend to remain separated from the rest of Malaysian society and to maintain a closely knit structure of discrete clans, dialect associations, and mutual aid groups bound together by a common culture and heritage that is an amalgam of Confucian, Taoist, and Mahayana Buddhist elements. Politically, they have been relatively inactive, partly because official policy for a long time excluded them from participation in the government, and partly because of their indifference to political concerns, which they did not feel were their own. In contrast to the Malays who settled in the area to farm the land and establish new homes, the Chinese came to make their fortunes and then return to their homeland. Later generations born in Malaysia, however, are becoming involved in political life and the determination of national policy in order to protect their economic power and interests (see ch. 13, Political Dynamics).

Although the Chinese had early trade and diplomatic relations with the area and formed a few permanent settlements after the Malaccan era, their great influx was associated with the need of British colonial enterprise after 1880 for a larger and more willing labor force than could be found among the Malays. Chinese response (originally all males, as women did not arrive in significant numbers until late in the 19th century) provided the bulk of laborers who cleared the jungles, constructed roads, established plantations, and expanded the mines. Tin mining was the activity most responsible for their movement into West Malaysia, and initially their settlements were concentrated around the mines in the Larut district, the Klang Valley in Selangor, the Kinta Valley, and Sungei Ujong in Negri Sembilan. In East Malaysia similar occupational patterns were followed, but large numbers of Chinese also engaged in sawmilling, fishing, the cultivation of gambier, pepper, and rubber, as well as in trade and commerce. They came to all parts of Sarawak and Sabah but settled mainly in the Rajang River basin of Sarawak, which in 1969 remained almost exclusively Chinese.

Malaysian Chinese, with the exception of one small group, came from provinces of southeastern China. The peoples of this area were divided into 10 or more related but distinct cultural groups speaking almost as many different, and usually not mutually intelligible, dialects. Each group to some extent remained apart, tending to form associations on the basis of speech and regional origin in China. The notable exception to southeastern China as a point of origin is a small settlement near Kota Kinabalu in Sabah, composed of immigrants from Shantung Province in Northern China.

Some of the distinguishable Chinese groups in Malaysia are the Cantonese, Hakka, Luichiu, and Tiechiu from various parts of Kwangtung Province; the Hokchiu, Hokchia, Henghua, and Hokkien from Fukien Province; the Hainanese from Hainan Island; and the Kwangsi from the province of that name. Two broad divisions exist within these groups. One consists of those Chinese who, regardless of origin and group dialect, sometimes speak Mandarin in their relations with other Chinese and spend their lives almost exclusively in the company of fellow Chinese. They are educated in Chinese schools and work in Chinese enterprises catering to Chinese customers or in Chinese labor groups under Chinese foremen in the tin mines or estates. They are concentrated in Johore, Perak, and Selangor but also are found in most other states. Family, territorial, and dialect specialization characterizes their trade, industrial, and commercial activities.

The second group consists of the more assimilated or acculturated Chinese who, although they generally adopt their immigrant father's dialect and profession, also have strong associations with Malaysia. They ordinarily are educated in English-language schools and speak English fluently, as well as some Chinese dialects and Malay. Members of this group can be found in all walks of life. Some are tin miners, fishermen, and farmers who, in West Malaysia, are almost indistinguishable from Malays except that they are non-Muslim and observe certain Chinese customs. Some are older, non-English-speaking businessmen who have cut their ties with China because they have a vested interest in Malaysia. Others, usually from the wealthier upper class, are insurance agents, schoolteachers, lawyers, printers, surveyors, auctioneers, and doctors. Those who have inherited their forefathers' property often become landlords, financiers, or industrialists.

Regardless of the group to which they belong, the Chinese are essentially the urban dwellers of Malaysia. Whereas about 85 percent of the Malays live in rural areas, approximately 75 percent of the Chinese live in towns.

The Indians

The Indian community, confined almost entirely to West Malaysia, constituted about 10 percent of the total population in 1969. It represents a relatively permanent and increasingly stable group.

The number of Indians was negligible until the middle of the 19th century, when significant migrations to West Malaysia first began. The impetus for this movement was provided mainly by agricultural development in the Peninsula, particularly the rise of the rubber industry. Indian society in Malaysia thus was, and remains, basically rural despite the modern general trend toward urbanization. The majority of Indians work on the large rubber, coconut, and oil palm estates of the west coast, and their two main areas of concentration are the rubber areas from Kuala Lumpur to Malacca and from the Kinta Valley to Penang. The remaining Indian population is found in urban areas scattered throughout West Malaysia.

Most Indian plantation workers are from southern India and include Tamils, Telegus, Chetis, and Malayalis. Some, however, are Punjabis and other northern peoples, or Sinhalese from Ceylon. The Tamils from Madras form the single largest group and, with the Telegus from Andhra, constitute the bulk of the tappers, weeders, and harvesters. Tamils also are found in west coast urban areas, particularly in Penang, where they are employed primarily as common laborers, construction and railroad workers, and as minor help in European offices.

The many Indian merchants who engage in dry-goods operations, news vending, moneylending, and the restaurant business are Tamils and usually employ other Tamils as their clerks. Many are Muslims, and their extensive intermarriage with Malay women on Penang Island has given the Muslim population there quite different characteristics from those on the mainland. Some Tamils have become doctors, lawyers, and teachers, thus attaining prominent roles in the social and intellectual life of the towns. Formerly the Tamils were known as Klings but, since the term has derogatory implications, it has been changed, both officially and unofficially.

The Malayalis from Travancore-Cochin are as a group better educated and more literate than the Tamils and Telegus. They usually are white-collar workers on the staffs of estates in rural regions or laborers in the towns. The Chetis, second only to the Tamils in number, are mainly engaged in the business of extending credit.

The northern Indians form a numerically small and relatively unimportant group in Malaysia. Primarily from the Punjab, they are not associated with the estate economy as exclusively as are the southern Indians, although they frequently serve as estate watchmen and policemen. The Sikhs, warrior people from the Punjab, are most distinguished as policemen but are also engaged in railroad work, dairying, and retail trade. Most of the northern Indians are professionals; others are engaged in commercial and financial occupations and in the railroad and dairy industries.

Over one-third of the Indian immigrants came from the lower castes in their homeland, but the differences between the various groups have largely disappeared in Malaysia. Caste distinctions are virtually unknown, and there is increasing intermarriage between Tamils, Telegus, and Malayalis. There also appears to be little intergroup antagonism, so that Indians of the Hindu, Islamic, Sikh, Roman Catholic, and Methodist faiths mix easily in their numerous social organizations. Exclusive voluntary cultural groups, such as an Andhra organization for the preservation of Telegu culture, can be found, but their impact is too small to disturb the relative homogeneity of Indian society. The northern Indians constitute a notable exception to this general ethnic unity.

Tribal Peoples of West Malaysia

There are three distinct groups of tribal people in West Malaysia, all of whom were well established in the area before the first Malays arrived from Indonesia. They include the Semang, the Senoi, and the Jakun.

The Semang

The Semang, believed to be the earliest inhabitants of Malaya, are descended from several tribes of Negritos who came to the Peninsula from mainland Asia. Their original habitat was the coastal forest and swamps around the mountain ranges of upper Perak, Kelantan, and Trengganu and the jungles of northern Pahang. As other peoples migrated into the area, the Semang were pushed into the interior, where they now live on remote mountain slopes of northern West Malaysia at bare subsistence level as nomadic hunters and gatherers.

Numbering less than 4,000, the Semang physically are short, almost dwarfish, and have negroid features. They speak a Mon-Khmer language to which has been added a few Malay loan words. Culturally, the Semang have been handicapped by the mutual antipathy that formerly existed between them and their neighbors. The Malay and the Jakun feared the alleged prowess of the Semang in witchcraft and magic, and the Semang, in turn, feared exploitation or slavery under the Malays. Most of this tension had been eliminated before 1969, but the Semang remain a circumscribed people facing racial and cultural absorption into Malay society.

The Senoi

The Senoi, who closely followed the Semang into Malaya, are the largest tribal group in the Peninsula and sometimes are erroneously referred to as the Sakai. The work *sakai* is derived from the Thai language and means serf, slave, or a barbarous race, and consequently, the Senoi are sensitive and precise about insisting on the designation Senoi. The Senoi language is closely related to Mon-Khmer used in Vietnam and Cambodia.

Mostly this tribal group is found in the mountains and the foothills of central West Malaysia, specifically in Perak, Kelantan, Pahang, Selangor, and Negri Sembilan. They usually are located in the valleys at the headwaters of principal rivers and their tributaries, where they live together in longhouses. The Senoi cultivate rice, millet, tobacco, tapioca, sweet potatoes, and bananas. In addition, they hunt and collect forest products and animals for trade or for their own use. Their number is variously estimated at between 24,000 and 70,000 and cannot be firmly determined. The Senoi have friendly relations with, and have been greatly influenced by, their Malay and Jakun neighbors.

The Jakun

The Jakun are a group who speak an archaic Malay language and inhabit the southern coastal areas and lowlands in the states of Selangor, Malacca, Negri Sembilan, and Johore. Their culture is similar to that of their Muslim Malay neighbors minus its Muslim and Hinduized accretions. They are represented by a number of scattered and distinct communities and subgroups that include: the Semalais, Semok, Beris, Mah Meris, Orang Selitas, Orang Kualas, Orang Bukit, Temuan, and Belandas of the Selangor and Malacca coasts; the Mantera and Biduanda of Negri Sembilan and Malacca; the Orang Ulu, Orang Kanaq, and Udai of Johore; and the Orang Laut or Sea Jakun of the west coast. More simply, however, the Jakun may be divided into the Orang Darat, who dwell on the land, and the Orang Laut, who are sea dwellers. The combined total of Jakun is estimated to be a little over 20,000.

The Land Jakun are slash-and-burn farmers who grow dry rice, sweet potatoes, tapioca, millet, sugarcane, beans, and occasionally tobacco and bananas. Their settlements are clustered around watercourses or are in hillside clearings and consist of Malay-type houses raised on piles with thatched roofs and bamboo or leaf walls. Each settlement contains a village with a recognized chief or headman. Even scattered and isolated families think of themselves as members of some community and subject to its chief. The most important member of the village, however, is not the chief but the shaman, who acts as an intermediary between the community and the myriad supernatural powers that influence every aspect of the Jakun's individual and social life.

The Orang Laut, although considered Jakun, almost constitute a group by themselves. They are migratory boat dwellers who frequent the islands and inlets of the Strait of Malacca and the entire west coast south of the Kra Isthmus. They also may be found on other islands eastward as far as Borneo. These Sea Jakun nominally are Muslim but retain many pagan habits. Little is known about their way of life. At one time they supplemented their fishing subsistence with piracy and now probably engage in occasional smuggling.

Indigenous Peoples of Sarawak

The main tribal groups in Sarawak are the Iban, Land Dayak, Melanau, Kayan, Kenyah, Kajang, Kelabit, Murut, Punan, and

Penan. These people ordinarily live in small village communities in the underdeveloped and sparsely settled parts of the interior, where they are self-sufficient for most social, economic, political, and religious purposes. Generally, the communities consist of one or more longhouses situated along rivers and streams, which provide the only means of transportation in many areas. They mostly practice a slash-and-burn dry rice agriculture, often supplemented by hunting, gathering, and fishing. There are a few groups, however, that have started to produce cash crops in order to buy cloth, tools, and kerosine lamps, but in most instances the basic tempo of their lives has not changed for centuries.

The Iban

The Iban also are known as Sea Dayak, so called by the Europeans who encountered them during their forays along the coast for trade and piracy. They constitute the largest indigenous group in Sarawak, accounting for approximately 32 percent of the total population. The Iban are probably fairly late arrivals, coming from the Kapuas area of Indonesian Borneo to concentrate originally in the Rajang area of the Second Division of Sarawak (see ch. 12, The Governmental System). During the last hundred years, however, the Iban have undergone extensive internal migration in a search for virgin jungle necessitated by their way of life and in 1969 could be found in all political divisions of the state. In spite of their great numbers and wide distribution, the group is quite homogeneous linguistically and culturally.

The Iban are a riverine people and veteran boatmen. Like most longhouse dwellers, they were slash-and-burn dry rice cultivators originally. Recently, however, they have been turning to the more sedentary cultivation of wet rice and cash crops, such as high-yield rubber, under government supervision and subsidy.

The Iban are known more colorfully as the original headhunters or "wild men of Borneo," although there is some evidence that they learned the practice from the Kayan. Some scholars hold that headhunting originated as an event concluding the period of mourning after a chief's death. Believing that the restless spirit of the chief was unable to find peace in the next world unless a loyal retainer was killed to attend him, the head of a sacrificial victim was placed beside his grave to signify that this last service had been performed. There have been relatively few headhunting murders in the 20th century among the Iban, except for an upsurge during World War II lasting through the Japanese occupation.

The Iban are monogamous and have a social structure in which rigidly defined classes are absent. Status is achieved by acquiring wealth and prestige. Most Iban adhere to animistic religious beliefs, but an increasing number near the coast are educated Christians who work as clerks, schoolteachers, and minor civil servants.

The Land Dayak

The Land Dayak constitute almost 8 percent of Sarawak's population but, in contrast to the Iban, have shown little interest in internal migrations, remaining largely in the inland areas of the southwestern First Division. They were not noted as seafarers, so that the designation Land Dayak was developed by the Europeans to distinguish them from the Iban. The term has little meaning to the people themselves, who prefer to identify themselves by their village and locality.

The Land Dayak are related to the Iban but tend to be milder. They thus were convenient prey for their more aggressive neighbors, forcing many to retreat upstream to higher ground and build fortress villages for protection.

Culturally, the Land Dayak are much less uniform than the Iban, exhibiting a great deal of variation in language and customs. There are similarities nonetheless that unify them as a group and differentiate them from other tribal groups. Their typical village, for example, always contains a central, circular headhouse, raised on piles and distinguished by a steep, cone-shaped grass roof topped by a crowning ornament. This structure serves as a guesthouse, as sleeping quarters for bachelors, and as a repository for village trophies. The land around the village is often a source of dispute with neighboring villages of different tradition or ancestry.

Christian missions have been active in the area for a long time, and some Land Dayak have adapted well to a change in religion. In some areas, however, missionary efforts have succeeded only in undermining native beliefs without replacing them with an adequate substitute.

The Melanau

The Melanau, numbering about 6 percent of the Sarawak population, are a coastal dwelling people, who have been described as a physical and cultural link between the less civilized people of the highlands and the more modern population of the lowlands. Physically, they resemble the Malays in that they have many of the mongoloid features, but the Melanau have heavier builds and broader shoulders. The Melanau women have a reputation for beauty, which formerly attracted slave-hunting pirates and still is a distinguishing attribute.

The Melanau are the main sago producers of Sarawak but also are large cultivators of rubber and wet rice. In addition, they are daring sailors and good fishermen, ironworkers, carpenters, and boatbuilders. The women are skilled in many handicrafts, particularly in plaiting baskets, mats, and sun hats.

The Melanau have come into close contact with the Malays and have been strongly influenced by them. The Melanau wear the Malay dress, although a few wear Western clothing. Originally longhouse dwellers, they now live in Malay-type villages of individual family huts. More significantly, many have been converted to Islam and are quite Malayanized; others have become Christians, largely Roman Catholic; and the remainder still adhere to ancient native beliefs.

The Kayan, Kenyah, and Kajang

These three tribal groups, together numbering only about 2 percent of Sarawak's population, are located primarily in the upper Baram River region but may also be found in the upper Rajang, Balui, and Kemena river areas. They are believed to have migrated from Indonesian Borneo, where their main populations still reside. The Kayan are the most uniform culturally and linguistically, although a few local subdivisions based on variations in dialect may be recognized among them. The Kenyah may be divided into the Real Kenyah, whose antecedents trace back directly to Indonesian Borneo, and other groups of uncertain derivation found in the Tutoh, Baram, Tinjar, and Belaga river areas. The Kajang are a residual category of several minor communities that are closely related to both the Kenyah and Kayan and whose elite groups intermarry with the aristocracy of both.

Physically, all three groups are short and powerful in stature. They were strong and courageous warriors who historically had been great rivals of the Iban until their power was broken by the larger group about a century ago. The Kayan and Kenyah, particularly, are considered to be wise counselors and fine artists, as well as outstanding singers, dancers, and craftsmen. They are very receptive to education, reserved, and modest.

Members of these tribes are basically longhouse dwellers whose architecture is noted for being conceived on a grand scale. A typical Kayan, Kenyah, or Kajang village, located at the juncture of two streams or at the bend of a river, usually but not always consists of a single longhouse. An unusual feature of those with more than one is the cultural and linguistic differences that exist between and among separate longhouses. The Kayan and Kenyah have an inherited aristocracy and are extremely class conscious. The door of the chief's quarters is quite large and is located in the center of the longhouse. The doors on either side then become correspondingly smaller as the rank of its inhabitants declines. The aristocrats also individually own caves of appropriate size along the Baram River, which contain the bird's nests so highly valued by the Chinese for soup.

The Murut and Kelabit

The category Murut embraces several different groups found in Sarawak, Sabah, and Indonesian Borneo, who are probably the least known and most inaccessible peoples in the area. The Murut of Sarawak who inhabit the remote uplands of the Fourth Division and the Fifth Division are not related to those of Sabah, and there is a clear difference of language between them. The Kelabit, occupying the same general region, are closely related to the Murut. Megalithic explorations in the uplands indicate that the Kelabit have lived there since the Stone Age and thus have been in longer continuous occupation of a single place than any other peoples of Borneo. The Murut practice shifting dry rice and tapioca cultivation; the Kelabit are wet-rice growers but also graze zebu cattle, buffalo, and goats. Both tribal groups are essentially longhouse dwellers, except in areas close to navigable rivers, where Malay influence has caused some to abandon the longhouse in favor of individual huts.

The Punan and Penan

The Punan and some of the Penan are nomadic peoples wandering in small family groups in the Baram Valley on the fringes of the Kayan-Kenyah-Kajang area. Together with the settled Penan, they total probably less than 4,000 persons. The Punan and the nomadic Penan do not build permanent homes and have no domesticated animals or agriculture. They are extremely silent hunters and experts with the blowgun, make fine rattan mats and baskets, and are noted as clever singers of melancholy songs.

The settled Penan trade various jungle products for external necessities, such as salt and cloth, at special government-supervised trading centers. They deal with Kenyah traders who have a traditional right to trade with specific Penan groups.

The relationship between the Punan and Penan is uncertain, and the Penan deny any association. There is, nevertheless, a great similarity in their languages, and both are remarkably alike in physical appearance.

Sabah Ethnic Groups

The main tribal groups in Sabah consist of the Kadazan (Dusun), the Murut, and the Bajau, each having one or more subgroups identified by locally imposed and accepted names. These groups are completely different from those of Sarawak, as the political boundary between the two states almost forms an ethnological barrier as well. There are, for example, no Dusun south of the border and no Dayak north of it.

The Kadazan (Dusun)

The Kadazan are the largest group of native people in Sabah, constituting approximately 32 percent of the state's total population. They are predominant along the western coast and plains, concentrated between Kudat and Beaufort in the interior valley of Tambunan, where they grow most of Sabah's rice. In early records they were referred to as Idaans, later termed Orang Dusun or (men of the orchards) by the Malay-speaking people. Some dislike this appellation, because it connotes a yokel, and increasingly refer to themselves as Kadazan. They have accordingly formed the Society of Kadazan to uplift their people socially, educationally, and economically and to create a common sense of racial consciousness.

A distinction generally can be made between the lowland or coastal Dusun and the hill or inland Dusun, which, in turn, appear to be delineated further into groups of subtribes that speak dialects more or less unintelligible to members of the other groups. Some of the subtribes are the Kadazan, Kivijan, Minobok, and Mangbok, names that been externally imposed by neighboring non-Dusun. Each subtribe represents a number of individually named villages and a local tradition that compose the basis of community identity. Unlike the Iban and Melanau of Sarawak, Kadazan communities are not always located near riverbanks.

The Kadazan, who are believed to have been derived from early native peoples that immigrated from Malaya, have been described as intelligent and interested in education. They have stoutly maintained their own distinctive language and culture. They were originally animist, but many recently have been converted to Roman Catholicism. The lowland Kadazan, as well as many in the inland communities, have abandoned the longhouse in favor of the individual hut.

The Bajau

The Bajau, most of whom call themselves Samah, represent about 13 percent of the population. They are found mainly on the east coast of Sabah and in Kota Belud on the Tempasuk River. Those on the coast have adopted Islam from the Malays.

The Bajau are descendants of the sea pirates who roamed the Sulu and Celebes seas in the 19th century. They are believed to be related to the Orang Laut of West Malaysia, especially those of

Johore from whom, they say, their legends have come. As pirates, they were considered savage and ferocious, but these traits seem to have disappeared.

The Bajau do not form a cohesive and uniform group. One section in the northern coastal region specializes in herding cattle and the cultivation of wet rice, coconut, and fruit trees. Those located on the east coast are still very similar to the more primitive Orang Laut and are subdivided into the Sea Gypsies, the boat dwellers, and the fishermen. They either live in their boats or in homes raised on stilts near or over the water. Not all of these groups can communicate with one another, although the language spoken by the settled Bajau and that of the Sea Gypsies are similar.

The Murut

The Murut of Sabah are among the more primitive people of southeast Asia and constitute about 5 percent of the state's population. They are concentrated in the high, inland country, follow a 7-year cycle of cultivation, and continue to use the spear, blowgun, and hunting dog. They come from the same stock as the Kadazan and use similar, mutually intelligible languages. They regularly identify themselves as a member of a particular subtribe, such as the Timigun, the Nabai, the Baokan, or the Semabu.

Until about 1900 the Murut lived in longhouses; but since this was largely a defensive measure, it began to die out with the establishment of district officers in Sabah under the British. Nevertheless, a number of Murut families in some areas continue to live together in a large house. The Murut practice shifting, slash-and-burn dry rice and tapioca cultivation in the jungles.

LANGUAGES

Historically, government linguistic policy has been a tolerant one in which the separate languages of various ethnic groups were recognized as valid for the transaction of official government and commercial business alike. Government financial aid, moreover, was provided for education in Malay, English, Chinese, and Tamil according to demand. In West Malaysian schools, Malay and English were compulsory subjects, although instruction in Chinese and Tamil was equally available on the basis of parental desire. In East Malaysia, English was the principal language in the educational system, but Malay, Chinese, and frequently some of the tribal tongues were also taught extensively (see ch. 8, Education).

When Malaysia was formed in 1963, however, the earlier liberal policy underwent change. The government, in an attempt to integrate the various ethnic components and imbue them with a sense of common identity, began to promote the greater use of Malay. This developed into formal policy in 1967 with the passage of the National Language Act, which made Bahasa Malaysia the sole, recognized official language in West Malaysia and prescribed its exclusive use in all official communications and documents with limited exceptions. In East Malaysia, English was to continue as an official language until, at least, 1977. The new legislation provoked much opposition from non-Malay elements, who interpreted the enforced use of Bahasa Malaysia as a move to subordinate their cultures to that of the politically dominant Malays. Much resistance also appeared, even among some Malays, because of the language's inadequacy as a vehicle for international communications and its lack of appropriate terminology to meet the requirements of modern technological and scientific society. Accordingly, a transitional period was established during which the continued use of English was authorized for some official activities until 1973, but other languages remained circumscribed and were sanctioned only for use in social intercourse.

In order to facilitate general acceptance of Bahasa Malaysia as a viable national language, a number of specific measures have been adopted and implemented during the transitional period. One of the most important has been the provision of increased financial support for the Dewan Bahasa dan Pustaka, a language and literature council that was first established as a corporate body in 1959. The mission of this agency has been to develop and enrich Bahasa Malaysia, to develop literary talent and publish new works in the national language, to standardize the spelling and pronunciation of words, to devise new and appropriate technical terms, and to prepare and publish an up-to-date Bahasa Malaysian dictionary. As a corollary to its work, the agency was largely responsible for an agreement between Malaysia and Indonesia in 1967 that coordinated their spelling systems and increased the mutual intelligibility of their written languages. In 1969 the Bahasa Malaysia dictionary of about 30,000 root words was nearing completion.

In the field of education, Bahasa Malaysia was made compulsory in schools at all levels and in all states. Other promotional devices include the annual observance of a National Language Month, in which the use of Bahasa Malaysia is stimulated in commerce, industry, and education through the use of popular slogans, such as "Bahasa Jiwa Bangsa" (language is the soul of a nation). The government also issues official circulars from time to time calling for the Malayanization of street, road, and city names; the use of Bahasa

Malaysia on shop signboards; the advertisement of job vacancies in the national language; and the requirement that telephone conversations between government officials avoid the use of any other language.

Bahasa Malaysia

Malay is the written and spoken language of many of the peoples of Malaysia, the Riau archipelago, the eastern parts of Sumatra, and the coastal regions of Borneo. It is similar to other Malayan languages of Indonesia, such as those of Madura, Bali, Macassar, and Buginese and Javanese, having had a common origin with them in the not too distant past. It is more distantly related to other languages of the Malayan branch of the Malayo-Polynesian family, such as those spoken in Taiwan, the Philippines, and Indonesian Borneo.

In West Malaysia, Bahasa Malaysia speakers are found in all regions of the Peninsula; in East Malaysia they are distributed generally along the coasts in both Sarawak and Sabah. It is used widely as a common vehicle among native tribal peoples in almost every group of which there is at least one person with some knowledge of the language. Historically, Bahasa Malaysia has tended to supplant the dialects of those peoples who have come under strong Malay influence, notably the Muslimized Jakun, Melanau, Bajau, and some Land Dayaks.

Dialects and Styles

Malay has a number of dialects, most of which result from regional isolation and divergence. There is little information about the majority of these, but among the better known are Jakun, Malacca-Johore-Riau, Pahang, Trengganu, Kelantan, Perak, Kedah, and Patani. Minangkabau, which is spoken in Negri Sembilan, is a separate and distinct language belonging to the Sumatran group.

Jakun, or archaic Malay, is spoken only by members of that group. It retains words that have disappeared from, or become archaic in, other dialects. Malacca-Johore-Riau is spoken in the southern and western part of the Peninsula, on the islands of the Riau and Lingga groups, and along part of the east coast of Sumatra. It resembles the Pahang, Perak, and Kedah dialects; speakers of each understand each other fairly easily, although subdialects are so local that an expert can place a man's distinct section or village on the basis of his speech. Trengganu and Kelantan differ greatly from many of the other dialects and are practically unintelligible to west coast Malays.

Patani differs primarily in its possession of numerous Thai loan words.

Five different styles, or modes of speech, are used in different circumstances. These are: a standard Bahasa Malaysia form; a trade or jargon form, sometimes called Baba or bazaar Malay; a court form; a traditional literary form; and a modern literary form.

Standard Bahasa Malaysia was used originally as a common language among speakers of different dialects. Based on the Malacca-Johore-Riau dialect, it was used especially by the British as the official Malay idiom. It is now firmly established in this role, is the form taught in schools, and is used for official and business purposes. Most Malays are familiar with standard Bahasa Malaysia and use it in conversations with strangers, although they revert to their own dialect in their own villages and homes.

Trade, or Baba, Malay is a corruption of standard Bahasa Malaysia used by the more assimilated Chinese, Europeans, and other non-Malays in the southern part of West Malaysia. It is understood by speakers of the standard form but is regarded by them as coarse.

The court form is essentially a high version of standard Bahasa Malaysia that is used when reference is made to royalty or to the better born or when in conversation with them. It stresses the deference and respect owed by the lower class speaker to his superiors. It is allusive, since direct statements are considered abrupt and impolite. It also abounds in special terms applied only to royal persons.

The traditional literary form is also high style, consisting largely of conventional and formal expressions of Sanskrit or Arabic origin that have not changed significantly since the 16th century. In letters between sultans and other high officials such expressions may constitute most of the text. The form is foreign to the Malay peasant, but educated Malays preserve the style with some modifications. It is particularly important in letterwriting, which traditionally follows a rigid pattern of etiquette.

The modern literary form is a recent response to the requirements of journalism and the influence of Western literature. It is more casual and is used primarily in newspapers and other forms of public literature.

Foreign Influence

Although Bahasa Malaysia is rich in expressions for minutely differentiating kinds of objects and actions, it has adopted many terms denoting abstract ideas and items of foreign origin. Sanskrit is the most important source of loanwords, providing terms for body parts, time, commerce, price, salable commodities, precious stones, ordinary metals, tools, musical instruments, family relationsips, elementary astronomical terms, various animals and plants, mental and moral states, and political entities and activities. Arabic loanwords are common for religious matters; and Tamil, Chinese, Portuguese, Dutch, and English have provided words in other spheres.

Writing System

Bahasa Malaysia may be written either in *jawi*, which is substantially the Arabic script, or in *rumi*, which follows the Latin orthography. *Rumi* has been established as the official form.

Early writings dating from about the 14th century were in *jawi*. This script was romanized into *rumi* by the Dutch, who gave Dutch values to the vowels, and by the English, who gave Italian values to the vowels and English values to the consonants. Neither the Dutch nor the English romanization, however, can be considered an accurate guide to modern pronunciation.

Chinese

The Chinese of Malaysia speak nine distinct, mutually unintelligible dialects reflecting the linguistic diversity of their origins in southern China. Six of the nine dialects are numerically important, including Hakka, Foochow, Cantonese, Hokkien, Tiechiu, and Hailam. The other three are Henghua, Luichow, and Kwangsi. The Chinese tend to settle in dialect groups, each forming a distinct village or neighborhood and often maintaining closer ties with their place of origin in China and with other communities speaking the same dialect than with their immediate neighbors. In addition, the patterns of dialect in some respects reflect different economic interests since many of the dialect groups are associated with particular occupations.

The need for some intercommunity form of linguistic communication was evident, and in 1918, when China adopted Mandarin as its official language, its use spread to Malaysian communities, where it was advocated as standard for Chinese commerce and education. The use of Mandarin, however, did not become universal. Many members of the older generation refused to adopt it, and it is the young people who have become most proficient in its use. This younger generation is large enough to make Mandarin an important medium of communication among the dialect communities at large.

The various Chinese dialects are characterized by the use of monosyllables, a relatively meager number of sounds, and the presence of tones. All are united through the unique Chinese system of writing with standard pictograms, ideograms, and phonograms, so that regardless of dialect, written Chinese is intelligible to all. With the exception of the communities from Western nations, the Chinese lead all other ethnic groups in literacy, and Chinese is the primary written language of the area's domestic commerce in which the Chinese hold a near monopoly. Since Malaysia was formed, increasing numbers of Chinese students have been learning English, some of them to the exclusion of their own written language. Many Chinese also speak Bahasa Malaysia and are completely literate in it.

English

English is the primary language of the small European segment of the population and forms a common language spoken with varying ability by the more educated elements of the various other Malaysian communities. Historically it has been an official language, and in 1969 it still remained the language of the courts and of foreign commerce in West Malaysia and of government, commerce, and education in East Malaysia. It is expected to remain in semiofficial status at least until 1973 (1977 in East Malaysia), when it is to be replaced by Bahasa Malaysia.

Throughout Malaysia, but especially in the eastern component, many Malays, Chinese, and Indians know English, and many others are showing an increasing interest in learning it for personal, economic, and social reasons. This is fostered by its continued inclusion as a regular subject in the curricula of most schools.

Tribal Languages

The small tribal populations of West Malaysia, except for the Jakun who speak archaic Malay, have monosyllabic languages related on Mon-Khmer in the Austro-Asiatic language family. The Semang speak two languages and at least 11 dialects; the Senoi speak four languages and 29 dialects. In East Malaysia, a large number of mutually unintelligible native dialects are found, all of which are modifications of the basic Malayo-Polynesian language family. Omitting Bahasa Malaysia which, like Chinese and English, has a wide interregional spread, there are five distinct linguistic communities. These are the Iban, Bajau, Dusun, Murut, and Kayan— spoken by the major ethnic groups of the same name. Two other important ethnic groups, the Melanau and the Land Dayaks, speak a number of small dialect divisions.

Except for the Bajau and the Dusun, who are found in the same territory in Sabah, the principal linguistic communities occupy fairly distinct areas, each tending toward linguistic homogeneity with little overlapping. Comunication within communities is largely interpersonal, and information travels by word of mouth; outside the communities, local dialects break down, and English and Bahasa Malaysia are generally used.

The Latin alphabet has been adapted to a number of the native dialects by missionaries working in the area. Among these Iban is most prominent, and those who read and write it constitute a sizable percentage of the population reported to be literate in native dialects. Other less homogeneous dialects in which there is some literacy include Melanau, Land Dayak, Dusun, and Bajau. Many of the tribal peoples who are literate are competent in English or Bahasa Malaysia rather than in their own dialects.

Other Languages

The language spoken by most of the Indians of Malaysia is Tamil, which, together with Malayalam, Telegu, and Kanarese, belongs to the Dravidian language family and has no relation to any of the other languages spoken in the country. The modern Tamil script differs from all other Dravidian alphabets in shape and phonetic value. It is adequate for representation of the vowels but poorly adapted for expressing consonants. About 40 percent of the Indian population is literate in some Indian language.

The language of the Thai in the northern part of West Malaysia is Siamese, which is entirely different from Bahasa Malaysia and is distinctly related to Chinese. The written script derives from the Devanagari alphabet of India, which varies greatly from the Perso-Arabic system (*jawi*) formerly used by the Malays. The circumstance of completely different languages and widely different scripts has kept the crossing of Thai and Malay cultures to a minimum. When communication is necessary, it is generally accomplished by using Bahasa Malaysia.

CHAPTER 5

SOCIAL STRUCTURE

Malaysia's traditional social structure, which was based on inherited status and subsistence agriculture procedures, had declined in importance by 1969. Malaysians in the 1960's were less willing than before World War II to accept the position in society to which they were born. A great expansion in education has been a major factor in raising such expectations of upward social mobility for large numbers of people. An accompanying trend affecting the entire population has been increased demand for cash and for such modern consumer goods as bicycles, outboard motors, radios, sewing machines, and professionally built houses. As a minimum, the rural villager in 1969 needed cash to provide his children with clothing suitable for school, a requirement that did not exist a decade before when rural children customarily went without education. The increased need for cash and the shortage of land available for rice cultivation have led to an ever larger portion of the rural farming population turning from subsistence agriculture to cash crops.

Large numbers of the expanding adolescent population have sought employment opportunities and scope for their new skills and interests in the larger urban centers. Urbanization (by which Malaysian census takers mean settlement in communities of larger than 1,000 inhabitants) has increased in the post-World War II period, with the larger cities attracting the largest numbers of new migrants from the countryside. Although urban areas remain predominantly nonindigenous, Malays and other indigenous groups have come to the capital city, Kuala Lumpur, in unprecedented numbers. The most recent census (1957) showed that, although the indigenous group was only 15 percent of Kuala Lumpur's population, as compared to 62-percent Chinese, the indigenous group had experienced during the previous decade a rate of increase substantially greater than that of Chinese, Indians, or others. Indications were that this increase in indigenous urbanization was accelerating in the late 1960's.

Independence, and the resultant changeover in government personnel from British to Malaysians, has had a significant impact on urban upper and middle class society. After independence the social and golf clubs that had previously been the exclusive preserve of the Europeans became the social focuses for senior civil servants, businessmen, and professional people of all races and ethnic groups; all members had English-language facility, wealth, and positions of importance in the political and economic life of the community and nation. British social institutions, such as the clubs, and the upper income neighborhoods have been retained intact by the new multiracial urban elite. The symbols of social status and leadership in matters of fashion also continue to come from a still-prominent group of British and other Europeans.

Within the Westernized Asian urban community, most of whose members attended multiracial English-language schools, there has developed in the past several decades a concern to establish a Malaysian national society to be based on a new, yet-to-be-defined, noncommunal Malaysian culture. The absence of any existing multiethnic Malaysian culture on which to build a national society and the distance that is felt between the urban Westernized upper group and the traditionally minded ethnic communities, which make up most of the urban and virtually all of the rural population, have prevented the establishment of a national society with a national system of values.

Civil service jobs and government-provided housing, formerly occupied by British career officers, were by the end of the 1960's in the hands of Malaysians. The dominant position of the Malays was guaranteed by constitutional provisions establishing ethnic quotas in civil service employment.

The high prestige of the civil service, attained because it had previously been the monopoly of the British and a few highborn, English-educated Malays, was maintained with the change in personnel. The social ranking within the upper group of civil servants is reflected in the rank order in the annual government Establishment List.

In East Malaysia, the people have only recently come to identify themselves with social units larger than the longhouse (multifamily dwelling), village, or local dialect group. In the 1960's they were becoming more aware of an identification with their ethnic group, their state, and their nation. The relative strength of these various bonds is still being tested. The indigenous Muslims have taken the lead in identifying their interests with national social goals.

COMMUNALISM

In 1969 society was divided, as it has always been, along communal lines. In West Malaysia the main communal groupings were

Malays, Chinese, Indians, and aboriginal peoples. In East Malaysia the main groupings were non-Muslim indigenous peoples, Chinese, and indigenous Muslims. Contact between members of different ethnic groups has been slight, even in urban areas, as a result of habits of separate education, residence, and shop patronage and concentration of different ethnic groups in different occupations. The tendency of occupations to be determined partly by ethnic considerations has led to income patterns also being affected by such factors. For example, during the 1950's in Kuala Lumpur, the Chinese residents had only one-quarter of their number in the lowest income bracket, as against one-third of the Malays and almost one-half of the Indians.

Measures have been taken to minimize divisive factors. If the plan announced by the minister of education in July 1969 is effectuated, all schools eventually will be conducted in the national language, and the possibility of cultural fusion into one nationality on a mass basis will be greater than it has been up to 1970. One change that has already occurred has been the reduction of the gap in literacy and education between the Chinese and the indigenous peoples as a result of the increase in school enrollment in rural areas (see ch. 8, Education).

Another change in the communal picture is that the bulk of all the communities is now Malaysia born and not new immigrants. Except in Sabah, immigration regulations have prevented the entry of unskilled laborers. Perhaps as a result of the permanence and stability of the various ethnic groups, as compared to before World War II, a shift has occurred in demands and expectations of the different groups. Formerly, the Chinese and Indians were noted for their lack of concern with the political life of the country in which they lived and worked, so long as their economic opportunities were not infringed. They have now began to indicate a greater interest in their adopted country and to seek a less restricted role in its political life. Malays in 1969 were moving away from concern only with the political aspects of the modern society to attempts at greater participation in the modern economy.

MALAYS OF WEST MALAYSIA

For the most part Malay society is rural and agricultural. The majority of Malays are engaged in subsistence ricegrowing and, on the east coast areas of the Peninsula, they have a virtual monopoly on fishing. Rubber small holdings are of great and increasing importance to the Malay rural community as a source of cash, for which the need has greatly increased in the past 20 years.

In addition to usually being farmers and residents in villages of smaller than 1,000 inhabitants, Malays throughout the nation share the same religion and basic national language. Within the broad category generally regarded as Malays fall also the Javanese, the Minangkabau, Batak, and Achenese Sumatrans, the Banjarese from Indonesian Borneo, and others who, though they share in the main outlines of Malay culture, differ markedly in cultural details.

Until the middle of the 20th century one of the most important distinctions within Malay society was the state from which one came within the Peninsula. The Malay states, each headed by a sultan, were the largest territorial units toward which Malays felt allegiance. With the Federation of Malaya in 1948 and, since then, with the gradual centralization and unification of government and communications in Malaysia, these state allegiances have declined in importance. The state of Negri Sembilan is distinctive in its social arrangements. There, Minangkabau Malays from Sumatra carried intact to the new country their unusual system of political and social organization based on matrilineal kin groups (see ch. 6, Family).

Social ranking among the Malays has traditionally been linked with urban or rural residence. Urbanites were assumed to be upper class, and rural Malays ordinary people. Until World War II this generalization was largely correct. The inherited upper class, which included sultans, persons of royal birth, descendants of the Prophet Muhammad, and aristocrats, as well as the courtiers, scholars, artisans, and other specialists needed to provide the amenities of court life, had always been urban residents. During the period of British control, a conscious effort was made to incorporate royalty and nobility into the government service. As a result, government servants partook of the prestige and urban way of life associated with the inherited upper classes.

Urban Malays were regarded as high in status but atypical and exceptional. This feeling was reinforced by the fact that the highest ranking members of the urban Malay elite have been for the past century eduacted at English-language schools and that urban areas in Malaysia have been, with the exception of a few towns in the northeast of the Peninsula, primarily Chinese in population and foreign in culture.

The tendency to regard all urban Malays as upper class has been modified by the increasing flow in the past two decades of young persons from the rural areas to the cities. The percentage of the Malay population in the teenage category has increased substantially in the past 20 years. This has been a cause of social tension, since there is little room in rural Malaysian society for unattached, dependent young people. Some of these young people are the first in their community to have had secondary-school education and find rural life too limited a field for their newly acquired talents. Others are motivated by a desire to take part in the modern way of life believed to be available in the cities. Improved urban-rural transportation and radio, motion pictures, and the like have created new wants among the rural youth. Many move to town to escape rural overpopulation and pressure on the land.

In this way, the urban areas have received an influx of impoverished Malay migrants, squatting in overcrowded rural-type houses in the Malay enclaves in the cities, many of them vainly seeking work. It was in such a neighborhood in Kuala Lumpur that the post-election rioting of May 1969 first broke out (see ch. 3, Historical Setting).

Rural Society

The traditional view of rural Malay society as a community of social equals has also changed. The growth of government bureaucracy and the spread of social services have brought to the villages a small group of new residents representing various government departments and bureaus: government schoolteachers and junior officials of health programs, irrigation and public works projects, and other government programs. These persons, because they are salaried, white-collar employees of the government with usually higher incomes than all but the wealthiest village landowners and who thus have the knowledge and the means to take part in the modern Westernized style of life, are thought of by the villagers as urbanites. While resident in the village, however, these government servants, especially the teachers, provide the greater portion of the leadership and effort in such modern social organizations as rural development committees, political party branches, and school and mosque committees. These temporarily transplanted urbanites thus form the modern village leadership, the cultural link between urban and rural Malay society. Their role, however, is generally limited to transmitting and implementing ideas and policies from the main offices in the city to the people in the country, and rarely the reverse. Unassimilated into village life, the modern educated group forms a new top layer in rural Malay society.

Within the village farming population, class differences are also developing. Whereas rural Malays formerly thought of themselves as belonging more or less to an unranked group of kin and neighbors, all ordinary people, they now grade themselves in three ranks—

wealthy people, ordinary people, and poor people. The great increase in rural population, the result in part of improved medical and public health facilities, has occurred without an equivalent increase in land available for use by the villagers. Land scarcity, overpopulation, and the increased need for cash have resulted in a widening gap between the wealthy and the poor in the village, with more residents landless and more acreage concentrated in the hands of a few wealthy landowners.

While this rural gap in wealth and style of living is negligible compared to the gap between urban rich and poor, it is widening and is felt by the villagers themselves to be interfering with traditional egalitarian practices, such as mutual unpaid cooperative projects in rice replanting and path mending. Except in cases of illness, death, or close kinship ties, help during planting and harvesting in the 1960's was paid for in cash or with a portion of the crop.

A landowner with a surplus amount of land above mere subsistence is under strong social pressure to allow a fellow villager who has insufficient or no land to lease or sharecrop the surplus acres. Many villagers, including housewives, gain income as seasonal farmhands, and an increasing number of farmers are entirely dependent on paid farm labor for their living.

The landowner with a surplus is regarded as the patron of his tenants and employees. He is socially obliged to provide the means of earning a living to as many as possible, even when it would be possible and more profitable for him to do the work himself. Often the object of the landowner's patronage is a member of his household. A survey of a village in Kelantan studied first in 1947 and again in 1963 showed a marked increase within each household of partial or total dependents. In 1963 the ratio of these dependents to full earners was five to one in half the households surveyed.

Whether close kin or not, the tenants, farmhands, and sharecroppers usually feel obliged to volunteer their help at family celebrations held by their patron and to support him in village disputes and in efforts to extend his influence over village affairs. Many teachers and other government servants living in rural areas have purchased village land and thus receive the double prestige of being members of the modern elite and landowning patrons.

The village—called by the imprecise term *kampong*, which can mean family compound, neighborhood, enclave, or village—is not of great importance as a social unit, although a sense of neighborliness is developed through the use of the same footpath, bus stop and general provisions shop. Adolescent boys, who spend their ample spare time together as a village group, have the strongest sense of village allegiance.

Islam plays a major role in social cohesion in rural Malay communities. The officials and teachers associated with the local village prayer house, at which daily prayers are held, continue to play a role in leading village opinion and organizing village activity in religious and secular matters, although their influence over secular fields is greatest if the religious leaders are modern in dress and way of life.

Traditional specialists in folk medicine, folk ritual associated with agriculture, and other animistic practices are still patronized by the villagers, but they do not earn enough income in this way to engage in such activities full time. Their prestige and their influence in affairs not directly related to their specialties have greatly declined with the modernization of the rest of the village leadership. In the northeast state of Kelantan, the most traditionally oriented Malay state, an anthropologist noted that in the 1960's in several villages, experts in *silat*, the Malay stylized art of self-defense, had considerable influence on their disciples in all aspects of village life.

The role of extended family ties in rural society is declining. The most important social unit and the basic unit for production and consumption is the nuclear family, composed of parents and unmarried children. Although villagers tend to marry fellow residents and are aware of blood and marriage ties with many fellow villages, these ties do not necessarily involve the villagers in closer relationships than would usually exist between neighbors.

In the place of territorial and kinship groupings of traditional rural society, the villagers have formed new social groups for modern purposes. Political party branches and committees established to carry out nationwide projects at the rural level have grown in number and importance. These committees and party branches provide the institutional framework within which the modern elite exercises its influence. A typical development committee has as its chairman the chief landowner resident in the neighborhood, but with the government schoolteacher its secretary and hardest working officer. The ideas incorporated in the committee plans often seem alien to the ordinary villagers and sometimes meet with apathy. The new urbanized elite is not usually consulted by the villagers in problems dealing with traditional rural pursuits, and the decline in traditional leadership has contributed to the virtual disappearance of spontaneous community cooperation in agriculture, fishing, and similar activities.

Urban Society

The decline of prestige of traditional leaders and of traditional ways of organizing society evidenced in rural villages is more pronounced in urban *kampongs*, the Malay enclaves of the cities. Kinship ties outside the family are of less importance, and the role of Islam is less prominent in binding these more secularly oriented communities together. Leadership is confined largely to political party and governmental bureaucrats, who are all educated people, with the most important and well-known leaders those with English-language education. As in the rural villages, however, modern leadership among urban Malays consists of implementing at the local level plans and policies devised at a senior level of the government or party. Few attempts are made by the leaders to encourage initiative from, or to represent the demands of, the urban mass.

The newest urban elite group is composed of the Malay-language-educated college and university students. Some of these young people are taking an active role in politics and have indicated, in organized demonstrations, that they question the allegiance of the present English-educated Malay leadership to the ethnic Malay community. In particular, the student activists feel more should be done to support and advance the interests of Malays as against the interests of Malaysia's Chinese.

Another urban group in the process of formation is the Malay business community. Out of 4 million Malays only approximately 20,000 were engaged in trade during the 1960's, most of them running village shops with a daily turnover of a few dollars. Government policies have been actively promoting the participation of Malays at all levels of private enterprise. In 1969 the government announced that all companies awarded "pioneer certificates," which gave them certain tax privileges, must in the future employ 46 percent *bumiputeras* (Malays and other persons of indigenous ethnic groups), of which 20 percent must be given executive and management positions. If suitable candidates were lacking, the companies were required to train the personnel themselves. The reluctance that has been shown by industry and private enterprise to employ Malay graduates of the various vocational and technical institutions contributed in 1969 to the dissatisfaction of the Malay college students.

In 1969 a small group of royal and aristocratic heirs continued to receive generous stipends from their state governments. This practice had been begun by the British as part of their system of indirect rule through the hereditary Malay ruling class. This hereditary elite has occupied the pinnacle of prestige in Malay society, combining wealth with the cherished symbols and emblems of traditional leadership, such as frequent formal ceremonies executed with careful attention to a complicated code of court etiquette, the exclusive right to wear certain colors, and to use and be addressed with certain words and expressions. The fact that academic secondary and university education for Malays was available, until recently, only to the hereditary upper class has meant that members of the upper ranks of the hereditary elite were the first to be able to qualify as modern leaders. Distant kin of the sultans and aristocrats without stipends have continued to be addressed by their appropriate titles, if they have them, but such persons have no influence beyond that earned by their other qualifications. Many titled Malays are mere subsistence farmers or fishermen.

Malaysians of any ethnic group who have achieved important positions in the government or have earned governmental recognition through social work or other means can receive honorary, noninherited titles from the state sultans or, of higher prestige, from the nation's reigning monarch. A recipient of the highest national title, similar to a life peerage, is addressed with the prefix "Tun." "Tan Sri" is the prefix to the next lower title granted by Malaysia's ruler, similar to a knighthood. A recipient of a knighthood granted by a state's sultan is addressed as "Dato."

CHINESE

Chinese society in Malaysia is characterized by its relatively uniform class origins (almost all the immigrants having been poor rural villagers in China), by the multiplicity and variety of its groups and organizations, and by its emphasis on individual achievement and economic and commercial activity. Voluntary Chinese associations reinforce the ethnic consciousness of the Chinese and provide aid and support in competing with other ethnic groups. Nationwide figures indicate that Malaysian Chinese are overwhelmingly urban in residence, and recent developments have increased this tendency. In East Malaysia, however, rural residents accounted in the 1960's for two-thirds of Sarawak's Chinese and more than one-half of the Chinese of Sabah. This difference in urban-rural distribution in East and West Malaysia has contributed to the social cleavage between Chinese of the two parts of the nation.

Throughout Malaysia, much of the Chinese population is distributed in communities that were formed on the bases of common place or origin in China and common dialect. In many cases all the Chinese in a given Malaysian community will have come from, or be the descendants of migrants from, the same village in China. The majority of the residents of the South China villages from which the immigrants came were members of the same extended kin groups, with one or two surnames shared among all persons living in a village. These kin ties and surname ties have continued to unite Malaysian Chinese, especially in rural areas.

Chinese-language education, however, is conducted in Mandarin, the Chinese national language, providing the growing numbers of Chinese-language-educated school graduates with a common language. The transformation within the past 50 years of the immigrant, almost totally illiterate population into one with more than 50 percent literacy is largely the result of Chinese private efforts and is likely eventually to loosen the dialect group ties. There are already a number of nationwide political parties and other organizations that cross dialect lines. Dialect affiliation, however, continues to play a role in competition for leadership and influence within multidialect organizations, such as statewide chambers of commerce and some political parties.

Among the educated, a significant social distinction is made between those who have received only Chinese-language education and those who have had English-language education. Although the English-language schools have always been predominantly Chinese in enrollment, because of their urban location and fees charged, most of the Chinese who attended schools have gone to Chinese institutions (ch. 8, Education). To be elected to the school committee of a privately financed Chinese school has been one of the highest honors the local Chinese community could grant a fellow resident. Wealthy local residents, with wide-ranging ties of kin, credit, or other association with their neighbors and with influential members of the Chinese urban elite, are usually chosen to serve on the school committees, regardless of whether they are knowledgeable on educational matters or illiterate. Policy is made by the school committee, which also has the job of finding the money to keep the school running. Teachers have little opportunity to influence educational decisions and have relatively low prestige, since they are regarded as salaried employees who can be easily dismissed by the school committee. In this respect, the Chinese social ranking system presents a great contrast with that of the Malays, since schoolteachers have an almost unrivaled position of prestige in Malay communities.

The small group of Chinese who received some English education have played a greater role in the national society than have the Chinese educated. In particular, the Straits Chinese (those Chinese families long resident in Malaysia who speak English or Malay among themselves) have played a major role, during and since the time of British rule, as representatives of the Chinese community, although in many aspects of culture and interests they are unrepresentative of the majority of the Chinese. The near monopoly of the English-educated Chinese on positions as officers of political parties has continued through the 1960's, confirmed by popular elections. Although most organizations for political or social purpose involving contact with non-Chinese are headed by English-educated Chinese, some of these organizations represent the interests of the non-English educated.

Voluntary Cooperative Groups

The outstanding feature of Southeast Asian Chinese society is its extensive development of voluntary cooperative organizations. These organizations, although organized along lines of kinship familiar to Chinese in China, were a new development arising from the new needs of overseas Chinese as they made the transition from traditional village farming to modern urban private enterprise.

There are more than 1,000 Chinese corporate associations in Malaysia that fall into the general category of benevolent associations. They perform many of the social and economic functions usually handled in modern Western countries by governmental organizations. The great majority of these organizations are local in character and are based on family, occupation, and dialect affiliation. Whatever their membership qualifications, their purpose is usually connected with economic benefit for the members. Most of these organizations do not attempt to represent the Chinese population as a whole. The dominant group in each dialect association and occupational guild is usually composed of members of one surname group, and the institutional structure of the association, and relations between its members, are controlled and manipulated by this leading group. This dominant group is usually also the wealthiest group within the association.

Guilds are sometimes almost indistinguishable from dialect associations since in many localities the members of a particular trade come from the same dialect group and even in some cases from the same village in China. Guilds, however, are always built around a single occupation, such as tinsmithing or watch repairing, whereas the dialect associations often include members of more than one trade. In activities connected with prices, wages, conditions of work, and apprentice training, the guilds take on many of the functions of modern labor unions. The form of traditional social organization existing since the mid-19th century in Chinese-owned tin and gold mines, known as the *kongsi* system, in which the workers and their employer live together communally, sharing the costs of food and lodging and splitting the profits in a fixed proportion between the headman and the others, is declining in usage.

Another type of social organization that has existed among

Chinese for centuries is the secret society. Originally religious or benevolent cooperative associations, the secret societies assumed a political and antidynastic character about the time of the Manchu conquest of China in the 17th century. Later, many of these organizations degenerated into criminal organizations. They have been illegal in Malaysia during the 20th century, and those that continued to exist were involved in organized crime.

Patronage Relationships and Social Status

The local Chinese Chambers of Commerce in the urban centers and statewide amalgamations of Chinese Chambers of Commerce served a quasi-legislative function during the colonial period, when they provided the recommendations for appointed representatives of the Chinese on government bodies, before the introduction in the 1950's (and in East Malaysia, the 1960's) of elected legislatures.

The practice of choosing a leader from the Chamber of Commerce to represent the Chinese ethnic group as a whole continued a custom, begun with the arrival of the first Chinese traders in Malacca, by which the government selected a wealthy businessman to represent the Chinese in their dealings with other ethnic groups and with the government.

The influence of a small group of wealthy businessmen has been considerable, therefore, in relations with the non-Chinese. It has also been great among the Chinese themselves because of the elaborate system of credit relationships within the Chinese community.

Rural farmers, who are almost entirely engaged in producing goods for sale rather than subsistence, are financed by local shopkeepers, ordinarily fellow association members and, in turn, the shopkeepers are financed by other Chinese businessmen.

In establishing credit, kin and other social connections with the debtor and hidden or overt high interest rates substitute for collateral for these high risk loans. Credit acquired from friends, fellow association members, and relatives is the chief method of accumulating capital. Thus a Chinese estimates his potential capital in terms of the number of people who might feel obligated because of social ties to make loans to him. The granting or refusal of patronage by a wealthy urban creditor can influence local decisions and leadership at the village level. A local man's influence and prestige are enhanced among his neighbors by the knowledge that he has a powerful "back mountain" (patron) behind him. The number of clients a patron has is the index of his power and social position in the community.

The control of Chinese employers over the job market is great. Between 80 and 90 percent of all private employers in Malaysia are Chinese, and employees are usually of the same dialect affiliation as their employers. The tendency for a Chinese to employ only Chinese, and usually only those of his own group, has contributed to anti-Chinese animosities by other ethnic groups and has been a cause of complaint within the Chinese community. This resentment has been aggravated by the persistence in the late 1960's of a high unemployment rate—10 percent in urban areas, according to 1969 estimates, with nearly half the nation's job-seeking women, adolescents, and young adults unemployed (see ch. 20, Labor).

Between the destitute Chinese, who sleeps in the local temple courtyard and depends on daily doles from the local dialect association or other association to which he can claim a connection, and the wealthy businessman living in a large Western-style or Chinese-style house, there is a wide range of social positions, determined by wealth and altering rapidly with personal changes in income. Professional, clerical, and other white-collar occupations fall midway along this spectrum, except where income or the lack of it brings a doctor, for example, to the highest rank or an unemployed teacher nearly to the bottom. Social status may be shown by the possession of expensive consumer durables, clothing and housing; by expensive hobbies, such as collecting rare orchids, jade, or porcelain; by publicized acts of charity; or by combinations of these activities.

New Villages

Between 1950 and 1960 the British relocated some 450,000 Chinese squatters and farmers (in addition to approximately 130,000 from other ethnic groups) into the New Villages, as part of the Emergency campaign to eliminate terrorist activities (see ch. 3, Historical Setting). In addition, an estimated two-thirds of a million persons—Chinese, Malays, and Indians—were brought together from dispersed quarters around estates and mining areas into other concentrated villages that would constitute defensible and more easily supervised units. Thus, an important source of food for the terrorists could be shut off, and their power of intimidation of individuals reduced. The Chinese affected included isolated mineworkers, pioneering Chinese settlers who left the cities during the Japanese occupation to become farmers, and urban workers living in shacks around the outskirts of towns. They were settled in approximately 500 villages, whose populations ranged from 44 persons on a few acres to 13,000 persons on 468 acres; 400 houses was considered the optimum size by the administrators.

The New Villages greatly increased the number of urban units in the Federation of Malaya. In addition to denying the guerrillas support, they improved the living standards of the rural Chinese by providing piped water, dispensaries, schools, and other social benefits previously scarce in the countryside. Many Chinese of the New Villages received for the first time legal title to their land. They also received improved awareness of the nation in which they lived; nearly three-fourths of the New Village adults became federal citizens.

Chinese urbanization was increased from 43.4 percent before resettlement to 75 percent afterward. With urbanization two-thirds of these resettled Chinese abandoned farming of food crops and raising of livestock.

In the 1960's, after the end of the Emergency that had led to their creation, the New Villages were still surviving, with an estimated rate of increase of population of about 3 percent per annum. The wire fences were gone, and representative-elected village committees or councils administered these new communities.

In July 1965 resettlement in New Villages began in parts of Sarawak in order to protect Chinese villages and to cut off rural Chinese support from the clandestine Communist organization's guerrilla activities, which were being carried out in concert with Indonesia during the Confrontation with Malaysia along the Kalimantan-East Malaysia border.

INDIANS

The Malaysian government classifies as Indians persons of ethnic groups indigenous to India, Pakistan, and Ceylon. These are concentrated along the west coast of the Malay Peninsula in Selangor, Perak, Johore, Penang, and Kedah.

Indians formed nearly 17 percent of Kuala Lumpur's population in the most recent census, compared with the national average estimated at about 10 percent. A substantial, and increasing, number of Malaysian Indians are urban residents, and the remainder live and work on the rubber estates of West Malaysia. Unlike the Chinese minority, however, the Indians in the 1960's did not constitute as much as half the Malay population anywhere in the nation.

Most Indian immigrants started out as temporary contract laborers on the rubber estates, but as they became more urbanized they have also become a more settled community. There was estimated to be by the 1960's a nearly equal balance between the sexes for the first time. Many Indians have become Malaysian citizens.

Urban Society

Urban Indian society is headed by the traders, the wealthiest group of Indians, who continue a tradition of trade between Indians and Malaysians, particularly in cloth and spices, going back thousands of years. Among these are South Indian Muslims, Tamil speakers, many of whom have intermarried with the Malay urban community and have a prominent position as intellectual leaders in the bigger cities, especially Penang. These Tamil-speaking Muslims are general merchants, dealers, and petty shopkeepers in urban centers and village markets. Within the Indian business community, a distinctive group from south India are the Chettiars, who have specialized in moneylending and banking. The Chettiars have remained closely tied by kinship and identification to Chettiars in India.

A group of Ceylonese Tamil-speakers, of whom there were 15,000 in the last census, has been concentrated largely in the government clerical services, especially the railway. These people—often called Jaffna Tamils after the province of Jaffna in northern Ceylon from which many of them came—feel that they are a distinct community from the majority of Malaysia's Tamil speakers who come from southeast India and have protested periodically against being classified with the other Tamils for census purposes and for purposes of political representation.

Another urban group, prominent in clerical jobs, are north Indians from Bengal and Uttar Pradesh. North Indians from India's northwest, Sikhs and Pathans, have been employed commonly as watchmen, cart drivers, and policemen, although there are also Sikh shopkeepers and moneylenders. Indians have also been prominent in some of the government services, such as the public works department and sanitation department, as unskilled laborers.

The Indian trading community, the leading group of Indian urban life, has generally kept aloof from the interests and problems of Indian estate laborers, the largest single group of Indians. Since Tamil speakers, the major Indian group, predominate in the lower paid occupations, they are regarded as a lower status group by some of the other urban dialect groups. Some of the urban Indians, especially the Muslims, have established firm roots in Malaysia, by intermarriage with Malays and many generations of residence in Malaysia. The absence of Indian-language schools above the primary level has meant that most resident Indians with high school education or above have attended multiracial English-language schools, and thus the intellectual elite has had much experience in coexisting with the other components of the nation's plural society. English-language-educated Indians have produced leaders for a number of multiracial organizations in West Malaysia. For example, an estimate of the membership of the National Union of Teachers, the influential union of English-language teachers, showed Indians providing 20 percent of the membership and more of the leadership.

Estate Society

The trade union movement has been one in which Indians have constituted the majority in West Malaysia, and the Indian workers of the west coast rubber, palm oil, and other agricultural estates have been the biggest group of trade union members. The estate laborers have been isolated from contract with rural Malays or other ethnic groups because of the estate practice of providing housing in "coolie lines," so that each estate resembled a small Indian village, with its own primary school and Hindu temple. A 1969 government regulation that would require all noncitizens to obtain work permits could deprive as many as 55,000 Indian estate workers of their jobs, thus reducing further the dominance of the Indians in estate agriculture.

Although traditional social distinctions such as those contained in the Indian caste system play a role in Malaysian Indian society, these distinctions are less important and confining than in the home areas from which the migrants came. The unwillingness to continue to abide by the social restrictions of the home areas has led to a permanent estrangement of some of the urban Indian residents from their homeland and has produced tension between recent and long-resident immigrants.

ABORIGINAL PEOPLES

Fifty thousand aboriginal people inhabit the interior jungles and hills of northern and central West Malaysia. Most have not converted to Islam or to the Malay way of life, but some have adopted over the years many habits and practices from the Malays, including a trend toward residence in single-family houses, away from the still-prevailing practice of residence in multifamily bamboo longhouses. The aboriginal peoples are noted for the emphasis within their communities on nonviolence, on the obligation to share one's goods with one's neighbors, and on noncompetitiveness. Social prominence and influence belong to the older people, because of their greater experience, and to people whose generosity and warmth have won them the friendship of their neighbors. Leadership, as such, is generally lacking since no one wishes to appear bossy, but there is usually a person in each large settlement appointed by the government to act as mediator between the government and the community from which he comes.

Government efforts to influence or change the society of the aborigines were few until after World War II, when a federal protector of aborigines was appointed. In the early 1950's thousands of aborigines were moved to fortified camps in the lowlands to protect them from the guerrillas and to deny the Communists their support. The resettlement program was abandoned when it was found that the change in climate, diet, and living conditions brought high death rates in the camps.

Instead of the camps, forts were established near major areas of aboriginal habitation, with police field force members stationed in them to provide protection against Communists.

In 1961 the government announced that it was engaged "in evolving a long-term policy for the administration and advancement of the aborigines. . . ." In a speech at the opening of the Federal Parliament in 1961 Malaysia's Supreme Head, the Yang di-Pertuan Agong, stated that the "ultimate objective must be to absorb these people into the stream of national life in a way, and at a pace, which will adopt and not destroy their traditional way of living and culture." A detailed policy statement by the Department of Aborigines of the Ministry of the Interior, issued in the early 1960's, gave as the long-run aim that the aborigines have "ultimate integration with the Malay section of the community" with special measures to protect their customs, institutions, property, and labor.

Between 1961 and 1965, M$2.5 million (3.06 Malaysian dollars equal US$1) was spent on projects especially for the aborigines. By 1965 there were 60 schools with 3,500 pupils in jungle areas, 100 medical posts, and two hospitals. The First Malaysia Plan for 1969 to 1970 set aside M$3.8 million for aborigine projects, among them agricultural development projects designed to encourage greater territorial stability and the gradual termination of the nomadic way of life.

INDIGENOUS PEOPLES OF EAST MALAYSIA

In East Malaysia the sense of ethnic identity, as distinct from identification with smaller localized communities, is a modern development, as is identification with state and nation. Historical and geographic features continue to create division and rivalry, such as between east-coast and west-coast Sabah Kadazans, First Division and Third Division Sarawak Malays, and Second and Third Division Sarawak Malays, and Second and Third Division Ibans (see ch. 12, The Governmental System).

A major cleavage within indigenous East Malaysian society is between the Muslims and the non-Muslims who, together with the Chinese, comprised a large majority in Sarawak and nearly one-half of Sabah's people. This cleavage has been demonstrated in elections, with Muslims tending to vote for Muslims and non-Muslims supporting other non-Muslims. It is also shown in the greater willingness of Muslim leaders to support federal policies aimed at national unification of language, education, and the like, whereas some non-Muslim indigenous leaders have led the effort to maintain a strict interpretation of the East Malaysian states' rights incorporated in the Malaysian Constitution of 1963 (see ch. 3, Historical Setting).

Non-Muslims

Sarawak

The indigenous peoples of Sarawak include different ethnic groups from those of Sabah. Occupationally, the range is great between the bands of nomadic Punans and Pennans, who have no agriculture and a low level of material culture, and the inland hill Kelabits, who have highly developed techniques of irrigated rice cultivation. Social structure is equally varied, ranging from the loosely structured and frequently changing communities of nomads to the more rigidly organized hereditary class systems of the Kayans, Kenyahs, and Melanaus.

Among the major Sarawak non-Muslim ethnic groups, the Ibans and the Land Dayaks, social status, although connected with inherited wealth and inherited possession of valued objects, such as ancient Chinese ceramic jars and brass gongs, is also dependent upon the personal achievements and abilities of individuals. A villager's abilities and achievements can be easily observed by his neighbors because the entire village lives in the apartment of a single longhouse.

The Ibans, or Sea Dayaks, as they are also known, are the largest single ethnic group in East Malaysia. Most Ibans live in raised bamboo longhouses of several hundred occupants, although some have adopted the Malay-style single-family house. Each family unit, typically a set of parents and unmarried children, lives in its own apartment (*bilek*) along the raised bamboo boardwalk that forms the street for the Iban rural settlement. Each longhouse has a headman, *tuai rumah*, whose position is as the intermediary between the longhouse and the government; he also can perform limited magisterial functions in his community. He is not an authoritative chief nor is he usually the son of the previous headman. The next highest administrative office among the Ibans is the *penghulu*, who represents a number of longhouses. The highest title among the Ibans is that of paramount chief, *temenggong*, a title held during the 1960's by Tan Sri Temenggong Jugah anak Barieng, an Iban of Sarawak's Third Division, who also held the federal title of minister of Sarawak affairs.

The indigenous non-Muslims of Sarawak, and especially the Ibans, have inherited a dominant position in landownership within the state from the time of Brooke rule. Of the 4,000 to 5,000 square miles that are suitable for agriculture, out of the nearly 50,000 square miles of Sarawak, Ibans hold approximately two-thirds, leaving only 1,600 square miles for all other rural residents to use. According to Iban custom, a family needs the exclusive rights to the use of 100 acres so that it can cultivate 5 acres a year, the minimum necessary to provide subsistence, rotating the plots annually over a 20-year period. Increase in population, which has led to returning to the not yet revitalized soil at shorter than 20-year intervals, has brought gradual depletion of the fertility of the soil and an increased desire among the Ibans to expand their customary landholding rights into new areas. Although several efforts have been made to legislate land reforms, these have been unsuccessful because of Iban unwillingness to give up any of their land to the Chinese and other coastal peoples who feel the land shortage acutely.

The urge to spread out into new land is an ancient one among the Ibans and has, over the centuries, driven them from their home areas in Indonesian Borneo north to Sarawak. This long-range migration is still continuing. When pioneering a new area of virgin jungle, a group of *bilek* families, perhaps six or more, clears the land, each family thereby acquiring the right to use that land as long as the family members or their descendants stay in that area. Gradually more families join their near and distant kinsmen, adding new apartments to the existing structure. A longhouse community consists of a group of these landholding families who each have exclusive use of a specific tract of secondary jungle to plant with hill rice, fruit trees, rubber, or pepper or allow to lie fallow. Eventually, as the land wears out, a pioneer group moves off to find new land to clear.

Although ritual observances organized by the specialist in charge of augury involve all the *bilek* families in participation and contributing food and offerings, other activities are generally carried out separately by the individual *bilek* families. Help in the fields given by a fellow longhouse resident is meticulously reciprocated, and there is no communal longhouse property other than the notched log that serves as the stairway leading from ground level up to the longhouse boardwalk.

Ibans and other non-Muslim indigenous Sarawak people have become active in political parties and have been appointed and elected to positions of importance in the state and national governments. Nonetheless, official occupations engage less than 1 percent of the indigenous population.

The literacy rate is low among members of indigenous Sarawak ethnic groups. The Iban paramount chief during the 1960's was typical of the older Iban leaders in being totally illiterate. The ability to speak English, the state's official language until 1973, has been equally rare. A younger group of educated indigenous non-Muslims has begun to reach maturity. Urbanization and English-language fluency among the young have been increasing.

Communication with other Sarawak peoples has usually been conducted in Malay and, although the interior people recall the slave raids of the coastal Muslims, there is little overt animosity between Muslims and non-Muslims. Among the Melanau, who include many recent converts from pagan beliefs to Islam, the ties of mutuality are still great between the Muslims and non-Muslims. Cordial relations between the indigenous inland peoples and Chinese are common, and in some areas there has been substantial intermarriage with Chinese.

Women have great influence in the life of Sarawak's interior peoples. The government has subsidized rural women's organizations aimed at teaching modern techniques to women to bring about improved living standards in the rural areas.

Sabah

The Kadazan (or Dusun) people number nearly 150,000 and are by far the largest ethnic group in Sabah. Within the Kadazan group there is a great variety of culture. Coastal Kadazans cultivate irrigated rice and, in the central interior hills and plains, slash-and-burn techniques are used. These different methods of cultivation of the staple crop have induced substantial differences in social organization. There has been considerable influence upon the Kadazans from coastal Muslims, Chinese, and Westerners. The habit of living in longhouses, which was common during the 19th century, has been largely abandoned in favor of single-family Malay-style houses raised above ground level. Kadazans are more market oriented than the other indigenous non-Muslims and set aside market days and market places for trade with coastal Muslims, a custom that may date back centuries to the arrival of the early Muslim traders. As among the Ibans of Sarawak, strong leadership and inherited social classes and titles are lacking, and women figure prominently in family decisionmaking.

Muslims

Nearly one-quarter of Sarawak's people and more than one-third of Sabah's people are Muslims. The Melanau group of Sarawak includes many converts to Islam, some of whom regard themselves as Melanaus and indigenous Borneans and some of whom see themselves more as part of Malay society in general including that of West Malaysia.

The Bajaus, Illanuns, and Suluks are among the Islamized peoples of Sabah who came originally from the Sulu archipelago in the southern Philippines. The Bajau sea nomads appear also to have connections with the nomadic Orang Laut, an aboriginal boat-dwelling people who congregate near the southern tip of the Malay Peninsula.

The Muslims of Philippine extraction are often grouped together under the overall heading of Bajau in Sabah and are usually called Moros in the Philippines. In the Philippines the Moros had been grouped in loose confederations that crossed ethnolinguistic lines to include Bajaus, Illanuns, and others in a shared system of social ranking. All members of a confederation acknowledged the political authority of a ruling chief (*dato*). This practice of recognizing each other's social ranks has carried over into Sabah, where the Bajaus (who numbered 60,000 in 1963) have often intermarried with Illanuns (approximately 4,000), with slightly higher status accorded the Illanuns because of their claim to descent from the Sulu sultans.

Inherited rank or descent from the Prophet Muhammad plays an important role in Muslim society in East Malaysia, making an easy transition for those pagan communities, such as the Melanaus, who have always had a developed sense of social ranking by birth. In general, the role of inherited position and rank is declining with the modernization of the economy. Although wealth usually is in the hands of persons who are well born by the standards of their community, improved social status through marriage is open to the wealthy commoner.

In the 1950's thousands of Muslims from the southern Philippines, Kalimantan, Celebes, and other parts of Indonesia came to Sabah to fill jobs as unskilled laborers. The Filipinos were the largest group, estimated in 1968 at 15,000. The timber and oil palm industries have become increasingly dependent upon Filipinos for labor. Most are temporary residents and live on the estates, separated from the indigenous people of Sabah. Because they are of the same religion and basically the same racial stock as the indigenous Muslims, those who seek it should find absorption into Sabah society easy.

CHAPTER 6

FAMILY

The most pervasive family forms in the country as those of the predominant ethnic groups. A Malay family may be either bilateral or matrilineal depending on whether kinship is traced through both parents or through the female line alone; a Chinese family is patrilineal; a native tribal family is usually, but not always, bilateral. Indian family patterns have little impact, both because of their limited number and of their relatively small influence within the society.

Laws concerning marriage and divorce are not uniform, varying according to religion, ethnic group, and the substance of laws passed by the separate states of the country. The Constitution of 1963 does not provide guidance in such matters except to declare that federal legislative powers do not extend to Muslim marriages or to the properties affected by them. Each individual state has promulgated some form of ordinance for Christian and Muslim marriages, as well as provisions covering persons who wish to contract civil marriages. Chinese marriages and those of the tribal groups, however, are usually performed and recognized according to religious rites or customary practices inherent in their respective cultures.

THE MALAYS

Bilateral Households and Kin Groups

Bilateral Malay families are essentially similar throughout the nation, although some inconsequential differences between the rural and urban family may exist as the result of the influence of Western modernism in the cities. The smallest family unit consists of the father, the mother, and their children; the basic functional unit, however, is the extended family, which usually consists of three living generations, including the parents, their married and unmarried children, and any grandchildren that may be born to them. Ordinarily, only one daughter, or one son if there is no daughter, remains in the family household and inherits the house and equipment. The other daughters may go to live with their husbands and parents-in-law or, like the sons, may establish new and independent households.

In the bilateral family the orientation of individuals is primarily toward age mates and cousins rather than toward ancestors or descendants. There is little sense of lineage, and only minor interest is displayed in descendants beyond living children or grandchildren. Family names do not exist. The cleavage between generations is emphasized by the respect and deference the younger are expected to show the older. Differences in age, even between members of the same generation, are important.

The extended bilateral family participates as a unit in the major Muslim festivals and in family ceremonies, as well as in its everyday economic and social life. It is also within the extended family that status and property are inherited. Inheritance practice varies greatly depending on whether customary law or the Muslim code is followed.

In cases where the Muslim code is used, the greater share of the property goes to male relatives. The rules state that one-eighth of a man's property is inherited by his wife. The remainder is divided among the children, the sons receiving two shares to each one granted to the daughters. If there are no sons, the wife receives one-eighth; the daughters share one-half of the remainder; and the other half is distributed among the deceased man's patrilineal relatives.

The operation of Muslim law concerning inheritance of family land is not rigidly observed, despite the almost universal adherence to Islam. In practice, the children, regardless of sex, usually receive equal shares. Quarreling about inheritance is considered to be in poor taste, and the religious rules are invoked only when some other agreement cannot be reached.

Although the household is the basic socioeconomic unit, another kinship group, called the *kaum*, or circle of relatives, is also important, because it brings related families or individuals together for reciprocal economic aid and joint participation in certain ritual functions. Beyond the extended family and the *kaum* there are more distant relatives who rarely participate in family activities.

The husband is regarded as the dominant partner in bilateral families, and the wife is expected to be shy and submissive. Traditionally, she walks a few steps behind her husband in public; in the home the man eats first and alone, the wife eating afterward in the kitchen with the children. In addition, a wife does not act as a hostess to male friends who visit her husband unless they are close relatives. A man and woman are not expected to show strong affection for each other either before or after marriage. If a man is overly demonstrative toward his wife, witnesses often suspect that she has bewitched him.

The young are expected to display affection and respect for their elders from whom, in addition to reciprocated affection, they receive guidance and discipline. Traditionally, the mother has the main responsibility for discipline and care while the children are young. As they mature she is assisted by a daughter, who also performs many other household chores. A son is expected to be spoiled by his mother and is supported by her in relations with his father. When a boy reaches adolescence the father assumes a greater disciplinary role. Among siblings, specific rights and duties are not rigidly formalized, but age carries a certain amount of authority.

Matrilineal Households and Kin Groups

The Malays of Negri Sembilan trace kinship through the female line, so offspring belong not to the father's descent group but to that of the mother. The primary social unit, therefore, is the matrilineal extended family. It may, and usually does, consist of three or four generations, including the mother, her children, her daughter's children, and possibly the children of her daughter's daughters. The household consists of the original mother, her unmarried children and married daughters, their unmarried children and married daughters, and the husbands of the married women.

A newly married couple moves into the home of the bride's parents and, although married sons go to live with their wives, they retain membership in their mother's extended family and take part in its activities. In his wife's household a man remains essentially a lodger, and, because the eldest son in each generation acts as the head of his sisters' families, controlling their economic transactions and landholdings, the husband must defer to him in matters pertaining to the affairs of the house and to his own children.

Every extended matrilineal has one or more elected elders who, in addition to keeping aware of family relationships, certain temporal transactions, and the quarrels and misdeeds of family members, are charged with enforcing the marriage code. This code forbids marriages between close kin as defined in the matrilineal system. Thus, a union between the children of two sisters is forbidden as being incestuous, but a marriage between the children of a brother and a sister is sanctioned and looked upon as most desirable. The elder is empowered to legitimize some milder forms of irregular marriage, but he has no jurisdiction over, or authority in, serious violations of the code.

In the same way that all members of a matrilineal family trace their descent from a common grandmother, various extended families claim a common ancestress many generations removed. This consolidates them into clans that, politically, may be divided into two groups. Members of the first group, called *waris*, are privileged because their ancestors, according to legend, married women of the early Senoi inhabitants and thereby obtained original land title and political power. Those of the second group, derived from later Minangkabau settlers, own land and have some political influence but lack the legendary claim (see ch. 4, Ethnic Groups and Languages). Clans of both types within a certain area constitute a *negeri*, or tribal organization, led by a chieftain elected from one of the *waris* clans. Every clan, therefore, is traditional and has its own territorial base, but only a few have *waris* status and the hereditary right to chieftainship.

Traditionally, all fixed property in a *negeri*, although owned individually by women, is held within the clan and may be used or exploited by its members. This property, called ancestral land, is inherited by the owner's daughters or, if she has no daughters, by those of her sisters. The extended family to which each owner belongs and the clan of which her family is a member have a sacred obligation to protect the integrity of ancestral land and to prevent its alienation outside the clan. Newly cleared and planted land, however, unless it has been specifically registered as ancestral land before clearing, is classified as acquired, and under the law it is inherited according to Islamic law, that is, from father to son. This dual inheritance system has led to many conflicts. Matrilineal leaders argue that Muslim law wrests control of clan property from its traditional woman agent and violates the clan obligation to preserve its integrity. Owners of newly cleared land—such as that for rubber cultivation—declare that, since it was not specifically registered as ancestral land before the importance of rubber as a cash crop was realized, its inheritance under traditional law is not applicable. In late 1969 no satisfactory settlement of the issue had been reached.

Malay Marriage and Divorce

It is important to Malay parents that their children, particularly the girls, remain chaste before marriage. Thus, although young girls and boys are allowed to mix freely until they are about 10 years of age, the movements and contacts of marriageable girls are very restricted. Malay boys are not as strictly controlled. The seclusion of women ends upon marriage, after which they enjoy relatively greater freedom, particularly in divorce and remarriage. Women usually marry when they are about 15 years of age; the men, before they are 20.

Although Islam permits more than one wife, monogamy is the general rule among the Malays. First marriages are arranged by the parents, because a young boy or girl is not considered competent to make a wise choice. Some parents attempt to follow their children's preferences, but young people are restricted by the lack of opportunities to meet members of the opposite sex.

In selecting a spouse, parents look for a near relative and the highest possible status. Muslim practice prefers marriage between first cousins, particularly with the father's brother's daughter in the case of a son. Generally marriage patterns vary according to social class. Lower class Malays tend to marry within the village or to members of nearby or related villages. Important considerations are wealth, the prestige of the family within the village, the official position of the father of the bride or bridegroom, the education and economic future of the bridegroom, and the education of the bride. Among upper class Malays, marriage within the class to preserve status is far more important than marriage within the village or area.

Marriage negotiations are usually initiated by the parents of the prospective bridegroom, who engage in discreet and indirect questioning to determine whether or not the proposal is likely to be well received by the parents of the selected girl. If a favorable reception appears probable, the two sides arrange a meeting at which female relatives of the prospective bridegroom ask for the girl. After the parents are in agreement, the consent of both children often is sought; if one objects, the match may be, but often is not, abandoned.

Details to be next considered, such as the amount of settlement to be made on the bride, the value of the wedding gifts, and the probable duration of the engagement, are regarded as matters too delicate for direct negotiation between the parties and are customarily referred to the village headman and other elders. Traditional Malay marriage consists of a number of marriage payments from the family of the bridegroom to that of the bride, the most important of which is that signifying the rank of the bride and her father. A man asserts his right to be considered of a given rank by asking or accepting a certain payment for his daughter. If his rank is in doubt, the village elder decides the issue. The cost of the wedding festivities is borne by the bride's family, but the bridegroom must also contribute. The headman fixes the amount of the contribution and sets the approximate date of marriage so that neither side can evade its obligations by prolonging the engagement indefinitely. When all these issues have been settled, the agreement must be confirmed by a formal proposal and a formal acceptance.

The Malay wedding ritual is very complex and consists essentially of two elements. The first involves traditional rites that continue for seven days; the second element is the religious Muslim ceremony. The religious ceremony is regarded as necessary to make the marriage legally valid, but the more ancient rites have lost none of their social importance.

The wedding begins with henna-staining ceremonies that last 3 days, at which time both the bride and the bridegroom are painted completely with henna, and their families entertain guests with feasts, Arabic hymn chanting, and special dancing. The 4th day is devoted to a ceremony in which the couple, dressed in royal garments, is enthroned in the house of the bride and sits in state during another wedding feast. The 7th day is marked by a ceremonial purification of the couple ending with the severance of a bridal cord that has been passed around their necks. The rupture of the cord marks the end of the ancient rites, but the marriage is not consummated until about a week later when the bridegroom takes up residence with the bride's family.

The Muslim ceremony probably is held at some time during the days of the other rituals and does not require participation by the bride. It consists only of a marriage agreement between the bridegroom and the bride's guardian (usually her father) and the exchange of the marriage payment. When these things have been accomplished, the couple becomes man and wife in the eyes of both religious and administrative law.

Initially, a newly married couple lives with the wife's parents and continues to do so until, as the family grows, the parental home ceases to be big enough. The couple then sets up an establishment of its own to the accompaniment of appropriate ceremonies. Before the assembled village the parents enumerate the articles with which they are endowing the new household, and the young people express satisfaction with all that has been done for them. These formalities are considered necessary to avoid disputes should there be a divorce requiring a proper distribution of family property.

The number of Malay divorces registered in any year is estimated to be about one-half the number of marriages registered in the same period. Incompatibility is given as the most common reason for divorce, but jealousy or the simple wish of husband or wife to be free to marry someone else is often stated. Polygyny also frequently ends in divorce for one of the wives because of conflict as to which female will exercise authority. Because divorce is as normal as marriage in Malay society, it is not considered evil or wrong and is seldom regarded as unfortunate. In modern Malaysia, however, there is rising dissatisfaction with the high divorce rate because of world opinion against it.

Divorce is regulated by Muslim rules, which do not require the participation of any official. Theoretically, all that is required is that the husband register the divorce and pay a small fee, after which he is permitted to remarry immediately. In practice, the husband informs his wife, either verbally or in writing, of his intention to divorce her. Such a pronouncement is called a *talak*. If he makes only one such announcement, it can be revoked by mutual consent within a 100-day period during which the wife may not remarry. After the 100 days expire, the divorce cannot be revoked. A triple *talak* divorce cannot be revoked at all, but the couple may remarry if the wife first consummates marriage with another man. This proviso is sometimes carried out by hiring a man to marry the woman after stipulating that he will divorce her the next day.

The wife also can initiate divorce by consulting a religious judge independently, but she rarely does so unless accompanied by a male relative. Religious judges tend to favor the husband's rights, and the woman must wait 100 days for the divorce action to become final. A divorced woman has a great deal of personal freedom and may remain unattached or remarry as she pleases. A young divorcee generally returns to her original family household; an older one may prefer to maintain her own residence.

For couples who have been married for some years, divorce is sometimes complicated, because property that has been acquired jointly after marriage must be divided equitably. The general practice is for each party to claim the forms of property most closely connected with his or her economic activity. Should the objects be very unequal in value, compensation in cash is given by the party taking the most valuable objects, or all the property is sold and the proceeds divided. When a husband or a wife has brought a substantial amount of property into a marriage, it returns to its original owner after the divorce. The burden of divorce is increased for women if there are children, since they stay with her until they become of age, after which they may live with either parent.

Malay Children

Malays, almost without exception, desire and look forward to having children. Unlike Muslims of the Middle East, they prefer girls to boys, because daughters are regarded as more likely to care for aging parents than are sons. Both girls and boys, however, are received with love and joy, and great care is taken to protect them from the numerous malignant supernatural beings and forces that Malaysians believe operate in the world.

In consonance with these attitudes, the adoption of Chinese as well as Malay children is a common practice. The foster parents of a Malay child are usually relatives who have no children of their own or who are wealthy enough to provide for the child better than his parents could. In such instances the parents may see the child in his foster home regularly. Circumstances vary in this respect, but in all cases the adopted Malay child is rarely completely separated from his natural parents. A Chinese child adopted by Malays, however, is unlikely to see his parents again. The unconditional character of this type of adoption favors the adoption of Chinese children into the Malay community.

In traditional Malay culture, pregnancy is a period for the observance of many rules, taboos, and magical precautions to protect the mother and her unborn child from evil influences. These activities are directed by a shaman, a practitioner to whom the unseen world is supposed to be responsive. At the time of birth also, the shaman performs certain precautionary rites, but the presiding authority is the midwife, who takes charge of the mother and child.

During early infancy, parents eagerly note signs of progress along recognized stages of development of the child. After about a week breast feeding is supplemented with mashed bananas and other fruits and with pulped rice. Weaning takes place in the second year; in time the baby is encouraged to crawl and later is helped to walk. Between the ages of 2 and 6 the child is allowed to amuse himself by playing games near the house and, as he gains capacity, to run errands for his parents. The very young boy or girl wears virtually nothing, eats simple food, and puts relatives to such little expense that large families are not considered an economic difficulty. At the age of 6 the child usually begins to receive some more or less systematic instruction from his elders.

Training of an occupational nature, other than that taught in regular schools, is informal. Most boys acquire technical knowledge and manual dexterity by assisting parents in their daily work; some may learn art or a productive skill by helping a village craftsman. Others concentrate on reading and writing, either for religious purposes or with a view toward becoming practitioners of traditional medicine, divination, or sorcery. Girls are generally better instructed than boys in proverbs, old maxims, folklore, tradition, history, and popular verse.

The conclusion of a boy's Koranic education comes around the age of 10, after he has acquired an ability to recite a few verses and is familiar with the daily Muslim ritual practices. The occasion is marked by the all-important circumcision ceremony, the elaborateness of which is matched only by that of the marriage ritual. It is highlighted by a great feast attended by many invited guests who are expected to bring contributions to the host. Sometimes these contributions constitute repayment of past obligations and are, in effect, merely a realization of assets. Others, however, are not repayments but create new debts on the part of the host, that are expected to be liquidated at some future similar occasion.

A Malay girl is taught something about the Koran but is not expected to attain the same standard of proficiency as her brothers. When her religious education is complete, she is dressed like a pilgrim to Mecca, her ears are pierced, and she is admitted to the community by a ceremony simpler and less public than that of boys. Adolescent boys and girls, having undergone these rites, are considered eligible for marriage.

Old Age and Death

Old age is not a period of idleness although, after years of rearing children, old people are customarily cared for by their sons or daughters. Many old men busy themselves doing odd jobs around the village compound; many old women, after they retire from active household management, continue to take care of grandchildren and assist in domestic chores. Some elderly people retain a measure of independence by collecting plants in the jungle, by making craft objects, or by peddling various items at the local market. They are treated universally with polite deference; their views are respected; and their advice is sought by their juniors.

The ceremonies attendant on death are of great importance in Malay culture, as not only the family but also the community as a whole considers the loss of a member to be a calamity. Prolonged and often very expensive funerals usually involve the entire village, which turn out en masse to aid the stricken family and to mourn with it. The entire event acts as a visible affirmation of the ties of family and reciprocal work groups, unites relatives and friends, and provides ritual observances reinforcing the solidarity of the whole local group in an atmosphere of shared grief and compassion. An overt display of grief is frowned upon, especially at the death of a spouse, although great sorrow may be shown at the death of a parent, a child, or even a good friend.

A dying person is attended by religious dignitaries who are required to be present at the deathbed of a believer and to prepare him for the afterlife by a sevenfold repetition of the unity of Allah, the cardinal principle of the Muslim faith. On the day of death, relatives begin to arrive to offer condolences and to leave a small sum of money. The Koran is chanted during the day and throughout the night and, if the family is wealthy, men are engaged for ceremonial prayer that may last a whole week. On the burial day the body is placed in a coffin and carried outside the house for a short funeral service. The bier is then lifted off the shoulders of attendants and carried away to the cemetery, followed by a procession of mourners chanting the Islamic declaration of faith.

After interment of the body, the family accompanied by a few friends returns to the house, and the Koran is chanted throughout the night. On the 3d day a funeral feast is held in honor of the departed. Similar feasts may be given on the 7th, 14th, 20th, 40th and 100th days after death. The 7th and 40th days' ceremonies are obligatory, and dire religious or magical punishment is believed to follow their omission. The 7th-day feast, which consists usually of chicken and rice, is held for the relatives. The more important 40th-day feast is held for the relatives and the praying men.

THE CHINESE

The Chinese Household

The Chinese household may consist of only one nuclear family, but more often includes the extended family and, occasionally, nonrelatives. The household consists of a group of individuals, whether related or not, who eat and sleep under a common roof and consider this shelter to be their home. This definition covers a number of aberrant arrangements, one of which records lodgers as separate households if they are unrelated by blood or adoption to any member of the household in which they are staying. Another arrangement, accounting for only a small portion of the Chinese population and becoming less common as immigration levels off, considers groups of unemployed maidservants or laboring women who live together as separate households.

The average size of urban and rural households is about five and seven persons, respectively. The household tends to be somewhat larger in East Malaysia, where it consists of the parents, their unmarried children, their married sons, the sons' wives and children, and sometimes a fourth or fifth generation. Wealthy parents customarily have at least one and sometimes several married sons living in their household, especially if there is a family economic enterprise in which the sons work together.

An extended household is created by an increase in the size of the nuclear family and by the extension of this family through the continued residence of a married child, who may be either a son or a daughter. The pattern of a married daughter and her husband remaining in the parents' home is accepted in Malaysia, but in China it would imply inferior status for the son-in-law.

The head of the family is either the father, the eldest son, or the son who is the most worthy and successful. A major concern of the Chinese family is the perpetuation of the male line and the assurance of having male descendants to carry out the necessary death rituals. Thus, boys are more desired than girls by Chinese parents, and the birth of a girl is sometimes considered to be unfortunate. This is especially true for a young wife whose status in her husband's family is often marginal until she gives birth to a son. In 1969, however, a daughter was welcomed if the family did not already have more than two girls and was not in economic straits.

The preference for sons also expresses itself in the adoption pattern. The Chinese, like the Malays, often adopt children, paying money as compensation to the natural parents of the child. The price of boys, since families do not willingly part with them, is quite high. Girls are commonly offered by the poor at no more than the cost of the mother's lying-in expense.

Economic factors affect the size of the Chinese household, as parents at the lower economic level may be forced to dispose of some of their children. The negotiation may take the form of "sale," in which total rights in the child are exchanged for money, or an immature girl may be given as a prospective daughter-in-law to another family. The more prosperous parents not only keep their own children but also may adopt others. The household is sometimes further enlarged by the presence of married sons who participate in the family business.

The Chinese in Malaysia practice polygyny, but this does not appreciably affect the size of households. The Chinese believe that it is difficult to keep peace and order between co-wives living together, so in polygynous marriages the husband usually maintains a separate house for each wife and her children.

The Family as a Socioeconomic Unit

The Chinese household in its extended form generally lacks the cohesiveness that traditionally characterized it in China. The head of the household is responsible, nevertheless, for the debts of his wife and for the action of other members. All members may contribute to a common fund for food, clothing, furniture, and certain types of ceremonial expenditure, but adult individuals keep the main part of their earnings for themselves. Economic activities, furthermore, are not confined to household enterprises. In rural areas some members of the household care for the land attached to the house, but others have wage employment away from home. In urban areas, where wage work and occupational specialization are more extensive, the household is even less an independent economic entity.

Although it is not an economic or administrative unit, the Chinese household is a self-conscious social entity. Family observances occupy a central place in the religious system and, despite the fact that old beliefs and practices no longer unite the family as firmly as before, the ceremonial respects paid to household gods and the ancestors still contribute to solidarity among the participants (see ch. 10, Religion).

The Chinese hold that all persons with the same surname descend in the patrilineal line from one ancestor, and they organize into surname groups on that basis. Explicit and implicit distinctions, however, are made between classes of surname relationships which, although not always clear cut, may be divided generally into immediate relatives, or kindred, and other persons bearing the same surname.

The kindred comprises those persons within five degrees of relationship on the male side, as well as the closest relatives on the mother's and wife's side who may have a different surname. Relatives living in Malaysia are known as local kindred; those remaining in China, or those who have returned there, are called home kindred. As time passes the home kindred are losing influence because it is difficult to maintain contact with them. Among the local kindred the surname unit is neither territorially compact nor a persisting and exclusive group with a corporate nature. Instead, it has come to be similar in many respects to the *kaum* found among the bilateral Malays.

The kindred of a man living with his parents consists of persons directly related to him and of their children or wives. The kindred of a wife are practically identical to those of her husband, for she is not a foreigner in her husband's group and usually maintains continuous and intimate relations with his, as well as her own, relatives. If a young married couple lives by itself, as is often the case, or with the wife's family, as sometimes happens, the couple's kindred group varies accordingly.

No leadership structure exists within the local kindred. No one person or small group of persons may represent the unit as a whole nor do members of a local kindred necessarily worship together or have a pattern for common action. Joint and mutual action by members of the group depends on personal factors.

The most inclusive surname group is that formed by all persons whose surnames are represented by the same written character, because only in the written language are they unequivocally identifiable. Such a group, which is often incorrectly called a clan, has a number of formal functions. It holds property, exercises extralegal functions, makes proper arrangements for worshiping the same mythical ancestor, and performs various other functions as an organization. Within a given region the eldest men of the eldest generation are the nominal heads and theoretically are responsible for setting dates for ancestor worship, settling disputes, and supervising other community activities. They are the managers and treasurers who come from wealthier families and sometimes are selected on the basis of social position rather than age.

Daily Family Patterns and Special Rites

The day of the typical Chinese family begins early. The woman arises first, offers incense at the household altar and the shrine of the household god, and prepares breakfast. If members of the family work away from the house she may also prepare lunch for them. At the conclusion of breakfast the men and the women who work outside the home leave for work together. Those remaining at home occupy themselves with housework and with the care of the vegetable garden and the domestic animals.

When the workers return at the end of the day, the family has its evening meal, an important occasion for talk and gossip. Games and other forms of amusement and diversion are structured along age and sex lines. The Chinese feel that husbands and wives have different interests and should pursue their pleasures independently. Accordingly, men and women tend to cluster in separate parts of the house. Only in the large urban amusement parks or motion picture houses are family outings noticeable.

The only important seasonally recurring events are of a religious nature and involve each household in certain mandatory rituals. A woman, particularly the senior female member of a household, is primarily responsible for carrying out these rites. The rituals consist of offerings to the household gods and to ancestors.

Both family and religion are emphasized in the major holidays. These are the New Year, the Feast of Tombs, the Dragon Boat Festival, the Rites for the Good Brothers, the Birthday of the Kitchen God, the Winter Festival, and the Departure of the Kitchen God. The New Year, on the 1st day of the 1st lunar month, is the most important. It marks the rebirth of life in general and is an occasion when each person resolves to change bad habits, pay off old debts, and start with a new slate. For the family it is a time of reunion when persons separated from their families return home and reaffirm the solidarity of the family institution.

The Feast of Tombs, on the 4th or 5th day of the 3d month, is an occasion for demonstrating personal devotion to the dead by making graveside offerings. The occasion is festive unless the grave is less than 1 year old, then it becomes a day of mourning and lamentation. Behind the rites is the belief that it is the duty of the living to care for the earthly dwelling place of the dead and to provide them with food.

The Rites for the Good Brothers, in the 7th lunar month, marks a period when the spirits are released from hell to roam the earth in search of food and other necessities. Since they are believed to menace peace, they are propitiated by colorful rites in which massive offerings of food, clothing, and entertainment are presented to them.

Marriage and Divorce

Chinese nuptial patterns may be polygynous and, when they are, provision is made for three statuses of wives: primary, secondary, and following. Usually, but not always, a man's first wife is one selected in an arranged marriage and is recognized as the primary wife. She is dominant in the family, enjoying unquestioned traditional and legal wifely rights. Beauty and charm are not qualities leading to her selection as much as are good health and a physique that promises abundant conception and easy partutrition. Her main role is to bear children to ensure the strength of the family and the continuation of the ancestor cult.

A man's motives for taking one or more secondary wives are usually amatory, and a secondary wife sometimes is hardly distinguishable from a mistress. If the man uses such an expression himself, even though he establishes her in a separate household of her own, it is clear he does not look upon her as a wife. She may, however, lay claim to that status if it is disputed. Legally, a secondary wife can sue for maintenance for herself and her children, can claim half the widow's share at the death of her husband, and has a secondary wife's rights to ownership in property. The prime legal disadvantage is her vulnerability to divorce, as her husband can repudiate her at will. Almost without exception, a secondary wife is socially inferior to both the husband and his primary wife.

The status of primary and secondary wives is mutually exclusive, but that of a following wife may cut across the others, because

132

the criterion on which it is based involves previous marriage. A married woman who becomes a widow or a divorcee and goes to live with another man is said to "follow" him, hence the designation, following wife. Such a union, although given social sanction in the community, has some derogatory implications evident in the phrase "dogs following one another" that is used in referring to it. Moreover, since the courts have not ruled clearly on such unions, the legal status of a following wife is unclear.

Chinese women appear to accept these forms of polygyny, although they generally prefer to be a sole wife. Nuptial practices and attitudes nevertheless are changing under the impact of modern influences. Many brides, for example, seem to prefer the long, white dress and veil of Western wedding practice to the traditional red Chinese costume. They also like to have an American-style wedding cake at the nuptial feast. In addition, notions of romantic love and free choice of partners as opposed to arranged marriages are becoming prominent among the younger generation. In practice, this results in a trend for betrothals to become a combination of free choice and parental dictation. If parents bring a prospective couple together, final approval rests with the young couple; if the couple initiates the match, veto or approval rests with the parents.

The advent of Christianity and the passage of civil marriage laws also tend to reduce the incidence of polygyny. Christian marriage, which provides an alternative to the traditional Chinese ritual, is popular and, of course, requires absolute monogamy. Civil marriage, which has considerable prestige and respectability because of its official nature and the formal documents it provides, is not only monogamous but also specifies that no woman other than a civil wife may claim a husband's property after his death. In effect, this reduces the legal status of a secondary wife to that of a kept mistress, a position that increasing numbers of women are unwilling to accept.

In 1969, however, the traditional Chinese wedding ceremony, at least in its broad aspects, was the form most often followed. It consists of a series of rites marking stages from betrothal to the induction of the bride into her husband's household. Betrothal begins with the exchange of photographs and horoscopes to test the probable compatibility of the couple. The matchmaker, usually an aunt or a close family friend, arranges for the young couple to meet. If they are agreeable to the match, gifts are exchanged and mutual family visiting begins. At this point the couple may see each other socially without a chaperone, and the engagement is considered binding. The wedding takes place within 1 year, the precise date often being set by a spirit medium.

Approximately a fortnight before the wedding the bridegroom's household sends gifts to the family of the bride, including some cash to be used for a part of her wedding outfit and jewelry. An additional sum, known as breast money, is also paid to the bride's mother. On the wedding eve, the bride and bridegroom go through a hairdressing rite in their respective homes; this ritual symbolizes their coming of age. Then, early on the wedding day, the bride goes in state to the house of her future father-in-law where, with the bridegroom, she pays her respects to the house deities, family ancestors, and senior members of the household. She then serves tea to the assembled group of relatives to indicate acceptance of her humble role in the family.

After the wedding ceremony itself, the bridegroom's family gives a lavish dinner for relatives and friends. Arrangements are made at this time for a group photograph of the bridal party to be taken. This picture is customarily framed and prominently displayed in the home through the years. On the 3d day of marriage and after the union has been consummated, the couple pays a return visit to the bride's family. If, in the meantime, the bride fails to furnish proof of her chastity, she may be dismissed immediately, the marriage dissolved, and the bride-price reclaimed.

Variants of the traditional ritual, known as New Weddings, are most prominent in the so-called mass and reformed ceremonies. In both of these types the betrothal and prewedding day practices remain unchanged, but the actual ceremony differs in form. In a New Wedding, it begins after the tea ceremony with a formal entrance of male and female guests, officials, the introducer or introducers, guardians, and the wedding couple, in that order. The marriage certificate is then read and signed by the couple and the officials. This is followed by ceremonial bowing and an exchange of rings by the bridal couple. The ceremony then concludes with a number of speeches, congratulations, and an expression of thanks by the bride and bridegroom. When such a wedding is conducted by a sponsoring organization simultaneously for more than one couple, it is called a mass wedding; when it concerns only one couple and no specific marrying organization is involved, it is called a reformed wedding.

Still other valid wedding forms exist. One of the simplest involves the mere preparation and signature of a privately made marriage certificate. Another, called a declaratory marriage, requires no more than an announcement in the Chinese press that a man and a woman have decided to live together as man and wife. A third form is the de facto marriage, established by cohabitation alone. Ordinarily a de facto marriage, if primary, takes place only when there is some impediment to a more formal union, such as, for example, when a previously married woman is unable to obtain a formal, legal divorce.

Divorce among the Chinese is neither as informal as the simple declaratory act among the Malays nor as involved as the legal process used by Europeans. Chinese who are married by the traditional rites separate by signing mutual consent agreements to end the relationship. This is accepted in Chinese society as tantamount to formal divorce. Mutual consent agreements apply only to primary wives; secondary wives can be repudiated at will by the husband. In East Malaysia mutual consent agreements are the only form of Chinese divorce.

Individual Life Cycle and the Family

Chinese infants, especially males, are petted and indulged but are introduced to the harsh realities of social environment as soon as possible. Early discipline is mainly in the hands of the mother, although the father may be called in if necessary. Child discipline ordinarily involves a great deal of shouting and remonstrance; physical punishment is avoided but may be employed if necessary. The Chinese father expects and insists upon discipline and respect from his children according to a prescribed code of deferential behavior that does not, however, prevent warm and intimate relationships between father and children.

Boys and girls play together in early childhood but draw more apart when they start school at about 6 or 7 years of age. When not going to school, boys are assigned numerous chores, such as helping in the family fields; girls usually care for their younger brothers and sisters or help with household tasks. As children pass into adulthood they are expected to continue to defer to the wishes of their parents, and the obligation to honor and support them in their old age remains compelling.

The ceremonial life of the individual, in addition to his role in observing rites connected with family gods, ancestors, weddings, and major holidays, involves formal rituals surrounding death. A major requirement of funeral ceremonies is an adequately large body of mourners to follow the hearse. The circle of kinsmen and friends usually is considered adequate to give the deceased his due but, when this group is relatively small, hired professional mourners may be required. The problem is met by mutual-aid or death-benefit associations organized on a surname basis to help with the expense and to ensure that a large number of association members will visit the house of the deceased to pay their respects and to join in the funeral cortege. Thus, even a man of moderate means or a relatively recent immigrant with few kinsfolk, can ensure that his coffin will be followed by a sizable number of mourners by belonging to a few associations.

Upon the death of a parent or a husband, a son goes to the house of a neighbor to get water for the ceremonial washing of the corpse. After that has been accomplished, members of the immediate family keep vigil, wearing unbleached calico clothes—the men unshaven, the women weeping for the dead.

While the corpse is in the house there is a steady flow of visitors, usually dressed in subdued costumes, black, white, and blue being the accepted colors for grief. As each visitor arrives, the mourners sit or squat in a line on mats beside the coffin, where they wail loudly. The visitor makes his obeisance before the corpse with incense and afterward may stay for refreshments.

On the day of the funeral, usually a Sunday, because most people are free to participate on that day, the coffin is placed on a decorated truck or hearse, and the procession moves off at a walking pace to the cemetery. At the graveside everyone disperses except the immediate mourners who stay on to participate in the last rites. These include lowering the coffin into the grave and consecrating it. Paper representations of houses, clothing, and food to aid the deceased in the afterworld are then burned at the graveside. Additional ceremonies are carried out on the 7th, 49th, and 100th days after death, after which deep mourning ends.

In Chinese concepts the dead do not cease being members of the family group but only move on to a more exalted place in family life where they are worshiped by the living. The ancestor rituals are conducted only by male descendants and their wives; hence, the salvation of a man's soul depends on his having male offspring to continue the ancestor cult.

TRIBAL PEOPLES OF WEST MALAYSIA

The Senoi

Both descent and inheritance among the Senoi are bilateral, and the basic family unit is the nuclear family of father, mother, and their children. The most important local group is composed of a village, sometimes several villages, ranging in size from 50 to 200 people. It is a corporate entity, because it holds title to a hereditary and specifically defined area of land, called a *sakaq*, where the village members have their farms. The *sakaq* group tends to be exogamous, and a member may change his group whenever he chooses, because the *sakaq* is an economic alliance rather than a kinship group. The extended family and the household, often identical, are of lesser importance than the nuclear family and the *sakaq* group. There rarely is economic cooperation outside the nuclear family. In addition, the Senoi who inhabit a particular river basin often form a loose group that develops certain dialectical habits, mistrusts other groups, and tends to be endogamous. These groups are also territorially and economically defined rather than being kinship entities.

Among the Senoi, marriage, when it is formalized at all, follows a simplified version of the Malay ceremony. Only about 4 or 5 percent of the marriages are polygamous. Theoretically, the Senoi prohibit marriage between second cousins but, in practice, the prohibition usually extends just to first cousins. The general residence pattern after marriage is ambilocal; that is, the couple generally lives with the parents of one spouse and then with the parents of the other.

Divorce rates are high, and long periods of separation between husband and wife can lead gradually to divorce. Either partner at this time can demand material compensation for wounded feelings. The children of a broken marriage go to whichever parent can, or will, pay for them.

All movable property is inherited by the children of brothers and sisters of the deceased, depending on the greatest need. Close relatives continue to use the land, although the surviving spouse has first claim to its produce. Among some groups the widow and her husband's relatives equally divide land acquired after the marriage.

The Semang

The Semang live in nomadic bands that range in size from 10 to 50 people. The basic kinship, and often the community, is the extended family, consisting of an elderly man and wife and their sons with their wives and children. Occasionally, related individuals or nuclear families join the group temporarily.

The only prohibitions on marriage are those between parents and children and between siblings. Marriage usually results from free choice. When an understanding is reached between a boy and a girl, the boy approaches the girl's father. If he agrees to the match, the prospective bridegroom presents him with a knife, a cloth, or sometimes a small sum of money, and the marriage is concluded. Residence after marriage tends to be ambilocal with some emphasis on patrilocal residence.

Divorce is frequent among the Semang, and most marriages are regarded simply as temporary unions. Usually, divorce does not occur until a new marriage is negotiated. The bridal gifts are returned if the wife initiates the divorce, but not if the husband does so. The children of a broken marriage may live alternately with either parent. Generally, inheritance is bilateral with some patrilineal bias.

TRIBAL PEOPLES OF EAST MALAYSIA

Although tribal peoples of East Malaysia form several ethnic groups, a general family pattern is characteristic of most of them. In the hinterlands they continue to live in longhouses (multifamily dwellings), cultivating burned clearings much as they have done for generations, but those touched by the cash economy of Western and Chinese business enterprise are changing slowly. Once direct producers of all they consumed, they are becoming less self-sufficient, relying on traders for many items of daily use, including part of their daily food staple, rice. In order to buy these items, they turn to the production of a few cash crops, or the men go to the towns, oilfields, or estates to work for wages. In such cases the relations of family members are loosened.

Political innovations that enlarge the sphere of political interest also work to draw the individual out of the narrow circle of family and village. Where once the education of children was informal and centered in the family, an expanding school system is teaching skills and values foreign to the older generation. Christianity is also altering beliefs about the supernatural, conceptions of marriage, and obligations within the family (see ch. 8, Education; ch. 10, Religion).

Households and Kin Groups

The basic family pattern, although varying in detail among groups, is one in which descent is traced through both the father and the mother. Only brothers and sisters have the same personal circle of relatives, and kinship is not reckoned beyond fifth cousins.

Among the Iban of Sarawak, a family group usually consists of two or more generations, although there is rarely more than one nuclear family of the same generation in a single household. The core of the household is a married couple and their children, but it may often be expanded to include a married child and his or her spouse and their children. Relatives beyond this group, that is, second through fifth cousins, are called an individual's *kaban*.

Marriage is preferred and practiced with *kaban* of the same generation and sometimes with first cousins provided they are not mem-

138

bers of the same household. Marriage with siblings or with close kin of a different generation is prohibited, but an Iban may marry a first cousin twice removed, or a third cousin once removed. The fact that a large percentage of Iban marriages are within the circle of recognized relatives results in a consolidation and interlocking of kindred who usually occupy longhouses in adjacent villages. All of the villages involved in such a relationship constitute a tribe, which usually is endogamous. The people who live in a longhouse thus are generally related to each other, with the closest relatives often occupying adjacent compartments.

Residence after marriage may be established in the compartment of either spouse's parents. If two married children are living in the same compartment at the time of death of the head of the household, they split the inheritance, and one couple moves into its own compartment. Children who marry into another compartment while the head of that compartment is still living acquire rights in the new household and relinquish all rights in their natal compartment.

The Land Dayak's household is similar to that of the Iban. Newly married couples may live with either spouse's parents at first, but eventually they establish their own household, leaving the youngest child to inherit the household of the parents and to support them in their old age. Most marriages among the Land Dayaks are between relatives and in the same village. Marriages outside the village are infrequent and constitute a relatively unimportant link between the villages concerned.

Among the Melanau, relatives outside the immediate family are classified as close or distant. Close relatives are all kin through third cousins. The status of fourth cousins is doubtful, and fifth cousins are considered distant relatives. Beyond fifth cousins people are strangers.

Incestuous relations for the Melanau are those between the immediate family or between closely related members of different generations. Relations between first cousins and between close affinal kin, such as between a man's wife and his brother, are ritually improper. Marriages between distant relatives of the same generation and with strangers are not desirable, but they are not forbidden. The ideal marriage is between second cousins, or within the circle of close relatives.

Among the Kayan-Kenyah-Kajang, the personal kindred of an individual extends to fifth cousins, but it appears that only marriage between first cousins is prohibited. The elite, however, insists upon marriage within its class to the point of ignoring the ban on marriage between first cousins. Also, since the elite is small in number, most members have to marry outside the village, even to a member of another linguistic community. The commoners usually marry within the village. Property is equally divided between persons of either sex, and even succession to the chieftainship may go to a woman.

The Kadazans (Dusun) of Sabah differ slightly from the general family pattern of the area in that they prohibit marriage between cousins to the fifth degree. Also, it appears that males are favored in some respects in the laws of inheritance. Residence after marriage varies between the lowland and the upland Kadazan. Generally, a young Kadazan couple in the plains will live with the girl's parents, whereas among the upland Kadazan, the young couple will reside with the boy's parents.

The Murut of Sabah place much heavier emphasis upon patrilineal inheritance than do the other tribal groups of East Malaysia. Most young people live in the village of the husband and, therefore, most of the persons in a small village are related through the male line. In such a village, marriage is likely to be with persons outside the village.

Marriage and Divorce

Marriage among tribal peoples is simple and is usually arranged by the parents, sometimes before the children are born, although later the wishes of the couple generally are respected. The marriage contract is commonly marked by a series of payments from the family of the bridegroom to that of the bride.

Among some groups, such as the Iban, a system of trial marriage is recognized; in other circumstances, a young couple may attempt to force their parents to approve the match by having the girl become pregnant. Marriage tends to be early in all groups, at around the age of 15 for girls and 17 or 18 for boys. Marriage is monogamous among most non-Malay tribal groups, and after the wedding both husbands and wives are expected to be faithful. Among some groups, however, polygyny is permitted by custom provided the first wife does not object. Polyandry is unknown in East Malaysia.

Divorce, although not common, can be obtained easily by either party at will on the grounds of incompatibility, illness, sterility, desertion, or adultery, with the repayment of the bride-price in whole or in part. In some cases a wife initiating divorce action must find a substitute for her husband. Both parties are free to remarry immediately after the divorce.

Ideally the relations between a betrothed couple are quite formal during a long period of engagement, and courtship begins after marriage. In practice, however, intimacy usually occurs earlier, and a number of marriages involve no ceremony beyond the couple setting up house together.

When a formal ceremony is involved, the bridegroom is escorted to the bride's house by a contingent of his friends. Firecrackers are exploded while the party waits for the bride to dress, and the guests are invited into the house. This period concluded, an elder reviews the marriage payments, which may be a specified weight of brass cannons—a medium of exchange that is particularly prized—but frequently may be paid in cash. Since marriage payments are usually made in installments that continue after the wedding, the elder formalizes plans for future payments. Among the Muslim Melanau, a formal Muslim wedding follows during which the bride remains behind draperies delineating her room. She is then brought out by her father and seated at the bridegroom's side, and an elder instructs them in the rights and duties of marriage. Marriage between different classes is common, but in theory the children of such unions are reduced one step in rank.

Marriage payments and the status or rank they signify play an important part in tribal marriages and may be typified by the practice among the Melanau. A man sets forth a claim to rank at the marriage of his daughter. This is not done easily for it involves a lavish expenditure of money for an extravagant wedding feast consonant with the rank claimed for the daughter. It also requires the sanction of the village elders, who have the decisive voice in matters of status and marriage payments. The father must also present certain insignia of rank to the bride, the most important of which are specific weights of brass. The father does not gain higher rank for himself, but it is recognized that his work is responsible for the higher status he can claim for his daughter and that it is his money that pays for the feast.

The Family as a Socioeconomic Unit

The Land Dayaks do much of their rice cultivation on a cooperative basis; the Iban will fight as a village if their land is encroached upon; the Murut clear their fields communally; but the general economic pattern of all is based on the family. Everywhere the nuclear family is the chief production and consumption unit, and among the Iban it is the landholding unit as well. Ownership and inheritance usually are on a more individual basis in other groups. Husbands and wives retain their individual ownership of land and other property acquired before marriage, jointly owning only that which comes to them afterward.

In the division of labor, men do the rougher, more dangerous, and more taxing work of clearing the land, hunting, heavy building, and trading at a distance from the home community. The women, assisted by the children, work continuously at lighter tasks associated more closely with home consumption. Children, particularly girls, fetch fuel and water. Women do some work in the fields, but most of their duties are centered on the house.

Although the family of mother, father, and younger children is the core, the household is often enlarged by the presence of other close relatives, such as a married son, a brother, or aging parents. Sharing living quarters and meals and united by close ties of kinship, the members of the household constitute the unit that, rather than the community as a whole, is responsible for the welfare of the old, the sick, and the orphaned. Related households assist each other in large projects, such as the construction of a house or the preparations for a wedding. Few refuse requests for help of this kind, since aid is reciprocal. Also, meals or feasts are provided by the family receiving help and the occasion is one of general sociability.

The tribal peoples of East Malaysia highly prize children, so the adoption of both boys and girls is common. Boys ostensibly are preferred, but girls are no less welcome, for at marriage they bring a bride-price, and too many boys for whom brides must be found are an economic liability. Respect for parents, elders, and persons of high status is inculcated in children. Physical punishment of children plays an important role in their rearing, as primary reliance is placed upon example, precept, admonishment, and the molding force of the child's experience in growing up.

CHAPTER 7

LIVING CONDITIONS

Malaysia, despite many serious health and social problems, is generally considered to enjoy standards of living that are among the highest in Southeast Asia. Food is plentiful, and nutritional deficiencies that do exist result from unbalanced rather than inadequate diets. A lack of housing in cities causes much crowding but is being overcome by large-scale, government-financed, low-cost housing development. In rural areas living structures are usually flimsily built and lack facilities for the disposal of human and household waste; nevertheless, they are quickly and cheaply constructed from an abundance of natural resources and at least afford adequate protection from the elements. In addition, medical and social welfare services are becoming increasingly available to everyone through extensive health and welfare programs of both the government and private organizations. Consequently, the average Malaysian is satisfied with his lot and does not consider life to be excessively burdensome.

THE ROLE OF GOVERNMENT

Major governmental interest in the health and welfare of its citizens is expressed in the activities of three cabinet agencies—the Ministry of Health, the Ministry of Welfare Services, and the Ministry of Local Government and Housing. The agencies operate under the concept that local authorities and private organizations are the primary forces in health and welfare services and that programs of the federal government are merely complementary or supplementary. In theory, therefore, the three ministries are looked upon as planning, coordinating, and advisory bodies for basic services that are performed by decentralized state and local authorities or by private interests. In practice, however, acute manpower and financial shortages make it necessary for the central government to subsidize local agencies and often to carry out major operational programs of its own. Thus the federal government operates most hospitals and medical facilities; assumes responsibility for programs to control and eradicate epidemic diseases; runs institutions and facilities for children and for aged, destitute, and handicapped persons; and takes the initiative and financial responsibility for most urban renewal and public housing projects.

The burden placed on national resources by these tasks is so great that all of them cannot be pursued with equal vigor, and a system of operational priorities is required. The order of precedence for them is not arbitrarily drawn but follows guidelines set forth in the First Malaysia Plan for 1966 to 1970, which is an outline of policies and programs for national development funded in the federal budget at a figure of about M$835 million (3.06 Malaysian dollars equal US$1) for the full 5-year period of its operation (see ch. 17, Character and Structure of the Economy). A rough estimate of actual priorities may be drawn from specific annual allocations of approximately M$150 million for medical and health services and M$20 million for welfare.

The Ministry of Health

The Ministry of Health, containing the Medical and Health Services Department and the Department of Chemistry as its major operating arms, is concerned with all matters of individual and public health. The Medical and Health Services Department administers and operates government general and special hospitals, clinics, dispensaries, and maternal and child health centers; carries out nationwide campaigns against major diseases, imposing quarantine on individuals and areas as required; licenses, supervises, and establishes standards for the medical and dental professions; operates rural, urban, and school health services; and is responsible for the initiation and development of sanitary measures and projects.

The Department of Chemistry performs duties related to the production, distribution, and use of foods, drugs, and poisons. Health inspectors of the department regularly visit shops, markets, pharmacies, and restaurants, where they are authorized to seize or impound any foodstuff or drug likely to cause a threat to health. The sale of certain drugs and most poisons is restricted to pharmacies licensed by the department. The Institute for Medical Research in Kuala Lumpur, with branch laboratories at Ipoh and Penang, is also under the direction of the Department of Chemistry. It conducts surveys and compiles statistics and reports on the causes and incidence of diseases that are used as planning bases for preventive and corrective programs of the Medical and Health Services Department. Laboratories of the institute perform research in bacteriology, biochemistry, pathology, malariology, nutrition, virus diseases, and medical zoology and provide training in these subjects for student technicians. The institute is also responsible for the production and distribution of various types of vaccines at a large pharmaceutical plant in Petaling Jaya.

The Ministry of Welfare Services

The Ministry of Welfare Services is a large and active agency organized on a functional basis to carry out all types of welfare services. Its various departments are concerned with child and juvenile welfare; the protection of women and girls who are destitute, homeless, or exposed to moral danger; the care of aged and indigent persons; the treatment and rehabilitation of the physically handicapped and mentally deficient; and the provision of emergency aid to victims of natural disasters. In carrying out these tasks, the ministry operates a probation service, homes, and several remand schools for juveniles; runs a number of institutions for the blind, deaf, dumb, and mentally retarded; conducts family casework; trains youth leaders and sponsors young people's organizations, awarding them grants-in-aid for such things as musical instruments, games equipment, and sports facilities; conducts research on problems of social maladjustment; and subsidizes a large part of the effort of private and religious groups engaged in similar activities.

The Ministry of Local Government and Housing

The Ministry of Local Government and Housing is involved in public health and welfare both as a planning agency and as an adviser to state and local governments in the fields of land use, slum clearance, urban renewal, and public housing. It also acts as the executive agent for many projects in the same areas. In these matters, the ministry's Department of Town and Country Planning is the major operating element. In cooperation with local authorities, it determines national requirements for housing and accommodations and develops plans and programs to satisfy them. This includes the construction of public housing developments in both urban and rural areas and the resettlement of whole groups of disadvantaged people into completely new villages and communities.

The most outstanding example of resettlement action was a project to improve the lot of squatters who had crowded into Kuala Lumpur as refugees during the Emergency (see ch. 24, Public Order and Internal Security). An area of about 4,000 acres, 6 miles outside the city limits, was selected and set aside for development as a new community. Low-cost homes and other facilities were built by the government, and thousands of squatters were moved in to occupy them. The project was so attractive that it quickly developed far beyond its original concept as a haven for squatters. New residents and enterprises moved in, building their own homes, shops, and industries. By 1969 the community had become the satellite town of Petaling Jaya, one of the most industrialized and thriving cities in West Malaysia.

HEALTH AND SANITATION

Vital Statistics

Vital statistics show that the continuous effort to ameliorate conditions of health and sanitation has been highly successful (see table 1). There was a slight increase in crude birth rates in Sabah, but this was offset by corresponding decreases in Sarawak and West Malaysia, resulting in an overall decline in birth rates for the country as a whole. Superficially, this might lead to a conclusion that the size of the population was becoming static, but decreases in the crude death rate and the rate of infant mortality were so significant that the population was actually increasing at an annual rate of over 3 percent. Life expectancy, moreover, which had been less than 50 years before federation, had risen to 58 years in 1969.

Major Diseases and Their Control

During the first half of the 20th century, the territory of what is now Malaysia was infested with fever and disease, but the general level of health in the country has since become second only to that of Singapore in Southeast Asia. Health conditions differed among various states and between urban and rural areas in all parts of the country and were particularly unfavorable in rural areas where primitive standards of sanitation fostered dysentery and other parasitic illnesses. As the result of vigorous control programs, however, epidemic diseases, such as typhus, cholera, smallpox, and dengue fever, which were the major causes of fatalities in the earlier period, have virtually disappeared. Campaigns to eradicate yaws, malaria, and tuberculosis were so successful that yaws was almost nonexistent; malaria was significant only along the border with Indonesian Borneo; and tuberculosis, although still a major health problem, was rapidly coming under control.

Table 1. *Vital Statistics for Malaysia, 1962 and 1968*

Area	Crude birth rates [1]		Crude death rates [1]		Infant mortality [2]	
	1962	1968	1962	1968	1962	1968
West Malaysia _____	40.3	37.3	9.3	7.6	59.7	47.9
Sabah _____	33.2	35.4	6.9	5.7	55.3	43.3
Sarawak _____	29.1	28.9	5.1	4.8	46.5	43.0

[1] Per 1,000 persons.

[2] Per 1,000 live births.

Source: Adapted from *United Nations Statistical Yearbook*, New York, 1969.

Diphtheria, whooping cough, bronchitis, and influenza were common. The lack of protein and vitamins in most diets caused considerable nutritional ailments and some malnutrition, and other diseases such as leprosy, poliomyelitis, and goiter also occurred. The major causes of death in 1968, however, were the organic and degenerative diseases, including heart ailments, malignant neoplasms, pneumonia, tuberculosis, and vascular lesions, in that descending order of frequency. Infectious and parasitic diseases, iron deficiency anemia, and bronchitis were also important causes of death (see table 2).

In achieving the general improvement in public health, the government, in cooperation with the World Health Organization (WHO), the United Nations Children's Fund (UNICEF), and other international agencies, adopted a multipronged attack. Of major importance and basic to all other efforts was a massive program of public education to inculcate an understanding of the causes and prevention of disease and to stress the importance of early detection and treatment. This program was supported by a constant and continuous flow of radio and television broadcasts, press releases, and articles to reach the public through all mass media; by an increase in public health personnel to provide similar information and instruction at public health centers; and, perhaps most importantly, by the institution of regular courses in health, hygiene, and sanitation in public schools.

Table 2. *Major Causes of Death in Malaysia, 1968*
(causing 100 or more deaths per year)

Affliction	Number of deaths
Degenerative heart and connected diseases _____	1,502
Malignant neoplasms _____	1,409
Pneumonia _____	1,400

Table 2.   Major Causes of Death in Malaysia, 1968—Continued

Affliction	Number of deaths
Tuberculosis	1,221
Vascular lesions	886
Helminthic infestations and infections	424
Various anemias	226
Diphtheria	210
Childbirth	147
Bronchitis	121
Intestinal obstructions	113
Malaria	113

Source: Adapted from *Demographic Yearbook, 1967*, New York, United Nations, 1968; and *United Nations Statistical Yearbook*, New York, 1969.

Specific methods of control included mass, and often compulsory, vaccination and inoculation against the major epidemic diseases, carried out by public health centers and mobile teams in rural areas for the general public and as a regular part of the school health service for children. It is estimated that almost 1 million youngsters of school age had been inoculated against major diseases by 1969. Quarantine regulations were strengthened and strictly enforced; port controls and quarantine of ships and imports were tightened; sanitary projects, involving better waste disposal and the provision of uncontaminated drinking water, were undertaken in both urban and rural areas; public housing projects to relieve congested and unhealthful conditions in urban slums and village longhouses (multi-family dwellings) were started; and several specialized campaigns to eradicate the more prevalent threats to public health were instituted.

Among the specialized campaigns against particular diseases, those concerning malaria, tuberculosis, and leprosy have been singularly successful. Malaria, endemic throughout the country, was unusually severe in Sarawak, where the eradication program began in 1963. The state was first divided into areas where the disease was either in the beginning, attack phase, or in the controlled, consolidation phase. Teams of locally trained personnel visited all dwellings in their assigned areas to detect active cases and to take case histories and blood slides of all persons affected. Passive cases were detected by hospitals and dispensaries in the course of their routine operations. When active cases were found, all homes in the areas were sprayed with DDT, and likely breeding places of mosquitoes were drained or treated with benzene hexachloride. Spraying was not performed in the consolidation phase unless a new active case was uncovered. Throughout the campaign mass media disseminated information on the disease and its eradication, and visiting teams explained the aims and reasons for the campaign to each household. Progress in rural areas was slow because of poor traveling conditions; but by 1965 major urban areas were considered nonmalarious, and the campaign as a whole has passed into the consolidation phase.

Tuberculosis became widespread during the Japanese invasion, when food was scarce and often spoiled and when facilities were not available for proper treatment and control. By 1960 tuberculosis had become one of the most feared diseases in the country, although it was 2 years later before a National Tuberculosis Control Program was launched. The aims of the program were to identify infectious cases through widespread, free X-ray examinations and tuberculin tests; to protect the population, especially infants and children, with BCG (bacillus Calmette-Guerin) vaccination; and to identify early cases, which could be treated outside hospitals. The plan involved the coordination and improvement of existing facilities and activities, but emphasis was placed on preventive measures. X-ray examinations were provided by hospitals and schools, both of which also administered vaccinations. An attempt was also made to vaccinate all newborn infants at hospitals and maternity and child health centers and by mobile teams that toured rural areas.

The greatest problems encountered in the campaign were those of educating people about the necessity for early examination and treatment and of segregating persons who were stricken. Working men, for example, often were reluctant to leave their jobs and spend long periods in hospitals far from home. Tuberculosis remained a major public health problem in 1969, but its prevalence was diminishing, largely because of efforts in increasing the number of outpatients, convincing employers not to discharge employees who were patients, and providing transportation for weekly checkups and treatment.

The campaign against leprosy, which is endemic in all regions, was marked by advanced methods of control and treatment that have greatly reduced its seriousness and by an educational and publicity program that has altered public attitudes toward lepers in general. Before improved services were made available, contraction of the disease usually meant a life of isolation. Pressure from the community often forced afflicted persons to live outside populated areas, where they had little means of supporting themselves and often became public charges. There was a tendency to regard those who had been afflicted as capable of infecting others and, even among lepers who had been cured, employment opportunities were negligible. By 1969, however, attitudes had changed. Although employment opportunities were still limited, the fear of lepers was disappearing, and many were able to live as productive members of society.

Control and treatment of the disease were concentrated in a number of leprosariums, such as the Rajah Charles Brooke Memorial Hospital near Kuching in Sarawak. This institution is the center for all leprosy patients in East Malaysia and can accommodate about 400 patients. It is a model of what modern leprosariums should be, profoundly affecting the attitudes of both the patients and the population with regard to lepers. It has become an institution in which the nation takes pride and to which tours of schoolchildren, visiting dignitaries, and others are regularly scheduled.

Most hospitalized lepers live in their accustomed manner in houses or longhouses within the hospital compound, but a ward is available to accommodate about 80 of the more seriously affected patients. Medical work is supervised by a visiting medical officer assisted by a permanent staff of hospital assistants, nurses, and aides. There is a well-equipped workshop that produces artificial limbs and provides therapy for patients. The institution also conducts training for a number of hospital assistants in the detection, treatment, and prevention of leprosy. Graduates of the courses are assigned to rural dispensaries throughout Sarawak to provide domiciliary care for lepers who cannot visit the hospital and to execute various phases of the control program in their areas.

When patients are discharged from the hospital, the governor of Sarawak presides over appropriate ceremonies, including the presentation of certificates of discharge, which are intended to be helpful in their rehabilitation and search for gainful employment. Other events, such as concerts to which the public is invited, are scheduled regularly to reduce the fear of lepers and to increase the likelihood of their acceptance in the community after discharge.

Medical Personnel

The availability of trained medical personnel, especially doctors, dentists, and registered nurses, in rural areas of West Malaysia and in all of East Malaysia is limited and considered to be less than adequate to provide optimum medical and dental service to all citizens. Official figures indicate that in 1968 there were only 1 physician for each 6,000, 1 dentist for each 11,600, and 1 registered nurse for each 1,600 members of the total national population. Shortages of other qualified personnel, such as laboratory technicians, radiographers, pharmacists, hospital administrators, and public health experts, were even more pronounced. Many hospitals in rural areas had to operate with only one or two resident doctors, and most dispensaries and clinics were run by hospital assistants, student nurses, and midwives. Consequently, indigenous medicine men were prominent everywhere, and many people depended on them to exorcise evil spirits, which they believed were responsible for disease (see ch. 10, Religion).

The effectiveness of professionally qualified personnel was further limited by their uneven distribution. A majority of the nation's total of about 1,700 physicians, for example, was concentrated in West Malaysia, where the ratio was 1 doctor for each 5,000 people. In East Malaysia the ratio was estimated to be 1 doctor per 11,000 persons in Sabah and 1 per 13,000 in Sarawak. In order to bolster the medical service, a large number of foreign doctors, particularly Koreans and Filipinos, were authorized to practice in Malaysia.

Before 1963 there were no facilities or programs for earning a medical degree in the country, and all doctors received their training at the University of Singapore or at some other recognized school abroad. In that year, however, a medical degree program was initiated at the University of Malaya, designed to provide a minimum of 50 doctors a year beginning with the first graduating class in 1969. In time this program is expected to mitigate shortages and provide a sufficient number of locally trained physicians to meet national requirements.

The Medical Registration Ordinance of 1966 regulates the medical profession by requiring all doctors to register before being admitted to practice. Applications for registration are submitted to the Medical Council in the Ministry of Health, which also issues necessary certifications. The council also promulgated a code of professional ethics for doctors, which it supervises, acting as a disciplinary agency with the power to void registrations for serious violations of the code. A considerable number of registered doctors were in private practice, but the great majority were employed in health services of the government.

The dental profession is regulated by the Ministry of Health through the Dental Board, which functions in the same way as the Medical Council. To be eligible for registration, a dental candidate must have completed a full course at some recognized dental school; since none existed in the country, most Malaysian dentists qualified in Singapore or elsewhere abroad. Many others, whose training was insufficient for registration but who had been practicing before the registration ordinance became effective, were allowed to continue but were not listed as "qualified" professionals. Such men were permitted to use local anesthetics but could not prescribe drugs such as antibiotics. In 1969 there were an estimated 450 dentists in the country, of whom roughly 35 percent were qualified. About 75 percent of qualified practitioners were in government service and were employed largely in school dental clinics.

The total number of fully trained nurses in 1969 was estimated to be approximately 6,000, about 5,000 of whom were in West Malaysia and 500 each in Sabah and Sarawak. Nurses, like doctors and dentists, were required to register and were certified only after passing examinations administered by the Nurses Board in the Ministry of Health. These tests were based on British standards, and their successful completion enabled a nurse to register anywhere in the Commonwealth as well as in Malaysia. Nurses' training, which also followed British schedules, was available in virtually all general hospitals operated by the government.

Other essential medical and health personnel were scarce but were becoming increasingly available from a variety of sources. About 60 pharmacists a year were graduated from appropriate courses offered by the Teaching Hospital in Petaling Jaya, and a few were trained at schools in Singapore. Most general hospitals provided training for hospital and nurses' assistants, physiotherapists, and medical administrators. Radiographers, laboratory technicians, and research specialists attended a special school operated by the Institute for Medical Research.

Three schools in West Malaysia train public health officials. The Rural Health Training School at Jitra in Kedah was established in 1953 to coordinate the training of assistant health nurses, midwives, and public overseers for duty in rural health centers. The Public Health Visitors School in Penang offers a 1-year course, including maternal and child care, personal and community health, dental health, and public health nursing in the first 6 months and special problems in child development, environmental sanitation, and nutrition in the second half of the course. Students are required to be registered nurses and to be qualified as midwives. The Public Health Inspectors Training School at Kuala Lumpur gives probationary public health inspectors one year of training, which, in addition to academic subjects, includes laboratory work, field visits, and all aspects of public health activities.

Medical Facilities

A majority of the nation's medical facilities are enterprises of the federal and state governments, although many small hospitals are maintained by large agricultural estates for their employees, and numerous other institutions are operated for the general public by private individuals or by charitable and religious organizations. The number of facilities was increasing so fast that in 1969 reported totals were incomplete and constituted estimates at best. Data concerning private institutions particularly was lacking. Government facilities included at least 85 hospitals with a combined capacity of about 35,000 beds, over 100 main health centers, about 350 subcenters, 500 or more fixed and mobile dispensaries, roughly 700 midwife clinics, and approximately 425 dental clinics.

Medical and dental services at government facilities usually are provided free of charge. Because the burden is so great, patients are treated on an outpatient basis as much as possible. Those requiring hospitalization are charged minimal fees in accordance with their ability to pay. Congested conditions, however, are being overcome by the implementation of the first Malaysia plan, which is aimed at the expansion of existing facilities and the construction of new facilities of all kinds. The goals of this plan called for the erection of several new hospitals and the ultimate availability of main health center for every 50,000, one subhealth center for every 10,000, and one midwife clinic for every 2,000 Malaysian citizens.

Government hospitals are designated as general, district, or special according to the type of medical service they perform. General and district hospitals are those providing general medical care and outpatient clinical service; special hospitals are those dealing exclusively with a single disease or disorder. The general and district hospitals usually are located in major cities, although some can be found in smaller communities in rural areas. The overwhelming majority are in West Malaysia, where there is at least one in every provincial capital.

The largest and most modern hospital in the country in 1969 was the Teaching Hospital established at Petaling Jaya in 1967. Equipped with the latest devices and equipment for diagnosis and treatment of disease and provided with a full staff of competent professionals, it has rapidly developed into a national medical center. In addition to extensive wards for inpatient care and numerous polyclinics for outpatient service, the Teaching Hospital's laboratories performed much of the work of the Institute for Medical Research and had quarters and facilities for about 750 student doctors, nurses, and medical technicians.

In East Malaysia hospitals were generally smaller and less completely staffed than those in West Malaysia but were equally well equipped and well run. The largest in Sabah was the 340-bed Queen Elizabeth General Hospital in Kota Kinabalu. Two other general hospitals were the new 290-bed Tawau General Hospital in east Sabah and the 190-bed Duchess of Kent Hospital at Sandakan.

Sarawak contained a total of six general hospitals, the largest and most complete of which was the 570-bed Sarawak General Hospital at Kuching. Other major institutions included the Sibu, Miri, and Somanggan general hospitals of about 250 beds each and slightly smaller general hospitals at Limbang and Sarikei.

The most prominent special hospitals in Malaysia included six leprosariums, five mental hospitals, and six tuberculosis sanitoriums. Among the leprosariums the Rajah Charles Brooke Memorial Hospital was the only one in East Malaysia. The largest of the five in West Malaysia was at Sungei Buloh, near Kuala Lumpur, which, in addition to providing care for lepers, was designated as the control center for the national antileprosy program. Other leprosariums, each with a capacity of about 200 beds, were located at Palau Jerejak, Tampoi (near Johore Bahru), Kuala Trengganu, and Kota Bahru.

Before 1966 the need for mental hospitals was acute, and their development was a matter of top priority in the first Malaysia plan. By 1969 their number had expanded to two in West Malaysia, two in Sabah, and one in Sarawak, having a combined total of about 4,500 beds. The two in West Malaysia were located at Rambutan (near Ipoh), and at Tampoi; the two in Sabah included the Buli Sim Sim Mental Hospital at Sandakan and a new one completed in 1968 at Kota Kinabalu; the single mental hospital in Sarawak was situated just outside Kuching.

The Lady Templer Tuberculosis Hospital in Kuala Lumpur is a private institution with about 250 beds. Details on the size, location, and operation on the nation's five other sanitariums, except that they are government owned and operated, are lacking. Presumably, however, they all follow procedures of treatment advocated by WHO.

DIET AND NUTRITION

Although the nutritional standards of Malaysia provide an average daily intake of about 2,400 calories and are relatively high when compared with the rest of Southeast Asia, an imbalanced diet causes many cases of beriberi, iron-deficiency anemia, and malnutrition. The staple diet of all ethnic groups is rice, much of which has to be imported (see ch. 18, Agriculture). In most parts of West Malaysia, rice is supplemented by fish, vegetables, some meats, and fruit when these items are available and when there is sufficient income to buy them. In East Malaysia and some of the more remote parts of West Malaysia, other crops such as tapioca, maize, yams, and sweet potatoes form the main supplements to rice. In all areas food is usually served at two main meals a day—the first consumed in the morning shortly after rising and the second late in the afternoon. Numerous light snacks are eaten between meals.

In urban areas large amounts of soft drinks and other beverages are sold. Non-Muslim people in rural areas make their own drinks, largely from rice. The Iban in Sarawak make a rice drink called *tuak*, which is smooth and sweet; other native groups make *borak*, a bitter rice drink. Because conditions surrounding handling and transportation in all parts of the nation are unsatisfactory, milk is of little nutritional significance in the diet; and even children receive little or no milk after weaning. There is a growing tendency, however, to use canned milk for infants and young children, and UNICEF provides powdered skimmed milk to some of the maternal and child health centers and to schools.

Food preferences in East Malaysia are somewhat different from those in West Malaysia. In Sarawak and Sabah, Chinese and South Indian dishes are favored by a majority of the population; in West Malaysia curries (usually without vegetables) are most popular. The curries are mild, contain much coconut, and are served with many kinds of *sambal* (little plates of either peanuts, salted fish, pickles, or banana slices). West Malaysians are also fond of *satay*, which consists of small pieces of meat grilled on a skewer and dipped in a hot sauce of ground peanuts and chilies.

For a variety of reasons, the diet in all regions lacks sufficient protein. In general the country raises only a limited amount of livestock, and not much animal protein is available, even to those who can afford it. The Chinese are fond of pork and raise pigs to provide it, as do the aboriginal peoples of East Malaysia; since the diet of these animals is in itself lacking in minerals and vitamins, however, the pork obtained from them is also nutritionally deficient. Because of religious proscriptions, Muslim Malays do not eat pork, and Hindus do not eat beef, and many do not eat meat at all. Malays, especially those in coastal areas, supplement their diet with fish or fish pastes. Goats, frequently seen in Malay and Dayak communities, provide a useful source of protein on special occasions, but they rarely form an integral part of the diet. In East Malaysia the inland peoples frequently do not take advantage of the vegetables and fruits that can be grown there, and attempts are being made to persuade residents to plant and consume them on a regular basis.

Because of the unbalanced diet, most children have some type of vitamin deficiency. Vitamin A and D capsules have been supplied by UNICEF but in such limited quantities that they do little to reduce the problem. In rural areas the absence of sanitation results in much helminthic infestation that also contributes to malnutrition. Improved dietary habits are taught in schools, and research on nutrition is carried out by the Institute for Medical Research. The impact of these measures on dietary habits was only slightly discernible in 1969.

HOUSING AND SANITATION

Housing

Housing in Malaysia differs between rural and urban areas and among the various ethnic groups that make up the population. Generally speaking, urban areas are overcrowded, and housing problems in them are serious. Although congestion is less intense in rural areas, incomes are low, and houses, except for the residences of large landholders, are small and rather flimsy in construction.

The extensive forest resources of the nation provide most materials essential for home building, although processed materials such as brick, shingles, concrete, and glass are coming into wider use. In addition, many of the dwellings in new public housing projects are of the prefabricated variety.

Rural Housing

Housing for rural people ranges from the simplest split-bamboo frame and thatched roof houses elevated on poles to substantial wooden dwellings with elaborate gables and tile roofs. The average house contains two rooms—one in front to receive visitors and the second in the rear forming a main living area. These houses also have a back veranda, where the cooking is done and other household chores are carried out. Houses characteristically lack water systems or sanitary facilities and are built with floorboards laid loosely apart to permit easy disposal of household waste. Almost invariably, poultry and livestock are kept in the space under the floor and serve as scavengers.

Furniture in rural dwellings is simple. Even in the more elaborate homes, it usually consists of little more than pandanus mats laid on the floor at night for sleeping, a few domestic utensils, and occasionally a wooden cabinet or chest for storing china, papers, and family or personal valuables. A number of shelves affixed to the walls accommodate a tobacco pouch, trays and materials used for betel chewing, photographs, and minor personal possessions.

Malays in rural areas, most of whom are small landholders, group their houses into *kampongs*, which are small, exclusively Malay villages from which inhabitants travel to outlying areas to work their plots. Rural Chinese, who also may be smallholders but more often work as farm laborers or operate isolated stores, ordinarily live in similar type houses in communities called New Villages, where they were concentrated and resettled during the Emergency to prevent them from aiding the Communist terrorists (see ch. 24, Public Order and Internal Security). Indians in rural areas are perdominantly estate workers and live in quarters provided by the estate management. These accommodations consist of a line of wooden, barracks-like rooms with thatched roofs that are built on stilts to provide cooking areas underneath. As these quarters deteriorate and become uninhabitable, the tendency on most estates is to replace them with similar structures made of brick with aluminum sheeting or tile roofs or, in some cases, with separate cottage-type quarters. All new construction must conform to minimum standards set by the Ministry of Local Government and Housing. In addition to requiring at least 160 square feet of living space with an additional 160 square feet for a veranda and an individual kitchen, these standards call for the provision of an adequate water supply, santiary arrangements, refuse disposal, and antimalarial works.

In East Malaysia the pattern of rural housing is somewhat different for indigenous tribal people, who commonly live in a unique type of dwelling called a longhouse. These structures, built of wood and situated along riverbanks, are raised on stilts and consist of a variable number of independent family compartments joined longitudinally one to the other under a common roof to form a single attenuated structure. A broad, public veranda runs the entire length of the building. The basic structure of the longhouse is built by cooperative labor, but each family owns and maintains its own compartment, including that portion of the veranda fronting on it. As many as 50 or 60 families, in effect constituting a small village, may reside in a single longhouse.

The longhouse is sparsely furnished. Inhabitants sit on bamboo or grass mats that cover the floor. The walls are draped with rolled-up hammocks, which are stretched between the walls at night. Shelves hold radios, brass bowls, china plates, and other personal items. In some Iban longhouses human skulls, treasured relics from the past, still hang from the ceiling. Sanitation in the longhouse is usually primitive; holes in the floor are the only accommodation for waste disposal, and pigs and poultry are kept underneath. Food is cooked on the veranda. Bathing and washing are done in the nearby river.

Urban Housing

The high rate of natural population increase, coupled with a growing trend toward urbanization, has caused much overcrowding in cities. Existing facilities are severely overtaxed, and many people, unable to find accommodations, are forced to double up in congested slums or to find shelter in ramshackle squatter areas clustered around the fringe of the city. The serious health and social problems created by these conditions have attracted the attention of private interests and the government alike, both of which have become deeply concerned with plans and projects to raze slum areas and to replace them with blocks of multistoried, low-rent apartments. In 1969 many such developments had been completed, but a scarcity of financing limited most of them to a few areas in Kuala Lumpur and Penang. Moreover, in all areas there was considerable resistance, especially among Malay families, to abandon traditional patterns of living and occupy quarters in which ethnic groups were mixed and where housewives found it inconvenient to patronize the many street vendors who hawked their wares through the streets.

The Chinese constitute the major ethnic segment of urban dwellers. From the wealthy businessman, called a *towkay*, to the myriad of small shopkeepers, taxi and rickshaw drivers, clerks, and street vendors, they control the economic life of the city. Those in the higher income brackets live in new high-rise luxury apartments in downtown areas or, in the suburbs, occupy spacious older, colonial-type bungalows with broad verandas, or newer, modern, ranch-type, detached homes. Those with lesser incomes reside in blocks of flats or substantial row houses in both the suburbs and the city proper. Low-income Chinese live in dormitories or cubicles on the upper floors of shops that line the narrow, crowded streets of the business districts. As many as 15 to 30 persons may live in one or two rooms of these tenements.

Urban Malays, who are usually employed in government service, teaching, the professions, or as industrial wage earners, tend to concentrate in sections where the traditional Malay way of life is perpetuated in terms of physical and social arrangements. Also referred to as *kampong*, the same term used in reference to Malay villages, the pattern in these areas is usually, but not always, a collection of substandard houses of wood and bamboo on stilts, connected by plank walkways. Only Malays may own property or operate a business in the *kampong*. The *kampong* is populated mostly by low-income Malays, and life revolves around a central mosque and an adjacent market. Other Malays, depending on their ability to afford the expense, live in homes or apartments like the Chinese, as do the Indians and other ethnic groups.

Sanitation

The Ministry of Health, operating through health centers in rural areas and local municipal authorities in urban areas, is responsible for environmental sanitary conditions in all parts of the nation. This involves the provision of potable water supplies, the construction and maintenance of sewers and other systems for waste disposal, the inspection and control of food handling, and public education in the necessity for clean houses, streets, markets, restaurants, and slaughterhouses.

Streams and ponds are the major sources of water for human use; but because most of these are heavily polluted, authorities have encouraged the digging of wells wherever possible. Most towns have a system of piped and fully treated water that is regularly inspected and capable of providing potable tapwater in business and residential areas. Population increases, however, usually outstrip the available supply, and considerable sums are spent each year in extending the service area. In rural areas, the customary practice of simply drawing water from a nearby stream is giving way under pressure from health authorities to an increased use of wells and, when this is impracticable, to the damming of streams to form settling areas from which water is drawn, given minimal chemical treatment, and then piped throughout *kampongs* or into the adjacent longhouses.

The disposal of human and household wastes is a major problem in all areas. Major cities have sewer systems but contain many congested sections that do not. In addition to extending services to these areas, there is an urgent need to improve existing purification systems to accommodate the increased load. By law local authorities are obligated to perform the tasks of street cleaning and, at private individual's expense, to collect and dispose of refuse and night soil. New buildings must be equipped with sewers or septic tanks, but older buildings usually have only a small cubicle with a latrine bucket in it. Even this type of sanitation is usually absent in remote parts of the country, where improvement is being attempted through a large-scale program to build pit latrines and to encourage the use of septic tanks.

WELFARE

Organization and Development

Historically, social welfare in the territory comprising Malaysia was considered to be the responsibility and function of individual families or of various philanthropic and community societies rather than an obligation of the state. The government occasionally made grants-in-aid to private organizations, such as the International Red Cross or the Boy Scouts, but did not participate directly in welfare services.

World War II and the Japanese occupation, however, greatly aggravated social problems and brought about a modification of earlier concepts and practices. In the postwar period thousands of families were left destitute; health conditions had deteriorated; the number of widows and orphans were multiplied; and traditional welfare services had reached a point where they were no longer capable of meeting the needs of the people. Accordingly, the returning British authorities found it advisable in 1946 to establish the Department of Social Welfare in the government of Malaya to assume a greater role in relieving public distress. The work of this agency gradually expanded until it was elevated to full ministerial status in the early 1950's. In the cabinet reorganization following the creation of Malaysia in 1963, it was designated the Ministry of Welfare Services and given operational authority for all official welfare activities and supervisory control of all private welfare activities in the nation.

In carrying out its mission, the Ministry of Welfare Services, like its predecessors, has always tried to maintain a planning and supervisory posture but, because of growing needs, it has had to assume many staff and operational tasks over and above the efforts of private individuals and organizations. In the area of staff activities, it conducts surveys and research into problems of social maladjustment to determine policies, programs, and priorities for welfare requirements of all kinds. In addition, it coordinates and supervises the activities of private agencies, providing them with financial assistance when necessary. In the direct operational field, it performs reformatory services for juvenile delinquents, including the operation of a probation system, approved schools, remand homes, and youth hostels. It affords protection to women and girls, including counseling and rehabilitation services and assumes responsibility for the protection and welfare of children and young persons in need, including the maintenance of residential institutions for orphans and measures for their adoption. It provides for the care of the aged, the blind, the deaf, the orthopedically handicapped, the mentally defective, and those suffering from crippling and chronic diseases and operates custodial and rehabilitation institutions for them. It also carries out emergency relief and aid for beggars, displaced persons, dependents of prisoners, and victims of natural disasters.

The establishment of the original Department of Social Welfare in 1946 was accompanied by creation of the Central Welfare Council to coordinate the work of private organizations and to integrate their efforts into programs developed by the government. Charter members of this council included such international organizations as the Red Cross, missions of the Anglican church and several other denominations, Rotary Clubs, Boy Scouts, Girl Guides, the Young

Men's Christian Association, and the Young Women's Christian Association. Later a wide variety of locally sponsored agencies affiliated with the council as active participating members. Among them were Junior Red Cross chapters, the Malayan Youth Council, the Malayan Association of Youth Clubs, the Discharged Prisoners Aid Society, the Malayan Association for the Blind, the Malayan Association for Retarded Children, the Sabian and Sarawakian counterparts of these groups, and a host of similar charitable societies and organizations. In 1969 the Central Welfare Council and its associated agencies, many of them expanded into national organizations with chapters in each state of Malaysia, were still active and provided the bulk of the manpower for welfare activities at local levels.

Funds for welfare work of the government are provided in that portion of the national budget earmarked for the Ministry of Welfare Services and by similar allocations of the individual states. Private organizations receive most of their funds from voluntary gifts and subcriptions but also are subsidized by state and federal governments through the Central Welfare Council. Another source of income is the Social Welfare Lotteries Board, established privately in 1951 to aid charitable institutions but later transferred as a promotional responsibility of the government. The board conducts a number of national lotteries, in which 60 percent of the returns is distributed in prizes and 40 percent is reserved for welfare work performed by voluntary affiliates of the Central Welfare Council.

Continuing Social Problems

Living standards in Malaysia are relatively high in comparison with neighboring countries though unemployment among the young is high. Annual per capita incomes vary among the states, being somewhat lower in East than in West Malaysia. The national average in 1968 had risen to M$930, and even subsistence farmers and laborers considered their scale of living to be adequate or at least tolerable. Social gaps in the nation's multiracial society are wide, and the preference given to Malays in social and political life and the generally better economic status of the Chinese results in tension among these and other ethnic groups.

Gambling, prostitution, alcoholism, narcotic addiction, and juvenile delinquency are continuing problems that have been reduced to minor proportions by appropriate preventive and corrective measures. Gambling (except for state lotteries) and the operation of brothels are illegal and adequately controlled by energetic police action. The use of narcotics, also outlawed, was confined mainly to opium smoking among an estimated 30,000 unskilled Chinese laborers. The number of addicts has been steadily decreasing under strict repressive measures, however, and in time is expected to disappear entirely. There has been some concern over the extensive use of rice wine during festivals and celebrations but, because of religious proscriptions in the largely Muslim population, alcoholism has seldom been a major problem. Juvenile delinquency was increasing, although in 1969 it had not yet reached alarming proportions. In combating the problem the government encouraged and supported the formation of youth clubs and hostels that provided recreational outlets for youthful enthusiasm and fostered the development of attitudes of responsible citizenship. When these measures were ineffective, the courts had recourse to at least five approved schools and a number of remand homes where juvenile offenders could be sent for residential care, training, and rehabilitation.

Excluding the expansion of medical services and facilities, the implementation of urban renewal projects, and the construction of public housing in rural and urban areas, which were designed to improve overall living conditions and contribute to public welfare in general, the major social problems facing welfare agencies were those involving individuals who for one reason or another were unable to or incapable of fending for themselves. Attempts to meet and solve these social problems were extensive and included separate and specific programs for victims of natural disasters, children, women and girls, and aged, blind, deaf, chronically ill, and other seriously handicapped persons.

Emergency Relief

Aid required for victims of natural disasters cannot be predetermined but follows standard practices once an emergency develops. Procedures used in dealing with the disastrous floods that ravaged the countryside of Perlis, Penang, Perak, and Johore in early 1967 and left an estimated 130,000 families homeless and without food, may be taken as exemplary. The government first declared a state of emergency in the area and set up centers to provide communications and distribute medicine, food, and clothing. These centers also acted as headquarters for military units that were mobilized to perform security and engineering tasks and for private organizations that responded with a multitude of services.

A Disaster Relief Committee, chaired by the prime minister and composed of other high-ranking government and civic leaders, was organized to direct operations. Among other things, the committee launched a national fundraising drive to collect money and gifts in kind for distribution through the relief centers in the stricken area. When the flood waters began to subside, rehabilitation measures were carried out. Materials for rebuilding homes, paddy seeds to replant crops that had been destroyed, livestock to replace those lost, and other forms of assistance were provided free of charge wherever necessary.

Similar types of action are taken in emergencies caused by fire, earthquake, and major crop failure. In the average year and in addition to monies collected by special fundraising campaigns, the government spends approximately M$3 million on various domiciliary programs in connection with emergency relief.

The Care of Children, Women, and Girls

The care of children is considered to be a matter of first priority in Malaysia. Social workers of the Ministry of Welfare Services in cooperation with Christian and Muslim leaders provide counsel and advice to families on family planning and methods of rearing their offspring. When cases of inadequate support, neglect, cruelty, or abandonment are uncovered, family workers are authorized to intervene and take necessary action to ensure the welfare of children involved. Workers sometimes locate foster homes or arrange for adoption by reliable families and at other times place children in one of the nine children's homes run by the government or one of the 26 maintained by private interests.

Other facilities for the care and welfare of children include a number of specialized institutions. The Spastic Children's Association operates two centers, one in Kuala Lumpur and the other in Penang, that give physiotherapy and special education to spastic children. There is also a class for spastics in Johore Bahru. The Selangor Association for Retarded Children administers and supports a school in Penang that offers classes for about 50 mentally deficient youngsters. The Malaysian Association for the Blind runs a school in Panang capable of accommodating about 200 children. In Penang, also, the Saint Nicholas School for the Blind, under the auspices of the Anglican mission, gives resident training to some 180 children. The Federation School for the Deaf at Penang, operated by private interests, offers primary education for those who are deaf and deaf-mutes.

The government also assumes responsibility for protecting women and girls from exploitation for immoral purposes and for their rehabilitation from a life of prostitution. Major facilities for this purpose are the Rehabilitation Center for Women and Girls at Kuala

Lumpur and an older institution of the Anglican mission, called Po Leung Kuk, located at Penang. Accommodations at these institutions are extremely limited and are capable of caring for a maximum of about 100 residents at any one time.

Care of the Aged

Malaysians of all ethnic origins have a deep respect for the elderly and devote much effort toward ensuring their comfort and well-being. Individual families regard the care of their parents and aged kinfolk as a firm obligation, to be accepted and discharged as a matter of honor. Most old people, therefore, continue to reside in the family household under the protection of their children and relatives. When, for any reason, this becomes infeasible, much of the concern for the aged is reflected in the welfare activities of the government and various private organizations, such as the Salvation Army.

The Ministry of Welfare Services has a large section to deal exclusively with problems of old people. Under its aegis nine old people's homes in West Malaysia and several in East Malaysia are operated. The ministry also has a service whereby elderly persons who have homes of their own but do not wish to enter one of the institutions are assisted with financial payments. In addition to facilities of the government, over 100 old people's homes are operated by private and charitable organizations.

Care and Rehabilitation of the Handicapped

A large number of government and private facilities exist to deal with the welfare of persons who are blind, deaf, chronically ill, or otherwise physically unable to lead normal lives. They include homes, centers, and facilities for the care, treatment, training, and rehabilitation of those so afflicted. In addition, other specialized organizations, such as the Anti-Tuberculosis Association, the Lepers Welfare Relief, and similar groups that do not operate formal facilities of their own, render valuable service by recruiting volunteers to work in existing institutions.

The Malaysian Association for the Blind is the most active organization catering to the needs of blind people. It operates the Princess Elizabeth School for the Blind at Johore Bahru in West Malaysia and similar institutions at Kuching and Kota Kinabalu in the eastern segment of the nation. The association also maintains the Kinta Valley Workshop in Ipoh and smaller centers for vocational training and rehabilitation of the blind at Kuala Lumpur, Temerloh, and

Kuala Besut. Another major institution for the blind is the St. Michael's Occupational Center at Penang, run by the Anglican mission. It provides a workshop for unemployed but trained blind young women.

The Federation School for the Deaf provides vocational training and rehabilitation for a limited number of adults as well as its regular educational courses for children and is the major institution for the deaf and deaf-mutes.

Government interest in caring for handicapped persons, excluding considerable financial aid to private institutions and basic responsibility for operating hospitals, sanitariums, leprosariums, and establishments that cater exclusively to children and the aged, consists of a variety of agencies and services that are wholly official responsibilities. In the area of residential care and treatment, the Cheshire Homes in Johore and Selangor and the Home for the Infirm in Penang are the most prominent. These institutions admit needy persons who are chronically ill and who would ordinarily occupy hospital beds but who no longer require hospital care. In addition to the two Cheshire Homes, two others were scheduled to be activated in late 1969.

In the area of rehabilitation, there are many centers organized, equipped, and staffed to deal with all types of disabling afflictions. The most comprehensive of these is the Rehabilitation Center for the Handicapped at Cheras, which provides postsurgical treatment, education, vocational training, and social services to blind, deaf, maimed, and otherwise incapacitated persons.

Social Security

There was no general social security system in Malaysia in 1969, but some rather comprehensive measures were in effect for various types of workers. Government employees were entitled to a pension when they retired and were protected against temporary or permanent disability during their working years. These benefits were provided on a noncontributory basis as a condition of their employment. Workers in private industry were provided medical care, treatment, and sometimes an indemnity for accidents sustained at work, and some received additional benefits under provisions of the Workmen's Compensation Ordinance of 1952. This act established the Employees Provident Fund, administered by the central government and maintained by equal, monthly payments from both employees and employers. Contributions were based on a sliding scale but at a maximum rate limited to 5 percent of earnings. Participants in the fund were paid a lump sum when they retired at the age of 55 years, or the same amount was awarded to their survivors in case of earlier death (see ch. 20, Labor).

The 1952 Workmen's Compensation Ordinance was replaced in July 1969 by a new Social Security Law. The new law made some changes in the Employees Provident Fund covering workers earning M$500 in industries that had five or more employees. These included a pilot employment injury plan to be tested among about 150,000 workers in five major cities and an invalidity (total disability) plan covering all Malaysian workers. The cost of the injury plan was to be borne entirely by the employer, and the invalidity plan was to be shared equally by the employer and the worker. Benefits available under both plans included medical care and treatment, with disability and dependents allowances as appropriate and, in the invalidity form, a pension, regardless of the age of the recipient.

CHAPTER 8

EDUCATION

Government policy in 1969 was devoted to the rapid transformation of Malaysian education into a uniform system with the national language, Bahasa Malaysia, as the main medium of instruction. This was the newest development in a 20-year-long effort to provide, through the development of a single multiracial school system, a common national identity and social cohesion. The disruption caused by communal disorders in May 1969 intensified government determination to hasten the unification of the school system along national, multiracial lines (see ch. 13, Political Dynamics).

The school system grew up divided along ethnic lines, each language stream completely separate from the others, until 1952, when the first comprehensive scheme of education for the Federation of Malaya was introduced. Texts, teachers, and curricula in the different language media of the secular and religious schools were, until the 1960's, almost exclusively foreign in origin and orientation. Although national uniform Malay medium instruction and domestically oriented curriculum content have been the goal of government policy since 1957, frequent compromises have been made as deemed necessary to satisfy communal or regional demands.

These communal hostilities, which threaten the nation's integrity, are regarded by the government as having been caused and perpetuated in part by the nation's history of an ethnically divided educational system. The new multiracial school system in the national language is recognized as an important, perhaps the principal, means of overcoming racial barriers in the society.

East Malaysia, which had been, in the postwar period until 1969, engaged in transforming Malay and Chinese schools into English-language schools, has required special treatment. As part of the agreement leading to the formation of Malaysia in 1963, a guarantee of English as the official language of the East Malaysian states until 1973 was written into Malaysia's Constitution. Sarawak, having nearly completed the transformation into English language schooling, was in 1969 not receptive to efforts to establish Bahasa Malaysia as the language of its schools.

In addition to using the educational system to help create a sense of Malaysian nationhood, the federal government's chief concern has been to provide trained manpower both for the present job market and for future industrial, technological, and professional needs. Education for these purposes in 1969 was expanding rapidly, partly as a result of aid from international organizations and friendly governments.

The secular schools receiving government funds include primary schools (first 6 years), lower secondary (3 years), upper secondary (2 years), sixth forms and colleges (2 to 3 years), and a university. A second university, University Kebangsaan, which is the first to be conducted in the national language, is scheduled to open in 1970. In the East Malaysian states of Sarawak and Sabah, the educational system is similar to that in West Malaysia, but there are differences in language of instruction and curriculum; and these states operate their school systems autonomously, although with federal funds. Curriculum content throughout the nation is moving toward uniformity.

A separate, private, Chinese-language secondary school system exists with curriculum content and political orientation regarded by the government as vulnerable to undesirable biases. The Muslim school system also is totally different from the secular educational system with curriculum content almost exclusively religious, and graduates of these schools have difficulty in finding jobs. The Muslim schools are the responsibility of the separate state governments, although federal activity is increasing in this area.

Expansion of basic schooling to all the people has continued. Whereas in 1950 only 35 percent of West Malaysians and under 20 percent of East Malaysians were enrolled in school, by 1966 approximately half the school-age population of East and West Malaysia were attending school. The expansion of educational facilities and adult education programs have had a great effect on improved literacy rates, which were up from 38.4 percent (1947 figures) in West Malaysia, 17 percent (1951 figures) in Sabah, and 17.6 percent (1947 figures) in Sarawak to 51 percent in West Malaysia, 24.3 percent in Sabah, and 25.3 percent in Sarawak by 1960.

HISTORICAL BACKGROUND

West Malaysia

Several types of Malay education existed in the pre-British period. The earliest was the training given specialists such as shamans and artisans in metals and weaving. There also was practical instruction by parents to teach children to fish, trap, and farm. Buddhist and later Muslim missionaries introduced Malays to learning from books.

Islamic education by the 19th century had become institutionalized. Beginning at 6 years of age, a child was given lessons in reciting the Koran in Arabic by the village religious teacher, either at home or at the local village prayer hall. These Koran schools were meant for the ordinary villagers, as were informal adult lectures on religion given at the nearest mosque.

For the potential religious teacher or officer for the religious courts or mosques, specialized education beginning in early adolescence was available at *pondok* schools. At a *pondok* (temporary dwelling) school, students boarded at their teacher's home or in huts set up nearby. The teacher received support in land and other gifts from the villagers. The students, instead of paying school fees worked in their free hours as farm laborers for the teacher. The curriculum was entirely religious. Students usually remained at the *pondok* school for from 5 to 10 years.

During the 19th century a number of English-language schools were established in urban areas by British East India Company officials and Catholic, Anglican, and American Methodist missions. By the 1870's English-medium schools were receiving grants from the British colonial government. The Malay College, which was an English-language boarding school established expressly for Malay boys of good family, a few trade and vocational schools, a technical college, and a school of agriculture had been established in British Malaya by 1941.

In general the English-language schools were used by the Chinese and Indian urban population. British policy forbade Christian missionaries proselytizing among the Muslims, and the urban location of the English schools discouraged Malays from attending them.

Most Malays had no schooling or went to rural Malay-language primary schools, the Sekolah Umum (public schools). Candidates for religious careers went to *pondok* schools or to a new type of school that became very popular in the 1910's called a *madrasah*, in which classes were conducted in Arabic. By learning to speak Arabic rather than merely to pronounce it as in the *pondok* schools, *madrasah* students became recognized as better qualified for religious careers than *pondok* graduates.

Free secular primary education in Malay became available to the rural populace in the late 1870's, when the British transformed the Sekolah Umum into the Government Malay Schools, paid for out of public funds. In the Government Malay Schools British policy was to provide 4 or 5 years of secular education of the most rudimentary type: Malay literacy (now for the first time in the Roman alphabet, known as *rumi* script), simple arithmetic, and basic rural skills such as basketmaking. The colonial policy was designed to prevent Malays becoming alienated from their rural environment. Higher education and English-language education were to be avoided, except for the few upper-class Malays who would need more than the three R's to take their place in the government.

Islam was removed from the required curriculum of the Government Malay Schools and made an after-hours, elective subject for which a fee must be paid. On an elective basis, however, Muslim teaching at the government school was encouraged as a means of attracting pupils. For many years the Government Malay Schools were not as popular as the Muslim schools. Secular learning was to some degree suspect, and the curriculum at the government schools did not prepare the graduates for improved employment opportunities, whereas graduates of religious schools might find jobs in the expanding Malay state religious bureaucracies. The only secondary schools conducted in Malay were two teacher-training colleges, one of them for women.

Chinese-language schools were established and paid for by the Chinese themselves. The earliest schools in the country were conducted in various regional dialects, but after China adopted Kuo Yu (Mandarin) as the national language, the overseas Chinese schools were quick to switch to Kuo Yu as well. Although English-language schools were 80-percent Chinese in student body in 1941, most Chinese still attended Chinese-language schools. The Chinese school system included primary (6 years), junior middle (3 years), and senior middle (3 years), roughly corresponding to primary, lower secondary, and upper secondary in the English language schools.

Chinese schools were not given government encouragement, because it was believed that the Chinese population was transient and it was felt by the colonial government that perpetuating the Chinese language among the permanent residents of Malaya would strengthen communal barriers. The result was that Chinese education remained oriented toward China. The texts and most of the teachers came from China, and opportunities for advanced education and recognition of degrees were in China.

Indian labor came to West Malaysia in a great wave in the late 19th century, mostly to work on the newly established rubber estates. In 1912 the introduction of a labor code to Malay brought a requirement that all estates provide 4 years of primary education for their workers. Tamil was the usual medium of instruction, but a few estate schools were conducted in other Indian languages. Small annual grants were given these schools by the government. The teachers and texts came from India, and the schooling, generally of a low standard, did not extend past primary school. No special classes for Indians were established to permit continuation of schooling in English-medium secondary schools, as was provided for Malays. Some Indians, however, lived in the urban centers and thus were able to use the English-medium schools. English education was attractive to the Indians, since it prepared them for clerical jobs in Malaya and also for jobs in India, which was until after World War II under British administration and used English as the official language.

For all its limitations, education progressed greatly during the first half of the 20th century. From 1900 to 1941 total student enrollment in Malaya increased at the rate of 7,000 a year, from 25,000 in 1900 to 312,000 in 1941, of whom nearly 130,000 were in Malay-language schools.

East Malaysia

In East Malaysia the quantity and quality of education were lower than in West Malaysia. In Sarawak, the second raja, Charles Brooke, established in 1902 a statewide system of primary schools in two languages: Malay-medium schools for Malays and Mandarin schools for Chinese. Raja Charles feared the possible cultural disruption for Asians of English-language education and, admiring and respecting the cultures of the non-Muslim interior peoples who had no written language, hesitated to introduce them to literacy too suddenly. The task of educating these interior peoples, he felt, was best left to the Roman Catholic and Anglican missions. The missions maintained English-language boarding schools in Kuching and established other boarding schools elsewhere, helped by government grants, but few people of the interior ethnic groups received any formal education until after World War II, although interest in education and literacy by the people themselves had been on the rise since the mid-1920's.

During the reign of Sarawak's third and last raja, the state school system included Muslims only. Chinese independent schools, however, received government grants. By 1932, 4.3 percent of Sarawak's budget was being spent on recurrent educational expenditures.

In Sabah, Catholic and Protestant missionary schools took the lead. By the start of the 20th century, there were mission schools in nine towns, catering almost exclusively to the Chinese community, which were conducted in English, and had a total student body of 450. No schools were established in the interior for many years. From 1915 until 1930 a small school (12 students) was run by the government in the Malay language to educate some of the sons of native chiefs. By the time this school closed in 1930, 10 other Malay language schools, with a total student body of 391 boys, were being run by the government education department.

Chinese-language education was begun and expanded by private Chinese money and effort. In 1909 there were already six Chinese schools, and soon thereafter they outnumbered all other types.

By 1940 the total student body in Sabah was 10,993. Over 1,500 of the students were in 28 Malay-language primary schools, where they learned rudimentary literacy and arithmetic, health, and gardening. Nearly 4,000 were in 52 mission schools, where they learned English. The Chinese-language schools were the most popular, with 59 schools and nearly 4,800 pupils, some of them girls. The government of Sabah looked to British Malaya for advice in educational policy, and of the 53 teachers in government Malay-language schools in 1940, 11 came from Malaya's teacher-training college.

During the Japanese occupation, English and Chinese schools were banned, but some continued surreptitiously. Malay-language schools were permitted, but the deteriorating living conditions of the population hampered education.

POLICIES AND PROBLEMS

Uniformity

British policy in Malaya after the war was aimed at creating a national educational system. In trying to achieve this, the colonial government was hampered by the individual states' insistence on continued control over education. With independence, secular educational policy and administration for Malaya came under the control of the federal Ministry of Education, making possible for the first time the creation of a uniform national education policy. Muslim schools, which by this time played only a minor role in education, continued as before independence under the various states' jurisdictions.

Statewide uniformity of standards in Sabah and Sarawak began to increase in the 1950's after the state governments assumed a greater portion of the financial burden of running their schools than formerly. Although financing of East Malaysian education has since 1963 become a federal responsibility, the state governments in 1969 continued to manage the East Malaysian school systems.

Radio and, in West Malaysia, television programs designed for schools have been used extensively to supplement texts and individual classroom instruction, providing a uniform curriculum. In parts of the country not easily reached by overland transportation, the portable transistor radio has provided a significant portion of classroom instruction (see ch. 15, Public Information).

Language

In West Malaysia, after the return of the British at the end of World War II, plans were drawn up to develop a multiracial school system to prepare the country for eventual independence. English and Malay were to be compulsory subjects. The eventual goal was education with the English language as the main medium of instruction.

To the educational planners, English had the positive advantage of being a useful world language for science and technology, as well as the negative advantage of being the language of no single ethnic group in Malaysia. Efforts to introduce classes conducted in English in Malay, Chinese, and Indian schools met with resistance from Malays, Chinese, and Indians. The Malays were anxious to establish their own language as the national language, and the other communities were determined to retain their individual linguistic and cultural heritage and identity.

In 1956 when Malayan independence was imminent, a committee headed by Tun Abdul Razak was established and instructed to recommend educational policy changes in order to establish a national system of education that would sustain and preserve the different languages and cultures while bearing in mind the intention of the government to make Malay the national language of the country. After independence, government policy, largely the result of the Razak committee recommendations, was to provide government-supported primary education in four languages—English, Malay, Chinese, and Tamil—and to require that all four meet certain national standards, including compulsory teaching of Malay and English as subjects and a common, nationally oriented curriculum content.

In 1957 the Alliance-controlled government pledged to establish Malay as the national language within 10 years and eventually as the main medium of instruction in the schools. The first Malay-language secondary schools were established in 1958, but English-language secondary schools have continued to receive government support. Support for Chinese secondary schools has come only from private sources, and there are no Tamil secondary schools.

A continuing interest in retaining English as a tool in educating manpower for modern technological and professional positions has been maintained by the government. In 1969 English-language instruction was the only type available in most fields at the University of Malaya and most college-level professional and vocational schools. Government-supported secondary schools teaching in English had 2½ times the enrollment of secondary schools taught in the national language, Bahasa Malaysia.

A new language policy, however, announced by the minister of education in July 1969 was aimed at making the national language the main medium of instruction at all levels by 1982. According to the plan, the conversion of English-language primary schools to the national language was scheduled to begin in 1970. English was to continue to be a compulsory subject. During the 1960's certain courses given in the national language have been introduced at all levels of the school system. Courses conducted in Bahasa Malaysia in mathematics, science, and technical fields at the University of Malaya were begun in the late 1960's and are anticipated in the new national-language-medium university, University Kebangsaan (national university), scheduled to open in 1970.

The Dewan Bahasa dan Pustaka (a language and literature council) has been active in supplying textbooks in Bahasa Malaysia for the schools, and efforts have been made to develop a standardized uniform spelling for Bahasa Malaysia and Bahasa Indonesia, the Indonesian national language that is a closely related Malay dialect. Given a standardized spelling system, Indonesian texts could be used in Malay language schools, as Indonesian teachers have been.

Education for Manpower Needs

According to a 1969 government statement, the chief aim of the government policymakers concerning education, aside from the determination to make Bahasa Malaysia the chief language of instruction throughout the school system, was that "educational output . . . [be] closely geared to the long-term manpower needs . . . for rapid industrial and agricultural modernization" (see table 3). The government has therefore been concerned with improving the science and mathematics programs in the academic schools and improving and expanding nonacademic vocational schools. Realizing that academic schooling is more popular with private schools because of its higher social status and relatively low equipment costs, the government has seen its role as primarily devoted to expanding government-aided education in the vocational and technical fields.

Occupational Level	1965 Supply	1970 Estimated supply	Additional requirements 1970–80 [2]	1980 Estimated supply
Agriculture:				
Professional _____	275	887	663	1,550
Subprofessional ____	1,035	2,969	2,304	5,273
Skilled _____	6,506	12,791	4,912	17,703
Total _____	7,816	16,647	7,879	24,526
Technical:				
Professional _____	1,300	2,594	1,938	4,532
Subprofessional ____	4,538	6,900	5,354	12,254
Skilled _____	61,068	84,176	32,324	116,500
Total _____	66,906	93,670	39,616	133,286
White Collar:				
Professional _____	6,363	11,093	8,286	19,379
Subprofessional ____	6,914	10,309	8,000	18,309
Skilled _____	40,381	56,171	21,570	77,741
Total _____	53,658	77,573	37,856	115,429
All Levels:				
Professional _____	7,938	14,574	10,887	25,461
Subprofessional ____	12,487	20,178	15,658	35,836
Skilled _____	107,955	153,138	58,805	211,943
GRAND TOTAL __	128,380	187,890	85,350	273,240

[1] These figures do not include the number of teachers, health service personnel, and scientists.

[2] Column is based on 74.7 percent of 1970 supply at professional level, 77.6 percent at subprofessional level, and 38.4 percent at skilled level.

Source: Adapted from "Educated Manpower," *United Malayan Banking Corporation Economic Review*, III, No. 1, 1967, p. 51.

The problem of fitting the educational system to the present job market has also received considerable governmental attention in 1969. Surveys were made of potential employers in some industries to determine what training should be given vocational students. The government had come to recognize that much of the secondary vocational education up to 1969 had led nowhere and resulted in a high proportion of youths between the ages of 16 and 25 being unable to find jobs.

In September 1969 the National Youth Development Corps was set up to train unemployed youths in rudimentary discipline and civics. Out of an initial 3,000 receiving training, 1,500 would, upon completion of the 3-month course, receive jobs as ordinary laborers for various government departments. The other 1,500, all of whom had the minimum qualification of a lower school certificate, would then join the National Youth Pioneer Corps, in which they would learn motor mechanics, electrical wiring, building construction, and other trade skills.

In August 1969 the minister of national and rural development announced plans to set up vocational training centers at industrial sites in five West Malaysian states to provide skilled labor for industry. Popular interest in education as a path to improved employment opportunities has also grown in the 1960's. A trend has been observed among ethnic community spokesmen to concern themselves more with efforts to increase the opportunities for their respective groups in higher education, government, and industrial employment and to devote less time than formerly to agitating for the retention of their respective traditional cultures.

Expansion of Enrollment

A major innovation since independence has been the speed with which the government has extended education facilities to more people (see table 4). The British policy had been to move only as fast in expanding educational facilities as the limitations of the budget would permit. On the one hand, suggestions that costs be lowered by double sessions, cheaper school buildings, and like procedures were regarded by the colonial government with suspicion, as likely to lower standards. On the other hand, requests to increase the portion of total expenditure spent on education were regarded as unsound budgetary policy.

Since independence the per capita expenditure on education has more than doubled in West Malaysia (see table 5). In East Malaysia between 1962, the year before Malaysia was formed, and 1967, per capita expenditure on education increased 68 percent in Sabah and 56 percent in Sarawak. Primary schooling in West Malaysia was made available for all children who wanted it in 1958 and free of all fees by 1962. In 1965 an additional 3 years of schooling were made available to all West Malaysian students desiring it, free in national-language schools and at reasonable fees for English-language students. In 1966 East Malaysians first received the right to free primary education.

Table 4. Percentage of Enrollment to Corresponding Age-Group in the Educational System of Malaysia, 1965-72

	1965 [1]	1966	1967	1968	1969	1970	1971	1972
Primary:								
Age group	1,394,643	1,422,589	1,450,543	1,486,334	1,522,124	1,557,918	1,593,708	1,629,502
Enrollment	1,217,309	1,272,700	1,322,400	1,369,200	1,405,200	1,449,500	1,486,900	1,530,000
Percent	87	89	91	92	92	93	93	94
Lower Secondary:								
Age group	608,068	633,543	659,017	669,869	680,724	691,570	702,419	713,271
Enrollment	231,555	299,617	386,588	452,550	506,657	550,064	593,947	625,486
Percent	38	47	59	68	74	80	85	88
Upper Secondary [2]:								
Age group	361,748	381,857	401,966	414,230	426,491	438,755	451,018	463,283
Enrollment	41,753	52,621	59,089	64,360	72,239	81,229	90,922	101,013
Percent	12	14	15	16	17	19	20	22
Post secondary [3]:								
Age group	324,831	345,044	365,256	381,447	397,634	413,823	430,015	446,202
Enrollment	14,482	13,950	17,450	18,031	22,973	24,780	21,368	24,798
Percent	4	4	5	5	6	6	5	6
University:								
Age group	792,769	818,877	844,990	903,182	961,373	1,019,565	1,077,756	1,135,942
Enrollment	2,835	3,603	4,852	5,997	6,783	7,691	8,573	9,439
Percent	0.4	0.4	0.6	0.7	0.7	0.8	0.8	0.8

[1] Figures for 1965 are definite; figures for years 1966-72 are estimated.

[2] Includes general, vocational, technical, and agricultural school's enrollments.

[3] Includes Form VI, technical and agricultural colleges, and all teacher training institutions' enrollments.

Source: Adapted from "Educated Manpower," *United Malayan Banking Corporation Economic Review,* III, No. 1, 1967, p. 50.

Table 5. *Educational Expenditure in Malaysia, 1957–66* [1]

Year	Total educational expenditure (in millions of M$) [2]	Total per capita educational expenditure	Population (in thousands)	Gross National Product (in millions of M$) [2]	Educational expenditure (percentage of gross national product)
1957	136	21.2	6,405	4,948	2.7
1958	150	22.7	6,596	4,758	3.2
1959	159	23.3	6,815	5,316	3.0
1960	179	25.5	7,018	5,886	3.0
1961	211	29.1	7,250	5,914	3.6
1962	262	35.0	7,494	6,231	4.2
1963	283	36.7	7,707	6,635	4.3
1964	337	36.3	9,278	8,021	4.2
1965	402	42.1	9,558	8,796	4.6
1966 [3]	425	44.0	9,664	9,239	4.6

[1] Prior to 1964 figures for West Malaysia only.

[2] M$3.06 equal US$1.

[3] Estimated.

Source: Adapted from "Educated Manpower," *United Malayan Banking Corporation Economic Review*, III No. 1, 1967, p. 49.

Nation Building Through the Schools

The use of texts and radio and television scripts made in Malaysia for Malaysians has contributed in recent years to the development of a national orientation of the curriculum away from the separate British, Chinese, Indian, and Arabic biases of the prewar schools. The gradual introduction of Malaysian standardized examinations to quality candidates for higher education and government service, replacing the previous standard examinations that were all written and graded in the United Kingdom, has also helped to promote the development of a nationally uniform Malaysia-oriented curriculum.

In 1969 concern continued to be expressed by government officials about the curriculum content and political orientation of the Chinese secondary schools, all of which were privately financed. During the Emergency of 1948–60, Chinese-language middle schools were considered to be on the side of the Communists, and the same charge has been leveled at Chinese schools in Sarawak in connection with the clandestine Communist organization activities there (see ch. 3, Historical Setting).

A close watch has been kept on the curriculum content of government-aided schools, including those at the university level. At the University of Malaya, access to books by Marx, Lenin, Stalin, and others has been restricted to students signing a special register of request.

University students entered politics to an increasing degree in 1968, with a demonstration at the Soviet Embassy by 100 students protesting the invasion of Czechoslovakia. Riot police, using tear gas, broke up the demonstration. In July 1969, 2 months after the riots following West Malaysia's federal elections, Malay students at the University of Malaya demonstrated against the continued political leadership of Prime Minister Tengku Abdul Rahman. At the end of August, a similar demonstration on campus in the presence of foreign delegates to an international conference on drama and music led to police action on the campus.

The postelection riots of May 1969 gave the government renewed determination to eliminate communĂ¢l barriers in the society. Multiracial schooling in the national language was seen as the major device to achieve the goal of Malaysian national identity and unity. It has been urged that parent-teacher associations form to work actively to promote neighborhood interethnic harmony. The government has required that racial tolerance and Malaysian national identity be taught in all government-aided schools.

Financing

Since independence, aid for educational programs from international organizations and from friendly nations, especially Great Britain, other Colombo Plan nations, and the United States, has been substantial. This aid has augmented the funds available from government revenues, which have fluctuated considerably with the rise and fall of the world prices of rubber and tin, making it difficult to plan effectively.

In May 1969, the International Bank for Reconstruction and Development (IBRD) approved a loan of US$8.8 million toward an estimated US$16.4-million plan of school construction and expansion, providing places for 10,900 new students, 8,100 of them in vocational, technical, or agricultural schools. According to the plan, East Malaysia is scheduled for expansion of its teacher-training facilities, general secondary schools, and its boarding accommodations for students from rural areas.

The development and expansion of domestic science classes will be assisted in 1970 by a grant of approximately US$220,000 from the Food and Agriculture Organization of the United Nations.

LITERACY

Literacy has made great strides in the 1960's throughout Malaysia. In West Malaysia an adult education program begun in 1961 had by 1967 given 850,000 illiterate adults 1 year basic literacy training, at a total project cost of M$57 million (3.06 Malaysian dollars equal US$1). By 1967 there were 10,000 classes with 6,500 teachers teaching literacy and other special education courses designed to benefit the adult rural population. An additional 125,000 adults were estimated to have received literacy training during 1968. Increased schooling opportunities for the school-aged population was, however, the chief means being employed to improve the national literacy rate.

Improvements notwithstanding, illiteracy remained a formidable problem in the 1960's, with almost one-half of the West Malaysians and three-quarters of the East Malaysians illiterate. Literacy was distributed unevenly between the sexes and among ethnic groups and geographic areas. Women were substantially less literate than men, although the gap was narrowing as the result of coeducation at the primary school level. Chinese had a slightly higher literacy rate than Malays, although not quite as high as Indians; according to 1957 figures for West Malaysia, Chinese literacy was 52 percent, Malay, 47 percent, and Indian, 53 percent. Literacy among the non-Malay indigenous people of Sabah and Sarawak averaged well below 15 percent. Ethnic differences in literacy rates were to a large extent the reflection of the settlement patterns. The urban people have had far superior access to schooling than rural people, and the nomadic aborigines living in the interior of the Malay Peninsula and parts of East Malaysia have remained almost entirely unlettered.

SECULAR EDUCATION

West Malaysia

Preschool and Primary

Private kindergartens and nursery schools, mostly in urban areas, all of them having female teachers, had a total enrollment of over 15,000 pupils in 1965. Free public education begins at age 6 with the 1st year of primary school (see fig. 7). Primary school continues through six grades, called standards. A student is promoted from one standard to the next without passing any countrywide examinations, but at the end of standard V an assessment examination, introduced in 1967, is given to students in the four primary school language streams: Bahasa Malaysia, English, Mandarin Chinese, and Tamil.

Primary school enrollment between 1965 and 1968 went from 1.2 million to 1.4 million students. Well under 10,000 of these pupils were in private schools (including Muslim schools). Primary education is compulsory for all children living within walking distance of a school.

According to plans announced by the minister of education in July 1969, English-language government-assisted schools were to be converted to Bahasa Malaysia beginning, a year at a time, with standard I in 1970. Selected subjects have been taught in the national language at the English-language schools since 1968, and by 1972 all but science and mathematics subjects and language courses were scheduled to be taught in Bahasa Malaysia.

Malay and English have been, since independence, compulsory in all schools, producing bilingual competence in English- and national-language schools and trilingual capabilities in Chinese and Tamil government-aided schools. At any national school Chinese or Tamil may be taught as a subject provided the parents of 15 of the pupils request it.

Although government-assisted primary schools are open to all races, language preferences in 1969 still divided the primary school populace according to ethnic group or, in the case of the English-language schools, separated non-Malays from Malays. Some opposition to the new language policy has already been voiced, with members of the English-language teachers' union, the National Union of Teachers, particularly vocal. An increase in the number of private primary school pupils may result from the removal of English primary schooling from the public school system.

Secondary

Secondary school beings with lower secondary school of 3 years duration, forms I through III, which since 1965 has been available at English- or national-language government-assisted schools to all West Malaysians who have completed primary school and, in the case of the English-language schools, can pay the school fees of M$5 per month. Until 1965 only a third of those leaving primary school had been able to find places in secondary school.

Private schools provide the only Chinese-medium instruction, and there are no Tamil secondary schools. In 1968 English-language schools had about 2½ times the enrollment of the Malay-language schools (see table 6).

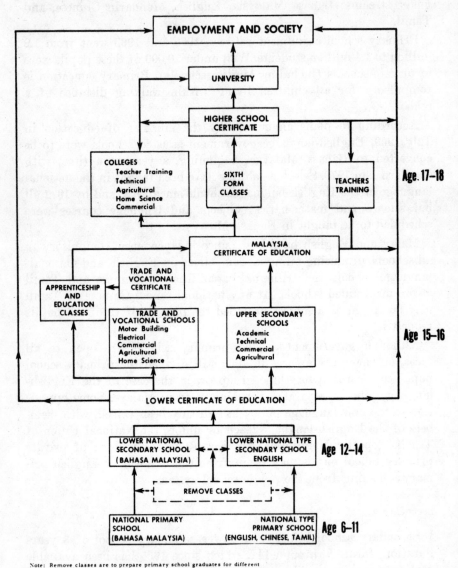

EMPLOYMENT AND SOCIETY

UNIVERSITY

HIGHER SCHOOL
CERTIFICATE

COLLEGES
Teacher Training
Technical
Agricultural
Home Science
Commercial

SIXTH
FORM
CLASSES

TEACHERS
TRAINING

Age. 17–18

MALAYSIA
CERTIFICATE OF EDUCATION

TRADE AND
VOCATIONAL
CERTIFICATE

APPRENTICESHIP
AND
EDUCATION
CLASSES

TRADE AND
VOCATIONAL SCHOOLS
Motor Building
Electrical
Commercial
Agricultural
Home Science

UPPER SECONDARY
SCHOOLS
Academic
Technical
Commercial
Agricultural

Age 15–16

LOWER CERTIFICATE OF EDUCATION

LOWER NATIONAL
SECONDARY SCHOOL
(BAHASA MALAYSIA)

LOWER NATIONAL TYPE
SECONDARY SCHOOL
ENGLISH

Age 12–14

REMOVE CLASSES

NATIONAL PRIMARY
SCHOOL
(BAHASA MALAYSIA)

NATIONAL TYPE
PRIMARY SCHOOL
(ENGLISH, CHINESE, TAMIL)

Age 6–11

Note: Remove classes are to prepare primary school graduates for different
language of instruction in government-aided secondary schools.

Figure 7.   Comprehensive educational system in West Malaysia, 1969

Source: Adapted from *Malaysia Yearbook 1968/1969*, Kuala Lumpur, Malay
Mail.

At the end of the lower secondary school, in form III, students
take the lower certificate of education examination in English or an
equivalent examination in Bahasa Malaysia. Successful candidates,

usually between 50 and 60 percent 'of all who take the examination, receive an academic certificate, the lower school certificate of education. Most students who continue past form III (in 1968 less than one-third of the primary school enrollment) then leave the academic stream for 2-year programs at vocational and trade schools of a non-academic type, leading to receipt of the Malaysian certificate of vocational education. Recipients of this certificate may then enter 5-year apprenticeship programs in several industries.

A small proportion of the form III graduates continue their general academic education in 2 years of upper secondary school, forms IV and V. A third option open to a small number of lower secondary school graduates is a combined program of general academic and technical training in engineering, agriculture, commerce, or domestic science. The demand for places in the academic or combined academic and technical upper-secondary schools greatly exceeds supply.

Government educational policy is to provide places eventually in the academic upper-secondary schools for 25 percent of the 15-year-olds (as compared to 13 percent in 1967); out of the 25 percent, 15 percent would be enrolled in schools with technical training.

Table 6. *Education in Malaysia by Type of Schooling from 1965 Through 1968*

Type	Number of schools	Number of teachers	Number of students	Female students [1]
Preschool:				
West Malaysia _____	n.a.	n.a.	15,053	42
Sabah [2] _____	33	50	875	46
Sarawak _____	47	108	3,442	45
Total _____			19,370	
Special (including handicapped):				
West Malaysia _____	4	93	832	37
East Malaysia _____	n.a.	n.a.	n.a.	n.a.
Primary (first 6 years): West Malaysia:				
Malay medium _____	2,331	21,176	606,846	303,677
English medium _____	406	8,262	310,429	128,468
Chinese medium _____	1,043	11,792	372,727	176,535
Tamil medium _____	679	3,096	81,872	42,509
Total _____	4,459	44,326	1,371,874	651,189
Sarawak (all English-medium except Chinese schools):				
Council schools _____	848	n.a.	78,364	32,510
Mission schools _____	135	n.a.	21,720	9,650

Type	Number of schools	Number of teachers	Number of students	Female students [1]
Chinese schools _____	217	n.a.	38,525	18,183
Private committee ____	3	n.a.	690	369
Unaided schools _____	10	n.a.	1,089	464
Total _____	1,213	4,151	140,388	61,176
Sabah :				
English medium _____	n.a.	n.a.	n.a.	n.a.
Chinese medium _____	n.a.	n.a.	n.a.	n.a.
Kadazan medium ____	n.a.	n.a.	n.a.	n.a.
Malay medium _____	418	n.a.	n.a.	n.a.
Total _____	623	3,895	104,871	43,455
Primary school totals:				
West Malaysia _____	4,459	44,326	1,371,874	651,189
Sarawak _____	1,213	4,151	140,388	61,176
Sabah _____	623	3,895	104,871	43,455
GRAND TOTAL _____	6,295	52,372	1,617,133	755,820
Secondary:				
West Malaysia :				
Malay medium _____	306	4,837	136,349	55,454
English medium _____	523	12,468	334,113	133,415
Chinese medium _____	50	724	19,507	6,443
Tamil medium _____	---	---	---	----
Total _____	879 [3]	18,029	489,969 [3]	195,312
Sarawak :				
Government _____	30	n.a.	7,393	2,241
Muslim schools _____	13	n.a.	5,510	2,316
Converted middle ____	10	n.a.	3,992	1,987
Unaided English _____	38	n.a.	12,876	4,865
Unaided Chinese _____	17	n.a.	3,176	1,037
Total _____	108	1,253	32,947	12,446
Sabah (all schools are either English or Chinese medium) :				
Government _____	20	n.a.	n.a.	n.a.
Grant-aided _____	34	n.a.	n.a.	n.a.
Non-aided _____	8	---	n.a.	n.a.
Total _____	62	690	16,508	6,152
Secondary school totals:				
West Malaysia _____	879	18,029	489,969	195,312
Sarawak _____	108	1,253	32,947	12,446
Sabah _____	62	690	16,508	6,152
GRAND TOTAL _____	1,049	19,972	539,424	213,910
Vocational and Professional Institutions:				
West Malaysia :				
Teacher training ____	18	392	6,010	2,586
Agricultural college __	1	33	548	65

Table 6. Education in Malaysia by Type of Schooling from 1965 Through 1968
—Continued

Type	Number of schools	Number of teachers	Number of students	Female students [1]
Technical college ____	1	64	913	50
Other _____	46	234	9,439	4,568
Total _____	66	723	16,910	7,269
Sabah:				
Teacher training colleges _____	2	n.a.	___ [4]	___ [4]
Teacher training centers _____	2	n.a.	n.a.	n.a.
Trade schools _____	2	n.a.	152	---
Total _____	6			
Sarawak:				
Teacher training colleges _____	3	n.a.	751	213
Commercial Institute _	1	n a.	44	43
Trade School _____	1	n.a.	136	---
Total _____	5		931 [5]	256 [5]
Universities:				
West Malaysia [6]:				
University of Malaysia	1	688	5,556	1,547
East Malaysia:				
Sarawak _____	---	---	417 [7]	n.a.
Sabah _____	---	---	n.a.	n.a.

n.a.—not available.

[1] Figures for female students in preschools and special schools are in percent; figures for female students in primary, secondary, vocational, and professional institutions are in actual numbers.

[2] 1961 figures.

[3] Includes 5 Malay-medium, 125 English-medium, and 50 Chinese-medium private schools with combined student body of 51,657.

[4] Total of 169 teachers, including 62 women, graduated in 1967.

[5] Full-time students; there also are 62 female part-time students at Commercial Institute and 58 part-time male students at Trade School.

[6] Malay-medium national university (University Kebangsaan) scheduled to open May 1970.

[7] Students at overseas schools at end of 1967.

In the second year of upper secondary, academic or academic and technical school, students may take the Malaysian certificate of education examination. A small proportion of those who pass that examination go on to preuniversity training in the sixth form, a 2-year academic program consisting of first year, called lower sixth, and second year, upper sixth. In 1967 there were approximately 500 students in six Bahasa Malaysia sixth forms, the remainder, approximately 20,000 students, were in English medium schools. The government planners anticipated that by 1982 all government-assisted secondary eduation, including sixth form, would be in the national language.

A larger proportion of holders of the Malaysia certificate of education than attend sixth forms attend colleges, institutions offering 12th- and 13th-year education in various fields. The recommendations of the Higher Education Planning Committee in 1967 were that places be provided for 16 percent of the 17-year-olds in teacher training, technical, agricultural, and other scientific and technical colleges and that an additional 4 percent of the 17-year-olds continue their academic education in the university preparatory sixth forms.

During the academic year 1967/68, the following public college-level vocational and technical institutions were in operation in West Malaysia: the Technical College in Kuala Lumpur with 68 lecturers and 752 students; the MARA (Majlis Amanah Ra'ayat) Institute of Technology with 19 lecturers and 551 students; and the College of Agriculture with 33 lecturers and 437 students. There were also a number of teacher-training institutions. Primary teacher training at Sultan Idris Training College and the Malayan Women's Training College, the two oldest Bahasa Malaysia secondary schools in the country, had 370 and 372 students, respectively. The Kota Bahru Teachers' College had 435 students, and 12 Day (i.e., nonboarding) Training Centers had a total of 3,904 students. There were three colleges for secondary school teachers in Penang, Kuala Lumpur, and Johore Bahru, with a total enrollment of slightly under 1,000.

The Language Institute, Specialist Teachers' Training Institute, and Technical Teachers' Training College, all in Kuala Lumpur, provided specialized teacher-training programs for 857 students. Twenty-eight regional training centers provided 3,639 students with an accelerated teacher-training program introduced in 1965 to help provide as quickly as possible the almost 4,000 additional teachers needed immediately as a result of the addition of three lower secondary years to the comprehensive school system.

In 1968 a college-level institution, the Tengku Abdul Rahman College, was established with the support of the Malaysian Chinese Association to help prepare students of all races for advanced education in the national school system, although primarily catering to the needs of graduates of Chinese secondary schools.

Graduates of sixth forms are eligible to take the higher school certificate examination. This examination is prepared and conducted jointly by the Cambridge Examination Syndicate (United Kingdom) and the University of Malaya. Candidates may take the examination in English, and gradually during the 1960's it has become possible to answer questions on some subjects in Bahasa Malaysia. The Ministry of Education has announced plans to take over sole control of the examination by 1970. By 1982 this examination will be offered only in the national language. The higher school certificate examination is the entrance examination for the University of Malaya, and successful candidates are also presumed qualified to apply for entrance to universities abroad. In 1968, for the first time, students might if they wish submit only national language papers at the higher school certificate examination for entrance to the University of Malaya.

University

The University of Malaya, established in 1961, has always been operated primarily in English, although courses in departments of Tamil studies and Malay studies have been conducted in the appropriate languages. Gradually courses conducted in Bahasa Malaysia have been introduced. In July 1969 the minister of education announced the government's plan to convert the university to the use of the national language as the chief medium of instruction and communication over the next 7 to 10 years. English would remain a second language of study, still compulsory in all government-assisted schools as it has been since the 1950's, and no course taught in English would be repeated in Bahasa Malaysia and vice versa.

Many students going overseas to universities have received government scholarships. In the academic year 1964/65, 5,000 students were studying at institutions abroad, 3,721 of them in Great Britain. Six hundred students had scholarships that year at institutions of higher learning at home and abroad.

Schools giving university degrees recognized by the Malaysian government as qualification for senior posts in the government civil service and various licensed professions, in addition to the University of Malaya and the University of Singapore, were for the most part British or Commonwealth universities and, since the mid-1960's, some United States universities. In the case of United States colleges and universities, there has been some reluctance to recognize their degrees at a par with degrees from schools run according to the Malaysian, British, and Commonwealth system of earlier and more exclusive specialization in one field of study.

At the new University Kebangsaan, the language of instruction will be the national language. In August 1969 the minister of education went to Indonesia to recruit faculty for the new university because Malaysia's present educational system has not produced Bahasa

Malaysia-speaking university-level teachers except in Malay and Muslim studies.

During 1968 and 1969 a proposal that there be a Merdeka University using Chinese as the language of instruction was made by Chinese educated leaders but was rejected by the government, whose policy has been to move toward multiracial education in the national language and away from separate education according to language of instruction. In July 1969 Deputy Prime Minister Tun Abdul Razak, then holding special authority as the Director of Operations, issued a regulation making it an offense to form, to contribute to, or to collect money for, any higher educational institution without the approval of the minister of education. The regulation, covering "college" level institutions and above, was explained by the government spokesman as preventing departures from the education policy that might encourage "disharmony among the various communities."

At the university graduate level, plans for a center for graduate and advanced research in the humanities and social sciences with an emphasis on Southeast Asia were disclosed by the vice chancellor of the University of Malaya in his annual report for the school year 1968/69.

East Malaysia

Although expenditure requirements for education in East Malaysia are met by central government funds, educational administration and policy are handled by the Sabah and Sarawak state governments. During the period of colonial rule in East Malaysia from 1946 to 1963, a movement toward emphasis on English-language education for all was begun. In Sarawak in 1962 Chinese-language secondary schools began to convert to English, although Chinese primary schools continued to use Mandarin Chinese. Almost all other primary and secondary schools in the 1960's either used English as the language of instruction or were in the process of adopting it.

In Sabah the process of conversion to English has advanced less quickly. The Malaysian minister of education announced in July 1969 that Sabah intended to conform to the West Malaysia plan of converting to Bahasa Malaysia.

Since January 1966 the first 6 years of school have been free, but not compulsory, to all East Malaysians. Sparse populations and the difficulty of overland communication, with few roads and river traffic limited to certain seasons of the year, resulted in the need for boarding schools for rural children. In many rural schools only the first

4 years of primary school were available in the 1960's. In Sarawak the number of primary schools increased from 850 in 1960 to 1,213 in 1968. The number of secondary schools increased during the same period from 40 to 108, and the total school enrollment went up 70,000 during the period.

In Sabah primary schools and enrollment have increased steadily. Between 1965 and 1967 the number of primary schools increased, from 556 to 623, with the enrollment changing from 86,413 students to 104,871. The increase in secondary schools and students in Sabah between 1965 and 1967 was substantial, with 20 schools added to the 1965 figures of 42 and enrollment figures rising from 11,422 to 16,508.

Secondary school, as in West Malaysia, is divided into lower secondary, upper secondary, and sixth form. The lower secondary school, or its Chinese equivalent, the lower middle school, is of 3 years' duration and is purely academic. Only one-third of the primary school students are able to continue their education, due to teacher and classroom shortages. At the present rate of expansion of school facilities, this ratio of primary to secondary enrollment figures will continue to hold. At the end of lower secondary school, Sarawak students take the Sarawak junior certificate examination; Sabah students take the Sabah junior certificate examination. Chinese schools have an equivalent examination.

Upper secondary school consists of forms IV and V, at the end of which students in Sarawak and Sabah take the Cambridge overseas school certificate examination. The number of students taking and passing this examination has increased substantially in the 1960's. The highest level of academic education provided in East Malaysia is the sixth form, a 2-year college-preparatory program at the end of which students take the Cambridge higher school certificate examination.

Academic education, being geared toward these British examinations, has less emphasis on local studies than does the national curriculum of the West Malaysian government-aided schools. Radio broadcasts and texts in various languages produced in East Malaysia provide some locally oriented education. Vocational, teacher, and professional training are in short supply in East Malaysia, although implementation of plans to expand in these areas as rapidly as possible has begun.

There was in 1969 no university education available in East Malaysia nor any plans to establish a university there. Scholarships to colleges and universities in West Malaysia and overseas are granted by the state governments, the federal government, Colombo Plan countries, and other governments and agencies.

Teachers

In West Malaysia as the student body has expanded, increasing between 1957 and 1968 by 350,000 in the primary schools and jumping from slightly over 100,000 to nearly 500,000 in secondary schools, many different schemes have been used to provide the additional teaching staff needed, while at the same time providing further training to teachers already in the school system so that they could introduce the new national curriculum.

The result has been that as the supply of teachers doubled during a 1-year period, training, salaries, and minimum qualifications have varied widely. Some of the older teachers have had to adjust to several consecutive major changes in curriculum and medium of instruction. The conversion of English-language schools to the national language will necessitate further training and adjustments for teachers. In 1969, as in the past, teachers of the various language streams have led the popular agitation concerning policies affecting communal education. As highly respected members of their respective communities, teachers by their support, or lack of it, have been able to exert considerable influence on national educational policy.

Efforts have been made to produce a uniform system of training and paying teachers. In 1967 a secondary teachers certificate examination was introduced. Candidates for the examination included 968 Malay-medium students and 2,119 English-medium students at the end of their training at Malayan teachers' colleges and regional training centers.

In East Malaysia teachers and teacher-training facilities were in great demand because of increased school enrollment. A 1967 government report estimated that 1,200 new primary teachers and 470 secondary school teachers would be needed by the end of 1970 in Sabah. Sarawak needed 1,000 new primary teachers by 1968 and 320 new secondary teachers by 1969.

A shortage throughout the nation of trained teachers for rural areas was the result of a nationwide preference of teachers for employment in urban areas. Use has been made of foreign, English-speaking teachers, especially United States Peace Corps, British, and Commonwealth volunteers and contract employees from various countries. For students being instructed in the national language, Indonesian teachers have been used to help meet the need for teachers able to teach science, mathematics, and advancd courses in other subjects (see tables 7 and 8).

Table 7. Number of Teachers Trained in Malaysia in 1967

Area	Number of teachers
West Malaysia:	
Primary school teachers _____	2,078
Secondary school teachers _____	1,815
Total _____	3,893
Sabah:	
Primary and secondary school teachers _____	169
Sarawak:	
Primary and secondary school teachers _____	326
GRAND TOTAL _____	4,388

Source: Adapted from *Malaysia Official Yearbook 1967*, Kuala Lumpur, Federal Department of Information, 1968.

Table 8. Number of Teachers by Qualification in Malaysia, 1968

Area	Number of teachers
West Malaysia:	
Trained:	
Normal classes _____	5,723
Malayan teachers colleges _____	8,486
Day training centers _____	15,426
Regional training centers _____	3,385
Language institute _____	1,714
Universities (Malaya and others) _____	2,142
Other institutions _____	18,571
Total _____	55,447
Untrained _____	n.a.
Sarawak:	
Trained:	
Graduates of teacher training institutions _____	473
Untrained:	
Passed secondary school _____	2,540
Below secondary school _____	2,728
Total _____	5,741
Sabah:	
Trained _____	1,750
Untrained _____	1,550
Total _____	3,300

n.a.—not available.

Further Education and Special Programs

According to 1960's figures, 1,371 further education classes were provided by the Ministry of Education at 187 centers employing 3,728 teachers and providing education for 42,078 students, who for various reasons had not been able to continue their education in regular schools. The full secondary school programs, forms I through VI, were offered, including preparation for the appropriate standardized examinations. There were also some classes devoted to technical and commercial subjects. Adult education, including literacy classes, were carried out by the Ministry of National and Rural Development.

Education for the handicapped was provided in 1967 at 15 governmental and private social welfare institutions. Integrated classes for the blind and for the deaf were run by the Ministry of Education. Sarawak and Sabah each had limited educational facilities for the blind. Approximately 700 persons of various ages, out of a registered handicapped population of over 11,000, received treatment, education, and training of various types during 1967.

Health records were kept in primary schools, and some medical services were provided for all pupils. Health education programs and public health projects, such as checks on rural pupils for intestinal worms, have been carried out by joint school health committees set up by the ministries of health and education.

A program for providing free hot meals had been carried out in 650 West Malaysian schools by September 1969. The Catholic Relief Services Organization was active in this program, distributing surplus American rolled oats, cracked wheat, and skimmed milk. The hot meals program was also carried out in Sabah and Sarawak with 23,250 students receiving hot meals in 1969.

MUSLIM EDUCATION

Religious instruction in Islam must be provided in all schools receiving government funds (except in East Malaysia) during regular school hours and as a compulsory part of the school curriculum if there are 15 or more Muslim students enrolled in the school. For Muslim students who do not receive religious instruction during school hours, afternoon religious classes are available, often held at the village prayer house or in the local Malay medium school building.

Islamic schooling leading to eligibility for employment as a religious teacher or as a religious official is carried out by *madrasahs* paid for by, and under the jurisdiction of, the states' religious departments or by *pondok* schools and *madrasahs* privately endowed and supported. At the *madrasahs*, instruction is given in the Arabic medium and consists of four years primary and, in a few cases, four years secondary education. Each year ends with an examination, and those passing the primary and secondary courses obtain appropriate certificates. Graduates of state-run *madrasahs* become recognized religious teachers. Graduates of *pondok* schools or private *madrasahs* must obtain special authorization from the sultan of the state in which they wish to teach before they may do so.

A 1956 government team surveying private Muslim schools found that students at these schools were for the most part dropouts from secular schools or had not been able to attend other schooling, that the texts came exclusively from overseas, and that Malay language and literature as a subject received almost no attention, nor did such secular subjects as arithmetic, geography, and history. In 1958 an office in the Ministry of Education was appointed to administer aid to nongovernment Muslim schools, provided they achieved certain minimum standards.

In 1955 the Muslim College at Klang was established to improve the general level of Islamic education. By setting an entrance examination with the subjects to be tested and the appropriate texts circulated to the Arabic schools and state religious departments beforehand, the central government hoped that the content of Muslim primary and secondary education would be improved and some standards of uniformity established.

At the Muslim College students have a 2-year preparatory course and a 5-year main college course. The preparatory course, designed to fill in the gaps in the students' different school backgrounds, includes science, humanities, mathematics, Malay, and English taught by teachers seconded from the Ministry of Education. The main course is divided into stages I (3 years) and II (2 years) ending with receipt of the higher certificate of the Muslim College (first given in 1959), qualifying graduates as teachers and officials for the religious courts of Malaysia.

In 1958 Islamic studies became a field of concentration at the University of Malaya. Some courses given at the Muslim College can be used toward a degree at the university and vice versa.

The problem of improving the standards and uniformity of the Muslim schools has been complicated by the fact that religious instruction is under the jurisdiction of the various states and not the federal government. The syllabus for the Muslim College, therefore, had to be approved by the Conference of Rulers, who have insisted on the retention of *jawi* (Arabic) script in Malay-language instruction (see ch. 12, The Governmental System).

The role of the federal government in religious instruction is increasing, however. In 1967 the financing of the Muslim College became the sole burden of the central government. The need for religious teachers to provide the compulsory religious instruction in the state-aided secular schools has brought about the introduction of examinations in Islamic religious knowledge as electives in the lower school certificate and Malaysian certificate of education examinations. These examination results are temporarily providing qualifications for religious instructors. Approximately 42,000 persons took the religious knowledge examinations in 1967. Many schools in 1967 still lacked religious instruction. In 1967 there were only 564 religious teachers in secular assisted secondary schools and 3,352 in assisted primary schools.

CHAPTER 9

ARTISTIC AND INTELLECTUAL EXPRESSION

The country's most significant movement in artistic and intellectual expression in 1969 was the conscious search for, and promotion of, a national culture. The pluralistic multiracial composition of the society supports a diversity of artistic traditions that, although interacting, have remained highly tangential. Malay culture has directly and indirectly incorporated varying elements from Indian, Muslim, Indonesian, Chinese, and Thai culture, among others. The Indian and Chinese communities in the country, however, have maintained cultural traditions reflecting more of their ethnic origins than indigenous cultural environment. This diversity is broadened by the frequent cultural subdivisions of the Chinese and Indians on the basis of village origin and occupation. Even residents of East Malaysian longhouses (see Glossary) practically within view of one another may speak different languages and support diverse traditions.

Extensive contact with external cultures has been an important element in harmonizing the traditions of even the most isolated ethnic groups; it has produced a thread of compatibility that runs through the tone and style in which the dominant Malay culture has restated these external traditions. As examples of the retention of these foreign cultural influences, glass beads, some of Roman and Middle Eastern origins, are highly valued among certain ethnic groups in East Malaysia, and considerable prestige is ascribed in many longhouses to collections of Tang and Sung pottery.

An active government role in promoting artistic activity is based in part on the view that the arts can be useful in the promotion of national unity, as reflected in the personal interest and engagement of the prime minister in artistic expression. Although the government is interested in the creative adaptation of the country to 20th-century concepts and media, much of its effort is directed toward the revitalization and preservation of traditional culture. At the end of August 1969 the country sponsored the International Conference on Traditional Music and Dance of Southeast Asia, in which orchestral and dance troupes from Cambodia, Thailand, and Malaysia were featured. As a result of the conference, educational and organizational facilities were proposed for Malaysia to aid the preservation of the cultural identity of the peoples of Southeast Asia.

The final form that will evolve from the country's search for a unified culture expressive of the country as a whole could not yet be foreseen in 1969. It will be dependent on the character of the expansion of academic facilities in the country and the removal of ethnic divisions in the intellectual community; it will however, necessarily incorporate traditional culture and include Malay, Chinese, Indian, and indigenous elements. The continuing evolution and perpetuation of this national culture doubtless will depend on the ability to unite these components in a style unique to the country but also reflective of international trends and developments. Significant developments in painting and architecture already have suggested that the country will be able to achieve such a blending.

THE LITERARY TRADITION

Traditionally, Malay literature reached the public in nonwritten form; it was related by voice, staged as drama or shadow plays, or was repeated in the form of a proverb. This vocal tradition resulted in the tendency to judge more in terms of the manner in which it was presented than in terms of the literary text. Malay attitudes toward literature have been changing. Contemporary Malay literature is usually identified with its author and presented in written form, and it is supported by a growing domestic demand.

Malay Prose

The development of Malay literature may be divided into three periods. The traditional period, displaying Indian and Muslim influences, includes all literature produced before contact with British literature in the 19th century. The transitional period, reflecting a marked turning toward the Middle East, includes all work produced after the beginning of British rule until the outbreak of World War II. The modern period includes those works produced since the war.

Traditional

Traditional Malay literature developed around the royal court and was the product of Indian influences from the first century A.D. until about the 13th or 14th century. Literature of the Indian period has survived only in manuscripts written in *jawi*, the Arabic script adopted at the time of the acceptance of Islam in the country in the 14th and 15th centuries.

The indirect route over which the two major literary sources passed before their arrival in the Peninsula brought not only variant versions, but also elements assimilated from each other or from cultures through which they had passed. Malay epic tales formed from these two traditions blend Hindu and Muslim names, gods, beliefs, local heroes, and prophets. An epic may have Muslim names but follow a plot based on a Hindu theme, or it may be joined with a *sejarah* (local history of a sultanate). The epics were passed on through either written texts or by oral tradition. In some cases they were staged as drama or shadow plays or were used for dance themes. By the 18th century their structure and texture had become formalized.

Pre-Islamic sources drew heavily on the Hindu *Mahabharata* and the *Ramayana* or from the Javanese cycle of Panji Tales. Muslim legends utilized in the Islamic period came from romances of such pre-Muslim heroes as Alexander the Great and King Solomon, stories of the Prophet Muhammad, adventures of characters sometimes rather fantastically related to the Prophet with little historical base, or tales concocted locally. The Muslim tradition also brought the Sukasaptati, Kalila dan Damina, and Bakhtiar tale cycles.

Hikayat Hang Tuah (Tale of Hang Tuah), which eclectically draws on both the Indian and Muslim traditions, is a 15th-century history that represented the first and only truly original Malay romance until the 20th century. Set in Malacca during the reign of Mansur Shah, it relates the adventures of the historical figure Hang Tuah, who began as a member of the sultan's bodyguard and rose to the rank of *laksamana* (admiral). His adventures present him as the perfect Malay hero—courageous, loyal to his sultan, devout, and romantically gallant.

Many critics believe the finest literary work in the Malay language is the 15th-century *Sejarah Melayu* (Malay Annals). The work provides a vivid account of medieval Malacca, draws from the oldest Malay romances and histories, and presents philosophic and ethical exhortations as the last words of dying heroes. Literary developments following the *Sejarah Melayu* tended to be chronologies of peninsular history.

Less formal than the epic tradition is a body of fables whose roots extend back to ancient, indigenous origins; many of these fables deal with the animals populating the peninsula. The tiger, the Malay king of beasts, is sometimes addressed as *dato* and is conceived as a dangerous, brutal foe. His frequent opponent, the bear, is more kindly. Elephants have an honorary position; crocodiles are feared, but they may provide certain protective functions.

Many of the fables center on the exploits of the mouse deer, a foot-high ruminant with a mouselike face common in Malaysia. Early cycles of mouse deer stories credit his skill and cunning in overcoming larger and dangerous foes. In later cycles, under the influence of Islam, the mouse deer is associated with King Solomon and assumes a more ethical role.

Transitional

An autobiographical account, *Hikayat Abdullah bin Abdul Kadir Munshi*, written in the 19th century, marks the beginning of modern Malayan literature. The change was greatest in terms of subject matter. Abdullah criticized traditional Malay society and moralized about human goodness and frailty. In the sphere of style and language, he did not depart radically from traditional usage, but his style was less cramped and his language showed greater originality. His literary style today is considered to mark the change from the historical to the modern.

Just before and after World War I, Malay writers who were inspired by the example of Abdullah began to appear in Indonesia. At the front of this modern literary expression in 1920 was a young Sumatran, Muhamed Yamin, who, experimenting with others with new forms of Malay poetic expression, formed an organization known as the Association of Young Sumatrans (Jong Sumatran Bond).

A Muslim socioreligious revival movement, initially appearing in the Middle East and especially in Egypt, began to have repercussions in Malaya in the mid-1920's. The movement was led by the religiously educated elite who wished to introduce modernization based upon Muslim teachings rather than on a total acceptance of Western civilization. In Malaya the press was the prime purveyor of the reform movement, and the journal *Al-Iman* was the first publication to act as its spokesman.

The Islamic movement in Malaya had a great influence upon Malay literature by introducing modern Egyptian literature. It is claimed by historians that Syed Sheikh Al-Hady, who was connected with the journal *Al-Iman*, adapted the first Egyptian novel, *Faridah Hanum*, into Malay in 1926, introducing the novel as a literary genre to Malay in the aspect of a fictional story about an ordinary man in contemporary life. Although *Faridah Hanum* was a romance about idealized characters and was set in Egypt, the problems treated were contemporary, concerning emancipation and education of women, premarital relations, and patriotism and national pride.

Around 1925 most literary works—primarily short stories—were first published in the newspapers. These short stories were used to discuss social problems, such as criticism of the social order, religious reform, and social progress, that reflected the concern of the religiously educated writers for the social or moral problems resulting from the spread of Westernization and its conflicts with the traditional moral code. Others, especially the Malay- and English-educated, emphasized political themes. One of the representative writers of this period was Abdul Rahim Kajai, considered the father of modern Malay short stories. Essentially a journalist, he wrote short stories, focusing on themes of social problems, that appeared in many newspapers in the 1930's.

In 1929 the first novel dealing with Malay characters in a contemporary setting appeared. Called *Kawan Benar*, it was written by Ahmad bin Abdul Rashid. Ishak Haji Muhammad, an English-educated Malay, also wrote novels as well as short stories concerning political themes.

The Malay-educated and those educated in religious schools did not know English and therefore were not familiar with Western literature or read only translated works and popular literature; mostly, they read Indonesian works, which were concerned primarily with the conflict between the old and the new order in Indonesian society. Representative of the Malay-educated writers influenced by Indonesian works were Harun Muhamad Amin and Abdullah Sidek. Literary activity in the 1930's centered around Persaudaraan Sahabat Pena, a literary society created in 1934, and represented one of the elements that helped to seed post-World War II nationalism.

Modern

During the Japanese occupation there was very little literary activity. Few novels were written, but short stories were printed regularly in the main periodicals, *Fajar Asia* and *Semangat Asia*, and in the newspaper *Berita Malai*. Many of them continued a great deal of Japanese propaganda, such as the story *Ubi Kayu* (Tapioca) by Samad Ismail, exhorting the people to plant more tapioca. Nevertheless, the literary changes occurring in the postwar period had their roots in the effects of the Japanese occupation, particularly in increased public awareness of modern Indonesian works.

After the Japanese occupation new literary styles did not make an immediate impact upon the society, and the pre-World War II literary traditions still retained a stronghold, especially in novel writing. Among the representative novelists of this initial postwar period was Ahmad Lufti, probably the last of Syed Sheikh Al-Hady's followers, who wrote over 10 short novels. His first two works did not deal with themes concerning contemporary problems; the others, however, were similar to the prewar didactic novels concerned with social ills and moral degradation from a religious point of view. Lufti's novels closely followed the popular topics of discussion in West Malaysia at this time.

A second postwar novelist of the prewar tradition was Harun Muhamad Amin, who displayed a flair for writing a story for its own artistic or aesthetic worth. His early novels were romantic stories. Ishak Haji Muhammad was another important writer of this period. His themes concern the fate of the common people in contemporary social and political conditions. On the whole, the novels of this period by other writers were generally short in length and regarded by foreign critics as poor in technique, mediocre in content and, particularly, badly presented.

While pre-World War II traditional were perpetuated in the novels, new life was instilled in Malay literature through short stories and poetry, primarily inspired by a new social and political awareness among young writers, who were affected by events both inside and outside the country. These new works were inspired by events such as the Malays' opposition to the Malayan Union (1946–47), labor unrest in Singapore, the Emergency (see Glossary), and the independence movement. The new literary drive was prompted not only by an increasing national consciousness but also by the desire to have a rich Malay literature. The political and social themes were not presented directly but were clothed in romantic and sentimental love stories, such as love for country conquering romantic love.

A definite consciousness of literary creativity and the development of new trends influencing contemporary writings can be dated from the formation of a writers' organization in Singapore called Angkatan Sasterawan '50—ASAS'50 (Generation of Writers of the Fifties). It was formed primarily to stimulate Malay literature by pooling the resources of young writers and to promote and safeguard the writers' interests. ASAS'50 treated political questions, social problems, language, and cultural matters. Its slogan was "Art for Society," emphasizing the belief of the group that literature should be used as a tool "for the betterment of society," and the organization possessed an underlying nationalistic tone.

The most productive period of ASAS'50 was between 1950 and 1954, when prominent members expounded their views through journals, newspapers, and radio. Leading members of the organization also were editors of the popular publications *Utusan Zaman* and *Mastika*. The works of the group included national idealization of the past, such as the two novels *Panglima Awang* and *Anak Panglima Awang* of Harun Muhamad Amin, but their major and lasting importance was their stress upon realism. Realism had been first introduced during the 1920's and 1930's, but it had not taken root. During the 1950's novels such as *Salima* by Samad Said and *Hari Mana Bulan Mana* by Salmi Manja concentrated on the realistic representation of social and political problems. The influence of this group continued through the 1960's despite the demise of the formal organizational structure that existed in the 1950's.

The dominant literary tone of the 1960's was a continuation of the realistic focus of ASAS'50. Writings were somewhat more autobiographical, and many novels originally published only in *jawi* were republished in romanized script. Newspapers and magazines played a continued but reduced support role. The major literary circle seemed composed of young writers publishing in *Penulis*.

Malay Verse

There is a large body of Malay verse passed on in both written and oral form. The earliest verse was not rigidly metrical but incorporated loose rhythmical patterns. Vestiges of these early verses can be traced back to segments of old Tamil verse inserted in parts of the prose text of the *Hikayat Raja-Raja Pasai* (Royal Annals of the Kingdom of Pasai), and they can still be found in village songs and ritual chants. The earliest type of verse that can be dated is a *shair* passage appearing on a Pasai tombstone from A.D. 1380.

A *shair* is a long narrative poem composed of quatrains. Each of these four-line rhyming units expresses an idea set in elaborate, romantic style. Usually there is a moral or didactic message woven into their total structure.

The Malays are very fond of proverbs, and there exists a wealth of proverbial sayings. Like proverbs elsewhere, they usually express the views of life of the simple folk living close to nature. Often they are cynical; nearly always they describe a disagreeable aspect of reality. By structuring what is disagreeable as a law of nature, they seek to make life's realities more bearable. Typical are the following: Can muddy water come from a clear well? Charcoal, even though it be washed with rose water, will not become white. A horse is by nature a horse and an ass is an ass. Fire when small is a friend, and when large is an enemy. Little fishes are the prey of large ones.

Some proverbs are but brief phrases (incomplete sentences in themselves), which are used in conversation; others are full sentences, sometimes with internal rhythm. Some appear in the form of a *pantun* (a brief poem), with a moral or didactic purpose.

The *pantun*, often similar to a folk-ditty, is one of the most cherished literary heritages of the Malays. It is heard at special occasions in Malay life, such as at weddings and festivals and during courtship, and it has also been adopted by other ethnic groups, especially the Chinese. The structure of the *pantun* is relatively simple. There are four lines (hence *pantun* is often translated "quatrain"), with the third line rhyming with the first, and the fourth with the second.

The first two lines and the second two lines form a parallelism, which usually is emphasized by the use of alliterative wording in the parallel lines (1 and 3, 2 and 4)—guideposts to the *pantun*'s inherent meaning. The first two lines usually are meaningless and simply provide the rhyming scheme for the last two lines, which convey the message commonly clothed in similes and metaphors. For example, a flower signifies a young girl, and a peacock, a beautiful woman. The message can be a riddle, a comment on life, an expression of an emotion or mood, advice to the lovelorn, or a reflection on history or customs.

The following examples are: first, an adapted or interpretive English rendering of a Malay *pantun*; and second, a literal English translation.

> The fate of a dove is to fly—
> It flies to its nest on the knoll;
> The gate of true love is the eye,
> The prize of its quest is the soul.

> Whence flies the green pigeon?
> From the swamp down to the rice-field
> Whence (comes) love?
> From the eye it decends to the heart.

The four ingredients of a good *pantun* are: a real connection between its two parts; the suggestion of this connection through the sound of words; cohesion, which comes not so much from rhyme as from assonance running through the entire line; and the slow and gradual—not instant—revelation of the meaning of the *pantun*.

Pantuns can be spoken, quoted, or sung during a dance; they are designed not to be recited or read, but sung by a chorus, with a choral refrain at the end of each line (during which the audience has time to think over the meaning). Rival choruses often engage in *pantun* contests. Often each chorus in turn sings only half a *pantun*, so that successive *pantuns* become intertwined, and the audience has an even harder time following the meaning. Ideal procedure during a *pantun* contest is to take up lines two and four of the opposing chorus' last *pantun* and use them as first and third lines of a new *pantun*. Thus, *pantuns* constitute both a formal and an informal element of Malay literature. Some are several centuries old, and new ones are constantly being created.

The *pantun* and the *shair* continued to be the most popular poetic forms through the 19th century. By the end of the 1930's, however, there was some experimentation with new poetic forms by writers educated in religious schools. Their words appeared largely in journals such as *Majallah Guru* and *Saujana*, published by Malay school-teachers' associations. The growth of this movement was slow and was interrupted by the outbreak of World War II.

Poetic expression in the postwar period has been marked by a rejection of traditional verse forms. Most poets have chosen free verse to present topical poems increasingly concerned with political and social issues in a style that alternates between the despair and the optimism of modern man. Included among the major modern Malay poets whose works had brought them recognition by the mid-1960's were Usman Awang, S. N. Masuri, Samad Said, A. S. Amin, S. I. Noor, and Salmi Manja.

Other Traditions

In addition to works in Malay, there are Malaysian works in Chinese, English, and Tamil. Translations of Malay works have been made into these languages, but less material has been translated from them into Malay. Despite attempts in the early 1960's, there has been little success in creating a unified literary movement including all four language groups.

Chinese and Tamil communities emphasize past traditions and have shown a greater interest in drama and poetry than in contemporary short stories and novels. National interest is sufficient to justify the selection of the University of Malaya in Kuala Lumpur as the site for such a gathering as the International Conference-Seminar of Tamil Studies in 1966.

Works in English did not appear until after World War I, and few works of lasting worth were produced. World War II and the Emergency stimulated several interesting but highly autobiographical works such as *Senja-Lion of Malaya* by Gurchan Singh in 1946 and the *Silent Army* by Chin Kee Onn in 1952 (see ch. 3, Historical Setting).

In the early 1950's a group of young undergraduates began writing avant-garde verse in English. Personal and apocalyptic, the verse reflected the youth and frustration of the writers. Their removal from the university setting and engagement in their respective professional fields brought the writing of most of them to an end, but successive graduating classes have left additional embryonic, but promising, works. Perhaps marking a more advanced step in the development of English writing in Malaysia is *Rib of Earth*, a collection of poetry by Edwin Thumbee.

Non-Malay groups in East Malaysia, such as the Land Dayaks, have a tradition of long unwritten narratives in poetic form that serve as chronologies and genealogies and also have a semireligious function. Their recitation usually lasts most of one night or may extend for several nights. Efforts to record and study this tradition have been undertaken under the direction of the curator of the Sarawak Museum.

PERFORMING ARTS

The performing arts have a rich and highly varied tradition in the country. Urban theaters, drama societies, touring companies, radio broadcasts, and village gatherings provide opportunities for expression of cultural traditions in this area. Costumes are frequently elaborate, although simple settings are used. Classic-style and slapstick comedy, historical drama, and modern social themes are all represented.

Malay Music and Dance

Literature and music are interwoven in Malay culture to the extent that music appears to have little independent existence, serving chiefly for the conveyance of texts or the provision of rhythm for dancing. Malay musical instruments include wind, string, and percussion. Among the wind instruments are flutes and flageolets (*suling* and *serunei*) and harmoniums of wood or bamboo (*gambang* and *gamboosh*). Another is the *buluh-parinda* (the languishing bamboo) or *buluh-ribut* (the bamboo of the storm), a sort of aeolian pipe which consists of a bamboo cane some 30 to 40 feet long that is stuck into the ground and "played" by the wind's rushing through holes drilled in the bamboo. The string instruments are violins (*rebab*), which the Malays borrowed from the Portuguese. Percussion instruments are *gendang*, drums of various sizes and uses. *Gendang raya* or *gendang panjang* are hung in the mosque; *gendang prang* are smaller war drums; *rabana kathira* are tambourines; and *nobat* are kettledrums, the use of which is confined to royalty.

The music is enharmonic, using quarter tones in contrast to the conventional Western full and half tones. Malay bands usually consist of eight performers—two drummers, two horn players, and four flageolet players.

Music forms a part of many occasions in Malay life and provides an important means of cultural transmission. The *orang bedikir* (religious singing), in which two choirs chant Koranic verses to each other, is perhaps the most popular form of village entertainment after a feast. Music plays a special role in shaman seances and at the installation of a sultan, when the new ruler must sit motionless while series of notes are played a certain number of times.

Malay dancing nearly always represents some story, message, or idea—a passage from a romance or a depiction of harvest, war, or marriage—and is nearly always a more or less formal performance, rather than a group activity, although the number of performers may be so large as to involve a sizable portion of those present. In all dancing of Malay and Javanese origin, not only the footwork but also the body motion, and most particularly the movement of arms and fingers, have specific significance. Dancing is very popular entertainment, and a dancing event may last from evening to dawn.

The dances have various names, and sometimes it is not quite clear just what the differences are between differently named dances and whether the differences refer primarily to choreographic peculiarities or to the occasion on which the dance takes place. The *ronggeng*, the most popular, traditionally is danced by two women. In addition to the dancing, it involves song and dialogue by the participants directed at each other and between them and the audience. The *ronggeng* evolved from Thai origins, with marginal incorporations of certain elements taken from traditional Malay dances, Chinese court dances, and Portuguese folk dances. It appears to be appropriate at all festivities and is often performed to Western dance tempos. Other dances include the *waygang*, of Chinese origin; the *topeng*, the *gamboh*, and the *joget*, which derive from Java; the *boria*, from India; the *hathrah* and *dabus*, from Arabia; and the *mayong*.

The dances that present selected scenes from one of the tales of the Panji cycle are called *topeng* (mask). The performers are masked, and their movements are accompanied and punctuated by Javanese music. Because of the spectacular elements of the performances and of the music, the text as recited or sung has become secondary in importance to the visual effect; and because of the cost of masks, the same mask is used regardless of the actual romance being presented—all tales have a common hero mask, a common heroine mask, and so on down the list of characters. Thus, the audience tends to identify characters, not by their lines, but by their appearance. Uneducated Malays are likely to lose sight of the specific identity of the respective heroes of the folk tales and to telescope the several heroes into one "arch-hero" or "arch-heroine" type. Often the hero of a specific play uses several names—another indication that in the text, as well as in the performance of the traditional romance, little attempt is made to bring out the personality of any character.

There has been a gradual shift (which now appears to be virtually completed) from amateurism to professionalism in dancing. A hundred years ago the dances were folk art, performed on occasion by nonprofessionals with special talent, but professionals have increasingly taken over. At public festivities it is now professional dancers alone who perform, with the exception of boys and girls who have had dance training and are often called upon to perform. It is not considered improper for little boys and little girls to dance together.

Muslim teaching has insisted that respectable women do not dance in public and certainly not with men. The Malay professional danseuse (*budak joget*, often called *ronggeng* after the name of the dance) seldom has long training and may have started dancing only when her reputation was beyond injury. Thus, she often lacks the youth, grace, beauty, and skill of her Indonesian counterpart; her attractiveness usually lies in her wit and in her memorized store of chants, songs, and texts that she sings in accompaniment to her dance. In the *ronggeng* it is permissible for male members of the audience to join in with one or another of the performing women, a feature that accounts largely for the popularity of this form of entertainment in both Malaysia and Singapore.

The Arabian *hathrah* is considered so proper that any pious Muslim may "safely" dance it. It is a lone dance, usually performed by boys to the accompaniment of Arabic words embodying religious sentiment, and an Arabian tambourine sometimes accompanies it. The *dabus* has mystical Muslim overtones and, when it is performed by religious fanatics, can lead to bodily harm for the dancers often stab themselves with *dabus* (awllike instruments) for the greater glory of Allah.

The dance called *mayong*, containing Thai and Hindu elements, has been traced to the lost kingdom of Ligor, a state of the upper Malay Peninsula, which, though documented to have existed as late as the 15th century, has not been geographically identified. A *mayong* company usually consists of four main players, a dozen or so musicians who play flutes, gongs, and drums, and supernumeraries. They perform on platforms or on the ground in huts, with illumination from lanterns and colored lights. The performance usually is based on a plot drawn from a cycle of 12 stories that form a separate body of Malay romance and that never have been published in written form, as far as it is known. *Mayong* also are presented as shadow plays.

Wayang Kulit

One of the more popular media for the presentation of Malay epics, romances, and dramas is *wayang kulit* (shadow puppet shows), whose origins are Javanese. The shadows of leather and wood puppets are cast by light onto a screen, which separates the audience from the performers. The performance does not rely on the puppets' actions alone; the handlers accompany the action with words and music. At least two persons are involved, one to handle the puppets and one to recite the dialogue.

The performance of a shadow play may go on for weeks. Malay audiences do not expect to be shown the whole tale at one sitting;

they want to sample the performers' acting rather than learn a story—since they already know all the stories well. Thus, a spectator often will come late to a show and leave early. In addition, the show is not spoiled for him—it is in fact enhanced—by sudden interruptions in the basic plot, when the two stylized clowns Semar and Chemuras (or Turas) appear to divert the audience by improvised, disrespectful talk about gods and demons. The plays are accompanied by drums, gongs, and Malay violins. Nightly puppet shows are held in Kota Bahru, capital of the state of Kelantan.

Other Traditions

Chinese music, like Chinese drama, takes two forms—classical and modern. Chinese music is performed by amateur societies as well as by the China Society, which also leads in promoting interest in the Peking Opera and in organizing the visual arts. There is a great deal of interest in the composition and performance of string music for quartet and smaller combinations and other collective musical activity.

Chinese classical drama is performed in urban theaters and by touring companies. It is very similar in form to Western opera in that there is a close relationship between vocal and instrumental music. In the Chinese classical form the outstanding feature is the predominance of percussion instruments in the rhythmic accompaniment supporting the lines and action of the players. Also characteristic of classical Chinese drama are the elaborate dances and the rhythmic and complex formations simulating the highly regimented art of self-defense known as Kun-tow and reproducing battle formations that are integrated into the play. Although period costumes are used, only a minimum of props and scenery is employed since the audience is expected to know some of the symbolism of the actors' standardized gestures and postures. Modern Chinese drama, on the other hand, is very similar to Western drama in the use of dialogue as opposed to mime.

Reflecting a lively interest in Western music, modern Chinese music contains many Western idioms; it often is played and performed with Western instruments—the piano, violin, and saxophone—replacing the traditional Chinese drums, flutes, and fiddles. Most popular of modern music are the Cantonese and Mandarin songs with Western orchestration that are introduced through the medium of motion pictures.

Considerable interest exists in Indian music, and the Hindustani and Tamil songs from motion pictures are particularly popular. Recitals of classical music and the presentation of historical and cultural

Indian plays are projects supported by the Indian Fine Arts Society. Ceremonial music is still played by temple musicians and on special occasions.

The dance is probably the most vital and important form of artistic expression in East Malaysia. Dances are an integral part of every festivity. Some have religious significance and are used for ingratiating the rice spirits or for driving away evil spirits causing disease or poor harvests. Dances are held to honor visitors and, on other social occasions, for pure entertainment. While women who dance are usually professionals, almost all the men in a village participate.

The most popular dance form is a solo performance done more often by men than by women. Male dancing is taken very seriously, and good dancers achieve a great deal of esteem and widespread fame. The Kayans and Kenyahs, in particular, are noted as the greatest exponents of the dance in northern Borneo (see ch. 4, Ethnic Groups and Languages). With an eager audience looking on, solo male dancers succeed one another, doing the same dance but with variations according to the individual's interpretation. The classic dance of the Bornean aboriginal peoples represents a headhunter's combat. Since traditionally the most esteemed art was fighting, the dances praise the virtues of the fight and extol valor in war.

The other local dance forms are similar to those found throughout Southeast Asia, but they have not reached the elaborate refinement identified with court dancing. Emphasis is placed on small movements of various parts of the body, particularly the hands and shoulders. Much of the dancing involves no movement of the feet. Impromptu versifying and the recital of old and new tales often accompany the dances. The dance orchestra consists of drums and gongs of various sizes and a few stringed instruments.

Among the Kayan and Kenyah, old men perform comic dances that are studies of birds and animals, the most notorious of which is the monkey dance. The performances of these dances are clownish, and no detail, however intimate, is omitted. One type of dance, which may even attract people from neighboring villages, is the *dingdang*. It involves one or more couples who face each other and chant verses while rhythmically shuffling back and forth. The art of this dance consists in spontaneous composition of topical humorous verses, preferably with members of the audience as subjects of the banter. Another characteristic type of dance, brought to northern Borneo from the southern Philippines, is performed by two dancers who take turns singing a story.

History and legends are recited in song. Most native groups have a rich and constantly developing lore or mythology and historical sagas, some of which may take days and nights to recite. Frequent themes among the Kelabits, for instance, are headhunting and trading expeditions, wars with sky spirits, and extermination of cannibal ogres. Important current events also are memoralized in song and added to the historical lore.

The Kayan and Kenyah, in addition to being the finest dancers, are noted as splendid singers. Like their dances, many of their songs are ancient. Their music is very melodious and often is played on their characteristic instrument, the *sapeh* shaped like a medieval viol. The *sapeh* has two or three strings, which sound similar to the notes of a harpsichord. The favorite songs of the Kayan and the Kenyah are drinking songs in the form of sagas extolling the virtues of a quest. A drinking song contains many verses improvised by a soloist; the phrases of the chorus, however, are fixed and repeated often throughout the song.

Western musical styles are becoming increasingly evident in present-day Malay and Chinese popular music, and Western classical forms are performed in urban centers. Philharmonic societies perform works by Beethoven, Borodin, Brahms, and Britten. The Drama Department of the University of Malaya has shown an interest in experimental theater, and tour groups such as the French Corps de Ballet receive enthusiastic welcomes.

VISUAL ARTS

Painting

Development of painting as realistic representation has taken place largely in the post-World War II period. The Muslim prohibition against the representation of living things blocked traditional Malay artisans from realistic representation, and painting was chiefly a decorative art. Painting by Indian and Chinese artists was executed in the styles and media of their respective cultures and did not reflect indigenous development. No gallery collection existed, and opportunities for academic training were limited.

Painting since the war has embodied a wide range of styles and media and represented not only an interest in international trends, but also the gradual emergence of a national culture. Both the new National Art Gallery and private galleries offer collections of indigenous paintings, and training facilities have been expanded. Malaysian artists are exhibiting abroad, and in 1969 59 works by 22 of the country's artists appeared at a Sao Paolo exhibition.

Four basic schools of painting have become discernible. The first school works in the styles and media of Western academic tradition and tends to focus on genre painting. The best known exponent of this school is Muh. Hoessein, who is the country's leading portrait painter. His studies in oils and pastels of the human face have a fresh clarity and naturalness and focus on facial and body lines with little concern for background detail or spatial movement. Among his better known works are *Aidah*, *Chomel*, *Azizah*, and *Little Secret*.

Traditional Chinese landscape painting is the source of inspiration for the second school of painting. This school is less interested in color than in the linear relationships and projection interreactions between natural and spiritual worlds. *Poppies* by Chen Wen Hsi and *Kampong* by Phoon Poh Hoong are typical of this school.

The third school of painting includes a wide range of basically abstract works that frequently experiment with color intensities and hues. At one extreme, represented by *Where Are We* by Cheong Laitong, are nonobjective intellectualizations about man and the modern world; others, such as *Fishing Nets* by Ho Kai Peng, are linear but more representational. Of all the country's painting, the works of this abstractionistic school are the most responsive to international art movements.

The fourth school is the most representative of the country's emerging national culture. It is devoted to the retranslation of batik techniques ordinarily used for making clothing with traditional patterns into pictorial murals and wall hangings that depict the new nation and its people. Such is the work of Seah Kin Joe. His batik paintings combine subtle shading and color variations with complicated compositions that possess internal movement, balance, and cohesion. His most famous work is a five-paneled, 8½- by 25-foot mural entitled *Joy of Living*, commissioned for the Hotel Malaysia in Singapore.

Sculpture

The country has seen only limited sculptural development. Marble and bronze works have no tradition in the country, and the small, antique bronze statuettes and castings found in the excavations of early sites are not of indigenous origins. During the colonial period sculptured friezes, swags, and busts appeared on some of the more elaborate urban structures, but they were almost exclusively the work of foreign artists. Of the handful of contemporary sculptors in the country, most of whom work largely in a Western academic style, the majority are Indians. The small statues and heads of Dora Gordine are considered by many to represent the best locally worked sculpture in the country.

ARCHITECTURE

Interaction between environmental, cultural, and historical factors has mitigated against the development of a single, distinctively national architectural style. The scarcity of easily quarried rock and the limited labor force provided by a low-density population has restricted traditional construction to moderate-sized timber structures. The preponderance in the population of newly arrived ethnic groups who brought and maintained their own architectural tradition and the concentration of urban settlements in coastal areas exposed to intercultural exchange and interaction led to the development of eclectic, multiple styles.

The only existing traces of structures built before the 15th century are ruins of stone temples and gravesites constructed between the fourth and the 15th centuries during the period of Hindu influence (see ch. 3, Historical Setting). Several of these sites, such as Gua Cha, are being excavated and reconstructed and have proved to be of considerable historical importance. Although not exact duplicates of Indian prototypes, these structures represent an importation of culture rather than the development of an indigenous tradition of stone construction.

The emergence of a distinctively indigenous style of architecture was stimulated by the construction of timber palaces and mansions for Malay royalty and court officials. The first of these structures that can be documented was constructed in the second half of the 15th century for the sultan of Malacca. These structures incorporated elements from Thai and other cultures, but they were Malay in their execution. They were constructed for a period of over 400 years, but termites, fire, and wood rot have left few examples standing. The oldest example, Istana Among Tinggi, which was rebuilt and restored by the government at Seremban in the 1950's, dates only from the mid-1860's.

Built of Chengal and Penak woods, these multiple-storied structures were built on low platforms and were frequently left unstained and weathered. Carved panels and borders, pierced stair railings, and carved semicircular fretworks provided rich ornamentation played against simple backgrounds and demonstrated a subtle handling of line, form, and texture.

The timber court palaces of the Malays represented a cultural development that affected only a marginal portion of the country's population. The average Malaysian timber dwelling follows age-old *kampong* (see Glossary) traditions that include both individual family dwellings and longhouse compounds. Building techniques vary throughout the country from simple huts woven of saplings and palm fronds to hand- and machine-dressed timber structures with thatched or corrugated metal roofs. Exterior decoration is the exception. The structures are placed on stilt-supported platforms and ventilated by natural airflows.

The construction of masonry structures was one of the major urban developments of the 19th and early 20th centuries. The structures ranged from simple-line, two-storied, balconied or shutter-façaded structures that combined shop and dwelling facilities to more elaborate, multiple-storied banks, hotels, and government buildings whose stucco and stone fronts presented eclectic combinations of Palladian, Moorish, Hindu, Chinese, and other architectural elements. The construction was more reflective of British attempts to adopt European architecture in terms they thought suitable to Asia than of indigenous stylistic developments.

During the 1950's the level of construction in the country considerably increased. War damage, which in Sabah flattened the major urban areas, and the growing need of a new state for housing, social service, and administrative facilities produced diverse and widespread construction needs. Particularly during the early 1960's, the immediacy and scope of these needs resulted in a greater focus on function than on aesthetic considerations. The importance of the period of the 1950's for the country's architectural development lay in an exposure to new materials, techniques, and design concepts. In addition to schools and housing projects, major government projects included the Merdeka Stadium and the Kuala Lumpur airport. Private construction brought commercial facilities, hotels, and gas stations.

After the embryonic 1950's architectural developments in the 1960's reached a higher level of sophistication in technique and design. Multiple-storied structures used cantilevered support systems, cast concrete forms, and metal and glass modular units. Sculpturally designed façades and glass walls sought to merge national traditions with international trends and concepts. Interiors alternated vibrant colors, warm woods, and contrasting textures.

In 1969 the country could boast a wide range of new and impressive structures. The tall, pierced shaft of the Houses of Parliament Building is tied to the ground by lateral lines of lower level corridors and a pavillion entrance. The new National Museum in Kuala Lumpur, designed by Ho Kok Hoe, is fronted with murals and carved wooden doors and has a mosaic floor and a roof that reflects designs found in the Malay timber palaces. The rolling campus of the University of Malaya features structures in the style of Le Corbusier, such as the Great Hall and the 750-bed technical hospital whose 15-story ward block merged post-and-beam and T-block diaphragm support systems and offers piped medical service lines. The National Mosque,

212

featuring a 245-foot minaret which is reflected in a pool and a parasol-shaped concrete roof over a mausoleum that can accommodate 8,000 worshipers, makes wide use of traditional symbolism. Recently constructed churches, such as the Kuching Cathedral and a small shoreside parish church in Butterworth, combine streamlined traditional elements such as *belian* (iron wood) shingles and raised platforms with reinforced concrete shells.

Architectural advances in the 1960's have also been evidenced in such functional projects as the Cameron Highlands Hydro-Electric Scheme, the new wharves at Port Swettenham, and the Klang Gates Dam. Urban planning in Kuala Lumpur has demanded not only schemes for future expansion but also means to resolve past mistakes and to simplify the increasing intricacy of interlocking urban development.

DECORATIVE ARTS

Highly colorful decorative arts are produced by ethnic groups throughout the country. The patterns used vary widely; in some cases they are derived from nature, with flowers and leaves; in others they are based on geometric or abstract designs. Craftsmen produce fragile items, such as lanterns and kites for festival use, and more durable wood and metal items. The relative cheapness and utility of manufactured articles have somewhat reduced the importance of crafts throughout the country. The continued production and transfer of craft skills are being encouraged by government, educational, and private organizations.

Wood and Matting

Wood carving is largely limited to carved house beams or items that are later painted; the major exception is carving done for the tourist trade. The Dayaks carve demonic masks with exaggerated features used for ceremonial purposes and dances. The Malay fishing boats along the east coast of the Peninsula down to Pahang were traditionally fitted with *bangau*, carved projections designed to hold spars, masts, poles, and anchors when not in use and usually carved in abstract or stylized forms representing dragons, seahorses, hornbills, or characters from a *wayang kulit*.

Wickerwork is used for the construction of walls that form the inner divisions of houses and for mats placed on the floor for various social and functional activities. Decorations are incorporated into the mats by weaving strands of varicolored palm leafstalks or by dyeing, offering cross or diamond patterns. Wicker baskets and trays of elaborate designs and varied shapes are also found. The Punans produce particularly high-quality wicker with elaborate black and white patterns.

Pottery

The importation of modern, manufactured glass and hardware items has displaced what seems to have once been a relatively well-developed pottery industry. The handsome Province Wellesley red and Johore and Perak black ceramics once available are no longer being produced. Today Selangor is the pottery center of the country, and the pottery industry is dominated largely by members of the Chinese community.

Metal

Tin is a popular metal for decorative and practical purposes and is used in its pure form or combined with other metals. It is used as an inlay on wood and for items such as betel-nut mortars. Selangor pewter is produced in contemporary designs and has become internationally competitive. Bronze is worked into daggers, swords, cannons, censers, trays, tools, and bowls.

Iron formerly was worked for agricultural tools, as well as for the *kris* and knives. The *kris* (of Indonesian origin) has two styles—those with a hilt forming one part with the blade and those with a wooden hilt. Characteristic of both kinds are the waves of the blade, the construction of which is a difficult and time-consuming process. Blades generally are etched with a mixture of rice, sulfur, and salt and often are rubbed with arsenic as an additional process. It is the *kris* hilt that is most decorated. Its handle, if not of the same piece as the blade, may be of wood, horn, gold, or silver. A great deal of decoration also is lavished on the sheath, made of various kinds of materials. Animal patterns often are employed, with monkeys being especially popular; Arabic lettering also is used for its decorative effect.

Work in gold and silver is done in four forms—respoussé, filigree, niello, and inlay. Repoussé involves beating out the design from the reverse side of thin metal; filigree is a technique involving use of thin metal wires to form designs; and niello utilizes sulfur to blacken designs incised in the metal. Finely worked boxes for tobacco, betel nuts, and limes, and sweetmeat bowls and trays were produced in the courts of the rajas and sultans. Gold and silver jewelry is produced throughout the country for all classes, sometimes as a form of savings.

Frequent motifs are adaptations of nature such as leaves and centipedes. Iban wedding headdresses are made of delicate hammered leaves.

Textiles

Pineapple, plantain, palm, and cotton fibers used for spinning in the past have been replaced by imported threads. Silk is imported from China, as it has been in the past. Embroidery of various kinds is done in the Peninsula. Lace is manufactured in Malacca, and its Portuguese name, *renda*, indicates that it was adopted from the Portuguese.

Malays love color, preferring brightness and contrast, and color schemes in fabrics are achieved by weaving various patterns, such as tartan plaids, checks, and stripes. Weavers in Trengganu dye the silk thread and then weave it into intricate patterns. Gold leaf is used for gilding luxury fabrics; in Pahang it is glued on, in a process derived from the Punjab of India.

Batik, made through time-consuming, alternate dyeings of fabric with wax shields, is popular throughout the country. Attempts have been made to produce machine-made batik commercially to compete with Indonesian production, but the handprinted process is preferred. Dayak craftsmen produce ceremonial wall hangings called *pua*, whose patterns are obtained through the predyeing of certain threads before the weaving of the fabric. The Bajau create a distinctive thick cloth with a broad red and black design woven through with silver thread.

Other Forms

Clothing and personal body decoration to a certain degree constitute an art form among the aboriginal peoples of East Malaysia. The advance of Western civilization has resulted in the increasing popularity among the indigenous peoples of Western-style clothing and hair styles; on ceremonial and ritual occasions, however, traditional garb continues to be worn, and body decorations such as tattooing are still observed on many of the older natives. Aside from the common sarong-type skirt or dress, the Balah Iban women on special occasions wear an interesting costume that covers them from head to toe in hats and robes of closely meshed colored beads. The hats are described as looking like pincushions from which protrude hundreds of long spikes threaded with small colored beads; from the ends of these spikes hang artificial flowers, ribbons, marbles, and silver coins. The dress consists of a beaded, long-sleeved robe that covers the woman from neck to ankles. Attached to her back is an apron of smaller beads with two or three bells hanging from the hem. In addition, the outfit consists of a silver belt with bells worn around the waist, beaded cravats, silver necklaces, and sashes worn with silver threads that crisscross the chest.

Tattooing is a common form of personal decoration. The Iban males traditionally had throat tattooes and also could have one joint of one finger tattooed blue for each head taken. When the number of heads taken exceeded the number of joints on both hands, the pattern was continued down the back of the hand. In addition to the tattooes, the Iban male could wear one hornbill feather in his traditionally uncut hair for each head he took. The Kayan and Kenyah women tattooed a blue-black pattern on their arms from their elbows to their fingers and on their legs from their toes to sometimes as high as their hips. Another beauty custom among Kayan and Kenyah women was to pierce their earlobes and stretch them to beyond their shoulders. Several thick brass rings were hung in the loop of each ear lobe, and a woman's reputation for beauty grew with the length of the earlobes and the number of rings in them.

THE INTELLECTUAL IN SOCIETY

Although social cohesion is based on effective communication, in a transitional, multiracial society such as that of Malaysia there are many obstacles to the free flow of communication. For example, the rooting of the educational system of a country in colonial traditions may set inhibitions toward experimentation and intuitive thinking, and the academic field may reinforce existing ethnic tension and competiton.

The country's university complex has a potential for unifying the intellectual elite, but this had not yet been realized in 1969. Malay students tend to focus on government careers and congregate in Malay and Muslim study programs. Chinese students at the University of Malaya are usually training for jobs in industry and study in the schools of engineering and science. Interaction patterns may be so minimal that ethnic separation is not ended but carried on in a new, less observable way.

Both the depth and number of facilities available for scholarly activities are increasing. In 1969 the University of Malaya, the country's major academic center, included schools of agriculture, the arts, engineering, science, medicine, education, and economics and administration. Graduate and, in some cases, postgraduate programs were available (see ch. 8, Education). The medical program was one of the best in Southeast Asia.

216

There is a growing interest in social anthropology, particularly in East Malaysia. Museums in the country have long suffered from competition from European collections and have been frequently housed in structures not originally designed for museum purposes. Gradual replacement or remodeling of these facilities and the building up of national collections are in progress. The new National Museum incorporates the most advanced display concepts and facilities.

Included among the major national academic societies in 1969 were the Arts Council of Malaysia and the Malay Historical Society. Professional societies included the Society of Architects, the Bar Council, States of Malaya, the Institution of Engineers, and the Malay Zoological Society. Representative of major academic and professional publications were *Pengasoh*, the *Sabah Society Journal*, the *Sarawak Museum Journal*, *Intisari*, and the *Kajian Ekonomi Malaysia*.

THE ROLE OF GOVERNMENT

The government's active role in the promotion of artistic and intellectual expression ranges from research grants and programmed study at the University of Malaya, for whose development M$30 million (3.06 Malaysian dollars equal US$1) was provided under the First Malaysia Plan for 1966 to 1970, to the sponsoring of local and regional competitions. Much of the government's activity is directed through Dewan Bahasa dan Pustaka (a language and literature council), and government efforts focus heavily on the restimulation of traditional forms of expression.

Under the First Malaysia Plan, M$3.3 million was to be provided for the construction of multipurpose centers whose programs include music, dance, drama, arts, and crafts. The government also tries to promote a revival of craft skills through the marketing of rural handicrafts and through grants to performing groups.

In many academic and technical areas the government maintains offices to provide a corps of trained personnel for public and, sometimes, private projects. The work of government staff architects, for example, ranges from blueprint planning of schools and housing projects to the more complicated and sophisticated problems of cost studies, projecting the benefits of compact versus open planning, integrating and preserving traditional structures into development plans and needs, and dealing with the general problems of increasing urban complexity.

CHAPTER 10

RELIGION

Religion is a major element in the plural nature of Malaysian society. It accentuates communal divisions arising from ethnic differences, and it directly affects political life, foreign relations, and many social institutions. At the same time, religion and culture form a bond of unity for Malays that does not exist among other ethnic groups in the country.

The predominant religion, Islam, is the faith of the Malays and of a much smaller number of ethnic Chinese and Indians. Since census figures do not include religious affiliation, there are no accurate statistics. In West Malaysia Muslims account for slightly more than half the population, and the proportion of Muslims in East Malaysia is believed to be from 33 to 38 percent; for the country as a whole, the Muslim proportion is estimated at about 44 percent of total population. Buddhism, Taoism, and Confucianism are professed by most of the Chinese, who make up some 35 to 40 percent of the nation's population.

There are perhaps 50,000 or more Indians, mainly low-caste farmers from southern India, who are followers of Islam, but the large majority of Indians in the country are Hindus and Sikhs. Together the Indians and a smaller number of Pakistanis, who are mostly Muslim, comprise an estimated one-tenth of the total population. Most Christians in the country live in Sabah and Sarawak, where they have been estimated to number some 15 percent of the East Malaysian population. There are few Indians or Pakistanis in East Malaysia, and the majority of the non-Chinese, non-Muslim, and non-Christian populations in East Malaysia are mostly animist or pagan.

Islam is the official religion of the country, but freedom of worship for other faiths is guaranteed. This freedom does not extend to the proselytizing of Muslims. In practice there is a high degree of religious toleration. There is a close interrelationship between government and Islam, and there are certain special obligations placed upon, and political advantages granted to, followers of that faith. Under the Constitution special position is accorded to Malays, who are defined as those who profess the Muslim religion, habitually speak the Malay language, conform to Malay customs, and were born in Malaysia before independence or are children of parents so born.

The same religious and cultural forces that unite the dominant Malay group discourage or prevent intermarriage with non-Malays and therefore act as a barrier to assimilation of the large Chinese minority, the lesser number of Indians, and other ethnic groups. Nevertheless, practical considerations have minimized the role of religion in the country's political life, even though it remains potentially explosive when added to racial and ethnic controversies.

Each of the nonindigenous major religions has undergone modifications in its Malaysian environment and has diverged in important respects from its original form in the homeland from which it came. Change also has been produced within indigenous religions by exposure to Islam and Christianity over several centuries.

HISTORICAL BACKGROUND

The earliest religion known to have been imported was Hinduism, which by the beginning of the Christian Era was established in the coastal regions of lower Burma, the Malay Peninsula (particularly the Kra Isthmus in modern Thailand), Java, and what is now South Vietnam. The cult of the Hindu god Siva became established throughout Malaya and Borneo. Personifying the powers and aspects of change in the universe, Siva was identified with fertility, the earth, and agriculture. Sri (or Lakshmi), Brahma, and Vishnu also were of importance. Before this time indigenous Malays were animists.

Buddhism was first introduced in the Malay Peninsula after the third century A.D. in its Hinayana form, but this was displaced in the 12th century by the Mahayana form. Mahayana Buddhism soon merged with the still flourishing Hinduism of the area to become Tantric Buddhism, characterized by the worship of the power of fertility of the Divine Mother (Sakti).

Islam largely displaced Hinduism and Tantric Buddhism during the 14th and 15th centuries, but some Hindu concepts and institutions remained—including divine kingship and reincarnation, or rebirth into a new existence after death. Hinduism exerted its greatest influence in a more indirect manner: its long presence in Malaya, the depth of its roots, and the nature of its philosophy created the climate in which the Muslim system first came to be accepted in the country. In the late 1960's Hindu influence still was quite apparent in the ceremonies of the Malay courts and in Malay art and literature.

The main current of Islam, in its development in the Near East after the death of Muhammad (A.D. 632) and before its expansion into Southeast Asia (ca A.D. 1350–1500), was that of Sunnism. The words and sayings of the Prophet, as set forth in the Koran and the Sunna, were central to Muslim thought and action. The Koran, containing God's revelations to Muhammad, concerned itself largely with broad ethical principles; these were explained, enlarged, and illustrated in the Sunna. Four versions of the Sunna came to have general recognition as being definitive—those of Abu Hanifa, Malik ibn Anas, al-Shafi'i, and Ibn Hanbal—and were used for guidance by different Sunnite groups.

The Islam that first reached the Malay Peninsula was a heterogeneous system from which the Malays selected concepts most meaningful to them. Many of the adopted Arabic religious terms acquired new meanings. The early teachers came first from southern and western India—Gujerat, Malabar, and the Deccan. The later teachers, from Persia, Yemen, and the Hedjaz, were largely merchants who made conversion simple, adapting their creed to fit Malay interests. They said that they could heal sickness and drive away spirits. They married the daughters of communal chiefs and through them influenced the communities.

For Hindu magic the Muslim merchants substituted Muslim magic. Against the heroes of the Hindu epics—the *Mahabharata* and the *Ramayana*—they created a fictitious picture of Alexander the Great as a predecessor of Muhammad in a war for monotheism and even went so far as to make Malay rulers his descendants. In the Malay shadow plays, they substituted the marvelous adventures of Amir Hamza (another mythical hero of Islam) for the old repertories from the Hindu epics. From the Persian they translated many tales of the Prophet and his companions. They promised that the constant reader of the Koran or of a pious tract would acquire the same merit as warriors who died in holy war.

Sunnites and Shiites, the latter being members of the major dissident sect of the time, alike argued their viewpoints before the Malays, and the Malay sultans compounded the situation by sponsoring contests on theological points. In general, the Malays tended to adopt the more mystical elements of Muslim thought, reinterpreting many of them and combining them with other borrowings. By the end of the 16th century the end product came to be a Muslim religion largely Sunni in form, but with Shiite elements and Sufi (Muslim mysticism) spirits, resembling nothing else in Islam outside of Southeast Asia and India.

The religious systems transposed to Malay soil by the Chinese and Indians also changed. Confucianism and Taoism originated in China before the beginning of the Christian Era, and Buddhism came in from India several centuries later.

Confucianism traditionally has appealed to the educated; Taoism, in its popular form, to the peasantry; and Buddhism, in various forms and at different times, to both. Most Chinese immigrants to Malaya,

Singapore, and Borneo were from the lower economic levels of south and central China and concerned themselves only with rites of kinship solidarity, with ancestor worship, and the rituals directed to such household and personal spirits as the guardians of the door and stove and the gods of health and luck. Since nearly all the Chinese immigrants were in the same socioeconomic category, their religion became a "people's religion," without philosophical speculation. There is also an insistent eclecticism in their approach to religion, which results in the ordinary Chinese being able to weave the fabric of his religion with strands taken from various traditions.

The Indian population of Malaya, including Hindus, Sikhs, and Muslims, arrived for the most part at the end of the 19th and the beginning of the 20th century. There is some evidence that the religious life of the Hindus has been greatly affected by separation from the localized cult systems of South Indian life—such as those of village, boundary, and land deities, which create a bond between the villager and his place of abode and labor—but more general aspects of the traditional religion, such as the Hindu pantheon, appear intact. The Indian Muslims appear to differ little in their religious views from the Malay Muslims.

MOSQUE AND STATE

Conversion of the early Malay rulers to Islam first gave that religion a political role that is not enjoyed by other faiths and that has continued to the present. The only special protection accorded to other religions is furnished by constitutional guarantees against interference and against taxation to support Muslim institutions. Special provisions also are made for the states of Sarawak and Sabah because of their primarily non-Muslim populations. Muslims have special obligations under law as well as special rights, and they have a separate system of courts and pay special taxes. Practicing Muslims alone are subject to Muslim law governing certain matters.

Under the Constitution the ruler of each state (with certain exceptions) is the head of the Muslim religion for that state. Religious questions pertaining to the country as a whole are decided by the Conference of Rulers (see ch. 12, The Governmental System).

In Penang and Malacca, which have no hereditary Malay rulers, the appointed governors exercise no responsibilities for the Muslim religion. Instead, these duties are assumed by the Supreme Head of Malaysia. He is the religious head of the state from which he is elected and in certain cases may act for the Conference of Rulers in religious matters affecting the country as a whole. Because of opposition from non-Muslim majorities in East Malaysia, neither Sarawak nor Sabah has a religious head. The constitutional provision that reserves to other states of the federal system the power to enact legislation on religious subjects does not apply to East Malaysia, unless the states there enact such measures by a two-thirds' majority of their legislative assemblies. Sabah and Sarawak also are exempt from a requirement that instruction in the Muslim religion be provided to Muslims in all government-assisted schools with more than 15 Muslim students, and the federal government may not give financial aid to Muslim institutions in East Malaysia without state government approval.

The general guarantee of freedom of worship in Malaysia is made subject to public order, health, and morality. Religious organizations and groups are given the right to own property and to operate their own institutions and schools. Discrimination solely on the ground of an individual's religion is prohibited.

In each of the Muslim states, the supervision of religious affairs is the responsibility of the religious affairs department. These departments are responsible for issuing opinions or rulings on religious questions and supervising such religious matters as collecting from Muslims the annual tithes required by law from Muslims. The Constitution reserves to the Muslim states nearly all power to legislate concerning Muslim affairs, including regulation of such matters as inheritance, betrothal, marriage, divorce, dower, maintenance, legitimacy, guardianship, and trusts.

In West Malaysia key government servants, if Malay, are given positions of authority on Muslim advisory and administrative bodies, with the result that the interlocking relationship between mosque and state is closer than is evident in the formal structure of either. Also, the law requires that Malays fill four-fifths of the positions in the civil service (three-fourths in the foreign service), and consequent favoritism toward Malays by government offices is a commonly expressed complaint of non-Malays.

In addition to special tax liabilities, Muslims are subject to a variety of penalties for violating the religious and moral code of Islam. These include failure to attend Friday prayers, consumption of intoxicating liquor, wifely disobedience, various sex crimes, contempt of religious authorities or of Islam, and others.

Malays also enjoy special privileges accorded by law. In addition to the government service quota system, Malays are also given special quotas for government scholarships and for entrance to upper-level educational institutions. Permits and licenses for certain trades and businesses are reserved for Malays under a quota system, and large areas of land are designated for exclusive ownership by Malays. Although these privileges are not specifically accorded to followers of Islam, the effect is the same because of the constitutional definition under which only Muslims are Malays.

MALAY MUSLIMS

Malays are Sunnite Muslims of the Shafi'ite school. The basic principles of the Malay religion are the Five Pillars of Islam: the declaration of faith in the omnipotence of Allah and in the divine messengership of the Prophet Muhammad; ritual prayers with ritual purification; distribution of alms; fasting in the month of Ramadan; and the pilgrimage to Mecca. Malays consider themselves true Sunnites, even though the Five Pillars of Islam were modified, reinterpreted, and changed in emphasis in the Malayan context. Islam appealed to the Malays because, as first introduced, it had strong mystic elements, and mysticism has always been important in Malay religion. Only recently have Sunnite traditionalism and Western empiricism gained any great ascendancy among educated Malays.

Traditional Concept of Existence

As conceived by the Muslim Malay, existence involves the action of three factors—*nyawa* (life soul, *maya* in Sanskrit), *roh* (intellect soul, from the Arabic *ruh*), and *semangat* (activating, or vital force). The typical Sunnite Malay regards the *nyawa* as emanating from the primal light and manifesting itself as the individual soul of a person or of an object. Such souls are usually external, visible, miniature in size, and identical in form for all objects of the same class. The soul of a house may appear as a cricket; that of a boat, as a firefly, snake, or person (depending upon its quality or size); that of a camphor tree, as a princess or a cicada; and that of a man, as a firefly or bird. The *nyawa* is a "life soul" in the sense that it remains associated with an individual even though he may be asleep, unconscious, or extremely ill, and in the sense that its final departure means death and physical disintegration. Also each *nyawa* has inherent characteristics, which its body may assume. It can exist apart from the body, for the Malays talk of the "soul" of the unborn, of the unconceived, and of the dead. The *nyawa* may be the soul that in Malay thought undergoes reincarnation or transmigration. It is not the entity, however, that lives immortal in heaven or hell, for the blows of the inquisitor angels fall on the actual human body; it is a new and incorruptible body that enjoys the Muslim paradise.

Malay mystics deny the existence of individual souls. Instead they talk of the "all-soul of the universe" (*nyawa rahmani*), an aspect of the supreme being or godhead (Allah or Al-Rahma), which permeates all nature and all things and which consists of the soul of all plants, animals, human bodily lives, and spiritual lives.

The *roh* is the agent of intelligence or knowledge and has inherent in it thought, reflection, intelligent consciousness, and sense of personality. It is without form, like a vapor, and its definite departure from the human body means death. Mystics, who believe in the unity of all things and the illusive character of heaven and earth and who reject the idea of personal souls, use *roh* for aspects of the divine intelligence or all-soul (*roh rahmani*) and may speak of the "soul of intelligent self-consciousness in animals."

The *semangat* is a mystical power that activates the qualities inherent in the *roh* and *nyawa* combined into a physical body. It acts as an energizing agency, but it is impersonal and devoid of individual will or spirit. It is possessed in various degrees by all things, and there is no "rank, condition, or degree" to distinguish the *semangat* in man from that in rice or in an animal. It is not thought to be immortal in the sense that a soul or body may attain immortality, but certain objects, such as stones and plants, and certain parts of the body, such as the teeth and hair, are prized as having it to an abnormal degree. The vitality or power in the hair shorn at a girl's first tonsure is considered so strong that it is buried at the foot of a barren tree so that it might bear fruit as luxuriant as her tresses. Saliva, too, is full of man's vitality, so that traditionally there was a special courtier to guard a royal cuspidor, and it is customary to spit on a baby to give it power and strength.

Everything connected with the body where vital force is present must be protected from the sorcery of enemies. A lover who takes strands of a girl's hair thus secures or attracts part of her *semangat* in order to weaken her and make her more tractable, and a woman's blood may be used by a disappointed lover to hurt her. Clippings from hair or nails are hidden or destroyed for fear that possession of them may give an enemy control over their owner's *semangat* and endanger his life. The *semangat* exists even in one's shadow. No one should walk upon a person's shadow, and the modern magician, to vaunt his power, will declare his shadow to be "the shadow of one beloved by Allah and the Prophet and angels forty and four."

In the Malay concept, *nyawa*, *roh*, and *semangat* occupy the physical body and apparently also can enter into the composition of incorporeal bodies, for the Malays believe that power from spirits enters into angelic bodies and that angels die.

The Spirit World

In accord with their concept of the spiritual basis of the illusory physical world, the Malays visualize the existence of innumerable spirit beings, arranged hierarchically in the order: angels, demons, and *hantu* or *jinns* (evil spirits or ghosts). The angels are largely Muslim but not entirely. Four angels, in the form of a bull, tiger, eagle, and man, support the throne of Allah; and cherubim cry incessantly "glory to God." Four archangels watch over the welfare of men: Jibra'il, the angel of revelation; Mika'il, the angel of mercy; Israfil, the angel of judgment; and Azra'il, warder of the angel of death, who will conquer all except the archangels. There are also throne-bearing angels. The angel called Ruh is the spirit who will implore mercy for the faithful on judgment day. Two inquisitor angels, Mankar and Nakir, visit the dead in their graves and inquire if they are believers. Four angels are attendant over man. Nineteen angels are guardians of hell; Malik is their chief, and Iblis, the fallen rebel angel, also called Siva or Saktimuna, is commander of the infidel *hantu*.

The Hindu deities are little known to the average Malay, but they remain of great importance to the mystics and magicians. Siva is known to all Malays as Batara Guru (lord teacher)—at once the white spirit of the sun and the black spirit of the earth—and also is known to the general populace as Nataraja (lord of dancers); as Rudra (storm god and leader of dead souls), the specter huntsman or raja of ghosts; and as Kala (the destroyer). Siva, Vishnu, Sri, the wife of Vishnu (often mistaken for the consort of Siva), Brahma, and Krishna regularly are invoked to protect the peasant clearing land for rice planting.

The demons of Muslim mythology are little known to the Malays, but *hantu* are thought to be everywhere, having been released on earth to plague mankind. They can assume the shape of men, horses, dogs, pigs, snakes, and insects. Some can fly; some can eat, drink, and marry. Their color varies according to their habitation. The *hantu* of the earth, dark forests, and lowering clouds are black and are the most dangerous; those inhabiting the sky are green; those in fleecy clouds and the shimmering sea are white; those in the fire and sunset are yellow. The *hantu* may cause disease, the intensity of which varies with the closeness of contact. Those of the air cause windborne complaints and dropsy, blindness, hemiplegia, and insanity. The *hantu* of the black earth cause vertigo, with sudden blackness of vision. Those of fire cause hot fevers and jaundice, and the white *hantu* of the sea cause chills, catarrh, and ague.

In addition to these spirits, there are the ghosts of the recent dead, apparently representing the *nyawa* but also possessing *semangat*. One class is benevolent, consisting of the spirits of chiefs or rajas, founders of settlements, and magicians, all of whom are attached to some place or clan (as in Negri Sembilan). Another class consists of the ghosts of the vengeful dead—those who were murdered, perjured, or unwanted, and those who died in childbirth. These are very dangerous and act as vampires. Finally, there is a class of spirits used as familiars by magicians and shamans. Sometimes they are inherited, but they may be obtained by a spirit-quest in the jungle or by being conjured up at night from the newly dug grave of a stillborn child.

The Five Pillars of Islam and Injunctions

To the typical Sunnite Malay, two aspects of his relationship with the spiritual world are of overwhelming importance: the preparation of his body for the final day of judgment, so that he may enjoy the heavens of the blessed; and the protection of his body, soul, and vital power from the evil spirits inhabiting his world. For these purposes he depends primarily upon the practices and prayers of Islam, particularly upon the Five Pillars stated in the Koran. The Malay approach to these practices is untraditional. Since the prayers and words associated with Islam are thought to derive from the godhead himself through Muhammad, they have an efficacy and a power in themselves. They are so holy that their very utterance will dismay and rout the evil spirits. Most Malay religious practice takes the form, therefore, of ritualistic recitation and repetition of Muslim chants. The other obligations required by Islam often have been reinterpreted or reduced to an indispensable minimum.

The Koran contains a number of injunctions. Drinking alcoholic beverages and eating pork are forbidden; idolatry is an unforgivable sin; ostentatious waste, pride, haughtiness, the wearing of gold and silver, and the taking of interest are condemned. The Malays obey the injunction against the eating of pork but freely accumulate gold and silver jewelry. They feel at least cautious about modern economic transactions involving the taking of interest but in practice may resolve the issue by making a clear distinction between the exploitation of individuals through personal loans with exorbitant interest and the impersonal interest from organizations. Finally, although Islam forbids gambling, it is traditionally an important part of Malay culture and is viewed as far less serious a sin than usury.

Ritual Practices

The Malays safeguard their existence in the physical everyday world through many other ritual ceremonies that reflect both Muslim and more ancient traditions. The most important are associated with birth, first tonsure, puberty, marriage, and death. It is believed that evil spirits are especially active on such occasions and that the *semangat* of the persons concerned must be strengthened. Almost all the ceremonies involve *kenduri* (a special feast) prayers, attendance by *imam* (religious leaders), and *gurus* (religious teachers), and certain dishes associated with religion. For a marriage or a death ceremony, there is often a feast, with a specific Arabic prayer and a specialist for every stage of the occasion. There may also be ritual feasting associated with the veneration of saints, to ward off evil, during or after taking a trip, or on any other occasion demanding special recognition. During the Muslim part of the service, the people seem very devout and pious, but the *kenduri* is the Malays' favorite religious vehicle and plays a more vital part in their religious and social life then any of the orthodox Muslim rituals.

One life cycle rite associated in the Malay mind with Islam, and highly regarded, is circumcision. Possibly because the Muslim practice was in line with previous Malay concepts, the custom was accepted without question or modification and appears to have an importance at least equal to that observed in other Muslim communities.

Worship of Saints and Ancestors

All traditional Malays venerate honored and deceased ancestors. Until recently a Malay ruler looked to his ancestors for the protection of his person and his state, visited their tombs after his installation or before any great enterprise and, if sickness afflicted a member of the royal house, set a cooling potion for the patient overnight upon an ancestral grave. The Malay magician still seeks the aid of dead magicians, founders of dynasties, and chiefs. To this belief Shiism added that of the veneration of Muslim saints, so that Malay Muslims now can turn to them for aid while still keeping their old Hindu and Buddhist saints. Persons desiring the aid of the ancient saints in solving the problems of life go to the proper tombs and make a vow that they will do certain things if the saint will aid them. Incense, rice, and flowers are taken to the tomb as an offering. The person making the vow usually has his head washed at the sacred spot as a symbol of devotion and purification, and the food is hallowed by the local village teacher of Islam, who knows some Arabic. This adds the necessary blessing of Islam to lift the ceremony a degree above the ordinary veneration of spirits.

Sacrifice

The Malay peasant, believing that every object is the repository of a spirit and every phenomenon the manifestation of a spirit, employs sacrifice as a simple and effective means of propitiating these entities. In the state of Pahang, villagers sacrifice an animal so that its blood dropping on the ground may cause a downpour of rain to cease; if an animal cannot be procured, they cut their own hands or feet. Rice, plantains, and cigarettes are cast on a rock to conciliate the spirit of rapids in a stream. The actor throws a quid of betel onto the roof of his playhouse for the white *hantu* of the air and buries another for the black *hantu* of the soil. The miner presents black rice and portions of a black fowl along with other food, cooked and uncooked, to the spirits of a tin mine. Rice planters erect an altar in their fields and propitiate the spirits of the dark soil with the flesh of a black goat. The cock offered to Siva should be yellow, and the goat sacrificed as an animal sacred to a Muslim saint or a revered ancestor should be white.

The humblest offering is selected in accordance with traditional rules. For some offerings there should be seven kinds of rice. Five was another sacred number, and some Malay offerings contain five quids of betel, five cigarettes, and five tapers to light the spirits to their fare. Even the position of an offering—its exposure on a beach, its burial in the soil, or its suspension from a tree—is significant. A Selangor fisherman seeks to placate the spirits of earth, beach, and sea by hanging three receptacles for meat, vegetables, betel, and cigarettes—one on the shore, one on a shoal halfway to the fishing ground, and one on his trap. When a house is about to be built, the head and feet of a goat or buffalo are deposited around the main pillars, possibly on the ancient theory that they guard the space between them from the incursion of evil powers.

Another basis for Malay sacrifice is the belief that the *semangat* of supernatural beings weakens unless it is coerced or strengthened by offerings of food. Thus, the sacrifices attendant upon rice cultivation are of enormous importance. The sacrifice made to the spirits at the beginning of the harvest is conducted by a shaman, who—as the accredited medium for communication with the sky father (Siva), the earth mother (Sri), the other gods of the Hindu pantheon, the spirits of ancestors, and the *hantu* of Islam—is employed to hold a seance to invite all of these to a feast. At this time he sacrifices an albino buffalo (to the Malay a sacred animal) that is without blemish, offering it up to "the ancestral spirits, genies, and goblins, owners of the earth and water of the district."

Periodic sacrifices are made also by districts or states to provide sustenance for the guardian spirits of the territory. The spirits of districts are regarded as subservient to the guardian spirits of the state, which used to command state sacrificial ceremonies to conciliate beneficent powers every third, fifth, and seventh years. In Perak the sacrifices also were used to decoy spirits to the open sea, the offering being placed on rafts that drifted down the rivers. Such state ceremonies were conducted by the state shaman, the assistant state shaman, and other assistants and elders.

Astrology

Most Malays believe that the course of human events is influenced by the celestial bodies and that harmony can be achieved between man and the universe by observing celestial omens and mystic numbers. The ancient Malay state was conceived as an image of the heavenly world of stars and God, with the palace representing the holy mountain—Mount Meru—and the sultan representing an incarnation of the god (usually Indra or Vishnu) or angel presiding over the lowest "earth" or heaven. The official structure also reflected the celestial order. Until recently, in the states of Perak, Negri Sembilan, and Pahang there were four dignitaries below the sultan, 16 lesser officials, and 32 minor noblemen. In the past the Malays also followed Hindu astrological belief in dividing the day into five ominous times and the lunar month into 28 houses of the moon, all of which could be lucky or unlucky for certain purposes. Each day is believed to be under the influence of a certain planet and thus auspicious in certain regards. Astrology is generally highly regarded among the rural population, as well as among large elements of the urbanites.

Amulets

Amulets, used widely for protection against evil spirits, are usually objects thought to be natural receptacles of a strong vital force, such as a stone, candlenut, cockleshell, or an unusual whorl in the wooden sheath of a *kris* (sword). Other objects may acquire power through magic, such as a protective thread to tie around the wrist, incense to scare demons, holy water to be waved over the sick and the newly married, yellow turmeric, red betel, and black ashes. Certain objects that acquire power by association with Islam or with things thought to be associated with Islam include amulets inscribed with magic squares, cabalistic letters, the signs of the planets or of the zodiac, the names of the angels, and the Excellent Names of Allah. Magical potions also are employed at times.

Mystical Practices

A number of other religious practices are carried out by medicine men, magicians, shamans, and devotees of mystic Sufi sects or orders. The most important and most common tool of such practitioners is the magical incantation or invocation, which has the power to produce a supernatural response. It is kept secret and is in rude metrical form. The incantation begins with a recitation of the story of creation, then invokes the gods, and concludes with the modes of union between God and man. It usually begins and ends with the Islamic profession of faith but also contains much Hindu and Sufi imagery.

230

Malay shamans, magicians, and followers of Sufi mystical orders practice numerous forms of divination. They read omens in the stars and planets, divine by observing the breath, look at the fingernails of little boys, read signs in a bowl of water, and study dreams. In the past the Malay sultans and the shamans were believed to be possessed by foreign spirits. It was thought that the sultan was the incarnation, or the representation on earth, of a deity. Although this Hindu belief has now been largely forgotten or discarded, the rites associated with it continue to be practiced, particularly during the installation or coronation of rulers. The Malay shaman was thought to be the receptacle of a god or spirit only during the brief duration of a seance.

The services performed by the shaman are varied. The hereditary state shamans call forth the guardian spirits of districts or states for periodic cleansing ceremonies or make sacrifices to the spirits of the state regalia. The ordinary shaman exorcises evil spirits of disease or spirits engaged in sorcery. The members of the Sufi orders demonstrate their power and Allah's grace by a trance dance, in which they apparently attack themselves with knives and other weapons yet survive unscathed.

In recent times there has been a tendency for the more extreme forms of mysticism to be replaced by an expression of piety in conjunction with the daily prayers. The worshiper sits on the ground, with his hands on his knees and his eyes shut, listening to Muhammad. He aids concentration by using a rosary of 100 beads that symbolize Allah and his 99 names. He is then transported in spirit out of this world as he continues to utter the attributes of Allah, and he becomes able to look back upon the world.

Muslim Law and the Adat

The Malays regulate their lives, to some extent, according to the dictates of the code of Muslim law (*shariat*), as interpreted by the school of al-Shafi'i. Responsibility for the interpretation and application of Muslim law on the local level, however, is vested in a *kadi* (Muslim judge) rather than in a community council of religious scholars, as laid down by Shafite principles. Each Muslim state ruler acts as a court of last resort on matters of religious law.

Malay customary law, or *adat*, still has great vitality in such spheres as family and inheritance. Muslim law and *adat* differ on certain basic points. *Adat* transmits arable land that is only part of an estate to a single heir; Muslim law regards the estate as a whole. *Adat* leaves the estate undivided as long as there are minor children or a widow; Muslim law permits the next of kin to require the distribution of the estate. *Adat* recognizes adoption and permits the one adopted to inherit; Muslim law does not recognize adoption and denies the adopted any inheritance. *Adat* provides that brothers and sisters share alike; Muslim law grants the men twice as much as the women. *Adat* gives a daughter precedence over the parents and brothers of the deceased; Muslim law permits her only a share of the estate. *Adat* permits children of the deceased to inherit by representation; Muslim law does not recognize the principle that the issue of a deceased person may take or inherit the share of an estate that their immediate ancestor would have taken or inherited, if living. *Adat* lets paternal and maternal halfbrothers share alike; Muslim law grants the larger share to paternal relatives. *Adat* makes a distinction between property inherited from previous ancestors and that acquired by an individual (as in Negri Sembilan); Muslim law makes no such distinction. *Adat* provides a widow with a reasonable life interest in the estate; Muslim law permits her to receive only a fourth or even one-eighth of the estate, depending on the circumstances.

Religious Functionaries and Institutions

The Malays have a simple religious hierarchy. The sultans as the "defenders of the faith" are the highest religious officials. A sultan appoints the state *kadi*, who in turn appoints the various *kadis* of the local mosques. The other local religious officials associated with the mosque—the *imam* and the *khatib*—may be picked locally on the basis of their qualifications. The local *kadi* administers both the Muslim law and the *adat*, frequently confusing or intermingling the two systems, and registers Muslim marriages. The *imam* acts as the presiding elder of the mosque and leads the congregation in prayer. The *khatib*, who acts as a preacher and addresses the congregation, is the reader of the *khutbah*—the discourse or text for recital, containing praises of Muhammad and prayers for Islam and for the rulers. The *bilal* is a religious functionary, under the *kadi*, *imam*, and *khatib*, who calls the faithful to prayer and has charge of the mosque building.

The mosque is the social and religious center for the community that it serves. Each mosque community has a certain amount of unity and cohesiveness, sustained through common participation in mosque services and other local religious activities. The mosque community also adheres to a common system of *adat* that may differ in slight details from the systems followed by neighboring communities. In rural areas the mosque community may consist of a single *kampong* (village) or of a group of closely situated *kampongs*.

Malay mosques are built in the architectural style of religious structures common to Southeast Asia, rather than that of the mosque of the Near East. Multiple pitched roofs rising one above the other are the distinguishing feature, and mosque looks rather like a pagoda with three or five superimposed roofs. Minarets are not common, although some newer mosques have them. The call to prayer is given by means of a drum, also used in the month of Ramadan to mark the period of the daily fast.

Every Friday in the mosque the common prayers are preceded by a sermon, usually consisting of conservative notions of proper conduct and religious duties. The main themes of these sermons stress religious as opposed to worldly activity and attribute "backwardness" of Muslim nations in comparison to the West to actions of those who profess Islam but do not live up to its teachings. The solution is stricter observation of religious duties, more Koranic study, and avoidance of Western knowledge and ways. Since in many areas these sermons still are read in Arabic, most Malays do not understand them. Nevertheless, the radio in Malaysia, for example, carries extensive religious programs on Thursday evening and Friday, and many of the popular songs are concerned with religious themes. Some of the more common themes are: "the world is a testing ground," "the world is temporary and perishable," and "one's fate is determined by God."

Most Muslims receive religious instruction as children, but such instruction usually emphasizes rote learning of the Koran rather than moral or theological knowledge. For more advanced instruction Muslims attend Arabic-language schools, some of which are associated with the mosques but may also be found in *kampongs* that lack mosques.

In general, Muslim law and doctrine and some form of mysticism are taught. Most students do not pursue the course to graduation but learn a few elementary things, such as part of the Koran, the prayers, and the ritual ablutions. The few who complete their courses celebrate with a *kenduri*. Graduates look for positions at a mosque or religious school, but if unsuccessful they become village magicians or shamans. There is constant rivalry between the school, and the mosque, each attempting to exert greater influence on the local religious community. The rivalry is often particularly sharp between the guru of a religious school and the *kadi* of the mosque.

Below the level of the mosque are village halls of prayer, where the villagers make their daily prayers and where elementary instruction is given in the Koran. The men and women teachers usually have attended a religious school for two or more years and have little more than an elementary education. They are primarily responsible for the strength of Islam in Malaya. In intimate contact with the common people, they give the basic instruction in Islam that is an essential part of every child's education. The instruction ordinarily consists only of memorization of large parts of the Koran; nevertheless, it formally establishes the children in the community of Islam. The local teachers also represent their village at the nearest mosque and conversely represent the mosque to the village. They collect the religious tax and remit part of it to the higher officials and are ever present in the village in an official capacity, attending all celebrations, marriages, funerals, ritual slaughterings, and ritual banquets.

The amalgam of aboriginal, Hindu, and Muslim elements that is peculiar to the religion of the Malays continues to have a profound hold on the great mass of rural and urban Malays. Educated Malays have been influenced greatly by the modernism emanating from al-Azhar University at Cairo and by secular education. As early as 1900, Mohammed Abduh of al-Azhar preached a puritan ideal of religion freed from superstition and advocated an educational approach that, for the Muslim world, would switch the onus of causing disease from *hantu* to microbes. The traditional Sunnite authorities, however, remained so rigidly conservative that in 1934 a tract on free will was burned because it had been compiled at the insistence of a Malay modernist from the al-Azhar University. These authorities still frown on acceptance of interest even from banks, companies, and cooperative societies.

Malay modernism has been most strongly stimulated by the secular education imparted by the English. For a time the modernists followed the Ahmedia movement started in the Punjab in 1900 by Mirza Ghulam Ahmed Kadiani. Later, they became interested in the Muhammadijah party of the Netherlands Indies (now Indonesia), which interpreted the Koran in the light of modern knowledge and aimed at the physical and intellectual advancement of the race. In a bid to command popular support, they took the word *tasawwuf* (the "mysticism" of the Sufi) and applied it to a system of ethics bearing on practical life.

Even before World War II, the Muslim theory of the brotherhood of all believers had been reinforced by the spread of democratic ideas. Far from claiming the possession of divine attributes, a Malay ruler sees himself as the servant of Allah and of his people. Another indication of a broader approach toward religious tradition is that, since the war, some peninsular Malays profess neutrality toward all religions and even are inclined to extol their Hindu past as a golden age of freedom and self-government.

Muslims in East Malaysia

In Sarawak and Sabah Muslims in practice display widely differing degrees of orthodoxy. They are exceptionally liberal and tolerant in their outlook on life and, except among the most orthodox, attach-

234

ment to Islam does not preclude persistence of "pagan" beliefs in spirits and the continued practice of some non-Muslim customs. Malay peasants sometimes continue to rely upon the services of spirit mediums for the treatment of illness, and they may perform propitiation rites to spirits that influence the rice harvest or the fish catch.

Even further removed from orthodoxy are those groups that only recently or partially have been converted to Islam, such as the Melanau, the Bajau, and the Illanun. Among these groups attendance at the mosque and other prayer observance in general is infrequent, except among the aged. The fast during Ramadan also is not strictly observed. The cult of spirit mediums still flourishes, although there is a tendency for their influence to be less among some Muslims who gradually are losing touch with the occult knowledge required for the conduct of the traditional rites. The adoption of Islam tends to make these groups less isolated than their pagan counterparts through their realization of belonging to a large community of believers in East Malaysia. It is difficult, however, to ascertain to what extent Sarawak and Sabah Muslims feel a bond of solidarity with other Muslims. The wealthier ones, who are able to make the pilgrimage to Mecca, are made aware of ties with the rest of the Muslim world.

Indigenous culture in East Malaysia to a considerable extent has held its own in the face of prolonged contact with Islam, which has had less impact on the society. Muslim law, for instance, is operative in the Muslim population almost exclusively in the sphere of family life, although even here such matters as inheritance are based on a combination of English common law and local customary law. Apparently, most weddings among Muslims are conducted according to the requirements of Islam.

Under the impact of Islam, traditional social institutions seem to have undergone little change. The principal Muslim innovation has been the establishment of the mosque as the community center of religious life. The architecture of Muslim schools and places of worship is unpretentious. According to Muslim teaching, it is more important to have the proper ideas about God then to obey Allah's injunctions in daily life. There is a strong mystical element in this emphasis upon thought as opposed to action.

Conversion traditionally has been superficial by orthodox Muslim standards. Apart from the profession of faith, circumcision (which long has been practiced among many of the indigenous peoples) and the prohibition against eating pork are the only requirements for adhering to the Muslim faith in East Malaysia. Attempts of religious leaders to remold East Malaysian patterns into greater conformity with Islamic orthodoxy have not on the whole met with lasting success. Nevertheless, widespread laxity in various observances, such as prayer and fasting, has not proved to be incompatible with loyalty to Islam in principle nor with profound respect for Muslim learning and piety as ideals. East Malaysian Muslim scholars who have made the pilgrimage to Mecca are greatly revered.

THE CHINESE

Among the Chinese the three main religions—Confucianism, Taoism, and Buddhism—are not sharply differentiated, and the religion of most Chinese is likely to embrace elements of all, emphasis depending in part on the area of China from which the family originally came. Confucianism unites and strengthens family life; Taoism seeks freedom from materialism; and Buddhism preaches a doctrine of reincarnation, purgatory, and obligation of ancestral worship.

The Spirit World

A large body of Malaysian Chinese view the universe as having myriads of incorporeal spirits, usually remaining in the spirit world but also wandering through, or appearing in, the world of man. The two worlds are separated by a boundary line, the distinction between life and death. The spirit world is divided into three parts: the upper heaven, the western heaven, and the lower spirit world. The upper or supreme heaven is headed by the Jade Emperor, from whom all final authority emanates. Under him are various ministers (such as the god of war and his sworn brother); the heads of the three religions (Confucius, Buddha, and Lao-tzu); and numerous others, including the gods of ten directions, of five directions, of the celestial bodies, of the stars, of thunder, of the zodiac, of gates and kitchens, and of all natural objects on earth. The western heaven is headed by Buddha (or sometimes by a woman, the Golden Goddess), who is under the Jade Emperor and also has a large group of gods under him. The exact relationship of the upper and western heaven is not expressed clearly.

The lower spirit world is the realm into which the spirits of the dead enter and are dealt with according to their record on earth. The supreme ruler of the lower world goes over the records with the help of 10 judges. Those who have led good lives are rewarded with titles, leisure, and comfort. Exemplary characters may become gods in the upper or western heavens or may be reinstated into another existence on earth in which they attain honor and luxury. The wicked are punished by severe torture, such as being sawed in half or boiled in oil. They may be banished permanently into hell, reincarnated into another life beset with poverty and degradation, or reincarnated as worms, rats, or other lowly animals. The punishment suffered by the spirit in the lower world may be mitigated or increased, respectively, by the good deeds or misdoings of its descendants. Prayer services at which hired priests officiate are among the good deeds. The spirit's destination in the next reincarnation also may be improved or prejudiced in the same way.

The spirit world and the human world are closely related. The spirit world is based upon the existence of the world of humans, and the human world in turn is supervised and guided by the spirit world. They exchange personnel, endorse the same virtues, condemn similar evils, and express mutual approval or disapproval. The gods of the spirit realms, however, do not know automatically of happenings in the profane world but learn about them through emissaries and lower functionaries, whose duty it is to record such happenings as they occur and report them to the responsible authorities. The lower functionaries include the day-inspecting gods and the night-inspecting gods, who report their findings to the heralding gods of the higher world of spirits. These in turn report the findings to the Jade Emperor and also to the kitchen gods, whose divine function is to watch over the behavior of the members of each household, particularly the women, and who ascend to heaven on the 24th day of the last month of the year to make their report to the supreme ruler. In the eyes of the functionaries from the spirit worlds the positive virtues include filial piety; fraternal harmony; sexual fidelity; industriousness; frugality; honesty in business dealings; harmony with neighbors, other members of the community, and members of the same surname group; and adherence to certain standards of loyalty, justice, ceremonial appropriateness, and shame. Negative qualities include licentiousness, indulgence in liquor, excess wealth, anger, violence, excessive pride, and blasphemy against the gods and heaven.

The Chinese believe that spiritual reward or punishment may come in one's lifetime, as well as after death, or may be visited upon one's children. Thus death by lightning, sudden and violent illnesses, and serious accidents are generally regarded as punishments originating from the spirit world. Conversely, wealth and good fortune usually are held to be rewards from the spirit world for good deeds performed by the recipient or his ancestors.

The Souls, Death, and Ancestor Memorialism

Many of the Chinese believe that every person has a body and three souls. At death the three souls go their separate ways. One takes up residence in the ancestral plaque (or a substitute) kept by each family on the house altar. It is this soul that is the object of ritual attention in domestic worship. Another soul is believed to linger at the grave, and the third is believed to go to the underworld to be tried and punished in the 18 departments of hell for its sins on earth and, eventually, to be reborn on the wheel of life. The Chinese in Malaysia, however, do not carry through consistently the concept of the soul of man as made up of three separate elements, for they also think of an ancestor as a more or less unitary personality. The function of the funeral rites is to aid the soul of the deceased in its journey in the underworld, where it must be provided for and protected from too strict an application of bureaucratic principles of judgment. When, year after year, the living visit the grave, they make offerings to the earth god, who is charged with watching over the peace of the soul residing there. Despite the apparent contradiction, it is the same personality that is thought to reside in the tablet, plaque, or photograph and this is memoralized when offerings are made at the house altar.

The Chinese in Malaysia differ greatly from those in China in their attitude to the ancestral plaque. In theory it is necessary to secure the soul in the plaque by the ritual of dotting it in, and a soul which has been so dotted can exist as that soul in no other place. In China such a plaque (actually a tablet) is handed down from eldest son to eldest son, and it is incumbent upon all descendants to come together in the house where the original tablet is kept and to engage in rites of kinship solidarity before it.

In Malaysia this practice apparently rarely takes place; instead the Chinese practice ancestor memorialism, an extension of filial piety, after death of the parents. Just as it is unthinkable during life to neglect one's parents or immediate ancestors, so it is unthinkable to neglect and forget them after their death. As an expression of continuing filial piety for deceased parents, therefore, children offer them ritual attentions. A part of whatever is given to the gods is given to the ancestors. Whenever daily incense is burned and whenever offerings are made on the 1st and 15th of the month, special festivals, and occasions of rejoicing, the ancestors receive their share; and on the anniversaries of their death special attention is paid to them. The ancestors are venerated or memorialized on all occasions when offerings are made to the gods of the family altar and, since the gods and the ancestors are on the same shrine, the ritual action carried out before it applies to both the gods and the ancestors. Nevertheless, the Chinese do not worship their ancestors in the same sense that they worship their gods, because the gods and ancestors occupy different positions in the invisible worlds and fulfill different functions in the material world.

238

Religious Practitioners and Syncretic Sects

The most frequent and important rites are those practiced in the home, commonly carried out by the women of the household, primarily by the senior female, who bears the main responsibility for them. Since children often are made to help the women in the simple daily and monthly rounds of lighting incense, it is common to see little boys playing their part, but adult male members of the household take little direct interest in religious affairs in the home. Women, particularly the older ones, abstain from eating meat on the 1st and 15th days of the month and on other fixed days.

In southeastern China the temple served as a rallying point or as a social center for the community. The temples in Malaysia have the same names as those in China, which have fixed social units, such as those temples in the towns devoted to the God of the Ramparts and Ditches and those in the countryside devoted to the Earth God. Although the gods of these temples have jurisdiction over a relatively fixed area, the congregation is not defined as being from a specific area. In the countryside a local temple may maintain a more fixed relationship to the people who live near it, but on the whole individuals may worship in the temple of their choice.

Temple priests usually are associated with the cults of the various deities, and the cults are sponsored by associations. A benevolent or regional association may have a section dealing with death and burial benefits and may support a temple in its graveyard. It also may have another section for those interested in the cult of a specific deity and may support another temple for this purpose. The cults and the priesthoods associated with them may be Buddhist or Taoist. Mahayana Buddhism and Taoism are represented by separate priesthoods, which offer their services to anyone who will pay their fees. The demand mainly is for funeral rites. These two religions are not clearly distinguished in temple organization, since the strictly Buddhist or Taoist temple is a rarity in Malaysia. In most temples both Buddhist and Taoist images are found, although they are often placed in separate rooms or shrines.

Taoist priests in Malaysia commonly belong to subdivisions of their religion that allow them to marry. Buddhist monks and nuns, on the other hand, live in monasteries and nunneries. There are two types of monasteries: the first is called "the monastery for all the world," and it is the only institution in which monks and nuns can be ordained; the second type is called a monastery "for sons and grandsons," which consists of a Buddhist "family" composed of a master and his or her disciples. A nunnery usually contains women other than nuns who have adopted the Buddhist faith by attaching themselves to a teacher and taking certain vows binding them to sexual abstinence and a vegetarian diet.

Members of syncretic religions form an important part of Buddhist life in Malaysia, and sectarian organizations enjoy a great deal of freedom, since there is no Confucian elite to pronounce upon their orthodoxy. Many of the initial syncretic religions had a history of political activity, especially in southeastern China in the 19th century, where the best known was the Great Way of Former Heaven (Hsien T'ien Ta Tao). The main concern, however, of syncretic religions was spiritual—to achieve Buddhahood by the cultivation of spiritual powers through performing yogalike exercises and reciting secret incantations. The leaders of such religions believed that they held heaven's mandate and that they were incarnate Buddhas. Maitreya, the Buddha to Come, was the chief figure associated with salvation, and often a religious leader would claim to be Maitreya on earth sent by chief deity—a female known as Venerable Mother—in order to end incorrect teachings or an unorthodox government. The Chinese sectarian organization best known in Malaysia was the White Lotus. Buddha influence is believed to have three cycles: Blue, Red, and White Lotus. The White Lotus cycle is the final one before the end of the universe, and in it Maitreya appears seated on a white lotus to lead all members to salvation.

Among other types of religious practitioners are spirit mediums, differentiated as to function, who are resorted to widely for communication with the spirit world. In the major functional branch the medium is possessed by gods, which are asked for advice and help, especially on matters of illness and other misfortunes. In the minor branch a female medium will try to tell her clients whether the ancestors, particularly the recently dead, are happy and in need of any of the things that humans can supply in the form of food, clothing, money, and shelter. The clients also will inform the ancestors, through the medium, of family events and try to gain their permission for marriages.

Fortunetellers are primarily in demand for the determination of auspicious days for various activities. They also determine the magical compatibility of couples as a preliminary to betrothal. The horoscope is most commonly employed, but divining blocks may also be used.

Ritual Practices

The Chinese express their piety by a quiet adherence to the positive virtues sanctioned by the spirit world. More overt manifestations of religious feeling appear in the domestic rites before the household

gods and ancestors and in special rites at certain times of the year
—New Year, Feast of Tombs, Dragon Boat Festival, Month of Good
Brothers, Birthday of the Kitchen God, the Winter Festival, and the
times of death or marriage. Some of the calendar observances, such as
the Dragon Boat Festival, are the occasion for large-scale public rites
or celebrations, but such public acts are not of primary importance
from a religious viewpoint. More spectacular rites involving self-
mortification by inserting needles through the body, rolling on beds
of sharp knives, walking on coals, or hitting oneself with an ax are
occasionally practiced by special cults; they are, however, very
unusual.

Chinese ritual is essentially family centered, and it is the family
or household rites that have the greatest significance; this is true even
in the death ceremonies, though the community as a whole at this
time offers support to the bereaved family in its attempt to carry out
the duties of filial piety. Of all the rites, marriage has suffered most
from the heterogeneity of Malaysian Chinese society that has resulted
in the weakening of the traditional kinship structure and the ties of
the chain of ancestors (see ch. 6, Family).

THE INDIANS

The majority of Indians in Malaysia are Hindus who worship a
plurality of gods and who adhere to a comprehensive range of ideals,
rituals, and beliefs. The orthodox Puranic Hinduism of the present
day is divided into six sects, the most important being Sivaism and
Vishnuism.

The Indians who migrated to Malaysia brought a religion connected with cultivation of the land, the welfare of the family and kin
group, and the deification of the place of family or kin group residence. Migration to Malaysia weakened this pattern, if only because
of the impersonal nature of employment on the large rubber estates
and the lack of familiar deities associated with the land.

An attempt has been made to continue some of the old forms in
the new setting. Each estate has at least one temple dedicated to a
god—usually derived from the Hindu pantheon—serving as a guardian deity for the estate workers. If one of the gods seems unpropi-
tious, however, the workers have no hesitancy in abandoning it and its
temple and turning to another deity. If workers are moved from one
estate to another, they easily transfer their worship to the deity installed at the new estate, even possibly from a benevolent Vishnu to a
terrifying Kala.

The estate temples and the temples in urban areas are tended by
Brahman temple priests, who care for the shrine, accept offerings made

to the deity, and otherwise act as intermediaries between the people and the god. The temple is regarded not as a place for communal worship but as the abode of a deity. The worshipers take no part in the temple ceremonies and merely enter the temple to attain spiritual uplift and blessing and to give offerings to the god through his priests. There are also Brahman domestic priests, who attend to the domestic religious needs of Indian families, and Brahman religious teachers. The priesthood, however, is not very large in Malaysia, and there is only 1 priest or monk for every 1,250 persons.

The average villager worships Vishnu, Siva, Kali, and other gods as need or custom dictates. The Brahman priests and teachers adhere to one or another of the various Hindu philosophies, according to their individual preference. They alone are concerned with the finer philosophical points and carry out the rituals associated with their adopted deities.

CHRISTIANITY

There are more than 300,000 Christians in Malaysia. Christian missions entered Malaysia soon after 1874, but they did not achieve even limited success until after World War II. They were most successful with the Chinese and Bornean indigenous peoples, less effective among the Indians, and not at all successful with the Malays. Conversion to Christianity, as is true also in the case of Islam, is often highly superficial and does not preclude the persistence of traditional indigenous beliefs.

Indigenous peoples, for example, tend to accept ritual and taboolike prescriptions that are in accord with their own conception of religion as largely a matter of obligations and prohibitions. No close connection is made between belief and ritual. Roman Catholics are most numerous, followed by Methodists, Anglicans, Presbyterians, and some Seventh-Day Adventists.

Although small in number, the Christians have had a profound effect on cultural, social, economic, and medical development through the establishment of hospitals, missions, and religious and secular schools that teach in the English language. The schools were particularly important to the Chinese, offering them their only route into the professions and white-collar positions and creating a large English-speaking and English-oriented Chinese group. As a Malaysian school system is established and developed, the importance of these Christian schools may decrease in West Malaysia but probably not in Sarawak and Sabah.

THE EAST MALAYSIAN INDIGENOUS PEOPLES

Basic Concepts

Animist cults, surviving from the distant past, claim the adherence of over half of the population of East Malaysia and constitute an underlying current within Islam and Christianity. These animistic cults reveal East Malaysia's ancient connections with the adjacent islands and mainland, since their religious patterns are similar to those common throughout Southeast Asia. Christianity and Islam are relatively recent arrivals, and their growing support is a result of their prestige and organized strength.

Although there are innumerable variations in details of outlook and practice and although none of the indigenous religions has formulated rigid theories of the origin and nature of the universe or of the various supernatural beings and their relation to man, native East Malaysians share basic concepts and beliefs, which are expressed in ritual rather than in systematic theology. All groups believe in a great number of nonhuman spirits, such as those of animals and of natural objects as trees, rocks, mountains, and waterfalls, which must be placated if they are angry, supplicated if various enterprises are to be successful, and thanked if they are to be favorable or neutral in the future.

The spirits of the dead, particularly of deceased chiefs, have the power to affect the living. Enormously diversified, spirits range in nature from positive malevolence to potential benevolence, and many are neutral and exercise variable influence. As a result, life is guided by a complex of rituals, omens, and taboos in order to propitiate this bewildering array of spirits. In particular these rituals surround the times of birth, death, illness, travel, and harvest. Violations of these rules entail bad luck, disease, or death, whereas their correct observance brings prosperity and health or at least wards off disaster. Emphasis is upon performing the proper ritual at the right time and avoiding actions that may bring the displeasure of the spirits upon an individual, the household, or the village. Often similar rituals are practiced in different villages, but the supporting ideology varies. Nevertheless, the prevalent assumption is that everyone shares the same basic beliefs, which make the rituals meaningful.

Indigenous religious belief and man's relations with the gods, spirits, and demons are strongly focused on the problems of living in this world rather than in the hereafter. Although there is belief in an afterlife, it is conceived as being similar to the present one. Ideas of rewards and punishments after death for acts on earth are vague and, when present, hint of Hindu and Muslim influence. The chief concern is to keep the spirit world, particularly the spirits of ancestors, which for good or ill are involved in human affairs, favorable to the living. In many of the rituals, the people directly evoke their deities, and the accompanying emotional reaction appears often to be one of anxiety. On the other hand, the approach to many of the festivals that accompany serious rituals is one of great joy.

Every living person is thought to have a number of souls, some of which may wander away in sleep or sickness, bringing misfortune to their owners. Throughout the area, it is the business of religious practitioners or spirit mediums (known by a variety of names, such as *dayong*, *dukun*, *sunduk*, and *manang*) to retrieve these lost souls and to communicate with the spirits. There may be more than one spirit medium to a village, or there may be none if no one has been called to the role. These mediums officiate at ceremonies, often to the accompaniment of songs and dancing, and they generally are the medical practitioners of the community, since most indigenous East Malaysians believe that disease is a result of the activity of spirits or demons who must be appeased or that illness is caused by the wandering of one or more of the individual's souls that must be recalled to cure the illness. In many cases the mediums are women, usually indoctrinated into the calling by older mediums. They do well economically and are apt to be second in prestige only to the local headman, whose office also carries with it some features of religious leadership. The headman must see that omens are heeded, taboos observed, and ceremonies held at the proper times and places.

Ritual

Indigenous practices throughout East Malaysia, with minor variations from group to group, are fairly uniform. The basic units of religious observance are the village community and individual households. One of the most important and widespread of communal ceremonies is that held annually to drive away spirits causing disease. Under the direction of a medium, the unfriendly spirits of a village are enticed onto a raft laden with food and gifts, which then is pushed into the current, carrying the spirits far away.

Many rituals are connected with burial and are to assure that the dead will arrive safely in the afterworld and not return to bother their kin. Before burial, care is exercised to protect corpses from evil spirits, and various rites and sacrifices are executed to prevent their souls from lingering among the living. Elaborate ceremonies also attend the cultivation of ricefields among most indigenous groups. Some believe in the existence of rice souls that account for the quantity and quality of the rice harvested. These spirits must be protected, placated when angry, and propitiated by a series of rituals.

The practice of headhunting, now prohibited, traditionally called for specific rites, many of which still are prevalent. The taking of heads did not have the same significance for all groups. For some the object was to acquire the potential force of the dead man's spirit, which resided in his skull. A supply of heads might be essential for the fertility of the fields and for human well-being in general. Other motives were revenging real or imagined wrongs, supplying a spirit companion for a dead person of importance, or simply acquiring individual prestige in this world and high status in the next.

Other means of combating the caprices of a nature abounding in spirits include scrupulous attention to omens and observances of taboos. Typical omens that indicate whether a given venture is likely to succeed are the conduct of certain birds and the markings on a pig's liver. Elements that indicate the significance of omens are, for example, the kind of bird it is, the time and place it was seen or heard, and the direction of its movement. Adverse warnings are taken seriously, and an entire village may risk starvation rather than tend the fields in the face of contrary omens.

Traditional patterns of life are reinforced by various taboos that restrict or prohibit certain actions. Among the important ones are those against incest and the eating of particular animals. Tabooed animals vary from group to group, but the crocodile commonly is revered and widely known as "grandfather." Many tribes will not kill crocodiles, and the folklore represents them as having once been men. If a taboo is violated, sacrifices are made to avert evil consequences. Incest, in addition, is thought by some groups to bring danger to the whole community and formerly was punishable by death.

Among the Kadazan (also called Dusun), the largest ethnic group in East Malaysia, the details of religious rituals are considered to be the business of priestesses, and the majority of the people remain relatively indifferent about such matters. The main role of a priestess is to conduct the various agricultural, communal, and personal ceremonies and rituals. Each priestess has her own familiar, which may be one of the many kinds of spirits. The control of a familiar, however, is only an initial means of communication of a priestess with the spirit world. Some priestesses hold classes for aspirants in which long lists of formulas are taught. A learner usually is visited first by her familiar during participation in seances, and at that point she becomes a spirit medium as well as a priestess. Some priestesses, however, who are able to conduct ceremonies have not been able to communicate with spirits and therefore cannot participate in seances. Each village may have as many as five or six priestesses.

The Kadazan believe in a great array of deities and spirits. The main deity, together with his spouse, is the creator of the seven heavens, the earth, and man. His many descendants are quite active, mainly as familiars of priestesses; but the main diety does not have much to do with life on earth, and prayers rarely are addressed to him. The spirits are divided into good and bad; the majority of them are bad spirits, the most important of which are the soul-stealers and disease-carriers. Each spirit has a specific abode, physiognomy, and role, and practically every accident or illness is caused by the actions of a particular spirit. Some spirits must be regularly placated, particularly those connected with livelihood activities, such as the water and rice spirits.

The Iban (Sea Dayak) conceive of several hundred gods, all of whom intervene in human affairs and are anthropomorphically envisioned. The Iban ritually approach their gods pragmatically, using sacrifice and propitiation as the principal means of getting the gods to act in a desired manner. The main feature of Iban rituals is the invocation of the relevant gods (since most of the gods have specialized interest) by commissioned experts before a shrine built in the gallery of the longhouse (multifamily dwelling). Such rituals are quite lengthy and can run for as long as 5 days and nights. All the relevant gods must be present at the shrine before the ritual can proceed, which involves the chanting of numerous words to describe the trip of the gods from the sky. Most of these rituals are performed for a specific *bilek* (apartment of the longhouse), family, or individual; however, of extreme importance is the communal ritual performed on the founding of a new longhouse.

Religious and magical ritual among the Iban supports three kinds of specialists: spirit mediums, augers, and the experts who perform the major rituals invoking the gods. All Iban, however, participate in these rituals, particularly since all activities have their special associated rites. The Iban is not passive before the gods and spirits, but rather he manipulates and cajoles them.

Among the Land Dayak, in contrast to the Iban, the most influential of active deities are the spirits of the ancestors, especially those of the most recently dead. The Land Dayak believe in a series of afterworlds, through which the ancestral spirits must pass before reaching their final resting place. It is during this journey that these deceased ancestors take an active interest in the present world and may be invoked to give help in return for favors. When a spirit reaches the last of these two or three afterworlds, it completely severs its interests from the cares of this world.

There are two categories of ancestral spirits among the Land Dayak. One consists of the spirits of fathers and mothers, possibly also grandparents and great-grandparents, of the participants in a ceremony. The second contains a group of named ancestors chosen not on the basis of their kin relationship to particular people but on the basis of distinctions won during their lifetime on earth, such as their reputations as rice planters, priests of the ancestral cult, and wise men in council. These named ancestors may have been dead for quite a long time and may be from villages other than the one involved. The named ancestors are considered to be more powerful than the ordinary ancestral spirits, but the latter are mentioned always in the general invocations, even at communal ceremonies.

Ceremonies to invoke protective deities are conducted on either a household or village scale by one or more old men skilled in the ritual. Commonly these men are priests of the ancestral cult, and there may be as many as six or more to a village. These priests are ranked informally, and the most skillful will conduct the more important village ceremonies. A man may become a priest if he is related, by birth or by marriage, to an older person who has been a priest. A great many men are thus qualified, but few actually become priests, since it takes a great amount of time to learn the long and detailed invocations. Basically, a priest has no special prerogatives but, since there are few opportunities for prestige in the egalitarian Land Dayak culture, the priesthood is a prestigious office.

CHAPTER 11

SOCIAL VALUES

Historical, political, and economic factors, many of them still affecting society in 1969, have reinforced the tendency of Malaysia's different ethnic groups toward separate development and minimal social contact between one another (see ch. 3, Historical Setting). Interethnic contacts are usually superficial, and stereotyping and distrust of persons outside one's own group have developed. This has made it difficult for Malaysians to put their sense of allegiance to their multiethnic nation ahead of allegiance to their respective groups.

The value systems of the Malays and the Chinese are the two most prevalent in the country. These are viewed as governing behavior toward members of a person's own group only, behavior toward outsiders being governed by other considerations, such as self-interest. Malay values give the highest priority to getting along with others, and Malay social behavior is concerned with ways of showing mutual respect between persons according to a carefully calibrated scale of social status, with highest status given to a traditional hereditary ruling group. Chinese values are primarily oriented toward contributing to the success and prestige of the patrilineal family, with effective competition and skill at accumulating wealth receiving the greatest social rewards.

Major differences between the two value systems, such as the difference in the ways Malays and Chinese view the pursuit of wealth, and minor differences in manners and tastes exacerbate Malay-Chinese mutual suspicion. These differences tend to make any manifestation of social unrest a potential opportunity for the outbreak of intercommunal violence.

Nevertheless, a small, influential group of multiracial composition, including the leaders of the national government, has succeeded in partly overcoming the interracial distrust as a result of various shared experiences. During the 1950's and 1960's this group has worked actively to promote racial tolerance and mutual understanding. These leaders have imposed restraints upon themselves and upon others in an attempt to avoid stirring up potentially explosive communal feelings.

THE COSMOPOLITANS

In the urban centers, most particularly the federal capital and those other cities where a significant number of bureaucrats live and work, a social group composed of people who have experienced multi-racial English-language education, are in the highest income bracket, and have occupational or social connections with the highest levels of government can be distinguished. Malays, Chinese, Indians, and others who participate in this group have, in many respects, more in common with one another than with the more parochial members of their respective ethnic groups. The shared beliefs, values, and style of living of this urban group have created, at the highest level of Malaysian society, lines of interethnic communication that are notably absent at lower levels.

The effectiveness of these cosmopolitans in creating interethnic harmony depends not only on their ability to have satisfactory personal relations with members of the other major ethnic groups, but also on their ability to represent their own communities in inter-ethnic bargaining for national power and influence. They are aware that if they lose sight of the aspirations of their respective ethnic groups in the course of adapting to the Western-influenced, multi-racial city life, with its English-language schools, multiracial government offices, and British-style golf and social clubs, they will be rejected by their respective ethnic communities. In such an event they would be impotent to lead the people at large, with their strong ethnic loyalties, into a national society. Therefore, they feel a need to determine afresh in each instance whether a situation should be dealt with according to the cosmopolitan, essentially British, code of values or according to the demands of ethnic group allegiance.

In determining which set of values to apply, pragmatic considerations are of far greater importance than ideological consistency. For example, there is a pride among the civil servants in a system of promotion through merit; even so, the promotion of oneself, one's friend, or a member of one's ethnic group is to be preferred to the promotion of a stranger through merit. Democratic concepts, such as belief in elections and in the idea of equal justice before the law, receive the support of the cosmopolitans but have occasionally been abandoned or suspended when the application of these ideals failed to yield results satisfactory to these leaders.

Pragmatism and the need to maintain social harmony are often given priority over loyalty to absolute moral or ethical standards. Moderation and flexibility are preferred to rigid adherence to conviction. In a recent sociological study of a small group of Kuala Lumpur bureaucrats, the suggestion was made that the relatively low status given to individual convictions stems from a belief that man is inherently motivated by self-interest and that, therefore, social chaos can only be avoided by the use of external sanctions, the most flexible and useful sanction being the desire for the good opinion of one's associates.

The cosmopolitans are selective when accepting cultural influences from the West. Western food, clothing, housing, sports, films, cars, and expensive household articles all have much prestige. Western-style education and facility in the English language are much admired and sought after. Nonetheless, it is widely considered undesirable for a Malay woman to wear Western-style clothing, and Chinese, no matter how Westernized, usually prefer Chinese to Western cuisine.

The belief in the desirability of "nation-building," a term often used by Malaysians for the establishing of a multiracial national society, is the single tenet that most clearly distinguishes the value system of the cosmopolitan group from that of the rest of urban society. The belief in the need to establish a national society stems from the awareness that no single ethnic group is large enough to successfully dominate the others in all spheres of human activity. It is felt therefore that, if the country is to survive, some form of interethnic assimilation or accommodation must be achieved.

Among a small group in some urban areas there had developed in the 1950's and 1960's a custom of paying formal calls at the homes of persons celebrating certain ethnic holidays. The annual 2-day holiday calling period is, for Malays, Hari Raya Puasa; for Chinese, the Chinese New Year; for Hindus and Sikhs, Deepavali; and, for non-Muslim indigenous peoples in Sarawak, Dayak Day. Although much of the holiday calling is done by persons of the same ethnic group, such as Chinese calling upon Chinese at the New Year holiday, the cosmopolitans have promoted the custom of persons of other groups also paying their respects on friends and acquaintances on these occasions. The social status of the participants is signalized by the number and importance of the callers. Persons of high social status expect to receive most of their visitors the first day, whereas lower ranking people receive callers the second day.

In the course of carrying out the government's efforts to reduce the economic imbalance between the Malays and the Chinese, the bureaucrats have become aware of the necessity for a revolution in the ranking of social priorities if the Malays are to catch up economically. The various special concessions made to Malays in order to give them the equivalent of a justifiable "gold handicap," to use the metaphor of former Minister of Finance Tun Tan Siew Sin, had not proved sufficient in themselves by the end of the 1960's to bring about sufficient economic improvement satisfactory to the Malays.

Deputy Prime Minister Tun Abdul Razak has repeatedly reminded Malay audiences that progress can result only from the "the diligence, determination and hard work of our people." Other English-educated Malays engaged in administering rural development programs have reiterated the necessity for Malays to change their attitudes. Government aid programs, the Malays have been told, "are useless to you without the full application of your own resources, both mental and physical."

The cosmopolitan Malay during the 1960's saw his role as leading his group toward a new and more economically rewarding set of social values in which hard work, even manual labor, business acumen, and thrift would be high in value as opposed to the traditional system, which ranked these traits as undesirable, unattractive, or antisocial.

GROUP IDENTITY AND LOYALTY

Apart from legal definition, the criteria for determining who is a member of an ethnic group vary among the different groups as a result of the differences in their respective value systems. Being a Muslim is the single most essential requirement for membership in the Malay community and participation in Malay culture. Speaking the Malay language and observing Malay rules of etiquette and social conduct are the other ways by which a Malay is identified. Biological and racial considerations are relatively unimportant in determining Malay ethnicity. Adopted infants of pure Chinese extraction and converts to the Malay religion and society from other indigenous ethnic groups are regarded, by themselves and others, as fully Malay. The criteria for Malay ethnic identify are all behavioral rather than inherited, because the emphasis in Malay society is on how one behaves.

Among Chinese the family is the source of most values, with great prestige accorded the father as family head. Chinese ethnicity is shown first of all by having a Chinese surname, which indicates that one has been accepted into a Chinese family by the male family head. Birth and race are, by themselves, not of overriding importance in determining who is Chinese. The man who sells his baby daughter to a Malay family for adoption (a common practice among poor Chinese) subsequently regards the child neither as part of his family nor as Chinese.

Inherited membership in a caste is virtually the sole means of entry into Indian Hindu society. Intermarriage between the small group of Indian Muslims and Malays can either bring the Indian into Malay society or vice versa, the ethnic group of the husband being the determining factor.

Modern education, modern communications, and modern ways of doing things had come so recently to play a significant role in the life of East Malaysia's indigenous non-Muslims that on the eve of the 1970's it was not yet possible to identify the essential evolving criteria for membership in a particular ethnic group. How much community of interest will develop between subgroups, such as between Ibans and Land Dayaks or between hill and coastal Kadazans, also could not be foreseen.

The outward symbols of ethnic identity, such as elongated earlobes, tattoos, and the wearing of loincloths and other traditional clothing, are rapidly disappearing throughout East Malaysia. Among the Western-educated group, conversion to various forms of Christianity, often as a result of mission schooling, has alienated the converts from traditional pagan beliefs, with as yet undetermined effects on the society.

In general, East Malaysians distinguish between people of the interior, who are presumed to be non-Muslim and to share the broad outlines of society in common, and people of the river mouths, who are presumed to be Muslim and to have closer ties to Malay culture than to indigenous non-Muslim culture.

The Roles of Art, Religion, and Culture

In creating and maintaining ethnic group solidarity, pride in the group's culture plays a major role. The Malays take pride primarily in their Islamic religion, which they see as conferring moral superiority upon them as believers in the one true faith and as a strong link with a great and powerful international Islamic culture. Recent efforts to activate this international link have included increases in numbers of pilgrims to Mecca, various Islamic conferences, and an annual Koran-reading contest, the final stage of which is held in Kuala Lumpur before a large audience with the contestants judged by Koranic scholars from Saudi Arabia. Many Islamic influences work to cement Malay cultural solidarity and to exclude the non-Muslim from the social network of the Malays. Among these influences are: a shared interest in gaining facility in reading Arabic script; a code of dietary restrictions that makes it almost impossible for Muslims to eat food prepared by non-Muslims; the gathering of the men in the neighborhood prayer hall for daily prayers; the weekly gathering at the mosque for Friday evening prayers; and the shared ordeal of the month-long annual fast (during which day is turned into night and night into day for the purposes of eating and sleeping). Other Islamic institutions that contribute to Malay exclusiveness are: the Islamic law courts; the Islamic taxes; the Islamic police, whose job is to enforce dietary and social prohibitions; and the Islamic professional pursuits, such as judgeships, mosque officerships, and teaching jobs.

Chinese cultural solidarity has a more secular basis than does that of the Malays, although there is considerable patronage of Chinese temples and of dramatic performances staged to commemorate temple holy days, by which Chinese neighborhood solidarity is cemented. The Chinese take pride in their secular culture, their secular theater, and their traditional painting, but the chief symbol of Chinese cultural solidarity is the ability to speak a dialect of the Chinese language and, ideally, to read Chinese. Pride in the Chinese written language as a symbol of a great civilization that can trace its roots back 5,000 years and in the language as an ingroup symbol has resulted in considerable friction with the Malays in the late 1960's when Malay became the official national language.

The Malays also take pride in their language and literature, particularly in the proverbs and adages embodied in their customary law, which serves as sources of authoritative precedent. Much of the concern with social ranking and courtesy that plays such a major role in Malay behavior is expressed verbally in uniquely Malay terminology.

Among the non-Muslim East Malaysians there has been considerable resistance to the establishment of Malay as the national language because they fear that the establishment of the Malays' language as the nation's would be the first step in the one-sided cultural assimilation of all indigenous groups into Malay society. English has been guaranteed until 1973 as an official language of East Malaysia and is preferred by some of the non-Muslims as an official language to Malay. Although English is considered harder to learn, it is regarded also as culturally neutral.

Pride in tribal languages and a special sense of solidarity with persons who speak the same language are evident among East Malaysians. Oral literature is important as a major source of traditional culture among some of the East Malaysian groups. Some traditional oral Dayak epics are of more than 48 hours in duration. Eloquence and verbal wit are highly prized among the East Malaysian indigenous leadership.

Indian cultural solidarity is also activated by the promotion of classical and modern Indian culture. The performing arts are the chief source of Indian cultural pride, although there is also considerable interest in Indian classical literature in Sanskrit and Tamil. Religion also plays a role in cultural solidarity among the Hindu majority, although caste distinctions and philosophical differences within the Hindu community are divisive factors (see ch. 10, Religion). The Muslim and Sikh minorities are excluded from the religious and cultural solidarity of the Hindu Indians.

Priorities of Loyalty Within Ethnic Groups

Ethnic solidarity of Malay, Chinese, Indian, and Dayak groups increased substantially in the post-World War II period. It is strongest when one group is confronted by another. For example, Malay solidarity increases whenever there is felt to be a threat from the Chinese. Such confrontations are infrequent, because contact between ethnic groups is slight at all but the highest urban levels, whereas divisions within ethnic groups are often of great day-to-day importance to the communities involved.

In one west coast Malay community studied during the late 1960's, persons of Minangkabau extraction were accorded prestige for being the descendants of the original inhabitants of the village. In the same community Javanese were regarded as being of the lower class because they had come originally as contract laborers. There was a question in the minds of some villagers as to whether the Javanese were truly Malays, since they had some very distinctive cultural traits. Banjarese (Malays from southern Borneo) were regarded by other Malays of another West Malaysian village as socially inferior.

Comparable divisions affect Chinese society. The results of a comparison of two Chinese rural settlements in West Malaysia in the 1960's, one of which contained only one dialect group and the other of which contained various such groups, suggest that neighborliness, cooperative activity, and the settling of minor disputes between villagers are harder to achieve in multiple-dialect communities.

The other ethnic groups, the Indians and the various groups of East Malaysians, are still more sharply divided among themselves. Solidarity is rare except in cases where the threat from outsiders is widely and strongly felt, as was the case in East Malaysia during the period of the Indonesia Confrontation (see ch. 3, Historical Setting).

VALUES AMONG TRADITIONAL COMMUNITIES

With the exception of the cosmopolitans, Malaysians view ethics, morals, and other social values as governing behavior within their own group and inapplicable outside it. Thus, although there are in Malay and Chinese society many similar ideas and values, such as the high value played on kin loyalty and on loyalty to friends and a preference for settling disputes and solving problems through the use of a respected mediator rather than through formal legal means,

255

these values are not usually applied by Malays to Chinese or by Chinese to Malays. The area within which ethical, moral, or personally felt restrictions on behavior apply is limited. Ethical or moral prohibitions seldom inhibit relations with persons not connected by ties of kinship or close association. Antisocial behavior toward persons of other ethnic groups is rarely condemned by the offender's own group.

The Malays

Within the society of the Malays, what is considered correct behavior is almost completely dependent on the social situation. Malays are always aware of the witnesses to any action and try at all times to behave appropiately in respect to their relationships with the witnesses. To be called *pandai* (clever) is the acme of praise and is applied to a person who carries off a given situation with finesse, satisfying the demands of the witnesses. To be *bodoh* (stupid, clumsy) is to be unable to properly assess, or rise to, an occasion—to be a bumpkin. Moral and ethical absolutes are not widely used; rather, what is thought to be proper behavior depends upon whom it affects.

A person is not hypocritical but, rather, socially suave, or *halus* (smooth, refined), when he changes his style of behavior or his opinion to suit a different occasion or audience. A dread of becoming *malu* (embarrassed, an object of public ridicule), a sentiment akin to stage fright, is a major factor in governing behavior. Public shaming is the major form of punishment inflicted on family members or neighbors who have misbehaved.

Styles of Behavior

There are three basic styles of behavior among Malays. One of them is the style of respect, which involves the mutual awareness of differences in generational rank and social status and which provides symbols, such as seating protocol, greeting gestures, status terminology in greeting and pronoun usage, conformity in dress to rigorous standards of modesty and grooming, that express in a formal way the mutual respect of the participants. This respectful style is often termed *halus* and is also used in social relations with all outsiders who are of equal or superior status.

At a level above *halus* style (with which all Malays are more or less able to cope) are the refined requirements of court etiquette, involving special word usage and protocol demands that are akin to religious obligations and taboos. The symbols of royalty, especially the crown and other regalia belonging to a sultan, require special handling, as their power is thought by some to be strong enough to strike dead on the spot a person who handles them improperly or without proper authorization.

The court style of behavior is the most exclusive of ingroup styles, since it is the monopoly of a small hereditary elite. Standard *halus* behavior, however, can be acquired by outsiders, as it is appropriate to relations with persons of unequal status who are not members of the immediate family or bound by ties of close friendship. Virtually all cordial relations between Malays and non-Malays are conducted according to the rules of *halus* behavior, with allowances made by the Malays for the relative lack of polish of the foreigner.

The basic minimal requirements of *halus* courtesy include sensitivity to the moods and needs of the others present, speaking softly and behaving with courtesy and gentleness, removing shoes before entering a house, consuming at least some of whatever refreshment is offered, avoiding placing one's head higher than that of persons of superior status, using only the right hand in eating and when passing things to other persons, avoiding touching the heads of children or any physical contact with persons of the opposite sex and, when at a gathering of men and women, congregating with the members of one's own sex. When a foreigner speaks Malay, behaves in a *halus* manner, and imitates Malay mannerisms, such as the way Malays point at persons with the thumb and not the index finger, he is regarded by Malays as having shown the kind of social sensitivity they most admire.

The third basic mode of behavior is called the *kasar* (rough, coarse) style and is used with intimate friends, close kin, and persons of substantially inferior social status. Thus, depending upon the situation in which it is used, *kasar* style can be an expression of the warmest affection or of the utmost contempt. As a style appropriate to intimate cordiality, it is usually used within the house, especially in the kitchen or back part of the house. The same close friends and relations who use *kasar* style in the kitchen will follow *halus* patterns when congregating in the front room or front garden for a wedding or other formal social occasion.

Kasar behavior is most often used by women. The typical occasion for friendly *kasar* behavior involving nonhousehold residents is during the cooking and preparation for a large feast to celebrate a wedding or similar family occasion. Cooking demonstrations have been used during the 1960's by various women's organizations, including multiracial organizations, as a means of reproducing, outside the home, the cordial kitchen atmosphere.

There is a tendency to associate the kitchen and cooking with friendship. Neighbors indicate the strength of the friendship between their households by exchanging cooked food or fruit from their own gardens. To give cooked food or fruit (which does not connote as close a social intimacy as cooked food) is a gesture of close friendship, and to eat it is a sign of social trust. To refuse or discard it is a hostile act. Fear of contamination of food owing to failure to follow Islamic dietary laws and fear of food contamination through sorcery make Malays hesitant to eat food not cooked by close friends or family members.

The typical environment for informal behavior among men is the local coffeeshop, which is the recreational center in the lives of men in the villages. Styles of speech and manners in coffeeshops are less informal than those prevailing in household kitchens but much less formal than those prevailing on public social occasions or at social functions taking place in the front part of one's house.

The salient characteristic of *kasar* behavior is the lack of concern with social hierarchy and the feeling of coziness that comes from being among one's own kind of people. Gaiety, calling people by nicknames, boisterousness, bustle, and earthy wit are typical of *kasar* behavior, as is a lack of concern for personal appearance and modesty. In these respects *kasar* behavior is in marked contrast to the great concern with dignity, refinement, and grooming that typify *halus* behavior. Some social rules, such as avoiding the use of the left hand when eating, apply regardless of the situation, and a wide range of behavior styles between the extremes of *halus* and *kasar* are used by the same people in different situations, everyone taking his cue from the highest ranking person present.

Achieving Social Prestige

Social prestige and relations of trust are built up slowly. Newcomers to a community, unless they are outstandingly superior in status by virtue of wealth, education, and association with the ruling elite, are not highly regarded or trusted. Persons whose potential mobility is great, such as rent-paying lodgers in urban areas or persons who work solely for cash wages, are also not regarded as full participants in community life. Having no firm ties to the community, they are deemed likely to put their own selfish interests above the good opinion of their neighbors. They are, therefore, regarded as not to be trusted.

Close family members and persons (often also relatives) who live in the same cluster of village houses or contiguous urban houses are the people whose opinions matter in most social situations. Deference also must be paid to persons of superior occupational and educational status and to wealthy persons. Such persons are occasionally called upon to mediate disputes. A friend or relative of one of the disputants will request the intervention of a person of higher status whose friendship or good opinion is valued by both disputants. The mediator's role is to attempt, in separate interviews with the contestants, to get each to concede something to the other side. A satisfactory compromise, in which neither side loses or gains all, is sometimes concluded with a peacemaking banquet given by the mediator and attended by both disputants.

Success in mediation rests on the fact that the contestants will make concessions for the sake of retaining the good opinion of the mediator that they would be unwilling to make for the sake of the good opinion of each other. It is a serious charge to say that someone is a *dalal* (fixer) who accepts money for his good offices in a dispute. Thus, an intermediary who receives a modest salary, such as a *penghulu* (headman of a subdistrict or a large village), is ambivalently regarded by the local community. In many areas the *ketua kampong* (hamlet or village headmen) have remained unsalaried because of the fear that a low salary would not compensate for the loss of prestige that would accompany taking money for services as a mediator.

In contrast to the *penghulu*, high-salaried persons have high prestige because of their ability to participate in the traditional princely or modern Westernized style of living. Government salaries are regarded as the most attractive form of wealth because of aristocratic associations. Relatively well-to-do salaried bureaucrats often exert considerable influence in the community, since they exhibit the traits associated with leadership and since their friends and neighbors hope to benefit from such a person's intervention on their behalf with powerful persons in the government. To be thought to have social connections with important persons is the single most important requirement for community leadership in urban areas and is also a significant credential in rural village leadership (see ch. 5, Social Structure).

Wealth coming from landownership or business is more ambivalently regarded. A common belief is that such wealth has been accumulated as a result of taking profits from one's neighbors and is, therefore, a mere step away from usury, which is forbidden by Islamic law and strongly condemned as antisocial behavior. A wealthy landowner who gives tenant-farming rights to less fortunate villagers, who gives frequent and large feasts and entertainments, and who thus, in essence, returns his wealth to the community from which it was acquired is given respect and loyalty by all the people who have benefited from his patronage. A wealthy person who does all his work himself, saves his money and reinvests it, instead of spending it on community entertaining, cannot achieve leadership and is highly unpopular in his community if his wealth is known to his neighbors.

Money acquired through hard manual work does not erase what

are considered the degrading means to gain it. An extended period of hard manual labor of any description is thought to be drudgery, and one can avoid it by being less greedy, by being clever or lucky, or by having good social connections. To be so lazy that one is conspicuously less well off than one's neighbors is also cause for community disapproval. Rather, a balance is sought between economic and social ambitions, and one tries to use wealth in socially approved ways. Money spent on one's house, a Malay's most valued material possession, and on clothing performs a social function, since it indicates one's concern for the regard of others. For a person of modest social origins, however, to imitate the lavish style of the upper class would, especially in the rural areas where everyone's social origins are known, be regarded as unacceptable arrogance.

Associates

Malays emphasize interpersonal relationships in all situations and usually shun institutionalized or long-term social groupings. Sharecropping arrangements, even those involving close relatives, rarely last more than a few harvests. The household is not a permanent unit of cooperation; it is not expected that boys will work for their fathers, and the pooling of family capital for an extended period of time is rare. One seldom seeks the help of the same mediator twice in a row, since different problems require that the mediator have different social skills and social connections. Ad hoc committees established for various purposes have increased greatly in the 1960's. These committees depend for their formation upon the social ties between members and last only so long as their objectives remain of immediate interest to the members.

Kin connections, although they are the ideal form of social ties upon which all friendly relations are patterned, also depend upon interpersonal contact. Malays wishing to maintain connections with family members living at a distance exchange frequent visits to one another's homes for several days at a time and attend faithfully at family festivals and in time of illness or death. The kin tie is not important unless it is kept alive by social intercourse. A Malay proverb says, "Better close neighbors than distant relatives."

Work and school associations play a limited role in social relations except when these underscore other ties, such as kin, neighborhood, or dialect. The closest non-kin friendships are usually formed by adolescent boys who have much freedom from assigned chores and parental supervision. Boys are expected to go off and have adventures before finally settling down to marriage and parenthood. The friendships formed through these shared adventures are close. Only among adolescent boys is there ever public display of affection, such as holding hands. Handholding between boys is not regarded as unmanly or improper. Between a boy and girl or a man and woman, however, handholding would be, if it were done, regarded as intolerably coarse behavior.

Social relations between the sexes are minimal. Men relax with men in the coffeeshops, women with women in each other's kitchens. Girls stay at home or with other girls, and boys go off to town with boys. There is constant worry about the possibility of being guilty of *khalwat*, the Islamically forbidden act of one person being in close unsupervised proximity to another person of the opposite sex who is neither spouse, parent, nor sibling. Being alone together is the offense, regardless of the intentions of the offenders. The dread of *khalwat* has limited the job opportunities for women as clerks and secretaries and, in general, limits the social interaction of the sexes.

Although women are nominally the social inferiors of men, they play a major role in family decisionmaking. The forms of respect for the superior social status of men are always maintained, however. In rural communities, where most Malays live, women do all the housework and approximately half the work involved in rice farming and rubber tapping. Women keep control of the household economy and also have a say in plans involving major spending, owing to the common practice of keeping the family savings in the form of gold jewelry, which is technically the private property of the wife. Since the social ties between women provide the basis for rural social and economic cooperation, rural areas are, in practice although not in theory, territories of female dominance. The failure, in some rural Malay communities, of a government program in the 1960's designed to change the methods of rice farming was blamed by some observers on a failure to convince the rural women of the benefits to be gained by adopting the new methods.

Urban areas give more opportunity for employment, recreation, and prestige for men. An adolescent boy who stays at home in his village and never goes to the city is regarded as slightly effeminate, whereas it is common for adolescent girls living in a city to be sent to live with grandparents in the home village to protect them from the dangers to their virtue and reputation thought to be prevalent in cities.

Relations With the Supernatural World

A belief that there is a cosmic social pattern within which to fit and about which to keep informed is widespread among Malays. Various spirits of saints and ancestors, nature spirits, and spirits of sacred objects, especially family objects inherited over several generations, also fit into this cosmic pattern. This belief is currently less important in Malay value orientations than formerly and seldom motivates positive action. Rather, it is after the failure of a plan or procedure that fate, the will of God, the intervention of unlucky spirits, or appropriate spirits that have not been placated are discovered to have been somewhat responsible.

One result of the widespread belief in spirits is an interest in sympathetic magic—a belief that it is possible to magically influence phenomena and events by a process of remote control using magic tools, such as miniature images of the object or person to be affected. Fear that magic is being used against oneself, especially a fear of food being magically contaminated, is common.

Fortune tellers, revelations in dreams, mediums, and horoscopes are relied upon by some, and special care is taken by matchmakers to insure that the dates and times of birth for prospective spouses are in harmony. An action for which there is strong personal motivation, however, will usually not be prevented by unfavorable omens.

The Chinese

An authority describing the Malaysian Chinese has written that they "regard themselves as part of the larger Chinese society and therefore aim at conforming to the values which they believe hold the wider Chinese society together." These values include the emphasis on the Chinese written language, Chinese family organization, and the recognition of the homeland as the source of their beliefs and ideas.

The underlying assumption that the social community that matters is not the place of residence but the far distant village of family origin in China has affected the social relations between Chinese and non-Chinese in Malaysia. It also has tended to divide the Malaysian Chinese into subsocieties based on criteria that are relevant to the home area in China rather than to their present residence in Malaysia. As a result of long residence in Malaysia, the cutoff of fresh immigration from China, and the change of government in their homeland, however, Malaysian Chinese had come in the 1960's to identify less with China than formerly, and their feelings of political allegiance to the homeland have greatly reduced in strength. The Chinese continued, however, to be slower to relate their social loyalties to conditions in the country of adoption.

Because the immigrant Chinese limited his social concern to seeking the good opinion of those at home (by sending letters and cash remittances to members of the extended family in China) and, in the new land, to seeking the good opinion of other migrants whose families had some tie of neighborhood, alliance, or dialect in China, he was able to limit the number of associates with whom he felt morally or socially obliged to share his belongings. More free of social claims on his goods and services than in China, the migrant Chinese, who usually maintained a bachelor life for some years after his arrival, was able to accumulate surpluses, cut down on socially oriented expenses such as good clothing and housing, make fairly risky investments with his surplus, work long hours and, in short, devote almost his entire attention to making money. The social ties he had with other Chinese migrants, being limited to those with whom he had much in common, were strong and permitted relationships of trust. Within this group, money could be borrowed and lent, resources pooled, joint enterprises set up, and other combinations for mutual advantage established with the strong likelihood that both sides would prove worthy of the trust relationship.

The importance of the family, which for a Chinese is an extended group of kin connected by blood or marriage through the male line, and of social bonds between families with a tradition of neighborliness or alliance in China made possible the establishment and continuation over long periods of time of formal organizations for mutual benefits built around a core of persons so connected. The organizational strength of Chinese migrant society has been especially conspicuous in Malaysia owing to the absence of this feature from Malay society. This organizational strength has been largely responsible for the superior economic position of the Chinese and for their reputation for clannishness (see ch. 5, Social Structure).

According to the traditional Chinese ranking of occupations, in descending order of prestige were scholars, independent farmers, laborers and, finally, merchants and soldiers. The Chinese migrants, almost all of them illiterate, were prompt to establish their own schools, with their own money where necessary, to provide literacy to their children. The Chinese have also been the group that has taken the greatest advantage of English-language education and are particularly conspicuous among Malaysians in the interest shown in secondary, advanced, and technical education (see ch. 8, Education).

The second-ranking occupation, that of independent farmer, has not maintained its position in the social hierarchy of the Malaysian Chinese. This is partly because of the existence of restrictions in favor of indigenous landownership, but it has been noted that, · even in those areas where landownership has been permitted, the Chinese farmer has often preferred to rent the land he farms and buy land elsewhere that is likely to give a better return on his investment. In this instance, economic advantages have displaced traditional Chinese value priorities.

Another change in social priorities occurring among Malaysian Chinese has been that the great economic power of the merchant has brought him from the bottom to the top of Chinese society. This reversal in priorities finds expression in the community-wide voting for membership on the local Chinese-language school board. The school board in many Chinese communities also acts as an institution for social administration and informal government. Membership on the board is the highest honor the community can grant a fellow resident and is often accorded to wealthy merchants, sometimes illiterate ones.

Since wealth is highly valued, so are the traits thought to bring about its attainment. Cleverness, ability to persevere toward long-term goals, industriousness, coolheaded unemotionalism, thrift and avoidance of waste of goods or other resources, as well as having good luck and knowing how and when to rely upon it, are all considered virtues.

Social Obligations

Chinese moral obligations are primarily to family members. The chief obligation is that of a son, his wife, and their children to a father, paternal grandparents, and so on, going back as far as memory reaches. These obligations are part of a religious cult of reverence for patrilineal ancestors. The child is made to feel that his debt to his father is unrepayable and that nothing he is asked to do for his father is an unreasonable demand. For a child to strike his father is to threaten the entire Chinese value system and is regarded by the whole community much the way murder is—as a dangerous antisocial act, potentially a threat to the peace of everyone. Children are supposed to be obedient and to be successful in competition in all fields in order to bring honor to the family and improve the family's economic and social status. Although the custom by which the funds of all wage earners in the family were pooled together and controlled by the senior male is no longer popular, sons are expected to work for their fathers; and capital investment plans often hinge upon the availability, or lack, of sons who can assume positions in the father's enterprise.

In addition to the patrilineal family ties which, among the Malaysian Chinese, do not extend as far as they would have done in the home village in China, the migrant Chinese have developed a network of social relationships based on friendship. These bonds of friendship, many of them associated with membership in formal voluntary organizations, are regarded as insurance against possible dangers from outside. The most desirable friendships are those between social equals and with social superiors. Friends are thought to be one's defense against misfortune, and the Chinese works to aid and promote the advancement of his friends, since the successful friend will be more effective in protecting and defending him if the need arises. A successful man, therefore, has a wide circle of friends.

A general suspicion of legalism, of formal rules of justice, and of government regulations, as likely to be applied against his own interests, has led the Chinese to try to cultivate friendship wherever possible. A friend, regardless of his occupation, is morally obliged to support his friend's interests, whatever the circumstances. If he cannot support his friends, at least he will never oppose them.

Relations With the Supernatural World

Chinese belief about the supernatural world is a result of the amalgamation of various strands of religious thought (see ch. 10, Religion). The universe is seen as amoral, a union of opposing forces, *yin* and *yang*, that must be maintained in perfect balance. Magic, alchemy, and mysticism can be used to restore the cosmic balance when required. In farming communities the need for supernatural help to ensure against agricultural calamities binds all villagers together in worship of the village's protecting spirits. Contributions for the maintenance of the temple where rites for the village spirits are held are obligatory for all village households, regardless of personal religious convictions, since otherwise community disaster could be blamed upon the dissident's lack of support. The ancestor cult, however, does not affect the community at large.

There is a belief in the existence of a type of personal luck that belongs to an individual from birth and is connected to his date of birth. The birth dates of prospective spouses are examined by experts employed by the families involved in order to ensure that the daughter-in-law does not bring bad luck on the family. A person thought to be unlucky is unpopular and is often blamed for the misfortunes of others with whom he has associated. It is considered wrong and foolhardy to go against one's luck. Fortune tellers, spirit mediums, and various divining tools to be found on every Chinese altar are used to predict the right course of action, the lucky number, the winning horse, or whatever answer is desired.

Other Value Systems

Indians

Through the ages Indian social values have been incorporated into a detailed code of rules, governing religious and ethical behavior, known as Hinduism. Religion gave Indian society its caste structure. Which caste a person was born into determined his choices of occupation, whom he could marry and associate with, and how he ought to behave. The secularization of Indian society and the introduction during the 20th century of a new stream of Hindu thought, which included among its precepts the elimination of caste restrictions, have affected Indians everywhere.

The Indians of Malaysia, most of whom are Hindus, have been moving to the cities from the agricultural estates at an ever-increasing rate. Estimates were that, in 1969, roughly half of Malaysia's Indians were urban residents, most of them engaged in manual labor and seeking where possible to move up into white-collar jobs. The urban Indian, thrown into contact with members of other communities, has found that the ties and restrictions of language dialect, custom, and caste are burdensome and almost impossible to adhere to strictly in an environment where his group is a small minority. Finding his traditional values unworkable without community support, the urban Indian has been more interested than the Chinese or the Malay in adopting Western values.

The Indian middle class, especially the English-language educated group, is the most secularized and the least attached to Indian traditional values. Members of this group feel embarrassment on behalf of the Indian community when popular traditional acts of penitence, such as fire walking and other spectacular acts of self-immolation, are practiced. Some efforts have been made by this group to have such practices banned by the government as offenses against public decency. In 1969 the conservative Hindu majority, in many ways more tenacious of custom than their counterparts in India, where many of these practices have been banned, continued their penitential rites.

Among devout traditional Hindus, self-control and behaving appropriately to one's position are the highest social values and are rewarded either in this life or in the next. Austerities of various kinds, especially fasts, are performed in order to increase one's self-control and one's personal power over nature, which can then be used to gain boons from the gods.

Indians regard social relations within the family as the ideal pattern for all social interaction. Traditionally, the Indian family has been composed of small household units, each dominated by the father, which were joined together in a network of cooperation with the households of the father's relatives, the senior male having the final say in matters of concern to all the households. Although the traditional family pattern has been weakened by migration, it remains the prototype for Indian trade union, political party, and other organizational structure, with small units of followers, each having a leader, clustering in alliances for mutual benefit.

Among the non-Muslim indigenous peoples, values differ greatly between groups. The Kayans have an elaborate system of etiquette connected with their inherited class structure, whereas the Land Dayaks are socially egalitarian.

The Semai of the interior hills of West Malaysia are noteworthy for the high value they place on social harmony and nonaggression. Among the Semai a person must share all he has and, if everyone does so, equitable distribution of goods over the long run is achieved. It is, however, highly improper to take notice of, or appear to be calculating, the balance between what one has given to and received from others. A person should share spontaneously and not count the cost.

In contrast, the Ibans, headhunters until the 1930's, have retained the warrior's respect for physical courage and manliness. In spite of their practice of housing the entire village in a single longhouse (see Glossary), they have a strong sense of personal property and an elaborate system of fines for infringement of property rules.

Among many of the interior ethnic groups of East Malaysia, value is given to certain inherited goods that are thought to have magic properties or to be the dwelling places of spirits. For example, ancient Chinese ceramics, including large Tang and Sung dynasty jars, are accorded places of honor in the longhouses. Most interior groups also attach great value to certain kinds of beads, some being very ancient, that are passed along through the family according to traditional rules of inheritance. The priorities of value of inherited possessions are changing, however, with the changeover from pure subsistence agriculture to the increasing dependence on cash crops. Traditional laws are not able to cope effectively with disputes involving modern types of inherited property such as rubber or pepper gardens. Also, the total cessation of headhunting and the conversion to Christianity among some of the interior groups of East Malaysia have weakened the people's reliance upon traditional laws and traditional values (see ch. 4, Ethnic Groups and Languages).

An interest in impersonal justice and a lawyer-like fondness for argument and skillful interpretation of legal precedent are common among many East Malaysian groups, including the Ibans and the Kadazans, the major non-Muslim indigenous groups of Sarawak and Sabah, respectively. There is also a common concern with augury and omens, such as certain animal noises and bird calls, and a fear that inattention to details of custom may bring disaster. Among some groups, taboos connected with these beliefs have resulted in high infant mortality rates and, occasionally, famine. After a series of calamities resulting from adherence to their traditional system of dealing with omens, the Kayans, in the early 1950's, began a reform of their community's code of customary law. By 1969 most Kayans had abandoned the old code in favor either of the new reformed system or of Christianity.

Social customs and religious rituals involving toasts and drinking of *tuak* (home-brewed rice beer) by both men and women are common among East Malaysian indigenous non-Muslims. In the 1960's, however, missionaries of some Christian teetotal sects converted a number of longhouse villages. Converts to Roman Catholicism and the Anglican church retain their custom of drinking *tuak* as part of longhouse hospitality and conviviality.

SECTION II. POLITICAL

CHAPTER 12

THE GOVERNMENTAL SYSTEM

The governmental system of Malaysia bears the imprint of indigenous tradition, as well as British colonial administration. It reflects also an attempt to achieve a political accommodation of its plural society.

The governmental structure basically conforms to that outlined in the 1957 Constitution of the newly independent Federation of Malaya, which provided for a federal system with a strong central government employing parliamentary democracy and an elected monarch as its titular Supreme Head called the Yang di-Pertuan Agong. The Supreme Head is elected for a term of 5 years by and from a group of nine hereditary Malay rulers who are members of the Conference of Rulers (Majlis Raja-Raja). He must act on almost all matters on the advice of the prime minister and his cabinet, drawn from and responsible to the bicameral Federal Parliament. The pattern is largely repeated in each of the 13 states of the federation that has either a hereditary Malay ruler or a federally appointed governor as head of state, a chief minister, an executive council, and a unicameral legislative assembly.

While the state of emergency regulations were in effect following the May 13, 1969, communal disturbance in Malaysia, parliamentary rule was suspended, and the country was governed by fiat under the National Operations Council (NOC). The cabinet was subordinated to the NOC.

Although standing outside federal and state legislative and executive organs, the Conference of Rulers plays a part in some of their activities. The Conference of Rulers has to be consulted on certain appointments and, depending on its composition, can block certain bills and make decisions as to religious acts and observances. It not only chooses but also can remove the Yang di-Pertuan Agong. It also can deliberate on any subject.

Malaysia is a looser federation than the one it superseded in the sense that Sabah and Sarawak have been granted special concessions concerning, among other matters, the head of state, language, religion, immigration, and the special position of the natives. The country, however, has retained the essential features of a strong central government in charge of defense, finance, foreign affairs, and internal security.

Most of the government's work is accomplished by a large number of government employees, nonpolitical civilians, and military officers pledged to serve the Supreme Head regardless of personal political views. Matters dealing with their assignments, remuneration, and promotions are entrusted to several nonpolitical service commissions. The Constitution favors ethnic Malays in some ways, especially in the fields of religion, education, and commerce, but does not impose discriminatory restrictions upon non-Malays.

BACKGROUND OF THE CONSTITUTIONAL SYSTEM

The constitutional evolution of the former Straits Settlements, the Federated Malay States, the Unfederated Malay States, and the Borneo territories into a unified nation encompasses the legacy of British tutelage as well as the indigenous political system (see ch. 3, Historical Setting). The political system of each of these elements developed in a different way. The Straits Settlements had crown colony status, which they kept until World War II.

The government of the Federated Malay States in 1896, with Kuala Lumpur as its capital, consisted of an executive and judicial branch; the legislative branch was added only in 1909. Each state retained its legislative powers, expressed through a state council, consisting of the ruler and representatives of the diverse groups that inhabited the state.

The power of the Council of State was advisory rather than legislative. Each state retained its hereditary ruler, who, although shorn of his powers, was given full formal honors. Malayan citizenship was not created, and the inhabitants remained subjects of their native states. The four states remained under the same basic system of government until after World War II.

The Unfederated Malay States, previously under Thai suzerainty (except Johore), did not come under British influence until the early 20th century. Their constitutional development followed lines similar to those of the Federated Malay States. There was a resident British adviser for each state with varying degrees of power and privileges, responsible to the high commissioner, who supervised the entire conglomeration of Malay territories.

The Muslim chieftains' governmental powers diminished under the British, but the traditional power they held through their titular roles as heads of the Muslims in their areas remained intact. British authority for their residents emanated directly from a series of treaties that invariably asserted the ruler's sovereignty while granting the administration of the region to the British in the ruler's behalf.

Indigenous tribal customs and local governments made important contributions to the area's constitutional development (see ch. 5, Social Structure). The British did not tamper with either the religious or the governmental structures, but by bringing a degree of regularity to government and permitting British officials to participate in it, the government institutions actually were strengthened.

Shortly after World War II, the British plan for the Malayan Union, which would embrace the Federated Malay States, the Unfederated Malay States, and the two Straits Settlements, but not Singapore, was abandoned after being placed in nominal effect for 2 years from 1946. Negotiations with Malay rulers and the United Malays National Organization for a revision of the constitution were begun in 1946 (see ch. 3, Historical Setting). Out of these negotiations a new constitution was framed and went into effect on February 1, 1948. The new nation was to embrace all of the areas included in the ill-fated 1946 plan, again excepting Singapore.

The principal constitutional instrument of the new government was the Federation Agreement of 1948, which recognized the sovereignty of each ruler in his state and revived the prewar protectorate relationship with Great Britain (see ch. 3, Historical Setting). Although the Malay rulers were able to regain many of the prerogatives they had previously enjoyed and qualifications for citizenship were tightened, the principle of a strong centralized government was mantained. Unlike the course of constitutional reforms in some other British dependencies, the Federal Legislative Council moved directly from an all-appointive body to one in which a majority of members were popularly elected.

The election of 1955 was a further important step in Malaya's constitutional development. The overwhelming and obvious support given to the Alliance Party added tremendous impetus to the rising demand for independence. In February 1956 at the Constitutional Conference meeting in London with the rulers of the Malay States and a delegation of the Alliance Party led by Tengku Abdul Rahman, the British government granted self-government to the Federation of Malaya, and the conference set August 31, 1957, as Independence (Merdeka) Day. With the agreement of the Federation's leaders, the conference also appointed a five-member constitutional commission, drawn from Commonwealth countries and of the United Kingdom and placed under chairmanship of Lord Reid.

The final draft of the Reid Commission, more than any of the previous constitutions, was a product of consultation and compromise. It represented the views of the British, the Malay rulers, and the Alliance Party. It was approved by the Alliance-controlled Federal Legislative Council in July and signed on August 5, 1957, by the United Kingdom and the rulers. This agreement terminated, as of August 31, 1957, the treaty relationship between the individual states and the Federation of Malaya on the one hand and Great Britain on the other.

The Federation of Malaya became an independent sovereign state within the Commonwealth headed by the Yang di-Pertuan Agong. Malacca and Penang had federally appointed governors as heads of state. Though amended in detail on several occasions, this constitution was subject to no drastic revision until September 1963.

Sarawak did not develop the formalized and concrete constitutional tradition of Malaya, but the long period of Brooke rule had provided it with a degree of stability and government responsibility. Administration was carried on by the raja (see Glossary) with the assistance of a small civil service. Legislative and financial powers lay in the hands of the raja. In the formulation of state policies, he had the advice of two state assemblies, the Supreme Council and the Council Negri, which were the equivalent of the executive and the legislative bodies. These two purely advisory bodies were loosely constituted without any defined functions. In 1941 Sarawak received its first constitution. It provided for the Supreme Council and the Council Negri, the latter composed of 25 members; 14 were official members appointed from the ranks of the Sarawak civil service, and 11 were unofficial members representing the divergent vested interests and peoples of the country. The Council Negri legislative and judicial powers allowed it to legislate the usual laws of government, to exercise ultimate authority over the expenditure of public funds, and to serve as guardian over the country's revenues. The Supreme Council, which included at least five civil service Council Negri members, served as an advisory committee to the governor, but he could choose not to consult it.

After Sarawak became a British crown colony in 1946, the Supreme Council and the Council Negri were allowed to retain their prerogatives and privileges. Ten years of British colonial rule culminated in the enactment by an order of council of the 1956 constitution, which provided a governmental structure with the flexibility characteristic of British colonial administrations.

The constitution continued the executive and legislative councils—

the Supreme Council and the Council Negri, respectively. Seven of the Supreme Council's 10 members were to be "associated with" the Council Negri. The governor continued to preside over the Supreme Council's meetings and, as previously, consulted the council and was obligated to advise it of his actions.

The Council Negri was composed of 44 members, of whom 24 were elected officials; the remainder were nominees of the governor and ex officio members. The elected officials derived their mandates from an electoral college that drew its authority from the local governments.

Before the formalized agreements that ultimately merged Sarawak into the country, further steps were taken in 1962 that liberalized electoral and constitutional processes. Further evolutionary constitutional reform was evident in early 1963, when the Council Negri raised the number of its elected members from 24 to 36 and moved toward a ministerial form of government.

Until its inclusion in Malaysia in 1963, Sabah had never had a formal constitution, but its long association with Great Britain gave it a number of ordinances that had acquired quasi-constitutional status. Originally, the region was governed by the British North Borneo Company. An appointed governor and an advisory council, composed of appointed representatives from various vested interests, maintained the necessary frame of government to negotiate year-to-year business. In 1946 when Sabah became a crown colony, an advisory board composed of representatives of various vested interests, including the British North Borneo Company, administered the territory.

The establishment of an executive council and a legislative council in 1950 brought the area closer to self-government. The legislative council, chaired by the governor as president, was composed of three high-ranking civil service officials, who were the ex officio members; nine official members, who were selected directly from the North Borneo civil service; and 10 unofficial members. The executive council was staffed by the three ex officio members of the legislative council, two official members of the civil service, and four members selected by the governor.

THE MALAYSIAN CONSTITUTION

The Malaysia Act of 1963 set up Malaysia by adding Singapore, Sabah, and Sarawak to the former Federation of Malaya and changing its name to Malaysia. Although not mentioned in the Constitution, the former federation came to be referred to as West Malaysia, and Sabah and Sarawak were called East Malaysia. In addition to the legal necessity to reorganize the legislature and the judiciary and citizenship provisions, there were also a number of constitutional changes arising from the political necessities of agreement on the entry of the new states.

Sabah and Sarawak, which were granted a special position, differ from the original 11 states in the way the Constitution governs the essential provisions in the state constitutions. Among these provisions were the powers of the state legislatures, the power of Parliament to legislate for them on land law and local government, financial arrangements with the federal government, the states' positions on official languages, and special safeguards for their constitutional positions. They are also excluded from the requirement of an official religion (Islam elsewhere in Malaysia) and of having Muslim education, and there are provisions relating to the practice of law and the position of their agricultural and forestry officials. Moreover, the Supreme Head had power to grant to Sabah and Sarawak further legislative and executive powers. This power was in 1965 extended to the states of West Malaysia.

Federal-State Relations

The country is strongly centralized. Federal jurisdiction is particularly evident in cases involving federal and state laws throughout Malaysia. There are, however, divisions in both the legislative and executive powers.

The Federal Parliament has full authority to legislate in matters dealing with external affairs, defense, internal security, civil and criminal law, the administration of justice and federal citizenship requirements, education, and immigration. (A limitation in the case of immigration is that Sabah and Sarawak must approve entry into their own states.) In addition, national development is a matter in which federal authority transcends, in certain circumstances, state rights. The Supreme Head, after consulting the state concerned and the National Finance Council, can set aside an area of land for development. The powers of the Federal Parliament, outlined in minute detail, also include authority to pass legislation dealing with such matters as plant disease, the federal capital's sanitation, and the control of agricultural pests. The Constitution, includes, however, a list of items in which legislative authority may be exercised by either state or federal legislatures. These categories include such matters as child protection, town and country planning, and public health problems. Nevertheless, in all cases federal legislation takes precedence over state law when conflict exists.

Among those matters wholly within the domain of the state legislatures are Muslim law, personal and family laws for those of the Islamic faith, and land laws. Economic or financial provisions of constitutions indicate the power relationship between federal and state governments. In West Malaysia, for example, the Constitution reserves all ordinary taxing powers for the Federal Parliament. The states may collect only the Muslim revenues and a few small taxes; therefore, they must look to the central government for grants to sustain their existence. Certain import and excise duties have, however, been allocated to the East Malaysian governments. As a further limitation on their finances, and thus on independence, individual states may borrow only from the federal government or from a bank approved by the government for a period of not more than 12 months (see ch. 23, Fiscal and Monetary Systems).

Fundamental Liberties

The Constitution guarantees a number of basic freedoms. Some of these are absolute, while others can be qualified by Parliament in certain circumstances. It contains a specific Bill of Rights that includes many major personal liberties which also characterize Anglo-Saxon jurisprudence. Basic liberties include the right of habeas corpus to protect against unjust detention and, in case of detention, the right to be dutifully and expeditiously notified of the reasons for detention and to be allowed counsel of one's choice, as well as speedy arraignment before a magistrate within 24 hours of apprehension. No person may be tried twice for the same offense unless a retrial is ordered by a higher court after the first verdict is set aside. A person is not liable to punishment for having committed an act made illegal after his actions. Citizens of the country are free to move about within its confines at will but are subject to laws relating to security, public order, public health, and the punishment of offenders. Banishment of a citizen is totally prohibited. Slavery and forced labor are expressly forbidden, but compulsory national service (such as conscription) and other service to the country, by an act of Parliament, may be made binding upon all residents.

Although Islam is specifically designated as the country's official religion, other faiths may be practiced in "peace and harmony." No one may be taxed to support a religion that is alien to his beliefs. Each religious group is empowered to regulate its own religious matters as it sees fit, to own property, and to establish and maintain its organizations and charities.

The Constitution delineates the procedure and guidelines that the federal government must follow when it finds itself obliged to pursue extraconstitutional measures to protect Malaysia from subversion. As drafted in 1957 the Constitution permitted Parliament to pass emergency laws when a substantial number of people, either from within or outside, threatened with violence the country, its people, or their property. In 1960 at the formal termination of the Emergency (see Glossary), the Constitution was amended to include four other conditions that would justify the invocation of extraconstitutional powers. They encompass exciting disaffection against the Supreme Head or any government in the country; promoting feelings of ill will and hostility between different races or other classes of the population likely to cause violence; to dislocate unlawfully the existing order; and to endanger the country's national security (see ch. 3, Historical Setting).

If, in the judgment of the Parliament, any of the five threats exists, it may pass an act of parliament granting specific powers to the Supreme Head. Safeguards of basic personal freedom may, in this matter, be set aside, although Parliament is empowered to revoke the specific powers by a majority vote.

If a state of national crisis comes about on very short notice, especially at a time when Parliament is not in session, the Supreme Head, acting on the request of the cabinet, may issue an emergency proclamation empowering him to assume extraconstitutional authority. The Supreme Head is then obligated to summon Parliament, and the latter may approve or disapprove the action taken. Thus the final decision rests with Parliament. Some of the powers conferred in the article are sweeping; for instance, Parliament could legislate on nearly all matters that the Constitution allocates to the states, and the elections could be suspended.

The 1960 amendments were fashioned to permit the federal government to deal with subversion similar to that which existed on the Peninsula from 1948 to 1960. As a result the federal government increased its authority in internal security matters and has basically strengthened its position in relation to personal liberties.

The need for emergency powers was well known to the framers of the Constitution because the government had battled against encroaching Communist subversion since 1948. This challenge was so serious that the Emergency Regulations Ordinance, promulgated in 1948 to preserve internal order and ensure success of the fight against the Communists, remained in force until 1960. The ordinance proved so effective that the government never implemented the restricting provisions of the Constitution.

In practice, although there was a state of emergency in force until 1960 and again from September 1964 onwards, few really drastic measures were taken, although local elections were suspended in 1965 (see ch. 3, Historical Setting). Emergency powers were again invoked, however, on two occasions—in Sarawak in September 1966, to justify the passing of a constitutional amendment that led to a change of government, and in May 1969, following the violent racial disturbance in Kuala Lumpur and other parts of Malaysia after the parliamentary elections (see ch. 13, Political Dynamics).

Citizenship

The citizenship provisions of the Constitution are both lengthy and complex. They are also the most frequently amended article.

The concept of Malayan citizenship originated only with the formation of the abortive Malayan Union in 1946. Before that, there was a state nationality and, later, in the case of many states, citizenship of the United Kingdom and colonies. The first laws of federal citizenship applied to persons who were state nationals or British subjects by birth in Malacca or Penang.

Malays have tended to emphasize that citizenship qualifications should consider the person's familiarity with the sympathy for Malay culture, particularly the language, and his undivided loyalty toward the Malay nation. Under provisions of the 1946 Malayan Union proposal, citizenship was to be granted to virtually all residents of Malaya. This concept of single citizenship, novel in the area, proved to be one of the fatal stumbling blocks for the 1946 union.

Laws granting citizenship were tightened in 1948 not as much as many Malays wished. A common federal citizenship was to be established over and above state citizenship. State citizenship does not appear to have retained any legal importance after Merdeka Day.

Apart from Malays, only second-generation Chinese, Indians, and other races would automatically qualify for federal citizenship. Immigrants would obtain papers on proof of 15 years' continuous residence (out of the previous 25 years) in the federation and on passing a "simple" Malay language test.

Under the 1957 constitution three basic categories were established for acquisition of citizenship. Citizenship was acquired "by operation of law" to individuals who had acquired citizenship before independence in 1957, to children of Malay parents, and to all persons born after independence. The second category was through registration of wives and children of citizens, or persons born in the country and resident there for at least 5 of the last 7 years, as well as those who had resided there for at least 8 out of the preceding 12 years. "Elementary" knowledge of the Malay language and good character were required as well as a declared intention to reside in the country. The third category was through naturalization of persons 21 or over, of good character, who possessed an "adequate" knowledge of Malay, had resided in the country for at least 10 of the last 12 years, and who intended to reside permanently in the country. These provisions were incorporated in the Constitution of Malaysia.

With the accession of Sarawak and Sabah to the new federation in 1963, Malaysian citizenship was also extended by operation of law to everyone born or naturalized in either state; citizenship may also be acquired on the Malayan terms that applied to naturalization.

The citizenship of all federal citizens may be terminated under certain circumstances, but where the termination is involuntary those who are citizens by operation of law must first be guilty of having committed some overt and deliberate act inconsistent with their claim of Malaysian citizenship. Federal citizens enjoy with other members of the Commonwealth the status of Commonwealth citizenship. They are, however, liable to lose their federal citizenship if they exercise any of the political rights (for example, voting in an election) applicable in the Commonwealth country in which they happen to reside.

The Special Position of the Malays

The ethnic Malays, who consider themselves the "sons of the soil" and who held under British rule a special position that preserved their political supremacy over non-Malay communities such as the Chinese and the Indians, have insisted that their interests be safeguarded through certain concessions and privileges. The Malays have maintained that if they were not specially favored in government employment, scholarships, and other matters, they would be completely overwhelmed by the competing racial groups, particularly the Chinese, who had obtained control of the economy and had dominated the professions. They maintained that they had not yet acquired an appreciable degree of economic power. At the same time provision of citizenship for non-Malays was increasing the voting strength and political power of non-Malays. Therefore, they argued, it was necessary to correct the imbalance in the living conditions and lives of the people in the country.

Thus, in spite of detailed provisions granting equality to all and favoring none, the Constitution has protective features benefiting Malays. Article 153 provides that "it shall be the responsibility of Yang di-Pertuan Agong to safeguard the special position of the Malays and the legitimate interests of other communities. . . . "

The religious faith of the Malays is supported inasmuch as the Constitution grants the individual states the right to legislate controls over proselytizing attempts among the Muslim by adherents of other faiths. State laws reserving land for Malays are sanctioned except in East Malaysia. Among his official functions the Supreme Head is empowered to ensure that considerable educational facilities are made available to Malays and that they receive the pertinent permits and licenses necessary for trade and business interests.

Malays insist that such privileges must be maintained until they decide that they are no longer necessary to survival. So far as Sarawak and Sabah are concerned, these special provisions apply equally to other indigenous residents in the same way as they apply to Malays and the aborigines of the Malay Peninsula.

Amendment of the Constitution

There are a number of different formalities to be observed for different types of constitutional amendments, but the applicability of these for each type is not clearly defined. Certain amendments can be made by Parliament alone, either by simple act or by an act passed by a two-thirds majority on second and third reading in each House. Certain amendments can be made by Parliament only with the cooperation of some additional person or body, such as the Conference of Rulers, the Yang di-Pertua Negara of Sabah, the governor of Sarawak, or the latter two heads of state. Certain provisions of the Malaysia Act 1963 have effect as if they were embodied in the Constitution and can be amended only in the manner appropriate to constitutional amendment.

In general a two-thirds majority is required, save in four categories of exceptional cases, when only an ordinary act is necessary. The amendments made so far have been the Constitution (Temporary Amendment) Ordinance 1958; the Constitution (Amendment) Acts, 1960, 1962, 1963, and 1964; the Malaysia Act 1963; the Constitution and Malaysia Act (Amendment) Act, 1965; and the Constitution and Malaysia (Singapore Amendment) Act, 1965.

STRUCTURE OF GOVERNMENT

The Central Government

The Supreme Head

The Supreme Head of Malaysia, His Majesty the Yang di-Pertuan Agong, holds office for 5 years or until his earlier resignation or death. Regulations require that the ranking hereditary ruler of the nine Malay states be first offered the succession at the end of the term, unless this ruler is a minor, has declined to offer himself for election, or the Conference of Rulers has by secret ballot voted against him as being unsuitable. The ruler who obtains at least five votes favorable to him is declared to be elected.

The Supreme Head is at the apex of the social pyramid within his country and has precedence over all other persons. As a constitutional monarch, his actual governing powers are extremely limited. Although all government procedures and acts are proclaimed and executed in his name, excluding the few matters in which he retains a personal discretion, the Constitution provides that in most functions he must act on the advice of the prime minister, Parliament, and the cabinet.

The Supreme Head summons the Parliament; he may also prorogue or dissolve it but only at the request of the prime minister. He may, however, refuse to dissolve Parliament, even against the advice of the prime minister. The appointment of a prime minister lies within his discretion. Although he has not had much opportunity to exercise his discretionary powers, the Supreme Head exercises influence in advising the cabinet, and he plays the important role of personifying the nation, thus constituting a focus for loyalty. He assents to all laws submitted to him, since he has no power of veto. He may address the houses of Parliament either separately or jointly. As supreme commander of the armed forces, he has the right of pardon and reprieve in military matters but not, except as specified by law, over other sentences.

The Supreme Head appoints the Lord President of the Federal Court and judges of the Federal Court and High Courts on the advice of the prime minister after consulting the Conference of Rulers and grants such distinctions as the Order of Chivalry.

Malaysia is a secular state, but the Supreme Head is the religious head of Islam in Penang and Malacca in addition to his own state. In all three he may issue pardons for offenses committed against Muslim law. He also acts as the spokesman for the Malay religious rulers in matters concerning the country as a whole. Elsewhere, the prerogative of mercy remains vested in the ruler of the Malay state.

During the time a ruler of a Malay state acts as Supreme Head, he selects a regent who becomes the active political leader of his state and ruler in his absence. The Supreme Head's approval remains mandatory for changes in his state's constitution, however.

The Deputy Supreme Head

The Deputy Supreme Head is the Timbalan Yang di-Pertuan Agong. He is elected by his brother rulers in the same manner as the Supreme Head. He exercises no power as deputy but is immediately available to fill the post of the Supreme Head and carry out his functions in the latter's disability or absence from the country. He is not permitted to exercise those functions during an absence of the Supreme Head that is expected to be less than 15 days unless instructed otherwise. In 1969 the Deputy Supreme Head once presided over the Conference of Rulers meeting at the request of the Supreme Head. On such occasions the deputy enjoys all the rights, prerogatives, and privileges of the Supreme Head.

The Deputy Supreme Head is likened to a permanent regent; but in the event of the Supreme Head's death or resignation, he does not necessarily succeed to the throne but takes over the exercise of sovereignty until the Conference of Rulers has elected a successor. The deputy, however, would be the first entitled to be offered the office of the Yang di-Pertuan Agong. At the last three elections—May 1960, September 1960, and September 1965—on each occeasion the deputy was elected the Supreme Head.

The Conference of Rulers

The Conference of Rulers consists of the hereditary rulers and the governors of states not having a ruler. The governors abstain when the conference selects and removes the Supreme Head, selects the Deputy Supreme Head, and decides matters concerned with the preservation of Malay and Muslim privileges, as well as the position, honors, and dignities of the rulers. With all members participating, the conference concerns itself with matters of national policy, high government appointments, and constitutional amendments. The conference has also been useful as a place in which the federal government can brief the rulers and their ministers on important political developments, such as the formation of Malaysia and the Indonesian Confrontation (see Glossary). It was also used in 1963 to settle, and announce the settlement of, the disputes between the sultans of Perak and Selangor and their respective state governments.

The conference makes its own rules by majority vote. Members are authorized to appoint a personal representative if they are unable to attend. It has a secretary (Keeper of the Ruler's Seal—Penyimpan Mohar Besar Raja-Raja). The conference is duly constituted when a majority of its members are present. It may meet at the request of the Supreme Head or by request of not less than three conference members, and it must meet automatically not later than 4 weeks before the expiration of the Supreme Head's term of office or whenever a vacancy occurs in that office or in the office of the Deputy Supreme Head of Malaysia.

The conference must be consulted in the appointment of the Lord President of the Federal Court, the chief justice and judges, the auditor general, the Election Commission, and the Public Service

Commission. The conference must likewise be consulted and concur in the alteration of state boundaries, the extension of Muslim religious acts and observances, to the country as a whole excluding Sabah and Sarawak, and in any bill to amend certain provisions of the Constitution. Consultation is mandatory in matters affecting the special position of the Malays as well as the indigenous peoples in East Malaysia.

The prime minister and chief ministers (called *mentri besar* in the states having a Malay ruler) attend all meetings other than meetings to elect the Supreme Head or the Deputy Supreme Head of the country.

The Prime Minister and the Cabinet

The cabinet (*juma'ah mentri*) is a council of ministers appointed by the Supreme Head to advise him in the exercise of his functions. It consists of a prime minister (*perdana mentri*) as chairman and an unspecified number of other ministers whom he selects from members of either House of Parliament. The cabinet is collectively responsible to Parliament.

The prime minister must be a federal citizen by birth, not by registration or naturalization. At the time of his selection he must be a member of the House of Representatives and, in the opinion of the Supreme Head, must command the confidence of the majority party in that House. If he ceases to command that confidence, he must either resign with this cabinet or request the Supreme Head to dissolve Parliament.

Each cabinet member must support, and must be supported by, the expressed views of his colleagues. If any member is "out of step" with his colleagues, he is expected to resign. Besides the cabinet minister's option to resign at any time, his appointment may also be revoked by the Supreme Head on the advice of the prime minister. A minister who is at the time of his appointment a member of a state legislative assembly must resign from the assembly before exercising the functions of his office.

The cabinet usually meets once a week. The prime minister or, in his absence, the deputy prime minister presides. The permanent secretary to the prime minister's department as head of the cabinet secretariat is responsible for summoning meetings of the cabinet, arranging the agenda, keeping minutes, and passing on the decisions.

The prime minister holds a dominating position in the cabinet, where he is first among equals. He has power to appoint and dismiss cabinet members. He advises the Supreme Head on the appointment of judges, the Public Service Commission, and the Election Commission, the filling of certain senior posts in the civil service, and on the bestowal of orders of chivalry and other awards. He is the chief negotiator with representatives of foreign powers. During Tengku Abdul Rahman's premiership, any program or project that needed to be emphasized or conducted with special drive was usually brought under his department, through which his position as party leader, his personality, and the part he played in obtaining independence for his country could be used most effectively.

The office of the deputy prime minister that Tun Abdul Razak has held in 1969 is not established under the Constitution or any written law. It exists by virtue of Tun Abdul Razak's unique relationship with Prime Minister Rahman and the high measure of confidence that he enjoys within the cabinet and the party. He is available to take over the administration in the event of the absence or disability of the prime minister, as well as to assist the latter in discharging his numerous duties.

Assistant ministers also are appointed from Parliament. They are not members of the cabinet but are subordinate to particular ministers. They assist in the running of the ministries, speak on subjects within the scope of the ministries in Parliament, and sometimes act on behalf of ministers who are out of the country.

With the formation of Malaysia, the duties of ministers and assistant ministers have multiplied. Under a constitutional amendment in 1964, parliamentary secretaries and political secretaries were appointed to assist them in the discharge of their duties and functions. Parliamentary secretaries must be drawn from members of either House of Parliament, but political secretaries need not be. Parliamentary secretaries differ from assistant ministers in being lower in rank and in having only parliamentary, and no administrative duties. In practice, the political secretaries seem to have been given mainly public relations duties.

The political secretary as an institution was in the pattern first introduced in Singapore in 1959. Like parliamentary secretaries, political secretaries are appointed and dismissed by the prime minister without the intervention of the Supreme Head. Political secretaries differ, however, from cabinet ministers, assistant ministers, and parliamentary secretaries in having their functions and remuneration determined by the cabinet instead of by the Constitution or act of parliament.

The National Operations Council

A special proclamation by the Supreme Head after the violent racial disturbance in May 1969 vested emergency power in the National Operations Council (NOC). Tun Abdul Razak, deputy prime minister at that time, was appointed director of operations by the

Supreme Head. The cabinet was named the "Emergency cabinet" and made subordinate to the NOC. Prime Minister Tengku Abdul Rahman, who is still theoretically in overall control of the government, served in an advisory capacity to the director of operations and was a member of NOC. The NOC was made up of a varying number of members, including the attorney general, the heads of the armed forces and police, and the prime minister. In June 1969 there were six Malays, one Indian member, and one Chinese. It coordinated the work of the civil administration, military, and police in an effort to restore peace. In many states there were also state operations committees with the chief minister and the state secretary generally serving as chairman and vice chairman, respectively, under the direction of the NOC. State executive councils, however, were subject to directives issued by their respective state operations committees. On the district level, the district officer was chairman of the district operations committee of his area.

The Executive Departments

The number of ministries may be increased or diminised, and functions may also be transferred from one ministry to another. Sometimes changes may have been designed to meet political needs (see ch. 13, Political Dynamics).

In mid-1969 14 ministers headed the 19 ministries in the cabinet (see table 9). In addition to the 14 cabinet ministers are three ministers without portfolio, who agreed to serve the government for the duration of the state of emergency (see ch. 13, Political Dynamics). The staff of each ministry was headed by a permanent secretary, who was a senior officer of the permanent civil service. The ministries were subdivided into departments and were also entrusted with the supervision of various government agencies subordinated to the ministries but not constituting part of it.

Sometimes a new department under a ministry may be set up to meet a need that has just arisen. The Department of National Unity, for instance, was created by the NOC in July 1969 with the primary task of assisting the director of operations who concurrently holds the portfolio of deputy prime minister. The Department of National Unity defines and formulates a national ideology that aimed at unifying the races.

Some ministers are given more than one ministry. The deputy prime minister, for example, was also minister of defense in 1969, responsible for the operations of the armed services as well as acting minister of finance. Similarly, the minister of labor was also acting minister of transport and minister of housing and local government. Occasionally, ministers without portfolio are appointed for certain distinctive purposes, such as to accommodate cabinet members sent abroad as diplomatic representatives, to manage the political party, and to perform other special duties. In July 1969, for instance, Tu Tan Siew Sin, the Malaysian Chinese Association president, was minister with special duties.

Table 9.   Ministries and Ministers of Malaysia, August 1969

Minister [1]	Ministry
Tengku Abdul Rahman _____	Prime Minister's Departments Ministry of External Affairs Ministry of Culture, Youth, and Sports
Tun Abdul Razak bin Dato Hussain [2] __	Ministry of Defense Ministry of Finance [3]
Tun Ismail bin Dato Abdul Rahman __	Ministry of Home Affairs
Dato Ganie Gilong _____	Ministry of Justice
Tan Sri V.T. Sambanthan _____	Ministry of Works, Posts, and Tele-communications
Enche V. Manickavasagam _____	Ministry of Transport [3] Ministry of Labor Ministry of Local Government and Housing
Dato Haji Abdul Rahman Ya'akub ____	Ministry of Education
Tan Sri Sardon _____	Ministry of Health
Enche Mohammed Khir bin Johari ____	Ministry of Commerce and Industry
Tan Sri Fatimah binti Haji Hashim __	Ministry of Welfare Services
Tan Sri Temenggong Jugah anak Ba-rieng _____	Ministry of Sarawak Affairs
Hamzah bin Dato Abu Samah _____	Ministry of Information and Broad-casting
Tuan Haji Mohamed Ghazali bin Jawi_	Ministry of Agriculture and Coopera-tives
Enche Abdul Ga'afar bin Baba _____	Ministry of National and Rural De-velopment Ministry of Lands and Mines

[1] Also included in the cabinet are ministers without portfolio Tun Tan Siew Sin, Enche Khaw Kai Boh, and Enche Lee Siok Yew.

[2] Also deputy prime minister.

[3] Acting.

Other Constitutionally Provided Bodies and Officials

Other governmental bodies exist that are not departments but over which general policy control is exercised by the government through a minister. These have a discretion in their day-to-day administration that is not permitted to a government department.

The National Land Council is one such body with legislative functions. It meets once a year at least, and more frequently if summoned by the chairman, to formulate national land policy, particularly that relating to such kinds of land utilization as mining, agriculture, and forestry, and to advise on any matter put to it by the federal or state authorities (see ch. 18, Agriculture). The chairman must be a minister appointed by the federal government, which also appoints up to 10 other members. Each state is represented by one member appointed by the ruler or governor. The chairman has an original but no casting vote. While the states have a voice in this body, the control lies with the federal government. Sabah and Sarawak are relieved of the necessity of following the policies of the National Land Council unless they choose to do so; while so relieved, their representatives on the council are not entitled to vote. Should either of these two states elect to be bound by the council, that state then acquired a vote in the body; however, the federal government also may add another voting representative, thereby keeping its voting control in the council.

The National Finance Council consists of 15 persons, including the prime minister, such other ministers as are named by him, and one representative from each state appointed by the ruler or governor. It may be summoned by the prime minister as often as he considers necessary and whenever the representatives of three or more states demand a meeting, but there shall be at least one meeting a year. It deliberates on any matter of financial policy put to it and must be consulted on certain matters, notably the raising of loans, the issue of grants to state governments, the assignment of taxes or fees to states, and questions of national development. The National Finance Council is not empowered to make policy that is binding on the federal government or the states.

The Election Commission reviews the division of the country into constituencies, conducts elections, and keeps electoral rolls. It functions in connection with both federal and state electoral matters. It consists of a chairman and three other members, appointed by the Supreme Head, with the advice of the Conference of Rulers. Originally this body enjoyed a substantial measure of independence. Its powers were reduced in 1962, however, when its ability to delimit the areas of constituencies were curbed, and the final decisions on boundaries were given to Parliament.

The commissioners usually hold office to age 65. They can be removed from office only by a special tribunal convened by the Supreme Head at the request of the prime minister.

The National Council for Local Government, which was established in a constitutional amendment in 1960, formulates national policy for the promotion, development, and control of local government and for the administration of any relevant laws. In particular, any projected legislation on local government can be examined with a view to securing uniformity. The composition and frequency of meeting of the council are the same as that of the National Land Council, except that the chairman shall have a casting vote in addition to his prerogative to vote on any question before the council.

The principal law officer of Malaysia is the attorney general. He is the legal adviser to the Supreme Head, the prime minister, and the cabinet. He also is the titular head of his profession. The attorney general must be a person qualified to be a judge of the Federal Court. He is appointed by the Supreme Head on the advice of the prime minister. The attorney general has the right of audience in any court or tribunal and takes precedence over any other person appearing before court. Either House of Parliament may appoint him a member of any of its committees.

The auditor general, appointed by the Supreme Head with the advice of the prime minister, after consultation with the Conference of Rulers, audits the accounts of the federal government and the states. His reports are given to the Supreme Head for submission to the House of Representatives. Reports relating to the accounts of a state are given to its ruler or governor for submission to the legislature. The auditor general is independent of the executive and cannot be removed from office except on similar grounds and in the like manner as a judge of the Federal Court.

The Parliament

Parliament consists of two houses: the Senate (Dewan Negara) and the House of Representatives (Dewan Ra'ayat). The 58-member Senate is made up of 26 elected members (two from each state) and 32 members appointed by the Supreme Head upon recommendation by the prime minister. The elected members are selected by their individual state legislatures and are frequently, but not necssarily, members of those bodies. The appointed senators are persons who, in the Supreme Head's opinion, "have rendered distinguished public service or have achieved distinction in the professions, commerce, industry, agriculture, cultural activities, or social service, or are representatives of racial minorities, or are capable of representing the interest of the aborigines."

The usual term of office of a senator is 6 years, regardless of parliamentary sessions or interruptions by dissolutions, but initially some were appointed for shorter periods so that all the senators' terms would not end in the same year. Parliament is empowered by the Constitution to increase the number of elected senators from two to three in each state, provided that they be elected by direct vote, but it can also decrease their number and remove appointed senators. The 1964 amendment, however, put the elected senators in a minority for the first time since the Constitution first came into operation; meanwhile the power to increase the number of elected senators had not been exercised.

The size of the House of Representatives, which can be altered by law, consisted in 1969 of 144 elected members—104 from West Malaysia, 24 from Sarawak, and 16 from Sabah. By temporary prescription the Constitution provided that parlimentary representatives from Sabah and Sarawak be selected by their state legislative assemblies. The representatives of the West Malaysian states are popularly elected. The first Malaysia-wide direct election of the members of the House was held in May 1969; however, the temporary suspension of parliamentary rule in the wake of the communal disorder that followed the elections precluded the newly elected members from taking their seats. Elections in East Malaysia were postponed. Tenure for members of the House of Representatives is set at 5 years, but it may be less if Parliament is dissolved.

Every citizen resident in Malaysia is qualified to be a member of the Senate if he is not less than 30 years old and of the House of Representatives if he is not less than 21 years old, unless otherwise disqualified by law. Residence, a qualification not defined in the Constitution, denotes a degree of connection with the country. Whether a person is qualified to be a member of either house of Parliament is a matter for the High Court of the region where the election took place.

If a member of either house is absent for a period of 6 months, that house may declare his seat vacant. No person can be a member of both houses, but a member of Parliament may be simultaneously a member of a state legislature. Persons who are appointed to the federal cabinet must resign their membership in Parliament.

Each house selects its own officers (president and deputy president of the Senate, Speaker and deputy Speaker of the House) and designates committees for the consideration of legislative motions. Originally the Speaker had to be a member of the House; this was changed by an amendment to the Constitution passed in 1964, and in November 1964 a nonelected member was chosen as Speaker. Each house makes its own rules, legislates by majority vote (the presiding officer voting only to break a tie—a prerogative that a nonelected Speaker does not have), and has a clerk with a staff. Members of Parliament enjoy parliamentary immunity and have traveling, postal, telephone, and medical privileges.

Parliament must be summoned by the Supreme Head at least once every 6 months. If a parliament is dissolved, a general election must be held within 60 days; the newly elected Parliament must meet within 90 days of the dissolution.

Most bills may originate in either house, usually with assistance of the appropriate ministry. Money bills originate only in the House of Representatives and must be proposed by a cabinet minister. Money bills, once signed by the Supreme Head, can become law without Senate consent, though the Senate has the power to delay them for a month. Other bills can bypass Senate consent if they are passed twice by the House in successive sessions—a year having elapsed between passages. Bills are given three readings—one when they are introduced, one when they are debated and voted on section by section, and one when they are finally voted on. A law, after being signed by the Supreme Head, must be published before it comes into force.

The Judiciary

The Constitution provides for a judiciary independent of the executive and legislative. It establishes the Federal Court, consisting of the Lord President and two chief justices of the High Courts and four other judges.

The judiciary, apart from religious courts, is an entirely federal service (see ch. 10, Religion). Courts subordinate to the High Courts are provided for, not in the Constitution, but by federal law.

One of the two High Courts is for West Malaysia and one for East Malaysia, and each is presided over by a regional chief justice. Each has not fewer than four other judges, to a maximum of 12 for West Malaysia and eight for East Malaysia, which had only four in 1969. Subject to original jurisdiction vested in the Federal Court for certain matters, the High Courts have unlimited jurisdiction in civil and criminal cases arising under federal and state law. Appeals go to the Federal Court, presided over by the Lord President, which has original jurisdiction in constitutional cases and advisory jurisdiction on constitutional matters referred to it by the Supreme Head. Appeal may be taken from the Federal Court to the Judicial Committee of the Privy Council in London, a procedure derived from membership in the British Commonwealth. The consent of the Supreme Head must be obtained for such an appeal, and the recommendation of the Privy Council is submitted to him without interference from either the British or the Malaysian government.

The independence of the higher ranks of the judiciary is secured by the legal qualifications laid down for appointment, the required consultations before appointment, the security of tenure and remuneration, and the restrictions on discussion of judicial conduct in legislatures. The Lord President and the judges of the Federal Court, and the chief justices and judges of the High Courts are appointed by the Supreme Head on the advice of the prime minister after consulting the Conference of Rulers. A 1966 constitutional amendment provided that, with minor exceptions, a judge of the High Court appointed to the Federal Court would cease to be a member of the High Court.

A judge can be removed from office on the ground of misbehavior or inability to discharge his judicial functions properly, but the procedure for removal was made cumbersome in order to safeguard judicial independence. The removal of the judge of the High Court or the Federal Court is placed outside the competence of both executive and legislature and entrusted, in effect, to a tribunal of judges and ex-judges.

By the 1957 constitution the final word in the selection of judges for appointment lay with the Judicial and Legal Service Commission, but this power was transferred to the prime minister in 1960 when the commission was temporarily abolished. (The commission was later restored, although the power transferred to the prime minister was not reclaimed). Before framing his recommendation to the Supreme Head, the prime minister must consult the Lord President of the Federal Court in all judicial appointments except that of a Lord President. In addition to the Lord President, he must consult the chief justices of the High Courts when appointing a federal court judge or chief justice, and the chief ministers concerned when appointing a chief justice for East Malaysia, and the chief justice concerned when appointing a judge to a High Court. In addition, before acting on the advice of the prime minister, the Supreme Head must consult the Conference of Rulers.

Among the functions of the judiciary is that of considering the validity of acts of Parliament and enactments and ordinances of state legislatures. The criterion is consistency with the Constitution. In terms of administration, the court system constitutes the Judiciary Department of the Ministry of Justice.

The Public Services

More than a hundred years of British hegemony bequeathed a distinctive British flavor to Malaysia's public services. Before independence in 1957, the public services were composed of two groups. At the top a relatively small and elite Malayan Civil Service, traditionally staffed by British and select Malay officials, presented the country with a professional phalanx of administrators. The Civil Service provided practically all the senior administrative officials of the federal government, with the lower reaches of the government staffed by other public servants.

In 1956, a year before independence, the White Paper on Malayanization issued by the government set the stage for the withdrawal of European, mainly British, civil servants. The exodus of the expatriate civil servants led to serious shortages of trained administrators. Vacancies were filled by promoting state civil service employees. A few were recruited directly from the state services of the former Unfederated Malay States. This policy resulted not only in filling high positions with men not qualified to hold them, but also created vacancies at lower levels for which competent and experienced replacements were not available.

At the outset the former Federation government had found it difficult to entice qualified young men into its ranks. Rapid economic growth in the area enabled private businessmen to offer higher salaries than the government could pay and thus obtain the services of many of the most able college graduates. Furthermore, the government, through its emphasis on Malayanization, denied itself in many instances the services of qualified Chinese and, to a lesser extent, Indian applicants. Nevertheless, the regular and secure salary offered by civil service and the prestige attached to holding an official government title have provided some incentive to young Malays to prepare themselves for government service.

In services requiring a general educational background, the Malays usually were in the majority, but in technical and professional services requiring a scientific, medical, or mathematical background, the Chinese predominated. Indians were particularly strongly represented in the railways, in public works, and in telecommunications.

Apart from Parliament and its staff, ministers, the higher ranks of the judiciary, the attorney general, the auditor general, employees of independent statutory corporations, and royalty itself, public servants are governed by one general and four specialist commissions. These are the Judicial and Legal Service Commission (for the government legal service, other than the attorney general, and the lower ranks of the judiciary), the Railway Service Commission, the Armed Forces Council, and the Police Force Commission. Public servants not subject to one of these four commissions are under the Public Service Commission. These commissions are responsible for the appointment, promotion, and discipline of members of their respective services. This does not include the special posts that the Supreme Head, a ruler, or governor designates to be within the realm of his personal appointment. Final selection, however, remains with the relevant commission.

Except for those who are members of these commissions by virtue of the offices they hold, all members are appointed by the Supreme Head with the advice of the prime minister and the Conference of Rulers. Their usual tenure in office is 5 years, and they can be removed only by a panel of judges and only for such grounds as misbehavior or inability to perform their duties adequately.

The service commissions have jurisdiction only over federal positions. All the states except Penang and Malacca are authorized to establish their own state public service commissions, and over half of them have done so. Sometimes federally appointed civil servants are assigned to entirely state-based operations. In such cases the employee remains under the jurisdiction of the government that hired him, but is paid by the one on whose project he is employed.

Civil servants are classified into four major divisions. Those in the first division have the highest educational or professional qualifications. They occupy the top administrative positions in the federal government and advise members of the cabinet and high state officials. At times serving in different states as district officers, they exercise considerable power on the local level. The second division includes executive or supervisory personnel and requires less rigid educational or professional credentials. Many of these federal junior officers, state civil employees, police officers, and various other personnel rise to the top echelon. The last two divisions overlap, but in general one includes such employees as stenographers and junior members of the police force, and the other, junior postal workers and less skilled office workers.

Civil service employees are by law denied the privilege of active political participation granted to other citizens. A civil servant may not solicit votes for any political party, nor may he hold party office. He is also forbidden to divulge official information for political reasons. His loyalty is expected to be to the incumbent government regardless of its permanence or his preferences. A federal civil servant, unlike a cabinet member, cannot be censured by Parliament for any lawful actions he might take at the command of the cabinet member.

State Government

Each of the 13 states is governed by the provisions of a written constitution, the dictates of its legislative assembly, and its state executive. States in West Malaysia are more closely linked to the federal government than Sabah and Sarawak in East Malaysia, which have been granted certain discretionary authority to protect their special interests.

Every state has an executive council (cabinet) to advise the ruler or the governor, headed by a chief minister. Each executive council is collectively responsible to the state legislature. A ministerial system is employed in Sabah and Sarawak. There are four political residencies in Sabah and five administrative divisions in Sarawak.

Rulers and Governors

The ruler or governor is the chief executive of each state. The rulers of the nine dynastic states of West Malaysia (Johore, Kedah, Kelantan, Negri Sembilan, Pahang, Perak, Perlis, Selangor, and Trengganu) are chosen by a variety of methods, laid down in each state constitution. Seven of the nine are called sultans. The ruler of Perlis has the title of raja, and that of Negri Sembilan is known as the Yang di-Pertuan Besar. Eight of the nine usually inherit their titles from the previous rulers of the state, who, in most instances, were their fathers; the Yang di-Pertuan Besar of Negri Sembilan is usually chosen from among nine local Malay chiefs. The nine rulers hold office for life, unless they become unfit. The heads of the states of Malacca, Penang, and Sarawak are governors, and that of Sabah is designated Yang di-Pertua Negara.

The governors of the state are chosen by the Supreme Head, acting on his own discretion, after consulting the state's chief minister. They need not be Muslims, although at the beginning of 1965 all of them were. Governors, who must be federal citizens by birth, are usually appointed for 4 years at a time and may be reappointed. A governor may resign at any time, but he can only be removed from office by the Supreme Head after a resolution has been passed by the state legislative assembly (by not less than a two-thirds majority of its total membership) calling for his removal.

Together with the Yang di-Pertua Negara of Sabah, the governors represent their states in the Conference of Rulers but do not participate in discussions relating to the status of state rulers or the election of the Supreme Head. They have similar functions to those of the dynastic rulers, but they are not the titular heads of Islam in their respective states.

The rulers and governors are not directly responsible to the political dictates of the populace. They do, however, act upon the advice of a state executive council, which is chaired by the chief minister and which retains collective responsibility to the legislature (see ch. 13, Political Dynamics).

The chief minister, who is the state's effective political leader, is appointed by the ruler or governor from the fully elected state legislative assembly. His function in a state is much like that of the prime minister of the federal government in the cabinet, and the procedure of his selection to, and his tenure of, office is similar.

Chief ministers accompany their rulers or governors to the Conference of Rulers, and the advice they tender to them is that which may be determined by the state executive council. The head of state, however, has a sphere in which he may act "in his discretion," which to some extent corresponds to the discretionary sphere of the Supreme Head, such as the appointment of the chief minister or the withholding of consent to a request for the dissolution of the legislative assembly. The nine rulers, however, have a wider field of discretion than does the Supreme Head, arising from their more permanent nature and from the fact that each is head of the Muslim religion in his state. Each may also act without ministerial advice on the making of a request for a meeting of the Conference of Rulers concerned solely with the position of the rulers or with religious acts and on certain other matters, including the regulation of royal courts and palaces.

The ruler of a dynastic state, as the titular head of Islam in his state, is granted discretionary pardoning powers in matters dealing with violations of Muslim law. In criminal offenses the ruler may commute sentences upon the advice of the state pardons board, which he chairs and the majority of whose members are appointed by him. Rulers also select and bestow honors and awards upon their citizens.

Legislative Assemblies

Constitutionally, the legislature of each state bears the same relationship to the state executive as the Federal Parliament bears to the federal executive. The state executive, for example, is responsible to the state legislature and cannot remain in office without the legislature's support. Harmony between the two bodies, however, is secured by the fact that the state executive and the majority of the state legislaure are members of the same political party.

All the states have only a single-chamber legislative body, presided over by a Speaker who is elected by the members from among their number (except in the case of Sabah and Sarawak). The Sarawak legislative assembly, the Council Negri, had 36 elected members and three nominated members in 1969. The elected members are indirectly elected through the district councils and divisional advisory councils. In 1969 the legislative assembly of Sabah contained 32 members, indirectly elected through the district council and the residency advisory councils, and five nominated members.

Each state legislative assembly has the right to order its own procedure, but in general the assemblies follow procedures similar to those employed by the federal legislature. Most state legislatuers meet only four or five times a year, and these meetings are usually very short except for the budget debate. The most important state function, land regulation, is the subject that is discussed at the greatest length. Three officials, the state secretary, the state legal adviser, and the state financial officer, may attend sessions; but their duties are purely advisory, and they cannot dictate policy or vote. Members enjoy parliamentary privileges. The term of an assembly is five years unless earlier dissolved. Persons employed by the federal government may not be elected to the state legislatures.

Executive Councils

On most issues the ruler or governor of each state is obliged to act on the advice of the state executive council. In Sarawak this body is called the Supreme Council; in Sabah it is known as the cabinet. In Sarawak the Supreme Council must have at least five members appointed by the governor, a majority of whom must be members of both civil service and the Council Negri, the legislative body. Although specific portfolios are not designated in the Constitution for these officials, there is a tendency among most states to designate government departments to members of the executive councils.

The executive council remains responsible to the people because it must command a majority in the legislative assembly of the state. When it loses that majority, it must either resign and be replaced by another executive council that can obtain a majority (as in Trengganu in 1961), or the ruler or governor must dissolve the assembly and cause new elections to be held.

The Judiciary

Lower courts, established by federal law, include sessions courts, magistrate courts, and *penghulu* courts, which exercise a limited and local jurisdiction. Muslim religious courts are established by the state legislatures and form a separate system. There is no state judicial system with general functions.

Both the magistrate courts and the sessions courts are situated in principal urban and rural centers and have civil and criminal jurisdiction. Civil cases come before one court or another according to the sum involved, and criminal cases, according to the seriousness of the offense. Only the magistrate courts have appellate jurisdiction.

The sessions courts are presided over by a president, who is appointed by the Supreme Head. He is a member of the federal legal service and is a qualified barrister or solicitor. The courts' criminal jurisdiction covers the less serious indictable offenses for which the maximum penalty does not exceed seven years' imprisonment and civil cases for which the maximum penalty is not over M$2,000 (3.06 Malaysian dollars equal US$1). Civil cases are usually heard without jury.

The West Malaysia magistrate courts consist of first- and second-class courts and have both civil and criminal jurisdiction, although of more restricted nature than that of sessions court. Second-class courts are usually identical with the assistant district officer and try few cases in the absence of a first-class court. First-class magistrate courts consist of either the district or circuit magistrates. The officers come from either the federal legal service or are seconded from the administrative to the judicial department for varying periods of up to 3 years. They are appointed by the rulers of the states in which they officiate on the recommendation of the chief justice.

First-class magistrate courts hear criminal cases for which the penalty does not exceed 3 years' imprisonment or M$2,000 and civil cases for which the penalty is not more than M$1,000. First-class magistrate courts also act as courts of preliminary inquiry in cases over which the High Court has jurisdiction and in cases involving unnatural death. In the states of Penang and Malacca, the coroner sits with the jury.

In each *mukim* (a subdistrict) in West Malaysia is a *penghulu* court in which the *penghulu* (*mukim* chief) has varied jurisdiction over minor disputes and misdemeanors relating to Malay customary law. Appeals from the *penghulu* courts are submitted to the district officer, who also has the power of revision. From the district officer, an appeal goes to the native court of appeal, which is composed of a judge of the High Court as president and two other persons appointed by the governor.

The *kadi* (Muslim judge) court of West Malaysia is a traditional state court, reflecting the ruler's role in Muslim affairs. It applies only to Muslims and has jurisdiction over such matters of personal status as marriage divorce, and inheritance. Appeals from the *kadi* courts may be taken straight to the state councils. Such courts continue to operate as much as they did before federation.

Both Sabah and Sarawak have their own systems of lower courts, but in December 1951 these two states combined the top level of their judiciary. After merger the Supreme Court was replaced by the High Court with two registries, one for Sabah and one for Sarawak. The High Court sits alternately in Kota Kinabalu, Sabah, and Kuching, Sarawak.

The High Court in East Malaysia has original and appellate jurisdiction over the more serious or important civil and criminal cases; over civil suits for recovery of debts of over M$500; over disputes about land titles; over suits concerning specific performances of contracts; and over all types of criminal offenses committed in any of the territories, perpetrated on the high seas on ships registered in one of the territories or committed by subjects of one of the territories on ships, whether registered or not. The court has the power to pass any sentence authorized by law, including the death sentence. It may hear and determine all appeals from decisions of the territorial courts in both criminal and civil matters.

The High Court is empowered to go beyond the precedents established by lower courts, when there are minor local variances of procedure and interpretation, and rests its decisions on its own precedents or findings even when these differ from the established practices in the particular territory from which the case was appealed. Appeals go to the High Court from the judgments of the first-class magistrates, sitting in either original or appellate jurisdiction, and from the judgments of second-class magistrates.

Below the High Court are three court systems: the district courts of Sarawak, which have civil and criminal jurisdiction; the magistrate courts of Sabah; and the native courts of both states. They apply law derived from English common law and local customary law.

Local Government

Local self-government was a new and largely still-developing institution in 1969, although some local boards of an advisory character existed before World War II. It has always been linked to the state governments rather than to the federal government.

In the rural areas the basic pattern was that of districts, each headed by a district officer, who before independence was a key figure in his area of jurisdiction. Drawn from the civil service, the district officer combined administrative, judicial, and policy functions in representing government to the people of the district. The district officer holds the power and duties of a magistrate, although he seldom acts in a judicial capacity. Appeals from *penghulu* courts may be submitted to him. The district officer is appointed by and responsible to the chief executive of the state, but also works closely with state and federal officials. He collects certain types of taxes and fees and can make small, temporary land grants under certain conditions.

Under the district officer is an assistant district officer who, besides assisting the district officer, generally has a specific responsibility for supervising a land office. Within the districts were the *mukims*, of which there are over 900 in West Malaysia administered by Malay *penghulu*. A *mukim* may include a large, sparsely inhabited tract of land or may be composed of one or several *kampongs* (villages) and the surrounding territory.

The *penghulu*, usually elected for life, is the liaison official between state or federal bureaucracy and the *kampong*. He is answerable to the district officer. He receives a salary in addition to remission of at least part of his land rent. He appoints a number of assistants (variously known as *naib* or *sidang*), who usually receive as remuneration remission of land rent. The smallest identifiable unit within the district—a small collection of houses, in most cases a *kampong*—elects a *ketua kampong*. He is considered an elected spokesman rather than a government official, and he receives no remuneration. Both the district officer and the *penghulu* hold regular meetings with their subordinates.

The Local Councils Ordinance of 1952 was enacted to stimulate the development of limited local self-administration. Although its wording permits wider application, its enactment was prompted by the creation of the New Villages (see Glossary) and other enforced concentrations of persons that were brought about under Emergency regulations during the Communist insurgency of 1948–60 (see ch. 3, Historical Setting). It provided that the district officer might, upon request by a "large proportion" of villagers, declare an area to be a local council area in which, subject to government approval, a council of between seven and 15 elected members might take charge of many aspects of government. The chief minister was empowered to appoint a certain number of members to the council to ensure minority representation where necessary. These councils could make rules and regulations concerning education, playgrounds, roads and highways, sanitation, health, general welfare, and other matters that might be referred to by its government.

The pattern of local self-government is somewhat different in the urban areas. Municipalities are fully autonomous bodies, having their own financial systems and holding property cooperatively; the structure consists of a municipal board, under a president, and an independent staff of public servants. The municipal councils of West Malaysia constitute the most highly developed system of local government in the country. Except in the capital, Kuala Lumpur, these councils are financially autonomous statutory corporations with a completely elected membership. Directly hiring the vast majority of their administrative and other employees, they require little assistance from state or federal civil servants. They supervise such diverse matters as public health, town planning, and cultural activities and finance these projects themselves.

Kuala Lumpur lost its partly elective city council under the provisions of the 1960 Federal Capital Act. Authority was transferred to a commissioner, who is assisted by the 11-man advisory board; six members are senior government officers (mostly secretaries or ministries), and five are unofficial members. The commissioner, who is appointed by the Supreme Head and operates under the direct control of the Ministry of Home Affairs, is not obliged to accept the recommendations of the advisory board; he must, however, express his reasons for rejecting its recommendations.

CHAPTER 13

POLITICAL DYNAMICS

The federal government, which in large measure executes policies of the ruling Alliance Party, continued in late 1969 to encounter obstacles to creation of a viable political system from among the diverse states and ethnic groups within the country. Deputy Prime Minister Tun Abdul Razak declared these obstacles to be communism and communalism.

Government leaders have been caught between commitment to preservation and promotion of the nation's basic Malay linguistic, ethnic, and cultural character on the one hand and commitment to national unity on the other. It is the former assumption that, when challenged by Singapore, led to the state's separation from Malaysia in 1965. Although committed to the principle of democracy, the federal government attached importance to the preservation of the federation. When its policies have generated opposition and increasing sentiment for state autonomy, as in East Malaysia, the federal government has asserted its authority and has employed its emergency powers.

Within this context, parliamentary rule has been suspended under a state of emergency, declared in May 1969, and a newly created National Operations Council (NOC) headed by Deputy Prime Minister Tun Abdul Razak exercised effective power. Prime Minister Tengku Abdul Rahman, however, remained the recognized leader of the federal government.

Because of the plural character of Malaysian society, political behavior has been largely determined by communal considerations that tend to penetrate almost all political issues; there are, however, other considerations that cross ethnic lines to mitigate communal divisions. Voting behavior and political affiliations follow primarily a communal but secondarily an economic or ideological pattern. The lines between separatism, alliance of separate ethnic groups, and noncommunalism often move back and forth as political necessity demands.

The governing Alliance Party undertakes to represent the three major ethnic groups in the country through its three components—

the United Malays National Organization (UMNO), The Malaysian Chinese Association (MCA), and the Malaysian Indian Congress (MIC). In 1969 there were indications, however, that these components of the Alliance have been losing some of the bases of their political support. The results of the 1969 general elections were interpreted as reflecting a resurgence of Malay nationalism and a corresponding weakening of the Alliance position. The emergence of the communally oriented Pan-Malayan Islamic Party (PMIP) as the strongest opposition party, with an appeal to Malay voters who demanded far more Malay assertiveness while opposing UMNO cooperation with the Chinese, created a dilemma for the UMNO. UMNO's dilemma arose from the fact that continuation of the Alliance required continued participation of the MCA. Moreover, while PMIP was free to exploit Malay sentiments, UMNO could not afford to alienate either Malays or the Chinese members of MCA, even though the influence of the latter had been severely weakend by the recent loss of more than half of its representation in the Federal Parliament.

Despite the fact that its support had been eroded both on the Malay and non-Malay sides, the Alliance government is survived in 1969 with a reduced majority, partly because the divergent policies of opposition parties impeded formation of a strong opposition coalition. The weakening of the Alliance position, however, has undercut the Alliance image as a model for an integrated Malaysia.

POLITICAL BACKGROUND

Political dynamics has been largely dominated by a high degree of ethnic and cultural pluralism. The British colonial policy of favoring the *bumiputera* (sons of the soil) Malays in the government services, while encouraging Chinese and Indian entrepreneurship in the economic sphere, further reinforced ethnic divisions already solidified by religious and linguistic divergencies (see ch. 4, Ethnic Groups and Languages; ch. 5, Social Structure).

These ethnic, religious, and cultural cleavages were not of vital importance during the colonial period. The responsibility of coordinating the interaction, or lack of it, among the communal elements was then in the hands of the British. As independence approached, the main ethnic groups and the British sought an arrangement that would reconcile various questions, the most difficult of which had communal overtones, such as citizenship, language, and the position of the Malay rulers. In addition, the three different systems of administration—Federated Malay States, Unfederated Malay States, and Straits Settlements—had to be merged into one political unit, the Federation of Malaya (see ch. 3, Historical Setting).

The compromises that resolved the difficulties were worked out mainly between the Alliance Party and the British and resulted in a bargain between the Malays and the Chinese elite. The Malays were to maintain their political ascendancy by retention of some of the traditional Malay features of government, such as state rulers, by greater voting power, and through advantages in the civil service. Citizenship qualifications for non-Malays were relaxed, thereby gradually increasing their electoral powers; they were also not to be interfered with in the pursuit of business. Since the bargain was not intended to be permanent, Chinese political influence was expected to increase, and Malays were expected to become more active economically.

The intercommunal compromises represented not only the constitutional situation but also Alliance policy, for it was that party that achieved them. The Alliance considered its political success in gaining independence for Malaya and in winning the general elections to be an endorsement of its communal policies. Conversely, Alliance leaders viewed attack on the compromises as an attack on not only the Alliance Party but also the very foundation of the nation as well.

The bargain or compromises, however, aimed to produce a mechanical balance between ethnic groups, not a fusion of attitudes or aspirations. An even more intricate, and no less mechanical balance was the compromise that led to the formation of Malaysia a few years later.

The bargain remained unstable, with Malays wanting to safeguard what they called their "special position" and establish dominance in the country's political and social life. Some sections of the Malay community grew increasingly dissatisfied with the benefits they derived from independence. Feeling politically insecure and economically depressed, they found it difficult to persuade non-Malays to accept a cultural uniformity based on Malay characteristics.

Because the Emergency, the period of Communist insurgency from 1948 to 1960, largely involved the Chinese, it has been common for Malays to identify the Communist threat as a Chinese threat, thus making the loyalty of the entire Chinese community suspect. As far as the Malays were concerned, military assistance to the government came almost entirely from the Malay community. The non-Malays for their part wished to extend the limits of what they regarded as their legitimate interests and, when the Chinese elements from the opposition parties challenged the special position of the Malays during the campaign for the 1969 general elections, extremists from both sides triggered off postelection racial violence.

Intertwined with contemporary Malaysian politics has been the problem of internal security. Twelve years of armed Communist rebellion, the hostilities during the Confrontation with Indonesia, a continuing Communist threat, and an intermittent occurrence of racial violence have forced the federal government to adopt strong security regulations and to justify the use of emergency powers. The federal government has considered itself to be restrained in the use of these powers. Some of the opposition party leaders, however, were arrested on the grounds of internal threats to security, and there were accusations that leaders of the Alliance Party used these emergency powers to stifle opposition.

POLITICAL ELITE

The political leadership has consisted of a very small group of men, mostly Malays, who have made the crucial decisions and have ensured that those decisions are enforced. These men are primarily representative of the Malaysian Civil Service but also include the select body of popularly elected government officials, the leaders and officers of political parties, the Malay royalty, and the chieftains of the various tribal communities in East Malaysia.

Individual membership in one group or another is not always perfectly definable because more often than not a party leader is also a cabinet minister, a tribal chieftain may hold an elected office, or a nobleman may occupy a key position in the government administrative or civil service. Elected government officials and party leaders, headed by the cabinet ministers and officeholders of the dominant Alliance Party, are the most influential in federal matters. Representatives of the affiliated Sarawak Alliance Party and Sabah Alliance Party have similar stature in their respective local areas. Leaders of opposition parties, except in a few states, have little influence upon either state or federal policy formation.

The political power of the senior level of the civil service is inherent in the fact that its members occupy key policymaking and operational posts in almost every ministry. The Ministry of Foreign Affairs, for example, is the only ministry in which civil service officers are not the permanent secretaries and, even within the ministry, senior civil service personnel are rarely subordinate in rank or authority to colleagues from any other branch of Malaysian society.

The elite group in the federal government has been remarkably stable. Of the 14 members of the "Emergency cabinet" in late 1969, four had held cabinet-level posts since 1955. These were Prime Minister Tengku Abdul Rahman, Deputy Prime Minister Tun Abdul Razak, Tan Sri V. T. Sambanthan, and Tan Sri Sardon bin Haji Jubir. The elite group in the federal government has been largely unified by Tengku Abdul Rahman (called the Tengku), whose influence on behalf of the acceptance of the Alliance system and the unity of the elite has been crucial, particularly in the face of the periodic conflicts over the role of the Chinese.

The Tengku has been Malaysia's prime minister since independence. Born on February 8, 1903, he is the seventh son of a Kedah sultan and a daughter of a Siamese Shan State chieftain. He attended a Malay school and a British school in Alor Star before going to a Siamese school in Bangkok. He later enrolled at Saint Catherine's College, in Cambridge, England, and was the first Kedah Malay to graduate from an English university (in 1925). Although he took up the study of law in his youth at Inner Temple in England, he did not become a barrister until 1949, at the age of 46. During the 1930's the Tengku worked in the Kedah Civil Service and served as district officer in various districts of the state.

During the Japanese occupation of World War II, the Tengku worked against the enemy and developed a sense of nationalism that later dominated his life. He cofounded UMNO with Dato Onn bin Ja'afar in 1946 and became its president in 1951. The Tengku is largely credited for bringing about the independence of his country and the creation of Malaysia. As prime minister, the Tengku has displayed pragmatism in domestic as well as foreign policy. In recent years he has increasingly delegated responsibility to others, reserving his energy for major issues, particularly in the field of foreign affairs.

Next to the Tengku in importance among the political elite is Tun Abdul Razak, who has been his deputy since 1957. Born in March 1922 in Pahang, where he started his career as a civil servant, Tun Razak earned a law degree in England in 1949. During the Japanese occupation, he joined Force 136, Malay Resistance Movement, "Wataniah" (see Glossary). Always active in politics, Tun Razak has had a hand in almost every important decision since 1957. He has been a leading UMNO official since 1951 and was a member of the Merdeka Independence Mission to London in January 1956.

More recently there have been signs of the rise to prominence of another leading Malay, Tun Ismail bin Dato Abdul Rahman, minister of home affairs, who acted as the head of NOC during the absence of Tun Razak. Tun Ismail has had key ministerial posts in the federal government, as well as in UMNO, and he was the first Malayan ambassador to the United States. Tun Ismail has taken a firm approach to racial problems and has opposed Malay chauvinism.

Among other elite groups the Malay royalty exercises a function that is primarily symbolic. Its members have great personal prestige but exert a minimum influence in the formation and execution of day-to-day policy decisions; they are politically important mainly to legitimize action taken by others (see ch. 12, The Governmental System).

Tribal chieftains in East Malaysia also have many symbolic functions of traditional ethnic and religious significance but, unlike the Malay royalty, they have retained considerable local temporal power and organize and lead political parties among their tribally oriented followers. Tribal chieftains have little impact on the shaping of federal policies, but they usually determine the political response of their own groups and thus have nationwide significance.

Most members of the military and police forces, the lower ranks of the civil service, trade unions, religious groups, and youth organizations do not seek a political role. The military forces do not have the tradition of political activism and under the Alliance government were not inclined to exercise political power. Because of the Emergency and the years of British rule, the Malaysian police force had engaged in some political activities (see ch. 25, The Armed Forces; ch. 24, Public Order and Internal Security).

The fact that the political elite are largely Malay results not only from the impetus of an early participation, when non-Malays were virtually excluded from political life, but also from the constitutional provisions that protect their position. In recent years operating policies designed to inculcate a sense of common citizenship and responsibility among all ethnic groups have been instituted. As a result, increasing numbers of Chinese, Indians, and other ethnic groups are entering the government. Some have already achieved ministerial status in the cabinet.

POLITICAL PARTIES

Before 1952 political parties were little more than pressure groups, seeking privileges and advantages for their ethnically oriented members, rather than organizations concerned with the form of operation of government. The exclusively Malay UMNO was created in 1946, not to gain a voice in government but to oppose British plans for the Malayan Union, which would have divested the Malay community of traditional rights (see ch. 3, Historical Setting).

After the establishment of the Federation of Malaya in 1948 and throughout the 1950's the development of political parties was retarded because of the Communist-created Emergency; nevertheless, since 1952 party politics have continued slowly to evolve. The 1955 elections for the Legislative Council of Malaya by direct vote of the electorate had a drastic and far-reaching impact on political parties. Leadership roles were assumed on the basis of popular support gained at the polls. There was a general strengthening and regularization of party structures, a clarification and restatement of issues, and the development of distinctive platforms on which to campaign for mass following. Loyalties often changed in the process, as did numerous alignments; many new parties were formed or splinter groups from old parties struck out on their own.

Ethnic considerations dominated political life, but such categorizations as economic status, levels of education, residence, social status, and age levels did cross ethnic lines. These factors served to moderate intensity of loyalty, to modify perceptions of the group, and to direct expectations from group membership. These factors tended also to affect party organization, party platform, and party leadership, as well as to provide the basis for internal party conflict.

The intermeshing of these factors is evidenced by the fact that parties that try to appeal to a noncommunal electorate lose some of their support to parties that do have communal ties. Parties that have appealed to only one community have been unable to win a majority in the Federal Parliament, however, and alliances of two or more communal parties have therefore come about. Parties that may be primarily engaged in interethnic political cooperation, an alliance of explicitly separate ethnic organizations, ethnic separatism (the PMIP being the foremost exponent), or noncommunalism often move back and forth between these positions as political necessity demands.

The greatest stimulus to political life and the formation of new political parties began in 1959 when the question of federation or separate existence was an important issue for the Federation of Malaya and the two Borneo territories of Sarawak and Sabah, as well as the British colony of Singapore. An attempt was later made by the Alliance Party toward organizational unity by welding state parties into federal entities. In the Federal Parliament the Sabah Alliance Party, the Sarawak Alliance Party, and the mainland Alliance Party joined together to form the Malaysian Alliance. The low level of political development in Sarawak and Sabah, in contrast to the competence of the Alliance leadership in West Malaysia, and the resources available to the federal government leaders, in contrast to the parochial division of the Alliance counterpart in Sarawak and Sabah, resulted in little regional influence on the politics of the Malaysian Alliance. This enabled the Alliance Party in West Malaysia to dominate the Federal Parliament, so far as the Alliance counterparts in East Malaysia were concerned.

Other than the Malaysian Alliance there has been no similar drive by other political parties toward organizational unity nor any attempt to weld state parties into federal entities. Parties in Malaysia insisted on their own separate identities, but techniques and procedures for mutual support and cooperation on nonracial issues were employed.

Similarly, because the ethnic composition of states is so sharply defined, state groupings are more important than federal groupings. State parties, in fact, rarely try to extend their influence beyond strict local boundaries. Incursions into Malaysia by the People's Action Party of Singapore, headed by Lee Kuan Yew, ended in mid-1965 with the separation of Singapore.

West Malaysia

Five political parties in West Malaysia represent the main political trends: the Alliance Party, the Pan-Malayan Islamic Party (PMIP), the Democratic Action Party (DAP), the Gerakan Ra'ayat Malaysia, and the People's Progressive Party (PPP). In addition, there are several minor parties that are noteworthy only because they exert some influence in small local areas.

The Alliance Party

The Alliance party had its beginnings in the electoral alliance between the United Malays National Organization (UMNO) and the Malayan Chinese Association to oppose the Independence of Malaya Party (IMP) in the Kuala Lumpur municipal elections of 1952. In 1954, when the number of seats in the Legislative Council was increased, the IMP threat began to affect the Malayan Indian Congress as well as the coalition of the UMNO-Malayan Chinese Association, and the Indian group then joined the coalition for the federal elections of 1955. The alliance victory, 51 seats out of the 52 contested, was so impressive that the alliance became permanent.

Subsequent attempts to merge the three constituent parties into a single organization, however, have not been successful. Members of each group, and particularly of UMNO, have resisted proposals to this end. Whereas the Alliance contests elections as a single body, its constituent parties have continued to function on communal lines, being responsible to their own members. The Alliance is thus an intercommunal organization.

Organizationally, there is an Alliance national council composed of 16 members each from UMNO and the Malaysian Chinese Association (MCA) and six members from the Malaysian Indian Congress (MIC). An executive committee of the council (who are also mostly members of the federal cabinet), made up of six UMNO, five MCA, and three MIC members, determines policy and selects candidates for national elections. Broad questions of policy are resolved among the constituent party heads and only then are decisions made. For example, the controversial national language bill of 1967 was subject to debate, compromise, and amendment in the Alliance National Council before its presentation to the federal House of Representatives. Once passed by this joint session of UMNO-MCA-MIC leadership, the bill's passage in the Federal Parliament was assured.

Once the Alliance National Council comes to a final policy decision, then it is the responsibility of each party's leaders to win compliance from its own rank and file. The rank and file need not be consulted but are expected to accept the party leader's decisions.

Most of the Alliance leaders are former civil servants, some with aristocratic backgrounds, professional men, and businessmen. Several of them have had long political careers. Alliance leaders are considered enlightened conservatives in their social and economic outlook. Since its founding, the Alliance has been dominated by Tengku Abdul Rahman, and Tun Abdul Razak has been his heir-designate.

Concern by the leaders of each component party for the interests of their own constituents has led to outright bargaining at the top level —the Alliance; when disagreements have developed, the Tengku has intervened. When compromise has not been possible, expulsion from the party has been one solution. Members of a party faction expressing dissatisfaction with Alliance decisions have often been disciplined by the party leaders.

The Alliance has proved successful for a number of reasons. Historically, it acquired a creditable record of support for Malayan independence and was in power when independence was achieved in 1957. The considerable financial resources of the MCA component combined with the popularity of Prime Minister Abdul Rahman have given the Alliance a character and vote power unmatched by any rival group. Its intercommunal policy, a source of strength from the time of independence, has suffered gradual erosion, however, and was one of the factors costing the Alliance support in the 1969 elections.

The major component of the Alliance Party is the UMNO. With branches in virtually every electoral district, UMNO has undergone a reorganization in 1959 and 1960 to gain greater control over state and local bodies. Dato Onn bin Ja'afar, cofounder of UMNO in 1946, tried to make it a multiracial party; when that failed, he broke away in 1951 to create the IMP. Since Tengku Abdul Rahman became president of the Alliance, he has been assisted by Tun Abdul Razak in the executive committee, which is the governing body of UMNO.

The second component of the Alliance is the MCA, which was founded in 1949 (as the Malayan Chinese Association) under the aegis of the Communities Liaison Committee, with Dato Tan Cheng Lock, a Straits-born Chinese, as president. Tan was a pioneer rubber planter and leading prewar Chinese spokesman. He was succeeded as president in 1958 by Lim Chong Eu, a British-educated physician from a well-known Penang family. Lim resigned from the Malayan Chinese Association in 1959 and was succeeded by Tun Tan Siew Sin, son of Dato Tan Cheng Lock. A Malacca politician, Tan Siew Sin has held cabinet-level posts since 1955. He was the minister of finance from 1959 through 1969.

The interests of the Chinese community at large have been the party's foremost interest. During the early years of its existence, the party represented varying shades of political opinions, but support was obtained mainly from the Malayanized sections of the Chinese community. The party, however, did not represent the Chinese to the same extent that the UMNO represented the Malays.

The MIC, the third component of the Alliance, is considerably smaller and less influential than either of its partners. Since 1955, when the party joined the Alliance, Tan Sri V. T. Sambanthan, a Tamil-speaking rubber planter and businessman, has been MIC president. Educated at Annamalai University in India, Sambanthan has held various cabinet-level posts and has been a member of the federal House of Representatives.

MIC was founded in August 1946 (as the Malayan Indian Congress) to represent the interests of the Indian community and to provide a medium for the expression of Indian opinion in Malaya. It was involved in left-wing activities in Malayan politics when it joined the All-Malaya Council of Joint Action (AMCJA), but later it resumed its legal existence as a communal party.

Although the MIC owed its importance in the Malaysian political scene in late 1969 to its membership in the Alliance, the inclusion of MIC within the Alliance also enhanced the latter's stature by making it representative of three major ethnic communities within the country. Indians, however, constitute no more than 10 percent of the country's total population and do not form a sizable portion of any federal constituency. Moreover, the MIC itself does not have a wide following within the Indian community.

Because of the relatively small number of potential voters the MCA and MIC could draw upon, these two components of the Alliance have had minority representation in the all-Alliance parliamentary ticket.

The Pan-Malayan Islamic Party

The Pan-Malayan Islamic Party (PMIP) has been Malaysia's strongest opposition party. It represents extremist views on race and religion in which far-leftist and far-rightist politics are combined. It espouses the slogan "Malaya for the Malays" and advocates the establishment of an Islamic theocratic state. Structurally, it is divided into two factions—one oriented to the political left and the other, relatively nonpolitical, placing greatest emphasis on religion. Members of the PMIP believe that for Muslims there should be no separation of religion and politics and that the economic difficulties of Malays are directly attributable to special treatment given non-Malays. They are adamantly opposed to the Malaysia concept and bitterly attack the UMNO for its association with the MCA and MIC. They seek to eliminate all non-Malay influences, particularly Chinese; to reserve all government positions for Malays; to make Malay and English the only authorized languages; and to deny non-Malay cultural or educational programs any government assistance.

PMIP was founded by a number of religious teachers led by Burhanuddin Al-Helmy, who is popularly known as an Islamic scholar and as a longtime champion of Malay nationalism and ties with Indonesia. He was arrested in 1965 on charges of conspiring with Indonesia to set up a pro-Indonesian government-in-exile.

Burhanuddin was succeeded by Dato Mohammed Asri bin Muda, who is also Kelantan's chief minister as well as member of the federal House of Representative. Like Burhanuddin, Mohammed Asri is an Islamic scholar; he is also a former teacher, newspaperman, and writer. He has served as Kelantan state assemblyman and Speaker of the assembly.

The PMIP did not, at the end of 1969, constitute a potent threat to UMNO's national dominance, but it was the party that offered UMNO its strongest external pressures. The PMIP has provided the one genuine alternative for Malays, including dissident UMNO factions seeking a communal representative but dissatisfied with the UMNO policy of interethnic accommodation. In general, PMIP's strongest support is found among the rural, less developed states of West Malaysia, primarily in Kelantan, Trengganu, Kedah, and Perlis. Islamic teachers are its staunchest backers. The party's chief election success has been in the state of Kelantan, where it thwarted Alliance attempts during the 1969 elections to wrest that state from PMIP's firm control with offers of economic progress.

In mid-August 1968 defections reduced the PMIP majority over UMNO in Kelantan's 30-member state assembly to three, but two of the defectors returned later to the PMIP fold. The PMIP had won control of the state assembly of Trengganu in the 1959 elections but later lost its majority owing to shifts in party affiliations among its members. In the 1969 general elections the party gained 12 seats in the federal House of Representatives, one short of its representation in 1959 but three more than were won in the 1964 elections.

The PMIP announced its support of the federal government efforts to maintain law and order following the postelection racial violence.

It nevertheless held to its aspiration to govern the country eventually with the support of the dissident faction of UMNO.

Democratic Action Party

The Democratic Action Party (DAP) is essentially a remnant of the People's Action Party (PAP) that was left on the mainland after the separation of Singapore in 1965. Having reconstituted itself as a new party in March 1966, the DAP remained popularly identified with the Singapore party and in the 1969 elections was catapulted into the position of second largest national party by winning 13 seats in the federal House of Representatives and 31 seats in the state elections.

The DAP has appeal to independent intellectuals and non-Malay voters, largely young and liberal Chinese. Like its parent body had done before the separation of Singapore, the DAP demands a Malaysian Malaysia, an end to the distinction between the *bumiputera* and other Malaysians, official recognition of Chinese, Tamil, and English languages and of foreign university degrees. With Chen Man Hin as national chairman, the party derives part of its support from Chinese guilds and clan associations that have ties with Singapore.

Labor Party

The Labor Party was founded in 1954 by trade unionists and academic socialists headed by Lim Kean Siew, a lawyer trained at Cambridge University and a member of the Federal Parliament. The party originally attempted to establish a noncommunal, ideologically based, socialist-oriented movement. Largely Chinese in membership, it included a number of radicals and a few moderates. To broaden its appeal beyond the urban non-Malay population, the Labor Party allied itself with the nationalist Party Ra'ayat to form the Socialist Front in 1957.

The Socialist Front, behind which the Labor Party operated until its dissolution in January 1966, was strongest in the urban districts of Kuala Lumpur and Penang but also had significant following in some Malay rural districts. In the elections of 1959 it gained eight seats in the federal House of Representatives and was the nation's third strongest party. Observers were led to expect the development of a strong left-wing opposition to the Alliance, since both the Alliance and the Socialist Front are intercommunal and compete on the basis of ideology. The Socialist Front, however, lacked the cohesive leadership at the highest level necessary to hold the combination together in the face of grass-roots conflict. Relations between its two component parties deteriorated as they split over issues on national integration, interpretation of the national language guarantee, disputes between the Chinese-speaking and English-speaking Chinese, and also a clash of personalities. In 1964 the two members elected to the Federal Parliament were both Labor Party members who had readopted their original party label. By December 1965 the Socialist Front was split.

The Labor Party lost its multiethnic image after the split with the largely Malay Party Ra'ayat. In 1967 the resignation of Tan Chee Khoon and David Ramanthan so nearly depleted the party of ranking leaders that it became practically defunct as a national organization, although its branches still remained active throughout the country. Efforts to refashion an electoral alliance with the Party Ra'ayat were made before the 1969 elections. The elections were boycotted, however, by the Labor Party on the ground that politically motivated arrests had crippled its ability to wage an effective campaign.

Party Ra'ayat

Founded in 1955 as a Malay party but later becoming multiracial, Party Ra'ayat has been the less important of the two partners in the Socialist Front. The party has been important to the Labor Party in a symbolic, rather than an electoral, sense. Its preeminent leader was Ahmad Boestaman, of Indonesian origin, who resigned in the second half of 1960. A member of the federal House of Representatives, Boestaman made a socialist appeal to the rural population, but he was arrested in 1963 on the grounds that he had developed subversive associations with Indonesian Communist Party leaders. The Party Ra'ayat, under its new president, Kassim Ahmad, entered the 1969 elections and won three state assembly seats, one in Penang and two in Pahang.

Gerakan Ra'ayat Malaysia

Malaysia's newest opposition party, the Gerakan Ra'ayat Malaysia (popularly known as Gerakan), was formed in March 1969. It is a coalition of three distinct factions: a breakaway group from the Labor Party headed by Tan Chee Khoon and the Malaysian Trade Union Congress official David Ramanthan; Lim Chong Eu and the remnants of his United Democratic Party (UDP), originally formed in 1962 after breaking away from the Malayan Chinese Association, in 1959; and the Alatas brothers and their former Party Negara faction.

Lim Chong Eu, a former president of the Malayan Chinese Association, was the chief moving force behind the formation of the party. Tan Chee Khoon, the secretary general of Gerakan, was elected to the federal House of Representatives as the Labor Party (Socialist Front) candidate in 1964 and had long been the leader of the right-wing faction of that party. The other two founders of Gerakan are university intellectuals—Syed Hussein Alatas of the University of Singapore, as Gerakan chairman, and Wang Gung-wu of the University of Malaya.

Gerakan was formed because of dissatisfaction and anxiety of certain Malaysian political and intellectual leaders over the Alliance handling of disturbances in Penang in 1967 and, especially, dissatisfaction over the Alliance approach to communal problems. A multiracial party, Gerakan favored a form of socialism within the framework of the Malaysian Constitution. The concept would entail direct government intervention in the economy, reduction of both Malay privileges and restrictions on non-Malays, and a nonaligned foreign policy. A gradual reorientation of the party to a more modernist Muslim-Malay direction was widely forecast with the departure of Gerakan's articulate Malaysian Chinese leader, Wang Gung-wu, who became a professor at an Australian university. Gerakan generally has supported the actions of the federal government in maintaining law and order after the postelection violence; in turn, they have expected a free hand in the government of Penang.

People's Progressive Party

The People's Progressive Party (PPP) was formerly the Perak Progressive Party, which participated in the 1955 general elections. It is largely confined in the state of Perak and particularly the municipality of Ipoh, which it controls. PPP, however, had not managed by 1969 to control the Perak state government; nevertheless, it has sufficient following in Perak state to win and maintain some seats in the federal House of Representatives. In the 1969 elections, however, despite efforts at electoral agreement with DAP and the Labor Party, its representation was reduced from five to four seats. PPP has been led by two brothers of Ceylonese origin who are both astute lawyers and politicians, D. R. Seenivasagam, who has represented the party in the Federal Parliament, and S. P. Seenivasagam.

The PPP is socialistic in domestic matters but has made no radical economic proposals beyond the eventual nationalization of tin and rubber. Although officially multiracial, the main appeal of the party has been to non-Malays, particularly the Chinese community, which forms the bulk of its support. It has been protective of Chinese interests largely on the issues of language and education. PPP also opposed those measures that provide for the "special position of the Malays." It has been relatively neutral in foreign affairs and strongly anti-Malaysia, but during the Confrontation it was a firm supporter of the federal government's foreign policy because of its dislike of the Sukarno government's treatment of the Chinese in Indonesia.

East Malaysia

In East Malaysia Sarawak was almost wholly apolitical until after the Malaysian proposal was made, at which time it developed parties that gradually polarized around the federation issue. The Sarawak United People's Party (SUPP), for example, was opposed to federation, whereas Party Negara Sarawak (PANAS), after a brief hesitation, supported it. At first the political parties that cropped up tended to be racially based, as in West Malaysia; by October 1962, however, all except SUPP had formed a Sarawak United Front—renamed Sarawak Alliance Party in January 1963—to work, among other things, to bring about the formation of Malaysia. Politics in Sarawak soon assumed a pattern similar to West Malaysia, although more complex.

Sarawak Alliance Party

The Sarawak Alliance was made up in 1969 of three racial components: the Dayak Party Pesaka, the Malay Party Bumiputera, and the Sarawak Chinese Association. It was independent from, but patterned after and affiliated in federal matters with, the Alliance Party in West Malaysia. The Sarawak Alliance is largely Dayak-dominated.

The Party Pesaka, with a claimed membership of 140,000 has been the leading member of the Sarawak Alliance coalition. It has stood for Dayak power and privilege, to which the other members of the coalition tacitly consent. Pesaka was organized by Dato Temenggong Jugah anak Barieng in June 1962 after breaking away from PANAS. Temenggong Jugah, a traditional Iban chief, was serving as *penghulu* (see Glossary) of the Merirai area in Kapit when he organized Pesaka. While serving as chairman of the Iban Sarawak Conservative Party, he also became an elected member of the federal House of Representatives.

Temenggong Jugah's political strength has been in part drawn from the allegiance of a number of traditional Dayak leaders, particularly from the Rajang River area. Pesaka's secretary general since 1964 has been Thomas Kana, a highly articulate and multilingual Iban who was a former administrator of the Shell Oil Company.

Party Bumiputera resulted from the merger of two distinct Malay parties, the Barisan Rakyat Jati Sarawak (BARJASA) and the Party Negara Sarawak (PANAS), in 1966 at the instance of the Alliance Party leaders in order to strengthen the Sarawak Alliance. With a claimed membership of 100,000, Party Bumiputera has increased Malay influence within the Sarawak Alliance. BARJASA's secretary general, Abdul Taib bin Mahmud, assumes that same office in the new coalition. Of Muslim Melanau extraction, Abdul Taib bin Mahmud received his law degree from an Australian university and has served as judge associate in the Supreme Court of South Australia. Bumiputera's chairman, also from BARJASA, is Dato Haji Abdul Rahman bin Haji Ya'akub, a lawyer trained in Europe who was a member of the federal House of Representatives and minister of education in 1969. Abang Othman bin Abang Haji Moasili, chairman of PANAS, has been given a portfolio in the Sarawak government. A veteran of 26 years' service in the Sarawak constabulary and a member of Kuching's hereditary Malay ruling class, Abang Othman has also been a member of the Council Negri, the legislative body in Sarawak.

BARJASA, in contrast to PANAS, represented the predominantly anticession faction of the Malay community (those against the Brooke's cession of the territory to the British in 1946), who were mostly the educated element and the Dayaks. BARJASA has been antagonistic toward PANAS and oriented toward the federal government. Among BARJASA's membership are Muslim Melanaus who have become assimilated into the Malay community, such as Awang Hippni bin Pengiran Annu, who was minister in the Sarawak cabinet.

Although noncommunal in principle, PANAS, the other element of Bumiputera, is basically Malay in membership. Organized in April 1960 by Datu Bandar and Abang Haji Mustapha to counter the mass enlistment of Chinese into SUPP, PANAS claims the support of a number of prominent Dayak leaders, several well-known Chinese, and Temenggong Jugah anak Barieng, before he broke away from the party. PANAS aimed its main appeal at those Malays who had favored the cession of Sarawak to the British crown.

During the first half of 1963 PANAS was one of the pro-Malaysia parties that formed the Sarawak Alliance, but because of a dispute over the distribution of seats it broke away, although remaining pro-Malaysia. In the elections of that year PANAS temporarily collaborated with SUPP (with which it had differences over federal matters) and hoped to divide the 10 seats in the Council Negri between them. The arrangement enabled SUPP, with 24 percent of the votes in the contested seats, and PANAS, with 15 percent of the votes, to have representation in the Council Negri.

The third and last member of the Sarawak Alliance coalition is the Sarawak Chinese Association (SCA). With Malay Chinese Association encouragement, Ling Beng-Siew, a wealthy Sibu timber baron and former member of the Council Negri and Supreme Council, resigned from PANAS to found the SCA in August 1962. SCA was formed as a haven for conservative, anti-Communists and pro-Malaysian Chinese, many of whom were repelled at the radical stand of the SUPP. Several leading Chinese, most notably Teo Kui-Seng, a Kuching businessman and SUPP cofounder who served as its assistant secretary general, added to SCA ranks. From the outset, however, the party, with only about 5,000 members, has been hampered because it reflects mainly wealthy business interests.

Sarawak United People's Party

The Sarawak United People's Party (SUPP) is Sarawak's oldest party and most formidable opposition group. It received more votes than the Alliance in the elections of 1963; because of weighting procedures designed to curtail Chinese influence in government, however, SUPP had only five seats in the Council Negri, a condition that had not changed in late 1969.

SUPP was founded in June 1959, largely by leading Chinese, as well as a few Dayaks and Malays. Although it intended to be multiracial in its recruitment of membership, initially attracting considerable support from non-Malay indigenous groups, particularly Ibans, SUPP depended primarily upon Chinese membership and support. Although the key post of secretary in local SUPP branches has often been held by a Chinese, an indigenous Sarawakian usually serves as chairman.

SUPP has been torn by factional strife, largely ideological, between those primarily in the top rank, including its chairman, Ong Kee Hui, and its secretary general, Stephen Yong. Both men favored multiracial national politics, whereas those at the district and precinct levels of the party are implacably anti-Malaysia and sympathize with the aims of the Labor Party or the Barisan Socialist Party in Singapore. Those at the district and precinct levels of the party are the faction that has largely provided legal cover to the Clandestine Communist Organization.

A split in the party was narrowly averted in 1965 when the extremists in SUPP were reluctant to join with the party at the Malaysia Solidarity Convention. At the annual meeting of the central committee of the party the moderates, including Ong and Yong, found themselves in a minority and walked out.

Despite the factional troubles and decimation of its leaders who were charged with threats to internal security, SUPP has been successful in gaining Dayak and Malay adherents in several areas where there was dissatisfaction with the alleged interference of the federal government in Sarawak affairs. SUPP has continued to advocate an independent Sarawak in which full political parity is granted to all ethnic groups. Inherent in the program also is the possibility of an amalgamation with Sabah and the creation of a separate federation limited to the Borneo territories. After Singapore's separation from Malaysia in 1965, SUPP demanded a referendum to determine the wishes of the state as regards continued membership in the federation.

Sarawak National Party

The Sarawak National Party (SNAP) was organized in 1961 by Iban leaders in the Second Division (see ch. 12, The Governmental System). It is largely a communalistic Dayak party, although it has increasingly become multiracial. It has continued to compete with the Party Pesaka for influence among the Dayaks. SNAP's membership of 60,000 is mostly in the first, second, and fourth divisions. Dato Stephen Kalong Ningkan, an Iban Dayak, has been SNAP secretary general and its leading spokesman. A one-time hospital assistant with the Shell Oil Company in Brunei, Ningkan had risen in Sarawak politics because of his ability to recruit Ibans into the party. He is a founding member of the Dayak Association in Sarawak, and his supporters regard him as a staunch defender of state and native rights.

In 1963 SNAP was part of the Sarawak Alliance, with Ningkan as secretary general; it bolted from the coalition in 1966, however, and has since remained in opposition, along with SUPP, to the Alliance. In October 1968 the party suffered a major loss when one of its top leaders and its main financial backer, Dato Wee Hood Teck withdrew from SNAP.

Sabah Alliance Party

In Sabah the Sabah Alliance Party (SAP) was the only party of significance at the close of 1969. SAP is dominated by the United Sabah National Organization (USNO), which has virtually absorbed, although indirectly, the few independent parties that existed previously. The other component of SAP is the relatively minor Sabah Chinese Association, whose president, Peter Loh, became a prominent political figure as the chief minister of Sabah in 1966.

USNO is the party of the Muslim-Malay element of the population, although it declares itself to be multiracial. It has had the moral and material backing of the UMNO since its beginning. The dominant personality of USNO is Tun Mustapha bin Dato Harun, who is Moro (Sulu Muslim) by birth, a member of the royal clan of Sulu, and traditional chief from the Kudat area. During the Japanese occupation in 1943, Tun Mustapha escaped to the Philippines to join the guerrillas there and emerged with the rank of captain. In 1959 he was sent by the British North Borneo government to Britain to

316

study English and politics. Before assuming the post of chief minister, which he continued to hold in late 1969, Mustapha was Sabah's Yang di-Pertua Negara, or head of state.

In the elections for a new state legislative assembly held in 1967 USNO captured 12 seats and gained two additional seats uncontested on nomination; winning five more seats (including two won by the Sabah Chinese Association and three by candidates entered not by USNO itself but by the Alliance as such), USNO controlled the new government. It also held the most seats (six) in the federal House of Representatives of any Sabah party.

The United Pasok-Momogon Kadazan Organization (UPKO) was the principal representative of the largest racial group in Sabah until its party members were virtually absorbed by USNO in 1968; it has retained, however, the potentiality for revival as an independent and active organization. UPKO itself resulted from the merger in 1964 of the United National Kadazan Organization and the United National Pasok-Momogun Organization in order to strengthen the political power of their combined following of Kadazans and Muruts in a joint position of asserting states' rights.

In the 1967 Sabah legislative assembly elections, UPKO gained the same number of seats as USNO (12), against the combined opposition of USNO and the Sabah Chinese Association; however, it was excluded from gaining a position in the Sabah government when it failed to agree on USNO's terms. Because of USNO's erosion of the political strength of UPKO, the UPKO national council announced in December 1967 the decision to dissolve the party.

The other component of SAP is the Sabah Chinese Association, which is the Sabah counterpart of the Malaysian Chinese Association (MCA). Peter Loh, its head, is a Sandakan-born Roman Catholic, who had been a leader of the Sabah National Party, a Chinese party. The Sabah National Party was previously constituted under the name of the Borneo Utara National Party, which in turn was made up of two Chinese-based parties—the United Party and the Democratic Party.

Sabah's Indian community, comprising less than 1 percent of the population, is represented by the Sabah Indian Congress, which had successfully claimed the right to be included in intercommunal negotiations.

INTEREST GROUPS

Traditionally, expression of special interests in Malaysia has not taken place through groups organized specifically for the purpose. The Malays used instead the traditional social leaders, mainly teachers and religious leaders, because of their political influence. The Chinese utilized various guilds, clans, societies, educational groups, and chambers of commerce. Except for these, there are few effective pressure groups in the country. The chambers of commerce constitute important pressure groups. The Chinese Chambers of Commerce, for example, are closely aligned with MCA, with occasional overlapping of the leading officeholders of the two organizations; these two organizations, however, are not necessarily identical.

Since the dominant religion is Islam, no Malay party could afford not to support Islam. In the northeastern states of Kelantan and Trengganu, cooperation between certain religious teachers and the PMIP has greatly strengthened the appeal of the party. Interest groups in East Malaysia are not yet very highly developed. The main exceptions are the Chinese Chambers of Commerce and the trade unions in the larger towns in Sarawak. In addition, SUPP has also exercised influence in the Kuching Chamber of Commerce. The Clandestine Communist Organization also makes use of affiliated groups such as the Sarawak Farmers' Association and the Sarawak Advanced Youth Association.

PARTY POLITICS

In order to retain power, the Alliance Party has sought to weld its component parties into a single organization. The leaders of the Alliance have insisted that these components enter into compromise among themselves and that they subordinate potential conflicts to the compelling need for unity. Competition among these components has been in part a controlled competition for individual distribution of political rewards, sometimes in the guise of struggle between conflicting communal groups. Economic status, levels of education, residence, social status, and age levels have helped, however, to moderate the intensity of communal loyalties, at the same time providing other internal conflict.

Opposition parties in their common effort to unseat the Alliance have aimed their attack at both the Alliance as a whole and the component parties. Generally, the opposition parties have tried to discredit one particular component of the Alliance by claiming that it has sold out the interest of its communal group to the others.

The government has discouraged criticism in the Federal Parliament from members of the Alliance. As a result, the level of participation in debates and question periods has been low, especially among the Alliance rank-and-file members. Most of the questions have come from the opposition and from representatives of Sarawak and Sabah.

Leaders of the federal government found such constraints useful in expediting the separation of Singapore in 1965.

Communal Problems and the Alliance

Pressures that had built up among the more militant right-wing Malays in UMNO resulted in the decision to end Singapore's connection with Malaysia. In addition to the Malayan Chinese Association rivalry with PAP among the Chinese community, a considerable number of Malays saw in Lee Kuan Yew's concept of a Malaysian Malaysia a threat to their privileged position as *bumiputera* (see ch. 3, Historical Setting).

Communal feelings that led to the Singapore crisis were aroused by the language issue, which was brought to a critical point by the fact that Malay was to become the sole official language in 1967. This issue had also played a crucial role in the breakup of the Socialist Front, and the Malayan Chinese Association, particularly its youth organization, was also profoundly affected. The Chinese community asked not only that Chinese be given an official status but, also for wider use of Chinese in all government departments and statutory bodies. UMNO leaders could not ignore the opposing views of PMIP, particularly in the four predominantly Malay states of Kedah, Perak, Trengganu, and Kelantan where the two parties compete for the same voters. The PMIP has gained considerable inroads in these states since 1967. Dissatisfaction with UMNO's policy regarding languages resulted in the resignation of Dato Syed Ja'afar Albar as secretary general of UMNO.

Other specific issues, with communal overtones, also threatened the unity of the Alliance. In 1967 a conflict over the chief ministership in Perak forced the Tengku to intervene by replacing the chief minister. In Malacca, Abdul Ga'afar bin Baba's resignation as chief minister to accept a higher post touched off a dispute in UMNO and within the Alliance. The dispute arose over the replacement of the Speaker of the state assembly, whom Abdul Ga'afar chose as his successor. Some UMNO assemblymen refused to endorse the candidate selected by the Alliance, who was a member of the Malayan Chinese Association, and proposed in his stead an UMNO assemblyman. The dispute occurred despite the previous gentlemen's agreement between the Tengku and the Malayan Chinese Association to the effect that, if the governor of Malacca was a Malay, the chief minister should be a non-Malay and vice versa.

Another crisis broke out with the Alliance over the question of filling the post of deputy prime minister when Tun Abdul Razak succeeds the Tengku in the future as expected. The issue was touched off by a public disagreement in December 1967 between the Malayan Chinese Association official newspaper and that of the UMNO. When the UMNO newspaper questioned the right of a Chinese to be deputy prime minister, Tun Razak temporarily squashed the dispute; but both Malayan Chinese Association and UMNO members alike view the succession crisis as far from resolved.

The assumption by Tun Razak of the chairmanship of the National Operations Council (NOC), which was created to deal with the state of emergency in the country in 1969, brought widespread speculation that the Tengku, who has been under pressure from Malay extremists, was being gently eased into retirement. Although NOC is vested with extraordinary powers and is a body to which the federal cabinet is subordinate, the Tengku is still the recognized leader of the federal government and has retained sufficient control of the Alliance Party. In July 1969 a leading dissident party member in UMNO was expelled because of charges that he tried to organize opposition to the Tengku's leadership. Despite the demands from UMNO extremists to keep MCA members from the emergency cabinet of 1969, the Tengku managed to appoint three MCA party members as ministers without portfolio, one of whom, Tun Tan Siew Sin also serves in the NOC.

Political Opposition in Malaysia

There was no single opposition with a recognized leader in the entire country in late 1969. Early in 1963 the opposition parties formed a united front in order to oppose the creation of Malaysia, headed by Abdul Azziz bin Ishak, who had been a former charter UMNO member and had held various cabinet-level posts. The opposition, however, did not remain united for long on any major issue, largely because of wide policy differences between the various parties.

The growth of opposition has been stifled by restrictions of the federal government that opposition parties must not resort to unconstitutional means or work in conjunction with Communist front organizations. The existence of the Internal Security Act and the awareness of the arrests made under it in the past have influenced the tone and temper in the Federal Parliament and the relationship between the federal government and the opposition. Moreover, because of the communal situation in Malaysia, the federal government bans the use of words that are likely to generate feelings of ill-will or hostility between the different communities in the country. This standing order has been criticized by the opposition as capable of wide interpretation, which could stifle debate.

In the second half of 1960 the opposition parties made efforts to avoid public conflict for fear of weakening their position at the polls. In February 1966 a conference at Ipoh laid the foundation for at least nominal unity. The PPP, UDP, Labor Party, and DAP participated, but the Party Ra'ayat and PMIP, the two Malay opposition parties, did not. Although no formally organized opposition emerged from the conference, some cooperation in distributing candidates among some opposition parties contributed to the electoral upset of the Alliance in the 1969 elections.

REGIONAL ISSUES IN EAST MALAYSIA

Sarawak and Sabah have been particularly sensitive to such political issues as Malaysianization of the civil service, conversion to the national language, the status of Islam, special rights and privileges for Malays or indigenous people, and economic development programs. On all of these issues the federal government has sought to bring the two states into line with its policies, on the ground that uniform policies for the entire country were essential to nation-building. Within Sarawak and Sabah the federal government has sought to ensure the political ascendancy of those who are more sympathetic to federal policies. In disputes with political leaders over states' rights, the federal government has sometimes drawn on its federal powers over such matters as federal patronage, internal security, trade, commerce, labor, and emergency powers as well as the allocation of development funds.

Federal-state relations have been a central issue of Sarawak politics. The federal government has provided support within the state for those favoring its nation-building policies. The complicated political configuration of Sarawak has enabled the federal authorities to play a decisive role in the coalition alignments that have characterized Sarawak politics. Political disputes over issues have usually been accompanied by a contest over political alliances, with the federal government playing a significant role in the negotiation of intra-Alliance agreements in the attempt to isolate proponents of state autonomy.

Sarawak Alliance Party

In June 1965 there was a realignment of parties in the Sarawak government. The immediate cause was the land reform legislation that the Sarawak chief minister introduced to ease the acquisition of legal title to land by the Chinese. BARJASA and Pesaka strongly opposed the measure. The former withdrew from the Sarawak Alliance, of which Chief Minister Ningkan was then secretary general, and several important SNAP leaders, including Tawi Sli, switched over to Pesaka. BARJASA and a substantial number of Pesaka members then tried to form a "Native Alliance," which would include PANAS, to take over the government. Before the union could be consummated Ningkan withdrew the proposed legislation, whereupon Temenggong Jugah, chairman of Pesaka, declined to join the anti-Ningkan group and with his party following withdrew his support from the proposed "Native Alliance."

In the cabinet reshuffle that followed, Ningkan remained chief minister; PANAS, which rejoined the Alliance, and Pesaka were both alloted cabinet posts; and BARJASA members also returned to the Alliance and regained their portfolios. Meanwhile, Ningkan, who did not believe that communal policies in West Malaysia were appropriate for Sarawak, continued to resist efforts to speed up Malaysianization of the Sarawak civil service, preferring instead the Borneanization of state administration. He also resisted increasing pressures to accept Malay as the sole official language for Sarawak in 1967, expressing favor for the idea that Chinese, Malay, and English be official languages for Sarawak. Moreover, he objected to federal funds being provided for the support of Islam and firmly supported the "special position" of Sarawak as defined by the Malaysia Agreement (see ch. 12, The Governmental System).

Conflict between the federal government and Ningkan came to a head in early 1966. A serious political crisis was touched off when Ningkan dismissed Abdul Taib bin Mahmud from the cabinet. The Tengku demanded Ningkan's resignation, on the basis of a "no confidence" letter signed by half of the Council Negri members. Ningkan refused to resign. Meanwhile, the Malaysian Alliance National Council in Kuala Lumpur nominated Tawi Sli, a Pesaka member and an Iban, as the new chief minister. Later, the governor of Sarawak, Tun Abang Haji Openg, at the instance of the federal government leaders, dismissed Ningkan and installed Tawi Sli as the new chief minister.

Tawi Sli is regarded by his colleagues as notably modest and retiring. He was chairman of the Batang Lupar District Council when he was named chief minister. With the support of Pesaka and BARJASA, he tried to gain a majority in the Council Negri by using the offices at his disposal to induce individual members of PANAS, SNAP, and SCA to join his government. He eventually succeeded, although SNAP broke with the Sarawak Alliance in July.

Ningkan meanwhile contested in court the legality of his dismissal and won his case in September 1966. When he resumed office as chief minister, the federal government declared a state of emergency in Sarawak, contending that the political situation in that state was being exploited by Communists and subversive elements. An emergency session of the Federal Parliament was called to amend the Sarawak Constitution so that the government would have the legal basis to take further action. The amendment was made; and the governor of Sarawak dismissed Ningkan for the second time and returned Tawi Sli to the chief ministership, with a cabinet made up of persons from all major communal groups.

Under the new party alignment, Pesaka became the keystone of the Sarawak Alliance. SNAP, however, continued to make inroads into Pesaka's base of support and made substantial gains in the 1967 state elections.

In their concern about the stability of the Alliance, federal officials managed to unite the two Malay parties, BARJASA and PANAS, to form the Party Bumiputera. The merger also increased Malay influence within the Alliance, which made cooperation with Pesaka and the SCA more difficult. In order to counter SNAP inroads among the natives, Pesaka leaders undertook a more militant stand within the Alliance on behalf of native interests.

Sabah Alliance Party

Sabah in 1969 was virtually a one-party state. Because of the lack of an identifiable opposition, the Sabah Alliance Party (SAP) has not operated as a unified party. It has served more as a mechanism for postelection negotiations in which each party's demands have been balanced against their strength at the polls. The Alliance carefully controlled the electoral process through negotiated agreements among its member parties on the basis of their performance in the local elections; these agreements also included distribution of offices in the Sabah government. Until the merger of UPKO with USNO in 1968 the stability of the Alliance had been constantly shaken by political conflict between the Alliance leaders, Tun Mustapha of USNO and Dato Donald Stephens of UPKO, who represented the two most important rival groups of the native community and were proponents of different policies.

Stephens, a wealthy timber magnate of Kadazan-Australian parentage and a journalist, played a prominent role in negotiating the terms for Sabah's participation in the formation of Malaysia; however, like Ningkan, he opposed the Malaysianization of the civil service, the emphasis upon the Malay language and the Muslim faith, and federal intervention in immigration, taxation, and the appointment and removal of high officials. On these issues, Stephens has frequently clashed with Tun Mustapha and his USNO supporters who favored working closely with the federal authorities.

A series of crises within the Sabah Alliance began in June 1964, when a new slate of party candidates for an enlarged legislative assembly had to be chosen. USNO, which won the largest number of legislative seats, challenged UPKO's retention of the post of chief minister, then occupied by Stephens. Through the Tengku's mediation, Stephens was allowed to remain as chief minister, but greater weight was given to USNO in the cabinet. Later that year Stephens, who was under pressure to Malaysianize the civil service, appointed John Dusing, a Kadazan, to the key post.

The appointment, however, was rejected by the head of state, Tun Mustapha. His action irritated UPKO leaders, who interpreted it as interference in politics, contrary to the general assumption that a head of state should be apolitical. Under a formula proposed by the Tengku, Stephens consequently was replaced as chief minister by Peter Loh of the Sabah National Party, and a UPKO member, G. S. Sundang, was named deputy chief minister. Stephens was appointed to a federal ministry.

With federal assistance, based in large measure on patronage and agreement favoring Chinese interests, a political coalition was forged between USNO and the Sabah National Party, which hitherto had been neutral in the USNO and UPKO dispute. The move effectively isolated UPKO from a position of power, and its leader, Donald Stephens, was temporarily removed from power and the local political scene.

After Singapore's separation from Malaysia, Stephens and UPKO took the position that under the changed situation the terms for Sabah's participation in Malaysia should be renegotiated. Swift counteraction by the federal authorities undermined UPKO's political support and induced Stephens to resign from the cabinet.

Demands were also made on UPKO to dissolve and for its members to apply for membership in USNO. When the demand was rejected, USNO threatened to expel the party from the Sabah Alliance unless Stephens and UPKO Secretary General Peter Mojuntin resigned from all leadership positions in the party, which they did.

In the 1967 state elections Stephens resumed the presidency of UPKO in order to compete for seats with USNO in what they called "friendly contests." In the ensuing election campaign, however, UPKO issued a party manifesto that revived all the longstanding grievances about federal intervention in state affairs. USNO in turn hinted at disloyalty. UPKO won 64,767 votes as against 64,638 for USNO. Both parties gained 12 seats each, but USNO, which had picked up additional seats, maintained its control of the new government. USNO, the Sabah Chinese Association, and the federal authorities were determined that, unless UPKO consented to USNO's terms, they would prevent UPKO from gaining a Sabah government from which it could upset the political balance. UPKO did not consent and instead withdrew from the Sabah Alliance and became an opposition party.

While UPKO was in the process of coordinating strategy with Sarawak's SNAP for resisting federal encroachment upon states' rights, Tun Mustapha succeeded in inducing UPKO leaders to defect to the Sabah Alliance. In January 1968 the unification of UPKO with USNO was announced. By being absorbed into USNO and regaining access to the Sabah government, UPKO leaders hoped eventually to undermine USNO's pro-federal orientation; Alliance leaders hoped that the inclusion of UPKO in the Alliance would minimize the possible outbreak of communal violence or serious political instability.

RESULTS OF 1969 GENERAL ELECTIONS

In the 1969 West Malaysian general elections, the Alliance Party was returned to power, but with a reduced majority in Parliament (see table 10). The Alliance also suffered setbacks in the state elections. Voting was postponed in one constituency in Malacca, and the whole election process in East Malaysia was postponed after communal violence had broken out. Out of the 103 constituencies in West Malaysia, the Alliance won 66 seats. With the 10 Alliance candidates returned unopposed in Sabah, the party was assured of a majority in the federal House of Representatives. The opposition parties won 37 seats, more than double the number they had held in the previous Federal Parliament.

Table 10. Results of Federal Elections of Malaysia, 1964 and 1969 [1]

| | Number of seats in House of Representatives | | Percentage of poll | |
	1969	1964	1969	1964
Alliance Party:				
United Malays National Organization (UMNO)	51	59	34.2	38.4
Malaysian Chinese Association (MCA)	13	27	13.0	18.6
Malaysian Indian Congress (MIC)	2	3	1.2	1.5
Total	66	89	48.4	58.5
Pan-Malayan Islamic Party (PMIP)	12	9	23.8	14.6

	Number of seats in House of Representatives		Percentage of poll	
	1969	1964	1969	1964
Democratic Action Party (DAP) _____	13	1 [2]	13.7	2.0 [2]
Gerakan Ra'ayat Malaysia _____	8	1 [3]	8.6	4.3 [3]
People's Progressive Party (PPP) _____	4	2	3.9	3.4
Party Ra'ayat _____	--	(Part of Socialist Front)	1.2	(Part of Socialist Front)
Others _____	--	2 [4]	0.4	17.2 [5]
GRAND TOTAL __	103	104	100.0	100.0

[1] 1969 federal elections in West Malaysia only.
[2] People's Action Party—PAP, Singapore only.
[3] United Democratic Party—UDP.
[4] Socialist Front.
[5] Socialist Front equals 16.1 percent.

The Alliance lost 22 seats in the parliamentary elections; on the state level, it was unable to wrest Kelantan from the PMIP, lost Penang to Gerakan by a considerable margin, and failed to get a majority in Perak, winning 19 out of the 40 seats. In Selangor, which contains the federal capital, the Alliance and the opposition parties tied, each winning four seats. The Alliance, however, won control of the state assemblies in Pahang, Perlis, Trengganu, Johore, Negri Sembilan, Kedah, and Malacca.

Of the 282 state seats in West Malaysia, the Alliance won 167 and the opposition, 115. Among the opposition, the PMIP had 40; the DAP, 31; Gerakan, 26; the PPP, 12; the Party Ra'ayat, 3; and independents, 3. The MCA, which has been weak in urban Chinese electorates, lost more than half of its seats. Of the 33 candidates it put up (three of whom were unopposed), 20 were defeated—nine in Perak, five in Selangor, three in Penang, two in Negri Sembilan, and one in Malacca. In these states the DAP, the PPP, and Gerakan had previously reached an agreement in conducting elections. Interpreting its defeat as a rejection of its leadership, MCA announced that it would not participate in the new Alliance government, although it would continue to support it.

Communal considerations have not ceased to be politically irrelevant in the voting pattern. A significant increase in vote was recorded by PMIP, whose championing of Malay resistance to supposed encroachment by other races was a factor in increasing its share of the total vote (24.3 percent). The Malay vote was split between UMNO and PMIP, as no more than 54 percent of the Malay electorate, which turned out in greater numbers than non-Malays, voted for UMNO candidates. Many of those Malays, who were discontented with the Alliance and fearful of losing their special rights if other opposition parties won power, turned to PMIP.

CHAPTER 14

FOREIGN RELATIONS

The Malaysian government has followed a policy of independence in foreign affairs, while adopting neither a passive nor a neutral stance. Foreign policy has been influenced by a number of special considerations: membership in the British Commonwealth, the 12-year struggle against Communist terrorists, a plural society, a dependence on trade, and the country's strategic geographic location in Southeast Asia.

During the early 1960's Malaya (after 1963, Malaysia) made a determined effort to widen diplomatic contacts among Asian and African countries, in part to counteract Indonesia's adverse propaganda during the Confrontation (see Glossary) but largely because Malaysia wished to belong to the Afro-Asian community. Influential Alliance Party members in the Federal Parliament had urged during the second half of 1965 the "widest diplomatic representation possible with countries, irrespective of their ideologies." Malaysia's foreign policy gradually shifted away from primary orientation to Great Britain and the British Commonwealth. Great Britain's decision to withdraw its forces from the Malaysia area in the early 1970's accentuated this trend. In the late 1960's Malaysia expanded its contacts further by establishing formal relations with Communist countries in Europe, including the Soviet Union. A friendly Soviet Union was counted upon to provide a counterweight to Communist China, but Malaysia joined either other staunchly anti-Communist countries in forming the Asian and Pacific Council (ASPAC) in June of that year.

Despite the establishment of diplomatic and commercial ties with the Soviet Union and Communist countries in Eastern Europe, policy toward the People's Republic of China (Communist China) had not changed by 1969. The government continued to fear Communist China's expansionist ambitions and its influence over the large Chinese population within Malaysia.

Despite its Western ties, the country considers itself nonaligned and is a member of the nonaligned group of Asian and African countries at the United Nations (UN) and in international conferences.

Although its orientation in general has been pro-West, Malaysia has avoided identification with the West more than is necessary for immediate tactical purposes, such as in the struggle against local communism or to ensure national security. It shared with other Asian and African countries at the United Nations and other international conferences an anticolonialist posture and opposition to racial discrimination and apartheid policies; it differed with them over other issues when such action was dictated by its traditional anti-Communist stand and consideration of national interests.

CONDUCT OF FOREIGN POLICY

Administrative Organization

Before independence in 1957 the foreign relations of Malaya were managed by the British Foreign Office and British officials elsewhere in the world. Malaya, however, has commissioners stationed in London, Australia, India, and Pakistan, and a number of nations established consulates in Singapore, Kuala Lumpur, and Penang. The British offered some preindependence training to a small number of civil servants, usually seconded from the Malayan Civil Service, by posting them in foreign quasi-diplomatic assignments or by providing other training of a diplomatic nature.

Because of a shortage of qualified personnel, the country has been slow since independence in opening diplomatic missions abroad. The earliest representation went to Commonwealth countries and the United States; five other Asian, two Middle Eastern, and two Western European missions had been opened by September 1963 when Malaysia was created. By the end of 1969, the country was maintaining 25 embassies abroad, in addition to consulates in five additional cities. Where there are no Malaysian missions available communications and inquiries were channeled through the legations of other Commonwealth countries, usually those of Great Britain. Twenty-seven countries maintained permanent embassies or legations in Kuala Lumpur in 1969, while 12 other countries enjoyed accreditation to Malaysia without resident mission.

The internal organization of the Foreign Affairs Service is patterned after that of the civil service, with which it was merged in 1966. Senior posts (Branch A, corresponding to Division I elsewhere in the public services) are occupied by holders of either an A.B. (honors) from a recognized university, a first- or second-class pass in the bar final examination, or a third-class pass in the bar final examination and a degree from a recognized university (see ch. 12, The Governmental System). Recruitment policy also gave ethnic Malays a 3 to 1 preference over non-Malays. Only about 100 officers in Branch A filled the senior posts in embassies, consulates, high commissions, and the foreign ministry in 1969.

The principal officers below the foreign minister are the permanent secretary for foreign affairs, deputy secretary for foreign affairs, chief of protocol, principal assistant secretary, and assistant deputy secretary. The Ministry of Foreign Affairs is divided into separate geographic divisions: the United Nations; South and Central America and Africa; Southeast Asia, Australia, and New Zealand; South and East Asia; Commonwealth and Europe; and Asia, West Asia, and North America. Each of these divisions is headed by a principal assistant secretary, except for the division for South and East Asia, which is headed by an assistant secretary.

The Administrative and General Affairs Division is under the deputy secretary. The Political Division, the Administration, Supply, and Finance Division, the Consular and Communications Division, and the Economic and Regional Cooperation Division are each under a principal assistant secretary. The Information Division, on the other hand, is under an assistant secretary, and the Protocol Division is under a chief of protocol.

Formulation of Foreign Policy

Foreign policy is formulated at cabinet level, and Parliament enacts laws implementing agreements with foreign powers. The Constitution does not specify where the power to declare war lies. External threats may justify the invoking of emergency powers, in which case the immediate power lies in the hands of the Supreme Head of Malaysia, Yang di-Pertuan Agong (see ch. 12, The Governmental System).

The Alliance Party has dominated foreign policy formulation since independence. The military is expected to be nonpolitical, and the corps of senior officers is regarded as a British-oriented elite. Trade unions are not affiliated with political parties, and their leaders have not sought to lobby in the federal government on foreign policy.

Since 1957 foreign policy has been determined largely by Prime Minister Tengku Abdul Rahman (called the Tengku) who concurrently held the portfolio of minister of foreign affairs. In recent years Deputy Prime Minister Tun Abdul Razak has assumed an increasing foreign policy role, although for the most part the Tengku has continued to make the crucial decisions. A majority of diplomats and senior foreign affairs advisers have been Malays. The most vigorous and most influential of them has been Dato M. Ghazalie bin Shafie, the permanent secretary to the foreign affairs ministry since 1960.

Domestic Political Factors

One of the historic realities that has exerted a continuing influence on the substance and application of Malaysian foreign policy has been the country's plural society. A roughly even balance exists between Malays and non-Malays, with Chinese constituting the great majority of non-Malays (see ch. 4, Ethnic Groups and Languages).

Although government policy has sought to make politically united Malaysians out of the diverse communities, a portion of each community has nevertheless tended to identify itself with its national and cultural homeland. A sense of nationhood, depending on a history of shared experiences, has so far not been well developed, since Malays and Chinese do not share a common heritage. Chinese attachment to Chinese tradition and culture and to China itself as a world power, irrespective of ideology, has remained a strong element. To a certain extent, the Indians have not significantly weakened their sentiment toward India, which they demonstrated in their overwhelming contribution to the "save democracy" fund launched by the Tengku in 1962 when India was attacked by Communist China.

Chauvinistic Malays often have a pronounced bias in favor of Indonesia and an antipathy toward the Chinese. In addition, the ultranationalistic Malays among members of the Pan-Malayan Islamic Party have condemned some aspects of formal ties with Great Britain and have objected to any such bias in foreign policies. Thus, in formulating and executing foreign policy the political elite, most of whom are Westernized Malays, have found it necessary to consider the feelings of the other communities and the more traditional members of their own community.

Historic Influence

Because independence was gained at a time when the country was engaged in a violent struggle against the Communist terrorist activities, foreign policy has been resolutely anti-Communist. To that extent, Malaysia has been inclined to favor the West. According to the Tengku, "where there has been a conflict between the two ideologies—Western and Eastern ideologies—then, we side with the Western ideologies or the Western understanding of democracy."

The existing pro-Western orientation, however, has deep historic roots stemming from Malayan colonial experience with the British. Throughout the period of British hegemony, the British were scrupulous in observing the constitutional position of the Malay rulers, and in general British-Malay relations were cordial and mutually advantageous. The British were regarded by the Malay community as the paternalistic protectors of the Malay way of life, and the British administration, for its part, was distinctly Malay-oriented. This overall cordiality left its impression on the Malaysian leaders.

A contemporary political byproduct of the colonial experience has been participation in the British Commonwealth of Nations. Whatever the exact responsibilities and privileges of membership might entail, the country has taken an active part in its Commonwealth affairs.

Experience with the Emergency left an indelible mark on the country's foreign and domestic policies (see ch. 3, Historical Setting). Communists, overwhelmingly Chinese, launched guerrilla terrorism that lasted from 1948 through 1960, cost the equivalent of nearly US$600 million, and claimed some 11,000 lives. The fact that it was Communist-directed and supported and was predominantly Chinese in composition has had considerable influence in determining policies in the international scene.

MULTILATERAL RELATIONSHIPS

United Nations

The Federation of Malaya was admitted to membership in the UN on September 17, 1957, by a unanimous resolution of the General Assembly sponsored by the members of the Commonwealth. Active participation and cooperation in UN peace efforts have characterized the country's membership in that body. Malaysia was a member of 12 of the 14 specialized agencies of the UN in 1969, Malayan troops served under the UN flag in the Congo from 1960 to 1963, and the country purchased UN bonds to support the UN operations in the Congo. The Malayan delegate opposed attempts of the Soviet Union to weaken the secretary generalship after the death of Dag Hammarshjöld and supported the appointment of U Thant to the vacated post. Malaya agreed to permit a UN survey team in 1963 to assess the attitudes of the people of Sabah and Sarawak toward the idea of federation. Because of Malaysia's active support of the UN, it was elected to a nonpermanent seat on the Security Council in 1965, a development which precipitated Indonesia's temporary withdrawal from the UN.

In another context, the country's activities in the UN reflect to some extent cross-purposes arising from membership in the Commonwealth, identification with the Afro-Asian group, opposition to colonialism and apartheid policies, and the need to maintain the posture of nonalignment. Nevertheless, the country's votes and statements were in 1969 by no means falling consistently with a pattern of Afro-Asian nonalignment policies. In casting its vote on cold war questions, the country was in agreement with the average Commonwealth voting record on about three out of four occasions and with its Southeast Asian neighbors about two out of three times.

Regional Groupings

Southeast Asia Treaty Organization

Despite its anti-Communist stand, independent Malaya declined membership in the Southeast Asia Treaty Organization (SEATO). The government viewed its defense agreement with Great Britain as a suitable and satisfactory alternative to SEATO membership because it provided protection without as much political involvement; another consideration was the unpopularity of SEATO with India, Indonesia, and some Malays. In addition, Malaya did not wish to provoke Communist China. Even Confrontation did not result in any overt change in the country's attitude toward SEATO.

Association of Southeast Asia

Initially formulated by Prime Minister Rahman and Philippine President Carlos P. Garcia during the Tengku's visit to the Philippines in January 1959, ASA was aimed primarily at economic and cultural cooperation, although leaders in other Southeast Asian countries, particularly in Indonesia, Cambodia, and Burma, have maintained that ASA is a "political" group.

The conflict with the Philippines over Sabah, the former British North Borneo, all but deactivated ASA after 1963, although the idea was kept alive by Prime Minister Rahman's strong interest. ASA was briefly reactivated when the foreign ministers of the member countries met at Bangkok in August 1966.

Malaysia-Philippines-Indonesia Regional Concept

Another form of regional cooperation involving Malaysia was the MAPHILINDO (Malaysia-Philippines-Indonesia) concept, which envisioned a loose confederation of these three countries of Malay ethnic origin. This concept was promoted by President Sukarno, Philippine President Diosdado Macapagal and the Tengku in 1963 at the Manila Conference. Within Malaysia, it was particularly attractive to the Malay racial component, which shares some common problems with Indonesia and the Philippines in relation to their ethnic Chinese populations.

Asian and Pacific Council

In early 1966, when Confrontation was waning and British retrenchment east of Suez was defined, Malaysian foreign policy displayed interest in new regional cooperation. It joined the Asian and Pacific Council (ASPAC), which was formed in June 1966 under the initiative of South Korea and made up of anti-Communist countries strongly aligned with the United States—Australia, the Republic of China, Japan, New Zealand, the Philippines, Thailand, South Korea, and South Vietnam. Malaysian contacts with these countries increased through the standing committee composed of the ambassadors of member countries residing in Bangkok.

Association of Southeast Asian Nations

On May 31, 1967, even before the resumption of diplomatic relations in August of that year, Deputy Prime Minister Razak, supported the proposal of Indonesian Foreign Minister Adam Malik for a new regional association in Southeast Asia. Originally, Malaysia sought merely to expand ASA to include Indonesia and Singapore, but Indonesia insisted on the formation of a separate organization. The Association of Southeast Asian Nations (ASEAN) was formed on August 8, 1967, in Bangkok. In addition to Indonesia and Malaysia, the new organization's membership included the Philippines, Thailand, and Singapore.

ASEAN basically pursued objectives similar to those of its predecessor, ASA, a point which prompted Malaysia to request the dissolution of ASA. Malaysia cooperated with ASEAN and was host to several committee meetings in Kuala Lumpur, but the country remained somewhat skeptical about the organization's future, largely because of the uncertain course of Indonesia and the numerous differences that still plagued Malaysia's bilateral relations with Singapore and the Philippines. Malaysia had made it a condition of its attendance at various ASEAN conferences that the Philippines would not raise the Sabah issue at such meetings. As a result of such reservations, Malaysia in 1969 tended to emphasize improvement in bilateral relations as a necessary prerequisite to the longer term regional solution.

Malaysia was host to the third ASEAN ministerial meeting in December 1969, at which the normalization of Malaysia's diplomatic relations with the Philippines was announced. This announcement and agreement to some 98 committee recommendations gave ASEAN a much needed boost.

BILATERAL RELATIONSHIPS

Great Britain and the Commonwealth

United Kingdom

Malaysia has enjoyed close formal relations with Great Britain, especially in defense, and an intricate network of informal relations based upon trade, investment, shared social and political values and, until recently, the continued employment of expatriates in civil military services.

Although the extent to which the British officially encouraged or even inspired the plan for the federation of Malaysia is still disputed, the public initiative lay with Prime Minister Rahman. Once the merger proposal had been announced, it was 4 months before the British government accepted it, contingent on a satisfactory investigation of Borneo public opinion and on guarantees of continued access to the Singapore bases. By July 1962 Great Britain had formally committed itself to federation within the ensuing 12 months. The Marquis of Lansdowne was appointed chairman of a committee to draft the terms of entry for the Borneo states, and most of its recommendations were incorporated in the Malaysia Agreement signed in London on July 9, 1963. The Tengku's concession to Indonesia and the Philippines at Manila in early August to allow a postponement of Malaysia's inauguration for the sake of a UN inspection team in Borneo reportedly annoyed the British government. A new high commissioner, however, was appointed to handle Anglo-Malaysian relations after Malaysia Day.

The creation of Malaysia was, however, followed by Indonesia's policy of Confrontation against the new federation. Great Britain committed itself fully to the support of Malaysia.

Malaysia has moved gradually away from its earlier intimate relationship with Great Britain. Prime Minister Rahman articulated this in his Independence Day speech of 1966, declaring that Malaysia should "be regarded by her neighbors as a specifically Asian country and not as a creation and protege of Britain." Soon afterwards, the Malaysian dollar severed its ties with the pound sterling, and certain commodities were made ineligible for the Commonwealth trade preference. The country also has turned to new sources of capital, principally international financial institutions.

Differences over Singapore's separation and British defense aid, Malaysian accusations of British interference in Sabah and Sarawak, and negotiations with Indonesia led to some anti-British feeling on the part of Malaysians, which was reciprocated by the British. Malaysia expected full support from the British in its dispute with

Singapore. Although the British apparently attempted to remain neutral in the dispute, some Malaysians believed that Great Britain was siding with Singapore and had been applying pressure to come to terms with Prime Minister Lee Kuan Yew both before and after separation. The British, on the other hand, appeared to feel that Malaysia had pushed Singapore out of the country without consulting Great Britain.

With the formal end of Confrontation, Great Britain moved rapidly to reduce its military presence in Malaysia and to formulate its plans for withdrawal "East of Suez." Britain's announcements in mid-1967 and January 1968 of a timetable for withdrawal upset the Malaysian government. Both the Malaysia and Singapore governments have expressed hope that some formal defense agreements with Great Britain can be continued.

In order to discuss the impact of the British military withdrawal and to formulate a new defense arrangement, five-power defense talks (consisting of Malaysia, Singapore, Australia, New Zealand, and Great Britain) were held in Kuala Lumpur in June 1968 and in Canberra in June 1969. Malaysians were still concerned over the prospect of British withdrawal despite assurances by British Defense Minister Denis Healey that the mobility of British forces would facilitate their deployment to the Far East after 1971, if necessary, and the pledge by British Conservative Party Leader Edward Heath that his party would reverse the British Labour Party withdrawal decision. Prime Minister Rahman accordingly issued a statement that his country has "to find an alternative arrangement for the security of the area."

Other issues with Great Britain related to the economy and to the Malaysianization of Sabah and Sarawak. Malaysians, whose economy suffered from the devaluation of British sterling in late 1967, were somewhat piqued with the equivalent of approximately US$70 million in aid offered by the British government to offset the effects of the withdrawal, in contrast to the equivalent of approximately US$140 million offered to Singapore. In trying to implement the government policy of Malaysianization in Sabah and Sarawak, Malaysians complained that numerous British expatriates in those states had stimulated resistance to Malaysianization.

Informal relations with Great Britain continue but are declining in importance. British ownership in the plantation economy continues on a large scale and, although the country severed its ties with the pound sterling in 1966, Malaysia's vast sterling reserves remained on deposit in London banks. Many cultural, educational, and linguistic links and the juridical link to the Privy Council all tend to reinforce past ties. Some Alliance Party members, however, have recently sought to discard the Privy Council link in favor of a mechanism outside of the Commonwealth, an action that would make subsequent ties to the Commonwealth purely formal.

Australia and New Zealand

Strategic and sentimental considerations underlie relations with Australia and New Zealand. Geographic proximity, the shared legacy of British colonial administration, and the English language have enabled many Australians and New Zealanders to help influence the political, social, and military institutions of Malaysia. Technical assistance, especially under Colombo Plan auspices, has been highly successful on the level of cross-cultural contact and has produced an influx of Malaysian students into Australian or New Zealand academic institutions.

Australia has not only considerable private investment in the country but also has become Malaysia's fifth largest trading partner (see ch. 22, Foreign Economic Relations). The country also has received an influx of Australian tourists. New Zealand, on the other hand, apparently enjoys a better image in the country than does Australia because of its "white Australia" policy, which the Malaysians deeply resent.

Fundamental concern for the country's security has been shared by Australia and New Zealand. This concern originated from the Japanese invasion of 1941 and 1942 and was later reinforced by the Emergency. In 1959 the two Pacific neighbors formally associated themselves with the 1957 Anglo-Malayan Defense Agreement through exchange of letters between their respective high commissioners in the former Federation of Malaya. Australia and New Zealand cautiously approved the Malaysia merger proposal in mid-1961, but they were little involved in the early Anglo-Malayan negotiations concerning the project and they were not informed or consulted by Malaysia before its break with Singapore in 1965.

The official Australian and New Zealand policy of accommodation during the initial period of Confrontation hardened following intensified Indonesian military activity. Australia offered military support to Malaysia on September 25, 1963, 5 days after New Zealand had entered into a similar commitment. The two Pacific neighbors had several thousand armed service personnel in Malaysia and Singapore when the Bangkok Peace Agreement was signed.

Both the Australian and New Zealand governments welcomed the end of Confrontation. It was especially important for Australia, which was anxious to normalize its relations with Indonesia. The separation of Singapore from Malaysia and the British military retrenchment in the Malaysia area, scheduled to occur by 1971, posed difficult problems for the Australian and New Zealand governments, and they called for reassessments of their defense commitments with Malaysia, which were to expire in 1971. Although Australia did not enter binding defense commitments with Malaysia in 1969, it did offer a generous amount of military, economic, and technical aid.

Singapore

Singapore is closely tied to West Malaysia by geography, economics, and personal relations, but differences in ideology, economic competition, racial suspicion, and a personality clash between leaders of the two governments caused tension and eventually led to the separation of Singapore from Malaysia on August 9, 1965 (see ch. 3, Historical Setting).

The separation agreement between the two countries promised close cooperation in defense, foreign policy, and economic affairs, but it remained largely unfulfilled in 1969. The agreement reference to defense underlined the essential interdependence between the defense of Malaysia and the defense of Singapore. A joint defense council was to be set up. Malaysia was to assist Singapore in external defense, and Singapore would "contribute from its own armed forces such units thereof as may be considered reasonable and adequate for such defense; each party will undertake not to enter into any treaty or agreement with a foreign country which may be detrimental to the independence and defense of the territory of the other party."

Implementation of the agreement has been impeded by a series of differences. Malaysia objected to Singapore's conducting separate negotiations with Indonesia, which led to Singapore's recognition in 1966. On the other hand, arguments over defense administration led to Singapore's withdrawal from the joint defense council in March 1966. It was this council that had rejected Singapore's plan for resumed barter trade with Indonesia in late 1965.

By October 1969 no definitive defense arrangements had been made, despite the sense or urgency lent by impending British withdrawal, the five-power talks on defense in 1968 and 1969, and bilateral talks conducted between their leaders. There were economic problems as well, and the Independence of Singapore Agreement 1965 rescinded the reference in the Malaysia Agreement to a common market (see ch. 22, Foreign Economic Relations).

Southeast Asia

Indonesia

The end of Confrontation marked a new phase in Malaysian-Indonesian relations. In addition to sharing ethnic and cultural roots, Malaysia and Indonesia in 1969 were following similar policies toward communism, suppressing local Communist activity but maintaining friendly ties with Communist countries other than Communist China. Indonesia's increasingly close association with the Western countries facilitated the rapprochement of the two countries.

The cordial relationship of the late 1960's contrasted with the period between Malaya's independence in 1957 and the ensuing conflict in 1963, which was characterized by a series of strained relations between the two countries. Indonesia had expressed overt disbelief in Malaya's determination to stand on its own feet and in its intention to remain a friendly and cooperative neighbor. Indonesia felt greatly offended, for example, by the fact that Malaya failed to support its claim in the UN for the incorporation of West New Guinea in 1957 and that the British in Malaya and Singapore provided bases and refuge for Indonesian rebels involved in the antigovernment revolt on Sumatra in 1958. While official Indonesian statements stressed cooperation between the two nations, hostility was expressed by such acts as the obstruction of Malay and Singapore shipping in the Malacca Strait and harassment of Malayan nationals in Indonesia.

Nevertheless, with some misgivings on both sides, the two countries signed the Treaty of Friendship in 1959. During the Indonesian delegation's stay in Kuala Lumpur, however, and Indonesian gunboat raid into Malayan waters, an incident which had not been uncommon since 1957, clouded the negotiations. The treaty remained an ineffective document, and all other attempts at cooperation ended in frustration and failure. As far as the Malayans were concerned, relations were strained most by Indonesian political subversion (see ch. 13, Political Dynamics).

In 1961 Prime Minister Rahman made an attempt to reconcile Indonesia and Dutch interests in the West New Guinea issue. Although his plan was quite similar to the formula on which the conflict was ultimately resolved, Indonesia rejected his role as mediator. Instead, it intensified its propaganda campaign to recruit volunteers for the liberation of West New Guinea from among the Indonesian-oriented segments of Singapore and Malaya.

The October 1965 countercoup in Indonesia did not produce a change of policy towards Malaysia until March 1966, when Sukarno was made to abdicate his executive powers in favor of General Suharto. It was then that Indonesia began to disengage from its policy of Confrontation.

On May 15, 1966, the Indonesian government proposed direct peace talks with Malaysia at foreign minister level. The ministerial meeting took place from May 30 to June 1. Differing national aims and interpretations as to the substantive essence of the quarrel seemed at first to preclude any agreement. Malaysia insisted that its origins and continuation as a legal entity were never at issue, especially since the UN had ascertained that the majority of the people in Sabah and Sarawak favored the merger with the former Federation of Malaya. Indonesia, on the other hand, demanded that adherence of Sabah and Sarawak to Malaysia must be based "upon the will for freedom of the peoples concerned."

Indonesian Foreign Minister Adam Malik and Malaysian Deputy Prime Minister Razak signed the peace agreement restoring relations in Bangkok on June 1, 1966. Indonesian ratification was delayed for 2 months, however, because of Sukarno's obstruction. On August 11, 1966, Razak and Malik appended their signatures to what President Sukarno described as an "improved version" of the Bangkok Peace Agreement. Elections held in Sabah in April 1967, which resulted in a victory for the pro-Malaysia Alliance Coalition, were accepted by Indonesia as fulfilling Malaysia's obligation under the Bangkok Agreement as far as Sabah was concerned. The elections in Sarawak scheduled for 1969, however, were postponed (see ch. 13, Political Dynamics).

On May 11, 1967, Malaysia and Indonesia resumed full diplomatic relations. The liaison offices that had been maintained in the capital cities after Confrontation ended were raised to full diplomatic missions. Even before the two countries recognized each other diplomatically, however, they had exchanged cultural and goodwill missions in 1966, and their delegations had met in Kuala Lumpur to agree on a common spelling for their related language.

In early March 1968 Prime Minister Rahman made a goodwill visit to Djakarta. The visit was the occasion for a proposal to renew the 1959 Treaty of Friendship, which virtually had been abandoned. One result of the Tengku's visit to Indonesia concerned the territorial waters of Malaysia and Indonesia, particularly in the Straits of Sumatra and Malacca. Accordingly, the two countries in 1969 signed an agreement delimiting the continental shelf between them in the Strait of Malacca, the east coast of Malaysia, and the Sarawak coastal areas. The agreement would facilitate the granting of concessions and exploration of mineral resources. The agreement was preceded by consultation talks necessitated by Malaysia's recent decision to extend its territorial water limits from 3 to 12 miles (in order to match Indonesia's 12 miles) that would cause overlapping of boundaries at some points, such as where the Strait of Malacca is only 20 miles wide.

Malaysia's desire for good relations with Indonesia has been reinforced by the wish to enlist Indonesia cooperation in regional security arrangements. As early as June 1966, one of Malaysia's influential leaders and minister of home affairs, Tun Ismail bin Dato

341

Abdul Rahman, said it would be impossible to check encroachment of hostile forces in Southeast Asia without the cooperation of Indonesia. Indonesian spokesmen, however, repeatedly have stressed the country's preference for closer economic cooperation and regional unity, rather than security ties. Indonesia would prefer to confine its security cooperation in the border regions with Malaysia. In an agreement signed on March 11, 1967, the two countries agreed to cooperate in border security arrangements to deal with the "common enemy—Communist groups operating the areas" and joint measures to deal with piracy in the Straits of Malacca.

Indonesia also increased its technical and cultural cooperation with Malaysia in recent years. Indonesian teachers have been sent to West Malaysia, and offers were made in 1969 to train Malaysians in science and technology. A flourishing Indonesia trade and tourist traffic to West Malaysia are handled by a consulate in Penang, and another one was to be opened soon in Malacca. Malaysia, for its part, waived visa requirements for Indonesian visitors, a privilege denied Filipino visitors since the strain in Malaysian relations with the Philippines became acute in 1968.

Philippines

Communication is facilitated between the Philippines and Malaysia by the English language, as members of both nations speak English mainly. Their governmental systems are both based on the principles of Western democracy, and they both have gained their independence peacefully, retained close ties with their former colonial rulers, and are distinctly Western-oriented. The Philippines promptly extended diplomatic recognition to Malaya upon its independence in 1957, but it was 4 years before the two countries agreed to exchange ambassadors.

Despite their common interests, the dispute over parts of Sabah territory, which the Philippines has officially claimed since 1962, continued to strain their relations in 1969 (see ch. 3, Historical Setting). The Philippines insist that the Sultan of Sulu, in using the Malayan word *pajak*, signified leasing the disputed territory to Great Britain in 1787, whereas Malaysia maintains that the word really expresses "cession" and that they, therefore, as legal heirs to the British possession, have undisputed right to the territory.

Diplomatic relations, which were broken in 1963, were resumed at the consular level in May 1964. Full diplomatic relations were not restored, however, until June 1966, but even earlier the Philippine government had undertaken a role as intermediary between Malaysia and Indonesia. Malaysia, for its part, encouraged rapprochement with the Philippines by supporting the Philippine bid for selection as headquarters of the new Asian Development Bank, although the Tengku had originally favored its establishment in Ceylon. Moreover, the government of the state of Sabah was cooperating with the new Philippine administration in eradicating smuggling.

In December 1967 Deputy Prime Minister Razak made a visit to the Philippines. The implementation of the antismuggling agreement that had been signed in the early part of the year was discussed, as were problems related to Filipino labor in Sabah.

In June 1968 the Philippine and Malaysian delegations met in Bangkok to have talks on Sabah. After 5 weeks the Philippine delegation announced that the period of "clarification" of its claim was over and that talks should proceed in a manner to settle the dispute. The Malaysians then rejected the claim on political and historical grounds. President Marcos then ordered, but did not effect immediately, the return of the embassy staff from Kuala Lumpur with the exception of one officer.

A cooling-off period agreed to by Philippine Secretary of Foreign Affairs Narciso Ramos and Deputy Prime Minister Razak at the ASEAN meeting in Djakarta in early August was disrupted by a Philippine bill redefining the country's national territory, which Malaysia interpreted as asserting sovereignty over Sabah. Despite warnings from the Malaysian government, President Marcos signed the bill into law in September 1968. This triggered Malaysia's suspension of diplomatic relations with the Philippines and government-sponsored demonstrations in Sabah and West Malaysia. A special session of the lower House of Parliament in mid-October unanimously passed a resolution condemning the new Philippine act.

In mid-October President Marcos attempted to arrange summit talks in Tokyo in order to establish some understanding with Malaysia. The Tengku agreed, on condition that it would not be a cover for reopening the Bangkok talks and that the claim would not be discussed. Before the talks could be held, however, Philippine Secretary of Foreign Affairs Ramos made a speech in the UN General Assembly in which he denied Malaysia's authority over Sabah.

Malaysia has appeared concerned that the breakdown in relations with the Philippines could kill hopes for turning ASEAN into an effective regional organization and saving it from the fate that overtook its predecessors, ASA and MAPHILINDO. Malaysia left the door open for mediation within the framework of ASEAN, and diplomatic relations of a sort continued to exist, although conducted through the countries' respective missions in Bangkok. Relations were finally normalized at the ASEAN conference in December 1969.

Thailand and Malaysia share common tradition and common political problems. Disputes between them have stemmed from territorial claims, minority grievances, the conduct of joint anti-Communist border patrols, and the threat of a canal across the Isthmus of Kra.

Thailand regarded the states of Kedah, Perlis, Trengganu, and Kelantan to have been forcibly ceded to Great Britain in 1909. It temporarily recovered them during World War II, but diplomatic pressure by the British at the end of the war forced their return to the Federation of Malaya.

The Thai-Malaysian border has remained a troubled area largely because of the separatist elements in Thailand's four southern provinces, which are predominantly Muslims and ethnic Malays, and Communist guerrilla activities along the border. Malaysia has repeatedly denied Thai allegations of encouraging these separatist sentiments. Communist guerrillas, believed to be rebel followers of Chin Peng, the Communist leader during the Emergency, have occasionally attempted to exploit the separatist movements. Moreover, Malaysian Communists have maintained a liaison with Thai Communists.

Cooperation between the security forces of the two countries in suppressing Communist rebels operating along their border regions was sought by the Tengku during his first visit to Bangkok after independence, and an agreement was signed in 1959. In March 1965 the two countries signed a second agreement for further strengthening collaboration in their counterinsurgency operations in the area. A Thai-Malaysia Joint Border Committee decided in 1969 to sanction the movement of the respective national forces up to 25 miles into each other's territory during joint operations.

Personal relationships between leaders of the Malaysian and Thai governments are excellent. Prime Minister Rahman's mother was Thai, and his early education was in Bangkok. Deputy Prime Minister Razak and Thai Foreign Minister Thanat Khoman also have developed a close friendship.

During Confrontation Thailand sought to help restore normal relations between Malaysia, on the one hand, and Indonesia and the Philippines, on the other. After Malaysia broke diplomatic relations with both Indonesia and the Philippines in September 1963, Thailand agreed to represent Malaysia in both Djakarta and Manila, and 2 years later, after the Malaysian rupture with Pakistan, Thailand assumed similar responsibilities in Rawalpindi.

Thai Foreign Minister Thanat Khoman brought the foreign ministers of Indonesia, the Philippines, and Malaysia together in February 1964 in Bangkok. Consular relations between the Philippines and Malaysia were resumed in mid-June 1964, largely through the mediatory efforts of Thanat Khoman.

Whereas the Thai foreign minister's attempt to bring Sukarno and Rahman together in early 1965 was unproductive, the next undertaken was more successful, for it produced the crucial Razak-Malik meetings of May 31 to June 1, 1966, in Bangkok, as the result of which they agreed to normalize relations.

Malaysian tourists traffic into Thailand has been increasing in recent years, and during Confrontation Thailand was Malaysia's major trading partner in Southeast Asia (see ch. 22, Foreign Economic Relations). Thailand also serves as one source of Malaysia's rice imports.

Burma

Relations with Burma, which welcomed the formation of Malaysia, have remained cordial. Because of its strict neutralist policy, Burma declined participation in ASA in 1961 and, while maintaining the friendliest of formal relations with Indonesia, it declined to submit a joint communique with Indonesia that might have been construed as a criticism of Malaysia.

Burmese government policy of minimizing contact with the outside world precluded it from diplomatic relations with Malaysia until 1964, when ambassadors were exchanged; before that, Burmese interests were represented by its consulate general in Singapore. In late 1965 Deputy Prime Minister Razak led a goodwill mission to Rangoon, and in April 1968 the chairman of Burma's Revolutionary Council, General Ne Win, visited Kuala Lumpur, the first visit by a Burmese head of government to Malaysia.

North and South Vietnam

Malaysia has displayed understanding of the predicament of South Vietnam because of its own experience with Communist guerrilla terrorism and of external threats directly or indirectly inspired by communism. It has consistently regarded the war in Vietnam as part of the pattern of worldwide Communist, particularly Chinese, aggression. It has remained convinced that the military defeat of the Vietcong revolutionaries would best serve Malaysia's national interest. Malaysian government leaders have felt, however, that too close an identification with the South Vietnamese regime would discredit the Malaysian image before neutralist Afro-Asian countries.

Formal relations had been established between Malaysia (then Malaya) and South Vietnam at the ministerial level in 1959, after

Prime Minister Rahman's official visit a year before. In that visit, the two heads of state expressed "complete identity of views." In 1960, when their diplomatic mission was raised to embassy level, the late Vietnamese President, Ngo Dinh Diem returned the Tengku's visit. The Tengku paid a second visit to the country late in 1961, when the two chiefs of state conferred on the Communist threat to South Vietnam. Subsequently, Malaysia sent advisers to give the South Vietnamese the benefit of its successful experience against Communist insurgency.

Malaysia's Vietnamese policy was not altered significantly either by the overthrow of the Diem regime in November 1963 or by Confrontation. Some of its aid program was temporarily suspended, but in July 1964 Malaysia gave a cordial reception in Kuala Lumpur to a goodwill mission headed by General Tran Thiem Khiem (appointed South Vietnamese premier in mid-1969). Malaysia also endorsed intensified American prosecution of the war and welcomed the visit to Kuala Lumpur of Prime Minister Nguyen Kao Ky (vice president in 1969) in October 1965. Despite its conflict with Indonesia, Malaysia in 1965 was training more than 2,000 Vietnamese counterinsurgency troops.

While providing various forms of assistance to South Vietnam, Malaysia has stopped short of becoming militarily involved in the war itself. At the UN its representative has called for Vietnam peace negotiations based on the principle "that all states have the right to an independent existence without interference from other states."

Malaysia has no formal relations with North Vietnam, other than trade in nonstrategic commodities. The late President Ho Chi Minh and Premier Pham Van Dong once linked the issues at stake in the Vietnam struggle with Indonesia's "crush Malaysia" campaign. In 1969 when Ho Chi Minh died, the Tengku called him "one of the great men of the century."

Laos

Although Malaysia and Laos shared similar attitudes toward regional security problems, especially those affecting the war in Vietnam, there has been little formal contact between them. Malaysia, however, has maintained diplomatic ties with Laos through the Malaysian ambassador to Thailand, concurrently accredited to Laos. In June 1966 Laos was the only neutral country that sent an observer to the meeting of ASPAC member countries. Both governments supported the American policy in Vietnam, including the level of military operations.

The first official contact between the two countries occurred in May 1962, when two leaders of the Laotian government, Prince

Boun Oum and General Phoumi Nosavan, made a formal visit to the Federation of Malaya. After the visit the federation government offered training in counterinsurgency operations to Laotian provincial governors.

Trade relations with Laos have significantly increased in recent years. Loatians found a major market for their important export, tin ore, in Malaysia where it is brought for processing (see ch. 22, Foreign Economic Relations).

Cambodia

Cambodia and Malaysia had not exchanged diplomatic missions by 1969. The Cambodian consulate general in Singapore continued to function after Malaysia's formation, but since the separation of Singapore Malaysia has had no resident representation.

Despite its entente with Communist China, Cambodia maintained correct relations with Malaysia. Profound differences in approaches to security problems and nonalighment divided the two countries. The Cambodian head of state, Prince Norodom Sihanouk, spurned Prime Minister Rahman's invitation to join a Southeas: Asian friendship treaty in late 1959 and also displayed initial reservation concerning the formation of Malaysia. The Cambodian representative to the United Nations Decolonization Committee of Seventeen, however, defended the merger proposal against severe criticism in late 1962, at a time when Sihanouk was making a state visit to Malaya and when Cambodian relations with Thailand and South Vietnam had seriously deteriorated. Although Prime Minister Rahman offered his services to the UN observer, Nils Gussing, in March 1963 in helping to settle the Thai-Cambodian border dispute, it was not until January 1964 that Sihanouk, during an unscheduled visit to Kuala Lumpur, requested the Tengku to mediate, suggesting Kuala Lumpur as a venue for discussions. No such discussion took place, however. On the other hand, the meeting between Philippine President Macapagal and Prime Minister Rahman, which Sihanouk had arranged during his visit to Kuala Lumpur in January, took place in Phnom Penh in February 1964. After the meeting the Philippines avoided identification with Indonesia in Confrontation, although it persisted with its Sabah claim.

Other Asian Countries

The People's Republic of China

Communist China has been one key point of reference for Malaysia policymakers because of the large ethnic Chinese population in the country. Irrespective of what regime rules mainland China, Malaysians fear Chinese influence within the country. The government has been particularly concerned, however, with the militant ideology of Communist China that encouraged leftwing subversives in Southeast Asia, both Chinese and non-Chinese.

Although Malaysia has increasingly established diplomatic relations or contacts with Communist countries in Eastern Europe, it has shown no disposition to change its basic policy towards Communist China. Malaysia has held to the "two Chinas" policy on the ground that neither the Communist China nor the Republic of China on Taiwan can represent China as a whole. It has favored in principle the admission of Communist China into the United Nations provided that the Republic of China should be protected as a political unit, that it would continue as a United Nation's member, and that a vote for admission of Communist China would not imply political recognition.

Despite the absence of diplomatic ties, trade and travel between Malaysia and Communist China have been allowed. Malaysia usually issues reentry permits to nationals wishing to visit relatives in the Chinese mainland for a short duration, and family remittances have been allowed. Immigration of Chinese from the mainland, however, has been forbidden.

The Republic of China

Despite the common antipathy of Chinese communism shared by Malaysia and the Republic of China, Malaysia had remained largely aloof in its position towards the government in Taiwan, and relations occasionally have been strained by the Chinese loyalty question. The Taiwan government's efforts to enlist the loyalties of overseas Chinese have angered various Malaysian leaders. In 1969 Malaysia protested to the Republic of China when some Malaysian Chinese students in Taiwan complained that they were regarded as nationals of that country and had been asked to swear alliance to it.

In the early 1960's the Malaysian Chinese Association, a component party of the Alliance Party strengthened its links with the Republic of China. A Republic of China consulate was opened in Kuala Lumpur in November 1964, several hundred Chinese Malaysian students flocked to Taiwan, and doctors from that island in turn were working in Malaysia. In addition, trade between the two countries has since increased substantially. A Malaysian consulate opened in Taipei early in 1967.

Japan

Japan recognized the Malaysia merger and maintained its large diplomatic mission in Kuala Lumpur, even during the period of Confrontation, but the Japanese were careful to emphasize their impartiality and their wish to maintain good relations with both disputants. The Japanese and the Malaysian governments share some views, but suspicion of Japan on the part of certain important elements of Malaysia's population, especially the Chinese, born of wartime experience, precluded closer bonds. Subsequently, Japan has tried to improve its image through economic and cultural means.

Japan showed restraint in openly advocating Malaysia's admission to the second Asian-African Conference scheduled for June 1965 in Algiers, but its vote on Malaysia's behalf was forthcoming. Japan also was precluded from dispensing substantial loans or grants to either disputant, although there was no interruption in Japanese trade with Indonesia. Once Confrontation ended, Malaysia received in November 1966 a Japanese loan of M$150 million (3.06 Malaysian dollars equal US$1) to assist the development plan. In September of the following year, in an agreement signed with Malaysia, Japan was to grant that country M$25 million and to provide technical help by way of a goodwill gesture to help atone for the Japanese occupation during the war. Scholarships for Malaysian students were offered to Malaysia, and since 1965 the Japanese government has sent to that country the Japanese Overseas Cooperation Volunteers, similar in function to the Peace Corps of the United States. These gestures have generated good will towards Japan.

The Republic of Korea

Malaysia shares a bond of friendship and a common anti-Communist posture with the Republic of Korea (South Korea). After ambassadors were exchanged in 1962, Deputy Prime Minister Razak led a five-man mission to Seoul in November of that year to sign a trade agreement. A Malaysia-Korean Cultural Agreement was proclaimed in Kuala Lumpur during the visit in September 1965 by the South Korean Prime Minister Il Kwon Chung. In early May 1969 the Yang di-Pertuan Agong and his wife paid a visit to South Korea to strengthen the friendship of the two countries.

In recent years South Korea has lent several medical doctors to Malaysia. Malaysia's anti-Communist line and recent interest in regional defense arrangements have strengthened the ties of the two countries. In June 1966 Malaysia joined ASPAC, an organization which was sponsored by South Korea. Malaysia has not officially recognized North Korea (the Korean People's Republic).

India, Pakistan, and Ceylon

In addition to association with the Pacific members of the Commonwealth, Malaysia also has many ties with fellow Asian members—India, Pakistan, and Ceylon. All three maintain high commissioner offices in Kuala Lumpur.

Ethnic ties link India and Ceylon with Malaysia's Indian and Ceylonese minorities. Because of this factor, the Malaysian government has been keenly sensitive to the currents of Indian foreign policy and, to a lesser extent, Pakistani and Ceylonese opinion. Opposition to anti-Asian racial policies wherever practiced links Malaysia with these three Asian Commonwealth partners.

Indian experience of nonalignment, even before the outbreak of hostilities with Communist China in 1962, made a strong and favorable impression among Malayan leaders. After India's split with Communist China, Malaya, which had opposed the Communist Chinese occupation of Tibet, was clearly concerned about an aggressive, expanding China.

Malaysians do not regard the Indian minority to be as much of an economic or political threat as they do the Chinese immigrants and so have adopted a generally hospitable attitude. During the period of Confrontation, India was slow to take a firm public stand on Malaysia's behalf, so that in May 1963 the Tengku referred to India as a "third party neutral" eligible for a mediatory role. After the death of Prime Minister Jahawarlal Nehru, India seemed to identify itself more with Malaysia. At both the preparatory meeting for the Algiers Asian-African Conference in April 1964 and the Cairo Conference of nonaligned states in October of the same year, the Indian leaders lobbied on Malaysia's behalf.

Malaysia in turn has consistently fully backed India in its border conflict with Communist China and supported India as one of the members of the preparatory committee for the Muslim summit meeting held in Rabat, Morocco, in late September 1969. Malaysia sought the inclusion of India in the conference over the vigorous objection of Pakistan that India is not a Muslim country.

Malaysia has received technical assistance from India. Training facilities have been provided for Malaysian military personnel in defense training institutions since 1965, and several Indians have been seconded to the Royal Malaysian Navy. Following the state visit of Prime Minister Indira Gandhi to Kuala Lumpur in June 1968, India offered to provide facilities for Malaysians in industrial, technical, and vocation institutions in India and to assist Malaysia in establishing an institute of technology. Plans were also made to finalize a trade agreement. In June 1967 the two countries entered into an agreement for the operation of air services between them.

Despite bonds of Islam, Malaysian relations with Pakistan have been quite different from those with India. The apparent leaning of Pakistan toward Communist China and Indonesia in 1964 and 1965 sharpened Malaysia's sympathies for India, despite Malaysian attempts to stay neutral in the dispute over Kashmir. Pakistan finally broke off relations with Malaysia in October 1965, in protest against what it claimed to be anti-Pakistan remarks by the Malaysian permanent representative to the UN during the UN Security Council debate on the Indian-Pakistan hostilities. Three months before the break, Pakistan's foreign minister, Z.A. Bhutto, had tried to oppose Malaysia's attendance at the proposed second Asian-African Conference.

A decision to resume diplomatic relations between the two countries was announced on September 1966. The decision was in some measure facilitated by the good offices of the Shah of Iran, the resignation of Bhutto in May of that year, and the cessation of hostilities between Indonesia and Malaysia.

Relations between Pakistan and Malaysia have steadily improved, and trade and commerce between them has substantially increased. Even during the disruption of diplomatic relations, Malaysia allowed Pakistani businessmen to engage in trade in the country.

During the dispute over the formation of Malaysia, Ceylon's official attitude was at first one of strict noninvolvement. Ceylon did not withhold diplomatic recognition of Malaysia, however, and supported India's proposal to invite Malaysia to the proposed second Asian-African Conference in 1965. A friendlier exchange between the two countries developed after Prime Minister Dudley Senanayake replaced Mrs. Solomon Bandarnaike, who was regarded by Malaysians as less sympathetic. Deputy Prime Minister Razak visited Colombo in April 1965, the first official guest of Senanayake's government. A resident high commissioner was soon appointed, the first having been withdrawn in late 1961.

In April 1967 the Tengku paid a 5-day visit to Ceylon at the invitation of its prime minister. In that meeting the two countries agreed to cooperate in stabilizing the price of one of their major industries, rubber. They also expressed identical views with regard to the solution of the situation in Vietnam. When the Ceylonese prime minister returned the Tengku's visit in October 1968, the Tengku made a statement of support for Ceylon's membership in ASEAN should Ceylon decide to join the organization. In order to facilitate trade and commercial relations, the two countries signed an agreement against double taxation in September 1969 in Kuala Lumpur.

Africa and the Middle East

Outside the framework of the UN, Malaysia has not identified itself closely with Afro-Asian solidarity and, even within the UN General Assembly and its committees, anticolonial utterances of Malaysian delegates have been marked with moderation and reasonableness. The Muslim religion, Commonwealth membership, and a record of friendship with most nonaligned Southeast Asian states helped to provide Malaysia with a niche among the Afro-Asian states, especially via such spokesmen as the United Arab Republic (Egypt), India, and Nigeria.

Nevertheless, Malaysia occasionally has found itself critical of its Afro-Asian colleagues, particularly concerning their indifference to such Communist aggression as the Chinese aggression in Tibet and the Soviet repression in Hungary. Many of the Afro-Asian states, on the other hand, questioned Malaysia's credentials—a country which had won its independence peacefully and remained on close terms with its former colonial ruler—and were equally critical of Malaysia's support of United States' Vietnam policies.

Malaysian propaganda initiatives in Africa started with Lee Kuan Yew's goodwill tour of 17 African countries in early 1964. In the latter part of that year, Deputy Prime Minister Razak visited Mediterranean Africa. In that visit an agreement was made with both Algeria and Morocco to exchange ambassadors and then announce support for Malaysian participation in the second Asian-African Conference in Algiers scheduled for June 1965.

In April 1965 Razak visited Ethiopia and the Commonwealth countries of Nigeria, Tanzania, Kenya, and Zambia. An embassy was later opened that year in Addis Ababa, headquarters of the Organization for African Unity, and a high commissioner office opened in Lagos. Several East African leaders had reaffirmed their recognition of Malaysia as a sovereign state and supported its admission to the second Asian-African Conference. Malaysia's drive for acceptance by the Afro-Asian countries was focused on organizations and conferences that espoused the cause of Afro-Asian solidarity or that emphasized nonalignment foreign policies.

Before Confrontation Malaysian diplomatic interests with Muslim countries were largely limited to Egypt, where Malay theological students gravitated to al-Azhur University in Cairo, and to Saudi Arabia, which attracted Malay pilgrims to Mecca. Once Confrontation was launched, Malaysia had to compete with Indonesia for support of Muslims elsewhere in the Afro-Asian world.

The diplomatic competition was focused in Cairo, where United Arab Republic President Nasser was trying to maintain a careful neutrality. The government did not withhold recognition of Malaysia, however, and full diplomatic relations were maintained at Kuala Lumpur at the ambassadorial level.

Deputy Prime Minister Razak toured Mediterranean Africa, while the Malaysian Supreme Head made state visits to several Muslim countries. Malaysia's diplomatic ties with other Muslim countries have multiplied since 1965. In 1965 a Malaysian diplomatic mission was opened in Morocco and Nigeria, which is partly Muslim. The Malaysian ambassador in Cairo was concurrently accredited to Sudan and to Lebanon in 1966; shortly afterward, Malaysia and Iran agreed to exchange representatives. The Shah of Iran helped in restoring Malaysia's diplomatic relations with Pakistan in 1966. Shortly after signing a treaty of friendship with Malaysia, the Shah of Iran and Empress Farah paid a state visit to Malaysia in early 1968. Algeria, whose struggle for independence from France has been consistently supported by Malaysia in the UN, has no resident ambassador in Kuala Lumpur. Its ambassador to India, however, was concurrently accredited to Malaysia in 1967. Diplomatic contact with Kuwait which signed a trade agreement with Malaysia in 1969, and with Jordan has been maintained through the Malaysian ambassador in Saudi Arabia, who is also concurrently accredited to these countries.

The absence of diplomatic relations with particular countries has not greatly hampered friendly exchanges with Muslim nations. A delegation from the Republic of South Yemen visited Kuala Lumpur in early 1969, and the two countries agreed to exchange diplomatic relations. The Tunisian Foreign Minister, Habib Bourguiba, Jr., visited Malaysia in July 1969, the two countries arranged to sign a cultural agreement and consular agreement on the abolition of visas.

In addition to diplomatic interest, Malaysia has recently attempted to increase its commercial ties with Muslim countries. Plans were announced in 1969 to open a trade office in Beirut, which will cover the Middle Eastern countries, and another one in Nairobi, for the East African area. A 17-man Malaysian trade mission left Kuala Lumpur in September 1969 to visit various capitals in the Middle East, including Iran, where Malaysia was taking part in the Second Asian International Trade Fair.

In addition to increased bilateral contacts, Malaysia has recently actively initiated or participated in a number of conferences of Muslim countries. In December 1966 Prime Minister Rahman proposed the formation of a commonwealth of Muslim nations, but his proposal received only lukewarm support.

Malaysia had vigorously denounced Israeli occupation of Arab territory taken during the Arab-Israeli hostilities in June 1967 and in the UN General Assembly had consistently voted draft resolutions opposing Israeli occupation. The Malaysian stand so enhanced its image among Muslim countries that it successfully acted as host to the International Islamic Conference, held in Kuala Lumpur, from April 21 to 27, 1969. The conference, attended by 23 nations, passed resolution condemning Israeli "agression" and calling on all Muslim nations to unite in recovering Palestine from Israeli. In addition to supporting the conference resolution, Malaysia allowed the Al Fatah Palestine Liberation Front, an Arab guerrilla organization, to set up an office in Kuala Lumpur to collect funds and enlist support for the recovery of Jerusalem and other Arab-claimed territories.

Malaysia was also one of the seven states that composed a commission to prepare the summit conference of Muslim countries held in Rabat, Morocco, in late September 1969 to discuss joint action against Israel over the burning of the Al-Aqsa Mosque in Jerusalem, the third holiest place of Islam. Prime Minister Rahman, personally represented his country in the conference.

The United States

United States interest in the political and economic affairs of independent Malaya before its merger into Malaysia was comparatively slight, even in the field of private investment, mainly because Malaya was firmly established in the sphere of interest of Great Britain and because of the lack of large-scale trade with that country. The area was consequently excluded from American defense responsibility or cultural influence.

Malaya had denied landing rights to American military aircraft, and until 1960 they were not permitted to fly over Malayan territory even on routine missions. In the years immediately preceding the Malaysian merger, Malay leaders and business circles harbored grievances against the United States capability to influence world prices of rubber and tin, Malaysia's major exports. This attitude was even more evident in 1961 when the United States began to sell its rubber stockpile abroad and in 1962 when it began to unload a 50,000-ton stockpile of tin. At times the government interpreted such United States actions as efforts to undermine the country.

The United States was a latecomer to the Malaysia-Indonesia dispute. Throughout 1962 the United States government welcomed the Malaysia merger plan as an act of decolonization and regional stabilization. In 1963, the first year of Confrontation, however, the United States, which was by then deeply involved in South Vietnam and had a large-scale assistance program underway for Indonesia, described its policy as one of "noninvolved cordiality." The breakup of Malaysian-Indonesian relations and the ensuing mob violence in September 1963 aroused the United States to lodge an official protest to the Indonesian government and to announce a temporary halt of all new economic aid to that country.

Meanwhile, in January 1964, the United States engaged in several diplomatic moves to bring the three MAPHILINDO countries together. President Lyndon B. Johnson, who appealed to Sukarno for concessions on Malaysia, describing the dispute as an obstacle to the improvement of Indonesian-American relations, sent Attorney General Robert F. Kennedy on a special mission to all three capitals. In spite of the fact that the United States suspended military assistance to Indonesia, abandoned plans to grant it a stabilization loan, and later stopped technical aid and surplus food shipments, the Malaysian government became increasingly critical of the United States.

Moreover, when the United States offered to lend Malaysia US$10 million at 5 percent interest to purchase aircraft, Malaysia rejected the American offer as too costly, and sections of the Alliance Party called for a review of relations with the United States. By early 1965, a US$4-million loan for the purchase of military equipment manufactured in the United States was extended under more favorable terms, and the Malaysian government launched a US$25-million bond issue in New York in April, which was oversubscribed. Other forms of American aid also were accepted by Malaysia. This favorable turn in Malaysian-United States relations occurred at a time when relations with the British were undergoing a reappraisal in Malaysia and was enhanced by President Johnson's brief stopover in Malaysia in early 1966 and the temporary restriction of the sale of stockpiled rubber and tin.

Prime Minister Rahman consistently supported United States policy in Vietnam; his support did not waver despite the brief strain in Malaysia's relations with the United States in late 1964 and the unpopularity of the Vietnam stand among neutralist Afro-Asian countries, whose support Malaysia had sought during the Confrontation period.

Non-Communist Europe

Overseas trade and diplomatic representation in non-Communist Europe remained significant in Malaysian foreign policy in 1969. Malaysia was especially interested in strengthening its ties with the members of the European Economic Community and had previously expressed interest in associate membership in that body. Malaysia's relations with France had been cordial, but, when France was under Charles De Gaulle, his posture of independence from Anglo-American policies in Southeast Asia caused some irritation in Malaysia. French attitudes were nonetheless important to Malaysia, especially in its bid during 1964 and 1965 for support from French-speaking states in Africa, some of which still look to France for advice and information.

A Dutch embassy has functioned in Kuala Lumpur since 1957. In November 1966 a new Malaysian ambassador presented his credentials at The Hague, relieving its resident ambassador in Bonn of concurrent accreditation. The Dutch government maintained an officially neutral policy on the Malaysia dispute with Indonesia.

Malaysia had its first ambassador to the Federal Republic of Germany in 1962, and West Germany has a resident ambassador in Kuala Lumpur. The West German government avoided public comment on the Malaysian dispute with Indonesia during Confrontation but did not discontinue its sizable economic aid program to Indonesia. Malaysian leaders have made several visits to Bonn, and West Germany has been the continental European country most valuable to Malaysia in recent years. West German aid to Malaysia has been concentrated mainly on cooperation in the field of infrastructural development in addition to providing soft loans for various construction projects, technical grants, and assistance.

No diplomatic relations existed with Portugal in 1969. In June 1965 the Portuguese consulate in Singapore, which was then the only formal link with Malaysia, was closed on orders from Kuala Lumpur. This occurred at a time when Malaysia's UN delegation was attacking Portuguese colonial policies in Africa (see ch. 3, Historical Setting). There are still several thousand Eurasians of part-Portuguese ancestry in southern Malaysia, but economic and political links have lost much of their earlier importance.

Malaysia maintains diplomatic relations with seven other non-Communist countries in Europe—Italy, Switzerland, Belgium, Denmark, Austria, Sweden, and Norway. The first five operate resident missions in Kuala Lumpur, but in 1969 Malaysia had been able to afford only a diplomatic mission to Rome, opened at the end of 1965, and a trade commissioner to Vienna. Malaysian exports to Italy have been only slightly less than the value of exports to West Germany (see ch. 22, Foreign Economic Relations). Switzerland has long enjoyed commercial and banking interests in Malaysia. The Malaysian ambassador in Paris has been concurrently accredited to Switzerland since 1961.

Sweden's ambassador in Bangkok has been concurrently accredited to Malaysia. Relations with Belgium have been cordial, except for the period from 1960 to 1961, when a Malayan battalion joined the UN peace-keeping operations in the Congo. Norway has concurrently accredited its ambassador in Bangkok to Malaysia. Malaysia has no diplomatic relations with the Republic of Ireland, but it has extended to the Irish some of the privileges usually reserved for citizens of Commonwealth countries.

The Soviet Union and Eastern Europe

The Soviet Union opened a diplomatic mission in Malaysia in 1968, less than a year after the two countries agreed to exchange ambassadors. There was no serious obstacle to establishing diplomatic relations with the Soviet Union.

Late in 1964 Prime Minister Rahman announced that his government would have no objection to establishing formal ties with Communist governments. The Tengku's gesture was more pronounced in February 1966, when he described Chinese-style communism as the main threat in Southeast Asia and said that his country would "support any retaliatory moves against Peking's influence" in the region.

Relations between the two countries were initially commercial, being based on a large Soviet purchase of Malaysian rubber. An official Malaysian trade delegation visited Moscow in November 1966, and an exchange of resident trade missions in early 1967 preceded the formal establishment of diplomatic relations.

The Soviet minister of foreign trade returned Razak's visit in February 1969 for talks with Malaysian government and business leaders on increasing trade between the two countries. The visit by the Soviet official paved the ground for the arrival in Kuala Lumpur in September of a nine-member Soviet trade mission led by the first deputy minister of foreign trade to discuss trade relations and the opening of the First Russian Trade and Industrial Exhibition in the Malaysian capital from September 23 to October 12, 1969.

While cultivating Soviet friendship, Malaysia expressed regret over Soviet action in Czechoslovakia during the Czechoslovak crisis in 1968 and urging the withdrawal of these troops. The whole tenor of its criticism, however, was generally restrained.

Malaysia's restraint was similarly demonstrated when Razak rejected suggestions in September 1969 that the Russian naval presence in the Indian Ocean at that time posed a threat to the security of Malaysia and of the region. Razak asked the Soviet Union to spell out the proposed Asian collective security pact, presumably aimed against Communist China, which was vaguely suggested in June of that year by the Soviet Communist Party Chief, Leonid Brezhnev, and repeated later by Prime Minister Alexei Kosygin.

In the fall of 1969 a Malaysian trade mission led by the minister of commerce and industry toured Bulgaria, Romania, and Yugoslavia for the purpose of expanding trade and economic cooperation between Malaysia and Eastern Europe. In Bulgaria the Malaysian mission attended the Twenty-fifth International Trade Exhibition at Plevdiv at the invitation of the Bulgarian government. The two countries have formally established economic relations in early 1968 but have not made any arrangements for exchange of diplomatic realtions.

Malaysia established diplomatic relations with Romania, on a nonresident basis, on March 22, 1969. At the same time the Romanian deputy premier was in Kuala Lumpur to sign a trade agreement that provided a most-favored-nation status to each other's produce and agreement to establish commercial representation in each other's capital.

Yugoslavia agreed to exchange diplomatic representation with Malaysia in 1967. A Malaysian embassy was to be opened in Belgrade, and the Yugoslav ambassador in Djakarta has been temporarily accredited concurrently with Malaysia in 1969. A trade agreement was signed between the countries in June 1969 on similar terms as the accord with Romania. The Yugoslav government invited Malaysia to send an observer to the consultative meeting of nonaligned nations in Belgrade that took place in July 1969.

CHAPTER 15

PUBLIC INFORMATION

The potential for public information in Malaysia is well developed and includes both private and governmental media. In mid-1969 there was an active and relatively free press, extensive radio and television networks, a growing motion picture industry, and a variety of other formalized audio and visual media. Apart from the increasing number and impact of these forms, word-of-mouth communication still constitutes one of the most powerful and important channels in illiterate rural areas and among the native tribesmen of Sarawak and Sabah and, to a lesser extent, among the ethnic communities in the urban areas.

Following the May 13, 1969, communal disturbances, an emergency government was established having special powers. These powers include censorship authority, including the power to suspend publications which violate censorship regulations. This authority had been used sparingly by late 1969, but its existence has been a restraining influence on press freedom. It is not known how long the emergency government or its powers will exist.

Most newspapers, periodicals, and books are privately owned and published, but the government plays an important role in providing educational and informational materials through the issuance of daily news releases for press, radio, and television; the publication of tracts in the vernacular; and the operation of translation services that make selected foreign and domestic articles available in the various local languages and in all media. Radio and television services are entirely owned and operated by the government, as are most of the local film production facilities. The distribution of films and the operation of motion picture houses are functions of private enterprise, although the government employs numerous mobile units that tour rural areas and show selected educational and documentary films in connection with other informational activities.

The quality and quantity of various information media have been limited by many factors. The lack of a common language is one of the most important and has inhibited the rise of a strong and united press able to influence the majority of the population. To overcome this handicap, many newspapers publish editions in more than one language. Daily radio and television programs are divided into specific language segments. Illiteracy, especially among ethnic groups other than Chinese, has further reduced the influence of the printed word. Among these groups, radio, television, and films are perhaps most influential. Television was still limited to a few cities in West Malaysia in 1969, and radio, although audible in all parts of the country, is often subject to interference from bad atmospheric conditions.

The effectiveness of each public information medium varies according to the composition and location of the audience. Among the urban Chinese, who constitute the most literate group in the country, the press is the most effective source of information. Even among the rural Chinese, the press is very effective, because Chinese newspapers, which often are the only ones found in rural areas, are numerous and usually carry news of special interest to the local dialect groups. Among urban Malays and Indians, the press, radio, and television perhaps have equal effect. Among non-Chinese rural peoples, the radio and word of mouth constitute the principal sources of information. In many places, especially among the aboriginal populations of Sarawak and Sabah, the recent acquisition of radio receivers and the improved literacy rate create a great faith in the content of broadcasts and the press medium.

Malaysia is subjected to a vast amount of foreign information. Much of it is Communist propaganda transmitted over strong short-wave radio stations located in Peking, Moscow, and Hanoi that are clearly heard throughout the country and often are used as sources of news for clandestine Communist newspapers. Much information also is available from free world transmitters in Japan, Australia, the United Kingdom, and the United States, all of which are audible in Malaysia. In addition, the British Broadcasting Corporation, by special arrangement with the government at Kuala Lumpur, operates 14 shortwave transmitters at Tebrau (near Johore Bahur) to bolster its Far Eastern service. Broadcasts from these stations, although beamed, programmed, and prepared in appropriate languages for various segments of the Orient as a whole, are heard and understood by many Malaysians. The Royal Australian Air Force also operates a small, low-powered station for Commonwealth forces stationed at Butterworth Air Base in Penang that has a large local audience. Finally, the free world countries maintain cultural and information offices in several large Malaysian cities.

THE ROLE OF GOVERNMENT

Freedom of Expression

Freedom of expression in all media of information is guaranteed by the Constitution. It is not, however, considered to be an absolute right and may be qualified by the authority of Parliament to impose such restrictions as are deemed necessary or expedient in the interests of national security or the maintenance of peace, tranquillity, and order in the society. Most of the bases for determining acceptability or restriction are drawn from provisions of the Internal Security Act of Malaya, which was extended to cover the entire country in 1963.

The government contends, moreover, that the various channels of public communications must serve as vehicles of persuasion for its policies, especially those aimed at consolidating the various components of the country and of promoting the formation of a unified Malaysian state. It also uses these channels to combat opposition both from within the nation, as expressed by Communist threats during the Emergency (the 1948–60 period of Communist insurgency), and from outside the country, as expressed by Indonesian belligerency during the confrontation with that country (see ch. 24, Public Order and Internal Security).

Within these parameters, the government allows a considerable degree of criticism, but it has not hesitated to impose limitations on publishers in time of emergency or internal stress. In mid-1969 it passed an amendment to the Internal Security Act specifically defining actions considered undersirable and subject to restriction. This amendment proscribes uttering, printing, selling, offering for sale, distributing, or possessing any matter likely to be prejudicial to public order, to incite or cause violence, to promote feelings of ill will or hostility between races, to counsel or lead to disobedience of law, to bring hatred, contempt, or dissatisfaction on any public official, or to spread false rumors, reports, or statements that might cause public alarm.

Government Organization

Official responsibility for public information activities is centered in the Ministry of Information and Broadcasting of the federal government at Kuala Lumpur. The ministry is a full cabinet agency organized into four functionally charged departments (information, radio, television, and film), a State Information Office in each state capital, and branch information offices in most administrative districts. Its mission is to disseminate information and government plans and policies to the people at all levels, particularly in rural areas, in order to promote common loyalty to the country, civic consciousness, and racial harmony.

The Information Department of the ministry is concerned primarily with providing materials for printed media and with the operation of mobile field information units. Elements at headquarters produce and distribute some 350 government press statements and an average of 3,500 press photographs each month. They also maintain a research and reference service that provides government publications, newspaper clippings, digests of press comment and editorial opinion, and other materials to government officials, the press, and students. Other elements of the department organize civics courses for groups of people; publish a weekly tabloid newspaper, *Warta Malaysia*, numerous booklets, tracts, and pamphlets, and the official annual yearbook; and produce posters, banners, displays, cutouts, models, and exhibits used in support of government programs.

Operation of the mobile field units, however, is the department's best known and possibly its most popular activity. These units, of which there were 138 in 1969 (114 housed in vehicles for land use and 24 in boats for river service), tour rural and isolated regions on regular schedules bringing news, information, and entertainment to people who otherwise would have to rely solely on radio. Each unit is equipped to show information and documentary films and to organize talks and group discussions. Each also is staffed to conduct civics courses that may last as long as 3 days for groups of 40 to 100 villagers. It is estimated that these units reach about 1 million people each year.

The Radio Department and the Television Department of the ministry control all technical and program operations of broadcasting stations in these media. They also, in conjunction with the Ministry of Finance, administer the system of licensing radio and television receivers owned by individual citizens.

The Film Department, known as Filem Negara, produces about 60 to 100 educational and documentary films each year, as well as a weekly newsreel. These films are produced in English, Bahasa Malaysia (Malay language), Tamil, Chinese, Iban, and Kadazan for use by the mobile units of the Information Department, by television stations, and by private commercial exhibitors. Filem Negara also rents personnel, facilities, and equipment to local and foreign motion picture producers who wish to make commercial entertainment films in Malaysia.

The State Information Offices, each under its own headquarters and State Information Officer, are purely operational and are charged with implementing directives issued by the ministry or by the government of the state in which they are located. They organize schedules of the mobile units, civic courses, exhibitions, speeches, and group discussions in their areas and distribute government press releases and other publicity material, such as posters, booklets, pamphlets, and leaflets received from headquarters in Kuala Lumpur.

Control

The production and dissemination of information is controlled by the government in a variety of ways, some of which are permissive whereas others are moderately restrictive or coercive. All radio and television stations and much of the local film effort are government owned and operated, so they are controlled directly and present no problems. Owners of radio and television receivers, however, are required by law to register their sets and to pay an annual fee amounting to M$12 (3.06 Malaysian dollars equal US$1) for radio or M$24 for radio and television combined. Privately produced and imported films must be reviewed and approved by the ministry's Board of Film Censors before they may be shown to the public. Any film, including those produced by the government, or any portion of a film that might conceivably be termed "undesirable" under definitions of the Internal Security Act of Malaya as amended, may be barred. The board's decisions are usually final, but they may be appealed and on occasion have been reversed.

Control of the press is achieved in three different ways, none of which involves outright censorship. Large portions of the domestic daily news are controlled at the source by the practice of issuing daily government reports and other handouts that form most of their content; second, all newspapers and other publications are required to register with the ministry, and none may be published, sold, or distributed without a government permit; and these permits may be suspended or revoked for the publication of so-called "undesirable" articles and stories. Thus, although a free press is guaranteed and generally practiced, publications that survive are those that usually adhere to and endorse government policies.

THE PRESS

Available information on the total number of newspapers in Malaysia was incomplete in 1969, but there were at least 40 daily journals of some significance. Twenty-two of these newspapers were published in West Malaysia and 18 in East Malaysia (Sabah and Sarawak). Newspapers published in West Malaysia, where nine had daily circulations of 20,000 or more, were larger than those in East Malaysia where only three had circulations exceeding 10,000 (see table 11).

Newspapers are published in all the major languages of Malaysia. Chinese- and English-language versions predominate, followed by Malay in both *jawi* and *rumi* script, and Indian in Tamil or Punjabi. No daily newspapers are published completely in the aboriginal languages, such as Kadazan, Iban, or Dayak, but these languages are used in certain sections of several East Malaysian journals. The English-language press, read by the educated class of all ethnic groups, is important as an interracial medium; the vernacular newspapers tend to perpetuate ethnic differences by voicing the demands and outlook of separate ethnic groups. Within the Chinese and Indian communities, there is further newspaper specialization serving the subgroups of these ethnic entities and, although all dialects of Chinese use the same script, some journals carry a special column in which they use local expressions to cater to specific dialect groups.

Table 11. Major Daily Newspapers of Malaysia, 1969

Title	Location	Language	Circulation
WEST MALAYSIA:			
Berita Harian	Kuala Lumpur	Malay	27,000
Chung Kuo Pao	____ do	Chinese	25,000
Eastern Sun	____ do	English	n.a.
Kin Kwok Daily News	Ipoh	Chinese	12,500
Kwong Wah Yit Poh	Penang	____ do	21,000
Majlis	Kuala Lumpur	Malay	3,000
Malay Mail	____ do	English	30,000
Malaya Samarchar	____ do	Punjabi	2,000
Malayan Thung Pau	____ do	Chinese	30,500
Nanyang Siang Pau	____ do	____ do	n.a.
Pardesi Khalsa Sewak	____ do	Punjabi	9,300
Penang Gazette	Penang	English	16,000
Penang Sin Poe	____ do	Chinese	17,200
Sevika	____ do	Tamil	2,000
Sin Chew Jih Pao	Kuala Lumpur	Chinese	n.a.
Sing Pin Jih Pao	Penang	____ do	32,000
Straits Echo and Times of Malaya	____ do	English	16,000
Straits Times	Kuala Lumpur	____ do	210,000
Tamil Nesan	____ do	Tamil	17,000
Utusan Malaysia	____ do	Malay	20,000
Utusan Melayu	____ do	____ do	55,000
Warta Negara	Penang	____ do	6,000
SABAH:			
Api Siang Pau	Kota Kinabalu	Chinese	3,000
Borneo Times	Sandakan	English and Chinese.	5,100
Daily Express	Kota Kinabalu	English and Malay.	13,400
Kinabalu Times	____ do	English	2,100
Overseas Chinese News	____ do	Chinese	12,100
Sabah Times	____ do	English and Chinese.	11,000
Sandakan Jih Pao	Sandakan	Chinese	6,000
Tawau Jih Pao	Tawau	____ do	2,500
SARAWAK:			
Chinese Daily News	Kuching	Chinese	2,400
Miri Daily News	Miri	____ do	7,800
Sa Chiew Daily News	Sibu	____ do	1,800
Sarawak Express	Kuching	____ do	2,500

Table 11. Major Daily Newspapers of Malaysia, 1969—Continued

Title	Location	Language	Circulation
Sarawak Tribune ____	____ do _____	English _____	3,600
Sarawak Siang Pao __	Sibu _____	Chinese _____	2,000
Sarawak Vanguard ___	Kuching _____	____ do _____	8,400
See Hua Daily News __	Sibu _____	____ do _____	8,000
The Vanguard _____	Kuching _____	English _____	4,600
Utusan Sarawak ____	____ do _____	Malay _____	n.a.

n.a.—not available.

Source: Adapted from *Editor and Publisher International Yearbook 1969*, New York, 1969; *Europa Year Book 1968*, II, London, 1968; and *Malaysia Official Yearbook 1967*, VII, Kuala Lumpur, Federal Department of Information, 1968.

The relatively low circulation of Malay- and aboriginal-language newspapers does not necessarily mean that these segments of the population are entirely without the benefit of the press. In practice, newspapers are regularly passed from hand to hand or are posted in community information centers in West Malaysian villages and in the longhouses (multifamily dwellings) of Sarawak and Sabah, so their readership is usually far greater than their actual press runs. In addition, many government pamphlets and periodicals printed in Malay and aboriginal languages from current and comprehensive substitutes for the more frequently appearing daily newspapers. The relatively low level of literacy among these peoples, however, gives a better opportunity for success for other means of communication.

No newsprint is produced in Malaysia, which contributes to the fact that most newspapers are small and usually contain less than 10 pages. Patterned after English models, page width runs from 14 to 17 inches and columns average about 2 inches. The style and quality of reporting varies greatly and, except for the larger journals, reflects a serious lack of trained newspapermen schooled in objective, factual journalism. There is no formal school of journalism in the country, although from time to time the Information Department of the ministry conducts short courses for prospective newspapermen.

Daily Newspapers in West Malaysia

The 22 major daily newspapers of West Malaysia have a combined circulation estimated to be about 550,000. Five of the journals are printed in English, eight in Chinese, five in Malay, two in Tamil, and two in Punjabi.

Among the English-language dailies, the morning *Straits Times* and the evening *Malay Mail*, both published by the British-owned Straits Times Press, Ltd., in Kuala Lumpur, are the most influential. The *Straits Times* has a circulation of over 210,000 (250,000 on Sundays) distributed nationwide and not only is the largest but also the closest approach to a great metropolitan daily in Malaysia. It is editorially conservative, supports the ruling Alliance Party, and enjoys a reputation for objective and competent journalism. The *Malay Mail* has a circulation of only about 30,000, but otherwise it is quite similar to the *Straits Times* and is highly respected.

The *Straits Times* normally contains 22 full-size pages of eight columns each and in appearance is comparable to most city newspapers in England. Banner headlines are infrequent, and advertisements are carried on the front page along with the major domestic and foreign news of the day. A unique front page feature carried in the center of the right-hand column every day is a small, two-inch space called "Stop Press." It is reserved for late bulletins that are printed in blue to make them more conspicuous. On days when news is routine and there are no bulletins, the space is left blank.

Interior pages of the *Straits Times* vary from edition to edition, but generally the first few pages are devoted to foreign and domestic news from the various press services. This is followed by two to seven pages of national and local news, one page of which is the editorial page. The next page usually consists of classified advertisements, after which come three or four pages of shipping news, market reports, and commercial news, and two or three pages of sports news. The back page contains late news and features from foreign news agencies and additional local stories. Special features include a "letters to the editor" section that appears on the editorial page, a crossword puzzle, radio and television program schedules, and several syndicated comic strips, such as "Peanuts," "Alley Oop," "Dick Tracy," "Li'l Abner," and "Bugs Bunny," scattered at random after page three.

Two other English-language newspapers of importance are the *Straits Echo and Times of Malaya* and the *Penang Gazette*, which had circulations of about 16,000 copies each and were published by the Straits Echo Press, Ltd., a Chinese company in Penang. Both are conservative and pro-West in editorial content. The *Straits Echo and Times of Malaya* is perhaps the more influential, because it also publishes an Ipoh edition of the same size, which gives it coverage of all northern Malaya. The Ipoh edition reverses the order in its title and is called the *Times of Malaysia and the Straits Echo*. The circulation of the *Penang Gazette* probably does not extend beyond the state of Penang.

Chinese-language newspapers in West Malaysia are published in

Kuala Lumpur, Penang, and Ipoh. Of the four published in Kuala Lumpur, two, the morning *Chung Kuo Pao* circulating 25,000 and the *Malayan Thung Pau* circulating 30,500, are of greatest importance. The *Chung Kuo Pao* has a definite Chinese bias, but is generally considered anti-Communist. Its influence is probably greater than that of its larger but younger competitor, because the latter publishes only four times a week.

One of the three Chinese dailies in Penang, the morning *Sing Pin Jih Pao*, is the nation's largest Chinese newspaper, with a circulation of 32,000. It belongs to the Sin Poh Amalgamated, Ltd., part of the Star chain of newspapers founded by the late Aw Boon Haw. The publication gets its Chinese news indirectly from Singapore, but also subscribes to the United Press International, the Associated Press, and Reuters. Its political policy is neutral. The other morning Chinese newspaper in Penang, the *Kwong Wah Yit Poh*, was established by Sun Yat-sen, the leader of the Chinese nationalist revolution, during his exile in Penang. It has a daily circulation of 21,000 and follows a moderate pro-Taiwan policy. The morning *Kin Kwok Daily News* of Ipoh has a circulation of 12,500 and is strongly anti-Communist and pro-Malaysia.

Only five Malay-language and four Indian-language daily newspapers are published in West Malaysia. Among the Malay journals, the *Utusan Melayu* of Kuala Lumpur enjoys the greatest circulation, 55,000. It is also widely read in Singapore. *Utusan Melayu*'s importance is considerable, as it provides an outlet for Malay nationalism promoted by the Pan-Malayan Islamic Party, with which it is believed to be connected. The *Berita Harian*, published in Kuala Lumpur by the Straits Times Press, Ltd., also has much influence. It is generally pro-Malay, although not as nationalistic as the *Utusan Melayu*. The other two Malay newspapers located in Kuala Lumpur have only limited local significance. The fifth Malay newspaper, the morning *Warta Negara*, is published in Penang and is geared to the rural Malay population. Its circulation is only 6,000. The four Indian-language newspapers, three of which are published in Kuala Lumpur and one in Penang, include the fairly important *Tamil Nesan* of about 17,000 circulation and the Punjabi *Pardesi Khalsa Sewak* of less than 10,000, both published in Kuala Lumpur. The other two Indian newspapers, the Punjabi *Malaya Samarchar* and the Tamil *Sevika*, published in Kuala Lumpur and Penang, respectively, are relatively small and uninfluential.

Daily Newspapers in East Malaysia

Press communications are particularly difficult throughout East Malaysia. Most of the literate people can be reached through Chinese, English, or Malay newspapers, but the various indigenous communities are best approached through their own language, the most important of which are Kadazan in Sabah and Iban in Sarawak. Knowledge of English is spreading among urban young people and is becoming a potential common language among Chinese, Malay, and indigenous groups.

The press in Sabah consists of eight daily newspapers, all but three of which are published in the capital city of Kota Kinabalu (formerly Jesselton). Four of Sabah's dailies are printed in Chinese and four in English. Two of the English newspapers have Chinese or Malay editions or sections; one of them has a Kadazan section.

The English-language *Daily Express* (with Malay edition) and *Sabah Times* (with Chinese edition) and the Chinese-language *Overseas Chinese News*, all published in Kota Kinabalu, with daily circulations of over 10,000 copies each, are the largest newspapers in East Malaysia. The Chinese-language *Api Siang Pau* and the English-language *Kinabalu Times* are smaller dailies published in the capital city. The *Sandakan Jih Pao* (Chinese) and the *Borneo Times* (English with Chinese edition) are published in Sandakan and have circulations of about 6,000 each. A relatively new publication, the *Tawau Jih Pao*, is a Chinese-language morning daily serving southeast Sabah.

Because of the relatively high literacy rate of the population of Sarawak, the Chinese-language press predominates, accounting for seven of the state's 10 daily newspapers. Three of the Chinese journals are published in Kuching, three in Sibu, and one in Miri. The remaining dailies, the English-language *Sarawak Tribune* and *The Vanguard* and the Malay-language *Utusan Sarawak*, are all published in Kuching. None of the newspapers has a circulation greater than about 8,500, nor are they truly competitive, since the distribution of each is restricted largely to its area of publication. The Chinese-language *Sarawak Vanguard* of Kuching, *See Hua Daily News* of Sibu, and *Miri Daily News* of Miri, circulating 8,400, 8,000, and 7,800 respectively, are the largest and probably the most influential in Sarawak.

Newspapers in Sarawak, especially those in the Chinese language, have been under very close regulation, because of the Communist threat in that area (see ch. 24, Public Order and Internal Security). Since 1962 several of the Chinese dailies believed to be under Communist influence or control have been closed, some of which have reappeared under different names. Consequently, the position of many newspapers is quite unstable. In June 1969, for example, the influential *See Hua Daily News* of Sibu was suspended for two weeks for "activities prejudicial to public order" and was in danger of being forced out of business completely. The suspension was lifted after 1 week, however, and in July it had resumed full operation.

Press Agencies

There is only one indigenous press service in Malaysia. It is a relatively new enterprise, the National News Agency (Berita Nasional Malaysia—BERNAMA), organized along lines similar to the AP in that its daily file consists of domestic news gathered by and exchanged among participating member newspapers. BERNAMA is unique, however, in that the government, through the Ministry of Information and Broadcasting, is a full-fledged and active member. Until July 1969 operations of the agency were confined to West Malaysia, but in that month service and membership were expanded to cover the entire country. BERNAMA's daily file is not large, consisting of local news judged to have national interest and government materials formerly distributed exclusively by official handouts.

International news and features are obtained from the various world press agencies that maintain branches in Malaysia. These include Reuters, UPI, Agence France-Presse (AFP), the Central News Agency of Nationalist China, the Pan-Asia Newspaper Alliance, and the United Press of India.

Reuters, the oldest agency in the region, enjoyed a virtual monopoly before 1941. It has a branch office in Kuala Lumpur and subordinate offices in Penang and Ipoh. Practically all the daily newspapers of Malaysia, including the vernacular press, subscribe to Reuters.

The UPI and AP did not begin operations in the territory that is now Malaysia until after World War II. Both have offices in Kuala Lumpur and Penang, and the UPI has an additional office in Ipoh. UPI service includes general news, features, and photographs; its principal subscribers are the Chinese newspapers. AP service, in addition to general news and features, includes special commercial news releases and a large airmail feature service. The rates of both these services are generally lower than those of Reuters.

The Central News Agency, an official agency of the Republic of China on Taiwan, distributes its file in Chinese to Chinese newspapers. The United Press of India maintains a correspondent in Kuala Lumpur who distributes its releases to the Indian vernacular press. The other agencies maintain offices in Kuala Lumpur to distribute their service to subscribers and to collect news of Malaysia for return to their homelands.

Some Malaysian dailies have arrangements with British and American newspapers and press syndicates for the acquisition of features and articles. The *Straits Times*, for example, reprints materials from the *Times* of London, and the *Malay Mail* reprints from the *London Daily Express*. Most of the larger English-language newspapers also maintain roving correspondents throughout Malaysia as well as permanent correspondents in the larger cities.

Periodicals

In addition to the daily newspapers, a great number of weekly, fortnightly, monthly, and quarterly periodicals are published, most of them in West Malaysia, and many by the government as well as by private interests. As a rule, those produced by the government are published by the Information Department of the Ministry of Information and Broadcasting, unless they are specialized publications of a particular governmental department. In all governmental publications the emphasis is on information, education, and indoctrination rather than on entertainment.

Periodicals produced by the private sector cater to a variety of interests. Some are basically news and information types similar to *Time* or *Newsweek* in the United States; others specialize in trade and commerce, labor, students, film, radio or television entertainment, or general interest and fiction. Like newspapers, Malaysian periodicals are printed in all major languages but, unlike newspapers, they are also numerous in some of the aboriginal languages. Precise data on periodicals are scarce and subject to change because of numerous publishing failures, so only scattered details on a few representative publications are available (see table 12).

ELECTRONIC MEDIA

Radio Malaysia

There are no private radio facilities in Malaysia, but broadcasting service is provided to all sections of the country by a single government-owned and -operated network known as Radio Malaysia. This system consists of 12 radio stations located at Kuala Lumpur, Penang, Ipoh, Johore Bahru, Kota Bahru, Kuala Trengganu, Kuantan, and Malacca in West Malaysia; Kota Kinabalu, Tenom, and Tawa in Sabah; and Kuching in Sarawak. Except for the three stations in Sabah, each of which has only one, all stations are equipped with two or three mediumwave transmitters, permitting broadcast of their programs on more than one frequency at a time. In addition, the stations at Kuala Lumpur, Penang, Kota Kinabalu, and Kuching have several shortwave transmitters for simultaneous broadcast of their programs to isolated portions of the country where mediumwave transmissions are poor or inaudible.

The eight stations in West Malaysia are linked into a network by an extensive microwave system; those in East Malaysia are incorporated

Table 12. Representative Malaysian Periodicals, 1969

Title	Location	Frequency	Language	Circulation
Anak Sabah	Kota Kinabalu	Monthly	English	5,300
Dolphin	Kuching	do	do	16,500
Guru	Penang	do	Chinese	10,000
Janobahari	Kuala Lumpur	Weekly	Tamil	25,000
The Malaya Nature Journal	do	Monthly	English	900
The Malayan Forester	do	do	do	n.a.
Malaysian Agricultural Journal	do	Quarterly	do	n.a.
Malaysian Government Gazette	do	Every two weeks	do	n.a.
Mastika*	do	Monthly	Malay	12,500
Nendak	Kuching	do	Iban	1,400
Opinion	Kuala Lumpur	do	English	n.a.
Panguan Raayat	do	Weekly	Malay	65,000
Pedoman Ra'ayat	Kuching	Monthly	Iban	6,500
Pembrita	do	do	Iban	6,500
Pengasoh	Kota Bahru	do	Malay	12,000
The Planter	Kuala Lumpur	do	English	1,700
Sarawak-by-the-Week	Kuching	Weekly	English, Iban and Malay	2,500
Sarawak Gazette	do	do	English	500
Sarawak Museum Journal	do	Annual	do	2,500
Sin Lu Pao	Kuala Lumpur	Monthly	Chinese	50,000
Solai	do	do	Tamil	3,200
Straits Budget	do	Weekly	English	n.a.
Suara Umno	Johore Bahru	do	Malay	1,500
Utusan Film and Sport	Kuala Lumpur	do	do	n.a.
Utusan Saracak	Kuching	Every three weeks	do	do

*Illustrated

Source: Adapted from *Editor and Publisher International Yearbook 1969*, New York, 1969; and *Europa Year Book, 1968*, II, London, 1968.

into the chain by rebroadcasting the signals of powerful shortwave transmitters located at Radio Malaysia's headquarters in Kuala Lumpur. Thus, the system operates as a true national network over which news, information, education, and entertainment originating in the capital may be received instantaneously and simultaneously in all parts of the Federation.

Although integral to and receiving the bulk of its programs from the network, especially those broadcast during prime listening hours, each of the 12 stations is a complete unit in itself, staffed and equipped to originate local programs for regional audiences. The station at Ipoh is typical and representative. In addition to its transmitters, the station consists of an auditorium to accommodate 200 people, a talk studio, three continuity studios, an editing room, a central tape recording room, a main control room, a record library, a canteen, and offices for its program and administrative staff.

Radio Malaysia offers two types of service for its listeners: the Home Service, which broadcasts over stations of the regular network, and the Overseas Service, which utilizes three powerful 100-kilowatt shortwave stations located at headquarters in Kuala Lumpur. The Overseas Service, identified on the air as Suara Malaysia (the voice of Malaysia), broadcasts about 8 hours a day in English, Indonesian, and Chinese (Mandarin) on beams directed to northern and eastern Asia, southern Asia, and Indonesia. Overseas programs are largely news, music, and informational and cultural features designed to provoke interest in and gain support for the Federation and the Malaysian way of life.

Stations of the Home Service are on the air 18 hours a day, from 6:00 A.M. until midnight. Program content varies slightly from station to station because of local listener preference, but a typical broadcast day averages about 70 percent music and entertainment, 6 percent news, 12 percent information and cultural subjects, and 12 percent education. Programs originating in Kuala Lumpur for the network are presented in English, Malay, Indian, and four dialects of Chinese; local programs in Sabah also use Kadazan, Murut, Indonesian, and occasionally Dusun, and those in Sarawak add Dayak and Melanau for specific ethnic communities in those states.

Many of Radio Malaysia's programs, especially those in the music and entertainment category, have had commercial sponsors since radio advertising was authorized in 1962. Most music programs, both network and locally produced, are recorded, but the 27-piece Radio Malaysia Orchestra, permanently based at the network control station in Kuala Lumpur, provides live daily concerts of classical, native, and popular selections for the network, and other stations encourage the appearance of local musical groups during non-network time. A weekly recorded program called the "Pick of the Pops" was highly popular among young people in 1969. Entertainment programs range from the daily morning "Breakfast Potpourri," a variety program featuring household hints and features of interest to women, through the "Children's Corner," offered nightly at 6:00 P.M., to an occasional panel game or a dramatic presentation on "Radio Theater." Segments devoted to storytelling in the classic oriental manner and live broadcasts of sports events also attract large audiences.

The importance given to news programs is evident in the practice of opening and closing each broadcast day with complete summaries of national and international events. Other news summaries, together with commentaries and analyses in all languages prepared at headquarters in Kuala Lumpur, are scattered throughout the daily schedule and are required to be carried by all stations. Other news programs of purely local interest are broadcast frequently by individual stations.

In the information and cultural category, a great variety of programs are broadcast. Daily lessons in English and the national language are featured to break down language barriers among the many ethnic groups. There is also a daily program offering legal advice called the "DA's Show" and a weekly feature on medicine and home remedies called the "Family Doctor." Much attention is attached to rural programming, because of the rising demand for knowledge in rural areas. One of the earliest and most popular of the rural programs is "Kebun Pak Awang" (Dad Awang's Farm), a half-hour weekly program of information and advice on latest farming methods and developments. Other well-liked programs include "The Science Magazine," a discussion of new scientific achievements; religious broadcasts; official speeches by high government leaders and reports of action by Parliament; audience participation broadcasts on controversial subjects; and tape recordings made in villages describing the lives and living conditions of various peoples and broadcast to create better understanding among the numerous ethnic groups of the nation.

Educational broadcasting, carried out as a joint activity of Radio Malaysia and the Ministry of Education, is highly developed to augment the formal curricula of most Malaysian schools. Officially called the Schools Broadcast Service, this series of professionally prepared lessons is broadcast four times a week (Monday through Thursday, inclusive) over the network and is required to be carried by all stations. The broadcast schedule involves a morning period of 1 hour and 30 minutes (9:00 to 10:30 A.M.) and an afternoon period of 2 hours and 30 minutes (2:00 to 4:30 P.M.) on Mondays,

Tuesdays, and Wednesdays. Both morning and afternoon periods are shortened to 30 minutes on Thursdays. The programs are written in Malay, English, Tamil, and Chinese segments and, in 1968, were used by about 3,000 schools.

Owners of radio receivers, regardless of the number each individual possesses, are required to register their sets with the government and pay an annual listening fee of M$12. This action is designed primarily to raise operating funds for Radio Malaysia rather than to serve as a control measure. A total of about 500,000 licenses was issued in 1969. Group listening in such places as the longhouses in East Malaysia and community centers, shops, village gathering. places, and restaurants in West Malaysia is common, so that the actual size of the radio audience may be twice that indicated by the number of licenses issued. Group listening is probably most wide spread in Sabah and Sarawak where the relatively high price' of receivers and the language of broadcasts act as limiting factors on sales.

Rediffusion, Ltd.

In addition to the regular broadcasting service provided by Radio Malaysia, privately owned and operated wire service is available to subscribers in Kuala Lumpur, Penang, and Ipoh. This service, called Rediffusion, Ltd., originates its own programs or relays those of the British Broadcasting Service or Radio Malaysia, delivering them by closed wire circuits directly into the homes or establishments of its clients. The service costs about M$5 per month.

Rediffusion, Ltd., programs consist of about 60 percent music with the rest divided among news, sports, and live studio entertainment. A small portion of the output is commercially sponsored. Programs are available over two networks: the Gold network, which is exclusively in the Chinese language, and the Silver network, which uses English, Malay, Indian, and Chinese. Both networks are very popular, as evidenced by the number of subscribers, which in 1969 amounted to 16,000 in Kuala Lumpur, 8,500 in Penang, and 4,200 in Ipoh.

Television Malaysia

Television is relatively new to Malaysia, having been inaugurated by the establishment of a single station at Kuala Lumpur in December 1963. Since then, Television Malaysia has expanded to a total of nine stations located at major cities in West Malaysia and fused into a single network by a system of microwave links fed and controlled from headquarters in Kuala Lumpur (see table 13). In mid-

1969 plans were under way to increase the number of outlets in West Malaysia and to introduce television service into Sabah and Sarawak by the erection of new stations in those states. The development program also included the provision of facilities to permit telecasting in color.

Table 13. Television Stations of Malaysia, 1969

Location	Channel
Batu Pahat	7
Ipoh	6
Johore Bahru	3
Johore Bahru	10
Kluang	9
Kuala Lumpur	5
Malacca	6
Penang	5
Taiping	4

Television Malaysia, like Radio Malaysia, is exclusively a government-owned enterprise operated as a function of the Ministry of Information and Broadcasting. Although help in organizing the system was provided by Canadian and United States technicians and advisers, all permanent staff members are Malaysian citizens employed by the civil service. Hours of operation total about 55 hours a week, but vary on different days of the week. Monday through Thursday, the network and all stations begin telecasting at 5:45 P.M. and stop at midnight; Thursday through Sunday, the opening hour is advanced to 3 P.M., but closing time remains at midnight.

The operating policy of Television Malaysia is to promote national unity through programs that inform, educate, and entertain all segments of the multiracial audience, so programs are regularly presented in English, Malay, Chinese, and Tamil. Since Malay is the sole official national language, however, efforts are made to popularize its use on television. At least two daily periods of instruction in Malay are featured, and all opening, closing, and other announcements are given in that language. In addition, all programs in other languages, including feature films and news, must have Malay subtitles.

About 45 percent of all network and local programs are live; the rest are film presentations. Much of the film is procured from international syndicates and includes motion picture entertainment features, short subjects, and animated cartoons. Documentaries on a variety of subjects are also provided by the United States Information Service and by other governments. Many presentations, however, especially local news, short documentaries on government operations and projects, and films concerning a variety of Malaysian cultural subjects, are produced by staff cameramen and technicians of the Television Department. In the area of news, for example, Radio Malaysia's own laboratories can process a roll of film in less than an hour, permitting events in Malaysia to be filmed, developed, edited, and telecast the same day.

Program substance includes all areas of conventional television fare, including news, special events, public affairs, music, motion pictures, and many of the familiar syndicated adventure, comedy, and situation series. An analysis of program schedules for the first week in July 1969, which may be taken as typical, indicates that straight aural and visual newscasts in the four major languages are presented five or six times a day. In addition, news "magazines" in Malay summarizing national and international news are telecast six times a week, and a monthly program called "Asiavishen," summarizing topical happenings in neighboring countries, is exchanged with fellow member nations of the Asia Broadcasting Union. Other regular features include a 5-minute period of national songs and an hour of animated cartoons for children, a twice-weekly program of Malaysian dances called "Puspawaran" and another of native music called "Bingkisan," and weekly presentations of reading the Koran, major speeches of high government officials, live broadcasts of sports events, religious and civic celebrations, and a program of popular music, called "Beat Club," for young people. Occasionally, a spectacular, such as the "Bob Hope Special," is added to the schedule.

Full-length motion picture features produced by major world studios are offered daily. During the sample week they included several from Hindi, Malay, and Chinese producers and three from Hollywood, starring John Payne, Maureen O'Hara, George Raft, Ellen Drew, MacDonald Carey, and Wendell Corey.

The bulk of the schedule, however, appeared to be made up of standard syndicated series designed for showing once a week on a fixed day and at the same hour. Most of these were the same as those appearing on United States networks and included the "High Chaparral," the "Lone Ranger," "Restless Gun," "Laredo," and "Bat Masterson" of the "western" type; "The Outsider," "Hong Kong," "Sergeant Preston," "Bold Journey," and "The Saint" of the adventure and private eye types; "Petticoat Junction," "Mr. Novak," and "Dobie Gillis" of the situation comedy type; and "The Outer Limits," "Suspense," "Celebrity Game," "Desilu Playhouse," and "Hollywood Palace" in other categories.

Owners of television receivers are required to register and pay an annual fee of M$24, which automatically includes the right to own an unlimited number of radio sets. In 1969 the total number of registered television homes was almost 500,000 but, because of group viewing, the number of Malaysians reached by the medium was considerably higher.

FILM

Films are highly popular and constitute an important medium of entertainment and information throughout Malaysia. Attendance is large in proportion to the population, especially in urban areas where there were over 400 commercial motion picture houses in 1969. Most of these theaters were concentrated in Kuala Lumpur and Penang, but many were located in other cities, and there was at least one in every small town. In rural areas theaters were virtually nonexistent, but large audiences were served by mobile units of the Information Department of the Ministry of Information and Broadcasting.

A majority of the large, first-run theaters were operated by two Chinese-owned chains: the Shaw Organization, which controlled 19, and the Cathay Organization, which owned 12 theaters in seven major cities of West Malaysia. Other theaters in these cities and those in smaller urban areas in both West and East Malaysia were also privately and largely Chinese owned, but usually were run as single, independent businesses.

Local production of entertainment features and short films was minimal, so most of these were imported from the United Kingdom, the United States, Hong Kong, and India, with an occasional one from some other country. Within Malaysia, film production was largely a government enterprise carried out by Filem Negara, a department of the Ministry of Information and Broadcasting, from modern studios in Petaling Jaya, near Kuala Lumpur. There were a few private producers, but their output was insignificant.

Filem Negara produced an occasional entertainment feature, largely as a source of foreign exchange, but concentrated on the production of documentaries, information and educational films, and a weekly newsreel covering domestic happenings. In 1968 production included 52 regular and five special issues of the weekly newsreel, 22 documentary and educational films, four semifeature dramatic films, and various trailers in support of national road safety, national solidarity, and other government programs. The documentaries included special coverage of visits by various foreign dignitaries: *Pesta Pulau Pinang*, a cultural color film about Penang; two films on health and youth training in Sabah; several films on sports; and a color film on the role of the Royal Malaysian Air Force. Among the semifeature dramatic films were the popular *Kesah Kampong Kita* series dealing with rural development and the *Tongkat Hitam* series on the theme of Crime Doesn't Pay.

Filem Negara productions are made available in 35-mm size for showing in commercial theaters and in 16-mm size for use by the mobile units. Their distribution is handled by the Federal Film Library operated by the agency and, in addition to commercial houses and the mobile units, are supplied to schools, clubs, associations, and other government departments.

INFORMAL MEDIA

Rumor and word-of-mouth information constitute effective media, although there have been few systematic studies of how they play their role. One study indicated that people tend to evaluate media mainly on the basis of personal relationship with the source of information. Lacking any general standards for evaluating the reliability of information, most tend to be unsure of impersoanl sources, fully confident of anything they receive in face-to-face situations, regard rumor and word-of-mouth data as reliable, and are much more ready to act on what "people said" than on data received through impersonal media.

Especially in the more remote communities, the role of travelers and peddlers as news sources is traditionally recognized, and information received from an "important" member of the community is valued more highly than that obtained from public sources. Among the Malays, especially in the villages, newspapers are read aloud to illiterate members of the community, and this news plus the information and gossip obtained from local notables and travelers are then spread by word-of-mouth. Local stores and coffee shops are rumor and information centers for all communities. Among the Malays the religious leaders, itinerant merchants, and travelers are important carriers of information, and families of the nobility are especially influential in forming public opinion.

News travels fast through the Chinese communities, mainly through such organizations as labor unions, societies, fraternal groups, and mutual protection bodies. Schools and youth associations are also very active transmitters. Many Chinese study abroad, and their impressions carry great weight when they return.

In other ethnic communities, the bazaars are probably most important in the informal transmission of information. Tradesmen, travelers, buyers, and government personnel meet and talk. Traders, boatmen, and porters act as middlemen in spreading news from bazaar to bazaar. Information is carried from each market center into the various dialect communities by bilingual individuals. Among the indigenous people in East Malaysia, the porches of the longhouses and village ceremonial centers are important gathering places where visitors are received and information is exchanged.

In the more remote areas of both East and West Malaysia, the "bamboo telegraph" is known to function rapidly. In this process of oral transmission, rumor is magnified, and translations into the various dialects frequently account for drastic changes in meaning and emphasis.

CHAPTER 16

POLITICAL VALUES AND ATTITUDES

On the eve of the 1970's, in seeking to create a Malaysian national identity, the Alliance government had formulated a national policy intended to blend Indians, Chinese, and Malays into an all-Malaysian culture, but one that is predominantly Malay. It has tried to achieve this goal chiefly by means of the national educational system and the Malay language. Continued communal orientation of the major ethnic groups, however, has not only hampered progress toward such an objective but has also inhibited the development of common political values and attitudes toward the nation, toward the government, or toward the Malaysian way of life.

At the end of the decade of the 1960's the government was guided by a Westernized elite, with the acquiescence of a population divided along several ethnic lines. Tengku Abdul Rahman, Tun Abdul Razak, Khir Johari, Tun Tan Siew Sin, and Tun V. T. Manickavasagam were among members of the elite who served simultaneously as national spokesmen, ethnic agents, and articulators of Western values.

Support by the people for a government that is paternalistic has been widespread, since such a system is compatible both with Malaysian tradition and with the realities—communal tension, illiteracy, a narrow range of loyalties, and the elite's monopoly of modernizing skills. The elite support for liberal democracy, however, is comparatively limited. Its leaders have adopted the concepts of democracy in an eclectic fashion, and only tenuously, lasting as long as they do not conflict with more deeply held values or endanger national stability and unity. Rather than put their faith in democracy, the leaders prefer to emphasize conciliation and compromise in politics.

Despite the growth of political groups and popular participation in political life, the masses have remained traditionally subservient to the rulers and the influence of the bureaucratic elite. An attempt has been made to secularize and rationalize state administration, but it has been tempered to accommodate Malay attachment to Islam and the rulers.

The federal government has instituted policies to foster political unity and national loyalty among the diverse regional and ethnic groups in the country. Since state loyalty has constituted a very integral part of politics, especially in East Malaysia, conflict between regionalism and the necessity to have a strong central government has become common.

MAJOR DETERMINANTS OF VALUES AND ATTITUDES

Islam

Islam has been a significant force in the political mobilization of the Malays. It has helped them to overcome parochial loyalties, stimulated popular participation in the political system, and contributed to political modernization. The conversion of the bulk of the Malay population to Islam took place without displacing existing political and social elites or challenging existing social values and practices.

The syncretic combination of the Sufi-Muslim tradition with the animist-Hindu-Buddhist element in Malay culture was achieved with little tension or conflict. Islam was interpreted to make it more compatible with the role of traditional leaders in society, as well as with the traditional beliefs, customs, and practices of the Malays (see ch. 10, Religion). Government leaders have been attempting to inculcate a pragmatic approach to both political and economic problems, but the value system inherent in Islam has not been substantially altered. In fact, the leadership has been more inclined to support the traditional Islamic value system than to challenge it.

The Muslim community, however, has been under constant pressures to change both its attitudes and behavior patterns. The country's economic growth, its modern communications system, and its educational system have resulted in an increasing number of Malays becoming Westernized, modernized, and increasingly secular in outlook. Nonetheless, the modernizing Malay elite, who are mindful of Muslim opposition to the separation of religion from state affairs, have sought to identify their secular attitudes and values with Islam.

Islam not only has served to legitimize authority but traditionally has been a stabilizing factor in the political system against civil strife and the collapse of royal authority. The roles of village officials and the local social status and ranking system were partly defined by the religious beliefs and attitudes of the village. They were legitimized in their office by religious rituals and by reference to religious sources of authority.

The main emphasis of Islamic values has been traditional and conservative, but it has been challenged by a modernist Islamic movement that espouses political and social reforms, popular democracy, and Pan-Islamic nationalism. Islamic orthodoxy, however, has been preserved and has had the effect of maintaining the symbolic unity of Islam in the nation. Those who accepted the new elements of religious and political faith did so with the feeling that they were not being converted to alien beliefs, attitudes, and values. On the contrary, they felt they had rediscovered their ancient cultural and religious heritage. Politics and religion are consequently closely linked with Malay society.

Colonial Rule and Recent Historical Experience

Since British colonial rule was relatively brief and largely indirect, Malay's colonial experience was less traumatic than that of some other countries. In the absence of deep-seated anticolonial bitterness, there were no intellectual elements capable of mobilizing such sentiment. Timely political concessions by the British, the ensuing struggle against a Communist rebellion, and the Indonesian Confrontation (see Glossary), prevailed upon Malays not only to refrain from turning to more extremist leaders but to cooperate closely with the British as well.

Power passed from the British to a local political leadership that was virtually identical in education, outlook, and social background with the local bureaucratic elite. This historical circumstance has led to the growth of a moderate and conservative leadership committed, in principle, to the achievement of a democratic state; however, a continuing crisis of unity and stability has led, in practice, to weakened democratic foundations.

Relations between the Malay and non-Malay communities have generally been characterized by a combination of active and passive coexistence, especially the latter. For the most part, collaboration has occurred only among the upper strata of Western-educated Malays, Chinese, and Indians, who are mostly civil servants. Because of their English-language education and modern, urban occupations, they share a common outlook and interpretation of events. Outside these strata, virtually three different political systems exist, each corresponding to a racial group. This is a principal reason for the emphasis on conciliation and compromise in political life.

THE WESTERNIZED ELITE AND THE ROLE OF GOVERNMENT

The governing elite has been Westernized by virtue of education, beliefs, and ideals, but a gap separates the political values of the elite from those of the mass of the people. The elite has shown support for a strong leadership in the government to maintain an orderly society. The leaders believe that an entirely democratic system might be a weak structure, unable to prevent men from exploiting one another.

Their expressed assumptions about human nature and environment do not lead them to expect either the political tolerance or the cooperation that would help sustain a fully democratic state. They believe that competition for spoils, the illiteracy and parochial loyalties of the masses, and the tensions and social distrusts make difficult the full functioning of a truly liberal democracy.

Freedom of speech, for example, seems more entrenched than the cannons of due process of law illustrating the selective way in which democratic ideals have been supported. Both beliefs are formalistic, however, and not only tend to give way when in conflict with more deeply held values but are also not permitted to endanger national stability or unity.

In contrast to what leaders consider the fragile base for democracy, the firm but paternalistic rule by a benevolent elite is considered to be more consonant with the pattern of both colonial and traditional regimes. Such rule makes assumptions about the environment that are regarded as compatible with Malaysian realities. The Westernized elite believes it rules by virtue of its superior qualifications; the masses, for their part, look to the Westernized elite, with their knowledge and organizational skills, for leadership. Both groups fear that popular rule might split the nation because of a constant threat of a communal conflict.

Having little part in the selection of leaders or the choice of policies, the mass of citizens are expected simply to follow the instructions of the ruling elite. The Alliance government has used its component parties to explain the government program and to elicit public support. The civil service has also been used as a direct link of the elite with the rural population.

As in the traditional and colonial rule, the people are expected to comply with political acts rather than to express an evaluation of their own, to acquiesce and not to exert pressure or criticize the ruling group. They cannot turn to political parties as the media of popular participation, since parties are not expected to solicit popular demands and channel them to the central government. The party system does not establish a communication link between the voter and his government; however, it does provide channels for eliciting loyalty, explaining government policy, and identifying the source of government favors.

Leaders have sought to promote unity and mutual confidence among communal groups through the schools, especially the national schools directly controlled by the state. The government hopes thereby to bring the ideals of Malaysian nationhood to future generations of children. The leaders believe that the government policy of having the state determine educational needs and standards will strengthen intercommunal bonds, as well as stimulate the development of the Malaysian national identity.

While promoting the idea of national unity, the leaders continue to adopt the principle of political selectivity. Among the rulers in nine of the states of West Malaysia and in the Malaysian Civil Service, Malays are given preference in recruitment. In East Malaysia preference is given to natives (non-Chinese). Rulers are chosen by largely arbitrary means limited to Malays, although some modification is possible based on achievement criteria. The choice of one of the rulers as the Supreme Head (Yang di-Pertuan Agong) of the entire federation of Malaysia follows a similar principle, since the selection is done by the rulers from among themselves. The pattern is not wholly fixed, as the senior ruler has not always been elected Supreme Head.

In the Malaysian Civil Service recruitment has been on the basis of not more than one non-Malay for every four Malays recruited. This restriction is embodied in Article 153 of the Malaysian Constitution, but it can be modified within categories bounded by communal preference.

The minister for national and rural development, the minister for home affairs, the minister for agriculture and cooperatives, and the prime minister must be Malay, but the minister of finance and the minister of commerce and industry have traditionally been Chinese. This arrangement is supposed to reflect to some extent the bargain between the Malays and the Chinese (see ch. 13, Political Dynamics).

Non-Malays dislike the four-to-one civil service ratio, but Malays regard it as symbolizing the essence of the bargain between the Malays and non-Malays. The Malays have made sure that their traditional rulers are retained in the federal structure of government, and they believe Malay control of the civil service must remain unchallenged if Malays are to remain masters of the country. Any attempt to unfreeze the bargain or to replace it with the achievement criteria is strongly resisted.

In a similar context, there have been elements of self-perpetuation in political succession, legitimized by election. For example, the administrative class selected by the British as their successor took over as political leaders of the new nation, and subsequent elections served to confirm this succession. National leaders have subsequently endeavored to develop loyalty more to institutions than to individuals in authority. In the past the loyalty that Prime Minister Tengku Abdul Rahman has personally commanded has been greater than the loyalty called for by his high office. The leaders fear that whoever succeeds the Tengku may not attract the same loyalty, affection, reverence, and obedience and have hoped that, as the pattern of government becomes established, loyalty will accrue more to the office than to the person.

Islam also plays an important role in the political process. The leaders have sought to establish a secular and rational government; in their interpretation of Islam and of what the actual powers of the Malay rulers ought to be, they tend to be secular and rational beyond that which the masses would prefer. Fearful of isolating themselves from the masses if they conform too strictly to the standards of government, moderate Malay politicians have had to temper their concept of rationality and secularism. The large-scale building of mosques and the frequent staging of Koran-reading competitions are evidence of the importance given to Islam by political leaders.

POLITICAL IDENTIFICATION

Despite the government policy of fusing the country's diverse communities into a common political identity as Malaysians, there has been a tendency among Chinese and Indian communities to look beyond the political borders of Malaysia. This attitude is especially reflected in the varying concepts of Malaysian nationalism, which generally has been described as a modified or attenuated Malay nationalism consisting of two component parts—a nucleus of Malay nationalism enclosed by the ideal of Malay-Chinese-Indian partnership, together with the indigenous peoples of East Malaysia. Some Malay leaders, however, equate Malaysian nationalism with Malay nationalism prefer to use *Melayu* (the Malay word for "Malay") instead of *Malayan* in every possible context. At the same time, some Chinese and Indians, in describing themselves as "Malaysians," refer to an altogether new political identity and refuse to consider it as similar to Malay.

Consequently, as 1970 approached, there appeared to be no unanimity about the meaning of Malaysian nationalism. Even though many Malays and a few Chinese and Indians already considered themselves first and foremost Malaysians, the bulk of the population remained uncertain what part of their present identity they would have to sacrifice before they could become Malaysians. A recognized authority has described the Malay as first of all a Malay, then a Muslim, and then a Malaysian; the Chinese first of all a Chinese, then a Buddhist or Christian if he is religious, and then possibly Malaysian; and the Indian first of all an Indian, then a Hindu or Muslim, and then possibly a Malaysian.

386

Malays, for their part, have a strong parochial identity with their state, which is symbolized more by the Malay ruler than by their religion. The Islamic concepts of *dar al-Islam* (the place of Islam) and *dar al-harb* (the place of war or abode of infidels) have defined those who were not included within the political system. Malays expect members of their community not only to be of the Muslim faith but also, as subjects of a particular state, to give professions of fealty and obeisance (*menghadap*) to the Malay-Muslim ruler. The process of conversion to Islam (*masok Melayu*) means the entry to the Malay community. Although less significant when compared to the period before World War II, the Malay attachment to the rulers and to Islam has remained strong because of the symbolic importance of these figures to Malays needing constant reassurance of their continued domination of the country.

The non-Malays generally have neither parochial identity nor regional loyalties; instead, they concentrate on safeguarding their interests at the national level. The Chinese in Penang and Malacca have made attempts to set themselves apart from the rest of the population on certain matters. Unlike the Malays, the Chinese and Indians do not display respect and loyalty for the sultans. They favor the limitation of the powers and privileges of the sultans when these are essential to the efficient operation of a centralized administration.

ATTITUDES TOWARD NATION AND GOVERNMENT

The leaders recognize that one aspect of the problem of nation-building is the transferring of loyalties from individual states, particularly in East Malaysia, to the country as a whole. Parochial attachment to the state has resulted in intermittent conflict between regionalism and the need to have a strong federal government. In addition, one of the main problems has been to attract the loyalties of various ethnic groups, which, other than the two states in East Malaysia, are not concentrated in any particular areas. In one respect this factor has made efforts at unifying the diverse ethnic groups less difficult, because the concentration of such groups would have intensified the feeling of distinctiveness.

National loyalty toward Malaysia was aroused during Indonesia's Confrontation with Malaysia. Many non-Communist Chinese resented the Indonesian treatment of Chinese in Indonesia. There were, nevertheless, many Malaysians who identified themselves with the Indonesian side. Among these were subversives in Sarawak, mostly Chinese, the defunct Socialist Front, and leaders of the Pan-Malayan Islamic Party. The subsequent emphasis on Malay culture has, however, undermined some of the unity that was stimulated by the Confrontation.

Most Malays believe that a common national culture should have as its nucleus traditional Malay culture. Most Chinese and Indians reject this position and suggest instead that the Malaysian nation should involve only a new political loyalty and not a denial of the multicultural basis of the present society. English-language-educated Chinese and Indians hold the view that cultural differences may remain, as long as most people accept more intensive modernization and come to share a common outlook that is not deeply anchored in any single traditional culture.

Through a series of elections at local, state, and federal government levels, more of the politically conscious Malaysians were being induced to affirm their loyalty to the nation and gradually to identify that nation with the political system, which they were learning to manipulate.

The Malays

The Malays consider themselves the true Malaysian group. To some extent, they view the Chinese and the Indians as aliens who are in Malaysia not by right but by leave of the Malays. Three interwoven factors form the basis of the Malay's special attachment to his homeland: a sense of kinship of the Orang Melayu (the Malay folks or Malay proper) ; a sense of traditional relationship to Tanah Malaya (land of the Malays), and a sense of historical continuity of the connection between Malays and the land they inhabit (see ch. 4, Ethnic Groups and Languages). They see Malaysia as one part of a larger Malay area, which should include the islands of Java and Sumatra. They also appear to recognize a secondary sort of linkage between themselves and the Thai, based in part on the historical connection between four of the Malay states and Thailand, and in part on the number of ethnic Malays who inhabit the southern Thai provinces.

The Malays see no contradiction between their recent history and their claims to primacy among Malaysia's peoples. Neither the century under the complete domination of the British nor the British grant of independence, with no military and very little political struggle on the part of the Malays, has affected the predominant Malay view that the land is rightfully and all theirs.

Although jealous of their varying degrees of state autonomy, Malays find themselves losing many of their prerogatives to the federal government. This basic change has evoked few complaints or conjectures, since Malays feel that they have secured their leadership in the new unity by insisting that the Supreme Head, most members of the Conference of Rulers, and the prime minister be Malay.

The Malays fear Chinese initiative, enterprise, and economic power, which they believe may be used to gain political power unless special precautions are taken. The British favored the interests of the Malays, by means, for example, of Malay land reservations and quotas to protect Malay business and professional interests in the face of Chinese business and economic expansion, and the Malay still looks to the government to protect him against economic exploitation by the Chinese.

Some Malays have a feeling of dissatisfaction with the present political leadership, expressed as criticism of high salaries, big expense accounts, and flashy perquisites of office. They have made the accusation that these manifestations are British inspired and violate Malay tradition, although no such criticism appears to have been directed against equally costly adornments of the state rulers. The prime minister has been berated for occasionally wearing the plumed hat that characterized British officials but which is not the traditional Malay headgear.

Traditionally, a Malay is a citizen by virtue of being a subject of the sultanate of the state in which he lives. The older *kampong* (village) Malay—in contrast with the less reverent younger generation—retains a strong loyalty to the sultan and the raja (see Glossary) group in general. This loyalty accounts for much of the general respect in which government authority is held by Malays. The people are keenly interested in the pomp and ceremony associated with the sultanate and in the general well-being of the ruler. They rarely express opinions or vote against the known wishes of their respective rulers. Malays have shown dismay that the country as a whole has been less able to maintain the trappings of a traditional Malay state, and some have expressed resentment not only because administration and policies of predominantly Malay states cannot be more pro-Malay but also because they are becoming increasingly more conditioned by communal interdependence.

To the Malay in more remote areas, government, especially the federal government, tends to be a far-off entity whose actions affect other people but appear to have little to do with his own life. In the cities the Malay finds himself drawn to, and more intimately affected by, government regulations and activity; even then, he may equate government with his ruler, for whom he has great reverence. The ruler, he feels, resides on lofty heights much beyond the reach of the common citizen.

The Chinese

Most of the Chinese who emigrated from China have kept much to themselves, maintained strong loyalties to their ethnic, social, and political organizations, and retained ties with their land of origin.

Only among the second and subsequent generations has their ethnocentricity weakened and a sense of loyalty developed toward the multiethnic political units in which they live. In terms of cultural orientation and to some extent political loyalty, the Chinese of Malaysia fall into three distinct types: the chauvinist Chinese, the British-oriented Chinese, and the Baba Chinese, who have adopted many of the attitudes of their new home.

A segment of the Chinese community, made up of those best described as Chinese chauvinists, believes firmly in the innate superiority of the Chinese, whether it be intellectually, culturally, linguistically, or in business acumen. They do not think of the government as theirs, even though some of them helped elect it. Malaysia may be their habitat, but it has not become their country. In their view the federal government runs the country largely for the benefit of the Malays, to which they do not object, provided that it does not interfere with what they consider their economic rights (that is, freedom to do business) and does not impede the maintenance of Chinese culture in Malaysia. Many, however, advocate a Chinese Malaysia and seek participation in political life, not because they feel real attachment to the country or its political destiny but because they want to safeguard their own position. Many of these would desire a Chinese Malaysia that was sympathetic to, if not linked with, mainland China.

The British-oriented Chinese are doubly alien to Malaysia; as Chinese the Malays consider them aliens, and most members of the Chinese community reject them because they aspire to emulate the British, maintaining British connections despite the end of the British rule. These people have largely shed Chinese customs and absorbed British, but not Malay, ways of life. They view with misgivings the participation of Chinese in the government coalition and appear to feel that by maintaining British loyalties and customs they have put the British in their debt and may some day call on the British government to protect them against the Malays.

Almost all of the Malaysian-oriented Chinese are Malaysian born, Malaysian or Commonwealth educated, and have been relatively successful within the existing system. Most are educating their children bilingually. Although proud of their Chinese heritage, they are also politically pro-Malaysian. For the most part, members of this small but growing community of Malaysian Chinese are to be found in the upper echelon of the Alliance, in the civil service, and among the affluent business community.

The Indians

In the past, the Indians, who at the end of 1969 constituted no more than 10 percent of the population, have sought to make their position secure by giving little or no trouble. Their political activities have always been more subdued than those of the Chinese, and they appear intent on remaining within legal bounds. Their role as moneylenders has made them as unpopular among Malays, as are the Chinese businessmen, but there are fewer Indians; although disliked by Malays, Indians, unlike the Chinese, are not feared. Because of their small number, they have little importance—politically, economically, or culturally; conscious of their limited strength, they do not aspire to much political power in Malaysia, but they seek to be represented.

The attachment that Indians in Malaysia feel for India is largely based on the sentimental ties that bind so many immigrant communities to their "old countries," and until recently the return migration of Indians was higher than that of Chinese. It is doubtful, however, that the typical Malaysian Indian views his community in the country as an outpost of India; he is well aware of its distance from India, geographically, politically, and culturally. The sophisticated Indian seems to view Malaysia with greater detachment than does his Chinese counterpart, and if he looks upon India as a great Asian power that can be—and in his view, should be—the spokesman of Asia, he does so only partially as an Indian. His ties to other Indians are weaker than those of the Chinese and subject him to less discipline. He is freer to acculturate himself and to grow real roots in Malaysia.

The Peoples of Sarawak and Sabah

The peoples of Sarawak and Sabah generally lack political experience. Both groups live in territories inhabited by diverse peoples with limited political participation at the national level. The British made little effort to foster self-government in either of these territories; consequently, native political institutions and consciousness, even on a state level, are of recent origin (see ch. 13, Political Dynamics).

Among the various ethnic groups of the area, the Chinese are the best educated and the most politically conscious. Some are newcomers; others are from families that have been in the area for generations. Old and new arrivals alike tend to retain loyalties to China as their cultural home and place of origin, and few have deep attachment to their place of residence.

After the Chinese, the Malays are the most politically sophisticated peoples of East Malaysia. They are acutely conscious of their former dominant position under the sultanate of Brunei and the Brooke rajas in Sarawak (see ch. 3, Historical Setting). They are inclined to look down on the Chinese and other ethnic groups. The Malay group consciousness is based largely upon the unifying force of the Islamic religion, combined with allegiance to the hereditary aristocracy.

The allegiance of the indigenous peoples has rarely gone beyond their particular longhouse (multifamily dwelling) or village. Many of the ethnic groups are broken up into numerous, more or less mutually exclusive and frequently hostile, subgroups with little or no consciousness of unity. Of these, the Iban (Sea Dayak) in Sarawak and the Kadazans in Sabah have come closest to a sense of group identity; this is especially true of the mission-educated clerks, junior civil servants, and teachers. The British made some attempts to integrate this ethnic kaleidoscope though such means as choosing the local authorities from various groups. This attempt did broaden somewhat the horizons of the village-bound indigenous peoples, but in its short history of operation it was hardly able to implant any general consciousness of national unity.

Malays from East Malaysia appear to have considerable rapport with peninsular Malays and Indonesian Malays. It was for this reason, at least in part, that the British were more successful in influencing the non-Muslim indigenous peoples.

NATIONAL SYMBOLS

Some symbols of national unity are purely Malay, consistent with the Malay hope that assimilation is to follow the Malay norm. The Supreme Head (Yang di-Pertuan Agong) is a potential focus for attracting national loyalties, although the title may be held for only 5 years, and eligibility for the office is restricted to the Malay rulers of the nine states.

The national language is also a Malay symbol, with little appeal to non-Malays. The flag and arms of Malaya and Malaysia bear no symbolic representation of the Chinese or Indian community in the country. Certain other symbols, existing or potential, however, are Malaysian. The rural development program no longer applied overwhelmingly to Malays after the New Villages (see Glossary), mostly Chinese, were included in the scheme. The program had symbolic and material attraction for Sabah and Sarawak when the Malaysia proposals were being discussed and has since been extened to these territories. The dispatch of Malayan troops to the Congo in 1960 had symbolic value in helping create national unity. The fact that the Tengku is partly Thai by birth and has adopted Chinese children is seen by some as a symbol of developing unity.

Malaysia's flag has a yellow, 14-point star with the yellow crescent of Islam in the upper right-hand quarter on a dark-blue field. The symbolism of the number 14 appearing in the Malaysian flag and coat of arms was to represent the unity of the original 14 states that had composed Malaysia. Since Singapore's separation from Malaysia in 1965, the symbolic representation of 14 was retained by simply adding the national flower, *bunga raya*, in the place of Singapore. There are still fourteen red and white stripes of equal width symbolizing the equal membership of the states of Malaysia. Each of the individual states also has a state flag; seven of the state flags contain the Islamic crescent.

The nation's coat of arms, originally designed for the 1948 Federation of Malaya, consists of a shield supported by two tigers (the tiger is the king of the beasts to the Malays). The crest is a 14-point star and a crescent, both yellow. On the red, upper one-third of the shield are superimposed five gold *kris*, or swords, denoting the five former Unfederated Malay States. The center of the shield has four, equal-sized panels of red, black, silver, and yellow (colors appearing in the flag of the four former Federated States). The lower portion of the shield contains three panels, which has been vacant until 1963, when designs symbolizing Singapore, Sabah, and Sarawak were added. Up to late 1969 no change had been made after Singapore's separation.

The outer quarters of the lower third of the shield portray, on the left, a device taken from the coat of arms of Penang (three blue feathers on a sky of yellow, topping a crenelated wave of blue, over blue and white waves) and, on the right, a Malacca tree, symbolizing the state of Malacca, presented on a green and white background. The legend below the shield, in black lettering on yellow, reads "Unity is Strength," in both Romanized and Jawi-script Malay. The coat of arms is used frequently as a seal on many high government orders, decorations, and proclamations.

There are three official versions of the Malaysian national anthem, "Negara Ku" (My Country). The full or royal version, which is taught in school, may be sung in public or played by an orchestra. It is also played as a salute to the Supreme Head or when the Royal Standard is broken to symbolize his presence. An abridged version, consisting of the first eight and the last eight bars, is used as a salute for the Supreme Head's consort, for the state heads of Malacca, Penang, Singapore, Sabah, and Sarawak, and for the Supreme Head's official representative. If the official representative is a state ruler, his state anthem is played as a salute to His Majesty's diplomatic representatives in foreign countries. The third version, or short version, of the national anthem consists of the final eight bars and is played at the end of public performances and entertainment.

The words of the "Negara Ku" are set to a Malay folk tune common to Malaya and Indonesia and were written at Merdeka (independence) in 1957. Translated into English, the words of the national anthem are:

My Country, my native land
The people living united and progressive
May God bestow blessing and happiness
May our Ruler have a successful reign
May God bestow blessing and happiness
May our Ruler have a successful reign.

SECTION III. ECONOMIC

CHAPTER 17

CHARACTER AND STRUCTURE OF THE ECONOMY

As the decade of the 1970's approached, Malaysia's economic system was in transition. From primary dependence on private enterprise, with governmental support for guiding economic development, the economy's movement was toward greater reliance on the role of government. The government was beginning to assume the primary responsibility for setting the economy's basic pattern, for the pursuit of policies implementing the pattern, and for solving economic problems. In assuming the role of economic leadership the government maintained the open and friendly attitude toward the private sector that had been its traditional policy.

From 1965, at the time of the separation of Singapore, to 1968, the gross national product (GNP) increased at the satisfactory average annual rate of 5 percent, and preliminary information for 1969 indicated that the country was enjoying a peak surplus on trade account, which is a pillar of the economy. Despite the overall progress, economic problems existed that impeded balanced growth and threatened social and political stability. Dissatisfaction over these problems manifested itself in open disturbances in mid-1969.

Imbalances in development that existed between urban and rural areas, between West Malaysia and East Malaysia—and more narrowly between the west and east coasts of West Malaysia—coupled with imbalances between ethnic groups resulted in marked income inequalities. In addition, the unemployment rate was high. New industries established from 1966 to 1969 had not provided enough new jobs to absorb the annual additions to the unskilled labor force nor to eliminate existing underemployment nor had they resolved the problem of major dependence upon a two-commodity (rubber and tin) economy.

In mid-1969 the government addressed itself to these root causes of instability and dissatisfaction, unequal distribution of income and unemployment, by embarking upon a new economic policy. The heart of the new policy was an accelerated industrialization program directed by the government. The major features of the program were the establishment of labor-intensive industries, the dispersal of industries from urban to rural areas, and the establishment of new plants in depressed areas in both West Malaysia and East Malaysia.

Although this redistribution of industry would tend to favor areas where Malays predominate, the goal is even development and correction of existing imbalances. The government is prepared to take the initiative in carrying out the program. It does not, however, negate the longstanding policy of encouraging private capital formation, both domestic and foreign, by the provision of incentives and services.

To implement the new economic policy the Capital Investment Committee headed by a minister with special duties and composed of senior civil servants and knowledgeable businessmen was organized in mid-1969. The functions of the committee are the undertaking of marketing and feasibility studies to identify suitable industries. After identification the government takes an active role in locating interested entrepreneurs and encouraging investment, using all available contacts, both domestic and overseas. If private enterprise is not interested, the government stands ready to establish desirable projects in contrast to its former passive role.

The private sector also is actively promoting economic expansion. At the end of 1969 the Sino-Malay Economic Cooperation Board was formed to help Malay businessmen become established in commerce or industry. The board, which is sponsored by the Chinese Chambers of Commerce and the Associated Malay Chambers of Commerce, is not a financial institution but one designed to act in an advisory capacity. Its purpose is to establish a permanent basis for cooperation between Chinese and Malay businessmen, to provide needed business services for interested Malays, and to arbitrate in business disputes between the two groups. Committees have been formed in all states, and the board invited the Associated Indian Chambers of Commerce to become a member.

The character of the economy is largely an outgrowth of developments during the colonial period. Its performance has been affected subsequently by both internal and external events such as the Emergency, the Confrontation with Indonesia, and the separation of Singapore (see ch. 3, Historical Setting). The country also faces an adjustment at the beginning of the 1970's because of the impending withdrawal of British forces.

The economy is based upon production and export of raw materials, especially rubber, tin, and timber and upon the import of goods for domestic consumption or for production facilities. For this reason it is vulnerable to changes in world economic forces and to the disparate trends in prices for raw materials and for finished products.

The importance of agriculture to the economy may be seen by the fact that it contributes about 30 percent to the gross domestic product (GDP) and employs 50 percent of the labor force. The First Malaysia Plan for 1966 to 1970 assigned about 30 percent of public development expenditure to agriculture, and the revised plan of 1968 continued to give it priority.

The agricultural sector is dualistic in character. Production consists of commercial crops, almost entirely for export, and food crops for domestic use.

Foreign investment and management have played an important part in the development of the country. Because of declining investment in rubber and tin facilities and because of investments made in oil refineries and other plants from 1962 to 1964, the inflow of foreign capital had decreased, and it was estimated that it accounted for no more than 5 percent of capital formation annually in the latter part of the 1960's. Renewed interest by foreign firms in exploring for minerals and mineral fuels in the 1970's promised an increase in the flow of foreign capital.

At the outset rubber and tin production were developed by foreign investment and management. The country is the foremost producer of both commodities, accounting for about 44 percent of the world supply of natural rubber and 43 percent of the total production of tin in the non-Communist world in 1968. Both because of the instability of world prices and the known decline in tin reserves, an objective of government economic policy has been the development of a wider range of export commodities including manufactured goods. Timber is the third most important export and is rising in volume and value. As an indication of the importance of foreign trade, export and import duties accounted for about 38 percent of the ordinary revenues of the central government in 1968.

The small size and fragmentation of the internal market have inhibited the establishment of large-scale industries for domestic production. Complete removal of interregional tariffs, which was underway in 1968 and 1969, however, would increase the market to a more efficient size.

Industry, including mining, manufacturing, construction, and public utilities, contributes about 23 percent of the value of the gross domestic product and, with the addition of transportation, provides employment for 19.5 percent of the labor force. Growth of manufacturing, which was still in a developing stage in 1969 and mostly consisted of light industries producing consumer goods and plants processing agricultural commodities, has been an objective of government policy since independence. A goal was the development of foreign exchange earning commodities for exporting, in addition to import substitutes that saved foreign exchange.

Diversity in racial composition has produced a specialization in economic activity. Traditionally, Chinese have gravitated to commerce, finance, and small-scale industry; Malays have engaged in subsistence agriculture, and Indians have become mostly plantation workers. An objective of economic policy is the mixing of racial employment in new industries according to the share in the population.

A transportation and communications system, an electric power system, organized financial institutions, and marketing channels are legacies from the colonial period. Although these services are inadequate in scope and in need of updating to meet the needs of the 1970's, they have provided an invaluable backbone for economic growth, one which many developing countries lack. Malaysia also has a history of a stable currency and a minimum of inflation.

In 1966 the First Malaysia Plan for 1966 to 1970 was announced and execution was begun. This was the first overall development plan, covering West Malaysia, Sabah, and Sarawak. Previously, each state had had its own development plan.

The board, overall objectives of the plan were: the promotion of the economic and social integration of the states of Malaysia and of the ethnic groups composing the population; the increase in per capita income and standard of living, laying special emphasis on low income groups; the generation of employment to keep pace with the growth of the labor force and a decrease in the unemployment rate; an increase in education and training facilities; and the diversification of the economy to moderate its dependence on two commodities, rubber and tin. To obtain these goals, sectoral development programs were prepared covering all phases of the economy, such as agriculture and rural development, all aspects of industry, transportation and communications utilities, education and training, health and family planning, and social and community services.

The First Malaysia Plan was carefully prepared to integrate the financial and manpower needs of sectoral programs. In addition to an estimate of the total expenditure required—including the distribution between the public and private sectors—an estimate was made of the geographic allocation of funds, thus determining the share to be devoted to West Malaysia, Sabah, and Sarawak. Specific sums, taking into consideration public and private expenditures, were allocated to each program. These were planned in phases over the 5-year period. The plan also contained an outline of the expected sources of public financing.

The ultimate responsibility for economic and social planning rests with the cabinet. Machinery for the preparation and administration of plans is lodged in the prime minister's department. In 1961 the central government organized the National Development Planning Committee and reorganized the Economic Secretariat into the Economic Planning Unit. The function of the National Development Planning Committee is the formulation, implementation, progress evaluation, and revision of development plans. The chairman of the committee is appointed by the cabinet. Membership consists of: the governor of Bank Negara Malaysia; representatives from the treasury, the Ministry of Commerce and Industry, the Ministry of National and Rural Development, the Economic Planning Unit, and the Department of Statistics; and appointed representatives from Sabah and Sarawak. The Economic Planning Unit is responsible for the staff work connected with functioning of the National Development Planning Committee.

The major ministries maintain planning and research divisions to support the work of national planning, and there is close communication among all agencies involved to ensure coordination in plans and performance. In addition, in 1967 an advisory committee, including representatives from private enterprise, employers' associations, and trade unions, was formed to channel information between government and private enterprise. Reports on the progress of programs are made to the National Operations Room by relevant ministries and agencies, and states also maintain committees for administering and evaluating development plans.

A midterm review of the First Malaysia Plan was undertaken in 1968 to evaluate progress made and reassess goals and strategy for the final 2 years. A survey of performance indicated that development expenditure by the central government had fallen short of the goal in 1968 because of lack of expected foreign financing for planned projects. Revisions were made in targets for some sectoral programs, and the conclusion was reached that there was a need to channel public development expenditure toward more directly productive projects during the last 2 years. Expenditures on development of agriculture, industry, essential infrastructure, and skills were stressed.

A second plan for economic and social development is in preparation, but details had not been announced in late 1969. The plan was expected to bear the imprint of the new economic policy inaugurated in mid-1969.

CHAPTER 18

AGRICULTURE

Agriculture dominates the country's economy. Despite a marked decline in rubber prices in 1967, agriculture provided 56 percent of the country's export earnings and generated about 30 percent of the country's gross domestic product (GDP). Rubber alone accounted for about 12 percent of gross domestic product. The agricultural sector, including forestry and fishing, provided employment for about 50 percent of the economically active population in West Malaysia and for about 75 percent in East Malaysia.

The country's land code and tenure system are the result of centuries of common practice and have been complicated by codification attempts based on diverse traditions. Available statistics on tenure, holding size, and many aspects of agricultural production are largely limited to West Malaysia.

Rice is the major staple food of the country. In 1967 West Malaysia produced about 80 percent of the country's crop; additional production in East Malaysia brought the total domestic crop to 70 percent of domestic needs. Self-sufficiency in rice production is a national goal.

Rural development is carried out by numerous government groups and is coordinated under the Ministry of National and Rural Development. Land development is the responsibility of the Federal Land Development Authority. The government provides extension service facilities and is actively engaged in drainage and irrigation schemes. Heavy emphasis is placed on community centers and local participation in program planning and implementation.

Under the First Malaysia Plan for 1966 to 1970, rural and agricultural development were given heavy stress and allotted 23.9 percent of the plan's budget allocations for public development. Among the major objectives were the opening of new lands for cultivation, increasing rubber productivity, expanding oil palm production, and continuing research programs, particularly in the areas of new crops and livestock production.

The country's soils, formed primarily from granite and Triassic rock, are highly acidic and low in mineral content. Centuries of decayed vegetation supplement forest soils and provide for a cyclic buildup of humus. Once cleared, however, the land is quickly leached to the humus by the heavy rains. In a few years once fertile land may become sterile unless it is constantly fed with fertilizers, which are, in turn, rapidly leached by the rains. River valleys offer rich soil deposits as do areas in West Malaysia fed by the weathering of the Penang volcanic range.

LAND UTILIZATION

Even though most of the economy is tied to the country's ability to produce primary goods, of which agricultural products represent a substantial portion, only 7,836,000 acres, or less than 10 percent of the total land area, was shown in 1967 as devoted to agriculture (see table 14). Swamps and tropical forests comprise over 75 percent of the total land of West Malaysia, about 75 percent of Sarawak, and 80 percent of Sabah. The only fully cleared parts of Malaysia are found in the state of Kelantan and in parts of the coastal plains of eastern Sarawak and Sabah.

Almost 80 percent of the total area cultivated in 1967 was devoted either to rubber or rice. Another 14 percent of the cultivated land was used for coconut and oil palm production. The total acreage devoted to fruit was more than three times that for vegetables, coffee, and tea combined. Miscellaneous food crops, such as sago, sweet potatoes, nuts, beans, melons, and sugarcane, made use of about 2 percent of agricultural land.

West Malaysia accounted for nearly 84 percent of all land devoted to agricultural production in the country. It accounted for 90 percent of lands in rubber, 85.4 percent of lands in oil palm, and 70.8 percent of lands in rice. According to available figures, Sarawak contained 77 percent of all land in pepper production.

Table 14. *Land Utilization in Malaysia, 1966–67*
(in thousands of acres)

Cultivation	West Malaysia	Sabah	Sarawak	Total
Crops:				
Rubber	4,342	259	303	4,904
Oil palm	335	57	---	392
Rice	904	96	277	1,277
Other food crops (sago, sweet potatoes, nuts beans, melons, and sugarcane)	112	9	36	157

Table 14. Land Utilization in Malaysia, 1966–67—Continued

Cultivation	West Malaysia	Sabah	Sarawak	Total
Beverage crops (coffee and tea) ---------------------	30	9	---	39
Coconuts ------------------	506	105	89	700
Vegetables ----------------	29	---	---	29
Fruit ---------------------	244	9	---	253
Spices:				
Pepper -----------------	2	---	7	9
Others ------------------	68	---	---	68
Other crops --------------	3	5	---	8
TOTAL ------------------	6,575	549	712	7,836
Type of Land:				
Total cropland* ----------	10.273	858	1,113	12,244
Forest area* ------------	31,280	23,350	35,275	89,905
Other land* -------------	9,147	5,180	11,954	26.281
TOTAL ------------------	50,700	29,388	48,342	128,430

*Figures are in square miles.

The amount of land under permanent cultivation in Sabah and Sarawak is small, reported in 1967 at 549,000 and 712,000 acres, respectively, and representing only about 1.9 percent and 1.5 percent of their respective land areas. The quality of land in both areas is poor and, despite government regulation, forest reserves are constantly challenged by shifting cultivation techniques and unlicensed land use.

LAND TENURE

Evolution of the Land Tenure System

The original Malayan customary law recognized only the right of the cultivator to the use of land because of his holding of it in the system of shifting agriculture. This customary law, comparable to that of Burma, Indonesia, Thailand, Borneo, and Sumatra, was appropriate to the natural ecological conditions in a dense monsoon forest. With a sparse population, abundant land, and tall forest vegetation demanding laborious felling before cultivation, the original rights were created by clearing and then cultivating the land and were absolute as long as the land was kept under cultivation or bore some other sign of continued interest on the part of the cultivator. In the case of wet rice, which is cultivated in the lowlands on permanent plots requiring the continuous investment of labor year after year, Malay custom allowed the cultivator to leave plots out of cultivation for a maximum of 3 years without forfeiting his rights.

With the establishment of regional monarchies, cultivators who had formerly lived in tribal units under chiefs became subjects of their local monarch raja (see Glossary) and were required by custom to pay him one-tenth of their crops. Their usufruct rights remained in effect as long as they occupied and cultivated their lands and paid their regular crop fees. Since abandoned land was forfeited to the raja and since he could seize either crops or land for nonpayment of the fees on cultivated land, there evolved the doctrine that the absolute rights to the soil, including cultivated, abandoned, and cleared land, were ultimately vested in the state in the person of the raja. In many districts of West Malaysia, forest land under state control is still known as the raja's land.

In time, the rights of the occupant cultivators evolved into grants in perpetuity from the state, subject only to taxes and certain cultivation regulations. Lands so held formed the category of alienated land —that is, alienated from state to private control—and land titles in this category were proprietary rights, which in effect constituted private ownership. The titles could be transferred by sale or inheritance and the lands either cultivated by the owner or let under various types of usufruct right to other cultivators.

The Modern System

The constitutional provisions, the distinctive religious, traditional and economic variations among the ethnic elements—Malay, Chinese, and Indian—and the Muslim law of inheritance combine to make the land problems peculiarly complex and account for the considerable difficulty officials have encountered in developing a unitary land code. In addition, the Japanese occupation during World War II left a legacy of unregistered land transactions; in some districts the registers were lost altogether. Dislocations during the Emergency (1948–60) compounded these problems and created new ones (see ch. 3, Historical Setting).

Although policy on land utilization has been primarily a state matter, state authorities have sought federal guidance in several areas. Both state and federal governments have agreed that land suitable for rice cultivation should not be alienated for other purposes and that land containing mineral or metal deposits should not be alienated for agriculture until the deposits have been exploited.

The Constitution of 1963 empowered the Federal Parliament to pass legislation promoting a uniform policy of land tenure and compulsory registration of titles and deeds. The National Land Council was established to oversee and coordinate the land utilization program and the development of a unitary land code; and the Office of the Commissioner of Land was appointed to serve as a federal advisory agency. The efforts of these two groups resulted in the National Land Code Acts of 1963 and 1965, both of which took effect in 1966 and placed all of West Malaysia under a uniform code. Implementation of the provisions of these acts is still taking place.

West Malaysia

All of West Malaysia has adopted the Torrens' system of Australia, under which public registration establishes the right of what amounts to ownership. Separate registers for smallholders are maintained in the majority of districts, and titles to incorporate town lands and estates of more than 10 to 15 acres are recorded in central state registers. Heavy personnel loads, however, frequently result in registration backlogs.

Alienation is subject to certain conditions and terms, such as the preservation of forest and wild game areas. The occupation of land without a state government grant of license is unlawful.

Land laws, as a rule, embody the old Malayan principle that title depends upon use. Perak, Selangor, Negri Sembilan, and Pahang, which constituted the former Federated Malay States, had a uniform land code that provided for the forfeiture of land if half of the area covered by the title was not cultivated for three consecutive years and prescribed fines for failing to plant at the proper time.

Kelantan, Perlis, Johore , Trengganu, and Kedah, the former Unfederated Malay States, followed the general pattern set by the Federated Malay States, but differences existed. Penang and Malacca, two of the former Straits Settlements, presented other variations.

An owner-farmer will normally hold land on a grant from the state in perpetuity under the law and be subject only to certain cultivation conditions and nominal annual quit-rents or water rates or both. Many farmers are owners in fact but not in name because their land titles are not up to date although they have a full legal claim to the land by inheritance or purchase. Some smallholders renounce their undivided shares of land registered in the title to allow another relative to cultivate them free. Many owner-farmers, upon retirement from active farming, will allow their children to cultivate the land free in return for old-age care but are shrewdly reluctant to transfer the title deeds.

In the use of land, owners of agricultural plots are bound by certain methods of cultivation. They may also be bound by conditions of the title; for example, rubber cultivation is often prohibited on land better suited to other crops. They also may be bound by provision of law, such as laws enforcing the proper cultivation of riceland or the conservation of soil on hills. State governments have also been able to encourage development of certain crops by reserving land for them and by granting special premium rates or rebates on rent; the pioneer cultivation of cacao, for example, was encouraged in this way.

The demand for land, stimulated by boom conditions for rubber and other crops in recent years, has given rise to more applications than the land offices can handle. Many applications have been outstanding for years. Moreover, in some districts the land office staff has been unable to prevent widespread illegal occupation.

Modern usufruct rights are dependent on individual agreements between cultivators and those proprietors who themselves do not wish to cultivate. Whereas the proprietary rights have been codified on European examples, the usufruct rights of the cultivators remain unwritten laws and in some respects are comparable with Indian and other Asian practices, although some aspects of the development of agricultural tenure systems are unique to West Malaysia.

Five basic types of agreements between farmer and landowner exist in West Malaysia, in addition to that wherein the farmer is given tenure rights directly from the state. Minor variations exist in different geographic zones and local terms vary between districts, but these basic types are well-understood and long-established forms of contracts throughout the main agricultural areas.

In the fixed-rent system (*sewa*), the tenant agrees to pay a specified amount of rent per local unit area or on the whole of the land he cultivates. The agreement covers a stated period, usually one year or one planting season, though it may be renewed annually for 10 or even 20 years. Normally *sewa* is payable regardless of the actual yield obtained, except in circumstances of drastic crop failure due to drought, flood, disease, or insect damage; in the event of crop failure tenant and landlord bargain for a lower rent or decide on part payment and carry over part of the rent as debt of the following year.

Fixed rents are payable in kind or in cash and are usually paid at harvesttime. The majority of fixed rents paid are in ricelands, particularly along the western coast.

The *pajak* agreement is an extension over a longer period than the annual *sewa* since the tenant agrees to pay a lump sum of the cash in advance to cover the whole period, usually between three and five years but occasionally as long as 12 to 15 years. The lease offers more favorable terms to the tenant by giving extra security of tenure and sometimes a lower annual rent per unit of area to compensate for cash payment considerably in advance. In *pajak susut* the tenant pays his rent in advance for a period of years, but the landlord reserves the right to terminate the agreement in the interim by refunding a portion of the original sum.

In the *pawah* or sharecropping system, the cultivator agrees before commencing to work the land to pay the landlord at harvest a fixed share of the resulting crop; the final amount actually paid is usually open to some negotiation. The *pawah* system predominates in the eastern coastal states where yields are generally lower than in the western coastal states. In the eastern coastal states the sharecropping system is highly developed with a wide range of shares and a wide choice for media of payment. The landlord's share, for example, ranges anywhere from 45 to 70 percent on the eastern coast. Pawah is found only in isolated cases on poor land and on the light, sandy soils of Perlis.

Under the *gadai* system, the landowner temporarily transfers the usufruct but not the proprietary rights to his land to another person in return for the loan of a sum of money. The period of this transfer usually is not specified.

The landowner entering into a *jual janji* agrees to pledge the proprietary rights to his land as security for the repayment of a loan at the end of a specified time. This arrangement resembles the British mortgage system.

In addition to forest reservations that are under special protection of the respective state governments, there are large areas, especially in the state of Kelantan, designed as Malay reservations. Land on such reservations can be alienated to Malays only. A Malay for this purpose is defined as a person "belonging to any Malayan race who habitually speaks the Malay language or any Malayan language and who professes the Muslim religion." The definition includes Indonesian and Thai immigrants. Originally these reservations were results of government efforts protecting the Malay smallholder against dealers, land investors, and moneylenders who held the land as security for their money; they came to have the purpose of protecting Malay ethnic interests against a threat of non-Malay domination on the Peninsula.

In parts of the states of Malacca and Negri Sembilan, there are special measures with nearly the same effect as that of reservations. These govern the registration of land held by matriarchal aboriginal tribes (see ch. 5, Social Structure).

Sarawak

The land tenure system of Sarawak attempts to achieve two objectives: to protect the native population from non-natives and to provide non-natives, particularly the Chinese, with enough land for effective economic development (see ch. 4, Ethnic Groups and Languages). Attempts at land reforms and proposals for changes in land restrictions in Sarawak became political issues in 1965. With the exception of a limited number of 999-year leases already in existence, most lease terms are for 60 to 99 years. Temporary installations are given shorter terms.

Before 1932 and 1933, when the Land Ordinance and the Land Settlement Ordinance, respectively, were introduced, distribution and control of land were in the hands of the raja, who could alienate land under perpetuity grants. As a supplement to the Land Ordinance, a Land Classification Ordinance was passed in 1949. This new legislation classified land into five categories and defined the rights to land by natives and non-natives.

The first of the five categories is native area land, which encompasses approximately 2,600 square miles. Occupancy is restricted to natives, and most of it is still under customary tenure. The second category is customary land, which includes all land held under native customary tenure. No titles are issued, and the rights are granted in the forms of licenses to use the land. Rights, earned by natives who clear and occupy the land, are transferable to the descendants. The third category is mixed-zone land, which can only be alienated when the rights have been surrendered. There are approximately 4,600 square miles of land classified as mixed-zone land, of which about 1,000 square miles are under Chinese and non-native control; the remainder is held by natives under native customary tenure. The fourth category, reserved land, includes all land kept by the government for various purposes, such as forest reserves and national parks. The fifth and final category, interior land, includes all land not falling into any of the other four categories. It comprises mostly uncleared forest and a very small amount of cleared land to which titles have not been issued.

After 1958 a new land code was legislated with the purpose of bringing together all the land ordinances that were in effect. The observance of the provisions in the Land Code rests in the hands of the Land and Survey Department. Other tasks of the department include alienation of land, registration of titles, dispositions affecting land, land surveyance and collection of land rents, premiums, license fees, and other revenues from land and mineral rights.

Sabah

Sabah has two types of land tenure: ordinary leasehold, available to any person upon the state's acceptance of application, and title by entry in the Register of Native Titles, confined to natives. All other land belongs to the state. No titles are awarded to natives practicing shifting cultivation in the hills. The property law is contained in the Land Ordinance, which was extended to Labuan Island in February 1963.

Title by entry in the Register of Native Titles confers upon the registered native a permanent, heritable, and transferable right of use and occupancy of the land. These rights are subject only to the provisions of the Land Ordinance, the tenant's participation in the performance of works of common benefit and the duty to cultivate the fields. Dealings in land held by entry in the Register of Native Titles between natives and non-natives are prohibited; however, land can be sold with the consent of the residents who are collectors of land revenue within their residencies. District officers and assistant district officers are assistant collectors of land revenue and deputy registrar of titles in their district. Registration of native title and field registers is done locally by the assistant collectors of land revenue, but dealings in all other forms of title must be registered by the registrar of titles at the state capital.

LAND DEVELOPMENT

Tenancy and Size of Holdings

There are no country-wide figures for tenancy and holding size. In 1969 the most recent available information for West Malaysia was based on the 1960 census of agriculture. Small holdings were classified as farms contiguous or noncontiguous with less than 100 acres of land. Any holding possessing 100 acres or more was classified as an estate.

According to the census figures approximately 60 percent of the rubber area was under estate production. The average size of all rubber estates was 800 acres; about 65 percent of the estates had less than 500 acres, and 10 percent had more than 2,000 acres. Forty percent of the rubber area was operated by smallholders, many of whom devoted only a small part of their land to rubber production.

Next to rubber, rice cultivation occupied the largest amount of cultivated land. Rice cultivation was almost entirely the province of smallholders, and the average rice holding was about 4 acres. Eighty percent of the land in coconut production was under smallholder operation. Estates in coconut averaged 1,000 acres each with several running over 3,500 acres. The production of oil palm was entirely on estates, with the average estate being about 2,000 acres.

The census figures revealed that about 75 percent of the farms in West Malaysia were operating under permanent ownership titles; about 20 percent were operating on a tenancy basis, and the remainder fell under a variety of temporary classifications. The ratio of owner-operated holdings was largest for those specializing in rubber and other permanent crops, and 90 percent of export-crop farmers held permanent title to their land. Less than 50 percent of the rice farmers held title to their land.

Considerable concern was evidenced by government officials during the 1960's over the fragmentation of estate land. Estates were being purchased and resold in lots of less than 25 acres to avoid being subject to the Employment Ordinance. Under the National Land Code Amendment of 1969, all land transfers of estate land are to be under the direct control of the Estate Board. Land transfers without the approval of the board will be rejected by the registrar of land titles.

Land Development Program

In order to help resettle rural people on their own holdings with high-yield crops the government maintains the Federal Land Development Authority. In addition to the opening of unused or undeveloped land to settlement for landless families, the Authority has set up infrastructure facilities including transportation and communication facilities and water supply systems. It has also attempted to ensure modern production and marketing facilities and social programs including schools and community development centers.

The Authority has attempted to follow the overall government guideline of agricultural diversification. Initially most of its projects concerned rubber cultivation, but by the mid-1960's a third of all projects initiated were in oil palm (see table 15). Between 1965 and 1967 no new rubber schemes were undertaken, but nine oil palm schemes were implemented. Most of the projects focused on West Malaysia. In 1967, 125,546 acres were in rubber, and 59,676 acres were in oil palm, giving a total main crop specialization of 185,222 acres. The development of subsidiary crops included 39 acres of fish ponds, 2,141 acres of wet-rice paddies, 774 acres of bananas, 213 acres of vegetables, and other crops for a total of 3,473 acres.

Between 1957 when the first scheme was initiated and 1967, 12,390 families were settled on 201,651 acres of new or redeveloped land (see table 16). By 1967, 16,429 new village sites had been established under the land authority, and 470 miles of village and access roads had been constructed. Also completed were 441 units of public and social services. Among these were 56 water systems, 44 postal agency units, 47 schools, 49 clinics, 39 community centers, and 28 bus service systems. The target figures for 1970 were 22,000 families on 270,000 acres. Based on an average of 6.2 persons per family, the total of persons settled by the Authority would be 136,400 and would represent about 2.3 percent of the population in rural West Malaysia.

Table 15. Schemes and Acreage of Land Planted in Malaysia, 1957–67

Year	Number of schemes			Acreage planted		
	Rubber	Oil palm	Total	Rubber	Oil palm	Total
1957–59	10	--	10	4,091	---	4,091
1960	4	--	4	10,509	---	10,509
1961	10	1	11	14,471	926	15,397
1962	11	--	11	24,673	1,749	26,422
1963	8	4	12	17,343	6,839	24,182
1964	8	3	11	22,398	8,317	30,715
1965	--	1	1	8,475	9,578	18,053
1966	--	1	1	14,442	14,032	28,474
1967	--	7	7	9,144	18,235	27,379
TOTAL	51	17	68	125,546	59,676	185,222

Source: Adapted from *Federal Land Development Authority Annual Report, 1967*, Kuala Lumpur, 1967.

Table 16. Settler Intake and Acreage of Developed Land in Malaysia, 1957–67

Year	Families	Cumulative total	Acreage developed (in thousands of acres)		
			Village site	Main crop	Total acreage
1957–59	1,191	1,191	657	4,091	4,748
1960	1,981	3,172	1,184	10,509	11,693
1961	715	3,887	2.967	15,397	18,364
1962	881	4,768	2,920	26,422	29,342
1963	2,043	6,811	3,655	24,182	27,837
1964	1,150	7,961	2,936	30,715	33,651
1965	1,294	9,255	286	18,053	18,339
1966	1,465	10,720	230	28,474	28,704
1967	1,670	12,390	1,594	27,379	28,973
TOTAL	12,390	12,390	16,429	185,222	201,651

Source: Adapted from *Federal Land Development Authority Annual Report, 1967*, Kuala Lumpur, 1967.

TECHNOLOGY

Technology varies widely throughout the country. In general, cultivation is by handtools. The most popular handtool is the *changkul*, which resembles a long, broad hoe. It is used for digging, weeding, and opening and closing irrigation channels. A three-pronged fork is also a popular handtool.

The transportation of materials and crops is frequently done with open baskets carried on the head or attached to a stick over the shoulders. Draft animals provided transport as well as power for plowing.

Mechanized equipment was not introduced until the post World War II period. During the early 1950's the government made considerable effort to increase the awareness of smallholders of the benefits of mechanization and to encourage its use by estate owners. Progress was slow, and by 1960 tractors were used in less than 10 percent of all estate and less than 2 percent of all farms. Presumably, these percentages were higher in 1969 but precise estimates awaited the next census scheduled for 1970.

The slow rate of adoption stems from several causes. Large machines and implements are not always suited to the topography, climate, and size of the holdings. Moreover, since labor has been relatively plentiful and comparatively cheap, the investment returns of mechanization even where feasible have not been high enough to serve as an incentive.

Available information concerning the use of fertilizer and insecticides is incomplete. The government actively has promoted research in these areas and has in many cases subsidized the costs of the adoption of commercially prepared fertilizers and insecticides. Public reaction was initially below government expectations but has been more favorable during the 1960's.

In 1966 a new division of food technology was set up under the Ministry of Agriculture and Cooperatives. Its main function is to conduct research on food processing, and it complements research being carried out by the Divisions of Agriculture, Fisheries, and Veterinary Service. Special training courses have been set up for farmers and their wives to instruct rural producers in the methods of processing and preserving foods and to disseminate new research findings.

Considerable attention is being focused on the development of drainage and irrigation facilities under the Ministry's Division of Drainage and Irrigation. In 1967 17 drainage schemes were completed, affecting 14,200 acres of land, and there were 32 other drainage schemes under construction. During 1967 62 irrigation projects were completed providing facilities for 33,070 acres of existing paddy land, opening up about 14,800 acres of swamp land and allowing double cropping on 38,949 acres.

The largest irrigation project undertaken by the division is the M$204 million (3.06 Malaysian dollars equal US$1) Muda irrigation project, scheduled for completion by 1970–71. The major focus of this project, composed of a 120-foot high and 1,250-foot long dam on the Muda River and a 210-foot high and 900-foot long dam on the Pedu River connected by a 5-mile tunnel, will be the double cropping of rice on 261,500 acres. The project is expected to nearly triple rice production in the area from 229,000 tons to 654,000 tons of paddy rice. The increase, equivalent to 267,000 tons of milled rice, compares to total domestic production of 600,000 tons of milled rice and imports of 300,000 tons and will lead the country well on its way to its goal of self-sufficiency in rice. Another irrigation scheme is scheduled for Kelantan, and drainage schemes are being affected in Sabah and Sarawak.

AGRICULTURAL PRODUCTION

Characteristic of the farming practices in Malaysia are the striking dissimilarities in the production methods of small holdings and estates. Whereas production on estates is organized on an industrial basis, small holdings are operated at subsistence or near-subsistence levels and follow preindustrial methods of cultivation. Production is a family affair of the relatively large household, even on a small plot of land, a fact which accounts for a relatively high ratio of people per acre of cultivated land. Market gardens, also operated by families, employ intensive production practices and are the most efficient small holdings.

The lack of adequate resources and capital are factors contributing to the low productivity and inefficiency of small holdings. Legal and institutional factors, however, such as fragmentation of forms into small uneconomical units, absentee ownership, and uncertainties of tenancy and sharecropping, are usually beyond the control of individual peasants and are largely responsible for inefficiency.

Subdivision and fragmentation of agricultural land are common in states where distribution of property is influenced by the Muslim law of inheritance. Under Muslim law, the estate of the deceased person must be divided equally among the immediate family, including wives and female children. Fragmentation leads to small, uneconomical holdings, increased indebtedness, and reduced productivity of the land. Because little income is derived from these holdings, the land-owner often seeks other employment, and the land is left to become a breeding ground for pests. Landownership is very important to Malaysians whether it is profitable or not; consequently, heirs usually cling to their share for reasons of prestige.

Fatalism is also a factor in the Malay's performance as a farmer. It is expressed by the concept of *rezeki*, which is a predisposition explaining the absence or small amount of control one has over something in terms of luck, thus neglecting to improve one's position.

Farming methods in West Malaysia are more advanced than in Sarawak and Sabah in terms of double cropping, systems of irrigation and drainage, mechanized machinery and equipment, fertilizers, and disease and pest controls. In Sarawak and Sabah the acceptance of more advanced farming methods has been slow because of the widespread practice of shifting cultivation, under which land is cleared by burning a section of the forest, farmed for several years until the soil is exhausted, and then abandoned for a time to allow the soil to rejuvenate while the farmer burns and plants a new area. The problems brought up by the practice of shifting cultivation include the destruction of forest reserves and erosion of topsoil, especially in the higher areas.

Under government auspices each state has a series of individual programs aimed at modernizing general production practices. These include drainage and irrigation facilities, disease and pest control, subsidies for the use of mechanized machinery and fertilizers, and adult education programs directed to the farmer and his family.

Commercial Crops

Rubber

Natural rubber was the most important single export in Malaysia through 1967. It contributed 12 percent of total gross domestic product or about 43 percent of the total contribution of agriculture to gross domestic product. About 4.9 million acres were in rubber production in 1967, 90 percent of which was in West Malaysia. Total production equalled almost 1 million long tons. Production in West Malaysia increased 2.8 percent over 1966 but dropped in East Malaysia. Average yields on estates in West Malaysia rose from 898 pounds in 1965 to 920 pounds in 1967. Smallholder yield rose from 772 to 790 pounds per acre.

The Para rubber tree was introduced into Malaysia in 1877 from seed taken from the Amazon Valley in Brazil and raised in London. The Para tree is characterized by its hardiness, which enables it to survive fierce competition from other species; good drainage, however, is necessary. The optimum density for high-yielding trees is about 129 trees per acre, but smallholders frequently plant 200 to 400 trees per acre. It takes 5 to 7 years of growth before tapping can be commenced.

414

During the early growth period, there is much work in the eradication of weeds, drainage where necessary, and measures to reduce erosion. The productive life of the tree is 35 to 40 years and the peak of its production is 7 to 8 years after initial tapping.

Although rubber production and the acreage devoted to it is on an increase, the government is attempting to increase crop diversity and to reduce the dependence of the economy on the price of rubber. The market for rubber faced crisis years during the depression of the 1930's, during the Japanese occupation in World War II, during the Emergency, and during the civil unrest of 1969. Moreover, in the third quarter of 1967, the price of rubber fell to US$0.474 a pound, the lowest price in 19 years. The price in 1969 had already nearly doubled the 1967 low (see ch. 3, Historical Setting; ch. 13, Political Dynamics).

One of the major problems has been the competition of synthetic rubber. In order to strengthen the position of natural rubber on the world market, the government in 1965 introduced standard Malaysian rubber (SMR). The key to this classification was the attempt to eliminate malpractices, increase quality, and achieve greater grading uniformity. A newly developed heavycrumb rubber was introduced, and by 1967, 78 percent of all rubber estates and 50 percent of small holdings in West Malaysia had been replanted with high-yield trees. The eventual goal is the increase of production and quality but the reduction of the dominance of rubber in the country's economy.

There are few rubber estates in Sarawak, and none are very large. In consequence, the rubber smallholders have not enjoyed the benefits of a substantial external private investment as has been the case on the mainland, nor have they received stimuli from estates for better management practices and technology. Much of the planted acreage is in old, unselected trees, and much of the new high-yield stock has not yet come or is just coming into its productive stage. Rubber is a key to Sabah's economy, with most rubber production along the western coast and the north-central interior.

Copra and Oil Palm

Under the national diversification program, oil palm is now considered the best dryland crop and has surpassed iron ore exports to become the fourth largest export, after rubber, tin, and timber. In 1967 the export of palm oil and kernel totaled M$134 million, making the country the world's largest exporter of palm oil.

The total acreage under oil palm in 1967 was 392,000 acres, an increase of 17.2 percent over the 1966 acreage. About 85.4 percent of this was in West Malaysia, and the remaining acreage was in Sabah. Considerable research is being carried out to breed better oil palm stock, control diseases, and improve management. The government is stressing the planting of oil palm through the Federal Land Development Authority schemes and private plantings and increasing their acreage devoted to oil palm.

The area under coconut cultivation for copra in 1967 was more than 520,000 acres, the majority of which was under smallholder production. The total copra production in 1967 was over 170,000 tons with about 80,500 tons of oil. The average yield per acre was between 1,600 and 2,000 pounds of copra.

Other Crops

Pineapples are grown throughout the country, but only in the states of Johore, Selangor, and Perak are they cultivated for the canning industry. Johore accounts for around 90 percent of the total production of the three states. Cultivation of the fruit is divided among estates and smallholdings. The Japanese occupation in the 1940's temporarily eliminated the pineapple-canning industry in Malaya, and most of the land devoted to pineapple reverted to jungle. After World War II the industry was rehabilitated (see ch. 19, Industry).

Pepper is grown by Chinese on smallholdings that average only three-fourths of an acre but are under the most intensive methods of cultivation. On the Peninsula, where areca nut and ginger are preferred for domestic consumption, pepper is of little importance. None of these spices is produced in commercial quantities. In northern Borneo, especially in Sarawak, pepper is an important export crop. Despite a fair decline in prices, the value of exports of white and black pepper from Sarawak has increased.

Pepper can be brought into bearing in 30 months, so that worldwide overproduction can occur rapidly, causing wide price fluctuations. Lack of capital discourages the aborigines from cultivating the crop, and the crop's propensity to price fluctuations hinders an even production by Chinese smallholders.

Manile hemp (abaca) is most widely grown in the area of Tawau in Sabah. The crop is highly susceptible to virus diseases, which in 1961 threatened to injure the production severely, but the disease was checked and continued production was assured.

Sago, a starch contained in the trunk of a large palm tree widely grown throughout the state, is the third of Sarawak's agricultural export crops, after rubber and rice. Export of sago has been rising steadily, but according to the Sarawak government, the condition "illustrates the lack of other economic activities open to the communities concerned." The product is of low quality.

Coffee production has had little allure with the instability of coffee prices in the world market in recent years. Cocoa, however, has been a profitable export crop. The quality grown in Sabah is good and is accepted at home and on foreign markets. Both lowland and highland tea are produced. The lowland variety produces higher yields than the highland tea, but it is less popular on the market because of its inferior quality. Tobacco is mostly planted for the local market and, with the establishment of a cigarette factory at Sibu, Sarawak, in 1960, a new incentive has been introduced to raise the quality and increase the quantity of the crop produced.

Food Crops

Rice

Rice is the staple food of the country and the second largest crop after rubber. In 1967 it occupied 1.27 million acres. Domestic production was about 1 million tons, or about 70 percent of domestic needs. The country hopes for self-sufficiency in rice production and, if targets are met for increasing paddy land through drainage, irrigation, and land development, the goal is scheduled to be achieved by 1970.

Efforts to increase domestic production have brought new hybrid varieties of paddy rice, greater fertilizer use, better management practices, and extensive drainage and irrigation programs. In 1967, 13 percent of the paddy fields of West Malaysia were being double cropped, and the double cropping figure for the country as a whole was 22 times higher than the 1957 area. The average yield in 1967 was 2,539 pounds per acre compared to 2,431 pounds during the 1966 season.

The Malaysian "Rice Bowl" is located in northwestern Malaya (Perlis, Kedah, Penang, and Perak) and accounts for over 55 percent of the total production. The northeast (Kelantan and Trengganu) accounts for over 25 percent, and another important area is in Selangor. Almost all the rice in the Peninsula is wet rice. Most of the rice planted in Sarawak is dry rice and is grown on the slopes of the interior mountains; there is little well-developed wet-rice-planting tradition in Sarawak. Farmers harvest only one crop per year although it is known that in the past two crops have been planted. In Sabah the main wet-rice-producing regions are along the western coast and inland. Dry rice is grown by aborigines in the hills and mountain areas, mostly using shifting cultivation.

Others

In addition to rice, a wide variety of crops are grown for local consumption. Of these, maize is the only important grain and is grown by smallholders. Sweet potatoes and cassava are among the most important of the root crops. Vegetables are grown in Malay and in Chinese market gardens. In elevated areas like the Cameron Highlands and in Sabah, vegetables associated with more temperate climates are grown and fruits such as strawberries. Tropical fruits such as rambutans and mangosteens are common in small holdings, and oranges are the main citrus fruit. Most of the 230,000 acres of fruit officially listed is canned for export. The fruit of the durian tree is one of the major fruits for domestic consumption.

Animal Husbandry

The country's tropical environment in general is not well suited to animal husbandry. Livestock raising offers a lower investment return than rubber and palm oil planting and in most cases supplements crop farming. The most commonly raised animals are buffalo, cattle, pigs, goats, sheep, and poultry. During the 1960's research and extension service efforts concentrated on increasing egg, poultry, and pork production, in which by 1969 the country had reached near self-sufficiency. By 1967 the value of the livestock industry had reached about M$350 million.

Except among the Indian population, the production of meat and milk has traditionally been secondary to the use of buffalo and cattle as draft animals. The buffalo and cattle stock of West Malaysia numbered 569,000 head in 1966 and represented about 85 percent of the country's buffalo and cattle herd. Small herds are found along the drier coastal stretches of Sarawak, and the Dayaks keep small numbers on a communal basis in the more fertile inland river basins. In Sabah cattle are raised mainly in the highlands and are generally not used for draft purposes.

The greatest advances have been made in poultry farming, which is frequently integrated with rubber planting. Between 1960 and 1964 improved breeding stock and management operations brought a 6-percent annual growth in the poultry flock. By 1969, 96 percent of the country's egg needs were locally produced and domestic poultry meat, estimated at 150 million pounds, supplied 98 percent of domestic needs.

Hog raising is an integral part of the Chinese garden market economy, except in Sarawak where mixed farming as such is little known. Cross breeding and artificial insemination have been used to upgrade the quality of local stock. The hog stock in West Malaysia numbered 599,000 head in 1966, and by 1969 national consumption of pork reached 210 million pounds.

Although representing but a small industry, duck raising is also common in market gardens, especially in coastal areas. Climatic conditions impede sheep and goat raising on a large scale, but small flocks are raised for meat for special occasions. The sheep and goat herds of West Malaysia in 1966 numbered 38,000 and 333,000 respectively.

Fishing

Over 1,000 species of fish are found in Malaysian waters. Over 250 species are used for food, but only 20 are marketed fresh, dried, or salted on a large scale. Annual per capita consumption in 1966 was about 75 pounds. Compared to meat, fish is relatively abundant. It is the second staple food of all Malaysians and provides 70 to 80 percent of the total animal protein produced and consumed.

About 302,000 tons of fish valued at M$259 million were landed in West Malaysia in 1967. This represented an increase of about 28 percent over 1966, the increase resulting largely from the adoption of trawling techniques. Estimates for Sabah and Sarawak listed 31,000 tons landed in 1966. Fishing engaged 62,000 people and contributed 2 percent of gross domestic product in 1967.

Fishing methods vary. Fixed traps along with different types of lines and nets are used inshore; for offshore fishing, troll lines and drift nets are used. Coastal fishing extending out to about 50 miles is relatively well developed. Plans were in operation to expand deep sea fishing through additional education facilities, but in 1968 the only deep sea fishing was being carried out by eight tuna vessels operated under a joint Japanese-Malaysian venture valued at M$1 million.

In 1969 Malaysian fisheries were undergoing a transition in which primitive methods were being up-dated. During the 1960's the total number of boats engaged in fishing decreased with the increased use of motor-powered boats. Between 1964 and 1967 the number of motor-powered boats increased annually by 5 percent and by 1967 had reached 65 percent of the total 20,000 vessel fishing fleet; slightly more than 75 percent of the motor boats are inboard.

Forestry

The country's tropical evergreen forest, banded by littoral forest land, provides oils, resins, gums, latex, medicine, fruit, barks, flowers, timber, charcoal, and firewood. Before the introduction of foreign capital, the indigenous population sustained itself without a serious disruption of the ecological balance. The initial imbalance brought by commercial harvesting of forest land culminated in government management of the country's timber resources.

In 1968 the country's nearly 89,000 square miles of forest land represented approximately 70 percent of the total land area. Reserves of 38,600 acres were being held by the government. Reserve land policy aimed at the conservation of existing forests on a long-range sustained-yield basis and water shed control. Reserve utilization and timber policy in the mid-1960's had become a political issue.

Annual yields vary widely throughout the country from 10 to 25 cubic tons per acre. The highest yields are in Sabah. Total production in 1967 equaled 8.9 million cubic tons, 44 percent of which was produced in Sabah. Growth in timber production and export during the 1960's surpassed all projections for the decade. Between 1961 and 1971 export earnings from log and sawn timber grew at average annual rates of 23 and 13 percent, respectively. Timber and forest product exports in 1967 were valued at M$602.5, which represented 16 percent of the country's total export earnings and stood third in importance after tin and rubber.

FINANCE AND MARKETING

Marketing for agricultural produce varies widely not only in scale but also in technical complexity. The mechanisms relied upon by smallholders contrast with those of estate production, and the limited marketing facilities available in rural areas represent a substantial obstacle to national development and integration of the national economy.

The collection and processing of agricultural produce is largely in private hands. Government operations only marginally augment the private sector and are largely attempts by government institutions such as the Rubber Research Institute or the Federal Land Development Authority to aid regional smallholder production.

Although smallholder production near population centers is frequently sold directly to consumers at local markets, the bulk of domestic production, particularly in West Malaysia, is handled through a series of middlemen and wholesale houses. Producers may be able to choose between mill agents, independent dealers, or cooperative societies for handling their crops.

West Malaysia, especially along the western coast, is far more developed than Sabah and Sarawak and possesses more advanced marketing and transportation facilities. The country's transportation system is one of the more advanced in Southeast Asia with varying levels of motor, rail, sea, and air facilities. Sea shipping offers both specialized vessels and regular schedules. Heavy reliance on traditional modes of transportation still exists, however, and certain areas are cut off from the national market and must rely on locally produced or preserved foods.

Institutional sources of credit traditionally have been insignificant, and capital flows from inheritances or personal savings have been marginal investment sources. The rural farmer has relied primarily on moneylenders and traders for loans at interest rates of 24 to 48 percent. Even with the advent of the cooperative movement in the 1920's, institutional credit remained scarce and represented a significant limit on agricultural and marketing development.

In order to encourage farmer participation in its extension program and its marketing and credit services, the government during the 1960's relied on both farmers' associations and cooperatives. The Farmers' Association Movement began in 1958 and by 1967 had reached 856 associations with nearly 45,000 registered members.

In the late 1960's attempts were made to streamline and increase the effectiveness of cooperatives through reorganization and consolidation. By the beginning of 1968, 1,603 rural credit cooperatives were registered, with a total membership of 583,000 and a working capital of about M$13.3 million. About one-fourth of the cooperatives were rice-milling societies with 50,000 members and a working capital of M$5.1 million. Certain urban-centered construction cooperatives have extended credit to farmers for housing construction.

The cooperatives were organized into rural bank authorities that as a whole formed the Apex Bank. Between 1958 and 1968 over M$28 million worth of loans were extended by the societies through the bank. Loans were at highly favorable interest rates and provided for the expansion of production and marketing facilities. Transportation, cold storage, poultry, and fishing facilities were major loan targets.

In September 1965 the Federal Agricultural Marketing Authority was established to supervise, coordinate, and improve agricultural production and marketing. It instigated a paddy and rice marketing survey in 1966 that analyzed all sectors connected with rice marketing, including farmers, market intermediaries, cooperatives, millers, wholesalers, retailers, and consumers. The culmination of the survey has been the establishment of a market scheme operated by the marketing authority that assures farmers of better market outlets, immediate cash payments, fairweight measure, and adequate supplies of sacking materials. Additional studies of coffee, copra, and vegetable marketing have been scheduled, and attempts at strict enforcement of licensing has helped fair marketing practices and the reduction of black market operations.

RURAL DEVELOPMENT

Development plans focusing on the forging of an integrated state system have had to handle problems at two different levels. On the one level are the more immediate, volatile problems stemming from ethnic diversity and mutual hostility. Particularly explosive throughout the 1960's was the rising tide of anti-Chinese sentiment that culminated in the 1969 riots and destruction of property (see ch. 3, Historical Setting; ch. 13, Political Dynamics).

Chinese investors have come to dominate various sectors in the agricultural economy, such as the processing and handling of crops, moneylending (shared to a degree with an element of Indian origins), and market garden production. Despite guarantees that are written into the legal systems whose sole purpose is the protection and preservation of the rights of citizens with indigenous Malay origins, there is considerable fear among Malays of a takeover by Chinese elements. This fear is underlined by the high percentage (35 to 40 percent) of Chinese in the population and reaches to the grass-roots level. Fear is seldom easily dispelled and creates problems whose destructive potential demands resolution but whose nature complicates solution.

On the second level are the continuing problems of bringing a multiplicity of isolated and diverse communities into interaction patterns that foster national awareness and interdependence. The government has built into its 5-year development plan (1966–70) rural development and community planning through a multiplicity of agencies whose coordination is the main responsibility of the Ministry of National and Rural Development. In addition to its coordination of development programs, the ministry is also directly in charge of the preparation of adult education and community development programs. Since 1966 the ministry has maintained a Research Division specializing in general development problems and in specific methods to increase program effectiveness. Throughout all its programs, the ministry attempts to utilize and support existing development machinery and the involvement of state and district personnel.

In addition to aiding the implementation of land programs under statutory bodies such as the Federal Land Development Authority, the ministry directly supervised the resettlement of certain areas of Sabah and Sarawak following the 1963 Confrontation with Indonesia (see ch. 3, Historical Setting). Usually, however, the ministry directly handles only the more important aspects of development schemes and turns over the completion of the program to the local authorities and programs concerned.

At the district level coordination is largely under the Community Development Program. The program uses village development committees to coordinate action groups at the village level and frequently yields access for government extension service innovations. In 1967 there were 2,212 village development committees. The goal is local planning and participation and the establishment of projects that the villagers can complete with the minimum of government assistance. Proposals are drawn up in village Red Books, and discussion is encouraged.

All programs from sanitation and environmental health projects to self-sufficiency in vegetable campaigns stress the importance of community-wide approaches and solutions. In addition, the Community Development Program offers special courses to help villagers participate more actively in community development and administration.

A national adult education program has been the advance guard of the Community Development Program since 1961. National language classes, aimed at the eradication of illiteracy, were working with 181,000 villagers in 1967. A constant effort is made to teach Malay and also to make those enrolled more development conscious. Vocational training and home economics programs advanced "functional literacy."

Since about 1963 the Muslim Pilgrims Saving Corporation has been in operation to invest the savings of those Muslims intending a pilgrimage in industrial and commercial ventures. The Muslim has the advantage of making profits as he accumulates his savings until he makes his pilgrimage; the capital in the meantime is aiding national development. Credit facilities and training programs including mechanics, construction, services, and management are available through the Council of Trust for the Indigenous People (Majlis Amanah Ra'ayat—MARA) established in 1966.

THE ROLE OF GOVERNMENT

The role of government in agriculture has been extensive. Well aware of the essential role of this activity in the country's overall development, the government allotted M$1,087 million for agriculture and rural development in the 1966–70 plan representing about 29 percent of public development expenditures provided for in the plan (see ch. 17, Character and Structure of the Economy).

The general guideline followed by the government had been to encourage community participation and local institutions rather than to enter the agricultural sector itself. It has promoted private investment with grants and has advanced the concept of self-sufficiency.

Shortly after independence the government established an extension service with field centers and research stations. Under this program the fisheries division of the Ministry of Agriculture and Cooperatives had supplied free fish to farmers to encourage farm ponds. Advance work is being carried on at the Veterinary Research

Institute in Ipoh on animal disease control and breeding stock improvement. An artificial insemination center has been established at Paroi to aid the expansion of artificial insemination services in the country. Significant progress has been achieved also in poultry and forestry research.

The Rubber Research Institute of Malaysia at Kuala Lumpur dates back to 1926. It has special soils, botanical, pathological, chemical, and statistical divisions. It also has a smallholders advisory service and an estates advisory service and provides publication and information services. The institute also operates regional schools and training programs.

The government has been actively engaged in irrigation and drainage projects, land settlement, community development, crop diversification, and the advancement of self-sufficiency in the production of certain food crops. It is the government that has fostered the cooperative movement and agricultural societies. Government efforts have attempted to expand marketing facilities and credit opportunities, always within the context of being the primer rather than the solitary source.

CHAPTER 19

INDUSTRY

Since Malaya's independence in 1957, a major national goal has been the remolding of the industrial base from one that met the needs of an export economy to a framework appropriate to a modern industrializing nation. In general, the policy followed was that of government cooperation with private enterprise, with a minimum of participation in operation.

In the late 1960's the salient influence in the development of industry lay in the increasingly dynamic and direct role taken by the central government in providing incentives for the expansion of industry at an accelerated pace and in determining the character, location, ownership, and employment makeup of manufacturing industries. The objectives were the redistribution of ownership and employment to reflect the multiracial character of the population and the dispersal of plants from urban to rural areas and from the more industrialized west coast to the less developed east coast of West Malaysia and to Sarawak and Sabah.

In 1967 industry, including mining, manufacturing, construction, and public utilities, contributed M$2.01 billion to the gross domestic product (GDP), which was M$8.6 billion (3.06 Malaysian dollars equal US$1). The share contributed by industry was 23.3 percent. Manufacturing, which was the most valuable sector, contributed 11.1 percent to the total gross domestic product; mining, 5.4 percent; construction, 4.7 percent; and public utilities, 2.1 percent. During the 5 years from 1963 to 1967, the value of industry's contribution rose 39 percent in contrast to an increase of 28 percent in the value of the gross domestic product. The value of all industrial sectors increased in absolute terms, but mining decreased in relative share.

Manufacturing industries mostly consisted of plants processing agricultural products and light industries producing consumer goods. The production of basic metals, however, was in a beginning stage in 1969. Production of cement and fertilizer was increasing but still not adequate to fill domestic needs. The production of transportation equipment was an assembling process.

As a base for industrialization, iron ore, bauxite, and tin were under exploitation, and deposits of copper had been discovered. Good coking coal was lacking, and sufficient petroleum had not been discovered up to 1969. The labor force was adequate in size but in need of training in skills.

POLICY AND ROLE OF GOVERNMENT

Industrialization of the economy, with emphasis on the expansion of manufacturing, was a major goal of government after independence. In encouraging industrial development, the government's policy was to leave operation of industry to private enterprise while the government served as a coordinator and furnished necessary assistance to the private sector.

To this end, the government maintained a stable currency and provided basic support services, which increased from time to time from 1957 to 1969. Consistently, government assumed the responsibility for providing the infrastructural facilities of power, water, transport, communication, and education, and for establishing guidelines for the organization and regulation of industrial enterprises.

As further encouragement to industrial development, an active program was initiated to develop sites known as industrial estates that were provided with roads, water, and power. In general, the construction of plants was left to industrialists, but for small industries unable to supply the necessary capital, Malayan Industrial Estates, Ltd., built plants for sale on easy credit terms. In 1967 the government set up the National Institute of Scientific and Industrial Research and the Standards Institution of Malaysia to establish product standards and to carry on research concerning materials, production methods, and markets. The National Productivity Center was established in 1961 with help from the United Nations Special Fund to train supervisory and managerial personnel. In 1969 another service, designed to promote joint ventures between Malaysian and foreign firms, was initiated. This service, known as the Register of Potential Investors, maintained a list of foreign and domestic firms and individuals desiring either capital or entrepreneurship to establish a new industry.

To provide incentives to invest in manufacturing, the Pioneer Industries Ordinance for Malaya was passed in 1958. This ordinance provided incentives through exemption from income tax and from import duties on equipment for a period of from 2 to 5 years for firms considered beneficial to the economy. Approval of applications for pioneer status was under the direction of the Ministry of Commerce and Industry, which had considerable latitude in determining the qualifications of firms for approval. At the end of 1966 there were 143 firms in operation holding pioneer certificates; of this total, 120 were located in West Malaysia, 12 in Sarawak, and 11 in Sabah.

In March 1968 the Investment Incentives Act, which replaced the Pioneer Industries Ordinance with a more comprehensive piece of legislation, went into effect. Incentives were offered in the form of pioneer status to firms that desired such designation and qualified for acceptance. Requirements, which were more carefully defined than formerly, included employment of a specified percentage of Malays and the availability of ownership to Malays. The government indicated that new pioneer industries should have at least 51-percent Malaysian ownership, thus limiting foreign ownership to a minority. Special investment tax credits were also made available to firms that did not qualify or did not want to become pioneer industries, and allowances were also made for expenses incurred in export promotion.

Tariff protection was used in some instances to encourage industrial development, but policies in this area were not well defined. In general, tariff protection was used sparingly and at the request of domestic manufacturers rather than being initiated by government. In 1968 automobiles, round steel bars, and plastic articles for household use were covered.

As additional assistance to industrial development, the government set up or participated in special financing service. The Malaysian Industrial Development Finance Limited was organized in 1960 to provide medium- and long-term loans for industry. The government and the national central bank, Bank Negara Malaysia, contributed only 20 percent of the capital of this institution. Private Malaysian sources provided 11 percent, and the remaining 69 percent came from foreign sources, a fact that limited equity participation by the institution in pioneer firms. Loans to manufacturing industries were increasing in late 1968, and their distribution was well diversified.

One of the most important steps taken by government was the organization of the Council of Trust for the Indigenous People (Majlis Amanah Ra'ayat—MARA) in 1965. The function of this organization was the encouragement of Malay participation in industry and business through the extension of financial and technical aid to firms that were predominantly Malay rather than Chinese or foreign and the initiation of educational and technical training programs for interested Malays. The council was able to provide both equity and loan financing.

To coordinate industrial development and the work of various agencies involved, the Federal Industrial Development Authority was established in 1965. It did not become active, however, until 1967 because of a long search for a suitable director. A major function of the authority was that of policy adviser to the government, and it also prepared industrial feasibility studies. Lack of definition of the role of various agencies involved in industrial development, however, hampered its effectiveness.

In mid-1969, after the establishment of the National Operations Council as an emergency measure, the central government took increasingly positive steps in the acceleration and direction of industrialization through the establishment of a new agency, the Capital Investment Committee. The main purpose of this committee was to speed up the granting of pioneer industry certificates by the elimination of time-consuming steps. Previously an applicant had had to deal with seven ministries involving 22 different sets of administrative procedures. Government members of the committee embarked upon an active program of identifying desirable industries and locations.

MINING

In 1967 mining and quarrying activities contributed M$471 million, or 5.4 percent of the value of the gross domestic product. West Malaysia provided M$464 million, or 98.5 percent of the total mining and quarrying contribution. In absolute terms, mining and quarrying declined in both 1966 and 1967 from M$606 million in 1965, which was the high point of the period from 1961 to 1967. The relative share in 1965 was 7.7 percent.

According to forecasts contained in the First Malaysia Plan for 1966 to 1970, the contribution of mining output to the gross domestic product was expected to decline by about 4.6 percent annually for the period of the plan because of the decline in known commercial mineral reserves. Prospecting, however, which was being carried out in 1966 by the Mineral Investigation Drilling Unit of the federal Department of Mines, indicated additional sources of metals already under exploitation and the existence of some that had not been exploited significantly. One goal of the First Malaysia Plan was the encouragement of Malay participation in mining. To implement this goal, the Department of Mines planned to provide financial and technical assistance to Malay miners.

Major minerals under exploitation in 1967 were bauxite, copper, gold, iron, manganese, tin, china clay, lime, marble, and a number of rare metals and earths (see table 17). Malaysia possessed supplies of most of the minerals needed for industrialization with the exception of good coking coal. Deposits of coal of lesser quality were known but were not under exploitation. Almost all mineral production was exported, and export taxes were an important source of government revenue. The future increase in industrialization would require the retention of a larger share of mining production for domestic use, with an attendant decrease in the quantity exported unless explorations should uncover new reserves that could be economically exploited.

Table 17. Production of Mineral Commodities in Malaysia, 1963–67

Commodity	Unit	1963	1964	1965	1966	1967
Metals:						
Antimony	metric tons	6	78	55	59	31
Bauxite	thousand tons	609	632	994	956	900
Copper						
(flotation concentrate)	metric tons	2,000	1,085	1,750	762	1,016
Gold	troy ounces	11,889	10,411	6,584	5,570	3,810
Iron ore[1]	thousand tons	7,381	6,569	6,983	5,855	5,436
Manganese ore[2]	metric tons	6,982	n.a.	1,591	58,788	85,105
Tin[3]	long tons	59,947	60,004	63,670	68,886	72,121
Smelter[4]	---do---	84,001	71,351	72,469	71,049	76,328
Titanium concentrate	metric tons	149,374	131,337	123,517	118,264	90,806
Tungsten ore and concentrate	---do---	7	5	10	6	24
Zirconium concentrate	---do---	262	147	571	786	472
Nonmetals:						
Cement	thousand tons	362	466	739	850	835
China clay	---do---	1	1	2	2	2
Lime	metric tons	166	226	190	132	160
Mineral Fuels:						
Petroleum (crude)	thousand 42-gallon barrels	373	352	351	346	328
Refined products	---do---	45,524	53,799	53,983	58,103	67,900

n.a.—not available.
[1] 60 to 64 percent iron.
[2] 30 to 40 percent manganese.
[3] 75 to 76 percent concentrate.
[4] Includes metal smelted from imported concentrates.

Source: Adapted from U.S. Department of the Interior, Bureau of Mines, *Minerals Yearbook, 1967*, IV : Area Reports, International, 1969, table 1.

Mining activities, which had been carried on for centuries, were in the hands of private enterprise. According to the constitution, state authorities have the right to permit prospecting for and exploitation of minerals lying within their boundaries, but the National Land Council has the right to formulate a general policy that applies to all state governments. Revenues from mining leases and permits and royalties from ores belong to the state where the activity is located, with the exception of that from tin, which accrues to the central government. Annually not less than 10 percent of the export duty on tin is returned to the state from which the output came.

Tin

Malaysia is the world's foremost producer of tin. In 1967 the country produced 72,121 long tons, or 43.1 percent of the total non-Communist world production of 167,200 tons. Production in 1967, which reached a peak for the postwar period, had been exceeded in only 4 other years: 1929, 1937, 1940, and 1941. For 1968, although final figures were not available in mid-1969, it was estimated at 72,500 tons. All output was exported, and in 1967 tin accounted for M$756 million, or 20.3 percent of total export value. Despite peak production in that year, the export value of tin had declined from M$872 million in 1965 because of a drop in price from M$11,797 to M$10,156 per ton. Preliminary information indicated a price upturn in 1968.

Tin had been mined in Malaya since very early times. Reference to tin mining had been made by Arab traders who visited there about A.D. 900, but it did not begin on a significant scale much before the second part of the 19th century.

Tin is a relatively rare metal found in only a few places, mostly in underdeveloped tropical countries. It has many industrial uses, is usually used in combination with other materials, and does not have readily available substitutes for most uses. Burgeoning industrialization in the 19th century, particularly the growing manufacture of canned foods using tin-plated steel containers, contributed to an accelerated growth in world demand, which was accompanied by an increase in supply.

Production of tin increased with great rapidity from 1870 to 1900. Malaya, because of propitious domestic circumstances that included the opening up of new fields, an increase in the labor force, technological changes in mining, improved transportation facilities, and an increasingly orderly environment, accounted for a large share of expanded supply. Output in 1890 was 42,000 tons, six times that of 1870 and slightly more than half of world production, whereas in 1870 it had accounted for less than one-fifth. From 1880 to the end of the 1960's, the country maintained its position as the premier producer of tin internationally.

All tin production in 1969 was in West Malaysia. From early times Perak had been the major producing state. In 1967 Perak, which contains the Larut and Kinta fields, active since the mid-1800's, accounted for more than 50 percent of total output. Selangor accounted for 30 percent, and the states of Perlis, Kedah, Negri Sembilan, Johore, Pahang, and Trengganu each accounted for a share of the remainder.

Initially tin mining was undertaken by Malays, and smelting was done by the Chinese. With the discovery of new resources in Perak and later in Selangor, however, Chinese immigrants flocked to the area for employment, and soon tin production, which was carried on by relatively uncomplicated methods, was dominated by Chinese capital, entrepreneurship, and labor. Conditions of extreme civil disorder that arose in connection with tin mining resulted in intervention by the British in 1874, and appointment of a British resident in each of the three major producing states, Perak, Selangor, and Sungei Ujong, which later became part of Negri Sembilan.

With the establishment of order, land surveys were undertaken, mine boundaries were fixed, regulations were established, and output was increased. Revenue from tin exports was used for the building of roads and railroads and the establishment of services, such as hospitals, schools, and postal and telegraph services. Improvement of the economic and social infrastructure, in turn, contributed to the discovery of new tin fields and an increase in output.

After the 1880's Western capital gradually became interested in Malayan tin mining, and technology became more complicated. Gravel pump mining, which was entirely mechanized, was introduced by the British and soon adapted by the Chinese, replacing their former wooden chain pumps, and the bucket dredge method from Australia was introduced in 1912. Increasing refinements in methods increased productivity, but they also brought higher capital investment requirements, with the result that budget dredge mining was developed by the wealthier European firms and those that included representatives of the United States, Canada, Australia, and New Zealand. With their more restricted financial resources, Chinese enterprises continued to employ the less capital-intensive gravel pump mining only, a cleavage which continued to exist through the 1960's.

In 1967 there were 1,072 tin mines in operation. Of the total, 66 were dredge mines producing almost 24,000 tons of tin content, and 960 were gravel pump mines that produced about 40,000 tons.

Gravel pump and dredge mines together accounted for 88.6 percent of total production. The remainder was produced by various processes, such as open pit, underground, and hydraulic mining. Small amounts were also recovered by washing gravel by hand, known as dulang washing.

Smelting of domestic production is carried on by the Eastern Smelting Company at its plant at Penang and the Straits Trading Company at its plant at Butterworth, on the mainland across from Penang. These are two of the seven major tin smelters in the world. There is also a third smaller smelter operated by the Oriental Tin Smelters that is controlled by a Japanese firm. To ensure operation at full capacity, tin ore was imported, processed, and reexported.

In the early part of the 20th century, the mining and smelting industry evidenced a trend toward financial integration that accelerated about 1930, resulting in control of the industry by a few firms, a number of which were based in Great Britain but international in scope of operations. The most important groups in Malaysia in the mid-1960's were Anglo-Oriental (Malaya), Ltd., Neill and Bell, and Osborne and Chappel, which as early as 1954, owned or controlled about 70 percent of dredge mining.

Malaysia is a member of the International Tin Council that, through the International Tin Agreements, since 1956 has acted to prevent wide price fluctuations. A buffer stock, to which each member is required to contribute a specific amount, is maintained, and the International Tin Council establishes prices at which tin from the stock must be bought or sold. In 1968 the council decided also to institute export controls that were continued in 1969. For the first quarter of the year, Malaysia's share of exports was fixed at 47 percent of the world total.

The future of the tin industry depends upon world demand, which is related to the growth of population, international industrial production, and competition from substitutes, which in the 1960's were becoming increasingly available as a result of product research. The long-run future is dependent upon potential supply of the metal, which is declining.

Because existing mines had been in operation for many years, encouragement of prospecting for new tin fields was an important objective of the government that initiated a dynamic mining policy in 1967. At that time offshore areas on the west coast of Malaya were opened to prospecting bids by the federal administration and the states adjacent. In 1968 licenses had been issued to three foreign-owned companies, representing British, United States, and Dutch capital. One license was issued to a company that was a joint venture of the government of Malaysia; the governments of the states of Penang, Perak, and Selangor; Riotinto Finance and Exploration, Ltd., of London; and the Bethlehem Mines Corporation, a subsidiary of United States Bethlehem Steel. The government of the State of Perak also opened a reserve of 90,000 acres for tin mining. Sixty thousand acres were set aside for prospecting by Malaysians only.

Iron

In 1967 there were about 30 iron mines in operation. The states of Pahang and Trengganu, where the only two large iron mines were located, accounted for 85 percent of output, and smaller amounts were produced in the states of Johore, Perak, Kedah, and Selangor. The two major mines were Bukit Besi, at Dungan in Trengganu, and Bukit Ibam, at Rompin in Pahang, both owned by the Eastern Mining and Metals Company. Ore from the Bukit Besi mine had been considered of good quality, but in the late 1960's quality and reserves had been declining. Reserves of the Bukit Ibam were more abundant, but the quality of iron was not the best. In December 1966 a new mine was opened at Lipis in Pahang by the Kokan Mining Company of Japan and local business men. It was expected to produce about 150,000 tons or ore annually, but no report had been made in mid-1969.

Iron ore mining had been developed by Japanese capital and entrepreneurship by World War I to ensure for Japan a source of industrial raw material that was lacking in that country. After World War II the mines were taken over from Japan and sold but, with the rehabilitation of the mines and the resurgence and growth of Japanese heavy industry, Japan was again the destination of almost all iron ore exported, which in 1967 was 98 percent of production.

Production of ore, which for the decade from 1958 to 1967 reached a peak of 7.3 million tons in 1963, fluctuated largely in response to export demand. The opening of a new steel mill at Prai in Province Wellesley in August 1967 as a joint Malaysian-Japanese venture increased the domestic consumption of iron. Unless production rose correspondingly, ultimately this would decrease the amount exported.

Bauxite

Bauxite mined in 1967 came from Telak Ramuna in Johore, West Malaysia. The amount produced was 900,000 tons, a decline from 956,000 tons in 1966. Almost all of the output was exported to Japan.

Known reserves of the Telok Tamunia mine in 1967 were about 20 million tons. Bauxite reserves of the only other known mine at Sematan in Sarawak, East Malaysia, had been exhausted in 1965, and there were no plans for exploration for new fields of this metal in 1969.

Copper

Before 1967 there were no copper mines in production, but small amounts of the metal had been recovered in connection with underground tin mining. As a result of a United Nations survey made in 1965, however, a deposit of copper was discovered in the Mamut Valley on Mount Kinabalu in Sabah. The deposit was estimated to contain 50 to 100 million tons of ore of commercially exploitable quality and was considered one of the most important discoveries in Southeast Asia. At the end of 1967 exploration rights were awarded to the Overseas Mineral Development Company of Japan. The enterprise was a joint venture with 50 percent local participation.

Other Minerals

A number of other metallic and nonmetallic minerals are produced in measurable quantities. Gold was mined in the Bau district in Sarawak in East Malaysia and was recovered as a byproduct of alluvial tin mining in West Malaysia. In 1967 Sarawak produced 2,521 troy ounces of fine gold, and West Malaysia produced 1,289 troy ounces of crude gold. Annual gold production in West Malaysia before World War II was about 40,000 troy ounces, most of which came from underground mines. From 1958 to 1967 it declined from 16,739 troy ounces to 1,289 troy ounces.

Production of manganese, which was a byproduct of iron ore mining, increased sharply from 6,982 metric tons in 1963 to 85,105 metric tons in 1967. Almost the entire output was exported to Japan for use in the rapidly expanding iron and steel industry.

Several metals, such as titanium concentrate, tungsten ore, and zirconium, useful in modern technological processes, were produced and exported. Xenotime, containing the rare-earth yttrium group elements, was produced in connection with tin mining and exported to Japan. Because of its high unit price, it added importantly to the income of tin miners fortunate enough to possess it. Other nonmetals

434

produced were china clay, lime, and marble. Sarawak, in 1967, also granted licenses for prospecting for silica sand.

Mineral fuels were not extensively exploited. Coal fields were known to exist on Labuan Island, off the coast of Sabah, but a survey by the United Nations Special Fund indicated that the coal had poor coking qualities and a high sulfur content. Coal for domestic use was imported from Australia and mainland China. The Nippon Coal Mining Company of Japan held a license to prospect for deposits at Silantek in Sarawak, and the firm was contemplating a feasible method of exploitation.

As of 1967 the only crude oil production came from the Miri field in Sarawak, operated by subsidiary companies of the Royal Dutch Shell group. Crude petroleum was imported from Saudi Arabia and Kuwait. In 1967 the government granted to two United States owned oil companies rights for exploring along the coast of West Malaysia. Several other United States firms had applied for exploration rights, and firms from the United States, Japan, and France were making surveys off the coast of Sabah. There were three refineries in operation in Malaysia, but capacity was inadequate to serve domestic needs, and refinery products were imported from a number of sources.

ELECTRIC POWER

In 1967 the total capacity of electric power in West Malaysia, including all sources, was 694,000 kilowatts, well over twice the installed capacity in 1961, which was 301,400 kilowatts. Total power consumed was 2.3 billion kilowatt-hours, slightly less than the 2.5 billion kilowatt-hours generated because of the loss of power in transmission. The increase in consumption from 1961 to 1967 was 91 percent. Information concerning installed capacity and power consumed in East Malaysia in 1967 was not available in mid-1969. Installed capacity in Sabah in 1967, however, was 187,000 kilowatts, and consumption was 35.3 million kilowatt-hours. Similar statistics for Sarawak had not been published.

A fairly adequate power system was instituted on the Malay Peninsula by the beginning of the 20th century, following in the wake of the European miners who arrived in the 1890's to exploit the tin deposits by more sophisticated methods than those locally in use. With spreading mechanization tin mining became the major user of electric power, a position it still held in 1967.

In 1967 in West Malaysia, which was more advanced in power facilities and consumption than East Malaysia, industrial and commercial enterprises accounted for 37 percent of power consumed, mining, 44 percent, and lighting and domestic use, 19 percent. Tin mining alone absorbed 42 percent of the total; the share, however, had declined from 52 percent in 1961 because of increased use by manufacturing and commercial firms.

Power is supplied by government-owned firms and private enterprises that sell to the public and by firms that supply only their own needs. In West Malaysia in 1967 the major producers of electric power were the National Electricity Board, a public enterprise, and the Perak River Hydroelectric Power Company, a private firm whose capital was owned in part by the federal government. A municipal plant owned and operated by the Penang City Council also supplied a small amount of power, and the total included the output of a few small licensed public suppliers. At the end of 1967 the National Electricity Board accounted for 71 percent of installed capacity, and the Perak River Hydroelectric Power Company accounted for 21 percent.

Generation of power is by thermal, hydroelectric, and diesel installations. Of the total power supplied in 1967, thermal stations accounted for 65 percent and hydroelectric plants for 28 percent. The remainder was provided by diesel generating stations that served towns and districts where the demand for power was small.

In 1965 the major thermal installations were the plants at Connaught Bridge and Malacca, those at Malim Nawar and the Batu Gajah near George Town in Penang, and a plant at Johore Bahru. Principal hydroelectric installations in operation were those at Cameron Highlands, Ulu Langat, Chenderoh, and Rahman.

Development of the electric power system to serve the growing needs of all segments of society was an important objective of botn a long-range plan extending to 1980, and the First Malaysia Plan. The program for the 5 years from 1966 to 1970 included an increase in total installed capacity, improvement of the existing transmission and distribution system, and a program of rural electrification. According to plan, installed hydroelectric capacity was to be increased by 136 percent; thermal capacity, by 84 percent; and diesel capacity, by 19 percent. A second important feature of the plan was creation of a national grid extending from Alor Star in the State of Kedah in the north to Kluang in Johore in the south that would be able to supply power during both dry and wet periods.

By the end of 1967 a thermal power station had been completed at Prai, and construction work had been started on one at Port Dickson in Negri Sembilan. Favorable reports had been received of the feasibility of the hydroelectric development of the Pergau River in Kelantan and of the upper Perak River, and priorities were established in projects to be undertaken. Progress had also been made in extension of the power network to supply the western coast of West Malaysia. The resulting integrated system had been named the western network. Electrification plans had been approved for 93 villages during the year. Part of the cost was to be provided by the federal government and part by the National Electricity Board. In addition, state governments had planned electrification of 40 other villages.

Over the duration of the plan, development expenditure for the electric power system was estimated at M$584.3 million, of which $M545 million was allotted to West Malaysia, M$15 million to Sabah, and M$24.3 million to Sarawak. In 1966 the International Bank for Reconstruction and Development made a loan of US$37 million to cover the foreign exchange costs of part of the program, and in 1967 the National Electricity Board transferred about M$20 million net revenue to the capital development account for use in financing projects. Implementation of the development program in West Malaysia was under the supervision of the National Electricity Board, which was the successor to the Central Electricity Board that had been created in 1949 for purposes of general supervision and operation of government-owned power stations. In East Malaysia power development was the responsibility of the Sabah Electricity Board and the Sarawak Electricity Supply Corporation. In addition to supervising the development plan and operating power stations, the National Electricity Board served as a regulatory agency in West Malaysia, issuing licenses to power producers and overseeing rates, which were fixed according to type of consumer and amount of power consumed.

CONSTRUCTION

From 1961 to 1967 construction was a dynamic sector of the economy. In contribution to the gross domestic product, it rose from M$218 million in 1961 to M$402 million in 1967, an increase of 84 percent, which substantially exceeded the increase of 45 percent in the gross domestic product itself. In share, it rose from 3.7 percent to 4.7 percent. Construction was overwhelmingly concentrated in West Malaysia, which accounted for more than 75 percent of the total in 1967. Activity was greatest in the State of Selangor, containing Kuala Lumpur, followed by Perak, Penang and Province Wellesley, and the State of Johore.

In mid-1969 comprehensive and detailed statistics on the component parts of the construction industry had not been published since 1965. The fragmented information available, nevertheless, indicated the buoyancy of demand for housing, industrial, commercial, and public buildings, and engineering projects. The need to increase the supply of housing units, relieve urban congestion, and eliminate slums was a spur to construction of both public and private housing. From 1961 to 1965 about 8,400 low-cost housing units were constructed in West Malaysia by the public sector that also was responsible for the construction of 4,837 units for public employees. At the same time, low-cost housing was undertaken by the public sector in Sabah and in Sarawak. Both detached houses and apartments were built.

Continuation of construction to eliminate the critical housing shortage was an important objective of the First Malaysia Plan that allocated M$150 million to West Malaysia, M$5 million to Sabah, and M$7.5 million to Sarawak for that purpose. Additional funds were allocated to the provision of housing for government workers.

Plans were outlined for slum clearance and the erection in Kuala Lumpur of low-cost housing using the prefabricated or industrial system of construction. By the end of 1967 a number of apartment houses about 15 stories in height had been built by this method. Two-room apartments in these buildings rented for M$45 monthly. More expensive dwellings also had been built in suburban areas adjoining Kuala Lumpur and other cities.

The value of nonresidential construction was increased by the erection of schools, including university and research structures, by the provision of facilities for tourists, and by many new factories. Shell buildings erected by the government to facilitate the quick expansion of industry were an important element in the total.

Extensive expansion of the highway system from 1961 to 1965, together with irrigation projects undertaken, added to the value of engineering construction that in 1965 exceeded the value of either residential or nonresidential building in West Malaysia. The program projected in the First Malaysia Plan provided for a continuation of the work undertaken in the previous 5 years, together with bridge-building, port improvement, and the extension of infrastructure facilities to industrial estates. By the end of 1967 progress had been made in the road and bridge construction program, and 17 drainage and 62 irrigation projects had been completed. The total value of engineering construction, however, was not available.

MANUFACTURING

Background and Organization

In 1967 manufacturing contributed M$955 million to the gross domestic product. From 1961 to 1967 the absolute contribution had risen steadily from M$487 million, and the share from 8.2 percent to 11.1 percent. As an indication of its importance to the economy during the period, the value of manufacturing had increased by 96 percent while the gross domestic product had increased by only 45 percent.

Historically, manufacturing had developed slowly from the processing of raw materials for export to the production of a few commodities for domestic use with local raw materials, especially those with high transport costs. After Malayan independence the government embarked on a program encouraging the establishment of manufacturing enterprises to provide import substitutes, mitigate dependence on the export of a few commodities, and add to employment opportunities. Despite accelerated government encouragement and the steady growth of manufacturing, industrialization in the mid-1960's was still in an early stage, and the contribution of manufacturing to the economy was not high compared with that in Taiwan, the Philippines, or Thailand.

Manufacturing has been located almost entirely in West Malaysia, which accounted for 87 percent of the contribution to the gross domestic product in 1967, slightly less than the share in 1962. Specifically, manufacturing was located on the west coast of the Malay Peninsula, particularly in and around Kuala Lumpur. Of the 10 industrial estates that were functioning in 1968, eight were on the west coast of the Peninsula, one was in Sarawak, and one in Sabah; only the one at Petaling Jaya near Kuala Lumpur was fully occupied. To provide more sites for manufacturing plants on the west coast of the Peninsula, two more estates were planned for that area; to encourage geographic dispersion, another estate was planned for the east coast of the Peninsula and one each for Sarawak and Sabah.

According to the 1963 census of manufacturing industries in West Malaysia, which was the most recent census available in 1969, only seven major industrial groups—food, wood, rubber, metal, nonmetallic mineral products, industries processing estate-grown agricultural products in factories, and the printing and publishing industries —employed more than 5,000 full-time workers each. Employment in individual plants tended to be small, with the average full-time employment of about 10 workers per plant. Establishments employing less than 10 full-time workers accounted for 82 percent of all establishments but contributed only 14 percent of net output; those employing more than 50 full-time workers accounted for about 4 percent of the total number but 60 percent of output. A survey made in 1966 indicated that only 14 plants had more than 500 employees each. All firms in Sarawak and Sabah had less than 50 employees per plant.

A large share of manufacturing capital formation is domestic. Historically, however, Malaysians have not been very active as manufacturing entrepreneurs, and an objective of government planning was to offer incentives to increase their participation in industry.

The value of manufacturing production in 1966, according to the survey made at that time, was M$2.01 billion, an increase of 8.8 percent from M$1.85 billion in 1965. The most valuable categories, in order, were: processing of estate-type products off estates, food processing, tobacco products, chemical products, wood products, rubber products, basic metals and metallic products, nonmetallic mineral products, machinery, beverages, and transportation equipment. All categories increased in value from 1965 to 1966. There were no changes in rank (see table 18).

Composition

The processing of estate-type products, which mainly consisted of rubber processing, was the most valuable category of manufacturing by a wide margin. In 1966 there were 143 establishments employing almost 9,000 full-time paid workers. From 1962 to 1966 establishments had decreased slightly in numbers but registered a small increase in employment.

Few details were available concerning the food, tobacco, and beverage industries. Among the food commodities produced, in addition to the canning of fruits and vegetables, were flour (including tapioca flour), monosodium glutamate, glucose, dextrin, bakery goods, sugar, and dairy products. In 1965 four new sugar. mills were planned, and by 1968 one integrated mill had gone into production. An increase in the canning of fruits and vegetables to reduce dependence upon imports was an important goal of the government development program. The output of tobacco products had increased from 1961 to 1967, and imports had declined. In 1966 a large brewery began operations, which increased the output and value of beverages.

In 1966 about 310 establishments were engaged in producing chemicals of different kinds. The most important commodity was fertilizer. A new fertilizer and chlorine plant with an annual capacity of 200,000 tons of fertilizer began production in 1967. The plant, which was a joint venture of the Chemical Company of Malaysia and the Imperial Chemical Industries of London, used ammonia byproducts from the Esso Oil Refinery and expected to produce fertilizer for rubber plantations. A new Esso ammonia plant also opened at Port Dickson in 1967.

Table 18. Value of Manufacturing in West Malaysia, 1965 and 1966
(in M$ millions)*

	1965	1966
Processing of estate-type products off estates ____	450	501
Food manufacturing _____	216	249
Tobacco products _____	186	198
Chemical products _____	161	171
Wood products _____	157	161
Rubber products _____	83	87
Basic metals and metallic products _____	73	79
Nonmetallic mineral products _____	41	43
Machinery manufacturing _____	28	32
Beverages _____	21	23
Transportation equipment _____	13	15
Miscellaneous _____	116	123
Pioneer firms not included above _____	305	330
TOTAL _____	1,850	2,012

*M$3.06 equal US$1.

The wood products industry was of significance not only for the value of output, but for the number of jobs it provided. In 1966 in West Malaysia, there were 471 establishments in operation with almost 14,000 paid full-time employees. The industry was also important in Sarawak, where there were 75 saw mills and planing mills employing 6,000 workers. In addition, Sarawak had 19 furniture factories employing 668 people in 1966; in the following year the number of plants increased to 32, but employment decreased slightly.

In 1967 West Malaysia had 13 plywood factories operating at full capacity and, in 1968, three more were in process of construction.

Prefabricated windows, doors, and houses were produced. Plywood and prefabricated wood products were exported, as well as used domestically.

Among the commodities produced by the rubber goods industry were sheeting and matting, foam rubber mattresses and other foam rubber products, tubing and hose, bicycle tubes, solid tires, and miscellaneous articles. Plants producing articles from rubber were of more than usual size, as 41 plants employed almost 7,500 paid full-time workers.

Although the basic metal and metal products manufacturing industries did not rank high in value of output, they ranked high in number of establishments and in employment, both of which increased from 1962 to 1966. In 1966 there were 331 establishments with 5,455 paid full-time employees.

Expansion of the basic metal industry was of particular significance to industrial development. In mid-1967 the first integrated steel mill, Malayawata Steel, Ltd., went into production at Prai in Province Wellesley. This was a joint Malaysian-Japanese venture, financed by the Yawata Iron and Steel Company of Japan, the Malaysian government, other Japanese and Malaysian investors, and the International Finance Corporation, an affiliate of the International Bank for Reconstruction and Development. Total investment was estimated at M$66 million. The plant used only domestic raw materials, including charcoal made from rubber trees. The most modern technological process was used for steelmaking. When operating at full capacity, the annual output was expected to be 124,000 tons of pig iron, 121,000 tons of steel, and 110,000 tons of rolled products. In 1967 two small rerolling mills were opened, and the following year another one was expanded. Completion of these facilities should reduce the dependence upon imported pig iron, most of which came from mainland China and Australia, and upon imported semimanufactured products that came from the closest industrialized countries.

The motor vehicle assembly industry developed from 1967 to 1968, aided by protective tariffs and import restrictions. In 1968 four assembly plants were in production, and two more were scheduled to open in early 1969. When in full operation, the plants were expected to produce ninety models of 37 different makes of foreign cars, based almost entirely upon imported components. Total output far exceeded the demand of the domestic market. The assembly operation, however, provided employment and training in skills.

The objective of the government was to encourage manufacture of component parts domestically and to make it advantageous, by taxation, for assemblers to use domestic parts. The government also was seeking a voluntary reduction in number of models produced.

The textile industry was very small. In 1967 there was only one large textile mill, operated by the foreign-controlled Textile Corporation of Malaya. The firm, which had pioneer status, started weaving in 1958 and spinning in 1964 and had an output of 35 million yards per year. Two new textile mills were in the planning stage.

CHAPTER 20

LABOR

The country's labor force, defined as those persons over 15 years old who are employed or actively seeking employment, stood at 2.7 million in 1967 and represented about 26 percent of the total population. About 50 percent of the labor force was engaged in agriculture, a reduction from the previous two decades as the result of shifts from agriculture to manufacturing and services. Unemployment in West Malaysia was estimated by the government at 8.8 percent, but at the same time East Malaysia was unable to meet labor needs of land clearing and lumbering.

A high correlation was still prevalent in the 1960's between ethnic groups and certain occupational categories. Malays and aboriginal peoples tended to work in agriculture and predominated among the smallholders. They have exhibited some aversion to working as wage earners on the large estates. Indians dominated the wage-earning group on the estates and the unskilled labor category in secondary industries. The Chinese have always gravitated to non-agricultural activities.

Labor legislation in Malaysia is among the most advanced, and wage standards are among the highest in Southeast Asia. The plight of the average worker in the country, however, varies from locality to locality and frequently from season to season. Wages are higher in East Malaysia because of the labor shortage. The country's dependence on basic commodities frequently results in direct wage fluctuations in response to shifts in the international market.

The separation of Singapore and its Chinese labor organizations from Malaysia in 1965 has resulted in a reduction of the political strength and activity of organized labor in the country. The government is attempting both to maintain what it feels is essential control over organized labor and to increase employment opportunities. In 1969 the government was operating an employment service, industrial training institutes, and resettlement programs.

Official statistical information concerning labor in the country usually takes the form of projections based on the partial censuses taken in 1957 and 1960. Most recent estimates are usually limited to West Malaysia and are often based on samplings and spot surveys. More

445

than 1.5 million workers classified as unpaid family laborers are excluded from the gainfully employed category, so that the total employment of women and children is lower in the work force estimate than would otherwise be the case.

STRUCTURE

Occupational Distribution

The 50 percent of the labor force engaged in agricultural production in 1967 compared with 65 percent in 1947 and 58 percent in 1962. Most of the decrease that took place between 1947 and 1967 occurred in the 1950's and resulted in the expansion of the service sector; the decrease that took place during the 1960's resulted mainly in the expansion of the manufacturing sector. In 1967, 8.5 percent of the labor force were in manufacturing, and 17 percent were in services. Trade occupied 11 percent of the labor force, and 8 percent were in utilities, construction, and transportation. The remaining 5.5 percent were in mining, quarrying, and other occupations (see table 19).

Table 19. Labor Force of Malaysia by Occupation, 1967

Sector	Number	Percent
Agriculture	1,350,000	50.0
Manufacturing	229,500	8.5
Services	459,000	17.0
Trade	297,000	11.0
Utilities, construction, and transportation	216,000	8.0
Mining and quarrying	81,000	3.0
Other	67,500	2.5
TOTAL	2,700,000	100.0

Source: Adapted from *Malaysia Official Yearbook 1967*, Kuala Lumpur, 1968.

Projections for the late 1960's, based on figures from the early 1960's, would place the government as the largest single employer of nonagricultural labor in both East and West Malaysia, although commercial enterprises as a composite provided greater total employment. The majority of government workers were engaged in the construction and maintenance of public works, in dockwork, and in the various ministries and government agencies. The number of wage earners in commerce in West Malaysia accounted for over 50 percent of all commercial workers, and the majority of workers in secondary industry were engaged in building and construction. Of the workers in manufacturing in West Malaysia, the majority were employed in textiles and general engineering; wood products and food processing companies employed the next largest groups.

Age and Sex

In 1965 more than 50 percent of the labor force were under the age of 20, and slightly more than 10 percent were over 50; this reflected the relative youth of the overall population and helps account for a preponderance of unskilled workers. A survey in West Malaysia in 1965 showed that in metropolitan areas about 24 percent of gainfully employed males were under the age of 25, and 65 percent were under the age of 40, indicating a greater concentration of unemployment in the younger age group. The respective figures for females were 39 percent and 73 percent, indicating that women begin their working careers at an earlier age and leave the work force earlier because of marriage and childbearing.

Projections based on 1960 census figures indicated that by the end of the 1960's female workers accounted for at least a third of the country's gainfully employed. The proportion was higher in East Malaysia than in West Malaysia. Women have come to represent a growing element in the labor force of West Malaysia, as rising unemployment among males has forced women to supplement family income. Although most women in West Malaysia are employed in agricultural production on estates, particularly as rubber tappers, many are also employed in manufacturing, particularly in the textile industry. Women have shown themselves to be highly productive textile workers and can enter into wage competition with men on a more equal basis in textiles than in any other industry. The remainder of women work primarily in commerce and services. Women in East Malaysia fit the same general patterns as in West Malaysia with a higher concentration in agricultural production.

Ethnic Distribution

Of the aboriginal population—principally the Dusun, Bajau, Sudan, Murut, Dayak, Iban, and Melanau—nearly all are engaged in agricultural pursuits, and the majority work for themselves or their families. Most cultivate rice, rubber, or sago; others are collectors of jungle products such as rattan, *jelutong* (a kind of latex), and *damar* (a resin). Fishing, frequently combined on a seasonal basis with farming, and coconut growing also are mainly aboriginal preserves. The sago and timber industries attract mainly the Melanau, whereas the Dayaks, when not busy with their ricefields, often work on the roads, as log extractors in the forest, or as unskilled laborers in the oilfields. Some Dayaks have been planting high-yielding rubber under government supervision and subsidy. Small numbers of the Sudan and Murut communities go into the police force. Less than half of the Bajau are engaged in agriculture; they enter in large numbers such industries as timber, rubber tapping, coconut growing, mangrove working, boatbuilding, and fishing. Government workers are also recruited from the educated of these groups.

In 1967 over 85 percent of the Malays in Malaysia lived in West Malaysia, where they constituted over three-fifths of the rural population, the majority cultivating rice and rubber as smallholders. Thus they accounted for the highest percentage of self-employed among the three major ethnic groups. Although the percentage of Malay women in the gainfully employed labor force is slightly lower than the average for all women, their percentage in the unpaid family worker category is higher.

Malays accounted for 25 percent of the wage-earning labor force, a disproportionate number in comparison to their percentage of the total population (about 39 percent) in 1965. In rural areas the wage-earning Malay worked on large rubber or oil palm estates, where they accounted for from 6 to 10 percent of the total estate labor. This percentage was increasing in the late 1960's as economic factors adversely affected the smallholding economy and as an influx of Malay women turned to wage labor. In the cities, Malay wage earners preferred building and construction work to manufacturing and were predominant in the government services. For mainly political reasons preferential treatment is given to Malays wishing to enter the government services. Even so, there are not enough qualified Malays to fill the available jobs open only to them.

The Chinese in 1967 had a large share in all occupations. Over half of the Chinese live in urban areas and dominate the nonagricultural sector of the labor force. Almost all retail trade is in the hands of Chinese merchants, streethawkers, and shopkeepers who represent a major proportion of the employees in finance, commerce, and communication. The labor force in the tin mines is predominantly Chinese as it is in the pineapple-canning industry, tobacco factories, brick and pottery works, engineering works, small foundries, rubber-processing plants, and Chinese-owned rubber plantations. Although the Chinese accounted for the largest number of laborers working for private employers, Chinese also accounted for from 80 to

90 percent of the employer category. There were few Chinese in government.

The rural Chinese were concentrated in the rubber, coconut market garden, and logging industries, with the majority found on small, Chinese-owned rubber estates and pepper gardens, which seldom employed more than 25 persons. There was little tendency for them to become smallholders.

The immigration of Chinese workers started with the opening of the Malayan tin mines about 1830 and became a flood after 1850. The workers arrived as indentured laborers, recruited by employers' agents in China. In the early period a coolie was advanced passage money and shipped to Malaya, where, little better than a slave, he remained indefinitely in debt to his employers.

Labor code provisions concerning the Chinese were numerous but, in comparison to the elaborate provisions governing Indian labor in Malaya, their scope was very limited. Inspection of places of work, housing and health standards, and supervision of wage payments were carried out by the officials of the protectorate and by health officers, but was generally ineffective because no definite standards of working and living conditions for Chinese labor had been established. This state of affairs was caused largely by the traditional noninterference of the Chinese government and by the traditional Chinese preference for hiring out on an individual basis and their dislike for governmental regimentation in the economic sphere.

The rapid influx of Chinese abated somewhat for several years after 1914, increased in the 1920's, and generally reflected fluctuations in the price of tin. There were no immigration restrictions until the depression, when a monthly quota was established. Some Chinese coolies were repatriated during the depression period, but repatriation soon ceased because of the Sino-Japanese War. In 1911 there were about 900,000 Chinese in Malaya; in 1941, 2.38 million. Since World War II, Chinese labor immigration has practically stopped.

The influx of Chinese to Sarawak and Sabah was also associated with the need of the British colonial enterprises in the mid-1800's for a larger and more willing labor force than the indigenous tribal people or the Malays could provide. The Chinese continued to immigrate as the economic structure became more oriented to large-scale Western enterprises. Throughout Malaysia the Chinese gradually evolved from indentured or recruited laborers to wage earners and self-employed workers and eventually came to dominate the nonagricultural sector of the economy.

Within the Chinese population, certain dialect groups have gravitated toward particular occupations. The Hakka commonly engage in agriculture, but they are important also in such urban occupations as tinsmithing. The Foochow people are found in every occupation, especially in pepper production; Sibu, where most of them are settled, has become known in China and in Sarawak as "New Foochow." The Cantonese are mainly laborers, but they also dominate the watch and clock trade, as elsewhere in Southeast Asia. The Hokkien concentrate on the export and import trade and generally control the financial affairs of the towns in which they reside. The Tiechiu dominate the grocery or shopkeeping trade in all of Southeast Asia.

Smaller dialect groups also fall into certain occupational categories. The Hailam operate most of the coffeeshops, and many also work as domestic servants and as sailors in European and Chinese employ. The Luichow have turned to charcoal making. The Chao An provide wharf laborers and building tradesmen. Those Chinese engaged in agriculture usually work in gardens or on estates until they have sufficient capital to have a small business of their own or to move closer to town.

Immigration of Indian labor to Malaya started in the middle of the 19th century. Indian workers were recruited under an indenture system, usually for a period of 3 years. The introduction of rubber cultivation in Malaya in 1877 and its subsequent expansion caused a large increase in the influx of Indian laborers.

The greatest influx of Indian labor to Malaya took place from about 1911 to 1930, rising to as much as 125,000 a year between 1920 and the depression of 1930. At the time of the most acute unemployment, many destitute workers were repatriated to India with Malayan government assistance. After the depression immigration dropped to 20,000 per year, and after 1946 it became necessary to restrict immigration to protect the standard of living and maintain local employment. The Immigration Ordinance of 1953 stated that only certain categories of newcomers—mainly relatives of persons already in residence—were permitted to immigrate, and immigration practically stopped. Under the federation agreements immigration remained a federal subject, though the states of Sarawak and Sabah were granted the right of approval of all entry into their territories.

In the late 1960's Indians made up a third of the wage earners in West Malaysia and over half of the employees on West Malaysian estates. The majority of the tappers, weeders, harvesters, and other groups on the plantations were Tamils from Madras; there were also some Telegus. The white-collar positions on estate staffs were mostly occupied by Malayalis from Travancore-Cochin, who generally were better educated than the other Indians. Indians in urban areas tended to work as unskilled laborers.

Only a small proportion of the gainfully employed were in the category that included Indonesians, Europeans, Sinhalese, and Filipinos. Most of these are unskilled, temporary immigrants who have taken up work in the timber camps, on estates, in public work labor gangs, and as unskilled labor throughout the country. This immigrant group, however small, is vitally important, especially in Sarawak and Sabah, where it supplies the bulk of the industrial labor that the other racial groups are either unwilling or unable to undertake.

Supply and Productivity

Official reports in 1969 showed an unemployment rate in major urban areas in West Malaysia of nearly 10 percent and in rural areas of 5.5 percent. Both figures represented an increase of .05 percent over 1962 estimates. Unemployment was highest among females and particularly among those workers between the ages of 15 and 24, about half of whom were unemployed.

In mid-1969, 134,634 workers were registered with the employment service of the Ministry of Labor; over 50 percent of this number were under the age of 21. Only 324 unemployed were registered in East Malaysia. Factory and transport workers, along with laborers, represented the majority of jobseekers.

Throughout Malaysia a shortage of skilled labor and a generally young labor force have been principal impediments to the development of high productivity and the ability to carry out increasing modernization and economic growth.

Industrialization, which is helping to provide employment for the rapidly growing population, is demanding more and more skilled labor. The supply of skilled workers, usually Chinese in origin, is inadequate in both East and West Malaysia. In rural West Malaysia rubber tappers, harvesters, and weeders are all considered skilled or semiskilled workers, and they constituted about 80 percent of the total number of estate workers in the mid-1960's.

In the states of Sarawak and Sabah, there was a shortage of unskilled wage earners, as well as skilled. In the 1960's the demands of the timber, rubber, oil, and governmental development programs were ahead of the supply of men willing and able to work in them. The majority of persons preferred to work their own small holdings, and the acreage planted by smallholders even increased from 1952 to 1962.

The government of Sabah has tried to solve the problem through several projects of controlled, large-scale immigration of skilled and unskilled labor. In the early 1950's some 1,500 Cocos Islanders and many Chinese, Javanese, and Filipino workers were brought in. In 1954 around 1,000 skilled and unskilled workers from Singapore and Hong Kong were imported to assist in urban construction work. Before the early 1960's, Javanese labor was imported to Sabah, and during the late 1960's the government sponsored migration from West Malaysia.

Despite the need, immigration of unskilled labor into Sarawak is resisted by the aboriginal elements in the population. Managerial and technical staffs are permitted to enter, but artisans, mainly in the building trades, may be issued temporary work permits when it can be shown that enough local men are not available for that particular job.

Paradoxically, the problem of a shortage of labor in Sarawak and Sabah is equaled in seriousness by the problem of underemployment in agricultural occupations. Because so few people are willing to leave the small family plots, the number of persons dependent and working on each small plot is increasing tremendously. As the rate of production per capita lowers, so does the return per capita. Government policy advocates a diversification of crops in order to prevent the bankruptcy of many smallholders when the world price of rubber or rice fluctuates.

CONDITIONS OF EMPLOYMENT

Wages

Wages fluctuate in relation to the degree of prosperity of the two major industries, rubber and tin, and according to race, sex, occupation, and place of employment. Generally, the Chinese command higher wages than either the Indians or the Malays because of their preference for piecework, their greater industriousness, and their higher degree of skill. Skilled labor in industrial occupations commands the highest wages; mining wages are higher than agricultural wages; and plantation wages are, on the average, higher than wages paid to the nonplantation agricultural workers. Men receive higher wages than women. Usually, wages are . lower and hours longer in the Asian-owned enterprises, and wages are higher and hours at or below the statutory limit in the European-owned enterprises and in government employment.

Before World War II, the Indian Immigration Committee of Malaya fixed wages for key areas in the rubber industry. Since the end of the war, wages in the rubber industry have been fixed by collective bargaining between the National Union of Plantation Workers and the Malayan Planting Industries Employers' Association, supposedly for each quarter according to an agreed sliding scale that relates to the average price of rubber during the preceding 3 months. Employers (generally Asian) who are not members of the association tend to disregard the scale.

Wages in the tin mines are generally higher than those of the rubber plantations, but they are not fixed by any system and are also subject to greater fluctuations. Piecework is prevalent, and the contractor system takes from one-tenth to one-fourth of the wages. Some miners work on a profit-sharing basis. Since World War II, the wage price bonus has been tied to the price of tin.

The wide diversity of conditions in industry, especially between large and small estates and between dredging and other types of tin mines, makes it impossible to give meaningful statistics of average wage rates, except in a few occupations. As an illustration, however, the average male machine operator in West Malaysia in 1968 in the soft-drink and tobacco industries received a monthly income of M$203 (3.06 Malaysian dollars equal US$1). Women received M$92 and M$169 in the respective industries. The average monthly wage in the tobacco industry for all workers under 21 was M$33. Clerical personnel in engineering operations averaged M$300, and truck drivers in sawmilling averaged M$279.

Indices of the relationship between wages and the cost of living are not available, and it is therefore difficult to determine the value of real wages. Before World War II, the Malayan worker's wages, though low, were higher than those in surrounding countries, and rice was plentiful. Until 1948 the increase in the cost of living over the prewar level was officially estimated as between 300 and 400 percent, whereas wages had generally increased only between 200 and 300 percent. Between 1949 and 1959 the cost-of-living index rose from 79 to 100 (1959 = 100); however, wages increased proportionately. In the early 1960's the cost-of-living index dipped to 99.7, while wages continued to rise.

Malaysian workers in 1969 were relatively well paid compared to workers in other Asian countries. Overtime work was paid at a rate of 1½ to 2 times the standard wage. Although the laws require that wage records be kept, that prescribed minimum wages be paid, and that company books be available for inspection, government inspectors uncover many abuses, especially in small, Asian-owned shops. Such abuses include hours worked longer than the maximum permitted and failure to pay higher rates for overtime or to give the statutory paid day of rest per week.

In 1947 the Wage Councils Ordinance was established that provided for ad hoc committees between workers and employers to help establish minimum wages and to settle individual wage disputes. Initially, these councils proved ineffective. In 1967 the wage councils were streamlined in order to enable easier enforcement of their decisions, and modification of the Employment Ordinance of 1955 extended coverage beyond laborers to all workers whose wages did not exceed M$500. As a result, a substantial portion of the wage-earning population could take their claims for wages and other matters connected with their contracts to the labour courts, with some hope of a settlement. In 1967 the labour courts in West Malaysia heard and decided 1,371 claims involving 1,954 workers, and claims worth about M$270,000 were ordered to be paid.

Working Conditions

By Asian standards conditions of work in Malaysia are relatively good. In a few enterprises, especially the small, Asian-owned businesses, very low and primitive standards are to be found; in others, the best modern standards may prevail. The average is generally satisfactory. Working conditions in government and municipal service are regarded as the best; wage rates, housing, and general conditions of health and safety are better than on the estates or in the mines, and government employment offers security of tenure, paid holidays, enforcement of benefits, and bonuses for continuous service. Working conditions in shops and restaurants are generally regarded as unsatisfactory by government inspectors, since the legal standards are most difficult to enforce there. Inspection of work conditions is generally less adequate in Sarawak and Sabah.

Free housing for its workers is provided by the estate management under a legal obligation resulting from the Indian government's insistence on benefits for Indian workers. The "coolie lines" barracks of the early estate-housing period have been condemned by the Malayan government and are gradually being replaced by modern detached-type houses. Free housing for mine workers is provided by many of the mineowners, although they are under no legal obligation. Planters are required by law also to provide free medical care for their laborers and education for the laborers' children. Many estates have their own hospitals, dispensaries, and schools. The standards of the hospitals vary from the very best on large estates to unsatisfactory on the smaller ones. Educational standards are generally lower than those of the government-sponsored schools.

The system of estate-provided health, housing, and education has meant in effect that such benefits have accrued predominantly to Indian labor. Other workers sometimes receive similar benefits, although their employers have been under no obligation to provide them. By and large, the Chinese workers have had to take care of themselves.

The government in 1969 was continuing its attempts to consolidate welfare legislation and advance the working conditions of the average worker. Hours of work, safety measures, accident and sickness compensation, and employment practices had all been at least in part brought under codification. All workers were under the Employees Provident Fund, and pension programs existed for government employees and workers in certain industries. Representative of protective legislation were the Workers Minimum Standards of Housing Act 1966, the Children's and Young Persons' (Employment) Act 1966, and the Factories and Machinery Act of 1969.

In 1969 the first stage of a comprehensive social security plan took effect, replacing the 1952 Workmen's Compensation Ordinance. The new program provides for a pilot employment-injury plan initially covering five major cities and for an invalidity pension plan covering the entire country. Government estimates placed the numbers of workers affected by the two programs at 150,000 and 800,000 respectively.

THE DEVELOPMENT OF TRADE UNIONISM

Trade unionism in Malaysia is largely a post-World War II movement. Before the war trade organizations were limited to company associations organized on a craft basis with limited membership and a social, rather than industrial, orientation. After 1945 the development of labor organization was relatively rapid, although the organization of labor was deterred, and is hampered still, by ethnic divisions, by widespread illiteracy among workers, and by the lack of leadership and experience. Labor unions have tended to development on ethnic rather than trade lines and on a small-shop basis rather than an industry basis. Characteristic of this growth was the emergence of a multitude of small unions competing among themselves for the affiliation of each group of workers. In the 1960's however, amalgamation and unification of the unions was taking place. In Sarawak and Sabah, where the labor movement was in its infancy in the 1960's, little cohesiveness was apparent among the workers.

Communists dominated the labor movement before World War II and, in the years that immediately followed it, broadened the scope of their activities. The subsequent disappearance of Communist leaders from the labor movement almost led to its complete destruction. Gradually, in the late 1950's the Communists again penetrated labor organizations, this time working in Sarawak and Sabah as well. In Sarawak and Sabah, where the Communists appeared in the early 1960's to have taken over the leadership of most of the unions, their ascendancy was no less spectacular but was less significant because of the relatively small proportion of labor involved in union organization.

Ethnic exclusivity has done much to determine the character of labor organizations. The Chinese, who were the first to organize, were the principal agents of communism. After the Emergency in 1948, Indians dominated the labor movement and, in the late 1960's, still retained most of the leadership positions. Malays and aboriginal peoples have only recently begun to play a part in labor organization, after years of noninvolvement. In the 1960's the majority of unions still tended to cater predominantly to one ethnic group, and longstanding friction between the unions constituted one of the principal barriers to the emergence of labor as a unified interest group.

The Labor Movement Before 1946

The evolution of the labor movement before 1946 was based on a different tradition for each of the large ethnic groups. The Malays did not participate. The Indians felt no need to organize until the 1930's, since they had been protected by special legislation and by the special agencies of the Malayan and Indian governments. The Chinese had begun labor organization in the 19th century and were the moving force behind the development of labor unions in the 20th century.

Chinese immigrants brought to Malaya two of their traditional organizations: trade guilds and secret societies. The guilds were particularly common among such established trades as tailoring, shoemaking, and carpentry and, as a rule, were limited to a particular regional group, such as the Hakka, Hainanese, or Cantonese. Various lodges of the Chinese secret Triad Society became powerful mutual-protection groups, covering among them the whole of the Chinese population and functioning in some aspects as trade associations. Both employers and employees belonged to the guilds and secret societies, and thus such questions as wage rates, hours of work, holidays, terms of apprenticeship, arbitration of disputes, and adjustment of claims were settled within each organization on a more or less "family" basis. For estate workers and those outside the guild pattern, employee-employer relations were based on customs and tradition rather than on contractual obligations.

The first legislation providing for the registration of societies (including those of labor character) was introduced in the Straits Settlements in 1889 and in the Federated Malay States in 1895, followed in both places by the Societies Ordinance of 1909. A 1928 amendment to the ordinance forbade registration of any society of proven subversive character and declared all such societies illegal. Under the ordinance many societies were organized, and a number of them, though primarily social, had as their secondary function the maintenance or improvement of members' status as employees; some of them became, in effect, labor unions.

Between 1924 and 1940 two political currents had fresh impact on Malayan Chinese labor—the nationalism of the Nationalist Party of

China (Kuomintang) and communism. The Kuomintang influence was quickly spent, and communism soon became the most important single factor in the development of the Malayan labor movement.

In the 1920's Communist infiltration found some support among Chinese immigrant elements, primarily the Hainanese and the Hakka. Agents began arriving who spread propaganda through night schools, "house" unions, and craft guilds. They infiltrated the leadership of many of the existing labor groups and began creating new ones. In 1924 the Communist influence became formalized by the establishment of the Nanyang Federation of Labor. Chinese seamen were organized in the Nanyang Seaman's Labor Union. The government in 1928 outlawed the Nanyang federation as subversive and later deported some of the alien leaders. In 1930, according to an official estimate, the Malayan Communist Party (MCP) controlled about 10,000 persons in various labor groups. In the next few years the MCP reorganized and concentrated on the long-range objectives of attracting Chinese, Indian, and Malay workers and establishing cells in industries. Whenever the Communists dominated a group, they called it a labor union.

The hardships of the 1930 depression period and the return of prosperity without accompanying wage increases brought a realization of the need to organize and a wave of strikes. In 1935 The Communists set up a number of front groups; one, the General Labor Union (GLU), became in the space of one year the most successful instrument the MCP has yet developed. Before 1936 strikes were only sporadic, but from 1936 to 1941 labor unrest was continuous. Political influence, primarily emanating from the GLU, became progressively evident. At first, unrest centered on desires for increases in wages to match the rubber and tin boom; in later years strikes were fomented in an attempt to cripple the British war effort. These strikes laid the groundwork for the development of the labor movement by showing that organized action brought results, which was a new idea in Southeast Asia. Communist infiltration was most successful among general laborers; skilled workers were least affected.

At the same time, the Indians were beginning to see the value of organization. Although there had existed a few social and educational improvement societies, few, if any, of these turned into labor unions, as better working conditions were obtained for Indian workers by legislation. The advent in India of a new nationalism inspired the middle-class Indians to spread the concepts of the Indian National Congress, the dominant party in India, through the local Indian press. The Central Indian Association of Malaya (CIAM) was formed, principally by the middle-class Indians. In 1941 this group attempted to gain control of the Indian workers and participated in the general strikes of 1941. Although the MCP attempted to interject Communist propaganda into this movement, the general sentiment was, rather, one of sympathy with the struggle for independence in India. The average lower-class Indian worker did not respond to this call upon his nationalism, and it was only after MCP agitation in the late 1930's that the Indian worker began to show the first signs of political self-consciousness. The tempo increased after the Japanese occupation.

In 1940, despite its involvement in the war, the colonial government effected the first labor union legislation, hoping for a gradual changeover from the associations to trade unions and the dissolution of those associations without strictly labor union functions. Labor union ordinances and trade disputes ordinances were passed by the Federated Malay States and the Straits Settlements in 1940 and 1941. The office of Trade Union Registrar was established in 1940 by the Federated Malay States. Also in 1940 the Malayan Industrial Court Ordinance provided for a system of appointed courts for the settlement of disputes and for a system of arbitration and courts of inquiry to be set up when required. The first body of this kind, the Interim Joint Council, which was not established until 1946, adjudicated disputes between government as an employer and government workers.

The legislation from 1940 to 1946 encouraged the organization of labor, but only as an economic and nonpolitical movement. It gave the government powers of control over the unions through the registration requirements and limitations placed on the use of union funds. Both employers and labor reacted adversely to the legislation; the employers resented legal recognition of the unions, and the labor groups felt the government was trying to restrict their activities through compulsory registration and to impose rules and regulations, which, however suitable for workers in Great Britain, were not easily understood by citizens of diverse legal traditions. No unions were actually registered until after the end of the Japanese occupation.

The effect of the war changed the attitude and, consequently, the direction of the labor movement. The Trade Union Federation was formed under the auspices of the MCP, which aimed at organizing labor against the Japanese. It assisted in fighting the Japanese after the capture of Singapore. Other Unions, such as the Stevedores Union and the Quarry Workers' Union, helped with the excavations required by the army to destroy the causeway to the mainland. The MCP guerrilla forces were encouraged, aided materially, and accepted as units in the resistance by the British. Indian workers formed the Indian National Army.

At the end of war the Malays, Chinese, and Indians of the area had seen disproved the myth of Western impregnability and had gained a new sense of their own worth and importance. Asian civil servants had performed the work that had been thought only Europeans could do. One of the results of this war effort was to give a new class-consciousness to the labor movement.

The Postwar Years

The years between 1945 and 1960 were characterized by unrest in the labor movement. The Communists were gaining increasing control and were thus creating government and employer suspicions about the whole movement. The majority of workers, with their sense of self-pride and dignity attained in wartime efforts, were anxious not to return to their prewar social and working conditions, particularly in relation to the British. In addition, racial separation and distrust had been further fostered by the Japanese, and recriminations concerning wartime activities were coming to the surface, particularly in Asian-owned enterprises.

During the few weeks in 1945 between the withdrawal of the Japanese forces and the arrival of the British, the Communist guerrillas— the Malayan People's Anti-Japanese Army ((MPAJA)—succeeded in organizing cells, which they called labor unions, for every type of trade and workers. Persisting even after the establishment of the British Military Administration (BMA), they gained control over almost all the unions in Singapore and many in the Malay states. All the Communist-controlled unions and groups were federated in the revived GLU, which, at the end of 1945 and the beginning of 1946, took advantage of the general unrest to organize a series of strikes. In January 1946 some 3,500 Communist agents circulated on foot, by truck, and by bicycle to ensure the success of a strike involving more than 150,000 persons. Again in February of that year, a new series of strikes involved all railroad workers, Indian estate workers, and various other workers.

It was at this time that the BMA policy changed from liberalism to firmness. When the BMA was established in 1945, it introduced a policy of complete freedom of speech and association and tried to avoid any suggestion of interference with the legitimate activities of the labor unions. The office of trade union adviser was created for the unions with no relation to the colonial government. Nevertheless, it was stipulated that the unions would have to comply with the 1940 legislation. It soon became apparent to the BMA that most of the unions were fundamentally subversive in character, and strict adherence to the legislation concerning union political activities was required.

By 1947 the MCP had gained control of a substantial number of unions in Malaya, many of them organized on a regional basis. Since the GLU was an organization operating in both Malaya and Singapore and therefore not acceptable for registration purposes, the MCP dissolved it and created a separate Pan Malayan Federation of Trade Unions (PMFTU). The organization exacted a high percentage of contributions from affiliated unions (up to 20 percent of the union funds), with the result that the member unions became dependent on their federation and thus easier to control.

During this period the Communist method of penetration was designed to keep under control a large membership of workers, many of whom were not particularly favorable to communism, and to maintain a semirespectable front for the benefit of the authorities. MCP policy was to allow most leadership positions to be filled by non-Communists but at the same time to place one or two party members in key posts. Either the president or the secretary and one or two full-time organizers were usually party members, but they were instructed to conceal their Communist connections. They took orders from GLU and were considered expendable. Real power was in the hands of a few Communist union members who held no official union office but ran the show behind the scenes, reporting directly to and receiving orders from the regional party body. Some served as necessary rank-and-file members to formulate "popular demands" and generate members' support for MCP-sponsored measures; others merely watched and reported to their party cells.

In early 1948 the Communist unions formulated a new mass-scale upsurge of labor unrest, based on the already worsening labor regulations caused by the extreme shortage of food, particularly rice; inflationary living conditions; and great variations in wage scales. Labor unrest quickly manifested itself in violent and widespread industrial and estate demonstrations and strikes. The problem of racial friction became more and more acute, particularly on the non-European-owned estates and enterprises. Adding fire to the racial friction were the suspicions and reactions toward collaborators with the Japanese. Indians and Malays particularly were accused of aiding the enemy. The Communists made a determined bid for power, using the unrest for their own purposes.

Labor union advisers on estates performed the functions of political bosses, levying fines and punishments on union and nonunion personnel alike for infractions against union rules. Some estates were completely taken over by laborers who had been laid off and refused to leave. The BMA, forced to take strong measures to curb the violence, forbade demonstrations and deported some alien Chinese leaders.

In their long-range plans to overthrow the government, labor was not the only agent used by the Communists to create instability. The police force, the military, and other groups were also the targets of infiltration or direct terrorism. Government countermeasures against these and other Communist activities culminated in 1948 in the declaration of the Emergency. At once, all the responsible officials of the PMFTU took to the jungle and either destroyed or took with them the accounts, documents, and funds of their federation. Within a few days the registration certificate of the organization was canceled. Leaders of most of the affiliated unions either fled or were detained; their registrations, too, were voided. The number of registered unions and their membership were abruptly cut in half.

The Emergency brought further restrictions on the activities of unions and increased government control. Laws passed in Singapore and Malaya in 1948 specified that all labor union officers, except the secretary, must be drawn from among persons actually working in the applicable industry; that no person convicted of extortion, intimidation, and like crimes may hold union offices; and that labor union federations were prohibited except on the basis of similar industry and occupation—a provision aimed at preventing the creation of wide, Communist-front organizations. The registrars of labor unions were given the power to freeze union funds if the union's responsible officers disappeared and to supervise balloting in union elections. A 14-day cooling-off period for strikes and lockouts in public utilities services was stipulated.

Union membership in the postwar years fluctuated with the fortunes of the labor unions. In Malaya there were approximately 270 unions before the Emergency. Between June 1948 and October 1949, almost half of them were dissolved, and membership was decreased by 70 percent. In Singapore the number of unions increased from 8 to 126 during 1946 and 1947, but decreased to 91 during the early years of the Emergency. By 1950 industrial disputes were few and purely economic. Most of the emerging unions were sponsored by the government or by employers. The Chinese, mistrusted by all, were reluctant to join the new unions.

In the early 1950's governmental restrictions on labor unions relaxed somewhat, and the Communists again tried to regain power. The MCP formed the underground All Races General Labor Union through which it planned to infiltrate the legal unions. This time the emphasis was necessarily on other racial groups as well as on the Chinese.

In the early 1950's labor activity centered on the Malayan Trade Union Congress (later renamed the Malaysian Trade Union Congress—MTUC), which set patterns to be reflected through the 1960's.

It was nonpolitical, non-Communist, and was principally devoted to improving working conditions and living conditions.

Relations between labor and government in Malaya in the late 1950's were not always cordial. The Alliance government, formed by the United Malays National Organization (UMNO), did not include labor representatives. In 1957 the Malayan Trade Union Congress accused the government of having an unsympathetic attitude toward the labor movement because of a UMNO proposal to introduce legislation barring aliens from holding union offices. Since almost all the union leaders were either Chinese or Indians and many of them were aliens, such a law would have been catastrophic to the labor movement. Malayan Trade Union Congress pressure prevented enactment of the law.

After the formation of Malaysia, Communist elements renewed their efforts to infiltrate the labor movement in West Malaysia but achieved limited success. With the separation of Singapore, where pro-Communist sentiment was greatest among the predominantly Chinese organizations, the remainder of Communist activity and influence in the country's labor movement was largely limited to infiltration of organized labor in Sarawak and, to a lesser degree, in Sabah, where it continues to receive careful government observation and control. As of 1969, little threat was felt imminent from Communist elements in the labor force.

Existing Legislation

In 1969 legal provision for the incorporation of labor organizations was contained in the Societies Ordinance of 1909 and in the Industrial Relations Act of 1967. Labor unions were still prohibited in 1969 from forming nationwide organizational structures, even though this was an option open to employers' associations.

The Industrial Relations Act represented the consolidation of labor legislation for all of Malaysia and replaced the various trade unions ordinances of West Malaysia (1959), Sarawak (1948), and Sabah (1947). Prior legislation establishing the right of labor to organize, strike, and bargain were incorporated in the 1967 act, as were the limitation of labor organization membership to workers in a common industry or occupation and the compulsory registration of all labor organizations. The act granted greater protection to workers to organize and provided the legal machinery to force employers to recognize the rights of legally registered unions. The act also increased government control over labor disputes in certain areas. It replaced the emergency provisions set up in 1965 during the confrontation with Indonesia, preventing strikes by certain groups of government employees and workers in industries classified as essential (see ch. 24, Public Order and Internal Security).

Labor Organizations

Worker Organizations

In West Malaysia at the end of 1967, there were 258 registered unions with a total membership of nearly 307,000. Through consolidation efforts, the total number of unions had dropped by 19 from the previous year; however, total union membership had increased during the same period by 22,000. The trade union structure was still highly fractionalized, with 226 unions providing only 18 percent of total membership. The 9 largest unions provided 51 percent of all union members. The two largest unaffiliated unions in 1967 were the National Union of National School Teachers, with a membership of 4,006, and the National Union of Engineer Employees, with 3,756 members (see table 20).

There were three labor federations: the Federation of Government Junior Staff Unions, with three affiliated unions; the Congress of Unions of Employees in the public and civil services, with 44 affiliated unions; and the Federation of Malay Teachers' Unions, with eight affiliated unions. The largest organization of labor unions, the Malaysian Trade Union Congress (MTUC), with 93 affiliated unions and 225,000 members, however, had not been allowed to register as a federation. Even though the MTUC represented 36 percent of all unions and 73.3 percent of all union members in West Malaysia, its legal status under the Societies Ordinance did not allow it to bargain for its members.

Table 20. Major Unaffiliated Unions of West Malaysia, 1967

Type	Name	Membership
Customs _____	Customs Services' Union _____	943
Educational _____	Educational Institutions Employees' Union __	1,347
Engineering _____	National Union of Engineering Employees __	3,756
Gold _____	National Union of Gold and Silversmith Employees _____	810
Government _____	Government Workers' Union, Kedah and Perlis	3,287
Do _____	Government Workers' Union, Kelantan _____	1,540
Do _____	Government Workers' Union, Negri Sembilan _	1,359
Kesatuan (teachers' union)	Kesatuan Kebangsaan Guru2* Lepasan Maktab/Pusat Latehan Harian _____	1,771

Table 20. Major Unaffiliated Unions of West Malaysia, 1967—Continued

Type	Name	Membership
Kesatuan (laborers' union)	Kesatuan Kebangsaan Pekerja2* Perusahaan dan Buroh Kasar Kerajaan _____	3,025
Kesatuan (union of state-government workers in public works) __	Kesatuan Pekerja2* Jabatan Kerja Raya dan Majlis Bandaran Trengganu _____	1,613
Kesatuan (government workers' union)_	Kesatuan Pekerja2* Kerajaan _____	1,726
Medical _____	Government Medical and Health Employees' National Union _____	2,431
Municipal _____	Municipal and Government Labour Union, Penang and Province Wellesley _____	1,617
Public Works Department ____	Public Works Department Employees' Union of Perak Union Building _____	2,343
Teachers _____	Malay Teachers' Union, Kelantan _____	1,749
Do _____	National Union of National School Teachers__	4,006
Technical _____	Technical Services' Union, Central Electricity Board _____	1,033

*In Bahasia Malaysia, plurals are formed by the superscript 2 following the word.

Source: Adapted from U.S. Department of Labor, Bureau of Labor Statistics, *Directory of Labor Organizations in Malaysia*, 1969.

The MTUC can trace its origins back to the formation of the Malaysian Trade Union Congress established in 1950. Through its participation in the National Joint Labor Advisory Council and other official organizations, it has been able to influence considerably labor and trade union policies. The major affiliates of the MTUC in 1967 by size were: the National Union of Plantation Workers, with 107,798 members; the National Mining Workers' Union, with 13,054 members; the National Union of Commercial Workers, with 12,451 members; and the Railwaymen's Union of Malaya, with a membership of 10,898 (see table 21).

The MTUC has been affiliated with the International Confederation of Free Trade Unions (ICFTU) since 1950. By 1965 it had

sponsored over 200 Malaysians for training abroad under groups
such as the ICFTU, the International Labor Organization (ILO),
the Asian Labor Education Center, the Colombo Plan, and the
United States educational exchange program. The MTUC and its affiliated unions also sponsor education programs at home for which
they have received government praise.

Unions in West Malaysia generally possess an educated leadership
and are nonpolitical and nonreligious. Although membership participation in union activities varies from union to union, the average
member is only marginally active. Some unions have tried to stimulate worker interest in union affairs through cultural and educational
programs, but most unions focus largely on the more practical issues
and common interests of its members.

Table 21. Major Affiliates of the Malaysian Trade Union Congress, 1967

Type	Name	Membership
Armed Forces	Federation Armed Forces Civilian Staff Union	4,581
Bank	National Union of Bank Employees	4,642
Clerical	Amalgamated Union of Employees in Government Clerical and Allied Services	1,690
Commercial	National Union of Commercial Workers	12,451
Electricity	General Electricity Board Junior Officers' Union	1,394
Do	National Electricity Board Employees' Union	3,952
Estates	All Malayan Estates' Staff Union	2,895
Government	Pahang Government Workers' Trade Union	1,679
Harbour	Harbour Trade Union	3,053
Hydro	Perak Hydro's Employees Union	1,542
Industrial	Government Industrial and Manual Workers' Union	1,582
Journalists	National Union of Journalists	38
Local Authorities	Amalgamated National Union of Local Authorities Employees' Federation	4,806
Mining	East Coast Mining Industry Workers' Union	6,553
Do	All Malayan Mining Industry Staff Union	844
Do	National Mining Workers' Union	13,054
Municipal	Penang Municipal Services' Union	1,371
Do	Kuala Lumpur Municipality Workers' Trade Union	1,819
Nurses	Malayan Nurses' Union	1,131

Type	Name	Membership
Perak	Perak Town Board, Town Council, and Municipality Employees' Union	1,639
Petroleum	National Union of Petroleum Industry Workers	1,438
Plantation	National Union of Plantation Workers	107,798
Port	Penang Port Commission Employees' Union	1,553
Postal	Union of Post Office Workers	1.071
Do	Union of Postal Uniformed Staff	939
Printing	National Union of Employees in the Printing Industry	1,184
Railwaymen	Railwaymen's Union of Malaya	10,898
Rubber	National Union of Employees in Companies Manufacturing Rubber Products	2,363
Teachers	National Union of Teachers	4,615
Technical	Malayan Technical Services' Union	3,072
Telecommunications	National Union of Telecommunications Employees	5,336
Transport	Transport Workers' Union	2,604
War Department	War Department Civilian Staff Association	3,680

Source: Adapted from U.S. Department of Labor, Bureau of Labor Statistics, *Directory of Labor Organizations in Malaysia*, 1969.

A relatively high percentage of union membership is made up of women, who by 1969 represented about one-fourth of the total membership. Surveys in the mid-1960's showed that Indians provided about half the membership of trade unions in West Malaysia, with Malays and Chinese constituting about 28 percent and 19 percent, respectively.

Trade unionism in Sarawak has developed steadily but slowly since the late 1940's. Most of the unions are small and urban centered, and they are predominantly Chinese in membership. Various elements in the Sarawak labor movement have been identified by the government and labor leaders as being under Communist influence or control. The largest union in 1967 was the Sarawak Public Works Department Workers' Union, with 2,008 members (see table 22).

Trade unionism in Sabah did not really take root until the early 1960's. This is reflective of the low degree of industrialization and predominance of workers in part-time or seasonal wage work as a supplement to their agricultural production. Ethnic difference may also have retarded the development of unionism. In 1967 the three largest unions were the Sabah Public Works Department Employees Union, with a membership of 1,200; the Sabah Teachers' Union, with 1,154 members; and the Sabah Commercial Employees' Union, with 1,048 members (see table 22).

Table 22. Major Unions of East Malaysia, 1967

Type	Name	Membership
Sabah:		
Commercial ___	Sabah Commercial Employees' Union _____	1,048
Customs _____	Sabah Customs and Excise Employees' Union	140
Electricity ____	Sabah Electricity Board Employees' Union __	459
Medical _____	Sabah Medical Services Union _____	704
Posts _____	Sabah Posts and Telecommunications Employees' Union _____	450
Printing _____	Jesselton Printing Workers' Union _____	126
Public Works _	Sabah Public Works Department Employees' Union _____	1,200
Railway _____	Railway Workers' Union _____	670
Shop Assistants	Sandakan District Shop Assistants' Union __	130
Shop Workers _	Taway District Shop Workers' Union _____	125
Teachers _____	Sabah Teachers' Union _____	1,154
Transport ____	Sabah Air Transport Workers' Union _____	133
Do _____	Sabah Land Transport Workers' Union _____	677
Sarawak:		
Bank _____	Sarawak Bank Employees' Union _____	100
Commercial ___	Sarawak Commercial Employees' Union _____	700
Customs _____	Sarawak Customs Services Staff Union _____	227
Government __	Senior Government Officers' Association of Sarawak _____	196
Lands _____	Sarawak Lands and Surveys Workers' Union_	466
Marine _____	Sarawak Marine Employees' Union _____	340
Medical _____	Sarawak Medical Services Union _____	673
Municipal ____	Kuching Municipal Council Staff and Workers' Union _____	122

Table 22.   Major Unions of East Malaysia, 1967—Continued

Type	Name	Membership
Port _____	Kuching Port Authority Staff Union _____	155
Postal _____	Sarawak Postal and Telecommunications Employees' Union _____	650
Public Works _	Sarawak Public Works Department Workers' Union _____	2,008
Radio _____	Radio Malaysia Sarawak Employees' Union __	106
Seamen _____	Sarawak Seamen's Union _____	655
SES Company_	SES Company Employees' Union _____	450
Native Teachers ___	Sarawak Native Teachers' Union _____	669
Teachers _____	Sarawak Teachers' Union _____	1,025
Transport ____	Kuching Transport Workers' Union _____	114
Water Board _	Kuching Water Board Employees' Union ____	206
Wharf _____	Kuching Wharf and Port Labourers' Union __	390
Do _____	Sibu Wharf and Port Labourers' Union ____	326

Source: Adapted from U.S. Department of Labor, Bureau of Labor Statistics, *Directory of Labor Organizations in Malaysia*, 1969.

Employers' Associations

The two most important employers' associations, both registered as labor unions, are those of the plantation industry and the mining industry. The Malayan Planting Industries Employers' Association (MPIEA) was formed in September 1947 for the express purposes of fixing wages and negotiating trade disputes. Standards established by the MPIEA are generally adopted by the whole industry. It has a strong central executive body, whose decisions are binding on members. Collective bargaining in 1948 between the MPIEA and estate workers' unions resulted in the signing of a collective bargaining agreement, the first in the labor history of Malaya. In 1964 the plantation workers and the MPIEA were again negotiating over a new wage structure for 300,000 rubber estate workers. The union's demands would amount to a 40-percent pay and fringe benefit increase. The issue has been turned over to the Department of Labor and Industrial Relations for investigation.

The Malayan Mining Employers Association (MMEA), established in 1946, represents all the European mineowners and about

15 percent of the Chinese owners. It was slow to start collective bargaining, since there was no union representing the united interests of mineworkers, and until 1956 it established wages and working conditions unilaterally. Its first contract with the Malayan Mining Employees Union, representing about 25 percent of the workers in the European-owned mines, was signed in 1956. Like MPIEA, the MMEA has a strong central executive body.

There are also a number of other employers' associations that deal, not with the labor unions, but with their members' professional problems. One of these associations is the Pan-Malayan Road Transport Operators Association.

The employers' associations have been planning to set up an employers confederation to serve as a spokesman for general management in the manner of the MTUC. In 1959 a preliminary step in this direction was taken with the establishment of the Federation of Malaya Industrial and Commercial Employers Consultative Association, a nonpolitical body, to serve management not already involved in other associations and to express policy for its members.

Employers in Malaya fought organized labor and were, to a large extent, responsible for the militant character of early union development. A large section of the employers' group, including almost all of the smaller Chinese employers, steadily refused to bargain with the unions and spared no efforts to discourage union activity. Many employers still maintain the attitude. Strong labor unions are mostly to be found in the government and municipal services, the European-owned enterprises, and the large Malayan companies doing business mostly with Europeans.

In general, the development of associations, the unification of policy, and the degree of coordination among individual employers have grown in proportion to the development and strength of the labor movement. Only in the late 1950's did a few employers' associations form for the sole purpose of neogitating with labor. All were opposed to the closed shop and fought any encroachments on presumed management prerogatives, such as the right to hire and fire personnel. The rubber and tin industries' associations have developed strong central governing bodies with authority to establish and enforce policy that affects the whole industry; they were also the most likely to be influenced by outside capital, through their London parent companies. Other associations had much less coordination and left individual members more freedom of action.

INDUSTRIAL RELATIONS

In the development of Malaysian labor relations, the weapon used almost to the exclusion of all others has been the strike. After

World War II, most unions, immature and without adequate knowledge of labor union methods, knew no other method for winning improvement of wages and conditions; moreover, satisfactory collective bargaining machinery was lacking on local, regional, and national levels. Most strikes were, and are, called for economic reasons, involving demands for wage increases or protests against arbitrary firing of workers.

Before the promulgation of the Emergency Act of 1964, which specified compulsory arbitration for essential industries defined under the Essential (Trade Disputes in the Essential Services) Regulations, the industrial relations system was based on voluntary negotiations between labor and management. The major function of the government was to provide conciliation and mediation services and to encourage the formation, maintenance, and adherence to joint agreements.

The Industrial Relations Act of 1967 repealed the Essential Regulations and represented a partial return to the concept of voluntary negotiation. In its consolidation of labor legislation and definition of labor rights, the act also established the government's clear right to intervene of its own motion in any labor dispute if the public interest so requires. The act provides for the establishment of an industrial court to which disputes may be referred by the minister of labor upon the joint request of the contestants or of his own motion. All collective agreements must be deposited with the industrial court, and the collective agreements recognized by the court are considered binding on the signatory parties.

During 1967 there were 161 trade disputes which, with 34 disputes from the previous year, brought to 195 the number of those pending. Of these, 162 had been settled, more than 100 with the aid of the Ministry of Labor. Forty-two disputes were referred to the industrial court, 7 of them at the request of the disputing parties.

Thirty-eight collective agreements were concluded, 28 of which were made after the Industrial Relations Act came into effect. The agreements affected 20,000 workers and brought wage increases of from 4 to 6 percent, as well as improving general working conditions. Forty-five strikes occurred in 1967, affecting 9,452 workers and resulting in a loss of 157,980 man-days. Seven of the strikes lasted more than a month and accounted for about 63 percent of the total man-days lost. Fifteen of the strikes were of no longer than a day's duration.

LABOR AND SOCIETY

The role of organized labor in Malaysian society had not been clearly defined by 1969. Elements composing the country's labor force had traditionally been nonactive, and organized labor was moving with considerable caution to avoid jeopardizing its potential role through disruptive activity that would, at a time of national crisis, bring government reprisals.

The MTUC and the other labor organizations at a minimum have been able to influence government policy and have helped to encourage the integration of the average worker into the still emerging society. This has been achieved through the advancement of wages and working conditions and through social action programs.

Organized labor in West Malaysia lacks the political vitality formerly provided by labor in Singapore when it was still part of Malaysia, and the small scale of political organizations in East Malaysia discounts their immediate potential. The Alliance Party has not won the wide support of labor, and during the 1969 elections labor tended to avoid identification with any national issue or party and focused on advancing the cause of labor on the local level.

The major social issue pressed by organized labor in the late 1960's was the advancement of equal rights and wages for women. In May 1969 the government promised to implement in August of the same year an equal pay schedule affecting 30,000 women at a cost of M$4.2 million. The annual cost of the equal pay schedule was programmed for M$11.4 million by 1972. Implementation of the new schedule, however, was delayed for administrative reasons and rescheduled for January 1970.

THE ROLE OF GOVERNMENT

In the government's relations with organized labor in the 1960's, two of its major concerns have been Malaysianization and employment. The government has defined its motivation as the desire to promote the welfare and well-being of workers and to integrate them into its program for national development and rapid industrialization. The government's experience with labor in Singapore before its separation and with Communist infiltration of the labor movement in East Malaysia has left it somewhat hesitant about allowing the development of strong centralized labor structures. Legislation increasing the rights of organized labor have also provided for government checks, and nationwide labor unions are still prohibited.

The government's involvement in long-term labor problems and issues stems from its position not only as policymaker but also as the major single employer and includes both legislation and policy pronouncements. As an employer the government issued in 1969 a new 10-point code of conduct for all civil servants and, in its advisory capacity, suggested that Chinese businessmen could take account of the government program for the reduction of the import sector and should shift from commerce to industry or be left out of the country's prosperity.

Malaysianization

Malayanization of the bureaucracy was planned before independence and before the creation of Malaysia for three phases, the last beginning in 1965, and initially was based on normal attrition. Retiring foreigners were to be replaced by Malayan citizens according to ethnic ratios established in the constitution. The schedule was accelerated through a program prematurely retiring and pensioning noncitizens, however, so that the Malayanization of the government services had been largely completed by 1962.

After the formation of Malaysia in 1963, Malayanization was re-termed Malaysianization. Malaysianization was not universally accepted, especially in East Malaysia where foreign nationals were in some cases preferred over personnel brought in from West Malaysia to supplement East Malaysian personnel.

Before 1965 there were no legal restrictions on the general right of foreigners to work in Malaysia except the control of entry permits, nor were there any specific trades or professions reserved for Malaysians. License controls were generally designed, however, to encourage the Malaysianization of the professions, and aliens were restricted from entry into positions for which there were qualified Malaysians.

In 1965 the government intensified its Malaysianization efforts and established the Standing Committee for the Malaysianization of Commerce and Industry. The committee was composed of cabinet-level officers and chaired by the deputy prime minister. The committee proposed the gradual Malaysianization of all technical, professional, and managerial personnel by 1980 and set about drafting schemes to train Malaysians for these positions. In addition, a standing committee chaired by the minister of commerce and industry was established to carry out Malaysianization through a gradual tightening of entry permit controls.

The labor force at large has been submitted to few controls save the general labor clauses protecting Malay rights and requiring training programs to train Malaysians to replace nonnationals within a reasonable period of time. In 1968, however, the Employment (Restriction) Act was passed providing for the registration of employed nonnationals and the introduction of employment permits for those gainfully employed in certain categories of trade and business. Registration permits cost M$10 and were expected to be valid for only

2 years. Applications were accepted during the month of July in 1969, and nearly 60,000 applications were submitted.

Employment

Just as pressing and difficult to solve as Malaysianization is the chronic unemployment problem that has existed for over a decade. The government structures much of its labor legislation and programs around this issue and uses it in part to justify its tightening controls over organized labor. Government demands have not always been happily received, and in 1969 organized labor was protesting the government's discussion of limiting overtime hours in order to promote more job positions.

The focus for government action in the Department of Employment and Training established in the mid-1960's. During 1967 and 1968 the department made substantial preparations for the expansion of its training program. By 1968 more than 1,000 trainees were enrolled; construction at Butterworth and Penang was underway; and a special grant from the United Nations Special Fund was pending. Further expansion was hampered in 1969 by a lack of teachers for the program, a third of which was staffed by volunteers from overseas. Private groups have been encouraged to set up special training programs, one of the more successful examples of which is the secretarial course set up by the MTUC education committee in 1968.

Under the First Malaysia Plan for 1966 to 1970, the government set a goal of creating 460,000 new jobs, 380,000 of which were to be in West Malaysia. Planned were 165,000 new jobs in agriculture, 55,000 in government administration and defense, 89,000 in service industries, 36,000, in manufacturing, and 42,000 in construction.

Under the assistance of an adviser from the ILO, the employment service operated by the Ministry of Labor was considerably overhauled in 1967. New procedures for registration, interviewing, and placement were established, and some of the 26 employment offices in West Malaysia were relocated. During the same year, under ILO assistance, an occupational research unit was established, and a new Malaysian occupational classification system was drawn up. Under the new system over 1,000 occupations commonly found in the country were defined, enabling a uniform understanding of titles used in development plans, training courses, statistical studies, and employment facilities.

Under the Ministry of Culture, Youth, and Sports, the government is attempting to train a pool of skilled youths for industrial employment. The National Development Corps was established in 1969 for 3,000 unemployed youths. Spiritual and physical training is to be augmented in the development corps with training in motor mechanics, electrical work, and other industrial skills. Direct placement into the labor force is to be provided.

The Malaysian Migration Fund Board was established in September 1966 to facilitate the movement of unemployed workers in West Malaysia to estates in Sabah. The federal government provides 70 percent and Sabah provides 30 percent of the program costs, but employers eventually will fund the operation. In 1967 1,069 workers and 1,217 dependents were sent to Sabah, 781 as field workers and the rest as tappers. Eighteen hundred workers were scheduled for migration in 1968.

CHAPTER 21

DOMESTIC TRADE

At the close of 1969 commercial activity represented the largest source of national income in the country. It surpassed the contributions made by either agriculture or industry to gross domestic product and was one of the major sources of employment in the country.

Major commercial flows are between rural, localized markets and urban trade centers and concern movements of primary products in exchange for consumer goods. Distribution within the country is handled through a complicated series of middlemen, resulting in price increases and, in some areas, shipping delays. Producers and consumers in rural areas are tied to local sales outlets by an extensive credit system, which in turn ties the local outlet to large firms and distributors. The government has advanced consumer and producer cooperatives as a means of counteracting this credit problem.

Various European and Asian nonindigenous ethnic groups have come to dominate certain aspects of commercial activity in the country. Malays have a low interest in commercial activity. Distribution of goods within the country is primarily in the hands of Chinese, who act as agents for import-export firms or as shopkeepers in urban areas and as merchant-moneylenders in rural areas.

The majority of the communication and service facilities are found in urban areas, primarily along the west coast of West Malaysia, where population density and industrialization are the highest. Although local markets rely heavily on traditional patterns and facilities, development programs are gradually changing the market structure. Major developments in the transport system since the end of World War II have been the emergence of an air transport network connecting East Malaysia and urban areas of West Malaysia, the general extension of the road network, the reconstruction of the east coast rail line, the upgrading of the east coast roads, and the completion of the East-West Federal Route II. Transport facilities in West Malaysia are basically adequate for present needs. Transport facilities in East Malaysia are geared mainly to the export of raw materials, particularly timber, and offer only a limited overland network.

Provisions for the expansion of consumer, transportation, and communication services represented just over one-third of the First Malaysia Plan for 1966 to 1970. The allocations for consumer and communication services maintained the relative percentages they had had in the period from 1960 to 1965. The allocation for the transport sector was cut in half, pending the completion of the transport sector surveys anticipated for the period. The United Nations began a study at the end of 1967, and the British government financed an additional study. In the fall of 1969 the government signed a regional transport survey agreement with the Asian Development Bank. The survey focus was to include eight countries in Southeast Asia.

COMMERCE IN THE ECONOMY

The role of commerce in the economy is reflected in its contribution to both national income and employment. Based on current factor cost, commercial activity in 1967 provided 34 percent of the gross domestic product. Figures breaking commercial activity into its components showed that transportation, storage, and communications provided 4.1 percent; wholesale and retail trade provided 15.1 percent; banking, insurance, and real estate provided 1.7 percent; and services provided 13.1 percent of the gross national product (GNP).

Official government figures showed that commercial activity employed about 36 percent of the employed labor force and was the second major employer of labor in the country (see ch. 20, Labor). Figures breaking commercial activity into its components showed that services employed 17 percent; trade employed 11 percent; and utilities, transportation, and construction employed 8 percent. In addition to this permanent, full-time employment, commercial activity also provided supplemental income for a substantial portion of the rural and village population.

MARKETING AND CREDIT PATTERNS

One of the major characteristics of the country's commercial sector is the small unit size of most commercial enterprises, particularly in retail trade. Supermarkets and department stores can be found in the large urban areas, but most retail units are composed of one man or a family peddling on a street or working out of a stall or small shop. Over half of those engaged in commerce are self-employed. Urban shops dealing in one particular kind of item may compete side by side; rural stores are frequently the only source of supply for their area and carry a wider variety of items.

A second major characteristic of commercial activity in the country is the close link that exists between the import-export sector and domestic trade. Large trade concerns simultaneously engage in import-export trade and in domestic trade both as wholesalers and retailers. Moreover, without the credit extended by these firms, most of the commercial sector would be hard put either to carry inventories or to grant credit in turn to their customers.

Producers and exporters seldom have direct contact but work through a complicated series of middlemen. Some large Western manufacturing firms have retail outlets of their own, but most rely on the use of agents, who are sometimes aided by a sales representative, rather than maintain local sales operations. Firms dealing in goods like office equipment and sewing machines maintain service outlets.

The integration of rural marketing into regional and national marketing is a function of the transport network available in an area. Almost all the surplus rice from the paddy land of the northwest section of West Malaysia and growing areas like Selangor and Perak is sold and consumed locally. Except for a small amount of tea, nuts, and pepper, almost all of the vegetables, fruits, and other food crops cultivated in market gardens in or near population centers are sold and consumed within the country. The vendor is frequently the producer. Fish is sold through local auctions, as well as through direct bargaining.

Many of the towns and villages have retail food markets provided by the state or local government. The market buildings have open sides, concrete floors, an adequate water supply, and good drainage and can therefore be efficiently cleaned daily. Retailers rent stall space and receive supplies of fresh vegetables, fruits (local and imported), fish, and meats from Chinese wholesalers or sometimes directly from the local producer. The markets are supervised and inspected by government agents, usually the police or a local sanitation board. Women sell much of the local produce and locally produced handicrafts, such as baskets, mats, tin and silver boxes, frames, sarongs, swords, and carved wood pieces.

Simple barter is uncommon, and even in rural areas most transactions involve money exchanges or credit accounts. Rural storekeepers sell most of their wares in return for local produce and, even if no money changes hands, running credit accounts are kept of the value of the items being exchanged. Except for brand name products in certain classes of stores, few items receive marked, uniform pricing. The buyer and seller arrive at a price by bargaining, both well-aware in advance of what the end price should be.

Credit facilities are more limited in rural areas and, as a result, rural interest rates are frequently higher. Particularly in smallholder rubber production, only one purchasing outlet is available to the producer. The local storekeeper is not only the sole purchaser but may also be the single source of goods produced outside the area and of credit with which to buy such goods. Rubber earnings will be used for foodstuffs, and hog and poultry earnings will go for extra items, such as clothing. The credit books may never be balanced, and a constant flow of credits and debits make both the shopkeeper and smallholder economically dependent on each other. The continuation of the process may result in an economic loss for the shopkeeper, justified in terms of clan loyalty, social merit, or face.

The government activity seeks to alleviate the restrictive credit situation through various development programs. Credit facilities as well as training programs for commercial activities are available through the Council of Trust for the Indigenous People (Majlis Amanah Ra'ayat—MARA). The Muslim Pilgrims Saving Corporation provides a mechanism for capital accumultation and credit expansion.

Banking unions, credit societies, and other cooperative societies have been created on state and district levels. Cooperative societies, particularly in rural areas, have been formed for village consumer purchases, milling of crops, paddy storage, rubber curing and sale, truck garden marketing, transport needs, construction, lumbering, farm mechanization, and land purchase. Figures for West Malaysia in 1968 showed a total of 2,830 registered societies with a total membership of 520,000. The most recent figures available for East Malaysia in 1969 show 400 registered societies in 1966 with a total membership of about 30,000.

CONSUMER, TRANSPORTATION, AND COMMUNICATION SERVICES

Consumer Services

The role of consumer services in the economy, including electricity, water, and sanitary services, rose steadily during the 1960's, from 3.8 percent of the gross domestic product in 1961 to about 7 percent by the late 1960's. The First Malaysia Plan allocated about M$807 million (3.06 Malaysian dollars equal US$1) for the development of these three services. Major development has been in West Malaysia.

In 1967 about 91 percent of the electric power in West Malaysia was supplied by government enterprises; the remainder was supplied by public firms selling to the public or producing power for their own consumption. The National Electricity Board was the largest public enterprise and supplied about 71 percent of West Malaysia's power needs (see ch. 19, Industry).

By the late 1960's there were over 200 water systems in West Malaysia, with a total rated capacity of just under 220 million gallons per day. Average daily service provided 161 million gallons for about 4.5 million people. About 30 systems provided a daily consumption in East Malaysia estimated at over 12 million gallons. Water is obtained from wells, boreholes, watersheds, and rivers. In some cases the water is used untreated, but it is often submitted to chemical coagulation, sedimentation, rapid gravity or pressure filtration, or chlorination. Water rates are not uniform throughout the country.

The more recently constructed systems and those systems recently expanded have sufficient surplus capacities to handle growing needs for some years to come. Some of the older supply systems, particularly in rapidly expanding areas like Kuala Lumpur and Penang, are rapidly reaching their rated full-utilization levels. Under the First Malaysia Plan M$202 million was allocated for the development of the water supply system; about 75 percent was scheduled for West Malaysia, and about 78 percent was scheduled for urban areas throughout the country.

Water Transport

Before the development of modern transportation, waterways were the country's principal means of communication and distribution. The rivers and tributaries penetrating the interior of the country provided a vital link between inland villages and the coast and were a major focus for commercial activity. Inland waterways are now of only marginal importance in West Malaysia, but they remain a major transport artery in East Malaysia.

Coastal trade is carried on by craft that vary widely in size and utilization of modern technology. The number of small craft engaged in coastal trade has been on the decrease since 1964. Figures were unavailable for East Malaysia, but in 1968 the number of coastal trade craft under 75 net registered tons that cleared West Malaysian ports was about 401,000, a decline of about 36 percent over the 1964 figures; the average small craft weight was just under 1 ton. About 3,200 coastal trade vessels over 75 net registered tons, with a total of 880,000 net registered tons, cleared West Malaysian ports in the same year.

Under the First Malaysia Plan M$113.7 million was allocated for port development; of this amount, 71.1 percent was for West Malaysia, 6.4 percent for Sabah, and 22.5 percent for Sarawak. Dredging and other improvements at minor ports represented 7.4 percent of the allocation for West Malaysia. The major expenditures were M$57 million for the Butterworth expansion program and M$4 million for construction at Port Swettenham, most of which was designated for berth facilities for deepwater vessels and storage facility construction (see ch. 22, Foreign Economic Relations).

Rail Transport

The railroad network in West Malaysia in 1969 totaled about 1,300 miles of single, meter-gauge track. It comprised a 488-mile west coast line, a 327-mile east coast line, and branch lines servicing port and urban areas. Both coastal lines connect with the Thailand State Railroad at the northern border, providing international passenger service connections, and merge in the south in a joint line to Singapore.

About 40 percent of the main line and switching locomotives in the late 1960's were diesel, and the remaining steam locomotives were all oil-fired. The rolling stock consisted of about 400 passenger coaches, including first- and second-class buffet cars, sleepers and day coaches, and about 6,600 freight cars. Workshop facilities were equipped to undertake heavy repairs on all equipment and to build new passenger and freight cars.

Between 1961 and 1967 the number of ton-miles handled increased 42 percent to about 658 million ton-miles and reflected a lengthening of the average haul. The total volume of goods showed no significant increase at the end of the 1960's over tonnage in 1961. Although the traffic of most goods increased during this period at about 10 percent annually, it was countered by a decrease in iron ore shipments. Two-thirds of the total tonnage consisted of six basic items: petroleum, cement, iron ore, timber, rubber, and rice. The total volume of passengers provided service declined between 1958 and 1968 by about 14 percent. The 348 million passenger-miles provided in 1968 also represented a decrease of 5 percent over 1958, counterbalanced by an increase in the average length of passenger trips.

The Malayan Railroad is a corporation within the Ministry of Transport and is administered on a commercial basis. Investment was highest during the 1960–65 period but, because of the level of development and awaiting the outcome of a general transport survey, investment under the First Malaysia Plan was reduced. Low operating efficiency and competition from road transport has resulted in a financial deficit, which between 1962 and 1968 had grown to a total equal to the M$20 million investment scheduled under the First Malaysia Plan. Plans for additional purchases of diesel locomotives and rolling stock were scheduled for the 1970–72 period.

The only railroad line in East Malaysia is in Sabah, running from

Beaufort to Kota Kinabalu. It is the only means of land transport through the Crocker Range. In 1967 the line carried 75 million tons 3.1 million freight-ton miles and provided service for 13,650 passengers. Stone and gravel were the major freight items, and the average haul was short.

Road Transport

The government estimated that in the late 1960's there were about 10,000 miles of roads in West Malaysia. About 3,000 miles were under federal jurisdiction, about 6,400 miles were under state jurisdiction, and the remaining mileage was under municipal jurisdiction. About 80 percent of all roads had bituminous surfaces. About one-fourth of the road network had been constructed between 1960 and 1965. Recent figures for East Malaysia were not available at the end of 1969. In the middle 1960's Sabah had a road network of about 1,300 miles, and Sarawak had a network of about 660 miles. Both areas were scheduled for road development by the late 1960's that would have increased their totals by about 65 percent.

Under the First Malaysia Plan, 8.6 percent of the total budget was allocated to road construction, with M$255 million budgeted for West Malaysia and M$134 million budgeted for East Malaysia. This was a reduction of nearly 40 percent over the 1960–65 period. Major development goals in West Malaysia were the improvement of existing federal roads, urban development, particularly in Kuala Lumpur, and new projects as required for the Federal Land Development Authority and other land settlement schemes (see ch. 18 Agriculture). Major goals in East Malaysia were the improvement of existing roads and major road construction, with heavy emphasis placed on proposals for a road system through the Crocker mountain range in Sabah.

The major problems encountered in road development during the 1960's were the lack of data on traffic patterns and growth needs, the lack of planning and coordination, divergent federal and state standards and specifications, and land acquisition difficulties. Road development in West Malaysia by the late 1960's met the basic needs of the economy. Heavy investment was still needed in East Malaysia, but the projected public investment in road construction for the country for the 1970's remained below the relative levels of the 1960–65 period.

The country has a relatively high ratio of motor vehicles (half of which are motorcycles)—50 per 1,000 people—and a marked annual increase in vehicle registration. Between 1960 and 1967 the number of cars and motorcycles increased respectively, 10 and 16½ percent annually, or about 1½ times as fast as the annual increase in the country's gross national product. The rates were higher in East Malaysia; the number of private cars, for example, increased annually 38 percent in Sabah and 19 percent in Sarawak. By mid-1969 there were about 561,800 officially registered motor vehicles in West Malaysia, including about 286,500 motorcycles, 200,000 private cars, 4,800 buses, 5,670 taxis, 48,900 trucks, and 15,930 miscellaneous vehicles.

In 1969 bus facilities were experiencing financial difficulties. By the late 1960's in West Malaysia there were over 800 bus routes and over 365 million passengers were carried annually. Tax problems and employment laws created rates that faced competition from taxicabs on long-distance runs. Even MARA, which has become the largest bus operator in the country, has encountered financial problems (see ch. 18, Agriculture).

Air Transport

Air transport in the country is provided by the Malaysia-Singapore Airlines (MSA), owned jointly by the governments of Brunei, Malaysia, and Singapore. The major cities of West Malaysia and many towns and administrative centers of East Malaysia are well linked by domestic and international connections. The capital is served by the Subang International Airport. Between 1960 and 1967 passenger-miles increased annually by 20 percent. In West Malaysia in 1968 there were 36,222 aircraft landings, 582,101 passenger embarkations and debarkations, 3,703 tons of cargo, and 1,103 tons of mail. Passenger embarkations and debarkations in East Malaysia in 1967, the latest date for comparable figures, was 339,535 in Sabah and 243,519 in Sarawak.

MSA has a record of efficient operation and balanced investments in runways, terminals, and telecommunication equipment. Net profits during the late 1960's averaged M$3 million annually. The shift to jets for major runs in 1969 resulted in a heavy need for investment in all-weather and night traffic control equipment and for the training of personnel qualified to handle the equipment. The M$21.5 million originally allocated under the First Malaysia Plan was increased to M$62.7 million, and annual revenue is expected to be adequate to meet all additional debt service requirements for the expansion, as well as to create additional reserves.

Communication Services

The country's postal service provides a great diversity of services, including the processing and delivery of mail, the payment of pensions and military dependents' allotments, the sale of certain communication licenses, the collection of certain utility service payments, the processing of postal money orders, and the maintenance of postal savings facilities. There is some overlapping of the different services provided by the post offices, mobile units, and postal agencies. Private agencies are frequently used to aid the extension of postal services in rural areas.

The most recent figures available for the late 1960's showed a total of 289 post office and 650 postal agencies, of which 79 percent and 83 percent, respectively, were in West Malaysia. Both parts of the country were using mobile postal units. Recent figures for total mail volume for the country were unavailable. Figures for postal savings at the beginning of 1969 showed 1.5 million depositors and total deposits of about M$240 million.

The country's telecommunication network includes telephone, telegraph, and telprint service and plays an ever-growing role in the commercial activity of the country. Advances made in the network during the 1960's stimulated both the efficiency and competitiveness of Malaysian commercial enterprise. The telephone service brought the largest revenues of all the telecommunication sectors in the late 1960's, yielding over M$50 million annually. There were over 120,000 telephones in service, and 87 percent of all the telephone exchanges were automatic. New equipment was being used throughout the country, and replaced equipment was being relocated in areas having more obsolete equipment or was used for temporary expansion purposes. Expansion of the country's microwave system was also being undertaken.

A major step was taken to link the country with international circuits in 1965 with the inauguration of the Southeast Asia Commonwealth cable (SEACOM), linking West Malaysia, Singapore, Kota Kinabalu, and Hong Kong. The extension of the cable to Guam in 1966 linked the country to the Japan-American Trans Pacific Cable and provided international circuits to Japan, the United States, and the United Kingdom.

In 1966 the country also joined the International Telecommunication Satellite Corporation (INTELSAT). Contracts were signed in 1969 for the construction of a M$6.6 million satellite ground communication station at Kuantan by a Japanese firm. The 97-foot-diameter dish antenna was scheduled to facilitate black and white and color television transmission as well as other telecommunication services. It also would link the country with countries not under SEACOM, particularly the Indian subcontinent.

In 1966 a new telecommunication training center was completed under the cooperation of the International Telecommunication Union (ITU) under the United Nations Development Programme. This center and the new broadcasting communication center, Angkasapuri, scheduled for final completion in 1970, have brought the country some of the most advanced traning and operating facilities in Southeast Asia.

DOMESTIC TRADE AND SOCIETY

The role played by commercial activity in society is complex and is only partly open to ready observation. Unofficial and informal groups, family and ethnic loyalties, traditional belief and obligation systems, regional variations, and the dual structure of the economy add to the usual difficulty encountered in identifying noneconomic factors associated with domestic trade.

Commercial activity provides a major channel for the flow and development of a modern national culture and its associated artifacts and symbols. The market plays a major role in rural and a supporting role in urban social communication. It is still affected by traditional cultural beliefs, and the intensity, range, and outcome of bargaining is affected by the relationship between the buyer and seller.

Except in small-scale rural marketing, Malays have traditionally not entered commerce. Various European and nonindigenous Asian ethnic groups have come to dominate commercial activity. The wholesale distribution of imported goods is controlled almost exclusively by Western or Chinese firms. Many of the Chinese firms are small and tied through credit arrangements to Western companies. The collection and initial processing of produce and primary goods, as well as most middlemen operations, are in the hands of Chinese. Indian merchants are found mainly in urban areas and deal with textiles, sewing machines, and dairy products (see ch. 11, Social Values; ch. 5, Social Structure).

The dialect and kinship groups of Chinese origin play an important role in commercial activity. In urban areas members of one group will trade with another member of the same group rather than with an outsider. In rural areas the producer and the merchant tend to be of the same dialect and kinship group.

TOURISM

Considerable interest was evidenced in the late 1960's in expanding the already growing role of tourism in the economy. By 1968 foreign exchange earnings had attained an increase of about 2.8 times that of 1965 earnings. The number of tourists declined between 1963 and 1965 but by 1966 had risen above previous levels. Figures showed

484

46,000 tourists in West Malaysia in 1966, as compared with 23,000 in 1965.

Tourism is the concern of the Department of Tourism under the Ministry of Commerce and Industry. The department is engaged in a wide variety of publications and programs. It has put out over 70 different types of publications, including press releases, brochures, calendars, and posters. It places advertisements in selected consumer magazines, trade journals, and travel supplements in the United States, Australia, Europe, and the North Pacific. Information centers are also provided.

In addition to information services, the department has sought special ways to encourage tourist trade in the country. It declared 1967 as the International Tourist Year and sponsored a series of exhibits, advertisements, and articles abroad. Car rental facilities became available for the first time also in 1967, as a result of government encouragement. In addition to providing special cultural centers and sponsoring cultural performances, the government has also set up training programs for tourist services. License fees and road taxes for tourist buses have been reduced, and special visa arrangements exist for short stays and in-transit stops by nationals of all the Commonwealth countries, the United States, and 15 other countries.

Programs have been restricted by financial limitations and have had to deal with inadequate domestic tourist infrastructure and international competition. Tourist accommodations outside Kuala Lumpur and Penang are scarce and, despite the advanced facilities at the Subang International Airport, much of the tourist trade was being diverted to Singapore in 1969. The government has initiated a special study to suggest coordinated public and private programs for the expansion of tourist facilities.

The department has encouraged the formation of tourist associations. By 1968 there were nine major tourist associations in the country. Tourist service groups representing all regions of the country met for the first time in 1968 to form the Federation of Malaysia Tourist Associations.

TRADE ASSOCIATIONS

A variety of trade groups and associations exists in the country. It includes chambers of commerce, trade associations, and unofficial groups. Such groups usually are regionally oriented and may be composed of local subgroups. In the late 1960's there were 16 officially registered chambers of commerce in the country. Among the nine in West Malaysia were included the Chinese Chambers of Commerce, the

Associated Indian Chambers of Commerce, and the Associated Malay Chambers of Commerce. Three chambers of commerce were listed in Sabah, two of which were Chinese organizations; four groups were listed for Sarawak, two of which were Chinese groups and one of which was Indian.

Figures for West Malaysia listed 12 industrial and trade associations. The major interests of these groups were timber, mining, rubber, and agricultural products. Figures were unavailable for East Malaysia.

In addition to the officially listed associations, there are unofficial, quasi-cultural groups among the Chinese and Indians, frequently formed on the basis of language or clan, that represent commercial interests on the local level. These groups usually restrict their activities to local issues and focus on a particular group interest in a community market. They represent credit and capital sources and work on the basis of trust and honor rather than legal contract (see ch. 5, Social Structure).

THE ROLE OF THE GOVERNMENT

Although government policy since independence has left commercial activity largely in the hands of private enterprise, the role of the government in commerce is important and has increased substantially since 1966 under the First Malaysia Plan. In addition to the policy of Malaysianization, major areas of government activity have been the expansion of credit, marketing, and service facilities under various development schemes; the operation of public transport and communication services; the operation of license controls and regulatory mechanisms; and national economic integration (see ch. 18, Agriculture).

The government's Malaysianization policy relies on both the use of entry permits, introduced in 1968 for those gainfully employed in certain categories of trade and commerce, and the training of Malaysians to replace technically skilled foreign labor. Responsibility for policy implementation falls under the Standing Committee for the Malaysianization of Commerce and Industry, composed of cabinet-level officers. This committee is under the chairmanship of the deputy prime minister (see ch. 20, Labor).

The government role in the transport system is coordinated under the minister of transport by virtue of the powers conferred on him by various regulatory acts. Air and railroad services are provided by public companies, as is a major percentage of bus service in the country. Road transport is controlled through various licensing processes but is in private hands. A standing committee was set up in 1967 to make recommendations for the establishment of a national shipping line, the nucleus of which would be two 10,000-ton freighters provided under a good-will agreement with Japan. There was no information available at the end of 1969 to confirm the establishment or progress of this project.

In addition to the provision of special facilities under general, national, or specific regional schemes, the interest of the government in the trading community includes the control of trading licenses and the encouragement of fair trading practices. Funds may be channeled into improvements in local markets or used for the construction of shops and open-stall facilities in urban areas. Typical of the latter plan is the M$600,000 trade complex with 72 shop units and open-market facilities announced in 1969 for construction in Kuala Lumpur.

Shopkeepers were required during the 1960's to place price tags on only four essential food items—rice, sugar, flour, and cooking oil. Overcharges and special discounts prompted the government in 1969 to warn that, unless shopkeepers priced all goods on a voluntary basis, pricing regulations might have to be implemented. Government concern has also been expressed over fair weights and measures.

CHAPTER 22

FOREIGN ECONOMIC RELATIONS

On the eve of 1970 Malaysia was in process of remodeling its historical pattern of trade and trading relations. The country had traditionally been dependent upon the export of two major raw materials, rubber and tin, for the foreign reserves required for the import of needed consumer and capital goods. Although rubber and tin were essential commodities in an industrializing world, they faced frequently fluctuating prices because of changes in world demand and the availability of substitutes, whereas the prices of manufactured imports changed only slowly. Because of this disparate behavior of export and import prices, the terms of trade were of great importance to the well-being of the economy.

A major objective of the First Malaysia Plan for 1966 to 1970 was an alleviation of this adverse situation. Government activities were directed toward the achievement of this goal by programs encouraging the diversification of natural resources exports and by investment policies encouraging an inflow of foreign capital and the establishment of industries with import substitution and export potential. Although 1968 was the last year for which comprehensive information was available, early fragmentary information for 1969 made public in September of that year indicated that exports had reached an all-time peak. All factors relating to the balance of trade and payments were reported as encouraging, and prospects for 1970 were described as good.

Traditional trading relations were also undergoing change. The separation of Singapore in 1965 had loosened ties with this close neighbor, and the removal of Commonwealth trade preferences in 1967 held potential for further changes in trading patterns in the future. At the same time closer trading relations were being established with countries of Western Europe and Eastern Europe, including the Soviet Union. Internally, the harmonizing of customs duties of West Malaysia, Sabah, and Sarawak was welding the country into a unit in international trade.

THE ROLE OF GOVERNMENT

The government has played an important role in foreign economic relations through measures taken to attract foreign investment and

489

aid as well as promotion and regulation of foreign trade. The government also has been active through membership and participation in international organizations bearing on the conduct of trade. Almost all activities relating to foreign economic relations are under the direction of the appropriate divisions of the Ministry of Commerce and Industry. Among the relevant divisions the most important were the Export Commodities Division, the Trade Division, and the Import and Export Control Office. In mid-1969 activities of the government increased in vigor and scope, and the government prepared to take an active rather than a passive role in determining foreign economic relations.

To attract foreign industrial investment, in competition with other countries of Southeast Asia that were pursuing an active industrialization policy, tax incentives were offered to foreign investors for the establishment of desired industries. Those industries with export potential or those that qualified as import substitutes were given priority, and in 1969 incentives were expanded to cover domestic as well as foreign entrepreneurs (see ch. 19, Industry). The Contact Center for Investors was established to assist in identifying desirable projects, and in mid-1969 the Capital Investment Committee was organized to conduct promotion drives to increase industrial investment.

Under the auspices of the Export Commodities Division of the Ministry of Commerce and Industry, the government established committees and boards to take an active role in all economic aspects of major exports or potential export commodities. The fields covered by such boards included commodity research and development, establishment of product standards, and conditions of production, manufacturing, and marketing.

To promote trade throughout the world in 1966 the government initiated the establishment of trade missions attached to overseas diplomatic missions. The first trade commissioners chosen were assigned to posts in Tokyo, New York, Stockholm, Sydney, Bonn, and Geneva. Participation in trade fairs and exhibits and the dispatch of special trade missions to foreign countries were also important methods of trade promotion. The conduct of these activities was the responsibility of the Trade Division of the Ministry of Commerce and Industry, and the trade commissioners attached to overseas diplomatic missions were officers of the ministry.

Of importance to the direction of trade were the reception of country trade missions and the foreign trade fairs and exhibits that were held in Malaysia. As an indication of the interest in increasing trade with Malaysia and rectifying a generally unfavorable trade balance, the Soviet Union held a trade fair in Kuala Lumpur from September 23 to October 12, 1969. The fair covered a wide range of products and attracted visitors from neighboring countries. Malaysia signed a contract for the delivery of a sizable order of fabrics and cotton textiles in 1970, which was in accord with the usual trade pattern between the two countries. Bulgaria also held an exhibit of machinery in Kuala Lumpur from October 26 to November 2, 1969. The exhibit included metalworking machinery, materials-handling equipment, tractors and other agricultural machines, and electric motors and equipment.

In addition, other trade promotions held in Kuala Lumpur toward the end of 1969 included a "British Engineering Week," two Australian exhibits of technical equipment and hospital equipment, exhibits of food and consumer products by Italy, France, Australia, and Denmark, and an exhibition by the United States featuring electronic scientific equipment held in September. Private Malaysian firms and government departments also visited a showing of cargo handling equipment, data processing equipment, and furniture equipment at the United States Trade Center in Bangkok.

The Trade Division of the Ministry of Commerce and Industry represented Malaysia at meetings of the General Agreement on Tariffs and Trade, the United Nations Commission on Trade and Development, the Economic Commission for Asia and the Far East, and the Commonwealth trade officials. The country also participated in conferences of the International Rubber Study Group and the International Tin Council.

FOREIGN TRADE

According to preliminary estimates in 1968 total foreign trade reached almost M$7.7 billion (3.06 Malaysian dollars equal US$1), a peak for the 9-year period from 1960 to 1968, during which trade rose from M$6.4 billion, an increase of slightly more than 19 percent. Except in 1961 and 1967, total trade value increased each year, although at highly varying rates, ranging from less than 1 percent in 1964 to 8.7 percent in 1968. Despite the wide fluctuations in annual growth rates, a surplus on trade account was maintained, and exports exceeded imports in value each year.

Detailed information concerning the share of West Malaysia, Sabah, and Sarawak in the value of total trade was not available in late 1969. According to estimates in 1965, however, West Malaysia accounted for almost 80 percent of trade value at that time, and the balance of trade was consistently favorable. Preliminary 1969 estimates indicated that West Malaysia had achieved an all-time record trade surplus of M$870.2 million during the first 8 months of the year.

According to the most reliable information available concerning Sarawak, imports had exceeded exports in value from 1960 to 1968 in each year except 1960, 1962, and 1968. The trade surplus of M$29.5 million in 1968, however, was well below the surplus in 1960, which was M$43.4 million. Detailed information on the foreign trade of Sabah after 1964 was not available, and during the period from 1960 to 1964 the state enjoyed a trade surplus in 1960 and 1961 and a deficit from 1962 to 1964.

Background and Organization of Trade

The geographic location of the Malay Peninsula was responsible for an early, although secondary, involvement in world trade. Because of its strategic position on an important trading route, the Peninsula attracted the attention of traders and was the focus of migrations, mainly from India, of peoples seeking commodities useful in their own countries or those that might be traded with other countries. The Peninsula was a good way station on trade routes, and control of the Strait of Malacca was considered of political as well as economic importance to empires that later were formed in Southeast Asia.

The founding of Malacca in the early 15th century was a step in expanding the role of commerce on the Malay Peninsula. The advent of Europeans in the 16th century—Portuguese, Dutch, and British— added to the trading groups and the commercial competition in the area (see ch. 3, Historical Setting).

Developments in the Western world in the 17th and 18th centuries determined the course of political and commercial events in Southeast Asia. Concomitant features of the burgeoning European industrial revolution were the need for additional sources of raw materials for increasing industrial production and expanded markets for finished products. Furthermore, the growing population and increased incomes added to the demand for consumer goods, which, in part, had long been supplied by Eastern countries. These circumstances focused the attention of Europe on the potential of Southeast Asia and enhanced the political and commercial rivalry of competing European nations. Replacement of sailing ships by steam-powered vessels requiring the establishment of fueling stations in ports along trade routes was another step linking Western commercial nations and enterprises with Southeast Asia.

Stable domestic governments in Asia and an understanding among European nations were essential to an uninterrupted flow of raw materials and the use of ports as transfer points for goods. To this end, Southeast Asia was divided into spheres of influence by the

Europeans. The Malay Peninsula ultimately came under British administration, which continued until 1957. British precedent was largely responsible for the establishment of free trade policies that were just being modified in the late 1960's.

Worldwide increase in demand for industrial materials and Western technology changed the pattern of production for export and left its mark on marketing methods in the Malayan area. Tin had long been produced for export in modest quantities by methods requiring only moderate investment. Production was mainly in the hands of the Chinese. In the early 20th century, however, new and more productive methods of extraction using the tin dredge were introduced. The new methods required higher capital investment and technological skill and were responsible for the entrance of large European firms into the productions and marketing fields (see ch. 19, Industry).

Rubber, which became the major export commodity, was brought into cultivation during the last quarter of the 19th century. In the beginning cultivation was conducted in conjunction with other commodities, mostly coffee, on estates owned by Western firms. With the advent of the automobile age in the early 20th century, the demand for tires increased the importance of rubber in world trade and brought about changes in the size of enterprises, the amount of capital required, the character of enterpreneurs, and marketing methods in Malaya.

New enterprises were estates of larger size than those established earlier. Many were publicly owned companies representing European, predominantly British, capital and managed by merchant agency houses established in Singapore. Agency houses, because of their experience and knowledge in the field of world trade and because of their capital resources, were able to provide integrated services of management, commodity marketing, shipping arrangements, insurance of cargo, and financing. Estates were also established by a few major rubber manufacturing concerns, and Chinese capitalists also organized rubber enterprises.

Not all rubber was produced on large estates; some was produced on small holdings and, in addition to European and Chinese, the Malays and Indians had some participation in ownership. The most recent information available on the ownership indicated that in 1962 European-owned estates accounted for 21 percent of the total number but 60 percent of total planted acres; the remaining estates were in the hands of Asians of varied origins, which other sources indicated were mainly Chinese. From 1958 to 1964 there was a trend toward reduction in the number of large European companies owning plantations producing rubber for export. During the period about 100 companies were absorbed by 27 existing concerns registered in the

United Kingdom. At the same time a large number of firms based in the United Kingdom were liquidated, and their estates were subdivided and sold to local buyers.

Other commodities that achieved significance in export trade were produced in different ways by a variety of ethnic groups. Palm oil was produced on estates mostly owned by European firms. The Chinese were prominent in investment and production of other commodities. The Malays enjoyed the greatest participation in the rubber industry.

Export of commodities produced by large estates and import of their requirements mostly have been carried on by the agency houses that manage them, and no intermediaries have been necessary. Large British trading firms that were active in Southeast Asia as early as 1828 were still active in the late 1960's and offered comprehensive services, including marketing, shipping, insurance, and estate management. Rubber, palm oil, and coconut products were exported through these channels and, in those instances where the estates were not managed by an agency house, an international trading firm took over the complete process, collecting export commodities from the estate and delivering imports. Export requirements of tin and iron mines were met without the use of intermediaries except in small degree. Rubber manufacturing firms with extensive estates managed their own exporting and importing and provided relevant services.

International trading agencies maintained correspondents throughout the world and locally served as manufacturers' agents for highly diverse products. Some foreign manufacturers of heavy machinery and engineering products maintained local branches to service their own products.

Collecting the export commodities of small-scale producers and distributing the import needs of small consumers assumed a different pattern that required the use of intermediaries in a complex trading structure (see ch. 21, Domestic Trade). Although most trade ultimately was centered in European-owned trading agencies, Chinese trading agencies also participated.

In the 19th century Singapore, a free port under British administration, became a focal point for East-West commerce. Cargo from the West was unloaded, divided, and reshipped to the Malay states and other countries. Commodities were also collected from the area, graded, packaged, and exported to Western countries. Singapore continued to play a role as an entrepôt, although after independence Malaysian ports increased in importance, and a larger share of trade was carried on directly with foreign countries. From 1958 to 1967 the share of both exports and imports from the Malay Peninsula passing through Singapore declined. In 1958 about 40 percent of such imports were from or via Singapore; in 1967 the share had dropped to 32 percent. Exports to or via Singapore dropped from 34 percent in 1958 to 29 percent of the total in 1967.

The principal ports of West Malaysia are Penang, on an island off the west coast; Butterworth, directly across from Penang on the mainland; and Port Swettenham, which is the port serving Kuala Lumpur, the capital, and in 1969 was the major port for rubber exports. Other ports are Malacca on the west coast and Dungan on the east coast; in 1969 Dungan was the major port for the export of iron ore. In East Malaysia, Sabah has two major ports, Sandakan, the shipping center for the timber industry, and Kota Kinabula, the capital. Principal ports of Sarawak are Kuching and Sibu. Labuan Island is a transshipment point for the Brunei Bay area. Expansion and improvement of port facilities was a goal of the First Malaysian Plan for 1966 to 1970.

There were five separate customs areas in 1969—West Malaysia, Sabah, Sarawak, Penang, and Labuan. Penang and Labuan were free ports. In March 1969 a limited single customs area for the whole country, excluding the free ports, was created. All commodities produced domestically, with the exception of a few categories produced in Sabah and Sarawak, were thereby permitted to move duty free among the three states. The minister of finance was given the authority to levy common customs duties on goods imported into any part of the country and to extend to Penang and Labuan any regulations considered necessary. In 1967 a start was made on the implementation of the act, and the minister of finance issued an order to bring about 60 percent of all items listed in the Malaysian Trade Classification and Customs Tariff under a common import tariff. In 1968, however, complete unification had not been achieved, and the work of harmonization was continued in 1969. Some internal tariff and trade restrictions still existed. In August 1969 it was reported that Penang had lost 90 percent of its free trade status and that new duties imposed would be further limiting.

Import duties in 1968 were imposed according to value and, in some instances, according to units. Almost all imports were subject to a surtax of 2 percent on the total cost, insurance, and freight. Commonwealth preferences had been removed from a number of imports. On January 1, 1969, the country adopted the Brussels Tariff Nomenclature, which was used by about 70 percent of all countries in international trade as a basis for classifying commodities. The new system replaced the Standard International Trade Classification, which had been in use since 1960.

Composition of Trade

According to preliminary estimates the value of gross exports in 1968 was M$4,113 million, an increase of slightly more than 10 percent over the 1967 value, which was M$3,723.7 million. In contrast, export value had declined about 3.2 percent from 1966 to 1967.

Almost all exports were raw materials, some of which had had a minimum of processing. Major export commodities, which consisted of rubber, tin, saw logs, sawn timber, palm oil, and iron ore, accounted for 75.7 percent of total value in 1968 (see table 23). Of lesser importance, but vital to the foreign trade of the country, were exports of coconut oil, copra, palm kernels, bauxite, pepper, and canned pineapples.

In volume exported, rubber, tin, saw logs, sawn timber, and palm oil increased from 1967 to 1968. Rubber and tin, which were the two most valuable exports of long standing and accounted for 53 percent of total export value, declined in unit value in 1968, while saw logs and sawn timber increased. The value per long ton of palm oil, of which Malaysia was the world's largest exporter, exhibited a downward trend from 1964 and dropped precipitously from M$624 per long ton in 1967 to M$424 in 1968. In every year except 1967, however, the increase in export volume more than compensated for the fall in price. Iron ore exports declined in volume from 6.3 million long tons in 1964 to 5.1 million long tons in 1968, mostly because of approaching exhaustion of the mines. Furthermore, the price fell from M$25.7 per long ton in 1964 to M$21.7 in 1968.

The contribution of minor commodities to total export value increased slightly in both absolute and relative terms, rising from M$111.2 million, or 3.3 percent of total value, in 1964 to M$161.8 million, or 3.9 percent of the total, in 1968. Over the period the performance of individual commodities was mixed. Coconut oil was the only commodity that increased in both volume exported and unit value, and total value more than doubled from 1964 to 1968. The unit value of palm kernels and of canned pineapple declined, but the volume exported increased sufficiently to overcome the price drop, and the total value of exports increased significantly in each instance. Although the volume of pepper increased, the price drop depressed total value. Copra and bauxite declined in both volume exported and price per ton. From 1967 to 1968, however, there was an upward turn in total value of each of the minor export commodities except bauxite and pepper.

Table 23. Gross Exports of Major Commodities of Malaysia, 1964–68 [1]

	1964		1965		1966		1967		1968 [2]	
	Volume [3]	Value [4]	Volume [3]	Value [4]	Volume [3]	Value [4]	Volume [3]	Value [4]	Volume [3]	Value [4]
Rubber ----------	913.6	1,395.8	950.7	1,461.8	997.1	1,473.9	1,026.7	1,274.6	1,152.6	1,353.2
Tin --------------	71.7	728.3	73.9	871.8	72.4	792.0	˙74.4	755.5	86.8	828.9
Saw logs --------	2,828.6	203.9	3,321.2	262.3	4,536.4	384.8	5,037.0	475.8	5,819.5	549.6
Sawn timber ----	499.4	90.5	521.0	95.4	496.3	81.5	606.0	107.0	784.2	149.3
Palm oil --------	124.1	81.1	140.9	107.3	181.7	120.1	185.9	116.0	281.1	124.4
Iron ore --------	6,317.0	162.5	6,634.2	161.3	5,680.7	136.2	5,245.9	122.1	5,086.8	110.2
TOTAL ---		2,662.1		2,959.9		2,988.5		2,851.0		3,115.6

[1] Fiscal year and calendar year begin January 1.
[2] Preliminary.
[3] In thousands of long tons.
[4] In millions of Malaysian dollars; M$3.06 equal US$1.

Source: Adapted from Bank Negra Malaysia Quarterly Economic Bulletin, December 1968, pp. 64–65.

The most important export commodities of Sabah were round logs, sawn timber, rubber, copra, hemp, and tobacco. Sarawak exported petroleum, rubber, timber, pepper, bauxite, and sago flour. Both states enjoyed the upsurge in timber exports in the late 1960's. West Malaysia was the source of almost all the manufactured goods exported, which included food products, beverages and tobacco, chemicals and chemical products, wood products, cotton fabrics, cement, rubber products, clothing, iron and steel products, footwear, and miscellaneous commodities. With the exception of beverages and tobacco and rubber products, all categories of manufactured goods manifested an upward trend in export value from 1964 to 1968. The contribution to the total, however, was relatively small, and it was considered highly desirable to increase manufactured exports to help alleviate the dependence upon rubber and tin.

Imports

In 1968 the gross value of imports, which included imports for processing and reexporting was M$3.5 billion, in contrast to M$3.2 billion in 1964 (see table 24). Although the value of imports increased about 11 percent from 1964 to 1968, growth did not keep pace with the growth of export value, which was 17 percent during the same period, thus leaving a comfortable trade margin.

In general, the importation of commodities was in response to consumer needs and the needs of export enterprises. In share of the total in 1968, the most important categories, in order of rank, were food, beverages, and tobacco; manufactured goods; machinery and transport equipment; and mineral fuels. Food, beverages and tobacco imports declined in absolute value and in share of the total from 1964 to 1968. All other commodity classifications increased in value during the 5-year period. The most significant changes in share were the increase in value of machinery and transport equipment, which accounted for 22.4 percent of import value in 1968 in contrast to 19.7 percent in 1964, and the share of mineral fuel, which rose from 11.4 percent of the total in 1964 to 14.1 percent in 1968. The most important component of the inedible crude materials category was tin ore, imported for smelting and reexporting, which made up about 51 percent of the value of the category and increased sharply from 1967 to 1968.

Direction of Trade

As a source of supply of scarce industrial raw materials and a user of manufactured and processed goods for consumption and investment, Malaysia carried on trade with countries all over the

Table 24. Gross Imports of Malaysia, by Commodity Classification, 1964–68 [1]

	1964		1965		1966		1967		1968 [2]	
	Value [3]	Percent	Value [3]	Percent	Value [3]	Percent	Value [3]	Percent	Value [3]	Percent
Food, beverages, and tobacco ---	950	29.7	873	26.0	839	24.8	852	25.6	841	23.7
Inedible crude materials ---	241	7.5	238	7.1	164	4.8	166	5.0	286	8.1
Mineral fuels ---	365	11.4	388	11.6	437	12.9	447	13.4	500	14.1
Chemicals ---	201	6.3	234	7.0	252	7.5	248	7.5	238	6.7
Manufactured goods ---	736	22.9	804	23.9	797	23.6	786	23.6	800	22.5
Machinery and transport equipment ---	631	19.7	729	21.7	800	23.7	736	22.1	793	22.4
Other imports ---	81	2.5	90	2.7	91	2.7	90	2.8	90	2.5
TOTAL ---	3,205	100.0	3,356	100.0	3,380	100.0	3,325	100.0	3,548	100.0

[1] Fiscal year and calendar year begin January 1.

[2] Preliminary.

[3] In millions of Malaysian dollars; M$3.06 equal US$1.

Source: Adapted from Bank Negara Malaysia Annual Report and Statement of Accounts, 1968, Kuala Lumpur, p. 70.

world. The direction and share of trade was shaped in large part by political and economic affiliations, geographic location, and the state of industrialization of the areas.

Because of the longstanding political and economic affiliations with Great Britain and as a member of the Commonwealth group of countries that customarily extended tariff preferences to other members, trade with sterling area countries, which included Singapore, the United Kingdom, Hong Kong, India, Australia, and others, had achieved a high degree of importance. In 1968 the sterling countries ranked first among trading areas, accounting for 38.8 percent of total value. Late in 1966 Malaysia removed tariff preferences from a wide number of imports from Commonwealth countries, which could be expected to influence the direction of ensuing trade in some measure.

The Far Eastern Countries, including Japan, Thailand, the People's Republic of China (Communist China), and others, ranked second as a trading area in 1968, accounting for 29.2 percent of the total. Ranking third was the North American industrial area, made up of the United States and Canada, that accounted for 12.9 percent. The fourth most important area was Western Europe, which included the countries of the European Economic Community (European Common Market)—the Federal Republic of Germany (West Germany), France, Italy, Belgium, the Netherlands, and Luxembourg. This area accounted for 10.5 percent of the total. The share of the Soviet Union and countries of Eastern Europe was 4.1 percent of trade value, and the remaining 4.5 percent was distributed among other nations of the world.

Trading areas ranked in the same order in 1968 as in 1967. During the year, however, there was some redistribution in share of the total. Trade with the sterling area declined from 41.1 percent of the total in 1967 to 38.8 percent in 1968, while the share of the Far Eastern countries rose from 27.7 to 29.2 percent. Trade with the United States and Canada rose from 11.8 to 12.9 percent of total value. There was relatively little change in the share of trade with Western Europe, which was 10.7 percent in 1967 and 10.5 percent in 1968. The Soviet Union and countries of Eastern Europe accounted for a slightly larger share, rising from 3.9 to 4.1 percent of the total in 1969.

In 1968 the ten most valuable trading partners, in order of rank, were: Japan, Singapore, the United States, the United Kingdom, Australia, Communist China, the Federal Republic of Germany, Thailand, the Soviet Union, and Italy. The composition of the list in 1968 did not change from that in 1967, and there was only one shift in rank. The Federal Republic of Germany rose to seventh from eighth place, replacing Thailand. Other valuable trading partners in 1967 and 1968 were the Netherlands, Hong Kong, Canada, and France. In 1968 Malaysia enjoyed a favorable balance of trade with Japan, Singapore, the United States, the Soviet Union, Italy, the Netherlands, Canada, and France. The value of imports exceeded that of exports for the United Kingdom, the Federal Republic of Germany, Communist China, Australia, Thailand, and Hong Kong, and a trade deficit existed.

Japan

Because of the complementarity of the production systems by which vital industrial materials were exchanged for manufactured and semi-manufactured commodities, a lively trade, both export and import, was carried on with Japan in 1968. The value of exports, however, which was M$755.0 million, comfortably exceeded that of imports, which was M$483.4 million.

In 1968 Japan, with its rapidly growing industries, especially the iron and steel industry and the automotive and electronic industries, and its lack of natural resources, was the third most valuable destination for rubber and the second most valuable destination for tin. It was also the sole market for iron ore and a major market for bauxite for the production of aluminum and for saw logs for the rapidly growing plywood industry. In return, Japan was the source of a wide variety of manufactured commodities, both consumer goods and capital goods.

Singapore

Because of its geographic propinquity to the Malaysian states and its position as a major free port on trade routes between East and West, Singapore had long ranked as one of the most important trading partners. From 1965 to 1968 the value of exports exceeded that of imports.

Traditionally, Singapore was an important destination for rubber exports. In 1968, however, rubber exports to Singapore declined significantly because of direct purchases by Communist countries. Singapore was also a major destination for saw logs, palm oil, palm kernels, coconut oil, pepper, sago flour, and canned pineapple. As a source of imports, it was a distribution point for commodities from all over the world.

Other Countries

In both 1967 and 1968 the United States ranked in third place as a trading partner. The value of exports substantially exceeded that of imports, and in 1968 a trade surplus of M$415.8 million, or 48 percent of the total value of trade between the two countries, existed. Rubber and tin were the most valuable exports. In 1967 and 1968 the United States ranked second as a purchaser of rubber and first as a purchaser of tin.

The Soviet Union ranked first as a purchaser of Malaysian natural rubber in both 1967 and 1968 but contributed only an insignificant amount of imports. The United Kingdom and the Federal Republic of Germany were important as sources of machinery, machine tools, and manufactured goods. As markets for exports, both countries were important purchasers of rubber and tin. In addition, the United Kingdom was an important market for palm oil, palm kernels, coconut oil, canned pineapple, and pineapple juice. The Federal Republic of Germany was becoming an increasingly important market for palm kernels.

Australia provided a source of meat, meat preparations, and dairy products and a market for rubber, tin, and sawn timber. Communist China was an important source of rice imports and an increasingly important market for rubber. From 1967 to 1968 exports of rubber to Communist China rose from 88,525 long tons to 128,881 long tons, an increase of 45 percent. Rubber exports to the Eastern European countries also increased significantly during the year, partly in response to trade agreements recently signed.

Trade Agreements

In the late 1960's a number of agreements were entered into establishing closer trading relations with the countries of Eastern Europe. In 1968 trade agreements providing for most-favored-nation treatment concerning customs duties and the issuance of import and export licenses were signed with Bulgaria and Romania. In the previous year similar agreements had been signed with the Soviet Union and Yugoslavia, and trade representatives had been established in Moscow, Belgrade, and Kuala Lumpur.

Trade relations with members of the European Economic Community and other Western countries were mostly regulated by multilateral arrangements made through the General Agreement on Tariffs and Trade and the United Nations Commission on Trade and Development. Removal of Commonwealth preferences had loosened trade ties with Commonwealth countries and in 1969 no information was available indicating the establishment of new trade agreements, beyond the special agreements with Australia and New Zealand, which had been in force since 1966.

BALANCE OF PAYMENTS

According to the preliminary statistics that were available at the beginning of 1969, the balance of payments position in 1968 showed an impressive improvement over 1967. In 1968 the overall balance on international payments showed a deficit of M$27 million, in sharp contrast to a deficit of M$247 million in 1967. Except in 1965, when there was a welcome surplus of M$134 million, a deficit had existed in each year from 1964 to 1968 (see table 25).

Improvement in the international payments balance was attributable in large measure to the increased surplus on merchandise account. In 1968 the net value of exports, adjusted for balance of payments purposes to exclude reexports, was M$4,044 million. The value of imports, excluding freight and insurance, was M$3,364 million, leaving a surplus of receipts over payments of M$680 million. This was the largest surplus recorded since 1960, when the unadjusted trade balance was M$846.4 million.

Table 25. *Balance of Payments of Malaysia, 1964–68* [1]
(in millions of Malaysian dollars) [2]

	1964	1965	1966	1967	1968 [3]
Net merchandise exports [4]	3,346	3,752	3,808	3,679	4,044
Net merchandise imports [4]	3,071	3,226	3,254	3,149	3,364
Merchandise surplus	275	526	554	530	680
Service receipts	461	512	481	460	437
Service payments	821	907	934	898	1,006
Service deficit	—360	—395	—453	—438	—569
Balance on goods and services	—85	131	101	92	111
Net private transfers	—201	—195	—196	—185	—180
Net government transfers	127	124	87	39	34
Balance on goods, services and transfers	—159	60	—8	—54	—35
Private long-term capital movement (net)	205	190	160	135	150
Official long-term capital movement (net)	19	94	7	126	98
Balance on current and long-term capital transactions	65	344	159	207	213

Table 25. *Balance of Payments of Malaysia, 1964–68* [1]—Continued

	1964	1965	1966	1967	1968 [3]
Movement in official short-term liabilities (net) _____	71	116	—11	—183	n.a.
Errors and omissions, including other short-term capital movements _____	—274	—326	—319	—217	—240
Overall surplus or deficit __	—138	134	—171	—247	—27

n.a.—not available.

[1] Fiscal year and calendar year begin January 1.

[2] M$3.06 equal US$1.

[3] Preliminary.

[4] Free on board.

Source: Adapted from *Bank Negara Malaysia Annual Report and Statement of Accounts, 1968*, Kuala Lumpur, p. 72.

In contrast to merchandise trade, in which receipts for exports customarily exceeded payments for imports, the service account traditionally showed an unfavorable balance. In 1968 the deficit of M$569 million exhibited an increase of almost 30 percent over the deficit of M$438 million in 1967. The increased deficit in 1968 reflected in part a decline in foreign military expenditure in the country attendant upon the gradual withdrawal of British military forces. The increased deficit resulted also from lower investment incomes from abroad, an increase in payments of profits and dividends by foreign-owned companies, larger freight and insurance payments on imports, and higher tourist expenditures abroad. Net private transfers, consisting, for the most part, of private remittances to the United Kingdom, India, Pakistan, and Communist China, dropped slightly in 1968. The drop in payments, however, was balanced by a similar drop in receipts from grants to the government. Over the 5-year period from 1964 to 1968, the gap between the inflow of funds from government grants and the outflow of private transfers widened significantly.

Long-term capital movements, consisting of reinvested profits of foreign-owned firms and other foreign investments and official foreign loan receipts, more than compensated for the deficit on current account of goods, services, and transfers; but the outflow of short-term capital in 1968 left a small overall deficit of M$27 million, which was met by drawing down the country's external reserves.

Early and fragmentary reports made public by the Department of Statistics in September 1969 indicated that the prospects for international trade and payments for the year were encouraging. Based on the increase in receipts from exports and a decrease in payments for imports during the first 8 months of 1969, it was expected that the trade balance for the year would show the largest surplus ever recorded. Moreover, the increase in reserves of gold and foreign exchange during the first part of the year had been satisfactory, and there was reasonable expectations of ending the year with a surplus in the overall balance of payments.

FOREIGN INVESTMENT

At the end of February 1969 foreign investment was valued at M$261.5 million; M$186.4 million was called-up capital, and the remainder consisted of loans. Foreign capital, which had contributed to the development of the country since the 19th century, had originally been invested in rubber plantations and tin mining by firms from the United Kingdom. By 1969, however, because of the worldwide growth of industry and the incentives offered by the Malaysian government, investment had diversified far beyond agricultural and mining ventures and involved 19 different countries. Ranked according to the value of called-up capital, the most important countries were the United States, the United Kingdom, Hong Kong, Japan, and Canada. The five countries together accounted for slightly more than M$173 million, or 93 percent of the total.

To meet the strong competition for foreign investment from other countries of Southeast Asia, the government established incentives for new ventures known as pioneer industries. Among the categories of industries established were those involved in petroleum refining, production of chemicals and chemical products, food processing, production of iron and steel, textiles, electrical appliances, wood products, and paper products.

FOREIGN ECONOMIC AID

Foreign economic aid has been received from a number of sources, although the country is not a major recipient of aid. In the late 1950's the British government made grants to assist in defraying the cost of the Emergency and to aid in the development of defense (see ch. 3, Historical Setting). By 1965 capital assistance valued at M$34.4 million had been received from Commonwealth countries, including Canada, Great Britain, New Zealand, and Australia.

By 1965 a consultative group, known as the Aid Malaysia Club, composed of prospective major creditor countries and sponsored by the International Bank for Reconstruction and Development (IBRD, also known as the World Bank), was established to assist achievement of the goals of the First Malaysia Plan, which was predicated upon the receipt of foreign loans and grants. The use of foreign aid, however, posed several problems, stemming from the lack of planning experience and insufficient machinery for plan implementation, the nature and size of projects involved, and procurement policy.

For the most part, aid proferred covered only the foreign exchange costs of projects, and the foreign exchange component of projects in rural development, road construction, and education was only a small part of total cost. Aid also was tied to the purchase of commodities in the offering country, and procurement policy had involved international competitive bidding with purchase from the lowest bidder. Commodities from donor countries were often not competitively priced. Although members of the group had offered M$600 million in the form of project loans and export credits, as a result of disappointing negotiations only M$87 million had been committed by the latter part of 1968. In mid-1968 funds were made available from Great Britain as special aid at the time of military withdrawal and as assistance in development programs, including rubber processing, oil palm and irrigation projects, the development of technical education, and the establishment of industrial estates. Part of the assistance was tied to procurement of commodites in Great Britain.

International financial institutions also provided economic aid. The World Bank concluded arrangements for a series of loans for its fiscal year 1968/69 with a total value of US$28.3 million. The loans were granted for development projects in electric power, water supply, telecommunications, and education. In mid-1969 the International Finance Corporation, which is a member of the World Bank Group of financial institutions, had made available economic aid with a total value of US$6.1 million, which was composed of operations loans and equity investments in the Tasek Cement Company and Malayawata Steel Company and an equity investment in the Malaysian Industrial Finance Corporation. A further commitment of US$230,767 for equity capital in the Malayawata Steel Company was made for 1969.

Technical assistance, including the supply of experts and provision for training, was supplied by aid from the Colombo Plan, an organization which had been initiated at a meeting of the Commonwealth foreign ministers in Colombo in 1950, the Peace Corps, and the Ford Foundation. In September 1969 it was announced that the Food and Agriculture Organization of the United Nations had allocated M$660,000 for use in 1970 for the expansion of domestic science facilities in the country. Private enterprises investing in Malaysia also provided technical training. An agreement signed in October 1969 with a Canadian firm, Cantrans Services, Limited, for the establishment of a forest products industry, consisting of a logging operation, a sawmill, and a veneer-plywood plant, included a provision for supervision and initial management and the training of 1,000 Malaysian workers.

CHAPTER 23

FISCAL AND MONETARY SYSTEMS

Government financial organization, the banking system, and currency system have been developing to meet national needs and to bring about uniformity of policy and administration throughout a federation of somewhat disparate elements. Policies governing the fiscal and monetary systems tend to be conservative. The government is dedicated to the achievement of the economic and social development goals outlined in the First Malaysia Plan for 1966 to 1970, while eschewing policies that would endanger existing monetary and financial stability to lead to inflation and increased unemployment.

The high degree of centralization that characterizes the fiscal system is advantageous in administering public finances efficiently and in carrying out major governmental objectives. Revenue collection and expenditures are centered in the Ministry of Finance, which also functions at the policymaking level. All revenues of the central government are paid into a consolidated fund, and expenditures are administered centrally. Although the central government accounts for the major part of public finance, the fiscal system of individual states also is centralized since all revenues accruing to the states are paid into a consolidated fund and administered centrally.

Bank Negara Malaysia, which is the central bank, is the head of the banking system and, since mid-1967, the sole source of currency issue. It also performs valuable services for the central and state governments. As head of the banking system, it regulates credit creation through control of bank reserve ratios, liquidity requirements, and interest rates. It conducts bank examinations and overseas compliance of the banking system with legal requirements. Monetary policies also have been of an essentially conservative nature aimed at holding the expansion of bank credit within safe limits and maintaining a sound currency.

The period from 1966 to 1969 has been characterized by the increasing involvement of the government in the direct shaping of economic development. Major fiscal problems have been those of reconciling growing current government expenditures and the need for development funds with a slower growth of public revenue that has resulted in budgetary deficits and the exhaustion of government surpluses accumulated in the past. In harmonizing the problems, the government has planned to rely in large part on private domestic investment and foreign aid and investment without undue use of inflationary credit from the central bank.

ORGANIZATION AND
MANAGEMENT OF PUBLIC FINANCE

In 1969 the fiscal system encompassed the financial activities of three levels of government—the central, state, and local or municipal (see ch. 12, The Governmental System). The major instrument of public finance was the budget of the central government. The fiscal year coincided with the calendar year.

Until 1963 Malaya, as an independent country, Sarawak, Sabah (then North Borneo), and Singapore maintained separate government budgets. After their federation into Malaysia in 1963, most public finances were incorporated into a federal budget, with certain reservations for state authorities. The financial activities of the Malayan states were largely taken over by the central government. Sarawak, Sabah, and Singapore retained a greater measure of fiscal autonomy. With the withdrawal of Singapore in 1965, the same pattern of public sector finance was continued. In addition to the budget of the central government, 13 states prepared budgets, and numerous local governmental units participated in varying degrees in the collection of revenue and planning for its disbursement. Local governments derived their fiscal status from state governments that had the power to confer financial autonomy on local units. This standing carried with it the right to draw up annual budgets and retain surpluses if such existed. In the event revenue were insufficient to meet local needs, state governments made grant-in-aid.

The basic principles for the conduct of public finance are contained in the sections that outline legislative and financial provisions in the Constitution, which was adopted in 1957 and last amended in 1964. According to prescribed legislative procedures, bills relating to money must originate in the House of Representatives and must be presented by a minister. When the bill has been passed by the House, it must be sent to the Senate. If it is not passed by the Senate without amendment within a month, it is then presented to the Yang di-Pertuan Agong, Supreme Head of the nation, for his assent.

The Constitution provides that no taxes shall be levied except under the authority of a law made by the Federal Parliament or by a state assembly. Certain fees and fields of taxation are reserved as revenue sources for the states. The states also receive revenue from the central government in the form of an annual capitation grant, a grant for the maintenance of state roads, and such other grants as may be made by law from time to time. By authority of the Constitution, states also receive a share of export duties on the tin and iron ore produced within their boundaries. The central government may pass laws to obtain revenue from any source not specifically reserved to the states or other governmental units. About 80 percent of the combined central and state government revenue accrued to the central government in each year from 1966 to 1968.

The Constitution provides that all revenue raised, except that raised from Muslim religious levies, must be paid into the consolidated fund of the central government or of the state. Expenditures provided for in the Constitution or other law, such as those for the maintenance of the Supreme Head, expenditures for pensions, retirement allowances and gratuities, expenses connected with the public debt, various grants to states, and salaries and expenses connected with specified public offices, are charged against the consolidated fund of the central government, and no further authorization is required for their disbursement. Other expenditures to be met from the consolidated fund, such as funds for defense, social and economic services, and general administration, are presented to Parliament annually in the form of a supply bill, which must be approved in order that funds may be appropriated for these purposes. If the amount appropriated in any 1 year is insufficient, a supplementary estimate showing the sums required is presented to the House of Representatives in an additional supply bill.

The Constitution confers upon the Yang di-Pertuan Agong the responsibility for seeing that a statement of the estimated receipts and expenditures for the year is placed before the House of Representatives before the beginning of the fiscal year. In practice, the minister of finance presents the budget estimates for the coming year, together with a report on the financial situation of the past year.

In 1969 a new budget format was put into use. For the first time the annual presentation was made in the form of a program and performance budget, delineating the programs to be undertaken during the year, with their cost and guidelines with which to measure performance at the end of the year. The purpose of the innovation was twofold: to bring about greater efficiency in the use of funds by the central government; and to provide a better method for coordinating current expenditures with the implementation of goals set forth in development plans, such as the First Malaysia Plan (see ch. 17, Character and Structure of the Economy). In preparation of the 1969 budget, eight governmental divisions adopted the new system.

Provision is made for the establishment of a contingency fund to meet unforeseen expenditure needs and for a state reserve fund. The Constitution also provides for the establishment of the National Finance Council, which serves the central government in a consultative role concerning financial affairs (see ch. 12, The Governmental System). The central government is not permitted to borrow except under authority of law, and states are not permitted to borrow except from the central government or, for a period not to exceed 12 months, from a bank approved by the central government.

The Constitution also provides for an auditor general, who is appointed by the Yang di-Pertuan Agong on the advice of the prime minister and with consultation of the Conference of Rulers. The function of the auditor general is the inspection of the accounts of both the central government and of the states and the preparation of an annual report. The annual report of the central government is submitted to the Supreme Head for presentation to the House of Representatives. A report on the account of each state is submitted to the ruler, or governor, for presentation to the legislative assembly.

The administration of public finances is the function of the Ministry of Finance through the treasury, which includes among its other divisions the Accountant General's Department, Customs and Excise Department, Inland Revenue Department, Finance Division, Administrative Division, and Organization and Methods Division.

In 1965 the ordinary budget of the central government, comprising ordinary revenues and recurrent expenditures, showed a small surplus of M$17 million (3.06 Malaysian dollars equal US$1). From 1966 to 1968 there was a growing deficit, although it was small in comparison with the budget. The overall deficit, which included that on the development budget as well as that on current account, increased from M$519 million in 1965 to M$665 million in 1968 and was expected to rise to M$692 million in 1969.

Expenditures

From 1966 to 1968 recurrent expenditures of the central government, as set forth in the ordinary budget, rose from M$1,712 million to M$1,957 million, an increase of 14.3 percent over the period. All categories of expenditures, except pensions, increased in absolute terms, with some changes in proportion but few changes in rank (see table 26).

Despite the administration's goal of holding the increase in current expenditures to about 6 percent annually, total expenditures of the ordinary budget rose significantly by 10.8 percent in 1967. The principal sources of increase were: expenditures for education, which increased 11.6 percent during the year; public debt charges, which increased spectacularly by 38.4 percent; grants to states, which increased by 8 percent; and general administration expenses, which increased 22.8 percent. Although charged to current expenditures, the increased cost of general administration was, in part, the result of the establishment of new missions abroad and contributions to international organizations and, consequently, was not of an annually recurrent nature.

Table 26. Recurrent Expenditures of Central Government of Malaysia, 1966–68
(in million M$)*

Ordinary Budget Expenditure	1966		1967		1968	
	Actual	Percent of Total	Actual	Percent of Total	Actual	Percent of Total
Defense and security ____	380	22.2	387	20.4	403	20.6
Economic and social services _____	705	41.2	748	39.4	783	40.0
Agricultural and rural development __	(27)	(1.6)	(29)	(1.5)	(34)	(1.7)
Commerce and industry _____	(3)	(0.2)	(4)	(0.2)	(6)	(0.3)
Transport _____	(15)	(0.9)	(18)	(0.9)	(19)	(1.0)
Post and telecommunications _____	(65)	(3.8)	(67)	(3.5)	(73)	(3.7)
Education _____	(361)	(21.1)	(403)	(21.2)	(401)	(20.5)
Medical services ___	(130)	(7.6)	(135)	(7.2)	(146)	(7.5)
Other _____	(104)	(6.0)	(92)	(4.9)	(104)	(5.3)
Public debt charges ____	177	10.3	245	12.9	258	13.2
Pensions _____	65	3.8	66	3.5	60	3.1
Grants to states _____	149	8.7	161	8.5	163	8.3
General administration _	236	13.8	290	15.3	290	14.8
TOTAL _____	1,712	100.0	1,897	100.0	1,957	100.0

*M$3.06 equal US$1.

Source: Adapted from Bank Negara Malaysia Quarterly Economic Bulletin, December 1968, p. 59.

In accord with the policy of restricting the growth of current public spending, the government in 1967 set up a special committee to review the spending and financial operations of ministries and departments to cut the cost of providing services. With the resultant improvement in efficiency and a slowing down in the rate of expansion of some categories, increase in total recurrent expenditures was held to 3.2 percent in 1968. This compared favorably with a growth of 10.8 percent in the year before and with the objective of holding expenditures to an annual growth of 6 percent but, because of unforeseen development, it fell short of the goal of restricting growth to 1.7 percent in 1968.

From 1966 to 1968 economic and social services consistently accounted for the largest share of expenditures, averaging slightly more than 40 percent annually. Among major expenditures defense and education fluctuated between first and second place and were followed, in order, by general administration, public debt charges, grants to states, and medical and health services.

Defense and security had accounted for a large share of the budgetary total because of external threats to national security, and it was anticipated that further increases would be necessitated by the withdrawal by the British forces. Governmental policy, nevertheless, was to restrain defense spending within limits that would not impinge upon plans for economic development and a higher standard of living. Expenditures for education had increased because of the extension of the educational period in West Malaysia and the governmental assumption of a larger part of the cost of public education in East Malaysia, as well as the addition of other services and facilities (see ch. 8, Education).

In the 1968 budget, which strove for fiscal austerity, expenditures for education declined both absolutely and relatively, and the costs of general administration were held to the 1967 level. Rapid expansion of medical and health services, however, accounted for an increase of 8 percent over the allocation in 1967 (see ch. 7, Living Conditions). Spending for defense increased by 4 percent.

The preliminary draft of the 1969 ordinary budget of the central government, as presented to Parliament in January of that year, estimated expenditures at M$1,925 million, a decline of about 1.5 percent from the 1968 total. Comprehensive details were not available in mid-1969. According to the announcement of the minister of finance, however, the allocation for education, which received the largest share, was M$433.7 million or 22.5 percent of the total. Preliminary estimates for medical and health services were fixed at M$149.6 million, or 7.8 percent of the total. The increase in recurrent expenditures of the Ministry of Defense was estimated at 2.2 percent.

Revenues

From 1966 to 1968, ordinary revenues of the central government rose from M$1,655 million to M$1,875 million, an increase of about 13 percent (see table 27). Revenues increased annually, although they failed to keep pace with the growth of expenditures, and there was a deficit on current account in each year in contrast to a small surplus in 1965.

Table 27. Ordinary Revenues of Central Government of Malaysia, 1966–68
(in million M$) *

	1966		1967		1968	
	Actual	Percent of total	Actual	Percent of total	Revised estimate	Percent of total
Domestic revenue _____	1,648	99.6	1,829	99.8	1,872	99.8
Direct taxes:						
Income taxes ___	(360)	(21.8)	(421)	(23.0)	(385)	(20.5)
Development tax	---	---	5	(0.2)	(43)	(2.3)
Tin profits tax __	---	---	---	---	(5)	(0.3)
Estate duty ____	(7)^	(0.4)	(10)	(0.5)	(7)	(0.4)
Total Direct Taxes _____	367	22.2	436	23.7	440	23.5
Indirect taxes:						
Export duties __	(223)	(13.5)	(195)	(10.6)	(200)	(10.7)
Import duties __	(381)	(23.0)	(466)	(25.4)	(503)	(26.8)
Excise duties ___	(134)	(8.0)	(151)	(8.3)	(167)	(8.9)
Other _____	(246)	(14.9)	(233)	(12.7)	(222)	(11.8)
Total Indirect Taxes _____	984	59.4	1,045	57.0	1,092	58.2
Tax revenue:	1,351	81.6	1,481	80.7	1,532	81.7
Nontax revenue:						
Commercial undertakings ___	(107)	(6.5)	(117)	(6.4)	(125)	(6.7)

	1966		1967		1968	
	Actual	Percent of total	Actual	Percent of total	Revised estimate	Percent of total
Currency surplus fund distribution _____	(40)	(2.4)	(72)	(4.0)	(57)	(3.0)
Other _____	(150)	(9.1)	(159)	(8.7)	(158)	(8.4)
Total Nontax Revenue ___	297	18.0	348	19.1	340	18.1
Foreign grants _____	7	0.4	5	0.2	3	0.2
GRAND TOTAL __	1,655	100.0	1,834	100.0	1,875	100.0

*M$3.06 equal US$1.

Source: Adapted from *Bank Negara Malaysia Quarterly Economic Bulletin,*
December 1968, p. 59.

The central government derived revenue from taxation, from the profits of commercial undertakings, profits from the currency surplus, and various other nontax revenues. Foreign grants, ranging from M$7 million in 1966 to M$3 million in 1968, were included in the total. Taxation was the source of at least 80 percent of revenue; and indirect taxes, composed of export duties, import duties, excise taxes, and miscellaneous others, accounted for almost 60 percent of total ordinary revenue. This situation left realized budgetary revenue of Malaysia vulnerable to the fluctuations of world prices for major export commodities, especially rubber, tin, and iron. The decline in receipts from export duties in 1967 was attributed to a fall in the price of rubber at the end of the year.

The management and collection of revenue are centered in the Ministry of Finance. The comptroller general of inland revenue, who is the head of the Inland Revenue Department, has charge of the management and collection of inland revenues, consisting of the income, development, tin profits, and payroll taxes, as well as estate duty and film-hire duty. He also administers the stamp duty offices in Alor Star, Ipoh, Johore Bahru, Kota Bahru, Kuala Lumpur, Malacca, and Penang. All inland revenue duties in West Malaysia are collected by the headquarters in Kuala Lumpur.

The comptroller general is also charged with overall responsibility for Sabah and Sarawak, where the heads of state are designated commissioners of inland revenue for their respective states. The commissioners are directly responsible to the comptroller general in all matters pertaining to assessment and collection of revenues in Sabah and Sarawak.

After a notification by the comptroller general that is due annually by March 31, each taxpayer must file a statement of income for the year. Employers are required to make an annual report showing all remuneration, in cash or kind, for certain classifications of employees. Assessments are made as soon as possible after the expiration date for filing returns, and the assessed tax is payable within 1 month after notice of assessment. The comptroller general is empowered to make exceptions under certain circumstances.

The Inland Revenue Department has an inservice training program for employees. Two federal counsels from the office of the attorney general, who are attached to the department, are responsible for drafting tax legislation and amendments and for other legal functions. The department has two rubber industry advisers and one tin industry adviser for consultation on technical phases of the industries. The investigation branch of the department is responsible for the detection of tax evasion.

Duties are levied on both imports and exports. These duties and exise taxes are administered by the Customs and Excise Department.

Direct Taxes

In 1968 the proceeds of direct taxes, comprising both personal and business income taxes, the development tax, tin profits tax, and estate duty, provided M$440 million, or 23.5 percent of the total ordinary budgetary revenue of the central government. From 1966 to 1968 revenue from direct taxes increased consistently in absolute terms; relatively, however, there was a slight decline from 1967 to 1968. Income taxes, which accounted for the overwhelming share of direct tax revenue, declined significantly from M$421 million, or 23 percent of the total in 1967, to M$385 million, or 20.5 percent of the total in 1968. The decline in revenue was attributable to the lower tax base in 1967, resulting from unfavorable rubber prices in that year, and to the lag in income assessment and collection caused by the increased work load of the Inland Revenue Department in the process of reorganizing the income tax system.

Income taxes in 1968 were levied on the basis of the Income Tax Act of 1967, which imposed a unifrom income tax throughout West Malaysia, Sabah, and Sarawak in place of the three ordinances that had existed formerly. Taxes are usually levied as of December 31 on the income of the previous calendar year. Exceptions are made in some instances, however, when the accounting year of a business firm does not coincide with the calendar year.

The Income Tax Act of 1967 contained rules for determining residence for both corporate entities and individuals and for establishing the base for taxable income. It also set forth the tax rates applicable to each classification. For corporate entities taxable income included gains or profits from any trade or business; dividends, including intercompany dividends; interest and discounts; rents, royalties, premiums, and other profits arising from property; and miscellaneous unspecified income. There was no capital gains tax nor tax levied on dividends issued in the form of stock. In determining the base for computing taxes, deductions were granted for rent on business premises, cost of repairs or replacement of equipment, cost of replanting an existing plantation, bad debts, obligatory contributions to an approved provident fund by an employer, and interest paid on money borrowed for income producing purposes. Provision was made for deduction of depreciation allowances in specific instances, and tax relief was also granted as incentive for pioneer industries and for export promotion (see ch. 19, Industry). After arriving at the taxable base, a flat rate of 40 percent was applied.

For the purposes of assessing personal income taxes, an individual is classified as a resident if he is a permanent resident or was in Malaysia for a specified length of time during the tax year. The law also provides for a classification as short-term resident for individuals who may reside in the country for a period of only 2 or 3 years. The status of resident is the decisive factor in determining the eligibility of an individual for personal reliefs and the benefits of graduated tax rates.

Taxable income for individuals is defined the same as that for corporations, with the addition of that derived from gains or profits from any profession or vocation; gains or profits from any employment, including allowances, perquisites, and benefits-in-kind; amounts received as compensation for loss of employment, certain retirement gratuities, pensions or annuities, and implied income from owner-used land and improvements. The income of a wife living with her husband is charged to the husband unless other arrangements are made. After determining total personal income, allowances for husband, wife, children, and earned income allowances are subtracted to arrive at the base for tax calculation. Tax rates are progressive and escalate gradually from 6 percent on the first M$2,500 to 40 percent on M$50,000. Amounts in excess of M$50,000 are taxed at the rate of 50 percent.

Other direct taxes consisted of the development tax, tin profits tax, estate duty, and stamp taxes. The development tax, which was initiated in 1967, was an additional income tax of 5 percent imposed on development income, which was defined as income from any trade, business, or profession and from the renting of property in Malaysia. The tin profits tax, promulgated in 1965, imposed a tax, in addition to income tax, on persons deriving income from tin mining operations. Stamps duties were imposed on documents such as mortgages, transfers of securities, bills of exchange, and other transactions. Rates varied according to the character and value of the document. Estate duties were levied on all immovable property in the country at progressive rates, which ranged from 5 percent on M$15,000 evaluation to 60 percent on estates valued at more than M$4 million.

Indirect Taxes

Indirect taxes accounted for the major part of ordinary revenue from 1966 to 1968, fluctuating slightly in share during the period. Indirect tax revenues of the central government were made up of export duties, import duties, excise taxes, and miscellaneous other taxes and fees. Revenues were paid into the consolidated fund of the central government. Import duties and excise taxes were administered by the Customs and Excise Department of the Ministry of Finance. In 1968 West Malaysia, Sabah, and Sarawak maintained separate export control systems, although the central government retained the right to legislate concerning exports from any Malaysian territory.

Revenues from export duties were a variable element, fluctuating both in absolute and relative terms according to world demand and price for major commodities. Revenue in 1967 reached a low point for the 3 years, but an improvement in rubber prices produced an upturn in 1968. Earnings in 1969 also increased because of a rise in sales volume in the first 6 months. The contribution of import duties increased from M$381 million, or 23 percent of total revenue, in 1966 to M$503 million, or 26.8 percent, in 1968. Imposition of import duties was used as a source of income and also as a tool to implement government policy and protect domestic industries. In 1968 import duties were increased on a wide number of minor items to increase revenue and on another group of commodities to encourage domestic production. In mid-1969 import duties were raised or imposed on 21 classes of goods to promote industrialization. Among the new ventures sponsored by an increase in import duties was the assembly of padlocks, bolts, and hinges by small units in villages.

Excise taxes, which were levied on a number of products manufactured domestically at specified rates per unit of production, were the source of substantial revenue. In 1968 duties were levied on petroleum products, beer, stout, and liquors produced in Malaysia at prescribed rates per gallon. In calculating revenue for the 1969 budget, new excise duties were imposed on petroleum gases, inner tubes for motor vehicles, veneer and plywood, other processed-timber products, primary cells and batteries, and electric light bulbs. New duties imposed were expected to raise additional revenue of M$1.8 million.

Nontax Revenue

In addition to revenues from taxes, receipts from commercial undertakings and government services, such as postal services, electric power, and telecommunications, added to the total, which also included rents on government property and miscellaneous sales. Any surplus from the management of currency was paid into the consolidated fund of the central government.

PUBLIC DEBT

At the end of 1968 the total public debt of the central government, domestic and external, was M$4,080.3 million, an increase of 35.5 percent over the total of M$3,011.1 million in 1966. Domestically held debt accounted for 85.5 percent of the total in 1968, a slightly larger share than the 83.4 percent in 1966. For the most part, public debt had been used for development purposes that were productive in character rather than for meeting deficits of ordinary government expenditures.

Domestic debt was represented by short-term treasury bills with maturities of 91 or 181 days and other short-term securities maturing in 2 or 3 years. Long-term debt was composed of government securities bearing 5-year maturities, 7-year maturities, and others maturing in 16 to 20 years and an issue of M$10.3 million national defense bonds. The longest term securities, which accounted for 67 percent of total domestic debt in 1968, had been issued for financing economic development. Commercial banks were the major holders of short-term debt. The Employees Provident Fund held about 63 percent of all long-term debt. Other holders included: insurance companies; the Post Office Savings Bank, which was the second largest holder; central government funds; commercial banks; and the central bank. The central bank held only a minor share of government debt. Expansion of the market for government securities was a major objective of government.

External debt was composed of drawings from the International Bank for Reconstruction and Development, foreign loans for commercial purposes, and other aid (see ch. 22, Foreign Economic Relations). The government had also raised revenue through issuing loans abroad about every 2 years, and in 1968 the central bank made an offering of securities of M$19 million in the capital market of the Federal Republic of Germany (West Germany).

Foreign debt in 1968 was the equivalent of 5.5 percent of the gross national product (GNP), not an immoderately large share compared with a number of other countries. Domestic debt, however, was the equivalent of 34 percent of the gross national product, a share which equaled that of domestic debt in the United States and Canada but was slightly less than that of Australia, which had a ratio of 37 percent of domestic debt to gross national product. Interest and amortization payments on the public debt ranked fourth among the recurrent expenditures of the central government. To implement the First Malaysia Plan, it was considered that further government borrowing from both domestic and foreign sources would be essential.

BANKING SYSTEM

Background of Banking

Commercial banking facilities that served the needs of the territories that made up Malaysia after 1965 and of nearby Singapore and Brunei began in the 19th century. The system developed to meet the needs of colonial powers engaged in foreign trade and mining, which were the major economic activities. Early banking facilities were branches of Western banks that were incorporated abroad and maintained overseas headquarters. Branch offices at first were located in Singapore and later in Penang. It was not until 1884 that the Chartered Bank of India established branches in Kuala Lumpur and in Taiping, both centers of tin mining. After the beginning of the 20th century, services were broadened by the establishment of banks by Malayan Chinese. Some of the institutions had headquarters in Malaya and some in Singapore. Although the number of domestic banks increased, in 1968 banks incorporated in foreign countries held 65.4 percent of total deposits.

Until 1958 there was no special banking legislation. Banking was carried on under the provisions of laws relating to companies in general. The Banking Ordinance of 1958, which came into force in January 1959, provided for licensing and regulation of banks in Malaya. In the same year the Central Bank Ordinance established the Central Bank of Malaya, which began operation in January 1959, establishing its head office in Kuala Lumpur. These ordinances formed the legislative framework for banking in Malaysia.

The banking system of Malaysia in 1969 had gradually evolved in response to the changing territorial composition of the country and the demands of modern economic organization. It was in the process of continued adaptation to current goals of development while maintaining stability and to political policies. After the establishment of Malaysia in 1963, the name of the central bank was changed to Bank Negara Malaysia (Malaysian National Bank). In 1965 amendments to the basic ordinances provided for the integration of the banking systems in West Malaysia, Sabah, Sarawak, and Singapore, extending the jurisdiction of Bank Negara Malaysia to all parts of the country and imposing uniform regulations on banks. New problems were created by the withdrawal of Singapore later in 1965, but by 1969 an accord had been reached on most problems.

Structure of Financial Institutions

The banking system in 1969 was composed of the central bank, commerical banks, financial institutions filling a specialized function, insurance companies, and a joint Malaysia-Singapore stock exchange.

Bank Negara Malaysia

Bank Negara Malaysia, which is the head of the banking system, has its head office at Kuala Lumpur and branch offices at Kuala Lumpur, Penang, Johore Bahru, Kota Kinabalu, and Kuching. The branch in Singapore was closed in April 1967. To facilitate transactions between the two countries, however, in March 1968 the central bank opened an account in Singapore currency with the accoutant general of Singapore, who opened a corresponding account in Malaysian currency with Bank Negara Malaysia.

The central bank performs functions relating to the central and state governments, the commercial banking system, and international financial institutions. It is charged with promoting monetary stability and a sound financial structure and with influencing the general level of credit availability to avoid excessive fluctuations in the economy.

The central bank held accounts and maintained banking services for the central government in all branch offices; in 1967 it also provided similar services to state governments of Selangor, Penang, Sabah, and Sarawak. The bank was empowered to make advances

to the central government up to a specified share of annual revenue
to meet temporary needs for funds. It also managed both short-
term and long-term domestic securities and issues of government
treasury bills, acted as agent for the central government in raising
market loans or investing funds abroad, and in general served as
adviser to the Ministry of Finance on relevant matters. The bank
administered the exchange control ordinance, and the governor of
the bank was the controller of foreign exchange for Malaysia. After
the establishment of a branch in Kuching in 1967, the bank also
administered exchange control for Sarawak.

In June 1967 Bank Negara Malaysia replaced the Board of Commissioners of Currency, Malaya and British Borneo as the sole
authority for the issuance of currency for Malaysia. From 1950 to
1967 currency was issued under an agreement that covered the then
existing Federation of Malaya, Singapore, British North Borneo,
Sarawak, and Brunei. The arrangement was continued for 8 years
after the establishment of a central bank in Malaya. With the
change in 1967, the bank began the issuance of the new national
currency and was charged with keeping reserves for preservation
of the currency. The bank took over part of the assets of the currency board, thus increasing bank assets from M$400 million to
M$1.2 billion. Currency liabilities increased from zero to M$750 million. To maintain the acceptability of the currency, it was required
that the bank should at all times maintain a reserve of approved
external assets of at least 35 percent of its deposit liabilities, or
slightly more than 80 percent of total currency in circulation. In
1968 reserves were well above the minimum legal requirements.

Seeking a smoothly functioning and stable banking system, the
central bank performs services for commercial banks. Since its initiation in 1959, the central bank has been responsible for providing
for the cash requirements of commercial banks and for accepting
surplus cash from them. It also provides them with the means of
transferring funds free between Kuala Lumpur and Penang, Johore
Bahru, Kota Kinabalu, and Kuching.

The central bank exercises control over the commerical banking
system in numerous ways. It is the holder of the bank statutory
reserves that, in 1968, were fixed at 3.5 percent of total liabilities.
The bank also was consulted on commercial banking policy and was
empowered to make recommendations concerning liquidity requirements and interest rates. In 1968 commercial banks were required
to preserve a minimum liquidity ratio of 20 percent against demand
and fixed deposits. Liquidity requirements for savings deposits were
changed in October 1968. After that time, banks were required to
hold at least 50 percent of their savings deposits in long-term gov-

ernment securities and housing loans. Powers of the central bank were also expanded in 1968 to include recommendations on commission rates and other charges payable to banks in addition to interest rates. The central bank conducts examination of commercial banks to ensure that sound banking policies are maintained and provisions of banking legislation carried out.

Bank Negara Malaysia represents the government in transactions involving international financial institutions. It is the official depository in Malaysia of the International Monetary Fund, the International Bank for Reconstruction and Development and allied institutions, and the Asian Development Bank.

Commercial Banks

In 1968 the country was served by 38 commercial banks operating 324 banking offices. Of the total, 16 were domestic banks with 167 banking offices, five were banks incorporated in Singapore with 61 banking offices, and 17 were banks incorporated in other foreign countries and having 96 banking offices. Banking offices tended to congregate in the more developed areas, such as Selangor with 83 offices, Perak with 43, and Penang with 38 offices. Although the more industrialized areas were provided with fairly adequate banking facilities, there was need for expanding services in rural areas.

Commercial banks accepted demand, fixed (time), and savings deposits. In 1968 total deposits were M$2.7 billion, an increase of slightly less than 35 percent since 1966. Demand deposits accounted for 35 percent of the total, fixed deposits for 47 percent, and savings deposits for 18 percent of the total. From 1966 to 1968 fixed deposits and savings deposits, both of which were interest bearing, grew more rapidly than demand deposits. Fixed deposits rose about 50 percent during the period, rising from M$842 million to M$1.3 billion. Savings deposits increased 42 percent, rising from M$340 million to M$484 million. Demand deposits increased slightly less than 16 percent in volume, rising from M$795 million to M$920 million. In mid-1968 fixed deposits drew interest ranging from 3 percent on deposits for 1 month to 6 percent on those for 9 to 12 months. Savings deposits, which could be withdrawn on short notice, drew 3.5 percent interest. Interest on all categories of fixed deposits and on savings deposits had increased by 0.5 percent during the 3-year period as an inducement to savers.

Commerial banks were permitted to make loans and to invest both in government securities and, under restricted circumstances, in shares of companies. Most commercial bank loans were short term. Credit extended to commerce accounted for the largest share of bank loans and advances during 1968, although it had dropped to 35.3 percent from 37.1 percent in 1966. Manufacturing, as the recipient of 18.2 percent of bank loans and advances in 1968, ranked second Credit to professionals and individuals ranked third, with 15.6 percent of the total. From 1966 to 1968 there was no dominant change in the pattern of bank lending, although the share extended to manufacturing rose during the period, while that of commerce declined. In mid-1968 the general interest rate on loans was 8 percent. The importance of foreign incorporated banks was evidenced by the fact that foreign banks, excluding those incorporated in Singapore, held 44.6 percent of all bank deposits and extended 50.5 percent of all loans and advances. From 1966 to 1968, however, domestically based banks had shown a steady increase in relative share.

In 1968 there was an amendment of the banking ordinance with the objective of increasing the stability of the banking and credit system. According to the amendment, foreign banks operating within the country were required to hold net assets of not less than M$2 million to ensure a continuing interest in the economy. To avoid a conflict of interest, a new provision required bank directors to disclose their interest in loans and advances made by their banks. Commerical banks were also required to submit to the central bank reports of loans and advances made to certain categories of borrowers.

Other Financial Institutions

In addition to commercial banks, there are a variety of institutions, both publicly and privately sponsored, that collect savings, make investments, and provide specialized types of financing. Such institutions are important as markets for government securities and as sources of investment funds that do not fall within the framework of commercial bank investment. In 1968 the Post Office Savings Bank held deposits of M$238.4 million, not quite half the volume of savings held by commercial banks. There was a total of 353 offices and approximately 1.5 million subscribers. Operation of the Post Office Savings Bank had just started in Sabah. Nine offices, with 1,600 subscribers, were established there during 1968. For the most part, the average per capita savings balance was small, being just M$161 for all of Malaysia. The average balance for Sarawak was M$345, more than twice the country average.

Total investments of the Post Office Savings Bank in West Malaysia and Sabah were M$241.5 million at the end of 1968. Investments in Sarawak were M$5.2 million. About 88 percent of invested funds in West Malaysia and Sabah were held in securities of the central government. Most investments in Sarawak were held in sterling securities. The rate of interest, which was 4 percent in mid-1968, had been raised from 3 percent in order to attract more savings.

The Malaya Borneo Building Society and the Muslim Pilgrims Saving Corporation accepted deposits and made investments. The Malaya Borneo Building Society, which was established in 1950, accepted fixed term deposits from the public; obtained loans, mainly from the Employees Provident Fund; and was an important source of funds for private housing in West Malaysia. The Muslim Pilgrims Saving Corporation was inaugurated in 1962 to accept savings from Muslims who planned a pilgrimage. Investment was mostly in the form of equities in companies.

The Employees Provident Fund, established in 1951, was one of the most important sources of development finance for the central government and was included in plans for financing the First Malaysia Plan (see ch. 17, Character and Structure of the Economy). Contribution to the fund was compulsory for employees earning from M$10 to M$500 monthly. The purpose was to provide a form of social security upon retirement. The fund originally operated only in Malaya, which later became West Malaysia. At the end of 1967 the Employees Provident Fund Ordinance was extended to East Malaysia, but the fund had not begun operation there at the end of 1968. In Sarawak three other provident funds—the Government Employees' Provident Fund, the Local Authorities' Provident Fund, and the Teachers' Provident Fund—were in operation. The major part of the funds of these institutions was invested in sterling securities.

According to the Insurance Act, 1963, which regulated the conduct of insurance companies, they were required to keep a minimum of 55 percent of their assets in authorized local investments, beginning in 1966. The share held in local investments, composed of loans and private securities, was well above the legal minimum. Government and other public securities accounted for 13.6 percent of total local assets in 1967.

A large number of cooperative societies with varying purposes operated throughout Malaysia. In 1968 it was estimated that 3,270 societies, with a membership of 564,062, were in existence; about 87 percent were located in West Malaysia. Cooperatives operated in both rural and urban areas. Most of them were thrift and credit societies, but some were marketing groups. In an endeavor to strengthen the functioning of cooperatives, a new regulation provided that membership of groups organized in 1967 and later must exceed 100.

Among the financial institutions with specialized functions were the Malaysian Industrial Development Finance Limited, which provided long-term financing for industrial enterprises, and the National Investment Company Limited, organized to assist Malay participation in commerce and industry. The Borneo Housing Development Limited was initiated in 1958 and was an important source of financing for housing construction in Sabah and Sarawak. The Borneo Development Corporation, organized in the same year, undertook industrial and commercial development projects in diverse fields. In 1955 the Sabah Credit Corporation was initiated to provide a source of finance for small- or medium-scale agricultural, fishing, or other rural projects. Interest-free loans from the Sabah state government provided the funds. In 1958 the Sarawak Development Finance Corporation was set up to provide loans for rural development in Sarawak. Resources of M$8 million in 1968 were composed of a M$6 million interest-free loan from the government of Sarawak and a M$2 million loan from the central government, bearing interest at the rate of 4 percent annually.

The Sarawak Development Finance Corporation had been reasonably successful in filling the need for agricultural financing, and in 1968 it established a subsidiary to develop facilities for the processing, storage, and marketing of agricultural produce. The corporation also took over responsibility for financing and administering the state's rubber planting program.

In early 1969 Parliament passed the Borrowing Companies Bill, which provided for the licensing and regulation of finance companies accepting deposits from the public. The bill regulated incorporation, minimum capital requirements, payment of dividends, conditions for making loans, and permissible types of investments for finance companies and placed them under control of the central bank.

Malaysia also has a stock exchange that is the source of a small and fluctuating but expanding volume of long-term investment funds. In 1968 M$67 million were raised through the issue of stocks and bonds. This was an increase over the M$49 million in 1966 and a sharp increase over 1967, when the value of new offerings was only M$22.6 million. The increase in value of issues was attributed to improved economic conditions in 1968. At that time, five Malaysian companies dealing in timber, tractors, milk products, textiles, and flour made offerings that were all heavily oversubscribed.

Malaysia and Singapore have joint stock exchanges with trading carried on in Kuala Lumpur and Singapore. Of the 190 companies listed in 1968, 88 were incorporated in Malaysia. The Malaysian listing was composed of 36 industrial and commercial companies, 5 property and development companies, 27 rubber companies, and 20 mining companies. Companies incorporated in Singapore, the United Kingdom, and Hong Kong were also listed. In addition, government securities of Malaysia were listed. The volume of trading, particularly in industrial shares, increased rapidly from 1966 to 1968. During the first 6 months of 1968, the turnover of industrial shares rose from 26,144 to 44,812 shares. There was a tendency toward speculative activity during the period.

During 1968 measures were taken to regulate the issuance of new securities by the private sector. The Capital Issues Committee—composed of the governor of the central bank and representatives of the Ministry of Finance, the Ministry of Commerce and Industry, the Registry of Companies, and the private sector—was formed to control the issue of securities by companies applying for listing on the exchange or new issues by companies already listed. The objective was to ensure the development of a sound securities market and provide the public with adequate and accurate information.

CURRENCY

The unit of currency is the Malaysian dollar, which is a nonconvertible paper unit having legal tender. The official par value is 0.290299 grams of fine gold, or M$3.06 is the equivalent of US$1. Bank Negara Malaysia has been the sole source of currency issue since June 12, 1967, and holds minimum reserves of gold and foreign exchange to the extent of 80.59 percent of currency liabilities. In reality, reserves have been much higher than the minimum legal requirement. The notes in general circulation are M$100, $M50, M$10, M$5, and M$1. Coins in circulation are 50 cents, 20 cents, 10 cents, 5 cents, and 1 cent.

Before 1967, currency had been issued by the Board of Commissioners of Currency, Malaya and British Borneo, and the value of the Malayan dollar was defined in terms of sterling as 2S.4d (2 shillings, 4 pence). Shortly after the separation of Singapore, negotiations were begun for the liquidation of the currency board; and on June 12, 1967, three new currencies—the Malaysian dollar, the Singapore dollar, and the Brunei dollar—with separate issuing agencies, came into existence. The currencies have identical gold parities and conversion rates in terms of United States currency—US$1 equals M$3.06—and they circulate interchangeably in the issuing countries. Assets of M$3 billion of the currency board were distributed as follows: Malaysia received 70 percent; Singapore, 22 percent; and Brunei, 8 percent. Assets were mostly in the form of sterling securities.

In the interest of a smooth changeover to new currency, the par value of the new Malaysian dollar in terms of gold remained the same as that of the old Malayan dollar, and Malayan dollars were exchangeable for Malaysian dollars. In November 1967 the pound sterling was devalued. Malaysia maintained the value of the new Malaysian dollar but, in consequence of the devaluation, the Malayan dollar, which was linked to sterling, depreciated to M$0.8571. In June 1968 Malaysia, Singapore, and Brunei fixed January 16, 1969, as the date on which the old Malayan currency would cease to be legal tender. At the end of 1968, about 95 percent of the total amount of old currency had been withdrawn from circulation, and only M$69 million remained in circulation in Malaysia, Singapore, and Brunei. Malaysia remained a member of the sterling area, although the link between the two currencies no longer existed.

SECTION IV. NATIONAL SECURITY

CHAPTER 24

PUBLIC ORDER AND INTERNAL SECURITY

Malaysia has often been subjected to forms of internal disorder that have harassed and disrupted the social, economic, and political life of the country. None has ever been decisive, although, on occasion, the difficulty has been serious enough to jeopardize the maintenance of constitutional government.

One significant challenge was a Communist threat to West Malaysia between 1948 and 1960 called the Emergency. It was a campaign of terror and armed insurrection that was defeated only after the application of maximum military and police controls and the thorough integration of the military-civilian-administrative sector into a united defense effort. A second serious threat began with the creation of Malaysia in 1963. This was a more powerful and complex challenge than the Emergency had been because it embraced a wider variety of attacks involving the active participation of external as well as internal elements. In addition to the Communists and various antifederation and racial extremists, who were essentially subversive in nature, the Republic of Indonesia launched an overt, officially announced policy of determination to "crush" Malaysia that was tantamount to a state of undeclared war. The Indonesian Confrontation continued unabated until the government of President Sukarno was overthrown and normal relations between Indonesia and Malaysia were resumed in mid-1966 (see ch. 3, Historical Setting).

The time and effort diverted to overcome these challenges had an adverse impact on the development of institutions of law and order. At the time of federation, for example, plans called for the unification of police forces in both East and West Malaysia into a single, national organization called the Royal Malaysia Police. Implementing action, however, had to be postponed until a new police act, replacing the separate police ordinances of the component states, was passed in August 1967. Similar efforts to modify the Malayan Penal Code and other basic documents and to make them applicable to the expanded federation also had to be laid aside temporarily, and in late 1969 their preparation was still in progress.

Despite these hindrances and delays, public order and internal security have remained under remarkably good control. The police forces in 1969 had been fused into a national agency, subject to federal policy, administration, and operational control. They were well organized and adequately trained to operate in close and continuing cooperation. Action against internal subversive elements was so effective that essential public services operated without serious disruption. Police facilities and efficiency were constantly improving, and the government was confident that, barring large-scale attack by external forces, public order and internal security could be fully maintained throughout the nation.

As the result of severe communal rioting that followed the national elections of 1969, an emergency was declared, and the government moved rapidly and effectively to restore order. Some constitutional guarantees were suspended, and the National Operations Council was given power to rule by decree.

POLICE

The Ministry of Home Affairs in the federal government is responsible for police activities throughout the nation. These responsibilities are carried out in accordance with the Police Act of 1967, which consolidated the police organization of West Malaysia, Sabah, and Sarawak into a unified force, called the Royal Malaysia Police (RMP). Control, administration, and direction of the RMP are exercised through national police headquarters in Kuala Lumpur under the command of an inspector general of police, who is the senior police official in the nation.

Historical Development

Before Europeans arrived in the area that is now Malaysia, only rudimentary forces for law and order were in existence, some of which stemmed back to the old Malacca empire. In the 16th century, for example, *Sejarah Melayu* (Malay Annals) noted a system of "night watchmen" created by the sultanate to guard against nocturnal prowlers and of a *balai*, or precinct station as it would be called today, to hear complaints of the people.

When Malacca fell to the Portuguese in 1511, the system of watchmen was abolished in favor of the colonial power's own forces, and a new policy based on the traditional authority of the *penghulu* (village headman or subdistrict chief) was put into effect. Each language group in an area was placed under the *penghulu*, who settled disputes, employed watchmen, and was responsible for maintaining local peace and tranquillity. The Dutch, who ousted the Portuguese in 1641, continued the *penghulu* system, as did the British during the first years of their hegemony over the area. The system never died out completely, and in modern Malaysia *penghulu* remain important adjuncts to law enforcement agencies through a limited authority to deal with local disputes.

From about the middle of the 19th century to the beginning of the 20th century, West Malaysia was a land of almost continuous disorder, punctuated by insurrections and rebellions in various states. Many local territorial chiefs employed armed retainers, who often ran rampant and terrorized the countryside (see ch. 3, Historical Setting). The problem of maintaining public order, therefore, consisted largely of dispatching armed patrols along the trails and paths between towns and settlements. Police consequently developed more along paramilitary lines than in forms commonly suitable for the simple suppression of civil crime.

The first such force in West Malaysia was the Perak Armed Police, established in 1867. It was followed by similar organizations in Negri Sembilan, Selangor, and Pahang. These forces operated until 1896, when the British amalgamated them into the single Federated Malay States Police. Subsequently, other forces were established as independent organizations in the remaining Malay states, and by 1920 a total of six separate police forces existed in the Peninsula. In 1946 the six forces were merged into the Malay Union Police, which was renamed the Federation of Malaya Police 2 years later. In 1958 the prefix *Royal* was authorized and, until Malaysia was formed in 1963, police forces in West Malaysia were officially designated the Royal Federation of Malaya Police.

The constabularies of Sarawak and Sabah had a similar origin and history, but their development was slower and less advanced in organization and facilities to deal with civil crime. Initially, all operations were carried out by the British colonial authorities from a single police headquarters in Brunei, with subordinate headquarters at Kota Kinabalu for Sabah and at Kuching for Sarawak. As in West Malaysia, operating forces were armed paramilitary units that patrolled areas between villages and towns, concerned more with the suppression of threats to internal security than with the enforcement of civil ordinances. The control of criminal elements was left largely in the hands of local *penghulu*.

The first change in the system occurred in Sarawak when that territory became a separate entity under the "White Rajas" (see ch. 3, Historical Setting). The paramilitary force for rural and jungle operations was maintained, but it was augmented by a new force exclusively concerned with civil crime; in 1932 these two elements were merged to form the first Sarawak Constabulary. Since the new organization was too small to cover the entire country, a number of village constables were appointed outside the constabulary to ·carry out police functions in minor stations.

Separate police responsibilities proved to be confusing, however, and in 1938 the village constables were disbanded and their functions reassigned to a slightly enlarged constabulary. Two years later a further reorganization divided the Sarawak Constabulary into two main units, known as Force A and Force B. Force A was given responsibility for all civil police duties; Force B, made up of paramilitary units, was assigned the mission of patrolling jungle and rural areas. This was the form of police organization at the time Sarawak was ceded back to the British in 1946.

British authorities did not reestablish a single police agency for all of British-held Borneo, nor did they attempt at first to reorganize the Sarawak Constabulary. Major effort instead was devoted to improving the quality and efficiency of existing forces. This subsequently involved the creation of a third police division concerned exclusively with the investigation and control of subversion and subversive elements that were becoming active in the area. Sarawak's Force A was designated the Regular Force; Force B was called the Field Force; and the new division was entitled the Special Force. An identical triangular organization was established in Sabah, the only difference being that its paramilitary division was called the Mobile Force instead of the Field Force.

While these changes and amalgamations were in progress a new factor was introduced into the society of West Malaysia, and to a lesser extent in East Malaysia, that altered the emphasis in all police organizations. This was the great influx of Chinese and Indian immigrants and the propensity of the Chinese to form huge, unassimilated communities that retained their own customs and organizations (see ch. 4, Ethnic Groups and Languages). After 1900 the Chinese, who were primarily urban dwellers, especially taxed police capabilities. Law enforcement agencies had to cope with urban criminal gangs, as well as with banditry and terrorism in the outlying areas.

Worst of all, perhaps, was the problem of suppressing the Chinese secret societies that formed the dynamics behind these new forms of crime. As a result, the police, while retaining strong paramilitary capabilities, began to develop larger and more sophisticated facilities for criminal investigation, detection, and apprehension. This generated an unusual degree of cooperation with military and civilian branches of government that, in 1969, still distinguished police operations.

The development of police and police organizations again underwent significant change during the 1948–60 Emergency, when the whole sphere of public order was thrown into chaos by the depredations of Communist terrorists. Police forces in West Malaysia were quadrupled, given greater authority under centralized state control, and directed to increase attention to the recruitment, training, and equipment of police personnel. It was during this period that police forces began to mature and emerge as modern, efficient agencies of law and order.

The amalgamation of Sabah, Sarawak, and the Federation of Malaya into Malaysia in 1963 was the occasion for the development of final plans to unify their separate police organizations into a single national police force to be called the Royal Malaysia Police (RMP). The name change was authorized, and the constabularies of Sabah and Sarawak were subordinated to federal authority for policy and supervision; but serious internal and external threats to the viability of the new nation, particularly armed opposition from Indonesia, resulted in the declaration of a general state of emergency that delayed further concrete implementing action for several years.

The situation began to stabilize in 1966 when the government of President Sukarno in Indonesia was ousted, the new regime at Djakarta halted active opposition to Malaysia, and normal diplomatic relations between the two nations were restored. Thus freed from the major external threat to national security, the government at Kuala Lumpur was able to give more attention to internal matters. A new police act to replace the separate police ordinances of all component states was promulgated in August 1967, and the RMP in its 1969 form was established.

Strength and Organization

The overall personnel strength of the RMP is approximately 38,000, of whom 28,000 are in the regular police forces and 10,000 are organized in a variety of specialized, paramilitary, and public order units. In addition, an estimated 4,000 civic-minded volunteers are enrolled in several reserve-type organizations for part-time duty in order to release permanent personnel for more important operational duties elsewhere, when and as required. The distribution of these forces roughly parallels that of the general population, so that about two-thirds are stationed in West Malaysia and the remainder are evenly divided between Sabah and Sarawak.

Top control of the RMP is vested in the federal Ministry of Home Affairs, but the administration, coordination, and direction of all police activities are delegated to the inspector general of police, who exercises his authority through police headquarters at the seat of government. This agency, officially known as RMP Headquarters, is organized on a directorate basis to carry out the fourfold mission of maintaining law and order, preserving peace and internal security, preventing and detecting crime, and apprehending criminal offenders. Included in this general mission are added responsibilities for providing the nation's fire services, for licensing vehicles and privately owned weapons, for furnishing escorts at ceremonial rites and during state visits, and for providing aid in time of national disasters.

RMP Headquarters consists of the office of the inspector general and five staff departments that control all administrative and operational activities of the force. The office of the inspector general, in addition to the inspector general and his aides, includes a section for research and planning and another for press and public relations, the deputy inspector general, and three deputy police commissioners who oversee the operations of the staff departments.

The five staff departments are: Department A, which is concerned with personnel, administration, and training matters; Department B, which directs police operations in the fields of public order and internal security, logistics, and marine affairs; Department C, which controls finance and supply; Department D, which constitutes the national office of criminal records; and Department E, which carries out counterintelligence and operations against subversive personnel and organizations. The activities of Department A and Department C are supervised and coordinated by one of the deputy police commissioners in the office of the inspector general known as the director for administration, supply, and personnel; those of Department B and Department D, by another called the director for internal security and public order; and those of Department E, by the third commissioner with the title of director for special operations.

Police operations are carried out on a territorial basis that divides West Malaysia into ten areas, called contingents, and East Malaysia into two segments, called components. Except for Kedah and Perlis, which together form one contingent, the boundaries of these areas are identical to those of individual states in West Malaysia and to those of Sabah and Sarawak in East Malaysia. Each contingent and component is directly subordinate to national police headquarters but is charged with raising and supporting its own regular police organization, which, in effect, constitutes a separate state police force in each area. Each also operates under its own headquarters commanded by a senior police official, called the chief police officer in the contingents and the commissioner of police in the components.

The organization of area headquarters in the components differs somewhat from that in the contingents. In Sabah and Sarawak, which have equal rank with West Malaysia as major political divisions of the nation, police headquarters are small replicas of the national organization in Kuala Lumpur. In West Malaysia, however, most staff planning and direction are performed directly for all contingents by RMP Headquarters, so that the five specialized departments are eliminated and the staff is organized around a few smaller sections devoted to the administration, support, and operational control of their subordinate units.

At the base of the operational structure in both contingents and components are neighborhood or community police stations that are manned by uniformed and plainclothes personnel to carry out conventional police duties. A varying number of stations, depending on population concentrations, make up a larger territory called a police division. All police divisions are subordinated to the headquarters of the contingent or component in which they are located to form the police force of that area. There is no fixed formula determining the number of police divisions in any particular force but, like the stations at the lowest operating level, they are established on the basis of population and territorial needs. Thus, in the contingents of West Malaysia, they range from three divisions in Malacca to 11 in Perak; in Sabah, there is one for each of the four political residencies; and in Sarawak, there is one for each of the five administrative divisions.

In addition to this regular police organization, selected contingencies and components may have one or more specialized units that are assigned to area headquarters for deployment anywhere within their respective territories. Some of these units, such as the Border Scouts in Sabah and Sarawak, are organic to the contingent or component in which they are raised. Other units, such as the Police Field Force (PFF), are federal forces detailed by RMP Headquarters to subordinate areas as needed. Operational control of federal units is exercised by the area headquarters to which they are detailed, but their command, administration, and support are retained by RMP Headquarters.

Specialized Police Units

The specialized paramilitary and public order units and forces supplement the work of regular police in the contingents and components where they serve. Major elements include the PFF, the Federal Reserve Units (FRU's), and the Marine Branch, which are federal organizations commanded by the inspector general and deployed at his discretion; and the Police Volunteer Reserve (PVR), various Auxiliary Police, Women Special Constables (WSC's), Border Scouts, and the RMP Police Cadet Corps, which are agencies of the separate components that activate them.

The Police Field Force

The Police Field Force (PFF) is the operational reserve of the RMP designed, trained, and equipped to seek out and destroy territories and criminals who seek refuge in the jungle, to patrol large tracts of sparsely settled and isolated areas, to assist regular police in public order situations beyond local ability to control, to provide guards and escorts for official personnel and state visitors, and to carry out such special tasks as the inspector general may direct. The force has an overall strength of slightly more than 6,000 men of all ranks organized into six Arabic-numbered light infantry units, each having a varying number of companies.

Number 1 PFF and number 2 PFF, of four companies each, are located in West Malaysia, where they are employed primarily in jungle operations. Number 3 PFF, of seven companies, and number 4 PFF, of four companies, perform comparable duties in Sarawak and Sabah, respectively. Number 5 PFF is essentially a public order unit whose four companies are deployed near urban centers in West Malaysia to provide guard, escort, and general police duties as required. Number 6 PFF is a specialized unit of two companies that garrisons five semipermanent jungle forts in Perak, Kelantan, and Pahang to provide a security screen against the infiltration of Communist terrorists from Thailand and to combat their operations in the northern jungles.

The Federal Reserve Units

The Federal Reserve Units (FRU's) are the public order reserve of the RMP consisting of six numbered units, of three troops each, and one lettered, independent troop. The force as a whole is controlled and administered centrally by the inspector general through the commander, FRU, at national police headquarters. Personnel for these elements are recruited from among members of the regular police and are then specially trained and equipped to deal with critical public order situations, such as the rioting that followed the elections in West Malaysia during May 1969.

Although the FRU's may be sent to any area of the nation, deployment of any unit is usually restricted to West Malaysia. FRU's 1, 4, and 5 were stationed near Kuala Lumpur in late 1969; FRU 2 was located at Kulai, Johore; FRU 6 operated out of Ipoh, Perak; and FRU 3 and "Z" Troop were assigned to Kepala Batas, Penang. The mission of these units is to suppress riots, disperse unlawful assemblies, and control large crowds that might become unruly. They also assist in rescue work during local and national disasters and aid local police in cordon and search operation, anticrime patrols, and the conduct of raids.

Police Volunteer Reserve and Auxiliary Police

The Police Volunteer Reserve (PVR) is an establishment of civic-minded volunteers in each police contingent of West Malaysia available for part-time police duties. Its members, recruited on a multiracial basis, are called to duty in time of need to relieve regular police of routine duties so that they may perform more important and urgent tasks. The overall strength of the PVR is estimated to be about 3,000 men of all ranks.

The Auxiliary Police is also a body of civilian volunteers in West Malaysian contingents similar to the PVR. It differs from the PVR only in size (total strength about 1,200) and in its concentration in rural areas. The Auxiliary Police is used mainly to assist regular police in maintaining law and order in villages and kampongs.

Women Special Constables

West Malaysian contingents abutting the Thai border are authorized a small force (about 75) of Women Special Constables (WSC's) for duty within the Border Security Area. These WSC's are trained to search and escort female prisoners during operations.

Special Auxiliary Police Units in Sabah

Special and auxiliary police units in Sabah include the Special Constabulary, the Police Reserve, and the Border Scouts. The Special Constabulary and the Police Reserve are both volunteer forces that function in identical manner to their counterparts, the PVR and the Auxiliary Police of West Malaysia. The Special Constabulary has an authorized strength of 600 and the Auxiliary Police a strength of 500. Elements of both units are scattered throughout all four police divisions of Sabah.

The Sabah Border Scouts is a paramilitary organization used to patrol the remote border areas with Indonesian Kalimantan. The Border Scouts also operate the border control posts at Tawau, Long Pa Sin, and Pensiangan, and the land crossing points at Ulu Moning, Kabu, Saliliran, and Bantul. They provide a police presence in these remote areas where civil administration is weak or nonexistent.

Special Auxiliary Police Units in Sarawak

Nonregular police units in Sarawak include the Auxiliary Police and the Border Scouts. The Auxiliary Police has a total authorized strength of 565, organized in four branches, to provide assistance for general police duties, protection of oilfields, antisubversive duty, and jungle patrolling. The Border Scouts, once a paramilitary force of about 1,200 officers and men, underwent change after 1963 when major responsibility for border security was assumed by the armed forces. In 1969 the Border Scouts had become a plainclothes, unarmed intelligence and antisubversive organization. Most Border Scout strength, however, remained concentrated along the border with Indonesian Kalimantan.

The Police Cadet Corps

The RMP Police Cadet Corps is a new organization, formed in mid-November 1969 and composed of volunteer students in secondary schools of West Malaysia. Its membership is drawn from male and female applicants of all races who, after serving a 2-month probationary period, become permanent members by passing an appropriate examination.

The activation order did not specify the ultimate strength of the organization but stated that its purpose was to inculcate a sense of responsibility for the maintenance of law and order among all students. In furthering this mission, cadets of the corps were authorized to help maintain discipline in schools, to promote harmonious relations between regular police and the public and, when necessary, to assist the police in certain minor public order situations as directed by the authorities.

The Marine Branch

The Marine Branch, sometimes referred to as the Royal Malaysia Marine Police, is a federal force of about 1,200 officers and men. It is controlled directly from RMP Headquarters through separate divisional commands for West Malaysia, Sabah, and Sarawak. The headquarters and operating base for the West Malaysian division is at the Royal Malaysian Naval Base in Singapore; that for the Sabah division is at Sandakan, and that for Sarawak is at Kuching. The mission of the force is to patrol Malaysian territorial waters to detect and prevent smuggling, piracy, illegal immigration, and traffic in firearms and other contraband; to enforce shipping ordinances; to engage in search and rescue operations; and to protect Malaysian fishing craft from hijackers and fishing grounds from poachers. The Marine Branch is equipped with about 400 motor vessels of various sizes, ranging from relatively large patrol craft of the "PX" class suitable for sea duty to small river and harbor motorboats that are little more than converted pleasure launches.

Personnel and Training

There are no racial or ethnic restrictions placed on eligibility for membership in any of the RMP forces; nevertheless, a marked ethnic division in them constitutes one of the major problems of the police.

Probably because police work was the first, and for a long time almost the only, government career open to Malays, recruitment of an adequate Malay force has never been difficult. Absolute figures are withheld for security reasons, but the latest report issued by the government indicates that at the beginning of 1969 the overall strength of the RMP consisted of about 39 percent Malays and 61 percent non-Malays.

The Chinese occasionally join the detective service but seldom enter the regular uniformed force because they dislike ordinary police work. Appeals are constantly made to attract more Chinese, and from time to time authorities have adopted a quota system in which only one-half as many non-Chinese as Chinese may be recruited. Response has been small, however, and most Chinese continue to shun a career in the police. Indians and Pakistanis, mostly Sikhs from northern India, are found at all levels in the contingents of West Malaysia and to a lesser extent in the components of East Malaysia. The junglewise Iban in Sarawak and native tribesmen in Sabah dominate most elements in those areas.

With some minor variations dictated by local conditions and availabilities in different states, there are three usual methods of entry into the police services, each based on the educational qualifications of the applicant. Candidates who have completed at least the 6th year of primary education may be recruited as constables; those who hold the overseas school certificate or the federation certificate of education may be accepted as probationary police inspectors; those with a degree from a recognized university, or who have passed the final bar examinations, are recruited as probationary assistant superintendents of police. An exception to these general prerequisites occurs in East Malaysia where, although literacy has been required since 1949, illiterates are encouraged to join PFF or the Border Scouts, in which jungle lore and tracking skills are considered more valuable than an ability to read or write.

Malaysia offers its police personnel training facilities and programs that are the equal of any in Southeast Asia. Each state has its own police training school in which basic courses in police methods and techniques are given to new recruits, and refresher, promotion, and specialized technical courses are available for those already on duty. In addition, there are a number of federally operated facilities controlled and supported directly from RMP Headquarters. These include the Police Depot at Kuala Lumpur, the Police College at Kuala Kubu Bahru, the PFF Training School at Cape Rambutan, and the Special Branch School at Kuala Lumpur.

The Police Depot offers basic and advanced courses in police administration and operations for all ranks and sometimes conducts unit training for public order units of the regular police. The Police College provides similar courses for officers only and, since 1968, has conducted a junior staff and command course for lower ranking officers, a senior staff and command course for officers of superintendent rank and higher, and a combined counterintelligence and prosecution course for officers assigned to that type of duty. The PFF Training School serves members of PFF units by giving them specialized training in military subjects, internal security, and jungle operations.

Police of all ranks selected for other specialized training are regularly sent to other government schools, such as those of the armed forces. Each year a considerable number of officers are also sent to training centers abroad, such as the International Police Academy in Washington, D.C., and police colleges in England, Scotland, Australia, and Japan.

Unit training also occupies an important place in the development of all police elements for which it is appropriate. Mobile units designed for mob control and suppression of strikes, riots, and demonstrations periodically engage in exercises to improve their efficiency in these matters. The various field and paramilitary forces, including the Marine Branch, regularly carry out command post exercises and, at least once a year, participate in field maneuvers with the armed forces.

Police Effectiveness

Most personnel of the RMP, regardless of the branch to which they are assigned, display high morale and pride in belonging to the service. The force is well organized and trained, living conditions are good, and pay is comparable to that which members might expect to receive in civilian life. Cases of police corruption are rare, and its incidence is kept low by swift and severe punitive action against all offenders. Internecine rivalries, either among units or between the leadership and rank-and-file members, have never appeared in sufficient strength to seriously affect the unity of the force. Consequently, the RMP as a professional agency has proved fully capable of coping with cases of individual crime, with riots and other threats to internal peace and security, and with the maintenance of public order and tranquillity.

The greatest hindrance to police work in the nation is the attitude of the public. In reality, as far as the police are concerned, there have been two publics—Malay and Chinese. On the basis of official reports, the Malays seem to be involved in serious crime less often than the Chinese, but most are indifferent to the police. Many of the Chinese have been openly hostile. Both Malays and Chinese tend to consider conviction for crime more a matter of bad luck than a disgrace or blot on their social standing. It may be significant that the Malay term for a policeman is *mata-mata* (meaning "eyes") and for a detective is *mata-gelap* (or "eyes in the dark"), words formerly used for the feared spies of local rulers.

The lack of public cooperation sometimes stems from a fear of retaliation. Cases have been recorded in which everyone among a crowd of persons present when a street crime occurred refused to identify the perpetrator. Because of these attitudes, the police admit that unpremeditated crime is almost impossible to investigate. They have relied heavily, therefore, on paid informants who are guaranteed protection from reprisal. Confidence in the ability of the police to protect a witness is strained when the criminal is a member of a secret society or when the informant is likely to be the terrorists' next victim. Even when guarantees are given, the fear of reprisal remains at least as strong as the desire to aid police or to have confidence in their ability to honor pledges of protection.

A major campaign to develop greater trust in police personnel has been diligently carried out since 1963. It is based on a simple plan of increasing the number of contacts between police and the public, in which actions to assist the people are given priority over those that merely enforce the law. Deeds of unusual helpfulness are recognized and rewarded by the authorities. This program has been extremely successful in improving general attitudes toward the police. Public esteem has also improved as the result of a demonstrable betterment in the public order situation since 1963.

CRIMINAL LAW AND PROCEDURE

Constitutional Rights

The federal Constitution guarantees fundamental rights to all Malaysian citizens and the basic rights of due process of law to all accused persons. Its provisions have been carefully drafted to provide for these rights and, at the same time, to allow the central authorities all powers necessary to deal with any national emergency. No person may be deprived of his life or property except in accordance with law, and complaints of unlawful detention are investigated by the courts, which may order the release of individuals if the complaints are justified. Persons arrested must be informed of charges against them, be granted the counsel of their choice, and be arraigned before a magistrate within one day of their arrest. These provisions do not apply to enemy aliens and may be abrogated when a state of emergency has been declared, such as occurred in the 1969 postelection riots.

In normal times various constitutional provisions provide that no criminal law may be retroactive and that no person may be subjected to double jeopardy. In addition, no citizen may be detained for more than 3 months unless an advisory board of three persons, appointed by the Supreme Head of Malaysia, has considered the case and reported that further detention is justified.

Criminal Law

The criminal law of Malaysia is defined in the Penal Code, written first for the Straits Settlements and gradually applied elsewhere. In 1963 it was extended throughout Malaysia and since then has been undergoing revision to accommodate traditional local practices in the three major components of the nation. In late 1969 the process had not yet been completed, and the existing code still formed the basis for most criminal action.

The Penal Code defines categories of offenses as those perpetrated against property, against the person, and against the state and public tranquillity and lists death, imprisonment, whipping, and fines as legally approved punishments. Imprisonment with hard labor and solitary confinement was abolished in 1952, and the number of offenses for which whipping could be imposed was reduced to only a few. An enactment of 1954, however, provided that minor offenders could be sentenced to "compulsory" work to be done during their leisure time.

The death sentence is mandatory only for murder. Attempts to murder or injure the head of a Malaysian state is punishable either by death or life imprisonment. Persons convicted of two other crimes—successfully inciting mutiny in the armed forces and causing the suicide of a child or an insane or intoxicated person—may be punished by death or life imprisonment but are usually punished by shorter terms of imprisonment. Reflecting the particular problem of gangsterism is a legal provision that, if one member commits a murder during a robbery, all other members may be given the death penalty.

The Penal Code permits the judge considerable freedom in passing sentence. For many crimes he may sentence the convicted offender either to life imprisonment or to a shorter term appropriate to the seriousness of his offense. With the exception of the penalty for gang robbery at night, for which a prison term of 14 years may be imposed, all prison terms are either for life or for a maximum of 10 years. Other measures include severe penalties for possessing or carrying firearms, ammunition, or explosives without a license and for consorting with another person violating these restrictions.

Criminal and Court Procedure

Criminal and court procedure is based on that of Great Britain. Crime is divided into two categories, seizable and nonseizable; in cases of seizable crimes any individual or policeman may arrest the offender without a warrant. Criminals apprehended for either category of offense are guaranteed a fair trial in one of the established courts having jurisdiction in the area where the crime was committed. Although persisting terminology and local custom are not yet uniform, there are three types of courts of original jurisdiction. Offenses of a minor nature that are punishable by terms of imprisonment not exceeding 1 year are tried in magistrate courts; those of greater severity warranting terms of up to 4 years are heard in sessions or district courts; those of a really serious nature are adjudicated by High Courts of justice (see ch. 12, The Governmental System).

Magistrates and the presidents of sessions courts sit alone and are competent to judge all cases legally within their jurisdictions. High Courts are presided over by a qualified judge, but the determination of guilt or innocence is made by a jury. In all court trials defendants may be represented by counsel, but such representation is not mandatory. Except in cases punishable by death, defendants are not entitled to free legal aid even though they desire counsel. If they cannot afford a defense attorney, they plead their own cases, after briefing by the presiding court officer on the points necessary to rebut the state's charges. In capital trials, the court appoints and the state pays for a qualified member of the bar to defend the accused.

In addition to the regular courts in West Malaysia, there are religious courts established under the laws of Islam, where criminal cases involving only Muslims are tried. A comparable system of native courts in East Malaysia exists to try cases arising from breaches of native law and custom in which all parties are natives.

The courts give special attention to offenders under 17 years of age. In disposing of their cases, emphasis is placed on treatment and correction rather than on punishment. In West Malaysia separate juvenile courts have been established, but in Sabah and Sarawak youthful offenders are tried in magistrate courts. Most juvenile cases, however, are handled without recourse to formal trial because of the prolific use of probation. The law requires that, before any court action is taken, juvenile cases must be referred to a probation officer, who makes a thorough investigation of the offender's home life and other data pertaining to his delinquency. The probation officer then may decide simply to place the juvenile on probation for a specified period of time; he may recommend that the offender be sent away from home for a short period of time and be placed on probation in a special hostel; or, at a last resort in serious offenses, he may ask the court to commit the offender to an approved correctional school.

Decisions proceeding out of court trials in criminal cases may be appealed if there is either a question of law or a dispute of fact. Appeals from magistrate and sessions courts are made to the High Court in Kuala Lumpur for cases tried in West Malaysia and to the High Court at Kota Kinabalu for those in East Malaysia. When appeals fail for any reason whatsoever, mitigation of sentences is still possible through the exercise of various powers of mercy vested in the Supreme Head or in the heads of the states. These individuals, at their own discretion, may grant pardons, respites, or reprieves of sentences for any crimes committed in their territories.

THE PRISON SYSTEM

Before 1950 policies and concepts regarding prisons and the treatment of prisoners were basically punitive. The idea that the best deterrent to crime was incarceration that made an offender's life hard and unpleasant governed all prison administration. Since then, however, this belief has been replaced by the concept that the reformation of prisoners through good treatment and training is the wiser course. Accordingly, prison practices in 1969 were based on principles enunciated in the Stanadrd Minimum Rules for the Treatment of Prisoners prepared by the United Nations.

The administration and operation of the prison system is a responsibility of the RMP. Policy is formulated and supervised by appropriate staff sections at police headquarters in Kuala Lumpur, and wardens and guards constitute a separate branch of the operating police force. Penal institutions are of diverse types, graded on the basis of the seriousness of the crime committed and the length of required incarceration. They range from walled compounds containing massive stone cell blocks offering maximum security to open farms or detention camps, called protective custody centers, where inmates work in the fields under minimum supervision during daylight hours. Regardless of type, however, all conduct strong educational programs and instruction in useful arts and crafts, and all carry out extensive welfare activities for prisoners, including after-discharge aid and employment service.

Major prisons in West Malaysia include the Central Training Prison at Taiping, to which prisoners serving long terms for serious offenses are sent, and four regional prisons, located at Penang, Alor Star, Kuala Lumpur, and Johore Bahru, which receive serious offenders serving shorter sentences. Another major institution is the Central Prison for Special offenders at Seremban, to which all political prisoners are sent. Those given light sentences for lesser offenses and in whom authorities place a measure of trust are sent to protective custody centers at Pengkalan Chepa, Kelantan, and at Kamunting, Selangor.

In addition to the general penal institutions, West Malaysia operates the Central Prison for Women at Johore Bahru; five local prisons for women at Kuala Lumpur, Taiping, Alor Star, and Pengkalan Chepal; and two local prisons for men, one at Kuantan for adults and the other at Sungei Patani for young prisoners. West Malaysia also operates three reform schools for juveniles, one for girls at Batu Gajah and the other two for boys at Telok Mas and Malacca.

There are four major penal institutions and one protective custody center in Sarawak. They include the Central Prison at Kuching for males, the women's prison at Kuching, general prisons at Sibu and Simanggang, and a protective custody center located about 6 miles from Kuching. In addition, there is the Sarawak Boys' Home, a reform school, at Sungei Priok.

Major institutions in Sabah consist of three general prisons, located at Kota Kinabalu, Sandakan, and Tawau; a new women's prison at Kota Kinabalu; and a protective custody center near Kota Kinabalu. Sabah has no separate institution for dealing with juveniles, but a reform school was scheduled to be built and ready for use in early 1970.

INCIDENCE OF CRIME

Available statistics released by the RMP on the incidence of crime are complete only through the year 1967. They show that the total number of crimes has steadily increased, rising from about 32,000 in 1963 to almost 52,000 in 1967 (see table 28). More recent figures had not become available by 1969.

Criminal offenses, defined as violations of either the Penal Code or other federal and state laws, are grouped into seven categories in official reports. Class I offenders are those committed against the person, such as murder, attempted murder, grievous hurt, kidnapping, and rape. The next four classes cover offenses against property, such as robbery, malicious destrictuion, extortion, forgery, and theft: Class II involves those carried out with violence; Class III, those without violence; Class IV, those consisting of malicious injury to property; and Class V, those having to do with currency. Class VI offenses are other violations of the Penal Code, and Class VII are violations of other state and federal laws. The bulk of crimes are those falling in Class III, followed in descending order of frequency by those in Class II, Class VII, Class I, Class IV, Class VI, and Class V.

Table 28. Criminal Offenses Reported in Malaysia in 1967

Category	West Malaysia	Sabah	Sarawak	Total
Class I _____	3,675	121	328	4,124
Class II _____	11,521	160	298	11,979
Class III _____	27,455	651	2,317	30,423
Class IV _____	467	16	79	562
Class V _____	25	1	30	56
Class VI _____	188	37	11	236
Class VII _____	3,520	494	526	4,540
TOTAL _____	46,851	1,480	3,589	51,920

Source: Adapted from Royal Malaysia Police Annual Report, 1969.

Most of the crime in Malaysia is organized rather than casual or individual. In West Malaysian urban areas especially, criminal gangs actively engage in robbery, extortion, smuggling, narcotics traffic, and various forms of gambling. A gang is defined by the law as a group of five or more persons associated for an illegal purpose. Police records list a total of 204 secret societies and criminal gangs, with a combined membership estimated to be about 3,000. All but four of these gangs are in West Malaysia. The number and activities of these gangs are reported to be gradually decreasing under concerted counteraction by the police.

INTERNAL SECURITY

Apart from foreign-backed subversion, the internal security of Malaysia has not been seriously challenged by a foreign power since friendly relations with the Republic of Indonesia were restored after 1966. A challenge to the validity of Sabah's membership in

548

the federation was raised by Philippine claims of sovereignty over that territory, but the problem was being considered through diplomatic channels in 1969 and was not expected to impair national tranquillity (see ch. 14, Foreign Relations). The only serious challenges in late 1969, therefore, were those arising from Communist terrorist and subversive activities.

Primary responsibility for maintaining the internal security of the nation, except for various paramilitary assignments of the armed forces, is vested in the RMP and is exercised specifically by the force's Department E, sometimes referred to as the Special Branch. The organization and operational details of this agency are cloaked in secrecy, but it is known that the national headquarters and those of the Sabah and Sarawak components are divided into special sections devoted to counterintelligence and the control of communism, terrorism, extremism, guerrilla forces, and subversive organizations and individuals.

The Communist Threat

There is no single, monolithic Communist party in Malaysia. The movement as a whole is united only in its dedication to a common international ideology. In practice, the party is divided into two otherwise nonintegrated groups: the Malayan Communist Party (MCP), which is operative in West Malaysia, and the nebulous Sarawak Communist Organization (SCO) which directs activities in East Malaysia. Both are officially illegal and are in direct communication with members of foreign Communist parties, particularly with those of the Chinese Communist Party, from which they receive, and to whom they render, maximum support and assistance.

Exchanges between the MCP and the SCO appear to be minimal for a variety of reasons. Both originated in their respective areas as separate and distinct and, although each has been amenable to cooperative effort when convenient, each is also understandably sensitive about its local responsibilities and prerogatives. More decisively, each seeks the establishment of separate political states in West and East Malaysia and is aware that the successful accomplishment of their objectives would make integration awkward and contrary to the international strategy of separate national party organization.

Local operating conditions further encourage separation of the MCP and the SCO. Both prefer the Chinese doctrine of violence to the Soviet-professed concept of peaceful coexistence, but the MCP has had little ability or opportunity to engage in either one. Its executive committee is in exile so that united front tactics are impracticable, and continued government suppression prevents the party from developing any significant strength in West Malaysia.

The SCO, however, has been spared most of the crippling reverses that weakened the MCP. It has been able to maintain a strong physical presence in East Malaysia, engage fully in united front activities, and develop much popular support among the influential Chinese community, especially in Sarawak. It exerts powerful political and economic influence through the area's second largest and best organized political.party, the Sarawak United People's Party (SUPP), through the Chinese school system, and through an ability to manipulate various labor groups (see ch. 13, Political Dynamics; ch. 8, Education; ch. 20, Labor). Of special importance is the SCO's youth front, the Sarawak Advanced Youth Association (SAYA) which, as a cross-society group, finds it relatively easy to recruit young dissidents into a large, aggressive, and active underground, known as the Clandestine Communist Organization (CCO). Trained, armed, and organized for guerrilla warfare, sabotage, intelligence, and all forms of subversive warfare, the Clandestine Communist Organization constitutes one of the most serious threats to internal security.

The net result in late 1969 was that the Communist threat in Malaysia existed as two distinct and separate regional manifestations. In both areas combined action of the RMP and the armed forces had demonstrated an ability to keep the situation under adequate control.

The Malayan Communist Party

Communism as an organized force came to West Malaysia in the early 1920's, emerging in a pattern that has characterized the party ever since. Early organizing attempts by British and Indonesian branches of the international movement were unsuccessful because their agents could not establish rapport with the local population. Agents from China, however, gained entrance to the Chinese community on racial grounds and played upon the strong emotional attachment most Chinese had for the land of their origin and on animosities they felt against the Malays. Communism thus began as, and has remained, a predominantly Chinese phenomenon.

During the first several years of its existence, the Malayan Communist Party (MCP) was occupied with recruiting and extending its organization and followed policies of penetration, infiltration, propaganda, and the creation of popular fronts. Although no mass support developed, the party was able to establish itself in the Chinese community, create a few fronts and Communist youth leagues, place some teachers in Chinese schools, and gain influence in labor organizations. Despite encouraging success in these operations, the MCP before World War II never became a decisive force and at most constituted only an occasional threat.

The outbreak of World War II and the invasion of the Peninsula by Japanese forces provided the Communists with an opportunity to improve their position. MCP leaders, posing as Malayan patriots, offered full cooperation in expelling the invaders. After some hesitation, the British authorities accepted and provided arms and training to men selected by the party for guerrilla duty behind the Japanese lines. After a few weeks of operations, these groups withdrew to the jungle, where they remained throughout the conflict. Raids against the Japanese were made when possible but were never very large or very important as far as effective resistance was concerned.

When the war was over, these elements came out of the jungle claiming major credit for a victory in which they really had played no decisive role. Because the slowness with which the British returned to the area left the MCP as the only well-organized group in Malaya, Communist elements took territorial control as the defeated Japanese relinquished it. The party kept good discipline in some areas and initiated terrorism in others, but at no time did they attempt to extend their control over the whole Peninsula. This was probably because of a split in their ranks over two policies proposed for use at the end of the war; one, called the Chinese line, favored an immediate attempt to seize power by force, and the other, known as the moderate policy, aimed at a return to agitation and front tactics along lines advocated by the international movement.

In the aftermath of the war, the MCP apparently accepted demobilization and turned in many of the weapons the British had given them. Relinquished weapons, however, were mainly those of non-Communist elements, while hard-core members retained their weapons, secreting them in previously established jungle bases as a hedge against the future. Meanwhile, the MCP was allowed to operate openly, although no formal action was taken to set it up as a legal party. Free to act without fear of police suppression and basking in a considerable popular favor because of their exaggerated claims to a war record, party members began to implement a moderate policy and to spread into all sectors of society. Efforts to penetrate and influence political parties met with little success, but the drive into youth organizations was extremely fruitful and that into labor was extensive and important.

These postwar successes imparted a sense of growing power among the rank and file of the MCP that resulted in a resumption of the old "Chinese line-moderate policy" controversy. Strong opposition arose among those who, pointing to the growing power of the Communist Party in China under policies of violence, found ample ground to criticize the existing MCP leadership. The controversy came to a head in February 1948, when the international movement prescribed a radical change for Southeast Asia that involved dropping united front tactics in favor of armed rebellion. The moderate secretary general of the MCP, Lai Teck, was discredited and replaced by the militant Chin Peng, who in 1969 still held that position.

Chin Peng immediately launched the MCP on a campaign of terror, sabotage, murder, arson, and armed rebellion that came to be known as the Emergency. The program was designed to unfold in three progressive stages. Beginning with small raids on rubber estates, mines, transportation facilities, power stations, and similar vital installations, the campaign was scheduled to advance to a second stage of larger attacks on military and police outposts. Once these were reduced and consolidated into firm operating bases, a final all-out war was to be initiated to overthrow the government. Accompanying this campaign of violence, the MCP began strident propaganda calling for an end to colonialism, expulsion of the British, and the establishment of an independent Malaya in which the Chinese might occupy a more prominent position.

The revolt got off to an auspicious start, largely because security forces were not yet organized or strong enough to contain the terrorists. The British, however, brought in strong military reinforcements; civilian vigilante corps were created to protect vital installations; a state of emergency was declared; and extraordinary powers were granted federal and local authorities to deal with the unrest. Gradually the situation was stabilized, and the insurrection never passed beyond the first phase.

Once these administrative measures were in operation, the government launched a two-pronged attack designed to isolate the Communist terrorists from the people and to dry up their sources of supply and intelligence. Residents from Communist-dominated sections were resettled in a series of New Villages in areas away from the jungle. These settlements were completely enclosed in barbed wire, provided with permanent military garrisons, and patrolled on a 24-hour basis to regulate all ingress and egress. This not only provided immunity from Communist extortion and reestablished a measure of confidence in the government but also, by granting the settlements considerable autonomy in government, blunted Communist propaganda about British exploitation of the people. More importantly, it supported the second prong of countermeasures by forcing the terrorists to emerge from their jungle hideouts and risk capture or annihilation in search of food supplies, and intelligence.

The Communists reacted by increasing their terrorism, which only embittered the victimized population and hardened popular attitudes against them. The guerrillas were forced to retreat deeper and deeper into the jungle where, disillusioned and discouraged, they deserted the insurrection by the hundreds. Finally, after his forces were reduced to a mere 500 and continued to be inexorably pressed by aggressive military action, Chin Peng fled northward across the border to a safe haven in Thailand. For all practical purposes the Emergency was over.

Since the flight of Chin Peng and the reestablishment of MCP headquarters-in-exile in southern Thailand, disruptive efforts of the party have been more of a nuisance than a serious threat to Malaysia's internal security. Armed Communist bands have engaged in sporadic raids across the border, and party members who remained underground in West Malaysia have agitated and fomented strikes, riots, and demonstrations to disrupt the economy and to discredit local and federal authorities. Party mechanisms have also supported attempts of the radical Pan-Malayan Islamic Party to create an all-Malay, Muslim, theocratic state embracing the whole Peninsula. During the brief period of Indonesian opposition to the creation of Malaysia, called the Confrontation, the MCP integrated its operations with those of Indonesia to form the nucleus of a northern attack force in case full-scale war broke out. Concerted government police and military countermeasures, however, were effective in keeping the situation under control.

In late 1969 the MCP appeared to have undergone little change in organization or strength. Its membership was estimated to total about 1,000, half of whom were in Thailand with Chin Peng and the other half at guerrilla bases in the jungles or operating undercover in front organizations throughout West Malaysia.

The Sarawak Communist Organization

Communism did not exist as a formal organization in East Malaysia until after World War II. Consequently, the Sarawak Communist Organization (SCO) has no long documented history comparable to that of the MCP; in fact, useful data was still so scarce in 1969 that its outlines were shadowy and obscure, visible mainly by inference from the nature and activities of its two powerful operating fronts and mechanisms—SUPP in overt political affairs and the Clandestine Communist Organization in all subversive activities. Apparently, the SCO has responsibility for all of East Malaysia because there is no evidence that separate parties exist for Sabah and Sarawak. Like the MCP, however, the SCO is predominantly a Chinese phenomenon oriented toward the Chinese branch of the international movement.

In the years following the end of the war, despite their war record and notwithstanding their superior education and capabilities, the Chinese were excluded from significant participation in the social and political life of the country. Young Chinese, especially, resented their status and concluded that their best hope for the future lay in closer identification with the revolutionary movement that was gaining the ascendancy in China. They therefore deepened and intensified liaison with Communist China, and it is probable that the SCO was secretly organized at this time.

Barred from operating legally, the Communists went underground and began an intense program of seeking power through united front efforts. They gained control of the Chinese school system and turned it into a major medium of Communist indoctrination. They agitated for expulsion of the British and the establishment of an independent, nonracial state in East Malaysia. In pursuance of these objectives, they organized numerous front organizations in all sectors of society, the most significant of which was SAYA. By 1956 SAYA had absorbed most of the other fronts and had established itself as an executive headquarters for all Communist activities in the area. Out of its hard-core membership a control organization was formed that became the clandestine Communist organization.

The strength of the Clandestine Communist Organization is applied in two major directions—in the political sphere through SUPP and in all other insurrectionary activities through its highly organized armed bands. Additional pressure is brought to bear through other organizations, such as the illegal Sarawak Farmers' Association, sports groups, and choral societies, but they are too weak to be significant and are employed primarily in supporting roles for agitation, propaganda, recruiting, and general promotion.

The Clandestine Communist Organization developed into a dangerous military threat in 1963 when a separate headquarters was established to conduct recruiting within the disgruntled Chinese student body after attitudes for outright revolutionary action had been nurtured by skillful propaganda and agitation. Recruits were organized into small units of about 30 men each and dispatched to the jungle to create operational bases and centers of resistance. When Malaysia was formed in 1963, these units were presented with training facilities and opportunity for joint action with Indonesian forces that had moved into Kalimantan as part of the Confrontation campaign. Some units slipped across the border, where they were trained in guerrilla tactics, sabotage, and agitation and also were equipped and supplied with arms and ammunition. Some remained in Kalimantan for joint action with Indonesian forces; others infiltrated back to turn their bases into outposts of terrorism and centers of refuge for raiders from across the border. They also maintained contact with Indonesian forces, from whom they received operational guidance, intelligence, supplies, and other support.

The end of Confrontation halted these operations, and joint action by Malaysian forces and those of the new Indonesian government liquidated most insurrectionary elements on both sides of the border. By 1969 serious threats to the internal security of both Sabah and Sarawak were under control. Nevertheless, an estimated 2,000 Clandestine Communist Organization effectives who, with the addition of non-Communist supporters, could field a force of over 3,500, backed up by about 25,000 civilian sympathizers, remained in jungle hideouts and required constant surveillance by security forces.

CHAPTER 25

THE ARMED FORCES

Armed forces available to Malaysia in 1969 consisted of its own land, sea, and air forces and similar British Commonwealth contingents physically present in Malaysia or in nearby Singapore. The presence of non-Malaysian forces in the country stemmed from a recognition that, although indigenous forces were able to maintain internal security under normal conditions, they could not, unless expanded, provide a defense against external attack or widespread civil disorder. Accordingly, a mutual defense agreement with the United Kingdom authorized Great Britain to retain its former colonial bases and to man them with Commonwealth forces. These forces had no authority in Malaysia other than that necessary for their own discipline, administration, and operation; they were, however, always available in case they were needed. Should such an eventuality arise, British units detached to aid Malaysia would be placed under the operational control, but not the command, of Malaysian military authorities.

This arrangement was scheduled for change as the result of military retrenchment by the United Kingdom and a decision to withdraw all Commonwealth units from Malaysia and Singapore by the end of 1971. In early 1969 they had already departed from East Malaysia, and sizable reductions had been made in those assigned to West Malaysia. The mutual defense agreement remained in effect, although just how it would be implemented after 1971 was unclear and the subject of much concern.

Preliminary talks held in late 1968 among Malaysia, Singapore, the United Kingdom, Australia, and New Zealand to determine future arrangements apparently were inconclusive. The United Kingdom reiterated that once British troops were withdrawn, they would return to Malaysia only under exceptional circumstances. In February 1969, however, Australia and New Zealand pledged continued military assistance on their own. Australia promised to station two air force fighter squadrons and to maintain one naval vessel in the area at all times; New Zealand declared that in addition to a second naval vessel, it would provide a force of transport airplanes. Each further agreed to make one battalion of infantry available to man a combined Australia-New Zealand force to be stationed permanently in Singapore. They stipulated, however, that these forces could be used only for "fundamental defense" of the area and were not to be employed for controlling internal disorders.

Malaysia meanwhile has been accelerating a modest expansion of indigenous forces to improve its own defense posture. The regular military establishments in 1969 had a total personnel strength of less than 40,000 assigned to the Malaysian Army, the Royal Malaysian Navy (RMN), and the Royal Malaysian Air Force (RMAF). Each component was a separate and coequal force, but the military establishment as a whole was controlled by a single joint staff in the Ministry of Defense. The only fully organized reserve force was the Territorial Army (TA), several units of which were normally on duty in the ground forces. The TA also administered a loosely organized and partially operational civilian guard of about 30,000 men called the Local Defense Corps (LDC). The RMN and RMAF had no effective reserves.

In addition to the regular establishment, there were several quasi-military police forces that could be made available in times of emergency. They included the relatively small Police Field Force, the Rolay Malaysia Marine Police, the Malaysian Aboriginal Paramilitary Force, and the Sarawak Border Scouts (see ch. 24, Public Order and Internal Security).

The multiracial character of the country's population and the historic domination of Malays have given an unusual ethnic cast to the armed forces. Recruitment was initially restricted to Malays and, despite concerted efforts of the government to instill a sense of common citizenship and the subsequent activation of multiracial units, Malays continued to dominate the forces in 1969. This was particularly noticeable in the army, where membership in the Royal Malay Regiment (RMR), which contained the bulk of all ground force strength, continued to be reserved for Malays only. All other army units, and the entire navy and air force were multiracial and generally conformed to specified racial proportions of 40 percent Malay, 40 percent Chinese, and 20 percent Indian and others. Only in the RMAF was there any significant departure from prescribed norms. Although the overall ethnic ratios were maintained, the RMAF officer corps contained 50 percent Chinese as against only 33 percent Malays; among enlisted personnel the percentages were reversed.

HISTORICAL BACKGROUND

Early Period

Early inhabitants of present-day Malaysia were grouped in numerous small, isolated states in Malaya and tribal groupings in Borneo that had little intercourse with one another. Since they had no important interests in common and no pressing need for one another, there was no welding of a national consciousness on which to found a unified tradition or create large military forces.

Some temporary cohesion, if not actual unity of the region, was established by the ancient empires of Langkasuka, Sri Vijaya, Majapahit, and Malacca. These powers dominated the area for varying periods of early history and reduced its small states to vassalage. They also provided some formal military experience by press-ganging many of the subjugated peoples into their conquering armies (see ch. 3, Historical Setting). Such service, however, was looked upon as a burden imposed by an intruder rather than as a duty or responsibility in response to self-asserted concepts of independent unity and did nothing to foster military thinking in a national sense.

After the last of these empires fell in the 15th century, a new consideration tended to reinforce traditional local dependence on the activities of small irregular forces. The Strait of Malacca and the South China Sea became strategic world trade routes plied by ships carrying great wealth. The small states in Malaya and Borneo all faced the sea and found it profitable to develop ports at river mouths from which to prey on this shipping or to exact tolls. Piracy became a way of life for many.

Small-scale guerrillalike warfare on land and piracy at sea bred warriors and local chieftains who could hold a small band together as long as they offered easy success, but they could not, and did not, produce large or disciplined forces united in a common aggressive or defensive purpose. They developed skills in man-to-man combat, but they had little in common with the growth of an organized military establishment. Such was the situation when the first Europeans arrived in the area.

Colonial Period

Superior European naval strength, which came with the empire builders, soon dominated the area and its waters, but piracy and internal bickering remained. Orderly development and trade in the region were seriously impaired by the chaos resulting from these conditions and, as British commercial interests increased, so did the demand for pacification. Throughout the years the United Kingdom dispatched increasing numbers of armed forces on permanent station, but it was approximately a century before they could put an end to piracy and the constant warfare among separate states and tribes.

By 1805 an effective Pax Britannica had been imposed, and the old system of factional armies went out of style. Even the almost universal practice of wearing the *kris*, the short, sometimes wavy-bladed sword that had been associated with the Malay warrior from ancient times, was prohibited by law. It remained, however, as a symbol of military virtue, typically representing individual rather than national or organizational accomplishment.

THE RISE AND DEVELOPMENT OF FORCES

Ground Forces

For many years volunteer indigenous personnel had been recruited for colonial forces, but it was not until 1932 that a self-contained indigenous unit was formed. There was not yet an independent, unified political system to which such a force could give its allegiance, but the fact that a local military force finally existed resulted in an upsurge of pride and a first consciousness of independent military responsibility.

At first recruitment for indigenous forces, based on the Malay-proclaimed principle of the "special position of Malays in their own country" was restricted exclusively to Malays. Chinese and Indian inhabitants of the region were not eligible because it was felt they had little attachment to Malaya and intended, ultimately, to return to their native countries. Personnel policies remained unchanged for 20 years before non-Malays were finally admitted into the ranks of newly formed multiracial forces. This set the precedent for a communal isolation in local armed forces that is clearly evident in the histories of how the various exclusively Malay or multiracial units that make up present-day Malaysian armed forces came into being.

The Royal Malay Regiment

The Royal Malay Regiment is the outgrowth of the first indigenous unit activated by the British. In 1932 25 young Malays were selected at Port Dickson in Negri Sembilan to form an experimental company and determine whether or not an indigenous force might be practicable. The group was given basic training and special instruction designed to qualify them to form cadres for future units. After a year the experiment was declared a complete success; 16 British officers and eight warrant officers were detailed to provide leadership; new recruiting was launched to bring the company up to battalion strength; and the Malay Regiment was officially activated.

When the extension of World War II to eastern Asia appeared imminent, additional Malay companies were raised to form a second battalion of the regiment. Both units served valiantly in resisting the Japanese invasion of Malaysia, but the force was dissolved by joining the British-supported guerrilla units in the jungle, known as Force 136.

After the war British authorities recalled those who had survived the jungle fighting and reactivated both Malay battalions. In 1948 the Peninsula was thrown into disorder by Communist terrorists in the 12-year campaign known as the Emergency (see ch. 24, Public Order and Internal Security). To help compose the situation, the Malay Regiment was expanded to three battalions in 1948 and, as the fighting continued, more battalions were activated so that total strength was increased to eight battalions by 1962. Meanwhile the Yang di-Pertuan Agong (Supreme Head of Malaysia) authorized the prefix *Royal* to be added to the official title of the regiment. Since 1962 two additional battalions, still exclusively Malay in composition, have been activated, bringing total strength of the RMR to 10 battalions.

The Malaysian Reconnaissance Corps

Origins of the Malaysian Reconnaissance Corps (MRC) go back to 1952, when a major change occurred in official attitudes concerning indigenous forces. At that time the Emergency was getting out of hand, and new forces were required to meet the threat posed by Communist terrorists in the jungle. It had become evident also that both Chinese and Indian ethnic groups, previously looked upon as transients, were in the area to stay and that many of them wanted to share in the defense of their adopted homeland. Since non-Malays were still denied admissions into the RMR, a new unit, called the Federation Regiment, was formed to accommodate them. Recruitment for the new organization was carried out according to a theoretical balance among ethnic groups in which personnel were admitted on the basis of 50 percent Chinese, 25 percent Malays, and 25 percent Indians and Eurasians. An attempt to adhere to these ratios, although they were strictly enforced at first, proved socially and politically inexpedient.

Malay recruits applied in numbers, but qualified Chinese, particularly those suitable for commissions, were slow in responding. Consequently, it was 1955 before the first battalion could be brought up to full strength. Two years later the Emergency was still critical, and a second battalion was added to the Federation Regiment, expanding it to a normal strength of two light infantry battalions.

Meanwhile, despite difficulties in recruiting Chinese, Indians, and other ethnic groups, it was decided that a light armored force, also multiracial in composition, should be added to support the infantry units of the regiment. One squadron, called the Federation

Armored Car Regiment, was activated at Seremban, Negri Sembilan. In 1957 this squadron was expanded to regimental size, and its road patrols played an important role in the Emergency. The Federation Regiment and the Federation Armored Car Regiment operated as separate units until 1960, when they were amalgamated and renamed the Federation Reconnaissance Corps. The combined organization was essentially an infantry-artillery unit that had to be retrained to fit its new role. When Malaysia was formed in 1963, the corps underwent a final name change, substituting the designation *Malaysian* for *Federation* in its official title.

Accompanying this development of the MRC's basic units in Malaya, a small multiracial volunteer force of British expatriates and Singaporeans was independently formed in Singapore in 1954. Gradually this organization expanded to squadron size and became a regular unit to assist in maintaining public order on the island. When Malaysia was formed, the force was absorbed into the MRC, moved to Ipoh in 1965, and officially designated the First Independent Reconnaissance Squadron of the MRC. In 1969 no further development of the MRC had taken place, and the basic multiracial character of its component units remained unchanged.

The Territorial Army

During World War II Malaya raised a large force of civilian volunteers called the Federated Malay States Volunteer Force (FMSVF) to oppose Japanese occupation of the land. Since it was intended to be merely a temporary wartime organization, recruitment was general, and no racial restrictions were placed on membership in it. When the war ended and the need for its services declined, the FMSVF received scant attention and became virtually moribund.

The advent of the Emergency brought a need for similar local forces to combat Communist activities, so in 1952 interest in the old FMSVF was renewed. It was converted into an organization of Home Guards charged with protecting *kampongs* and New Villages (see Glossary) against terrorist attacks. Recruiting among all civilian inhabitants of the areas that the Home Guards defended was authorized, and the organization rose to a strength of about 300,000 before the Emergency subsided.

Once the immediate threat had passed, the Home Guards began to disband, and in 1958 it appeared they might suffer the same neglect accorded their predecessor. This time, however, the government determined to avoid such a waste of experienced manpower. Remaining elements in each area of the country were regrouped into infantry battalions and support units to form a new and more formalized organization called the Territorial Army (TA). Units of the

562

organization were then assigned to the individual states of the Federation in which they originated to serve as local military forces. The TA retained this discrete form until 1962 when a number of its best units were federalized to provide a combat-ready reserve for the MRC. Remaining elements were kept intact in their home states where, after redesignation as the Local Defense Corps (LDC), they became the equivalent of local volunteer militia units. In 1969 no further development of, or changes in, the basic roles of the multiracial TA or LDC had taken place.

The Malaysian Rangers

The Malaysian Rangers was a relatively new organization that did not become an integral part of the regular Malaysian army until 1963. Its activation was inspired by the effectiveness of the Sarawak Rangers during the Emergency. These expert jungle fighters were created originally in 1862 by Sir James Brooke as an independent force to aid in pacifying tribal chieftains but later were incorporated into the Sarawak Constabulary (see ch. 24, Public Order and Internal Security).

In 1952 the Malayan government, which lacked jungle trackers of its own and believed that only the Iban (Sea Dayak) of Sarawak possessed appropriate qualities for the task, appealed to that protectorate for help in locating Communist strongholds in the jungles of Malaya. Sarawak responded by raising a permanent organization of Iban volunteers patterned after, and again called, the Sarawak Rangers. The group was then sent to Malaya, where it performed brilliantly and received much acclaim and many decorations and awards.

After the Emergency the Rangers returned to Sarawak, where they were incorporated into the British army as a colonial force liable for worldwide service. When Sarawak became part of Malaysia, they were detached from the British forces, incorporated into the Malaysian army and, with British help, began to expand into a new multiracial force of four battalions. The first battalion was raised in Sarawak of Iban from the old Sarawak Rangers. The cadre of the second was provided by the RMR and the MRC but drew its personnel from Sabah. The third and fourth battalions followed in 1965 and 1966, respectively, both being recruited on a Malaysia-wide basis.

Other Ground Force Elements

Malaysian ground forces also included a number of supporting arms and services, all of which were multiracial because they were developed either by grouping similar units formerly integral to the old Federation Regiment or by recruitment, which has always been open to all Malaysians. In direct support were the two Malaysian artillery regiments, the two regiments of Malaysian signals, and the five squadrons of Malaysian engineers. In general support were the Malaysian Ordnance Corps of various units that obtained, stored, issued, and maintained all weapons, ammunition, and vehicles; and the Malaysian Service Corps of specialized units for transportation, general supply and maintenance, port activities, and civic action projects, such as flood relief. The general support organizations were jointly organized and manned to serve the RMN and the RMAF as well as the army.

The Royal Malaysian Navy

The Royal Malaysian Navy came into being as a volunteer force to augment British naval forces during World War II. Most of its personnel served aboard ships of the British Royal Navy in India, Ceylon, and East Africa. This force was demobilized after the war was over but was reactivated in 1948 as an indigenous Malayan Naval Force under British command and control. It served in the area as a colonial defense unit until the Federation of Malaya became independent in 1957 when, both administratively and operationally, it was transferred to the new government, although physically it continued to be based and headquartered at the huge British naval base in Singapore. When Malaysia was formed, it changed its name to the Royal Malaysian Navy and moved its headquarters to Kuala Lumpur. Plans were made to establish a new naval base for its vessels somewhere in Malaysia, but in 1969 the ships remained at the Singapore base.

Most of the ratings in the RMN are Malays, but its rolls are open to Chinese, Indians, and other applicants as well. The force was expanded significantly during 1963 and 1964, and there was a noticeable increase of interest among all citizens for a career in the navy. As a result the proportions in effect in multiracial units of the navy more nearly approximated the overall ethnic ratio in 1969.

The Royal Malaysian Air Force

The Royal Malaysian Air Force is the youngest of the nation's armed forces. It was created in 1958 as the Royal Malayan Air Force with Malayan personnel who had been serving with the British Royal Air Force as flight personnel or with the Royal Air Force Regiment (Malaya) in guard and maintenance units forming cadre. The new force took over the former British airbase at Kuala Lumpur, which in 1969 still served as its headquarters.

Like the other forces, the RMAF substituted *Malaysian* for *Malayan* in its official title in 1963. As an independent national force, it has been expanding rapidly, recruiting all Malaysians regardless of racial background. The lack of technically qualified Malays was reflected in the fact that in 1969 Chinese formed more than one-half of the officer corps, but Malays continued to dominate enlisted grades.

The Role of British Forces

The fact that indigenous Malaysian units were initially creations of the colonial power is but one aspect of the role played by the British in the historic development of the forces. Of greater import is that both before and after federation, British personnel, facilities, and techniques so permeated indigenous organizations that they faithfully reflected British concepts, attitudes, organization, and operational practices. Before federation local elements were under a British tutelage so complete as to amount to full command control; since then, command has been passing to Malaysians as fast as qualified local leadership could be developed. By mid-1969 all key staff and command positions had been assumed by Malaysians. A number of Commonwealth officers and noncommissioned officers were still seconded to various tactical units, but generally they were assigned only as advisers and training specialists. Moreover, even these seconded personnel were scheduled to be phased out by 1975.

Powerful empire forces have also played a decisive role in defense of the area, although this also underwent change as the result of the mutual defense talks in early 1969. Thus, along with the assumption of full indigenous command, Malaysia was increasingly assuming primary responsibility for its own defense.

POSITION IN GOVERNMENT

Top Command

Supreme command of the armed forces is vested by the Constitution in His Majesty, the Yang di-Pertuan Agong. All activities of the defense establishment are carried out in his name and under his authority. The Constitution further specifies that all officers held the Supreme Head's commission and that he has the prerogative of mercy in military offenses triable by courts-martial. The power to declare war, however, is not his but devolves upon the cabinet, subject to the sanction of Parliament. Thus the armed forces are servants of both the crown and the people, with the latter exercising ultimate control through their elected representatives in Parliament, which determines the size and composition of the services and appropriate monies needed to support them.

Actual control of the forces is exercised by the National Defense Council (NDC), a body created in 1963 to streamline and unify the defense establishment. The NDC is chaired by the prime minister and includes the minister of defense, the home minister, and other selected civilian officials. The chief of the armed forces staff and the inspector general of police attend its meetings but are not considered members. The NDC decides the day-to-day policies, administration, discipline, and command of the armed forces, but it leaves implementing decisions to the chiefs of the various services within their own organizations.

Directly subordinate to the Supreme Head but subject to the decisions and directions of the NDC is the Ministry of Defense, which is the headquarters of the overall defense establishment. It contains the Armed Forces Staff under its own chief to coordinate and control the individual services and to provide combined logistic support for them. The chiefs of the army, navy, and air force, together with their staffs, are members of this joint body so that, while retaining full executive control of their own organizations, each service commander is also an official of the ministry.

Territorial Organization

Ground Forces

For territorial defense, Malaysia is divided into five areas, each of which is the responsibility of a numbered Malaysian Infantry Brigade (MIB). These organizations are headquarters only, established to control a varying number of assigned tactical units. Three MIB's are located in West Malaysia and two in East Malaysia.

The three MIB's in West Malaysia have headquarters at Sungei Besi, Ipoh, and Temerloh, respectively. Their areas of responsibility generally coincide with state boundaries. The MIB at Sungei Besi defends Kuala Lumpur and the states of Selangor, Negri Sembilan, Malacca, and Johore; another covers Perlis, Kedah, Perak, and Penang; the third is responsible for Pahang, Trengganu, and Kelantan. In East Malaysia MIB boundaries are established according to administrative division; one MIB is responsible for the three southerly administrative divisions of Sarawak, and the other, for the two northerly administrative divisions of Sarawak and all of Sabah.

The Royal Malaysian Navy

All of the Royal Malaysian Navy vessels normally are assigned to the main naval base at Singapore, called KD Malaya (KD, or

Kapal Di-Raja, meaning Ship of the King), following the tradition of naming naval installations as ships. The RMN also contains separate area commands for each of the country's two geographic segments. Naval activities in and around Malaya are commanded by the naval officer-in-charge West Malaysia, whose headquarters is at KD Malaya. The command contains a minor installation, KD Sri Penang, at George Town, Penang.

Headquarters of the naval officer-in-charge East Malaysia, KD Sri Labuan, is on the island of Labuan in Sabah. It has two subordinate installations, KD Sri Tawau in eastern Sabah and KD Sri Sibu in Sarawak.

The Royal Malaysian Air Force

The Royal Malaysian Air Force contained no subordinate territorial organizations but exercised full command of all its elements directly from Air Force Headquarters in Kuala Lumpur. Flying squadrons of the force were assigned in whole or in part to any appropriate base in either West or East Malaysia as needed.

Missions and Concepts

The primary missions of the armed forces include all necessary action to preserve the unity and integrity of the country. In 1969 Malaysia still contained a number of dissident forces and intruders that were remnants of Communist terrorist organizations in West Malaysia and of guerrilla bands that arose in East Malaysia during the confrontation with Indonesia. Their permanent pockets of resistance and mobile patrols were well hidden, and land travel to close with and liquidate them was difficult because of the rough mountainous and jungle terrain in both areas. Much of the search-and-destroy effort was carried out by specialized paramilitary units of the Royal Malaysia Police, but ultimate responsibility for internal security rested with the armed forces (see ch. 24, Public Order and Internal Security). Accordingly, and since the use of large formations and normal weapons in such operations was impracticable, the basic army combat force was the light infantry battalion, organized, trained, and equipped to operate in small patrol-size units in all types of terrain. These forces demonstrated a high degree of effectiveness in keeping disruptive elements under control.

The RMN contained no large attack ships, submarines, air arm, or marine corps, so it limited its activities to coastal patrols to intercept and turn back waterborne intruding parties and guerrilla resupply efforts. The sea frontier was constantly and effectively patrolled in a zone extending three miles from shore. The RMN was aided in this task by boats of the Royal Malaysia Marine Police (see ch. 24, Public Order and Internal Security).

The RMAF was a relatively new force equipped with a small inventory of rotary wing, transport, trainer, and tactical aircraft but devoid of strategic bombers or a modern antiaircraft defense system. It had no offensive capability nor was it fully able to patrol its own airspace, and the RMAF had to depend on Commonwealth air forces for the greater part of these tasks. Its mission, therefore, was restricted to minor transport duty and some air supply and logistic support to the ground forces.

Financial Support

Financial support for the armed forces is contained in the appropriation for the Ministry of Defense in an annual national budget in which the fiscal year and the calendar year coincide. For the fiscal year ending December 31, 1968, it amounted to M$548.3 million (3.06 Malaysian dollars equal US$1) and represented 19.4 percent of the total budget, or 5.7 percent of the gross national product. Figures for the 1969 appropriation were not available, but the minister of finance, in presenting estimates to Parliament, indicated they would reflect an increase of about 2.2 percent. This would continue a trend of annually mounting defense expenditures that had more than doubled since 1964. Despite increasing costs, it is estimated that the government can meet future requirements without undue strain on the total economy, although other needed developments may have to be somewhat curtailed.

Actual defense expenditures are made somewhat unclear by grants of both money and equipment provided to Malaysia's armed forces by the United Kingdom, Australia, New Zealand, and Canada. The extent of this aid is not readily discernible, but its monetary value probably exceeds that of the official budget figures.

THE ARMED FORCES AND MALAYSIAN SOCIETY

Manpower Sources

About 10 percent of Malaysia's total population in 1969 were males between the ages of 18 and 45 physically fit for military duty (see ch. 2, Physical Environment and Population). Roughly one-half of all eligibles were Malays; one-quarter were Chinese; and the remainder were Indians, Pakistanis, and others. Together they formed the basic reservoir from which personnel for the armed forces were drawn. In addition, more than 100,000 young men reach military age each year, and the services depend on these for the bulk of their new recruits. Since total requirements were low, the maintenance of the military establishment at authorized personnel strength had little adverse impact on the civilian labor force.

Procurement of Officers

There has been no military aristocracy, and there is no indication that one is developing in Malaysia. The idea of the armed forces as the servant of the civil power is too deeply entrenched by attitudes and values inculcated by British forces. The government in power has had considerable difficulty historically in attracting indigenous personnel for officer commissions. Among Malays, most young men qualified to become officers were already members of the raja class (see Glossary) which provided social status in itself and had its own social gradations unchanged by the attainment of military rank. The Chinese were generally disinterested in becoming members of a system in which promotion and assignment policies favored Malays and which offered no real career possibilities. The Indians did not care for a career in the military services.

In the search for officer candidates, Malaysia adopted the British practice of accepting applicants from both the ranks and from the regular school system. In 1953 the Federation Military College was established by the British at Port Dickson to prepare young men to take their places as officers of the armed forces and as leaders in the professional, commercial, and industrial life of the Federation. In 1961 this institution was moved to Sungei Besi, near Kuala Lumpur, and renamed the Royal Military College, it has continued as a major source of officers for all the armed forces.

The Royal Military College is divided into two separate schools, the Boys Wing and the Cadet Wing, with academic and military training. The Boys Wing admits boys between 14 and 16 years of age and gives them an essentially English public school education through the equivalent of high school. It has a total capacity of 300 students.

The Cadet Wing admits graduates of the Boys Wing and of equivalent civilian schools under 21 years of age. It has a capacity of about 150 students. Cadet courses vary in length depending on the service a student elects to join, but all courses qualify a successful graduate for a commission in either the army, navy, or air force. Graduates also compete for matriculation at the University of Malaya; the Royal Military Academy at Sandhurst, the Royal Naval

College at Dartmouth, and the Royal Air Force College at Cranwell, in England; and the Officer Cadet School at Portsea, in Australia. Most graduates, however, accept direct commissions into one of the three Malaysian forces.

Procurement of Enlisted Personnel

In 1969 personnel on duty in all three armed forces were volunteers, although a system of conscription was available for use if needed. Except for the Royal Malay Regiment, with membership restricted exclusively to Malays, personnel are recruited from Malaysian society at large without regard to ethnic origins or to the service component involved.

Applicants for all services must be 18 years of age (17 in the army with parental consent), physically fit, at least 5 feet-2 inches tall, and have completed the equivalent of an eighth-grade education. Because there are always more volunteers than required to fill the few vacancies, each service can be extremely selective, and only the best physical specimens are accepted. Initial enlistments are for 12 years (10 of active duty and two of reserve), but additional and repeated reenlistments for consecutive 3-year periods are authorized until the serviceman reaches the mandatory retirement age of 45. Most men in uniform, especially Malays from rural areas, like the economic security provided in the services and elect to remain on duty as long as possible.

The system of conscription came into being with passage of the National Security Ordinance in 1952. This measure called for conscription to meet personnel needs during the Emergency but, except for the requirement for registration, it was not put into effect until much later. The first and only callup did not take place until the fall of 1964 when a class of 14,000 was inducted as a temporary precautionary measure in the confrontation with Indonesia; even then, most of the class was assigned to civil defense organizations, and only about 3,000 found their way into the regular forces.

The National Security Ordinance has never been repealed, and in 1963 it was made applicable to the entire country. Its terms require all male citizens from 21 to 28 years of age to register for possible induction into one of the armed forces, the police, or civil defense organizations for tours of duty of up to 2 years. Final selections are based on the same criteria in effect for volunteer service, and very few categories of registrants are exempt from liability. Among those excused are senior government employees, members of the armed forces and the police, religious officials, the mentally disordered, and the physically handicapped, but even they must apply for formal exemption certificates. Sometimes when extreme hardship might be involved, other individuals may have their obligation to serve postponed temporarily.

Quality of Manpower

Malaysians as a whole make excellent soldiers from the point of amenability to training and discipline, military bearing and smartness, cleanliness and neatness, pride in the uniform, and care and handling of weapons. There are some qualitative differences among the various ethnic groups, but these are psychological rather than physical and affect attitudes rather than performance.

Although Malaysians are relatively small in stature, they are strong, well-adapted to their environment, and capable of sustained performance under extremely adverse conditions. All groups also seem to possess mechanical aptitude, although the lack of experience with machines makes training and supervision necessary for proper performance of such tasks as preventive maintenance of automobiles and other mechanical equipment.

Virtually all the active combat experience of the forces has been in jungle warfare, a type of conflict in which the Malaysian is recognized as among the most skillful in the world. Contrary to seemingly logical expectations, nevertheless, he does not come to the service naturally knowledgeable about the jungle. Both the village inhabitant of Malaya and the longhouse (multifamily dwelling) dweller of East Malaysia are residents of the clearings who probably have no more acquaintance with the jungle than is necessary to follow a well-defined trail between villages. The Iban of Sarawak is a jungle expert; his methods, developed into formalized unit tactics by the original Sarawak Rangers, have long been incorporated as major objectives in the training schedules of the entire establishment.

It is the consensus of most observers that the Malay will work hard at anything that is worthwhile and necessary by his standards, that affords social satisfaction, or that is "good sport." British leadership evidently was able to exploit these incentives to command respect for competence, fairness, and firmness, all of which are values characteristic of the Malaysian serviceman.

Mobilization Potential

The ability of the nation to mobilize its strength in time of war is not so much a function of manpower as it is one of facilities, equipment, and finance to support augmented forces. The navy and the air force have no organized reserves and, with no ships or aircraft in reserve, these services could not be increased much beyond their regular active duty strength. The army could call on the TA for additional units and on the LDC for personnel to bring its active duty elements up to full strength. It could also assume control of the sizable paramilitary forces of the police. Without considerable outside support, however, it would be hardpressed to arm and pay them or to provide them with training areas and facilities. Full unaided mobilization strength would be reached in one year's time and probably would not exceed 50,000 men in all three services combined.

With outside logistic support and the loan of instructors and training facilities from its Commonwealth partners, the army could probably double its normal size, and the navy and air force could increase by about 50 percent in one year. Mobilization could also continue, and the overall establishment could triple its combat strength and effectiveness in 2 years, at which time full mobilization would be reached.

ORGANIZATION AND COMPOSITION OF THE ARMED FORCES

The Malaysian armed forces in 1969 had an overall personnel strength of less than 40,000 officers and men, of whom about 90 percent were in the ground forces. The remainder were fairly evenly divided between the navy and the air force. Each component was organized into a conventional headquarters and staff at Kuala Lumpur controlling combat and support elements appropriate to its type of service.

The army was essentially a light infantry force of slightly under 35,000 men, whose combat units included several infantry battalions and a number of field artillery and reconnaissance units. Noncombat elements of the army consisted of variously sized units of engineer, signal, ordnance, quartermaster, and transportation types. Most of the noncombat units were employed to provide essential service and support to all forces.

The navy was the smallest of the three forces, having a personnel strength of almost 3,000. It was primarily a patrol force of approximately 60 vessels of all types grouped into squadrons on a functional basis. Patrol vessels formed most of the squadrons, but there were also a mine countermeasure unit and another composite element for survey and training.

The air force had a personnel strength only slightly larger than the navy with an aircraft inventory of less than 100 airplanes of all types. These planes included jet fighters, helicopters, and piston engine transport, training, and liaison types. The force was organized into squadrons based on the type and mission of aircraft involved.

TRAINING

Formal training installations for the Malaysian armed forces are extremely limited, but those that do exist are well organized, closely supervised, and enthusiastically conducted. Each of the three services has its own training center at which, in addition to all recruit training, a limited number of basic technical and specialist courses are provided for selected junior officers and enlisted men. Advanced technical and specialist training for all grades and ranks is not available in Malaysia and must be taken at appropriate training facilities of Commonwealth forces in the United Kingdom, Australia, New Zealand, Canada, or India and, since 1965, in service schools of the United States.

Apart from the Royal Military College, which prepares young men for commissions in all three services, the only known formal school for officers is the joint Staff and Command School, established at Port Dickson, Malacca, in 1968. Little was known about this institution in early 1969 except that it had a capacity of only about 35 students a year. Because of its newness and limited size, most staff college training, especially that for senior officers, was still provided by the United Kingdom, Australia, and India.

Army Training

Individual training in the army follows schedules and methods adapted from those of the British army and is carried out at the Military Training Center in Port Dickson, Malacca. All new recruits are inducted at this center where, regardless of ultimate assignment, they are formed into training units for recruit training that lasts for 17 weeks. This phase has no unique aspects but consists of conventional physical conditioning, drill, fieldcraft, weapons familarization, marksmanship, and methods of survival designed to accustom the recruit to life in the military service.

At the conclusion of recruit training, personnel are selected for permanent assignment to one of the arms or services, and their training thereafter begins to differ and specialize. Those selected for combat, or combat support elements, remain at the center for an additional six weeks' training in basic small-unit action and the fundamentals of jungle warfare. Noncombat personnel are given technical or specialist training supervised by their branch headquarters. For this purpose separate signal, ordnance and service corps schools are located at the center; enginerring training, however, is conducted by a special training squadron at the engineer base in Klang. The length of basic training varies with the requirements of the particular service involved.

At the end of basic training, all personnel report to their permanent units where they receive virtually all subsequent training on the job. There are no scheduled programs or facilities for advanced individual training for enlisted men in Malaysia. When such training is necessary, a few of the more highly qualified men may be selected to attend pertinent courses abroad.

Individual training for ground force officers follows a similar general pattern. Immediately after being graduated from the Royal Military Academy, newly commissioned officers also report to the Military Training Center and undergo a short course in basic jungle tactics, weapons, communications, leadership, and administration before reporting to their units. After 6 months' active duty, some may be selected to attend the new joint staff school, but otherwise specialist and technical training in subjects of interest to both combat and noncombat duty is obtained in service schools in Commonwealth nations or in the United States.

Unit training in the army is continuous and is carried out under the supervision of the brigade to which the unit is assigned. Schedules begin with small unit exercises and progress upward through company and battalion formations, concluding with an annual large-scale field maneuver in which naval and air force elements participate. Tactical doctrine for this training is essentially that developed in general British practice, modified to apply to jungle conditions in Malaysia.

Malaysian unit training is based on a summary of lessons learned during the Emergency, periodically brought up to date to conform to new conditions, weapons, and equipment. It emphasizes the use of surprise, rapidity of movement, simple planning, and the swift local concentration of forces. Great value is placed on secrecy, discipline, and stealth in the movement of small, lightly armed units in the jungle; on automatic reaction to fleeting contact; on ambush and assaults on enemy camps; and on the development of initiative, resourcefulness, and rapid decisionmaking by junior commanders who lead patrols and small units.

One of the most important features of unit training is qualification and maintenance of skill in the use of weapons. A range of 75 yards, is a long shot in the jungle, and seldom is more than one round at a furtive enemy possible. Consequently, in addition to known distance practice, much attention is given to quick, accurate shooting with all weapons at suddenly appearing targets. Because company and battalion weapons, such as mortars and machineguns, are seldom used in the jungle, retraining in their use is a continuing requirement to maintain proficiency.

Naval Training

Formalized individual training for all naval personnel is concentrated at the Malaysian Naval Training Center at KD Malaya, the major operating base of the RMN in Singapore. Facilities of the center are excellent but limited in scope and capable of providing only recruit training and a number of basic courses for enlisted men, and a single naval orientation and indoctrination course for newly commissioned officers. All training in 1969 was supervised by experienced advisers and instructors on loan from the British Royal Navy.

Recruit training follows standard British schedules that include naval discipline and practice, weapons familiarization, basic seamanship, and physical conditioning. At the conclusion of the recruit phase, men are selected for specific types of duty and undergo appropriate basic training in mechanics, gunnery, signals, navigation, radar and electronics, electricity, administration, and supply. No advanced training in any of these subjects is available, so after basic training all ratings are assigned to permanent stations and receive additional training on the job.

Newly commissioned officers are required to report directly to the center from the Royal Military College for a short course in naval indoctrination and orientation before proceeding to their permanent stations. All technical and specialist training of officers is obtained by attendance at naval service schools abroad. Staff training for naval officers is provided by the joint staff school in Port Dickson.

Afloat training is conducted exclusively in Malaysian waters and usually as a part of routine operations, although sometimes special training cruises are scheduled with Commonwealth naval forces. This training concentrates on developing skill in detecting, intercepting, and eliminating waterborne intruders. RMN units also participate in annual joint maneuvers with the army and air force.

Air Force Training

Individual training in the RMAF is carried out at different locations, depending on the type of training involved. Recruit training is centered at Sempang Air Base a few miles south of Kuala Lumpur; technical training is provided by the Kinrara Technical Training School in Kuala Lumpur; flight and pilot training is offered by the

Flight Training School established at the Alor Star Air Base in Kedah; some staff training is obtained at the joint staff school at Port Dickson, but in 1969 most staff training, especially higher level, was being assumed by air service schools of the Unites States Air Force.

Recruit training at Sempang Air Base is conventional in substance and covers an 8-week period. At its conclusion airmen are assigned to operational squadrons for further training on the job or are selected to attend courses at Kinrara for technical training in various specialties connected with their assignments.

The Kinrara Technical Training School is a sizable institution with a capacity of about 250 students a year. Its basic courses of about 20 weeks' duration cover virtually all technical subjects required by the air force, including separate courses in engine and airframe mechanics, engineering, electronics and radio, instruments, and air navigation. Graduates of these courses return to their units for duty, but after unspecified lengths of time they may return for advanced training in the same subjects. Advanced courses may last for as long as 9 months, and most air force noncommissioned officers are selected from among their graduates. In addition to purely technical subjects, the school offers several courses in management, control, and organization for junior officers and senior noncommissioned officers.

Aviation cadets for the Flight Training School are recruited from among young men between the ages of 17 and 25, in or out of the service, who have a school certificate showing credits in English, mathematics, physics, and general science and who successfully pass rather rigid aptitude and physical tests. Those selected first attend the Royal Military College for 1 year for schooling in military subjects and leadership before transferring to Alor Star Air Base for flight training. Qualification as a pilot normally takes about 42 weeks, during which time the cadet receives much classroom instruction in technical subjects, as well as a minimum of 160 hours actual flying time.

After graduation from the school, the new flyer is assigned to an operational squadron simply as a rated pilot. All pilot upgrading and conversion training to various types of aircraft used by the squadron is accomplished within the unit as a part of routine operational flight training.

LOGISTICS

The logistics system for all three component services of the armed forces is a staff and operational responsibility of the joint and unified Logistics Division of the Armed Forces Staff at headquarters in

Kuala Lumpur. At staff levels, the division formulates logistic policies and procedures, determines force requirements, maintains records, and takes authorized procurement action for the defense establishment as a whole. Its operational mission is carried out by two unified corps, within and controlled by the division, called the Malaysian Ordnance Corps and the Malaysian Service Corps.

The Malaysian Ordnance Corps

The Malaysian Ordnance Corps is sometimes referred to as the "Shopkeeper of the Armed Forces" because, except for a few items such as perishable subsistence and expendable office supplies authorized for local procurement by individual units, it receives, stores, issues, and maintains most rations, personal and organizational equipment, vehicles, ordnance, and petroleum products used in common by the three forces. The corps also provides housing and performs maintenance and repair services on material and equipment that is beyond the capability of using units.

The major supply installations of the corps are the Central Ordnance Depot at Batu Garrison, Kuala Lumpur, and the Armed Forces Ammunition Depot at Majidee Barracks, Johore Baharu. The ordnance depot handles all classes of supplies, equipment, and material; the ammunition depot stores and issues all types of ammunition and explosives. There are also smaller, satellite ammunition depots operated directly by the corps at Taiping in Perak, Kuching in Sarawak, and Tawau in Sabah.

Using units are responsible for the routine care, maintenance, and servicing of their own vehicles and equipment, but field and major depot maintenance and repair are the responsibility of specialized elements of the ordnance corps. Major repair is accomplished at the Central Workshop, which is located near the ordnance depot at Batu Garrison. Less difficult and extensive repair is performed at light workshops, one of which is located in each brigade area of the army. These smaller workshops also are assigned mobile repair detachments that visit army, navy, and air force installations in their areas to assist local units in maintaining their equipment in combat-ready condition.

Personnel and various technical units of the ordnance corps are formed into composite maintenance and repair detachments assigned to each army brigade headquarters. These detachments are tailored to meet the specific supply and service requirements of the forces within their jurisdictions. They man and operate general supply depots and petroleum and ammunition dumps throughout the brigade area. Each also contains a transportation company to support the brigade and, where necessary, they may be assigned a port detachment to operate port sections and a parachute packing, maintenance, and supply unit for air drop operations.

The Malaysian Service Corps

The Malaysian Service Corps is manned and equipped to provide all administrative services for the defense establishment, such as personnel and recordkeeping, professional services, and legal and religious activities. Personnel and operating elements of the corps, like those of the ordnance corps, are assigned to each army brigade to carry out their triservice missions.

GRADES, RANKS, AND PAY

Grades and Ranks

The Malaysian armed forces have adopted in toto the British grade and rank structure from recruit through general or its equivalent in the army and navy. Under British tutelage relations between enlisted men and officers have become very much like those in the British army. Specific evidence is lacking, but in the past young men of the raja class (see Glossary) apparently have not hesitated to enter the ranks at the bottom, nor have they shown any great ambition to attain commissions.

Pay

In 1969 the pay system for members of the armed forces was uniform in the three services and consisted of a base value for each grade and certain allowances. The entire schedule is revised periodically to reflect current economic conditions and is fixed after correlation with general civil service salaries and wages, as well as with previous military pay schedules. It is, therefore, the equivalent of, or better than, that available in the civilian sector.

Provision is made for pay increases within grade by automatic augmentations of the base that normally occur at 2-year intervals. In addition to base pay, each serviceman is entitled to a cost-of-living allowance arranged on a scale according to rank and a marriage allowance granted to both officers and enlisted men.

UNIFORMS

The uniforms of all Malaysian armed forces are patterned after, and are essentially the same as, those of their counterparts in the British forces, except for dress uniforms in the army. In combat, troops wear lightweight khaki British battledress with combat boots and helmets or helmet liners. For garrison and off-duty, the normal uniform is a short-sleeve khaki shirt, khaki trousers or shorts, matching visored service cap, and black low shoes and socks.

Dress uniforms in the army are of two types. Members of the Royal Malay Regiment wear a white uniform with a black, knee-length Malay sarong over it, black shoes and socks, and black caps that differ for officers and enlisted men. Enlisted men wear a black, overseas-style Muslim cap to which their regimental badge is affixed; officers' caps are also black but are of a visorless pillbox variety with a gold encircling band. The dress uniform for all other elements of the ground forces are similar but differ in two respects: the Malay sarong is omitted and the caps are red.

AWARDS AND DECORATIONS

Malaysian awards and decorations include three orders, six medals, and one award authorized by the federal government and a large number of others awarded by the governments of the individual states. In addition to these decorations various British Commonwealth awards, no longer awarded after 1957, remain valid and may be worn or displayed by Malaysian armed forces personnel upon whom they were conferred. Orders and awards of the federation take precedence over those of the individual states.

Federation Awards and Decorations

The three federation orders are the Most Exalted Order of the Crown, the Most Distinguished Order of the Defender of the Realm, and the Illustrious Order of Loyalty to the Malaysian Crown. The highest of these is the first named, which is purely honorary and has no military implications. It has only one grade and is restricted to Malayan rulers and governors, foreign heads of state, and certain very distinguished persons.

The second highest order is the Most Distinguished Order of the Defender of the Realm, awarded in five classes and a medal. It is the highest award for which military personnel are eligible and is conferred for exceptionally meritorious or faithful service to the country or to the person of the Supreme Head. The class of the order granted depends on the position or rank of the recipient and the level of his achievement. Its first two grades, grand knight and knight, automatically entitle recipients to affix the traditional Malayan titles "Tun" and "Tan Sri," respectively, to their names. The other grades, companion, officer, member, and the medal are for degree of service only.

The third order is the Illustrious Order of Loyalty to the Malaysian Crown, a relatively new order about which little information was available in early 1969, except that it was conferred in three classes. Presumably, it was awarded for meritorius service to the country of a high order but lesser in degree than that warranting the second order.

Below these orders are three medals for gallantry, three for service, and one award for lesser acts of gallantry. In descending order, the gallantry medals include the Supreme Gallantry Award, the Gallantry Award (Military), and the Gallantry Award (Civil). The Supreme Gallantry Award is conferred on military personnel, police, and civilians for acts of great heroism or courage involving extreme danger. It may be awarded in peacetime or in war. The Gallantry Award (Military) is conferred for heroism or gallantry of a very high order performed in actual combat. The Gallantry Award (Civil) is given to civilians for gallantry of a very high order and to military personnel for gallant acts performed in noncombat situations.

The three service medals include the General Service Medal, the Long Service and Good Conduct Medal, and the Volunteer Decoration. The General Service Medal is awarded to members of the armed forces who have served honorably for at least one year since 1957. The Long Service and Good Conduct Medal is conferred on military personnel who have served honorably in any of the services for at least 21 years. The Volunteer Decoration is given for any volunteer service.

The single Mention-in-Despatches Award is conferred on military personnel of any of the forces and on members of the police. It is granted for acts of gallantry in peace or war that deserve recognition but are not sufficiently high to permit the award of a higher decoration.

State Awards and Decorations

Each state has its own series of awards and decorations which generally follow the pattern of the federal system. The highest award is usually an order reserved for royalty, heads of state, or distinguished friends of the state. There is also an order of merit for distinguished lesser personnel; a medal or two for various degrees of gallantry, often divided into separate forms for military and civilian personnel, or for officers and enlisted men; one or two medals for meritorious service of significance to the state; and a final one for good conduct and length of service in the armed forces.

MEDICAL SERVICE

Because of a shortage of medical and dental personnel, health services in the Malaysian armed forces are limited. As for other logistical services, the joint Armed Forces Staff at headquarters in Kuala Lumpur is charged with providing medical and dental care on a triservice basis. In 1969 it had not yet been able to attract enough qualified officers, and many doctors and dentists still had to be seconded from British forces.

Medical officers were assigned to each major operating unit (regiment or battalion) in the ground forces and to each army garrison, naval shore establishment, and air force flying field or base. Sick quarters, including small hospitals of up to 40 beds, were established at most of these installations, and the air force operated a 60-bed hospital in Kinrara. Facilities at these establishments, however, were capable only of routine care and minor surgery. Patients requiring specialist care or long-term in-patient treatment had to be accommodated at civilian hospitals.

MILITARY JUSTICE

By mid-1969 Malaysia had not devised its own code of military justice as an independent nation. Procedures in administering military justice that prevailed under the British regime were at least temporarily in effect since the federal Constitution prescribed that, after federation, existing laws were to remain in effect until repealed. The National Defense Council (NDC) has responsibility for the command, discipline, and administration of the armed forces, but the Constitution gives the Supreme Head the power to grant pardons, reprieves, and respites from punishments meted out by local commanders or the NDC.

OTHER MORALE FACTORS

Rations

Meticulous attention is paid to the religious and other food requirements of all troops. Specific food demands of Malays, Chinese, and Indians are satisfied whenever possible.

Recreation

Malaysians are especially enthusiastic about sports, and the military system recognize their value for troop morale. Football (soccer) was especially popular, and company and battalion teams were formed for service competition, as well as for games with civilian teams. Track and field sports, swimming, and volleyball were also popular.

Motion pictures are one of the favorite forms of entertainment among all communities in Malaysia. All established military posts had motion picture theaters, and mobile units visited troops away from their home stations regularly.

Religion

The only religious leader known to be assigned to the forces was the *guru* (Muslim teacher), of which there was one per battalion. It is likely that military personnel are dependent on local communities for mosque services. If this condition obtains for the Malays, it is undoubtedly true that no more attention is given to the Chinese and the Indians, whose religious participation is principally in a family environment.

BIBLIOGRAPHIES

Section I. Social

RECOMMENDED SOURCES

Appell, G.N., and Harrison, Robert. "Ethnographic Profiles of the Dusun Speaking Peoples of Sabah, Malaysia," *Journal of Malaysian Branch of the Royal Asiatic Society*, XLI, No. 214, Part 2, 1968.

Arasaratnam, S. "Social Reform and Reformist Pressure Groups Among the Indians of Malaya and Singapore, 1930–1955," *Journal of the Malaysian Branch of the Royal Asiatic Society*, XL, Part 2, December 1967, 54–67.

Bastin, John, and Winks, Robin W. (comps.) *Malaysia: Selected Historical Readings*. Kuala Lumpur: Oxford University Press, 1966.

Beamish, Tony. *The Arts of Malaya*. (Malaysia Heritage Series.) Singapore: Donald Moore, 1954.

Cady, John F. *Southeast Asia: Its Historical Developments*. New York: McGraw-Hill, 1964.

Dentan, Robert Knox. *The Semai: A Nonviolent People of Malaya*. (Case Studies in Cultural Anthropology.) New York: Holt, Rinehart and Winston, 1968.

Elliott, Allan John Anthony. *Chinese Spirit-Medium Cults in Singapore*. London: Department of Anthropology, London School of Economics and Political Science, 1955.

Emerson, Rupert. Malaysia: *A Study in Direct and Indirect Rule*. New York: Macmillan, 1937.

Evans, Ivor Hugh Norman. *The Religion of the Tempasuk ·Dusuns of North Borneo*. Cambridge: Cambridge University Press, 1953.

Fauconnier, Henri. *The Soul of Malaya*. New York: Penguin Books, 1948.

Fennell, Thomas Rixon. "Commitment to Change: A History of Malayan Educational Policy, 1954–1957." (Doctoral dissertation, University of Hawaii, Department of Modern History.) Honolulu: 1968 (microfilmed dissertation No. 11925.).

Firth, Raymond. *Malay Fishermen: Their Peasant Economy*. (2d ed., rev.) Hamden: Archon Books, 1966.

Firth, Rosemary. *Housekeeping Among Malay Peasants*. (2d. ed., rev.) (London School of Economics, Monographs on Social Anthropology, No. 7.). London: Athlone Press, 1966.

Fisher, Charles A. *Southeast Asia: A Social, Economic, and Political Geography*. New York: Dutton, 1964.

Fraser, Thomas M. *Rusembilan: A Malay Fishing Village*. Ithaca: Cornell University Press, 1960.

Gullick, J.M. *Indigenous Political Systems of Western Malaya*. London: Athlone Press, 1965.

Hall, D.G.E. *A History of Southeast Asia*. New York: St. Martin's Press, 1955.

Hanna, Willard A. *The Formation of Malaysia: New Factor in World Politics*. New York: American Universities Field Staff, 1964.

Harrisson, Tom (ed.). *The Peoples of Sarawak*. Kuching: Sarawak Museum, 1959.

Higher Education Planning Committee Report. Kuala Lumpur: 1967.

Husin Ali, S. "Patterns of Rural Leadership in Malaya," *Journal of the Malaysian Branch of the Royal Asiatic Society*, XLI, Part I, July 1968, 95–145.

King, Neville. "Intellectuals' Dilemma," *Far Eastern Economic Review*, LX, No. 19, May 9, 1968, 293–294.

Larkin, John A., and Benda, Harry, Jr. *The World of Southeast Asia: Selected Historical Readings*. New York: Harper and Row, 1967.

Mabbett, Hugh. "Kampong to Capital." Pages 83–88 in *The Straits Times Annual for 1968*. Kuala Lumpur: Straits Times Press, 1968.

McGee, T.G. "The Cultural Role of Cities: A Case Study of Kuala Lumpur," *Journal of Tropical Geography*, XLVII, May 1963, 178–196.

"Malaysia." Pages 683–693 in *Encyclopedia Britannica*, XIV. Chicago: William Benton, 1969.

Malaysia in Brief. Kuala Lumpur: Federal Department of Information, Malaysia, May 1967.

Malaysia Official Yearbook 1967, VII. Kuala Lumpur: Federal Department of Information, 1968.

Malaysia Yearbook 1968/1969. Kuala Lumpur: Malay Mail.

Means, Gordon P. "Eastern Malaysia: The Politics of Federalism," *Asian Survey*, VIII, No. 4, April 1968, 289–308.

————. "State and Religion in Malaya and Malaysia." In M.M. Thomas and M. Abel (eds.). *Religion, State, and Ideologies in East Asia.* Bangalore: East Asia Christian Conference, Committee on Church and Society, 1965.

Mokhzani, B.A.R. "The Study of Social Stratification and Social Mobility in Malaya," *East Asian Cultural Studies* (Tokoyo), IV, Nos. 1–4, March 1965, 138–162.

"Mosque for Tomorrow," *Time*, LXXXVI, No. 8, October 8, 1965, 70–73.

Newell, William H. *Treacherous River: A Study of Rural Chinese in North Malaya.* Kuala Lumpur: University of Malaya Press, 1962.

Parmer, J. Norman. "Malaysia," Pages 281–365 in George McTurnan Kahin (ed.), Ithaca: Cornell University Press, 1965.

Population and Vital Statistics Reports. (Statistical Papers Series A, XXI, No. 2.) New York: United Nations, Department of Economic and Social Affairs, 1969.

Provencher, Ronald. *Two Malay Communities in Selangor: An Urban-Rural Comparison of Social Habitats and Interaction.* (Unpublished Ph. D. dissertation, University of California, Department of Anthropology.) Berkeley: 1968.

Purcell, Victor. *Malaysia.* New York: Walker, 1965.

Rauf, M.A. *A Brief History of Islam.* Kuala Lumpur: Oxford University Press, 1964.

Reece, Bob. "Communalism: Thoughts of a Premier Prince," *Far Eastern Economic Review*, LXVI, No. 41, October 9, 1969, 91.

Rice, Oliver (ed. and trans.), *Modern Malay Verse: 1946–1961.* Kuala Lumpur: Oxford University Press, 1963.

Robequain, Charles. *Malaya, Indonesia, and the Philippines.* New York: Longmans, Green, 1955.

Roff, William R. *The Origins of Malay Nationalism.* (Pustaka Ilmu, Yale University Southeast Asia Studies, No. 2.) Kuala Lumpur: University of Malaya Press, 1967.

Scott, James C. *Political Ideology in Malaysia: Reality and the Beliefs of an Elite.* New Haven: Yale University Press, 1968.

Sheppard, Haji Mubin C. "Four Historic Malay Timber Building," *Federation Museums Journal*, VII, 1962, 86–94.

Smith, T.E., and Bastin, John. *Malaysia.* (The Modern World Series.) London: Oxford University Press, 1967.

Sullivan, Frank. "Thoughts of an Art Collector." Pages 22–25 in *Straits Times Annual for 1965.* Kuala Lumpur: Straits Times Press, 1966.

Swift, M.G. *Malay Peasant Society in Jelebu.* (London School of Economics, Monographs on Social Anthropology, No. 29.) London: Athlone Press, 1965.

Taib bin Osman, Moh. "Trends in Modern Malay Literature." Pages 210–224 in Wang Gungwu, *Malaysia.* New York: Praeger, 1964.

Tregonning, K.G. *A History of Modern Sabah: North Borneo 1881–1963.* (2d ed.) (Pustaka Ilmu Series.) Singapore: University of Malaya Press, 1965.

Wales, Horace C. Quaritch. *Prehistory and Religion in Southeast Asia.* London: Bernard Quaritch, 1957.

Wallace, Alfred Russell. *The Malay Archipelago.* New York: Dover Publications, 1962.

Wang, Gung-wu (ed.). *Malaysia: A Survey.* New York: Praeger, 1964.

Wheatley, Paul. *Impressions of the Malay Peninsula in Ancient Times.* Singapore: Donald Moore, 1964.

Wilson, Peter J. *A Malay Village and Malaysia: Social Values and Rural Development.* New Haven: Human Relations Area Files Press, 1967.

Winstedt, Richard O. *The Malays: A Cultural History.* London: Routledge and Kegan Paul, 1965.

Wong, Elizabeth. "University Hospital." Pages 74–77 in *Straits Times Annual for 1968.* Kuala Lumpur: Straits Times Press, 1967.

OTHER SOURCES USED

Allen, G.C., and Donnithorne, Audrey G. *Western Enterprise in Indonesia and Malaya.* New York: Macmillan, 1957.

Annual Bulletin of Statistics, State of Sarawak 1968. Kuching: Department of Statistics, State of Sarawak, 1969.

Appell, G.N. "A Survey of the Social and Medical Anthropology of Sabah: Retrospect and Prospect," *Behavior Science Notes*, III, No. 1, 1968, 1–54.

Arasaratnam, S. *Aspects of Society and Cultural Life of Indians in Malaysia.* (Paper presented at the Cultural Conference of the Malaysian Society of Orientalists.) Kuala Lumpur: October 22–25, 1965 (mimeo.).

———. *Indian Festivals in Malaya.* Kuala Lumpur: Department of Indian Studies, University of Malaya, 1966.

Aziz bin Yahaya, Abdul. "Les Musées de Malaisie," *Museum*, XIX, No. 4, 1966, 237–241.

Bailey, C.H.R. "Report from Malaysia," *Liturgical Arts*, XXXIII, No. 3, May 1965, 62–74.

Barron, Louis (ed.). *Worldmark Encyclopedia of the Nations*, IV: Asia and Australia. (3d ed.) New York: Worldmark Press, 1967.

Bass, Jerome R. "Malaysia and Singapore: Moving Apart?," *Asian Survey*, IX, No. 2, February 1969, 122–129.

British Territories in Borneo. *Annual Report of the Geological Survey Department for 1958*. Kuching: Government Printer, 1959.

Brown, C.C. "Sejarah Melayu or Malay Annals," *Journal of the Malaya Branch of the Royal Asiatic Society*, XXV, Nos. 2 and 3, October 1952, 5–276.

Buck, Harry M. *An Introduction of the Study of the Ramayana in South and Southeast Asia*. Kuala Lumpur: Conference-Seminar of Tamil Studies, 1966.

Carow, Jay R. "With the Peace Corps in Malaysia," *American Institute of Architects Journal*, XLIV, No. 6, 1965, 61–64.

Chang, Min-kee. "The National Education System of Malaysia. Its Policy and Structure," *United Malayan Banking Corporation Economic Review*, III, No. 1, 1967, 28–33.

Cheeseman, H.R. (ed.) *Bibliography of Malaya*. London: Longmans, Green 1959.

———. "Education in Malaya 1900–1941," *The Malayan Historical Journal*, II, July 1955, 30–47.

Comber, Leon. *Chinese Secret Societies in Malaya 1800–1900*. Singapore: Straits Times Press, 1957.

Demographic Yearbook, 1967. (19th issue.) New York: United Nations, 1968.

Dhat, Kharak Singh. "Education and Problems of Malaysian Nationhood," UNITAS: *Revista de Cultural y Vida Universitiaria*, XXXIX, March 1966, 49–55.

Djamour, Judith. *Malay Kinship and Marriage in Singapore*. London: Athlone Press, 1959.

Dodd, Joseph W. "The Colonial Economy, 1967: The Case of Malaysia," *Asian Survey*, IX, No. 6, June 1969, 438–446.

Downs, Richard. "A Kelantanese Village of Malaya." Pages 105–186 in Julian H. Steward (ed.), *Contemporary Change in Traditional Societies*, II: Asian Rural Societies. Urbana: University of Illinois Press, 1967.

The Economist Intelligence Unit. *Quarterly Economic Review*, Annual Supplement. London: EIU, 1969.

"Educated Manpower, 1965–1980," *United Malayan Banking Corporation Economic Review*, III, No. 1, 1967, 49.

"Education Expenditure in Malaysia in Relation to Other Macro-Economic Data," *United Malayan Banking Corporation Economic Review*, III. No. 1, 1967, 49.

Enloe, Cynthia H. "Issues and Integration in Malaysia," *Pacific Affairs*, XLI, No. 3, Fall 1968, 372–385.

Estimates of Population for West Malaysia (1967). (Research Paper No. 1.) Kuala Lumpur: Malaysia Department of Statistics, March 1969.

Europa Year Book, 1968. London: Europa Publications, 1968.

Europa Year Book, 1969, II. London: Europa Publications, 1969.

The Far East and Australasia, 1969: A Survey and Directory of Asia and the Pacific. London: Europa Publications, 1969.

Far Eastern Economic Review Yearbook, 1969. Hong Kong: FEER, 1969.

First Malaysia Plan 1966–70. Kuala Lumpur: Malaysia Government Party Office, 1965.

Franke, Wolfgang. *The Structure, Concepts and Ideals of Chinese Culture*. (Paper presented at the Cultural Conference of the Malaysian Society of Orientalists.) Kuala Lumpur: October 22–25, 1965 (mimeo.).

Freedman, Maurice. "The Handling of Money: A Note on the Background of the Economic Sophistication of Overseas Chinese." Pages 38–42 in T.H. Silcock (ed.), *Readings in Malayan Economics*. Singapore: Donald Moore, for Eastern University Press, 1961.

———. "Notes and Comment: The Growth of a Plural Society in Malaya," *Pacific Affairs*, XXXIII, No. 2, June 1960, 158–168.

Freeman, J.D. *Iban Agriculture*, I: Iban Social Organization Kuching: Government Printing Office, 1955.

———. "The Iban of Western Borneo." Chapter 5 in George P. Murdock, ed. *Social Structure in Southeast Asia*. (Viking Fund Publications in Anthropology, No. 29.) Chicago: Quadrangle Books, 1960.

———. *Report on the Iban of Sarawak*. Kuching: Government Printing Office, 1955.

Gallagher, Charles F. "Contemporary Islam: A Frontier of Communalism," *American Universities Field Staff Reports*, Southeast Asia Series, XIV, No. 10, May 1966.

Garvin, Edwin N. *The Students*. (Reports on Education in Sarawak.) Washington: U.S. Peace Corps. 1963.

Geddes, W.R. *Nine Dayak Nights.* London: Oxford University Press, 1961.

Gerakan Raya Talking Point No. 1: Progress in Education. Kuala Lumpur: Federation Department of Information, Malaysia, 1969 (mimeo.).

Gerakan Raya Talking Point No. 2: Eradication of Illiteracy. Kuala Lumpur: Federal Department of Information, Malaysia, 1969 (mimeo.).

Gerakan Raya Talking Point No. 14: Government Aid to Chinese Schools. Kuala Lumpur: Federal Department of Information, Malaysia, 1969 (mimeo.).

Gilani, S.J. "Higher School Certificate Examinations in Economics," *Kajian Ekonomi Malaysia,* IV, No. 1, June 1967, 73–83.

Glick, Henry Robert. "Political Recruitment in Sarawak: A Case Study of Leadership in a New State," *Journal of Politics,* XXVIII, No. 1, February 1966, 81–99.

Gordon, Shirle. "Pondok and Our Peasantry," *Intisari* (Singapore), II, No. 1, 32–33.

"The Gravestone of Sultan Mansur Shah of Malacca!," *Malaya-in-History,* V, No. 1, February 1969, 37.

Great Britain. Central Office of Information. *North Borneo and Sarawak.* London: Her Majesty's Stationery Office, 1963.

Grossholtz, Jean. "An Exploration of Malaysian Meanings," *Asian Survey,* VI, No. 4, April 1966, 227–240.

Gullick, J.M. *Malaya.* New York: Praeger, 1963.

———. *The Story of Early Kuala Lumpur.* Singapore: Donald Moore, 1956.

Guyot, James F. *The Two Cultures and Malaysia's Development Revolution.* (Paper presented at the Annual Meeting of the Association for Asian Studies, Philadelphia.) Philadelphia: March 24, 1968 (mimeo).

Hanna, Willard A. "The Day of the Bumiputera, Part I: Motivating of Ethnic Malay," *American Universities Field Staff Reports,* Southeast Asia Series, XVI, No. 6, February 1968.

———. "Peninsular Thailand: The Thai Muslim Centers of Pattani and Yala," *American Universities Field Staff Reports,* Southeast Asia Series, XIII, No. 26, October 1965.

———. "Sabotaging Sabah," *American Universities Field Staff Reports,* Southeast Asia Series, XVI, No. 15, September 1968.

Harrisson, Barbara. "A Classification of Stone Age Burials from Niah Great Cave, Sarawak," *Sarawak Museum Journal,* XV, Nos. 30 and 31, 1967, 126–200.

Harrisson, Tom. "Borneo Death," *Bijdragen tot de taal-, land- en volkenkunde*, CXVIII, No. 1, 1962, 1–41.

———. "The Peoples of North and West Borneo." Chapter 11 in Wang, Gung-wu, *Malaysia*. New York: Praeger, 1964.

———. "Tribes, Minorities and the Central Government in Sarawak, Malaysia." Chapter 9 in Peter Kunstadter (ed.), *Southeast Asian Tribes, Minorities and Nations*. Princeton: Princeton University Press, 1967.

Harrisson, Tom, and O'Connor, Stanley J. "The Tantric Shrine Excavated at Santubong," *Sarawak Museum Journal*, XV, Nos. 30 and 31, 1967, 201–222.

Hayden, Howard. *Higher Education and Development in Southeast Asia*, I: Director's Report. Paris: UNESCO, 1967.

Hodder, B.W. *Man in Malaya*. London: University of London Press, 1959.

Hsu, Yun-tsiao. "Chinese Culture in Malaysia." (Paper written for the Cultural Conference of the Malaysian Society of Orientalists.) Kuala Lumpur: October 22–25, 1965 (mimeo.).

Husin Ali, S. *A Note on Malay Society and Culture*. (Paper presented at the Cultural Conference of the Malaysian Society of Orientalists.) Kuala Lumpur: October 22–25, 1965 (mimeo.).

Hussein Alatas, Syed. "The Grading of Occupational Prestige Amongst the Malays in Malaysia," *Journal of the Malaysian Branch of the Royal Asiatic Society*, XLI, Part I, July 1968, 146–156.

International Yearbook of Education, XXIX. Paris: UNESCO, 1968.

Jamuh, George. "Coastal Melanau Taboos," *Sarawak Museum Journal*, VIII, December 1958, 710–731.

Jamuh, George; Harrisson, Tom; and Sandin, Benedict. " 'Pelandok' the Villain-Hero—in Sarawak and Interior Kalimantan," *Sarawak Museum Journal*, X, December 1962, 524–534.

Jones, Alun. "Orang Asli: An Outline of their Progress in Modern Malaysia," *Journal of Southeast Asian History*, IX No. 2, September 1968, 286–305.

Jones, L.W. "Malaysia's Future Population," *Pacific Viewpoint*, VI, May 1965, 39–51.

———. The Population of Borneo: *A Study of the Peoples of Sarawak, Sabah and Brunei*, London: Athlone Press, 1966.

Kahin, George McTurnan. "Malaysia and Indonesia," *Pacific Affairs*, XXXVII, No. 3, Fall 1964, 253–270.

Kanapathy, V. "Education, Manpower, and Malaysian Economic Development," *United Malayan Banking Corporation Economic Review*, III, No. 1, 1967, 8–27.

Kennedy, Joseph. *A History of Malaya, 1400–1959.* London: Macmillan, 1962.

King, Frank H.H. *The New Malayan Nation: A Study of Communalism and Nationalism.* New York: Institute of Pacific Relations, 1957.

Kirkup, James. *Tropic Temper: A Memory of Malaya.* London: Collins, 1963.

Kuchiba, Masua, and Tsubouchi, Yoshiro. "Cooperation Patterns in a Malay Village," *Asian Survey*, VIII, No. 10, October 1968, 836–841.

"Language and Learning," *Far Eastern Economic Review*, XLIV, No. 8, May 21, 1964, 391–392.

Lee, Edwin. "The Emergence of Towkay Leaders in Party Politics in Sabah," *Journal of Southeast Asian History*, IX, No. 2, September 1968, 306–324.

Leigh, Michael B. *The Chinese Community of Sarawak: A Study of Communal Relations.* (Singapore Studies on Malaysia, No. 6.) Singapore: Malaysia Publishing House, 1964.

Lewis, Diane Katherine. *The Minangkabau Malay of Negri Sembilan: A Study of Socio-Cultural Change.* (Unpublished doctoral dissertation, Cornell University, Ithaca, New York, 1962.)

Ley, C.H. "Muruts of Sabah (North Borneo)." Chapter 10 in Peter Kunstadter (ed.), *Southeast Asian Tribes, Minorities, and Nations.* Princeton: Princeton University Press, 1967.

Liang, Kim-bang. *Sarawak, 1941–1957.* (Singapore Studies on Borneo and Malaya, No. 5.) Singapore: University of Singapore, Department of History, 1964.

Lim, Chong-yah. *Economic Development of Modern Malaya.* Kuala Lumpur: Oxford University Press, 1967.

MacDonald, Malcolm. *Borneo People.* New York: Knopf, 1958.

McGee, T.G. "Down But Not Out," *Far Eastern Economic Review.* LXIV, No. 23, June 5, 1969, 566–568.

McKie, Ronald Cecil Hamlyn. *The Emergence of Malaysia.* New York: Harcourt, Brace and World, 1963.

———. *Malaysia in Focus.* Sydney: Angus and Robertson, 1963.

Mahajani, Usha. *The Role of Indian Minorities in Burma and Malaya.* Bombay: Vora, 1960.

Malaysia. Department of Statistics. *Monthly Statistical Bulletin of West Malaysia.* Kuala Lumpur: May 1969.

"Malaysia: Another Year of Progress," *New York Times* (Special Supplement), August 30, 1964.

Malaysia into the Seventies; A Straits Times Special Feature. Kuala Lumpur: Straits Times, 1969.

"Malaysia's Social Problems: Monkey Business," *Far Eastern Economic Review*, LIX, No. 3, January 18, 1969, 106–111.

Miller, Harry. *A Short History of Malaysia.* New York: Praeger, 1965.

Milne, R.S. and Ratnam, K.J. "Patterns and Peculiarities of Ethnic Voting in Sabah 1967," *Asian Survey*, IX, No. 5, May 1969, 373–381.

Monthly Statistical Bulletin of West Malaysia, May 1969.

Morris, H.S. *Report on a Melanau Sago Producing Community in Sarawak.* London: Her Majesty's Stationery Office, for the Colonial Office, 1953.

Mullen, Vernon. *The Story of Sarawak.* (2d ed.) Kuala Lumpur: Oxford University Press, 1967.

Murphy, Henry B.M. "Cultural Factors in the Mental Health of Malayan Students." Chapter 8 in Daniel H. Funkenstein (ed.), *The Student and Mental Health: An International View.* Cambridge: Riverside Press, 1959.

Murray, Douglas P. "Chinese Education in Southeast Asia," *China Quarterly*, XX, October-December 1964, 67–95.

Naguib al-Attas, Syed. *Islamic Culture in Malaysia.* (Paper presented at the Cultural Conference of the Malaysian Society of Orientalists.) Kuala Lumpur: October 22–25, 1965 (mimeo).

Ness, Gayl D. "Modernization and Indigenous Control of the Bureaucracy in Malaysia," *Asian Survey*, V, No. 9, September 1965, 467–473.

Nimmo, Harry. "Social Organization of the Tawi-Tawi Badjaw," *Ethnology*, IV, No. 4, October 1965, 421–439.

Noor bin Hashim, Mat. "A Malay Child in a Religious School," *Intisari*, II, No. 1, 12–13.

Ongkili, J.P. *The Borneo Response to Malaysia 1961–1963.* Singapore: Donald Moore, April 1966.

Ooi, Jin-bee. *Land, People, and Economy in Malaya.* London: Longmans, Green, 1963.

Parkinson, Brien K. "The Economic Retardation of the Malays—A Rejoinder," *Modern Asian Studies*, II, No. 3, July 1968, 267–272.

————. "Non-Economic Factors in the Economic Retardation of the Rural Malays," *Modern Asian Studies*, I, No. 1, January 1967, 31–46.

Parmer, J. Norman. "Malaysia: Changing a Little to Keep Pace," *Asian Survey*, VII, No. 2, February 1967, 131–137.

———. "Malaysia 1965: Challenging the Terms of 1957," *Asian Survey*, VI, No. 2, February 1966, 111–118.

Payne, Pierre Stephan Robert. *The White Rajahs of Sarawak*. New York: Funk and Wagnalls, 1960.

Peacock, B.A.V. "Malaysian Prehistory: Some Current Problems." (Paper of the Department of History, University of Malaya [mimeo.].)

Peaslee, Amos J. (ed.) *Constitution of Nations*, II. (3d ed., rev.) The Hague: Martinus Nijhoff, 1966.

"Percentage of Enrollment to Corresponding Age-Group," *United Malayan Banking Corporation Economic Review*, III, No. 1, 1967, 50.

Polsky, Anthony. "Hot Cross Lines," *Far Eastern Economic Review*, LXIV, No. 24, June 12, 1969, 597–598.

Price, Waterhouse and Company. *Information Guide for Doing Business in Malaysia and Singapore*. N.pl.: Price, Waterhouse, October 1968.

Pringle, Robert M. "The Brookes of Sarawak: Reformers in Spite of Themselves." (London Cornell Project of East and Southeast Asia Studies. Conference held at the Chantecler Hotel, Ste. Adèle-en-haute, August 24–30, 1969.) Quebec: May 1969 (mimeo.).

———. *The Ibans of Sarawak Under Brooke Rule 1841–1941*. (Master's thesis, Cornell University, Ithaca, New York.) Ann Arbor: Microfilms, 1967.

Purcell, Victor. "The Chinese in Malaysia." Pages 190–198 in Wang, Gung-wu, *Malaysia: A Survey*. New York: Praeger, 1964.

———. *The Chinese in Modern Malaya*. (Background to Malaya Series No. 9.) Singapore: Donald Moore, 1956.

Rahman Ya'akub, Dato Haji Abdul. "Education and Bahasa Malaysia." (Text of speech by minister of education over television, Malaysia.) Kuala Lumpur: Malaysian Department of Information, July 21, 1969.

Ramsay, A.B. "Indonesians in Malaya," *Journal of the Malaysian Branch of the Royal Asiatic Society*, XXIX, Part I, May 1956, 119–124.

Rauf, M.A. "Islamic Education in Malaya," *Intisari*, II, No. 1, 14–31.

Rawlins, Joan. *Sarawak 1839–1963*. London: Macmillan, 1965.

Reece, Bob. "Some Teaparty," *Far Eastern Economic Review*, LXIV, No. 24, June 12, 1969, 598–599.

———. "Who's the Driver," *Far Eastern Economic Review*, LXIV, No. 22, May 29, 1969, 481.

Republic of Indonesia. Embassy in Washington. Information Division. *A Survey on the Controversial Problem of the Establishment of the Federation of Malaysia.* Washington: [1963].

Richards, A.J.N. "The Ibans." Pages 9–25 in Tom Harrisson (ed.), *The Peoples of Sarawak.* Kuching: Sarawak Museum, 1959.

Robbins, Burling. *Hill Farms and Padi Fields: Life in Mainland Southeast Asia.* Englewood Cliffs: Prentice-Hall, 1965.

Roose, Hashimah. "Changes in the Position of the Malay Women." Pages 287–294 in Barbara E. Ward (ed.), *Women in the New Asia.* Paris: 1963.

Runciman, Steven. *The White Rajahs.* Cambridge: Cambridge University Press, 1960.

Rutter, Owen. *The Pagans of North Borneo.* London: Hutchinson, 1928.

Sabah in Brief. Kuala Lumpur: Malaysia, Ministry of Information and Broadcasting, 1969.

Sandin, Benedict. *The Sea Dayaks of Borneo Before White Rajah Rule.* London: Macmillan, 1967.

Sarawak in Brief. Kuala Lumpur: Malaysia, Ministry of Information and Broadcasting, 1969.

Sarawak, the Object of Our Affection. Kuching: Peace Corps, Sarawak, July 1, 1966 (mimeo.).

Sather, Clifford. "Social Rank and Marriage Payments in an Immigrant Moro Community in Malaysia," *Ethnology.* VI, No. 1, January 1967, 97–102.

"Senoi-Semang." In Frank M. Lebar, Gerald C. Hickey, and John K. Musgrave (eds.), *Ethnic Groups of Mainland Southeast Asia.* New Haven: Human Relations Area Files Press, 1966.

Shaplen, Robert. *Time Out of Hand: Revolution and Reaction in Southeast Asia.* New York: Harper and Row, 1969.

Shuster, Donald E. *Teachers in Government Schools.* (Reports on Education in Sarawak.) Washington: U.S. Peace Corps, 1963.

Silcock, T.H. *Southeast Asian University: A Comparative Account of Some Development Problems.* Durham: Duke University Press, 1964.

Singh, Kernial. "The Saga of the Malaysian Squatter," *Journal of Southeast Asian History,* V, No. 1, March 1964, 143–177.

Skeat, Walter William. *Malay Magic: Being an Introduction to the Folklore and Popular Religion of the Malay Peninsula.* (Unabridged republication of work first published in 1900.) New York: Dover Publications, 1967.

Smith, T.E. *The Background to Malaysia.* London: Oxford University Press, 1963.

Snider, Nancy L. "What Happened in Penang?," *Asian Survey*, VIII, No. 12, December 1968, 960–975.

Starner, Frances L. "Malaysia's First Year," *Asian Survey*, V. No. 2, February 1965, 113–119.

State of Sarawak. Department of Statistics. *Annual Bulletin of Statistics, State of Sarawak, 1968.* Kuching: State Government Printer, 1968.

Statesman's Year-Book 1968–1969. (Ed., S.H. Steinberg.) New York: St. Martin's Press, 1968.

Stewart, Robert B. *In the Classroom.* (Reports on Education in Sarawak.) Washington: U.S. Peace Corps, 1963.

Swift, M.G. "Capital, Saving, and Credit in a Malay Peasant Economy." Pages 133–156 in Raymond Firth and B.S. Yamey (eds.), *Capital, Saving, and Credit in Peasant Societies.* Chicago: Aldine, 1964.

———. "Malay Peasants." Pages 219–244 in Richard D. Lambert and Bert F. Hoselitz (ed.), *The Role of Savings and Wealth in Southern Asia and the West.* Paris: UNESCO, 1963.

Swift, Michael. "Men and Women in Malay Society." Pages 268–286 in Barbara E. Ward (ed.), *Women in the New Asia.* Paris: UNESCO, 1963.

Taib bin Mahmud, Abdul. "The Role of Muslims in Nation-Building in the Federation of Malaysia," *Islamic Review*, LII, December 1964, 22–23.

Teeuw, A. "A History of the Malay Language, a Preliminary Survey," *Bijdragen tot de taal-, land- en volkenkunde*, CXV, 1959, 138–156.

T'ien, Ju-k'ang. *The Chinese of Sarawak: A Study of Social Structure.* (Monographs on Social Anthropology, No. 12.) London: Department of Anthropology, London School of Economics and Political Science, 1953.

Tilman, Robert O. "Malaysia: The Problems of Federation," *Western Political Quarterly.* XVI, December 1963, 897–911.

———. *Malaysian Foreign Policy: The Dilemmas of a Committed Neutral.* (Reprint Series No. 22.) New Haven: Yale University Southeast Asia Studies, 1967.

———. "The Non-Lessons of the Malayan Emergency," *Asian Survey*, VI, No. 8, August 1966, 407–419.

———. "The Sarawak Political Scene," *Pacific Affairs.* XXXVII, No. 4, Winter 1964–65, 412–425.

Tregonning, K.G. *The Britsh in Malaya: The First Forty Years 1786-1826.* Tucson: n.pub., 1965.

Tweedie, M.W.F. *Prehistoric Malaya.* Singapore: Donald Moore, 1955.

UNESCO Statistical Yearbook 1967. Paris: UNESCO, 1968.

United Nations Statistical Yearbook. (10th issue.) New York: UN, 1969.

U.S. Department of Agriculture. Economics Research Service. Foreign Regional Analysis Division. *A Survey of Agriculture in Malaysia,* by Robert M. McConnell. (Foreign-95.) Washington: 1964.

U.S. Department of Labor. Bureau of Labor Statistics. *Labor Development Abroad.* Washington: GPO, 1969.

United States. Department of the Interior. Board of Geographic Names. *British Borneo, Singapore, and Malaya.* (Gazetteer No. 10.) Washington: GPO, 1955.

van der Kroef, Justus M. "Chinese Minority Aspirations and Problems in Sarawak," *Pacific Affairs,* XXXIX, Nos. 1 and 2, Spring and Summer 1966, 64-82.

———. "Communism in Sarawak Today," *Asian Survey,* VI, No. 10, October 1966, 568-579.

———. "Nanyang University and the Dilemmas of Overseas Chinese Education," *China Quarterly,* XX, October-December 1964, 96-127.

Wang, Gung-wu. *A Short History of the Nanyang Chinese.* (Background to Malaya Series No. 13.) Singapore: Donald Moore, 1959.

Ward, Barbara E. "A Hakka Kongsi in Borneo," *Journal of Oriental Studies,* I, No. 2, July 1954, 358.

Wheatley, Paul. *The Golden Khersonese.* Kuala Lumpur: University of Malaya Press, 1961.

Wikkramatileke, Rudolph. "Variable Ethnic Attributes in Malayan Rural Land Development," *Pacific Viewpoint,* V, May 1964, 35-49.

Wilder, William. "Islam, Other Factors and Malay Backwardness: Comments on an Argument," *Modern Asian Studies,* II, No. 2, April 1968, 155-164.

Williams, Thomas Rhys. *The Dusun: A North Borneo Society.* (Case Studies in Cultural Anthropology.) New York: Rinehart and Winston, 1965.

Winstedt, Richard O. "A History of Classical Malay Literature," *Journal of the Malayan Branch of the Royal Asiatic Society.* XXXI, Part 3, June 1958, 1-261.

————. *Malay-English Dictionary.* (2d ed., rev. and enl.) Singapore: Marican, 1957.

"World Bank Loan to Malaysia," *International Financial News Survey,* XXI, No. 23, June 13, 1969, 185–186.

World Illiteracy at Mid-Century: A Statistical Study. (Monographs on Fundamental Education.) Paris: UNESCO, 1957.

Wright, Leigh R. "Historical Notes on the North Borneo Dispute," *Journal of Asian Studies,* XXV, No. 4, May 1966, 471–484.

Yip, Yat-hoong. "A Case for the Teaching of Economics in Secondary Schools in Malaysia," *Kajian Ekonomi Malaysia,* IV, No. 1, June 1967, 65–72.

Zain bin Abdul Majid, Mohd. "Teaching Economics in the National Language," *Kajian Ekonomi Malaysia,* IV, No. 1, June 1967, 84–92.

(Various issues of the following periodicals were also used in the preparation of this section: *Far Eastern Economic Review* [Hong Kong], January 1967–December 1969; *New York Times,* July 1–December 31, 1969; *The Straits Times* [Kuala Lumpur], July–December 1969; and *Washington Sunday Star,* July–December 1969.

Section II. Political

RECOMMENDED SOURCES

Bastin, John, and Winks, Robin W. (comps.) *Malaysia: Selected Historical Readings*. Kuala Lumpur: Oxford University Press, 1966.

Boyce, Peter. *Malaysia and Singapore in International Diplomacy: Documents and Commentaries*. Sydney: Sydney University Press, 1968.

Braibanti, Ralph (ed.). *Asian Bureaucratic System Emergent from the British Imperial Tradition*. Durham: Duke University Press, 1966.

Brimmel, J.H. *A Short History of the Malayan Communist Party*. Singapore: Donald Moore, 1956.

Catley, R. "Malaysia: The Lost Battle for Merger," *Australian Outlook*, XXI, No. 1, April 1967, 44–60.

Editor and Publisher International Yearbook 1969. New York: Editor and Publisher, 1969.

Emerson, Rupert. *Malaysia: A Study in Direct and Indirect Rule*. New York: Macmillan, 1937.

Enloe, Cynthia H. "Issues and Integration in Malaysia," *Pacific Affairs*, XLI, No. 3, Fall 1968, 372–385.

————. *Multi-ethnic Politics: The Case of Malaysia*. Berkeley: University of California Press, 1967.

Europa Year Book, 1968. London: Europa Publications, 1968.

Gehan, Wijeyewardene (ed.). *Leadership and Authority*. Singapore: University of Malaya Press, 1968.

Glick, Henry Robert. "Political Recruitment in Sarawak: A Case Study of Leadership in a New State," *Journal of Politics*, XXXVIII, No. 1, February 1966, 81–99.

Great Britain. British Information Service. *Malaya: The Making of a Nation*. (I.D. 1270.) London: Her Majesty's Stationery Office, May 1957.

Great Britain. Colonial Office. *Constitutional Proposals for the Federation of Malaya*. (Presented by the Secretary of State to Parliament, June 1957.) London: Her Majesty's Stationery Office, 1957.

————. *Report of the Federation of Malaya Constitutional Commission, 1957*. London: Her Majesty's Stationery Office, 1957.

Gullick, J.M. *Indigenous Political Systems of Western Malaya*. London: Athlone Press, 1965.

————. *Malaysia and Its Neighbours*. New York: Barnes and Noble, 1967.

Hanna, Willard A. *The Formation of Malaysia: A New Factor in World Politics*. New York: American Universities Field Staff, 1964.

Hanrahan, Gene Z. *The Communist Struggle in Malaya*. New York: Institute of Pacific Relations, 1954.

Jones, S.W. *Public Administration in Malaya*. London: Royal Institute of International Affairs, 1953.

King, Frank H.H. *The New Malayan Nation: A Study of Communalism and Nationalism*. New York: Institute of Pacific Relations, 1957.

Lee, Edwin. *Sarawak in the Early Sixties*. (Singapore Studies on Borneo and Malaya, No. 5.) Singapore: University of Singapore, Department of History, 1964.

Liang, Kim-bang. *Sarawak 1941–1957*. (Singapore Studies on Borneo and Malaya, No. 5.) Singapore: University of Singapore, Department of History, 1964.

Lockard, Craig A. "Parties, Personalities and Crisis Politics in Sarawak," *Journal of Southeast Asian History*, VIII, No. 1, March 1967, 111–121.

Malaysia Official Yearbook 1967, VII. Kuala Lumpur: Federal Department of Information, 1968.

Maryanov, Gerald S. "Political Parties in Mainland Malaya," *Journal of Southeast Asian History*, VIII, No. 1, March 1967, 99–110.

Means, Gordon P. "Eastern Malaysia: The Politics of Federalism," *Asian Survey*, VIII, No. 4, April 1968, 289–308.

————. "The Role of Islam in the Political Development of Malaysia," *Comparative Politics*, I, No. 2, January 1969, 264–284.

Milne, R.S. *Government and Politics in Malaysia*, Boston: Houghton Mifflin, 1967.

————. "Political Modernization in Malaysia," *Journal of Commonwealth Political Studies*, VII, No. 1, March 1969, 3–16.

Nash, Manning. "Tradition in Tension in Kelantan," *Journal of Asian and African Studies*, I, No. 4, October 1966, 310–314.

Parmer, J. Norman. "Malaysia," Pages 281–365 in George McTurnan Kahin (ed.), *Governments and Politics of Southeast Asia*. (2d ed.) Ithaca: Cornell University Press, 1965.

Rahman, Tunku Abdul. "Malaysia: Key Area in Southeast Asia," *Foreign Affairs*, XLIII, No. 4, July 1965, 659–670.

———. *May 13 Before and After*. Kuala Lumpur: Utusan Melayu Press, 1969.

Ratnam, K.J. *Communalism and the Political Process in Malaya*. Kuala Lumpur: University of Malaya Press, 1965.

Ryan, N.J. *The Making of Modern Malaysia*. Kuala Lumpur: Oxford University Press, 1967.

Scott, James C. *Political Ideology in Malaysia: Reality and the Belief of an Elite*. New Haven: Yale University Press, 1968.

Starner, Frances L. "Malaysia's First Year," *Asian Survey*. V, No. 2, February 1965, 113–119.

Tilman, Robert O. *Malaysian Foreign Policy: The Dilemmas of a Committed Neutral*. (Reprint Series No. 22.) New Haven: Yale University, Southeast Asia Studies, 1967.

Tregonning, K.G. *Malaysia and Singapore*. Melbourne: Chesire, 1966.

OTHER SOURCES USED

Armfield, Hugh. "Just a Mirage?," *Far Eastern Economic Review*, LXII, No. 49, December 5, 1968, 530, 567–568.

Bass, Jerome D. "Malaysia and Singapore: Moving Apart?," *Asian Survey*, IX, No. 2, February 1969, 122–129.

Braddell, Ronald St. John. *The Legal Status of the Malay States*. Singapore: Malaya Publishing House, 1931.

Bradley, C. Paul. "Communal Politics in Malaysian Borneo," *Western Political Quarterly*, XXI, No. 1, March 1968, 123–140.

———. "The Formation of Malaysia," *Current History*, XLVII, February 1964, 177–188.

———. "Malaysia's First Year," *Current History*, LXVIII, February 1965, 82–88, 114–115.

Brimmel, J.H. *Communism in Southeast Asia: A Political Analysis*. London: Oxford University Press, 1959.

Butwell, Richard. "Malaysia and Its Impact on the International Relations of Southeast Asia," *Asian Survey*, IV, July 1964, 940–946.

Carnell, Francis G. "British Policy in Malaya," *Political Quarterly*, XXIII, July 1952, 269–281.

———. "Constitutional Reform and Elections in Malaya," *Pacific Affairs*, XXVII, September 1954, 216–235.

———. "Malayan Citizenship Legislation," *International and Comparative Law Quarterly*, I, October 1952 (4th Series).

———. "Malayan Elections," *Pacific Affairs*, XXVIII, December 1955, 315–330.

Cheesemen, H.R. (ed.) *Bibliography of Malaya*. London: Longmans, Green, 1959.

Cowan, C.D. *Nineteenth-Century Malaya: The Origins of British Political Control*. New York: Oxford University Press, 1961.

Dodd, E.E. *The New Malaya*. (Report of the Fabian Colonial Bureau.) London: Fabian Publications, 1496.

"Emergency in Malaya: Some Reflections on the First Six Years," *World Today*, November 1954, 477–487.

The Far East and Australia, 1969: A Survey and Directory of Asia and the Pacific. London: Europa Publications, 1969.

Far Eastern Economic Review Yearbook, 1962, 1965, 1966, 1967, 1968, and 1969. Hong Kong: FEER, 1962 and 1965–69.

Federal Ordinances and Statutes, 1954. Kuala Lumpur: Government Press, 1955.

The Federation of Malaya Agreement, 1948. Kuala Lumpur: Government Press, 1952.

Gamer, Robert E. "Southeast Asia Political Systems: An Overview," *Journal of Southeast Asian History*, VIII, No. 1, March 1967, 139–185.

Great Britain. British Information Service. *The Federation of Malaysia*. London: Cox and Sharland, 1963.

Grossholtz, Jean. "Political Integration and the Management of Dissent in the Malaysian Political System." (Unpublished paper prepared for the Twentieth Annual Meeting of The Association for Asian Studies, Philadelphia, March 1968.)

Guyot, James F. "Political Succession and Political Development in Burma and Malaysia." (Paper prepared for a panel on Problems of Succession in Contemporary Southeast Asia at the Association for Southeast Asia meeting in Boston, March 1969.)

Hanna, Willard A. "Three New States of Borneo," *American Universities Field Staff*, Southeast Asia Series, XVI, No. 18, November 1969.

———. "Three New States of Borneo, Part III: Pragmatism in Sabah," *American Universities Field Staff*, Southeast Asia Series, XVI, No. 20, November 1968.

Hatta, Mohamed. "One Indonesian View of the Malaysia Issue," *Asian Survey*, III, March 1965, 130–143.

Hawkins, David, and Drummond Stuart. "The Malaysian Elections of 1969: Crisis for the Alliane," *World Today*, XXV, No. 9, September 1969, 394-403.

Hawkins, David C. "Britain and Malaysia—Another View: Was the Decision to Withdraw Entirely Voluntary or Was Britain Pushed a Little?," *Asian Survey*, IX, No. 7, July 1969, 546-562.

Hickley, Hugh. *Sarawak and Its Government*. Kuching: Government Printing Office, 1954.

Hill, L.C. *Report on the Reform of Local Government*. Singapore: Government Printing Office, 1952.

Hogan-Shaidali, S.A.E. "Communalism and Racialism in Malayan Politics," *Eastern World*, VII, September 1953, 20, 21.

Indonesia Intentions Towards Malaysia. Kuala Lumpur: Federation of Malaysia, 1964.

Jones, J. Mervyn. "British Nationality Act 1948." In *The British Yearbook of International Law 1948*. London: Royal Institute of International Affairs, 1949.

Kahin, George McTurnan. "Malaysia and Indonesia," *Pacific Affairs*, XXXVII, No. 3, Fall 1964, 253-270.

Keesing's Contemporary Archives: Weekly Diary of Contemporary Events, XVII, Nos. 1416-1430, January 1969.

Kementerian Luar Negeri. Malaysian Ministry of Foreign Affairs. *Kaki Tangan Dari Malaysia di-Perwakilan* [2] *Seberang Laut*. Kuala Lumpur: Kementerian Luar Negeri Malaysia, July 31, 1968.

Leifer, Michael. "Anglo-American Differences Over Malaysia," *World Today*, XX, April 1964, 155-167.

McGee, T.C. "The Malayan Elections of 1959: A Study in Electoral Geography," *Journal of Tropical Geography*, XVI, October 1962, 70-99.

McKie, Ronald Cecil Hamlyn. *The Emergence of Malaysia*. New York: Harcourt, Brace and World, 1963.

Malaya Federation of Local Councils. Kuala Lumpur: Ministry of Home Affairs, December 10, 1952 (mimeo.).

———. *Malaysia Report of the Inter-Governmental Committee, 1962*. Kuala Lumpur: Government Printer, 1963.

"Malaysia: Another Year of Progress," *New York Times* (Special Supplement), August 30, 1964.

Malaysia Official Yearbook 1967. VII, Kuala Lumpur: Federal Department of Information, 1968.

"Malaysia, Singapore, Brunei," *Quarterly Economic Reviews*. No. 1, 1966-No. 1, 1969.

Malaysia Yearbook 1968/1969. Kuala Lumpur: Malay Mail, n.d.

Maxwell, W.G., and Gibson, W.S. *Treaties and Engagements Affecting the Malay States and Borneo*. London: Truscott, 1924.

Middlebrook, S.M., and Pinnick, A.W. *How Malaya is Governed*. New York: Longmans, Green, 1949.

Miller, Harry. *Prince and Premier*. London: Harrap, 1959.

————. *The Story of Malaysia*. London: Faber and Faber, 1965.

Mills, Lenox A. *British Rule in Eastern Asia*. London: Oxford University Press, 1942.

Morais, J. Victor (ed.). *Who's Who in Malaysia*. Kuala Lumpur: J. Victor Morais, 1965.

Munthe-Kaas, Harald. "Dubious Down Under," *Far Eastern Economic Review*, LXV, No. 27, July 3, 1969, 5.

The National Operations Council: A Report on the May 13 Tragedy, Kuala Lumpur: October 9, 1969.

Ott, Marvin. "Malaysia: The Search for Solidarity and Security," *Asian Survey*, VIII, No. 2, January 1968, 127–132.

Parmer, J. Norman. "Constitutional Change in Malaya's Plural Society," *Far Eastern Survey*, XXVI, October 1957, 145–152.

The Penal Code of the Federation Malay States. Kuala Lumpur: Government Press, 1952.

Peretz, René. "American-Malaysian Relations: Substance and Shadows," *Orbis*, XI, No. 2, Summer 1967, 532–550.

————. "The Changing World of Malaysia," *Current History*, LII, No. 305, January 1967, 29–35, 51.

Purcell, Victor. *The Chinese in Malaya*. London: Oxford University Press, 1948.

Pye, Lucien W. *Guerrilla Communism in Malaya*. Princeton: Princeton University Press, 1956.

Republic of Indonesia. Embassy in Washington. Information Division. *A Survey on the Controversial Problem of the Establishment of the Federation of Malaysia*. Washington: [1963].

Shaplen, Robert. *Time Out of Hand: Revolution and Reaction in Southeast Asia*. New York: Harper and Row, 1969.

Sheridan, L.A., and Groves, Harry E. *The Constitution of Malaysia*. New York: Oceana Publications, 1967.

A Short History of the Malayan Communist Party. Singapore: Donald Moore, 1956.

Silcock, T.H., and Aziz, Ungku Abdul. "Nationalism in Malaya." In William L. Holland (ed.), *Asian Nationalism and the West*. New York: Macmillan, 1953.

Silcock, T.H., and Fisk, E.K. (ed.) *The Political Economy of Independent Malaya.* Berkeley: University of California Press, 1963.

Smith, T.E. "The Malayan Elections of 1959," *Pacific Affairs,* XXXIII, No. 1, March 1960, 38–47.

———. "Malaysia After the Election," *World Today,* XX, August 1964, 351–357.

Smyly, W.J. "Cobbold Report," *Far Eastern Economic Review,* XXXVII, August 16, 1962, 289–290.

Snider, Nancy. "What Happened in Penang?," *Asian Survey,* VIII, No. 12, December 1968, 960–975.

Statesman's Year-Book 1968–1969 (Ed., S.H. Steinberg.) New York: St. Martin's Press, 1968.

Stockwin, Harvey. "Defence Deals at Dinner," *Far Eastern Economic Review,* LX, No. 26, June 27, 1968, 655–657.

———. "The Law's an Ass," *Far Eastern Economic Review,* LXII, No. 43, October 24, 1968, 200–204.

———. "Malaysia-Lee Disengaged," *Far Eastern Economic Review,* XXV, May 1956, 65–73.

———. "The Nude Strikes Back," *Far Eastern Economic Review,* LXI, No. 29, July 18, 1968, 141–142.

———. "The Sum of Five Negatives," *Far Eastern Economic Review,* LXI, No. 39, September 26, 1968, 629–631.

———. "Suspiciously Like Nothing," *Far Eastern Economic Review,* LXI, No. 28, July 11, 1968, 116–117.

———. "Where There's No Will," *Far Eastern Economic Review,* LXII, No. 41, October 10, 1968, 115–117.

Taylor, W.C. *Local Government in Malaya.* Alor Star: Kadah Government Press, 1949.

Tilman, Robert O. "The Alliance Pattern in Malaysian Politics: Bornean Variations on a Theme," *South Atlantic Quarterly,* LXIII, January 1964, 60–74.

———. "Elections in Sarawak," *Asian Survey,* III, October 1963, 507–518.

——— "The Nationalization of the Colonial Services in Malaya," *South Atlantic Quarterly,* LXI, No. 2, 1962, 183–196.

———. "Public Service Commissions in the Federation of Malaya," *Journal of Asian Studies,* XX, February 1961, 181–196.

Tinker, I. "Malayan Elections: Electoral Pattern for Plural Societies?," *Western Political Quarterly,* IX, June 1956, 258–282.

Tregonning, K.G. "Malaya 1955 (Political Changes)," *Australian Quarterly,* June 1956, 20–35.

van der Kroef, Justus M. "Communism and Chinese Communalism in Sarawak," *China Quarterly*, XX, October–December 1964, 38–66.

———. "Communism and the Guerrilla War in Sarawak," *World Today*, XX, February 1964, 50–59.

———. "Singapore's Communist Front," *Problem of Communism*, XIII, No. 5, 1964, 53–62.

Vandenbosch, Amry, and Butwell, Richard A. *The Changing Face of Southeast Asia*. Lexington: University of Kentucky Press, 1966.

Wang, Gung-wu (ed.). *Malaysia: A Survey*. New York: Praeger, 1964.

Who's Who in Asia. (3d ed.) Hong Kong: Pan-Asia Newspaper Alliance, 1960.

Winks, Robin W. *Malaysia and the Commonwealtlh: An Inquiry into the Nature of Commonwealth Ties*. (Reprint Series No. 9.) New Haven: Yale University, Southeast Asia Studies, 1965.

(Various issues of the following periodicals were also used in the preparation of this section: *Far Eastern Economic Review* [Hong Kong], January 1967–December 1969; *Foreign Affairs* [Kuala Lumpur], 1966–March 1968; and *The Straits Times*, [Kuala Lumpur], May 1–October 15, 1969.)

Section III. Economic

RECOMMENDED SOURCES

Bank Negara Malaysia Annual Report and Statement of Accounts, 1968. Kuala Lumpur: Bank Negara Malaysia, 1969.

The Economist Intelligence Unit. *Malaysia, Singapore, Brunei: Annual Supplement 1968*. London: Spencer House, 1968.

The Far East and Australasia, 1969: A Survey and Directory of Asia and the Pacific. London: Europa Publications, 1965.

Federal Agricultural Marketing Authority Annual Report and Statement of Accounts, 1965 and 1966. Kuala Lumpur: FAMA. 1966.

Federal Land Development Authority Annual Report, 1967. Kuala Lumpur: Malaysia Government Printing Office, 1967.

First Malaysia Plan 1966-1970. Kuala Lumpur: Malaysia Government Printing Office, 1965.

Fisher, Charles A. *Southeast Asia: A Social, Economic, and Political Geography*. New York: Dutton, 1964.

Kanapathy, V. "The Place of Agriculture in Malaysian Economic Development," *United Malaysian Banking Corporation Economic Review*, II, No. 1, 1966, 6-29.

Lim, Chong-yah. *Economic Development of Modern Malaya*. New York: Oxford University Press, 1967.

Malaysia Official Yearbook 1967, VII. Kuala Lumpur: Federal Department of Information, 1968.

Malaysia Yearbook 1968/1969. Kuala Lumpur: Malay Mail.

Monthly Statistical Bulletin of West Malaysia, May 1969.

Ooi, Jin-bee. *Land, People, and Economy in Malaya*. London: Longmans, Green, 1963.

Puthucheary, J.J. *Ownership and Control in the Malayan Economy*. Singapore: Eastern Universities Press, 1960.

Sumitro Djojohadikusumo. *Trade and Aid in South-East Asia*, XII. Melbourne: F.W. Cheshire, 1968.

Zuzik, Michael B. *Labor Law and Practice in Malaysia and Singapore*. Washington: GPO, 1965.

OTHER SOURCES USED

"Aggressive Selling Now to get Investors for Malaysia," *Straits Times* (Kuala Lumpur), August 12, 1969, 13.

Allen, G.C., and Donnithorne, Audrey G. *Western Enterprise in Indonesia and Malaya.* New York: Macmillan, 1957.

Annual Bulletin of Statistics, State of Sarawak, 1968. Kuching: Department of Statistics, State of Sarawak, 1969.

"Application Forms for Employment Permits Available from July 1," *Siaran Akhbar*, June 28, 1969.

Asian Development Bank. *Asian Agricultural Survey.* Seattle: University of Washington Press, 1969.

Bank Negara Malaysia Quarterly Economic Bulletin, I, No. 4, December 1968, 3–15, 24, 25–34, 35–70.

"Banking in Exporting Countries," *United Commercial Bank Review*, XIX, No. 2, April 1968, 1–13.

Barlow, Colin. "The Marketing of Smallholders' Rubber," *Malaysian Management Review*, II, No. 2, December 1967, 27–40.

"Business as Usual," *Far Eastern Economic Review*, LXV, No. 35, August 28, 1969, 582–585.

Cobban, James L. *The Traditional Use of Forests in Mainland Southeast Asia.* (Papers in In International Studies, Southeast Asia Series No. 5.) Athens: Ohio University, Center of International Studies, 1968.

Comber, Leon. *Chinese Secret Societies in Malaya.* New York: Augustin, 1959.

"Contact Center for Investors," *Malaysia Industrial Digest*, II, No. 1, First Quarter 1969, 3.

Davies, Derek. "The Racial Balance Sheet," *Far Eastern Economic Review*, LXV, No. 28, July 10, 1969, 119–123.

Dubas, Floyd J. "Malaysia Takes Selling," *International Commerce*, LXXIV, No. 34, August 19, 1968, 2–5.

"Employers' and Employees' Welcome AMBO Report on Social Security," *Siaran Akhbar*, May 4, 1968.

"The Employment (Restriction) Bill," *Siaran Akhbar* (Kuala Lumpur), May 4, 1968.

An Even Better Deal for All. Kuala Lumpur: Alliance Headquarters, 1969.

Exchange Restrictions, Eighteenth Annual Report. (Exchange Restrictions Series.) Washington: International Monetary Fund, 1967.

Exchange Restrictions, Nineteenth Annual Report. (Exchange Restrictions Series.) Washington: International Monetary Fund, 1968.

Exchange Restrictions, Twentieth Annual Report. (Exchange Restrictions Series.) Washington: International Monetary Fund, 1969.

Far Eastern Economic Review Yearbook, 1962, 1964 1965, 1966, 1967, 1968, and 1969. Hong Kong: FEER, 1962 and 1964–69.

"First Advanced Courses in Management of Labor Relations," *Siaran Akhbar* (Kuala Lumpur), February 26, 1965.

"Forest Products Industry for Malaysia," *International Financial News Survey*, XXXI, No. 23, November 14, 1969, 370.

"German Loan to Malaysia," *International Financial News Survey*, XXI, No. 13, April 4, 1969, 103.

Goinga, Cornelis J.H. "Malaysia Sparks Interest," *International Commerce*, LXXV, No. 42, October 20, 1969, 19–21.

Golay, Frank H., et al. *Underdevelopment and Economic Nationalism in Southeast Asia.* Ithaca: Cornell University Press, 1969.

Grube, A.F. "The Mineral Industry of Malaysia and Singapore," Pages 501–515 in U.S. Department of the Interior, *Minerals Yearbook 1967*, IV. Washington: GPO, 1969.

A Guide to Investment in Malaysia. Kuala Lumpur: Ministry of Commerce and Industry, November 1966.

"Help For Malay Traders in Every State," *Straits Times* (Kuala Lumpur), October 22, 1969, 24.

Hill, R.D. "Agricultural Land Tenure in West Malaysia," *Malaysian Economic Review*, XII, April 1967, 99–116.

Ho, Robert. *Farmers of Malaya.* (Department of Geography Publication G/4.) Canberra: Research School of Pacific Studies, 1967.

Hunter, Guy (ed.). *The Effects of Industrialism on Race Relations.* Paris: UNESCO, for Institute of Race Relations, London, 1963–64.

International Finance Corporation Annual Report 1969. Washington: International Finance Corporation, September 29, 1969.

International Monetary Fund Annual Report 1969. Washington: International Monetary Fund, 1969.

Jackson, James C. "Oil Palm: Malay's Post-Independence Boom Crops," *Geography*, LII, July 1967, 319–321.

———. *Planters and Speculators: Chinese and European Agricultural Enterprise in Malaya 1786–1921.* Kuala Lumpur: University of Malaya Press, 1968.

Joaquim, R.P. "The Oil Palm Industry and the Malaysian Economy," *Journal of the Ministry of Commerce and Industry—Malaysia*, I, No. 3, November 1968, 33–36.

Kunstadter, Peter (ed.). *Southeast Asian Tribes, Minorities, and Nations*. Princeton: Princeton University Press, 1967.

"Labour Minister Opens Trade Union Secretarial Course," *Siaran Akhbar* (Kuala Lumpur), April 22, 1968.

Leigh, Michael B. *The Chinese Community of Sarawak: A Study of Communal Relations*. (Singapore Studies on Malaysia, No. 6.) Singapore: Malaysia Publishing House, 1964.

Mahajani, Usha. *The Role of Indian Minorities in Burma and Malaya*. Bombay: Vora, 1960.

"Malaysia." Pages 683–693 in *Encyclopedia Britannica*, XIV. Chicago: William Benton, 1969.

"Malaysia," *Labor Development Abroad*, XIV, No. 6, June 1969, 12.

"Malaysia Grows Steadily," *International Commerce*, LXXV, No. 47, November 14, 1969, 30–36.

Malaysia in Brief. Kuala Lumpur: Federal Department of Information, May 1967.

Malaysia Industrial Digest, II, No. 1, First Quarter 1969.

Malaysia: Information for Investors (A Summary). Kuala Lumpur: Federal Industrial Development Authority, 1968.

"Malaysia, Singapore, Brunei," *Quarterly Economic Review*, No. 3, September 1968, 5–10; No. 4, December 1968, 4–10; and No. 2, June 1969, 5–8.

"Malaysian Bill on Anti-Fragmentation of Estates," *International Financial News Survey*, XXI, No. 10, March 14, 1969, 79.

Malaysian Trade Review, 1967. Kuala Lumpur: Associated Chinese Chambers of Commerce of Malaysia, 1968.

Malaysian Trade Review 1968. Kuala Lumpur: Associated Chinese Chambers of Commerce of Malaysia, 1969.

"Malaysia's Budget," *International Financial News Survey*, XXI, No. 4, January 31, 1969, 30.

"Malaysia's Shipping Services," *Journal of the Ministers of Commerce and Industry—Malaysia*, I, No. 3, November 1968, 7–8.

Means, Gordon P, "Eastern Malaysia: The Politics of Federalism," *Asian Survey*, VIII, No. 4, April 1968, 289–308.

Monthly Statistical Bulletin of West Malaysia, January 1969.

Murphy, Mike. *Rural Development Handbook for Peace Corps Malaysia*. Washington: U.S. Peace Corps, 1965.

Ness, Gayl D. *Bureaucracy and Rural Development in Malaysia*. Berkeley: University of California Press, 1967.

"New Government to Solve Problems Facing Industries," *The Straits Times*, August 15, 1969, 7.

Ng, Anthony. "Big Jump in Exports," *The Straits Times*, October 17, 1969, 1.

————. "Chocs Shock: Duty Up By 400 Percent," *The Straits Times*, September 12, 1969, 1.

Peaslee, Amos J. (ed.) *Constitutions of Nations*, II. The Hague: Martinus Nijhoff, 1966.

Pick, Franz, *Pick's Currency Yearbook 1968*. New York: n.d.

Price, Waterhouse and Company. *Information Guide for Doing Business in Malaysia and Singapore*. N.pl.: Price Waterhouse, October 1968.

Provencher, Ronald. *Two Malay Communities in Selangor: An Urban-Rural Comparison of Social Habitats in Interaction*. (Unpublished Ph.D. dissertation, Department of Anthropology, University of California, Berkeley, 1968.)

Purvis, R.N. *Evaluation and Use of Under-Developed Agricultural Statistics: The Food Economy of Malaysia*. Ithaca: Cornell University Press, 1966.

Reece, Bob. "A Meaty Bone of Contention," *Far Eastern Economic Review*, LXII, No. 48, November 28, 1968, 486-490.

Report on Employment and Unemployment in Metropolitan Towns, States of Malaya 1965. Kuala Lumpur: Department of Statistics, December 1965.

Rubber Research Institute of Malaya. Kuala Lumpur: RRIM, 1960.

Rutter, Owen. *The Pagans of North Borneo*. London: Hutchinson, 1928.

Salim, Agoes. *The Market for Small Farm Rubber in Malaya*. Kuala Lumpur: Ford Foundation, 1965.

"Shock and Dismay Over the New Import Tariffs," *The Straits Times*, September 13, 1969, 23.

Smith, Eldon D. *Tenancy Among Padi Cultivators in Malaysia: A Study of Tenancy Conditions and Laws Affecting Landlord-Tenant Relations*. Kuala Lumpur: Ford Foundation, 1965.

Stanton, Jean E. "Rural Development in Malaysia," *Canadian Geographical Journal*, LXX, No. 3, September 1968, 84-93.

Straits Times Annual for 1968. Kuala Lumpur: Straits Times Press, 1967.

Suleiman, Ali. "Angkasapuri." Pages 17-19 in *Straits Times Annual for 1969*. Singapore: Straits Times Press, 1968.

Survey of Construction Industries, West Malaysia-1965. Kuala Lumpur: Malaysia Department of Statistics, 1966.

Swift, M.G. "Capital, Saving, and Credit in a Malay Peasant Economy." Pages 133–156 in Raymond Firth and B.S. Yamey (eds.), *Capital, Saving, and Credit in Peasant Societies*. Chicago: Aldine, 1964.

Tan, Tun Siew-sin, Malaysian Minister of Finance. *The 1969 Budget*. Kuala Lumpur: Malaysia, Federal Department of Information, 1969.

Thani, Nayagam, Xavier S. *Notes on Early Tamil-Chinese Trade*. (IATR [1966] SECTION: A. 13.) Kuala Lumpur: Conference Seminar of Tamil Studies, 1966.

T'ien Ju-k'ang. *The Chinese of Sarawak: A Study of Social Structure*. (Monographs on Social Anthropology, No. 12.) London: London School of Economics and Political Science, 1953.

U.S. Department of Agriculture. Economic Research Service. *The 1968 Agricultural Data Book for the Far East and Oceania*. (No. 219.) Washington: GPO, 1968.

U.S. Department of the Interior. Bureau of Mines. *Minerals Yearbook, 1967*, IV: Area Reports, International. Washington: GPO, 1969.

U.S. Department of Labor. Bureau of Labor Statistics. *Directory of Labor Organizations in Malaysia*. Washington: 1969.

Vining, Dale. "West Malaysia's Rice Irrigation Project," *Foreign Agriculture*, VII, No. 28, July 14, 1969, 9–10.

Voon, Phin Koong. "The Rubber Smallholding Industry in Selangor 1895–1920," *Journal of Tropical Geography*, XXIV, July 1967, 43–49.

Ward, Barbara E. (ed.) *Women in the New Asia*. Paris: UNESCO, 1963.

Wheelwright, E.L. *Industrialization in Malaysia*. New York: Cambridge University Press, 1965.

Wilson, Peter J. *A Malay Village and Malaysia: Social Values and Rural Development*. New Haven: Human Relations Area Files Press, 1967.

The World Bank Group in Malaysia. Washington: International Bank for Reconstruction and Development, January 1967.

World Bank International Development Association Annual Report 1969. Washington: International Bank for Reconstruction and Development, September 29, 1967.

"World Bank Loan to Malaysia," *International Financial News Survey*, XXI, No. 23, June 13, 1969, 185–186.

(Various issues of the following periodical were also used in the preparation of this section: *The Straits Times* [Kuala Lumpur], June–December 1969.

Section IV. National Security

RECOMMENDED SOURCES

"Anniversary of the Royal Malay Regiment," *The Malay Mail* (Kuala Lumpur), March 3, 1968.

Army, Air Force, and Naval Statistical Record, I. Wimbledon: Aviation Studies, January 1967.

Ewing, L.L., and Sellers, Robert C. (eds.). *Reference Handbook of the Armed Forces of the World, 1966*. Washington: Robert C. Sellers, 1966.

Fisher, Charles A. *Southeast Asia: A Social, Economic, and Political Geography*. New York: Dutton, 1964.

King, Frank H.H. *The New Malayan Nation: A Study of Communalism and Nationalism*. New York: Institute of Pacific Relations, 1957.

Malaysia Official Yearbook 1967, VII. Kuala Lumpur: Federal Department of Information, 1968.

Meadows, Martin. "The Philippines Claim to North Borneo," *Political Science Quarterly*, LXXVII, September 1962, 321–335.

Tan, Tun Siew-sin. *The 1969 Budget*. Kuala Lumpur: Malaysia Department of Information, Kuin Printers, 1969.

van der Kroef, Justus M. "Communism and the Guerrilla War in Sarawak," *World Today*, XX, February 1964, 50–59.

———. "Communism in Sarawak Today," *Asian Survey*, VI, No. 10, October 1966, 568–579.

OTHER SOURCES USED

Barron, Louis (ed.). *Worldmark Encyclopedia of the Nations*, IV: Asia and Australia. (3d ed.) New York: Worldmark Press, 1967.

"The Facts About Who Holds Those Top Government Jobs," *Malaysian Digest*, I, No. 8, October 14, 1969, 1.

Henniker, M.C.A. *Red Shadow Over Malaya*. London: Blackwood, 1955.

International Yearbook and Stateman's Who's Who 1968. (16th ed.). London: Burke's Peerage, 1968.

MacLeod, Alexander. "Racial Strife in Malaysia May Hamper Defense Talks," *Christian Science Monitor* (Eastern ed.), June 14, 1969, 4.

"National Language Drive in Sabah Offices," *The Straits Times*, September 25, 1969.

Ooi, Jin-bee. *Land, People, and Economy in Malay.* London: Longmans, Green, 1963.

O'Toole, E.H., and Sheppard, H.A.M. *Malayan Orders and Decorations.* Kuala Lumpur: Malaya Department of Museums, 1961.

Purcell, Victor. *Malaya: Communist or Free.* Stanford: Stanford University Press, 1954.

Royal Malaysia Police Annual Report. Kuala Lumpur: RMP, 1969.

Trumbull, Robert. "Plan for Defense of Malaysia Set," *New York Times*, June 20, 1969, C-2.

Winder, David. "Defense Gap Galvanizes Commonwealth in the Pacific," *Christian Science Monitor* (Eastern ed.), June 18, 1969, 2.

(Various issues of the following periodical were also used in the preparation of this section: *The Straits Times* [Kuala Lumpur], July–November 1969.

GLOSSARY

adat—Custom; customary law; customary behavior.

BARJASA—Barisan Rakyat Jati Sarawak. A Malay political party that became a component of Party Bumiputera.

bilal—Official of a mosque responsible for calling the faithful to prayer. Often also serves as mosque caretaker.

bilek—Compartment of a longhouse occupied by an independent household. *See* longhouse.

British North Borneo—Name for the British colony that became in 1963 the state of Sabah, a component of the federation of Malaysia.

bumiputera—Malaysian of ethnic group regarded by the government as indigenous, such as Malay, Dayak, or aborigine. Comes from Sanskrit word meaning "son of the soil."

capitan—Headman of a Chinese or other nonindigenous enclave, group, or organization.

Clandestine Communist Organization. Term used for the clandestine Communist subversive organization active in Sarawak.

Confrontation—Indonesian hostile confrontation with Malaysia, involving military action, mostly along the East Malaysia-Kalimantan border, during the period from 1963 to 1965. Officially concluded by treaty August 11, 1966.

DAP—Democratic Action Party. West Malaysian opposition political party with majority of membership Chinese.

dato—Title of distinction granted by the head of a component state of Malaysia. Traditional title of nonroyal district chief. Title of respect. Grandfather. A senior.

Dayak—Non-Muslim indigene from any of the interior ethnic groups of Sarawak and Indonesian Borneo. Sea Dayaks, or Ibans, are the most numerous Dayak group in Malaysia. Land Dayaks are another large Dayak ethnic group.

Dusun—*See* Kadazan.

Emergency—Period of Communist insurgency in the Federation of Malaya (West Malaysia) from 1948 to 1960.

Gerakan Ra'ayat Malaysia—Malaysian People's Movement. A West Malaysian political party.

guru—Teacher.

haj—Muslim pilgrimage to Mecca.

haji—A man who has made the *haj*. A *haji* retains the title in front of his name for life, e.g., Haji Anwar. The corresponding feminine title is Hajjah.

hantu—Spirit, ghost, or goblin.

Iban—Also called Sea Dayak. Ethnic group of Sarawak and neighboring areas in Indonesian Borneo.

imam—Presiding official of a mosque. Approximate equivalent of vicar.

Kadazan—Also called Dusun. Most numerous indigenous ethnic group of Sabah.

kampong—Village; hamlet; family compound; enclave; neighborhood.

kaum—Family group. Also faction, group, or party.

kenduri—Malay feast given in connection with a religious or life-cycle event, such as a wedding or circumcision.

khalwat—the Islamically forbidden act of being in close, unsupervised proximity to another person of opposite sex who is neither spouse, parent, nor sibling.

khatib—Reader in a mosque. Chief mosque official after the *imam*.

kongsi—Chinese organization or society based on rules patterned after traditional clan rules. As developed by migrant miners, a joint cooperative venture in which all laborers lived together, dividing living costs and sharing profits, with their leader, the *capitan*, receiving a double share.

Kuo Yu—*See* Mandarin.

longhouse—Multifamily or multihousehold raised bamboo or wooden rural dwelling in common use among a number of East Malayan non-Muslim indigenous ethnic groups and among some aboriginal peoples of West Malaysia. Consists of a variable number of separate family compartments (each called a *bilek*) joined longitudinally one to the other along a raised boardwalk. Although members of different *bileks* are often connected by family ties, each *bilek* operates as a separate household.

madrasah—Islamic school conducted in Arabic.

Malayan Union—Plan of the British in the period immediately following resumption of control after World War II to unite the Malay states and the Straits Settlements under a central government, with reduction of state autonomy. The plan was abandoned when it met with political resistance from Malay leaders.

Malaysian dollar—The monetary unit. 3.06 Malaysian dollars equal to 1 United States dollar.

616

Mandarin—Also called Kuo Yu. The Chinese national language.

MAPHILINDO—Stillborn grouping for collective defense of Malaysia, Philippines, and Indonesia originating out of meeting in 1963.

MARA—Majlis Amanah Ra'ayat, the Council of Trust for the Indigenous People. Organized in 1965 to encourage *bumiputera* participation in industry and business through the extension of financial and technical aid to firms that are predominantly *bumiputera* and the initiation of educational and technical training programs for interested indigenous persons.

MCA—Malaysian Chinese Association. One of the three political parties that make up the Alliance Party of West Malaysia.

MIC—Malaysian Indian Congress. One of the three political parties that make up the Alliance Party of West Malaysia.

mukim—Secular territorial division within a district under the administrative control of a *penghulu*. Also means the area served by one mosque of general assembly (the mosque attended for Friday prayers).

Nanyang—From Chinese word meaning "Southern Seas." Maritime Southeast Asia.

New Village—Communities established, fenced, supervised, and protected by the government for the resettlement of rural persons, most of them Chinese, who were thought to be vulnerable to attack or solicitation from the Communist guerrillas during the period of the Emergency.

Party Bumiputera—Political party, mostly Malay in composition, participating in the Sarawak Alliance government.

penghulu—Headman. Chief of a *mukim*, which may include one large or several small villages. (*See mukim.*) A salaried official, he is either elected by the residents or appointed by the government.

Pesaka—Party Pesaka. Political party participating in Sarawak Alliance government, predominantly Dayak in membership.

PMIP—Pan-Malayan Islamic Party. West Malaysian party in opposition to the Alliance and promoting Malay ethnic nationalist goals.

pondok—Islamic boarding school at which students, instead of paying school fees, work for their teacher as farm laborers in their free hours.

prahu—Small Malay sailing craft.

raja—Prince; ruler; governor. In the 19th century, sultan's deputy, usually of a royal lineage, who served as local ruler or district chief over a portion of the sultan's realm.

raja muda—Crown prince.

Sabah Alliance Party—Political party composed of several component parties, the United Sabah National Organization (USNO) being the largest.

Sabah Chinese Association—Political party.

SCA—Sarawak Chinese Association. Political party.

Sea Dayak—*See* Iban.

shahbandar—Harbor master and controller of customs.

Sherif—Title reserved for persons descended from the Prophet Muhammad.

SNAP—Sarawak National Party. Opposition political party of Sarawak, predominantly Dayak in membership.

Sri Vijaya—Empire consisting of seaports along coasts facing the Strait of Malacca and the Java and South China seas. Powerful from the seventh to 12th centuries A.D., its capital was near the present site of Palembang in southern Sumatra.

sultan—Islamic ruler who is both the sacred and secular chief of his realm. There are eight sultans in Malaysia, one from each of the states with a Malay royal house (except Negri Sembilan, whose royal house has different titles and powers).

SUPP—Sarawak United People's Party. Opposition political party of Sarawak, predominantly Chinese in membership and support.

Syed—Title reserved for persons descended from the Prophet Muhammad.

temenggong—Traditional title of one of the senior officials of Malay sultan's court. In East Malaysia, title given to paramount chiefs of several indigenous ethnic groups, e.g., Temenggong Oyong Lawai Jau, paramount chief of the Kenyahs.

UMNO—United Malays National Organization. One of the three political parties that make up the Alliance Party of West Malaysia.

USNO—United Sabah National Organization. Political party of Sabah, with predominantly Muslim leadership, and the biggest single component of Sabah Alliance government.

Wataniah—Name of Malay resistance group during the Japanese occupation.

White Rajas—The British White Rajas of Sarawak. First raja, Sir James Brooke, founded the dynasty in 1841. At his death, in 1868, he was succeeded by his nephew, Raja Charles Brooke. Third and last raja, Charles Vyner Brooke, reigned from 1917 to 1946, at which time he ceded Sarawak to the British crown.

yam tuan muda—Deputy king. Title invented by the Bugis overlords of the Johore-Riau sultans in the 18th century.

Yang di-Pertuan Agong—Supreme Head of Malaysia. National monarch elected for a 5-year term by and from the hereditary rulers of the nine Malay states: Perlis, Kedah, Kelantan, Trengganu, Perak, Pahang, Selangor, Negri Sembilan, and Johore.

Yang di-Pertuan Besar—Also called Yam Tuan. Title of head of state of Negri Sembilan, who is elected from a group of candidates of royal descent by an electorate composed of members of the state's hereditary ruling group.

INDEX

Capital Investment Committee: 396, 428, 490

capital punishment: 544

capitan: Glossary, 32, 44

Celebes: 36, 117

Celebes Sea: 11, 15

censorship: 359, 363

census: 1, 7, 8, 20, 47, 97, 110, 111, 219, 413, 445, 447; agricultural, 409; industrial, 439

central bank. *See* Bank Negara Malaysia

central government. *See* federal government

Central Indian Association of Malaya: 457–458

ceramics. *See* pottery

Ceylon: 349–351

chambers of commerce (*see also* Chinese Chambers of Commerce): 318, 396, 485–486

chemical industries (*see also* exports): 440–441

Chen Man Hin: 310

Cheng Ho, Admiral: 31

Cheng Lock, Dato Tan: 307

chief minister: 293–294

child welfare: 143, 144, 160, 163

childhood: 125–127, 129, 135, 143, 155

Chin Peng: 552, 553

China: 79, 93, 240, 332, 348, 390, 435, 550

China society: 207

Chinese Chambers of Commerce: 108, 318, 396, 485

Chinese Communist Party: 549

Chinese language (*see also* films; Mandarin; periodicals radio; schools; television): 73, 74, 93–94, 203, 262, 310; press, 360, 363, 364, 366–367, 368

Chinese of Malaysia (*see also* communalism; ethnic groups; family; labor force; social structure): 26, 41, 43–45, 46, 48, 51, 57, 78–80, 277, 291, 378; Communist threat, 65, 329, 333, 347–348, 550, 553; culture, 195, 207, 209, 210; dominance in economy, 385, 388, 389, 390, 396, 422, 448, 449–450, 475, 484.

Christianity and Christian missions: 4, 54, 85, 86, 88, 119, 133, 138, 169, 171, 172, 192, 219, 220, 242, 243, 253, 267, 268

circumcision: 127, 228, 235

citizenship: 54, 271, 274, 275, 277–278, 288, 293, 300, 301, 304, 389

civilian volunteer forces: Local Defence Corps (LDC), 558, 563, 572; Territorial Army, 558, 562, 572

Clandestine Communist Organisation (CCO): Glossary, 66, 67, 68, 110, 178, 315, 360, 550, 553, 554, 555

climate: vii, 8, 15–17

commerce: 5, 47, 321, 475–487, 489–507

common market: 339

Commonwealth (British): 2, 62, 187, 272, 278, 289, 329, 330, 333, 336, 338, 350, 352, 360, 390, 485, 500; citizenship, 278; defence forces, 557, 565, 568; relations, 338–339; trade preference removal, 489, 500, 502

communal conflict: 61, 70, 72, 109, 167, 249, 269, 318, 325, 381, 384, 422

communal cooperation: 384, 385, 386, 389, 396, 398, 422

communalism (*see also* Malay nationalism): 97, 98–99, 249, 299, 300, 301, 303, 305, 306, 307, 311, 316, 319–320, 322, 327

communications (*see also* films; newspapers; press; radio; television; transportation): ix, 9, 47, 52, 398, 410, 426, 431, 476

Communist China (Peoples Republic of China): 1, 64, 65, 332, 334, 340, 345, 347–348, 350, 352, 357, 500, 554

Communists and communism (*see also* Clandestine Communist Organisation; guerillas; Malayan Peoples Anti-Japanese Army): 2, 5, 60, 62, 66, 67, 69, 113, 178, 276, 298, 299, 301, 302, 304, 311, 320, 329, 330, 332, 333, 340, 342, 344, 345, 346, 357, 361, 368, 383; influence on trade unions, 455–463, 471; propaganda, 360, 457, 458, 552; terrorism, 561–563, 567; threat to security, 531, 534, 549–555

Communities Liaison Committee: 307

Conference of Rulers: 193, 269, 279, 280, 286, 290, 292, 294; composition and powers: 269, 281–282, 293, 388

Confrontation with Indonesia: 67–69, 70, 72, 110, 281, 336, 339–341, 355, 531, 554, 555; influence on economy, 396, 422; influence on foreign relations, 312, 329, 334, 335, 337, 338,

federal-state relations: 292, 321, 324, 325, 404

Federated Malay States (1896): 47, 52, 270–271, 300, 393, 405, 456, 458; structure of government, 270

Federation Agreement (1948): 60, 271

Federation of Malaya: 1, 26, 59–63, 64, 100, 110, 271–272, 273, 291, 300, 304, **305, 333, 341, 344**, 393, 523, 535

fertilizers: 402, 412, 414, 417, 425, 441

Filipinos (*see also* Philippines): 75, **117, 342, 343**

films: 359, 362, 363, 375, 377–378; documentaries, 362, 375; educational, 377

finance (*see also* foreign aid; revenue): ix, 336; institutions, 398, 522–528; organisation, 509–512

First Malaysia Plan (1966–1970): 5, 113, 144, 153, 217, 397, 398, 422, 428, 476, 506; in commerce, 478, 479, 480, 481, 482; in economic development, 397, 398, 399, 401, 481; finance, 511, 521; objectives, 398, 436, 438, 473, 489, 495, 509

First Russian Trade and Industrial Exhibition: 357

fishing: 99, 401, 412, 419, 421

floods (1967): 162–163

Food and Agriculture Organization (FAO): 179, 507

food processing industries: 418, 439, 440, 441

food production (*see also* land development; marketing): 401, 413–414, 417–419

Ford Foundation: 506

foreign aid (*see also* Asian Development Bank; defense; International Bank for Reconstruction and Development; International M o n e t a r y Fund): x, 490, 505–507; economic, 168, 179, 339, 349, 355, 356, 399, 419, 476, 505–506, 510, 516; technical, 338, 342, 349, 350, 356, 375, 426, 506–507

foreign exchange: 8, 377, 398, 484, 523

foreign information: 360, 369–370

foreign investment (*see also* British capital investments; Investment Incentives Act): 336, 338, 396, 397, 419, 426, 427, 432, 433, 435, 442, 443, 493, 505, 510; encouragement for, 489, 490, 505

foreign missions: 329–358

foreign policy: 339, 355; determining factors, 329, 332–333; formulation, 331; principles, 329–330

foreign relations: 283, 303; administration, 330–331

foreign reserves: 5, 337

forestry: 286, 401, 419–420, 424

forests: 402, 403, 404, 419–420; preservation, 403, 405, 407, 408, 414, 420

free education: 54, 169, 176, 180

free trade: 41, 494, 495

freedom of expression (*see also* press): 360–361, 362–363, 384

fruit: 402, 416, 418; for canning, 416, 418, 448

Funan: 28

– G –

Garcia, Carlos P.: 334

General Agreement on Tariffs and Trade: 491

General Labor Union (GLU): 457, 459, 460

George Town: 8

Gerakan Ra'ayat (*see also* elections): Glossary, 311–312

gold: 18, 214

government workers (*see also* public service): 446, 463

governors: 269, 281, 292, 293–294, 295

Great Britain (*see also* British capital investments; British early trade; British influences; British rule; British withdrawal; defense; foreign aid, trade): 179, 273, 329, 330, 332, 336–337, 344, 354, 355, 360, 377, **573**

gross domestic product (GDP): 397, 401, 414, 425, 428, 437, 439, 475, 478

gross national product (GNP): **395**, 476, 521

Gua Cha: 211

guano: 20

guerillas and guerilla war (*see also* emergency; Malayan Peoples Anti-Japanese Army): 60, 62, 66, 109, 110, 113, 333, 345, 458, 550, 552, 567

Gulf of Siam: 7

Gunong Korbu: 9

Gunong Tahan: 9

Gurney Sir Henry: 60

New Villages: Glossary, 109–110, 157, 298, 392, 552, 562

New Zealand (see also defense; trade) : 1, 69, 335, 337, 338–339, 431, 573

Nigeria : 352

non-alignment policies : 312, 329, 333, 334, 347, 350

North Borneo Alliance Party : 66

North Kalimantan National Army : 66

– O –

official language. See National language

oil palm (see also exports) : 8, 112, 117, 401, 409, 410, 415–416, 494

oil refineries : 397

oil wells : 8, 18, 435

opposition parties (see also elections; Pan Malay Islamic Party) : 300, 302, 311, 318, 320–321

orchids : 17

– P –

Padas River : 15

Pahang, State : 2, 9, 11, 18, 293, 405, 431; historical, 25; River, 9

painting : 209–213, 254

Pakistan : 330, 344, 349–351, 504

Pakistanis : 1, 3, 4, 21, 219

Pan Malay (see also Pan Malay Islamic Party) : 55

Pan Malayan Federation of Trade Unions (PMFTU) : 460

Pan Malay Islamic Party (PMIP) (see also elections) : 300, 305, 308–310, 318, 319, 321, 332, 367, 382, 387, 553

pantun : 201–202

Pangkor Treaty (1874) : 45

Party Ra'ayat (see also elections) : 55, 311–312, 321

peat : 12

Penang : city : 22, 111, 158, 310, 330, 342, 367, 370, 436, 473, 479, 495, 522; historical, 25; State, 2, 8, 11, 110, 162, 222, 272, 277, 280, 292, 293, 296, 312, 393, 405, 417, 433, 436, 437, 524

penal system : 531, 544–547

Penan : 84, 87, 114

penghulu : Glossary, 46, 47, 115, 259, 295, 296, 297–298, 533–533

Penulis : 201

Peoples Action Party (PAP) : 64, 69, 70, 71, 306, 310, 319

Peoples Pargressive Party (PPP) (see also elections) : 312

Perak : historical : 25; River, 9, 437; State, 2, 9, 16, 18, 110, 214, 281, 293, 312, 319, 405, 416, 417, 431, 433, 437, 524

periodicals : 199, 200, 202, 217, 359, 365, 370, 371

Perlis : 2, 293, 309, 344, 405, 417, 431; historical, 25

per capita income : 5, 161, 398

Petaling Jaya : 145, 146, 152, 153, 377, 439

petroleum (see also oil wells) : 426, 435

philharmonic societies : 209

Philippines (see also Filipinos) : 3, 15, 117, 334, 335, 336, 342–343, 347; controversy with, 2, 66, 72, 334, 335, 342, 347, 549

Pickering, W.A. : 46

pirates and piracy : 30, 32, 48, 51, 342, 540, 559

pitcher plant : 17

police : 291, 292, 532–543; Islamic, 253

policies and role of government (see also Malaysianization; nation-building) ; in cultural field, 195–196, 217; in defense, 565–567; in economy, 395–399, 401 (see also land development) ; 423–424, 425, 426–428, 452; in education, 167–168, 172–180; in foreign relations, 329–357; in labor, 445, 471–474; in public information, 360–363; in social welfare, 143–146; in trade, 486–487, 489–491

political parties (see also elections; individual parties; opposition parties) : 101, 103, 104, 106, 116, 302, 304–305; East Malaysian, 313–317; West Malaysian, 306–312

polygamy : 124, 129, 132, 133, 137, 140

pondok : 169

population (see also census) ; vii, 7, 8, 20–23, 219; increase, 7, 22, 157; teenage, 100

ports : x, 479, 495

Portuguese : 3, 31, 34–35, 41, 532

Port Dickson : 569, 573

Port Swettenham : 11, 213, 480, 495

Post Office Savings Bank : 520, 525

postal services : 482–483

pottery: 214
power: 426; electric, 435–437
prahu: Glossary, 11
press: 198, 359, 360, 361, 363–370;
freedom, 359, 360–361
press agencies (*see also* Associated
Press; Reuters; United Press International): 369–370
prime minister (*see also* Rahman):
269, 280, 282–283, 286, 287, 290, 292,
303, 388, 399
private enterprise: 104, 395, 396, 399,
423, 425, 426, 430, 436, 486, 507
Privy Council: 289, 337, 338
pro-West policies: 332
public debt: 520–521
public order: 531–548
public service: 270, 290–292
public service commissions: 291–292
Punan: 83, 87, 114, 214

– Q –

quarantine: 144, 148

– R –

racial tolerance: 62, 249, 301, 305, 307,
310
radio: 172, 173, 189, 200, 204, 233, 359–
363, 370–374; educational, 172, 373
Raffles, Thomas Stamford: 39, 40
Rahman, Tengku Abdul: during emergency, 72, 284, 302, 320; in foreign
relations, 331, 332, 334, 336, 337, 340,
343, 344, 345, 346, 347, 350, 351, 354,
357; in independence and creation of
Malaysia, 61, 62, 64, 67, 68, 271; personal history, 303, 392; political
leadership, 69, 283, 299, 307, 319, 322,
324, 381, 385, 386; in Singapore
secession, 70, 71
Rahman, Tun Ismail bin Dato: 303,
341
railroads: x, 51, 52, 475, 480–481, 486
rainfall: 8, 14, 15, 16
rainforest: 17
raja: Glossary, 77, 293, 389, 404, 408
Rajah Charles Brooke Memorial Hospital: 150, 154
raja muda: Glossary, 33, 40
Rajang River: 14, 79, 313

Razak, Tun Abdul: 72, 173, 188, 283,
299, 303, 319, 320, 331, 335, 341, 343,
344, 345, 349, 351, 352, 357, 381
Rediffusion Ltd.: 374
referendum (1962): 65
regionlasim: 321, 381, 387
Register of Potential Investors: 426
Reid Commission (*see also* Lord
Reid): 272
religion (*see also* Buddhism; Christianity; Confucianism; Islam; religion
and the state; Taoism): vii, 219–247,
253–255; freedom of, 275
religion and the state (*see also* law;
religious courts; tax): 222–224, 275,
280, 282, 582
religious courts (*see also* law): 545
religious reform. *See* Islam
reptiles: 19
Republic of China (on Taiwan): 335,
348, 369
Republic of Korea. *See* South Korea
research programs (*see also* Rubber
Research Institute; Institute for
Medical Research): in agriculture,
401, 412, 415, 418, 423–424; in national development, 422; in commerce, 490
Reuters: 367, 369
revenue (*see also* customs duties;
tax): 47, 57, 68, 397; collective expenditure, 509–520; from land, 408,
409; from mining, 430; from tin, 431
Riau islands: 36, 39, 40
rice: 54, 154, 401, 406, 409, 410, 413,
417–418; dry rice, 84, 87, 89, 417;
wet rice, 86, 404, 410
riots (1969): 70, 71, 101, 179, 283, 301,
309, 312, 359, 422, 532; influence on
economy, 415
rites and rituals (*see also* marriage):
Chinese, 131–136, 238, 239, 240–241;
death, 127–128, 135–136, 238, 239, 241,
244; Malay, 124, 127, 227–231, 382;
indigenous tribes, 243, 244–247
river systems: 479; East Malaysia, 12;
West Malaysia, 9–11, 402
roads and highways: x, 52, 438, 475,
481–482, 486
Royal Dutch Shell: 435
royalty: 42, 100, 302, 303, 382

Royal Malaysia Police (RMP) (*see also* police force) : 531, 532, 535–537, 547, 549, 550, 567

rubber (*see also* exports ; Rubber Research Institute) : 8, 17, 22, 47, 51, 354, 355, 356, 395, 396, 397, 401, 410, 414–415, 452, 494 ; cultivation, 406, 414–415, 493 ; estate labor, 3, 47, 110, 112 ; estates, 409, 414–415, 493 ; prices, 351, 401 ; products, 440, 442 ; small holdings, 22, 99, 409, 414, 415, 493 ; wages, 453

Rubber Research Institute of Malaya : 420

rulers : 269, 271, 272, 281, 292, 293–294, 295, 296, 300, 301, 381, 385, 387, 392, 393

rumi : 93, 363, 393

rural development (*see also* Ministry of National and Rural Development) : 392, 398, 401, 410, 421–423 ; committees, 101

rural living (*see also* local government) : 101–103, 156–157, 180, 295, 359, 360, 362, 367, 378, 384, 389, 411 ; economic aspects, 395, 396, 420, 475–478 ; employment, 448, 449

– S –

Sabah (formerly British North Borneo) (*see also* Philippine controversy) : administrative divisions, 13 ; British rule, 49–51, 62–63 ; indigenous people, 87–89, 113–114, 116–117 ; special constitutional provisions, 114, 270, 278, 279, 286 ; territorial expansion, 50 ; topography and vegetation, 14–15 ; United Nations survey, 67, 333, 336, 341

Sabah Alliance Party (SAP) : 302, 305, 316–317, 323–325

Sabah cabinet : 295

Sabah Legislative Assembly : 294

sago (*see also* exports) : 416, 448

Sambanthan, Tan Sri V.T. : 302

Sandakan : 15, 59, 368, 495

Sandys, Duncan : 64

sanitation : 145, 146, 148, 156, 159, 423

Santubon (mountains) : 12

Sarawak (*see also* Brooke rule) : administrative divisions, 50 ; British rule, 48–51, 62–63 ; indigenous peo-

ple, 83–87, 113–116, 234–236, 244–247 ; special constitutional provisions, 114, 270, 278, 279, 286, 322 ; territorial expansion, 50 ; topography and vegetation, 11–14 ; United Nations survey, 67, 333, 336, 341

Sarawak Advanced Youth Association (SAYA) : 318, 550, 554

Sarawak Alliance Party : 66, 302, 305, 313, 315, 316, 321–323

Sarawak Farmers Association : 318, 554

Sarawak Communist Organization (SCO) : 549–550, 553–555

Sarawak National Party (SNAP) : 316, 322, 325

Sarawak United Peoples Party (SUPP) : 66, 315–316, 553, 554

schools (*see also* education ; English language) : 147, 167–194, 182, 183 ; broadcast services, 373 ; Chinese, 56, 106, 168, 170–173, 178, 181, 186, 188, 265 ; Christian, 54, 242 ; curriculum, 168, 169, 170, 173, 178, 190 ; enrollment, 99, 168, 171, 174, 176, 177, 180, 181, 189, 190 ; health services, 144, 148, 152, 192 ; Indian, 56, 111, 173 ; Malay, 54, 104, 169, 170–173, 176, 190 ; primary, 112, 168, 169, 171, 180–181, 189, 190, 194 ; private, 54, 56, 168, 180, 181, 192, 193 ; public health, 152 ; secondary, 101, 168, 179, 181–187, 190, 192, 194 ; teacher training, 170, 172, 179, 186 ; technical, 169, 174, 175, 176, 179, 183, 185, 186 ; vocational, 169, 174, 175, 176, 179, 183, 186, 189

school committees : 101, 106

sculpture : 210

Sea Dayaks (Iban) (*see also* Dayak tribes) : Glossary, 49, 74, 83, 84–85, 113, 114, 115, 116, 138, 139, 141, 157, 215, 246, 253, 267, 315, 316, 367, 392, 563, 571

Selangor : 2, 110, 214, 281, 293, 405, 416, 417, 431, 433, 437, 522, 524

secret societies : 108, 456, 534, 543, 548

sectoral development : 398

Security Council (United Nations) : 69, 333, 351

Seenivasagam, D.R. & S.P. : 312

Segama River : 15

sejarah : 197

Sejarah Melayu (1536) : 30, 197, 532

self employment: 448, 476

Semang: 74, 82, 137–138

Senanayake, Dudley: 351

Senoi: 74, 82, 122, 136–137, 267

Senate: 287, 289

separation of Singapore: influence on economy, 396, 522; influence on labor organizations, 445

Shafie, Dato M. Ghazalie bin: 331

Shah of Iran: 351, 353

Shahbandars: Glossary, 33

shair: 201, 202

shaman: 83, 126, 168, 204, 229, 230, 231, 233

share-cropping: 102, 262, 407, 413

shifting cultivation: 84, 87, 89, 402, 414, 417

Shiism: 221, 228

shipping: 340, 420, 487

Sibu: 16, 21, 368, 495

Siew Sin, Tun Tan: 251, 285, 308, 320, 381

Sihanouk, Prince Norodom: 347

Sikhs: 81, 111, 222, 255; religion, 4, 219

silat: 103

silver: 18, 214

Simporna: 15

Singapore (*see also* defense): 78, 64, 305, 331, 335, 336, 337, 339, 340, 367, 393, 459, 460, 461, 471, 482, 489, 494, 501, 510, 521, 524, 527

Singapore secession: 1, 69–72, 299, 306, 319, 324, 336, 337, 338, 339, 347, 393

Sino-Malay Economic C o o p e r a t i o n Board: 396

slash-and-burn cultivation. *See* shifting cultivation

slums: 145, 148, 158, 438

smallholders (*see also* rubber): 405, 407, 409, 413, 416, 417, 420, 424, 448, 451, 477, 478

social customs: 249–268, 382

social clubs: 97, 98, 250

social problems: 161–162

social security: 165–166, 455

Social Security Law (1969): 166

social status: 78, 92, 98, 100, 108–109, 117, 251, 254, 255, 256, 305, 382, 569

social structure (*see also* social status): 26, 30, 42–43, 97–117, 382; of Chinese, 105–110, 252; of ethnic groups, 73–89; of Indians, 80, 110,

112, 252; of Malays, 78, 97–105, 249–252, 255–262

social welfare services: 52, 101, 110, 143, 144, 145, 159–166, 192, 338, 410, 454

socialists: 310–312, 315, 319, 387

Socialist Party (of Singapore): 64

Societies Ordinance (1909): 462, 463

soils: 401–402; conservation, 406

songs and sagas: 208, 209

South China Sea: xvi, 2, 7, 8, 14, 15, 559

Southeast Asia (*see also* MAPHIL-INDO): xvi, 195, 232, 243, 337, 339–347, 352, 357, 434; regional corporation, 63–64, 66, 67, 334–335, 341, 346; studies, 188

South East Asia C o m m o n w e a l t h (SEACOM) cable: 483

South East Asia Treaty Organization (SEATO): 334

South Korea: 335, 349

Soviet Union: 329, 333, 357, 500, 501, 502; aggression, 352, 357

spices: 402, 416

Sri Parameswara: 31, 32, 33

Sri Vijaya, Empire: Glossary, 28, 29, 559

state boundaries: 282

state government (*see also* federal-state relations): 45–48, 284, 292–297, 406, 408; authority, 274–275; organization, 510–512; structure, 269

standard of living: 110, 143, 161, 398

sterling area: 500, 529

stock exchanges: 522, 527

Strait of Malacca: 2, 8, 11, 25, 28, 30, 35, 340, 341, 342, 559

Straits Settlements: 2, 41–42, 43, 45, 270, 271, 300, 456, 458

Straits of Sumatra: 341

strikes: 72, 457, 458, 459, 460, 463, 470

Subang International Airport: 482, 485

Sufi sect: 33, 221, 230, 231, 234, 382

Sugut River: 15

Suharto, General: 340

Sukarno, President: 66, 67, 68, 69, 312, 340, 341, 344, 355, 531, 535

sultan: Glossary, 4, 33, 43, 46, 54, 77, 100, 204, 230, 231, 293, 387, 389

Sultan Hussein: 40

Sultan Mansur Shah: 33, 34, 197

Sultanates: 389

PUBLISHED AREA HANDBOOKS

550–65	Afghanistan	550–24	Lebanon
550–98	Albania	550–38	Liberia
550–44	Algeria	550–85	Libya
550–59	Angola	550–163	Malagasy Republic
550–73	Argentina	550–45	Malaysia
550–20	Brazil	550–161	Mauritania
550–61	Burma	550–79	Mexico
550–83	Burundi	550–76	Mongolia
550–50	Cambodia (Khmer Rep.)	550–49	Morocco
550–96	Ceylon	550–64	Mozambique
550–159	Chad	550–35	Nepal, Sikkim and Bhutan
550–60	China, People's Republic of	550–88	Nicaragua
550–63	China, Republic of	550–157	Nigeria
550–26	Colombia	550–94	Oceania
550–91	Congo (Brazzaville)	550–48	Pakistan
550–67	Congo (Kinshasa) Zaire	550–46	Panama
550–90	Costa Rica	550–156	Paraguay
550–152	Cuba	550–92	Peripheral States of the Arabian Peninsula
550–22	Cyprus		
550–158	Czechoslovakia	550–42	Peru
550–54	Dominican Republic	550–72	Philippines
550–155	East Germany	550–162	Poland
550–52	Ecuador	550–160	Romania
550–150	El Salvador	550–84	Rwanda
550–28	Ethiopia	550–51	Saudi Arabia
550–29	Germany	550–70	Senegal
550–153	Ghana	550–86	Somalia
550–87	Greece	550–93	South Africa, Republic of
550–78	Guatemala	550–95	Soviet Union
550–82	Guyana	550–27	Sudan
550–151	Honduras	550–47	Syria
550–21	India	550–62	Tanzania
550–154	Indian Ocean Territories	550–53	Thailand
550–39	Indonesia	550–89	Tunisia
550–68	Iran	550–80	Turkey
550–31	Iraq	550–74	Uganda
550–25	Israel	550–43	United Arab Republic
550–30	Japan	550–97	Uruguay
550–34	Jordan	550–71	Venezuela
550–56	Kenya	550–57	Vietnam, North
550–81	Korea, North	550–55	Vietnam, South
550–41	Korea, Republic of	550–99	Yugoslavia
550–58	Laos	550–75	Zambia